Output, Inflation and Growth

AN INTRODUCTION TO MACRO-ECONOMICS

[handwritten signature]

Glasgow University

1975

Output, Inflation and Growth

AN INTRODUCTION TO MACRO-ECONOMICS

SECOND EDITION

D. C. Rowan

PROFESSOR OF ECONOMICS,
UNIVERSITY OF SOUTHAMPTON

MACMILLAN

First edition 1968
Second edition 1974

Published by
THE MACMILLAN PRESS LTD
London and Basingstoke
Associated companies in New York Dublin
Melbourne Johannesburg and Madras

SBN 333 16628 0 (hard cover)
333 16629 9 (paper cover)

Printed in Great Britain by
WILLIAM CLOWES & SONS, LIMITED
London, Beccles and Colchester

To My Wife

Contents

Foreword to the Second Edition

THE revisions incorporated in this new edition are mainly those suggested by the numerous helpful critics among the book's users. Thus Chapter 10 (The Investment Function) and Chapter 17 (The Theory of the Price Level) have both been substantially revised while a new chapter has been written to provide a rather fuller account of the Quantity Theory of Money (Chapter 17*). At the same time a number of minor errors in Examples and Questions have been eliminated and references added to recent empirical work. I cannot acknowledge individually all those, both teachers and students, who have written to me pointing out possible improvements. I do, however, offer them all my sincere thanks. I can only hope they notice an improvement and, if they detect new or remaining errors, will continue to call them to my attention.

Most of the figures and tables have now been taken up to the end of 1970. However, where, as for example in Chapters 23–5, the data is illustrative of a method rather than primarily descriptive, I have left things as they were. At the same time I have not expanded Chapters 16 and 24 to take account of the new techniques of control adopted by the Bank of England in the autumn of 1971, since our experience of these new techniques is as yet too limited to permit us to draw useful conclusions.

Finally the book has benefited considerably from the criticisms and suggestions of Professor Thomas Mayer, who collaborated with me on the U.S. edition. To him I gladly acknowledge a deep debt of gratitude.

D. C. ROWAN

Foreword to the First Edition

THIS book was begun as long ago as 1955 when I held a lectureship at the University of Melbourne. Like most texts it developed from a lecture course – in this case an introduction to macro-economics – which I then gave. In 1956 I moved to the University of New South Wales (then the New South Wales University of Technology) and by then the first draft was nearly two-thirds complete.

At New South Wales it was, for various reasons, impossible to complete the text. The finished chapters, however, were used as the basis for an introduction to macro-economics which formed part of the first-year economics course for those reading for the Bachelor of Commerce degree.

In 1960 I returned to the U.K. and took up my present appointment at the University of Southampton. By 1964 it became possible to work on the book again and, by 1965, the basic draft was, at long last, complete. Since the end of 1965 I have undertaken considerable revisions.

In the task of revision I have been greatly helped by the constructive criticisms of those economists who have so generously read the book in whole or in part. So many economists have helped me in this way that I cannot thank each individually. I must, however, record particularly deep debts of gratitude to J. M. Fleming (University of Bristol); C. S. Soper (University of Melbourne); A. J. Hagger (University of Tasmania); E. B. Butler (University of Sheffield); and A. G. Ford (University of Warwick). Those defects which the book still retains must be attributed entirely to the shortcomings – and the obstinacy – of the author.

My thanks are also due to Dr Shipra Dasgupta, Mr D. Crossfield and Mrs E. Rick, who prepared many of the tables and diagrams, and to Mrs P. Dunn, who has so painstakingly and patiently typed the many drafts and revisions.

I am also particularly grateful to Miss Diana Marshallsay, who was not only responsible for the Index but who also gave me immense help with the checking of proofs.

Finally I must record my debt to the many undergraduates of Melbourne, New South Wales and Southampton who, over the eleven years in which the book has been in preparation, have taught me so much about the way in which introductory courses should be taught.

University of Southampton   D. C. ROWAN
January 1968

A Note on Statistics

MANY of the figures in this book employ published economic statistics relating to the British economy. In each case I have followed the usual practice and given a reference to the source whether official or unofficial.

Every care has been taken to make the figures and their reproduction as accurate as possible. Readers are, however, warned that because of minor differences in series, the inevitable revisions which are made from time to time in published economic data and the difficulties of reproduction, the figures should be taken as illustrative of economic behaviour rather than precise quantitative descriptions of it.

Acknowledgements

THE author and publishers would like to thank the following for their kindness in granting permission: The Clarendon Press, for material from 'The Interrelationship between Costs and Price Changes 1946–1959', by L. A. Dicks-Mireaux, from *Oxford Economic Papers*, 1961; H.M. Stationery Office, for material from *Economic Trends*; International Monetary Fund, for material from *International Financial Statistics*, Supplement to 1963/64 issues; The National Institute of Economic and Social Research, for material from the *National Institute Economic Review*; and *The Times*, for material from *The British Economy: Key Statistics*, 1900–66.

Preface

THE primary purpose of this book is to provide an introduction to macro-economics suitable for undergraduates in the first year of a degree course in Economics or Social Science. Despite this, the book should be useful to schools and other educational institutions and some professional bodies, for I have tried, as best I can, to keep the language and exposition simple and I have assumed that my readers have no previous acquaintance with the subject.

The approach of the book emphasises that economics is a social science which aims to develop testable predictions in terms of measurable concepts. Though it contains a good deal of theory, I have tried consistently to develop the view that theory is meant to be tested. To this end each chapter is supplemented by questions and exercises many of which require the reader to select data from published sources and use it to make simple tests of economic predictions or hypotheses. *This means that the student is asked not only to read through the book but also to work through it.* It also gives the student the opportunity to learn economics in the best of all possible ways – by working out problems for himself. By this approach I hope not only to encourage an appropriate methodological outlook but also to discourage the student from thinking, as many students do, that economic theory is empty and arid and applied economics mainly unstructured description only loosely related to theory.

Many students are drawn to economics initially by an entirely natural and creditable concern with social problems. Unfortunately many introductory courses, in their anxiety to give an adequate grounding in theory, devote little time to the application of theory to policy issues. The result is sometimes disenchantment. I have tried, by devoting the last four chapters of the book explicitly to short-run policy, to give the reader ample opportunity to apply the theory of the earlier chapters to policy problems. In these chapters I have placed the emphasis on the *difficulty* of conducting macro-economic policy rather than the capacity of a relatively simple theory to grind out apparently satisfactory answers to complex questions.

Economics is commonly studied by many students who do not continue the subject after completing their 'A' level examination or the first year of their university course. With this in mind I have tried to make this book self-contained in the sense that those who read and use it properly should be able to take an informed and critical interest in such valuable publications as *Economic Trends* and the *N.I.E.S.R. Review*. At the same time, since many students do proceed further in economics, I have sought to provide a suitable foundation for further work in macro-economics. In particular I have tried to avoid teaching, in the interests of simplicity, things which must subsequently be untaught. At the same time I have tried to avoid concealing difficulties.

Two problems inevitably face the writer of any introductory text: the first and most awkward of these is to decide what use to make of mathematics; the second is how far to describe the institutional framework within which the theory is developed.

As far as the first problem is concerned, the decision taken is to assume no knowledge of mathematics beyond that required for the G.C.E. 'O' level and, in particular, no knowledge of the differential calculus. This point is important, for many people are discouraged from any systematic study of economics by the belief that the subject is now accessible only to well trained mathematicians. Obviously those who possess a grasp of mathematical methods of analysis, the most powerful tools for thinking yet developed, are in an advantageous position. Nevertheless it remains true that 'O' level mathematics is enough for the whole of this book.

Not infrequently the fear of mathematics is misplaced. What looks like 'mathematics' is simply the plentiful use of symbols (rather than words) and the frequent employment of the notion of a function. Few students would regard as unintelligible the proposition that 'consumption depends upon income'. Many, however, regard as 'mathematics', and *therefore incomprehensible*, the statement $C = f(Y)$. I have attempted to eliminate this 'pseudo-fear' or 'symbol phobia' by two methods. The first is to devote a chapter to discussing and illustrating the use of symbols, functions and identities. The second is to use symbols and functional notation wherever I can in the hope, which my experience suggests to be not entirely unjustified, that growing familiarity with this means of expression (which is becoming increasingly common in the literature and the texts) will breed confidence in its interpretation. To some readers the result may seem excessively formal, pedantic or even forbidding. I believe it represents a sensible way of meeting an awkward and unavoidable problem.

As regards the description of institutions I have, after a good deal of cogitation, decided that this must be kept to a minimum. As a result there is very little institutional material (in the narrow sense) in the text. There is, however, a good deal in the questions and exercises in that, where appropriate, questions have been devised which require the reader to relate the theory of the text to the behaviour of particular groups of institutions. This may not prove to be the ideal decision, but in view of the high opportunity cost of including purely descriptive matter it is the one I find most strongly supported at the moment.

Structurally the book is divided in the following way. Chapters 1–18 develop a predominantly static model of the macro-economic system. Since most people who embark on economics think, instinctively, in dynamic terms, the static nature of the analysis is given continuous emphasis. Chapters 19–21 are explicitly dynamic. The first gives a short discussion of some aspects of economic growth, emphasising the supply side of the problem and making use of the familiar, but to many objectionable, concept of the production function. The second gives a brief account of the cycle; the third discusses the problem of rising prices with special reference to British experience. Finally, Chapters 22–25 seek to relate the analysis of the earlier chapters directly to problems of policy, not in the sense of providing solutions or showing, with full benefit of hindsight, how much better things might have been managed than they were, but in order to show the very formidable difficulties of conducting macro-economic policy in a dynamic world.

Analytically the book is planned to follow what might be called 'the principle of increasing difficulty'. In the early chapters basic ideas are spelled out in considerable detail; there are many illustrations and not a little repetition. As the book proceeds, the reader is assumed to acquire facility with economic analysis. Exposition becomes briefer and the demands placed upon the reader more severe but never, I hope, too severe.

Though the book is conceived as a whole it can be argued that the explicit introduction of dynamics coupled with the 'principle of increasing difficulty' make Chapters 19–21 unsuitable for inclusion in an introductory course. Those who take this view can, if they wish, omit these chapters. In doing so, however, they incur two severe costs. The first cost arises because, though Chapters 22–25 *can* be studied without Chapters 19–21, they present greater difficulty when treated in this way. The second cost arises because the omission of Chapters 19–21 removes from the course all discussion of growth, the cycle and rising prices – the three subjects which, at one level or another, students find continuously under debate in the daily press and on television. In my view the loss in realism and continuity resulting from the omission of Chapters 19–21 is not offset by any worthwhile gain in simplicity and I believe that most benefit will be obtained from the book by using it as a whole.

Just as the exercises are an integral part of the book, so too are the reading lists which follow each chapter. Wherever possible three types of references have been given: first, there are references which supplement the work of the text; second, there are references which provide an alternative approach to that presented in the text; third, there are references to more advanced treatments of problems discussed in the text.

The reading lists have been kept deliberately short. On the other hand, because of the strains at present imposed upon university and other libraries, alternative references have been provided wherever possible.

In addition to using these references systematically, readers are strongly urged to cultivate the habit of consulting both the monthly *Economic Trends* and the quarterly reviews published by the Bank of England and the National Institute of Economic and Social Research. The latter publication (referred to hereafter as the *Economic Review*) is available to students at a specially reduced rate of subscription. For those embarking on the study of macro-economics, purchase of a student subscription is very strongly recommended.

Economics, though a difficult and, at present, regrettably imprecise subject, is nevertheless exciting and rewarding. I hope that, if they use this book well, readers will find that some of the excitement of economics has communicated itself to them.

1 The Scope of this Book

THE social result of economic activity is the satisfaction of human wants. In any period of time, say a year, an immense *variety* of goods (cars, clothes, books and beer) and services (such as those of doctors, dentists, politicians and pop singers) becomes available in varying *quantities*. These goods and services satisfy the wants of those who purchase them. Obviously not all wants are satisfied by this economic activity for wants are virtually insatiable and resources are scarce. But if we think of the 'economic system' of a country in this way we can, subject to some obvious safeguards, regard it as a 'machine' for organising the production of goods and services which ultimately satisfy human wants.

The machine analogy is useful but has its dangers. It is essential to avoid too mechanistic a view of the economic system. This is best done by reminding ourselves that the annual flow of goods and services depends upon *human action*. Retaining our machine analogy we may think of economics as

the *scientific* study of the principles determining the operations of the economic 'machine'

which, since the 'machine' is really a complicated set of social and technical relations between human beings, can alternatively be thought of as

the *scientific* study of *man's behaviour* in the everyday business of earning his living.

This second definition forcibly reminds us that economics is concerned with human behaviour. Economics is therefore a social science – that is one of the group of disciplines which studies human behaviour. Others are sociology, psychology and anthropology. Each of these selects a particular aspect of human behaviour for study much as, in the natural sciences, physics and chemistry study particular aspects of the physical world.

This division of the social sciences into economics, sociology and psychology is not of course immutable. Its justification is simply convenience. The division has, so far, proved fruitful and helpful.

As long as it does it will be retained. As soon as it does not it will be
abandoned.

Both our definitions of economics contain the italicised adjective
scientific. The precise meaning we attach to this term is set out in
Chapter 2. For the present, however, it is sufficient to note that, in
terms of our machine analogy, the purpose of economics is to
explain

> *why* the machine (or economic system) operates to produce the
> results that we observe and not some other set of results.

In short the questions which concern economists, as social scientists, are questions involving 'how' or 'why'. As such they form part
of what is called *positive economics*. By contrast questions involving
the word 'ought' form part of what is called *normative economics*.
These distinctions are elaborated in Chapter 2. At this stage the
student is asked merely to note that there *is* a significant distinction
between the two types of question and to remind himself that much
popular discussion of economic questions belongs to 'normative'
rather than 'positive' economics. This, of course, does not mean that
normative economics is unimportant or that economists do not
discuss normative questions.

When, retaining our machine analogy, we ask the positive question
why does the machine operate as it does and not in some other way,
we are not being very precise. To make any progress we need to
clarify the meaning of the word 'operates'. What is it that the
economic system does that we seek to explain?

In the first place, as we have already noted, the economic machine
organises, in any period, the production of a flow of goods and
services. Suppose that we can measure this flow by a single magnitude
called 'output'. Since output satisfies wants and human wants are
insatiable we would like to have twice, three times or ten times the
annual flow of output we are currently (1970) obtaining. We cannot
because 'resources' are scarce. The available resources set an upper
limit to output. But, since it is a matter of common knowledge that
output fluctuates, it does not seem plausible to think that the flow of
output is always at the maximum level obtainable with the existing
resources. We can then ask:

> (i) what, in any given period (say 1970), determines the magnitude
>   or the flow of total output?

In the second place, as a casual reading of the newspapers will
remind us, output grows over time. In the last decade it seems that

output in the U.K. has grown rather more slowly and less steadily than it has in many other countries. Our second question is then:

(ii) what determines the rate at which output grows?

We introduced the concept 'output' as a convenient means of measuring the annual flow of goods and services made available by our economic machine. Since resources are scarce (in relation to wants) somehow or other the commodity composition of this 'output' has to be determined. If we want missiles we must, in general, agree to have less butter. Our third question is therefore

(iii) what determines the commodity and service composition of output in any period?

It is a familiar observation that there is more than one way of doing most things. Cats *can* be choked with cream. They can also be shot, drowned, starved, or poisoned. In the same way most commodities can be produced in ways which, from the economist's point of view, differ significantly. For example, forty men with thirty shovels and ten wheelbarrows can move the same amount of earth in a day as either four hundred men working with their bare hands or one man equipped with a bulldozer. It would be easy, but tedious, to multiply examples of this kind. Clearly where more than one method of production is possible the question arises:

(iv) what determines the ways in which resources are combined to produce goods?

Even the least curious observer of developed economic systems cannot fail to notice that some persons (who can often be classified into professional groups) obtain a larger share of the flow of goods and services per period ('output') than others. Dentists, on average, receive more than dustmen. Doctors, on average, receive more than drivers of delivery vans. Why is this? Or, to put the question in the form which we have hitherto used,

(v) what determines the way in which output is distributed between persons and groups?

It is these five questions which economists try to answer by discovering the principles upon which the economic system works. These questions, as the reader may readily convince himself, are common to all human societies.

The five questions listed have been set out, as the reader will have noticed, in what are called 'real' terms. That is we have spoken of the flow of goods and services – not its money value. In short, we have said nothing whatever about the absolute level of prices. Nevertheless the behaviour of the price level is a problem of considerable interest. Indeed, since the end of World War II there has probably been as much effort devoted to examining the determination of the price level, and its rate of growth, as to any questions in economics. Accordingly we add to our list of questions:

(vi) what determines the level of prices?

(vii) what determines the direction in which and the rate at which prices change?

These two questions, by definition, relate only to societies who use money rather than barter and whose prices are therefore expressed in terms of a monetary unit such as the pound, the dollar, the rouble, the franc, the mark or the rupee. They are therefore not necessarily common to all human societies as the first five are, for it is possible to conceive of a society which makes no use of any monetary unit. This point, however, need not worry us for in this book we are concerned only with the workings of the 'mixed' capitalist-collectivist economies of Western Europe and the United States. That is, we are assuming, though we shall not attempt to describe it in any detail, a particular type of institutional framework. Economies of this type express all prices in terms of an abstract monetary unit. They thus possess a price level. It follows that questions (vi) and (vii) are relevant to the frame of reference in which we have chosen to work.

Though we cannot discuss the institutional framework of the mixed economy in any detail it is worthwhile considering a few of its major features. Overwhelmingly its most important characteristic is the dominance of the market.

A market is an organisation which makes it possible for those who wish to buy to get into touch with those who wish to sell. Modern communities contain an immense array of markets some of them very highly specialised. There are 'money markets' in which those who have funds available for short periods offer loans to those who have a temporary need for money. The price at which these loans are made is the short-term rate of interest. There are highly organised markets in meat, fruit, vegetables, fish, wheat, tin, rubber, tea and in many other commodities. There are markets for services such as air freight space. In a broad sense there is a market for labour. There is, indeed, a market for virtually every good and service produced and demanded in a modern community.

In such a system of markets everything has a price. The price of labour, for example, is a wage or salary. With the money received from the sale of his (or her) labour the individual worker demands goods or services and can obtain them, up to the limit imposed by the income he receives and the wealth he possesses, in whatever combination he wishes. The market system thus makes it possible for an individual to specialise completely at his work and get in return whatever combination of goods and services he wants and can pay for. For this reason in modern communities it is rare to find an individual who makes, by himself, a complete commodity.

The prices ruling in the markets reflect the availability of commodities (or services) on the one hand and the community's requirements for them on the other. Suppose, for example, the community wants, and is willing to pay for, more washing machines than are currently being produced. The price of such machines tends to rise. As a result producing them becomes more profitable. The firms making them expand output and to do this bid for more labour in the labour market. Wages in the washing machine producing industry tend to rise relative to wages elsewhere and labour is attracted into the washing machine industry. In short the mechanism of the market provides signals in the form of profits (losses) which tell producers what kinds of output are to be expanded (contracted). In responding to these signals producers redeploy the productive resources of the economy by attracting labour (and other resources) into more profitable lines and withdrawing it (and other resources) from less profitable or unprofitable lines. Thus, as a consequence of individual decisions, reconciled by the market system, the pattern of production gets determined. By a similar process operating in the labour market so do wages and salaries, and, since each commodity has a price, the market system also determines not only what is to be produced but how much of what is produced is to go to each individual.

This, of course, is a highly simplified account of how any market economy actually operates. It is useful only at a very general level of discussion. How any market actually operates requires detailed and systematic study. For our present purpose, however, a simplified sketch is sufficient provided the reader is aware not only how simplified it is but also of the need, when studying any particular market, to confront our generalities with careful observation of what actually occurs.

Our economy, despite the degree of government intervention, government controls and government planning which justifies the adjective 'mixed', still conforms to a very large extent to the simplified picture of the 'market system' sketched above. Indeed what is remarkable is not the extent of government intervention and planning but the very restricted role they play in the modern 'mixed economy'.

Overwhelmingly our economic system is still based upon individual enterprise. To confirm this statement the reader has only to walk through the shopping area in any large city, note the immense variety of goods and services available, and ask himself what proportion of these arises out of the planned activities of state enterprise. The answer, obviously enough, is a very small proportion. Overwhelmingly the immense variety of goods and services needed to sustain contemporary urban life are available in appropriate quantities in modern urban communities as the result of many millions of individual decisions made effective by the market process.

Thus though the economic system may be said to determine the rate of output, the composition of output, the methods by which output is produced, the distribution of output and the rate of growth of output over time, it does so not as the result of *conscious direction* by a group of planners but as the result of many millions of individual decisions acting through (and being reconciled by) the market process. Broadly speaking no one concerns himself with our five questions. Producers pursue profit. Consumers arrange their expenditure, subject to the limits imposed by their income and wealth, to get that collection of goods and services which they prefer. Workers seek the highest price they can get for their labour. The result may not be ideal from some social points of view. But the market system demonstrably does work – as a visit to Selfridge's will confirm – and it is the market system, operating within the framework defined by law and social custom, which provides the answers to our seven questions.

Broadly speaking the seven questions set out above define the subject matter of positive economics which we examine against the particular background of a *market economy*. But just as it has been found convenient to subdivide the social sciences so economists have found it convenient to subdivide economics. As a result, in the technical language of economics, it is now usual to speak of *macro-economics* and *micro-economics*.

The former is that part of economics which studies the behaviour of *aggregates*. Examples of these are 'output', 'employment', 'consumption', 'investment', 'the general level of prices', 'exports' and 'imports'. *Macro-economics* thus seeks to explain the values these aggregates take in any period. Again speaking rather broadly, macro-economics may be said to embrace the Theory of Output and Employment, the Theory of the Price Level and the Theory of Economic Growth: that is, to be concerned with the questions we have listed as (i), (ii), (vi) and (vii).

The concentration on aggregates entailed in macro-economics results, again speaking broadly, in the deliberate neglect of those problems we have listed as (iii), (iv) and (v). We simplify our task of explaining the level of total 'output' by either assuming its commodity composition to be invariant or assuming that changes in its composition do not have a significant effect on its total. The justification for this procedure is that, within limits, it has proved useful.

By contrast *micro-economics* seeks to provide answers to the questions we have numbered (iii), (iv) and (v). It seeks to explain not the general 'level of prices' but the price of some particular commodity such as peanuts. Analogously micro-economics seeks to explain not the 'general level of output' but the output of particular commodities. Broadly speaking micro-economics embraces the Theory of Demand, the Theory of Supply and the Theory of Distribution.

We now begin to see how macro- and micro-economics complement each other. The former neglects individual prices and concentrates on the determination of the 'general price level'. The latter takes the general price level as given and seeks to explain the determination of a particular price in relation to all other prices. A precisely similar approach is made to problems of output: here macro-economics seeks a method of explaining the general level while micro-economics takes the general level of output as given and seeks to explain, on this assumption, what determines the quantity of a particular commodity which is produced.

In this book we shall discuss only macro-economics. This means that we shall consider only the Theory of Employment and Output, the Theory of the Price Level and the Theory of Economic Growth. This does not mean that micro-economics is of less moment. On the contrary a reference back to our questions (iii), (iv) and (v) will convince the student of the importance of this branch of economics. This decision to concentrate on one branch of the subject is again one of convenience. It is simply not possible to extract a quart from a pint pot. In the same way, within the planned length of this book it is not possible to deal usefully with the whole of positive economics.

SUMMARY

1. Economics is a social science which seeks to explain why the economic system operates as it does and not in some other way.
2. Every society, whatever the stage of its development, must provide answers to five questions. These are

   (i) What, in any given period, determines the magnitude or rate of total output?

    (ii) What determines the rate at which 'output' grows between any two periods?

    (iii) What determines the commodity and service composition of 'output' in any period?

    (iv) What determines the ways in which resources are combined to produce goods?

    (v) What determines the way in which 'output' is distributed between persons and groups?

3. In the 'mixed capitalist-collectivist' economies found in Western Europe and North America these questions are 'answered' by the economic system as the result of countless millions of individual decisions which are reconciled in the market.

4. Since mixed economies (as here defined) express prices in terms of a monetary unit there emerges the concept of a 'price level' and the derived concept of its rate of change. These lead to our questions (vi) and (vii).

5. The purpose of positive economics is to explain why the economic system provides the answers which it does to these seven questions and not some other set of answers.

QUESTIONS AND EXERCISES

1. We are often told that there is a serious national need for engineers, scientists and technologists. In a *market* economy what evidence would you look for to test this statement? Does 'need' mean 'shortage'? If not what does it mean?

2. If there was a 'shortage' of engineers how do you think the *market* system would tend to eliminate it?

3. The prices people are prepared to pay for goods and the costs of producing them determine what is produced. What is produced determines what enterprises are prepared to pay for different kinds of labour. Extend this argument to explain the relative incomes of (i) the top pop group; (ii) Lord Stokes; (iii) your doctor; (iv) postmen.

4. If it is true that producers are always pursuing profit how can this help to explain the *methods* by which a good is produced?

5. Discuss the contention that the market system works badly because a successful salesman receives a higher income than a great

physicist. What is meant by 'badly'? Is this question one for
positive or normative economics?

SUGGESTED READING

F. Zeuthen, *Economic Theory and Method* (Longmans, 1955) ch. i.
J. Robinson, *Economic Philosophy* (Pelican, 1962) ch. i.

2 The Process of Economic Analysis

IN Chapter 1 we defined the four main problems with which this book deals as being to explain

(i) what determines the level of output in any period;
(ii) what determines the rate at which 'output' grows between any two periods;
(iii) what determines the general level of prices in any period;
(iv) what determines its rate and direction of change between any two periods.

We have thus *selected* particular aspects of the economic system for intensive study. How are we to set about analysing these problems?

Since our aim is to develop a theory which explains the determination of output – that is why output is what it is in any period and not some greater (or smaller) magnitude – our first task is that of economic *description*.

Since we hope to develop a theory which will explain the facts we need to know what the facts are. The purpose of *economic description* is to give a systematic account of the facts which is, at one and the same time, sufficiently detailed for our purposes and sufficiently simple for us to comprehend it. Two processes are involved here: (i) the definition, in operational terms, of a set of concepts with which a complex economic reality can conveniently be described; and (ii) the use of these concepts to provide a description.

All this no doubt sounds somewhat confusing. We shall now try to clarify it by an example.

What the economic system produces, in any period of time we may use for accounting purposes, is a flow of dissimilar goods and services. In principle it would be possible to make a detailed list of the quantity of each good and service produced in any given period. But such a list would contain several millions of dissimilar items many of which would need to be measured in different units. The result would be comprehensive but not readily comprehensible. Moreover there is no obvious way in which the quantities of the various heterogeneous goods and services could be added together to produce a single total. What, for example, is the sum of 1·2 million cars, 97 million cabbages, 7 million 'books' (themselves not homogeneous),

3 new aircraft carriers, a new cathedral and 2 new atomic warheads? To deal with this difficulty we make use of an abstract concept of output. This has two characteristics:

(i) It possesses the capacity to satisfy human wants;† and
(ii) it requires the use of scarce resources to produce it.

This definition, it should be noted, is derived directly from the observation that all scarce goods – that is goods which command a price – share the common property of being able in some degree to satisfy human wants – a point which we established in Chapter 1.

Thus defined, output cannot be observed directly. All that *can* be observed is the flow of heterogeneous goods and services which are scarce (that is command a price) and which are produced in any period. In addition to our definition we therefore need to write down a set of rules which will enable us to say that a given flow of heterogeneous goods and services is equal to a particular flow of output. Once this has been done, output is, in principle, *measurable*: that is, the abstract notion of 'output' has been made operational. Provided we are prepared to undertake the work of measurement, or find someone to do it for us, we can then give a comprehensive, comprehensible and numerical description of the facts in which we are interested.

In the next two chapters we shall discuss in some detail the concepts (of which 'ouput' is only one) that we shall need to use to describe those facets of economic behaviour which interest us. We shall also discuss how these concepts can be measured. At this stage, however, we anticipate some of our later results by introducing a graph (Fig. 2.i) on which three variables are plotted against time. These three variables are

(i) the output of the United Kingdom for each quarter from 1950 to 1970;
(ii) the industrial output of the United Kingdom for each quarter from 1950 to 1970;
(iii) the percentage of the work-force unemployed for each quarter from 1950 to 1970.

We shall not now comment on this set of observations of recent economic events. The reader, however, is invited to make a list of those problems in positive economics which the figure suggests to him.

† Wants may be satisfied directly or indirectly. Hence a shoe manufacturing machine indirectly, by aiding in the process of shoe production, satisfies wants.

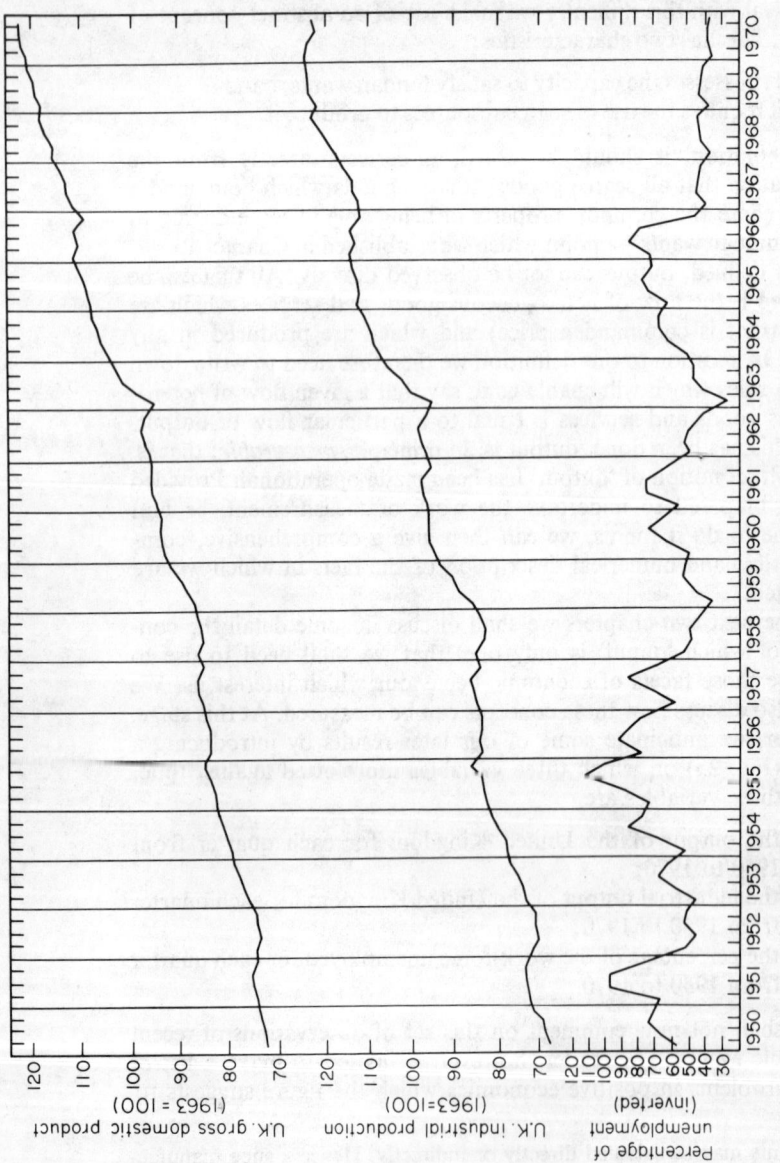

Fig. 2.i Quarterly estimates of the gross domestic product (1963 = 100), industrial output (1963 = 100) and of the percentage of the work-force unemployed of Great Britain, 1950–70

Sources: (1) Gross domestic product: 1950–5, *Studies in an Inflationary Economy*, F. W. Paish; 1955–70, *National Institute Economic Review*. (2) Industrial production: *Monthly Digest* (1950–71). (3) Unemployment: 1950–4, *London and Cambridge Economic Bulletin*; 1955–70, *Monthly Digest*

Economic description provides us with a systematic account of what we believe to be the relevant facts. Without some preliminary theory, that is without some notion of what it is we want to investigate, we have, of course, no idea what facts are relevant. Theory and fact in this sense are complementary not opposed concepts as the loose expression of everyday speech might lead us to suppose. Description, however, is not itself theory. For description can do no more than summarise for us, within the framework of a chosen conceptual scheme, what *has* happened. It does nothing directly to explain to us *why* whatever it was that happened actually did happen though it may suggest possible lines of enquiry to us. To explain events is the task of theory. What then *is* a *theory*?

Since economics is a social science, any economic theory must *contain hypotheses concerning the way in which human beings behave.* It is these hypotheses, which may obviously be correct or incorrect, which give economic theory its operational significance. These hypotheses must be expressed in terms of the conceptual framework in which the economic events are described. From these hypotheses by a process of logical deduction, we derive *predictions†* in terms of the conceptual framework which we have used to describe events. These *predictions* can then be tested against actual observations. If our observations conform to our predictions we may say that our theory is *not refuted by events.* We cannot say that it is 'correct' for other observations may, and eventually will, be made which force us to modify or abandon it. On the other hand if our *predictions* are not in conformity with observations our theory *is refuted* and must be abandoned or modified.

All this sounds very difficult and possibly rather dull. In some cases it *is* difficult though it is *never* dull. A simple example may aid in clarification. Suppose that we are interested in explaining the monthly production of beer. We first define beer in such a way that the monthly production of it can be measured: that is we provide an operational definition. This is not quite so simple as it sounds for beer, like goods and services, is not homogeneous. Our definition must be in some degree arbitrary. Armed with our definition we can measure 'beer' production in each month and plot it on a graph.

Let us assume that the resultant curve looks like Fig. 2.ii. How are we to develop a theory to explain the fluctuations in production revealed by this graph?

From our discussion of the workings of a market economy we can argue that beer producers will try and adjust the quantity of beer produced in any month to the quantity consumed. For if they

† Sometimes called 'theorems'.

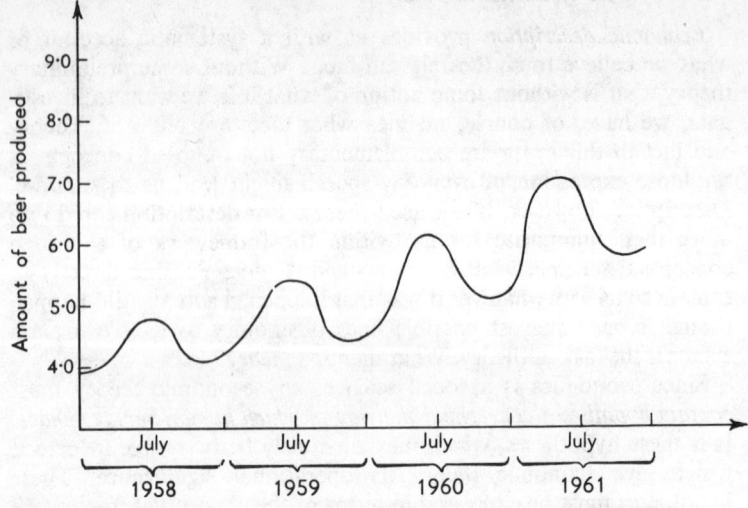

FIG. 2.ii The quantity of beer† produced (in million bulk barrels) over
a period of 4 years

produce more than this, either stocks of unsold beer will accumulate
(and deteriorate) or beer prices will fall. Either way producers will
make *less* profit than they otherwise would. Equally if they produced
less beer than the public wanted to consume the producers would be
forgoing profits. Since as we have seen producers pursue profits and
seek to avoid losses we may assume that they aim to produce the
quantity the public wants to purchase at the ruling market price.
Accordingly we may adopt the hypothesis that beer producers will
plan to produce in any month the quantity of beer they *expect* that
the public will want to buy. How do they form their expectations?

The main guide we have to the future is what has happened in the
past. We can thus think of *brewers in general* as adjusting their production of beer in each month to the consumption of beer in the
previous month. Hence, we can write our first hypothesis about
human behaviour thus:

beer production in January = beer consumption in December.

We now need to formulate some hypothesis about the beer-drinking decisions of *people in general* in order to explain consumption.

It is a familiar observation that public houses and bars are more
crowded in summer than in winter. We should therefore expect
some systematic seasonal variation in monthly beer consumption

† Hypothetical data.

due ultimately to variations in climatic conditions. It also seems reasonable to argue that, given the 'weather' conditions, people drink more beer when they are more 'prosperous'. But surely, given the 'weather' and the 'degree of prosperity', the more beer people will drink the 'cheaper' it is in relation to other forms of alcohol? If whisky cost, per pint, the same as beer would not people drink more whisky and less beer?

These considerations lead to a simple hypothesis about human behaviour which states that

the quantity of beer consumed in any month $\Big\}$ depends upon $\Big\{$

(i) the 'weather' in that month

(ii) the general degree of 'prosperity' in that month

(iii) the 'cheapness' of beer in relation to other forms of alcohol in that month.

We now have to give operational meaning to our notions of 'the weather' 'the general degree of prosperity' and the relative 'cheapness' of beer. This is not hard. In any month we can measure the weather by the average hours of sunlight or average daily temperature. Similarly since the 'general level of prosperity' is likely to be inversely related to the percentage of the work-force unemployed we can measure the 'degree of prosperity' by the reciprocal of this percentage. To measure the 'cheapness' of beer let us take the price of whisky as a proxy for the price of other forms of alcohol. Then the 'cheapness' of beer is measured by: price of whisky (per bottle)/ price of beer (per pint).

We now have three behaviour hypotheses. These are:

(i) beer producers (brewers) pursue profits and seek to avoid losses: hence they try to adjust production to expected consumption;

(ii) the rule they follow to do this is to make production in any month equal to consumption of the previous month;

(iii) consumption in any month depends upon:

    (*a*) average temperature;

    (*b*) the reciprocal of the percentage of the work-force unemployed;

    (*c*) the ratio of the price of whisky to the price of beer.

We can now use our theory – in which every variable is operationally defined – to generate a number of *predictions*. Some typical predictions are as follows:

if, in any month, with no change in the 'weather' (temperature) and no changes in the relative 'cheapness' of beer (price of whisky in relation to price of beer) unemployment rises as a percentage of the work-force then

(i) beer consumption in the *same* month will fall; and

(ii) beer production in the *following* month will fall by an equivalent amount.

Predictions of this kind can be tested against observations of what actually occurs. If the observations conform with our predictions we may continue to hold our theory. If they do not we must abandon it.

The example is, of course, artificially simplified. As a result the process of deducing predictions logically from the behaviour assumptions is extremely easy. It consists in saying:

$$\text{if} \left\{ \begin{array}{c} A \\ \text{increase in the} \\ \text{percentage of the} \\ \text{work-force unemployed} \end{array} \right\} \begin{array}{c} \text{occurs in} \\ \text{context} \end{array} \left\{ \begin{array}{c} C \\ \text{no change in average} \\ \text{temperature} \\ \text{no change in the ratio} \\ \dfrac{\text{whisky prices}}{\text{beer prices}} \end{array} \right\}$$

$$\text{then} \left\{ \begin{array}{c} B \\ \text{decrease in} \\ \text{beer} \\ \text{consumption} \end{array} \right\} \text{will occur.}$$

$$\text{If } B \text{ occurs then} \left\{ \begin{array}{c} D \\ \text{fall in beer} \\ \text{production} \end{array} \right\} \text{occurs one month later.}$$

An alternative way of putting the same thing is to say:

If, other things being equal (often written *ceteris paribus*), the percentage of the work-force unemployed in any month *rises*

then, in the same month beer consumption will fall

and, in the next month beer production will fall by an equivalent amount.

In many economic theories the chain of reasoning, though ultimately reducible to this form, may be much more complicated. We may for example have to argue that, *on our behaviour hypotheses,*

if A occurs in context C then Z will occur
if Z occurs Q will occur
if Q occurs R will occur
if R occurs S will occur
if S occurs B will occur.

Here again we can make the same predictions as before – *if A then B* – but only after a good deal more intellectual effort. But the greater complexity of the second example does not alter the fundamental nature of the process. This is the derivation of testable (or meaningful) predictions from hypotheses about human behaviour. It is because positive economics seeks to develop testable predictions of this kind that it can lay claim to the adjective 'scientific' – for the essential nature of scientific enquiry is precisely the development of predictions which can conceivably be tested by observation and experiment.

Two further points of great importance also emerge from this example. *Notice that the basic assumption of our method is that there is regularity in human behaviour – in this case human beer drinking behaviour and the production planning of brewers.* If there was no regularity, our behaviour hypotheses would be false. Beer consumption would fluctuate capriciously from month to month and no systematic explanation would be possible. The assumption of regularity is, of course, familiar enough in the natural sciences. Is it a reasonable assumption in the social sciences?

To answer this question consider what would happen if there were *no* regularities in economic phenomena. Not only would beer consumption fluctuate capriciously – so would the consumption of all other commodities. Business planning whatever producers tried to do would be virtually impossible. Now as a matter of common observation business planning, though difficult, is not impossible. Hence we may argue that regularity is present in sufficient degree to make some prediction conceivable.

The second point to notice is that, in expressing our behaviour assumption, we spoke deliberately of *people in general*. We are trying, in other words, to formulate hypotheses about group behaviour – *not individual behaviour*. Predicting individual behaviour is notoriously difficult even if we choose individuals whom we have known intimately for most of our lives. Predicting group or average behaviour is, however, far simpler. Why is this?

To see why consider the case of an insurance company which receives a proposal for life assurance from a man of 30. The proposal is to mature at age 60. Medical examination of the proposer shows no obvious physical defects. The proposer is, let us say, a librarian. Now the insurance company has no means of knowing at what age any particular proposer will die. Our librarian may be run over and killed ten minutes after the policy comes into force. Alternatively he may live to 90. On the other hand, from the statistics of deaths, the insurance company can easily calculate the percentage of 'average healthy' adult male librarians who die at any given age. These percentages can be plotted on a graph like Fig. 2.iii.

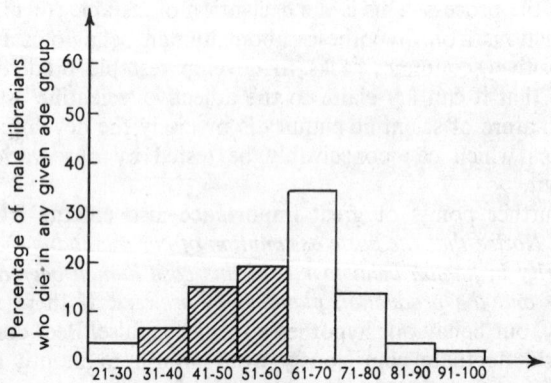

FIG. 2.iii The percentage† of 'average healthy' adult male librarians who die at any given age

The next step is simply to interpret these percentages as 'probabilities'. The *most* probable age bracket in which death occurs is, on this figure, shown to be 61–70. Equally the probability of the average adult male librarian dying before the age of 31 is 0·03. The insurance company can now readily calculate the number of cases per cent in which 30 year old males will die before the age of 61. This is the sum of the probabilities in the shaded area. All it then has to do is (i) charge a premium sufficient to cover this risk and leave it a margin of profit and (ii) write life policies for a sufficiently large number of librarians for the average behaviour to be applicable. In short, life insurance, indeed all insurance, can be conducted profitably because though it is impossible to forecast what will happen in individual cases, it *is* possible to predict what will happen, on average, in a large number of cases.

A similar situation exists in physics where the physicist, though he cannot predict the response of an individual electron to a given

† Hypothetical data.

stimulus can predict, with a useful degree of accuracy, the average response of a large group of electrons.

We may sum up what we have learned about the process of economic analysis so far as follows.

(i) The first stage is to *select* a problem;
(ii) The second stage is *economic description* which consists in:
    (*a*) *defining* operational (or measurable) concepts in terms of which the problem is to be examined;
    (*b*) *measurement*;
(iii) The third stage is to formulate, in terms of these concepts, *hypotheses* (or *assumptions*) about human behaviour;
(iv) The fourth stage is to derive, by logical processes, *conclusions* or *predictions* in terms of the concepts already defined.

These four stages are sometimes referred to as the development of a 'model' of the economy (or a part of the economy).

(v) The fifth stage is to *test* the *predictions* of the theory or model against observations.

If the predictions are shown to be in conformity with the observations the theory is *not* shown to be correct. *It is merely shown not to be incorrect.* We can continue to hold it until its predictions cease to correspond with observation. When this happens we need to develop a new theory or model which generates predictions consistent not only with observations which the old model *could* explain, but also with observations which the old model *could not* explain. Our new theory (model) must therefore be more general in its scope than the old.

From this it is easy to see that the advance of knowledge, in all sciences, takes place through the continuous testing and reformulation of theories. Each new theory is more powerful, in the sense of being able to explain a greater range of observations, than the theory it replaces. Reformulation, in short, is a necessary part of the advancement of knowledge. From which it follows that, when we develop a theory or model, we should not simply look around for observations which support it. Even the least useful of theories can be supported by *some* observations. Rather we should seek to expose our model to the most stringent tests our ingenuity can devise. Indeed the golden rule for anyone studying positive economic theory is to ask himself continually the question:

What *testable or falsifiable predictions* does this theory generate?

This, as we shall see in later chapters, is often a difficult question to answer.

We have now said enough about the process of economic analysis to make it clear that what we have called 'positive economics' deals with issues which can be settled ultimately only by an appeal to the facts. This indeed is the characteristic of what we earlier called 'how' or 'why' questions.

By contrast, 'normative economics' deals with questions which *cannot* be settled by an appeal to the facts. Consider for example the statement

The Government ought to raise taxes on cigarettes by 6p per packet of 20 in order to reduce lung cancer.

This, on analysis, consists of three propositions:

(i) *if* a tax of 6p per packet is imposed *then* cigarette consumption per year will fall by a certain amount;
(ii) *if* cigarette consumption falls by this amount *then* the incidence of lung cancer will decline;
(iii) it is *desirable* that the incidence of lung cancer should decline.

Proposition (i) is easily recognisable as a *prediction* about the way the economic system works. It is a proposition in *positive economics*. Proposition (ii) is similarly a *prediction* in human biology. Both these propositions can, in principle, be tested by an appeal to observation.

Proposition (iii) is, however, of an altogether different kind. It asserts that a reduction in the incidence of lung cancer is 'good' or 'desirable'. We may agree with this. *But if we do not the disagreement can never be settled by any appeal to the facts*. This is because Proposition (iii) is what is called a 'value judgment'. It reflects the 'value judgment' that one state of affairs is 'better' than another. In general, though possibly not in this case, many people will disagree over judgments of this kind. Their disagreements however cannot be resolved by observation or research.

It follows that normative propositions in economics involve not only propositions in positive economics, which can be tested by an appeal to the facts, but also value judgments which cannot. This does not mean that normative propositions are unimportant. They are of very great importance and we shall devote part of this book to the examination of some 'normative' issues. What it does mean is that the student, particularly in his reading of the popular and semi-technical press, should be careful to distinguish positive economic statements from value judgments. For the former he should demand evidence. For the latter he can merely offer agreement or disagreement. In the same way, he should draw the same distinction in his own thinking and writing and, where his value judgments are inevitably involved, seek to make it clear precisely what they are and where they enter the argument.

The terminology employed here seeks to distinguish between positive and normative economics because this distinction, though ultimately invalid, is useful pedagogically. The reader, however, must not fall into the trap of thinking that normative economics, as we have used the term, is in any sense inferior to positive economics. This view can all too easily be arrived at through excessive contemplation of the rather elementary examples used to illustrate what is meant by 'normative'. By definition normative propositions involve a value judgment and the value judgments involved are frequently unacceptable to the reader. At the same time the examples offered, in the interests of simplicity, often appear to require very little positive economic analysis. It is thus only too easy to assume that disputes over normative economic propositions are largely non-technical disputes over value judgments. Any assumption of this kind is entirely unjustified. Indeed some of the most promising (and most technical) modern developments in economics, including linear and other programming techniques, are concerned precisely with the problem of how best to reach a given objective and are thus, in the general sense, normative.

Properly speaking, therefore, normative economics is concerned with economic problems in which some objective (or target) is either given explicitly or implied. Thus if a businessman's objective is to maximise profits then given this target his problem is to discover how to do it. This is frequently a complicated programming problem.

By contrast, positive economics is concerned to describe, explain and ultimately predict what actually occurs in the economic system.

SUMMARY

1. Positive economic analysis of a selected problem consists of

   (i) Economic description which entails

      (a) the definition of measurable concepts;
      (b) measurement;

   (ii) formulation of behaviour hypotheses in terms of these definitions;

   (iii) generation of testable or falsifiable predictions (in terms of the definitions) from the behaviour assumptions;

   (iv) testing the predictions against observations.

2. Positive economics is thus concerned with issues which can, in principle, be settled by the examination of evidence.

3. The fundamental assumption of positive economics is that, on average, the behaviour of man in the everyday business of earning a living, exhibits sufficient regularity to make possible a predictive science of economics.

4. That there are observable regularities in economic behaviour is beyond dispute. What matters, however, is the degree of precision in prediction these regularities permit and whether positive economics can attain a useful degree of precision.

5. Normative economics consists of

   (i) predictions derived from positive economics which are, in principle, testable coupled with
   (ii) value judgments which cannot be tested.

QUESTIONS AND EXERCISES

1. Using the theory of beer production outlined in the text, generate *ceteris paribus* predictions for the results of (i) a 'heat wave' in July; (ii) an additional ten per cent tax on whisky in April; (iii) a social survey showing that beer is the most popular drink of the aristocracy published in March. In each case what is the precise meaning in terms of the theory of *ceteris paribus*?

2. What do we mean by saying that our predictions are in conformity with the facts? Plot on a graph the predicted values given by the table and compare them with the observed values. Plot also the difference between the predicted and observed values. Which is the 'better' theory? Why? Give your reasons. What can you learn from examining the errors?

Year	Actual value	Value predicted by:	
		Theory 1	Theory 2
1	100	100	101
2	51	51	50
3	43	44	42
4	43	44	41
5	47	49	49
6	62	64	61
7	81	83	82
8	111	113	112

3. Develop, on the general principles of our theory of beer production, an operational theory to explain the monthly production of automobiles in the United Kingdom. Use your theory to generate *ceteris paribus* predictions for the results of (i) an increase in the minimum deposit on hire purchase transactions; (ii) a reduction in purchase tax; (iii) a reduction in U.K. tariffs on imported cars. Treat each case separately and, for each prediction, give a precise meaning, in terms of your theory to *ceteris paribus*.

4. Can you develop an operational theory which would make it possible to test the proposition that 'The root cause of juvenile delinquency is simply broken homes'?

5. 'A tax on the television advertising of cigarettes, tobacco and alcohol could not fail to bring immense social benefits.' Analyse the propositions implied in this statement. Has it any meaning?

6. Is there any way of testing the following propositions?

   (i) Honesty is, in the long-run, always the best policy.
   (ii) The higher the rate of tax on increments in income the less the professional classes will be disposed to work.
   (iii) Virtue is always rewarded – in this world or the next.
   (iv) Woman are inferior (superior) to men.

7. Suppose you are the son (or daughter) of a brewer who tells you that he *neither* seeks to maximise his profits *nor* plans his monthly beer production to be equal to the previous month's consumption. Does his statement invalidate the theory put forward in this chapter? If not, why not?

8. According to Fig. 2.ii beer production has a general tendency (trend) to rise from 1958 to 1961, for each successive seasonal peak (and trough) is higher than its predecessor. Can this be explained in terms of the model in the text? If so how? If not what additions would you make to the theory to explain it? Give your reasons.

9. What are the obvious objections to the beer model in the text? How would you seek to improve it? In what way do your modifications change its predictions?

10. Assume that brewers commonly hold stocks of beer. On the basis of the model in the text – and Fig. 2.ii – graph the path of these stocks over time. Does this graph help you to answer Question 9?

11. 'No theory predicts with complete accuracy: there is always *some* error.' Do you agree? If so what is the difference between a 'prediction' derived from a theory and a 'guess'?

12. If the statement quoted in Question 11 is correct, how does science advance?
13. Meteorologists predict the weather. So do witch doctors. In what sense, if any, do they differ? If they do not is it correct to regard a witch doctor as a scientist? And vice versa?
14. 'That experience of privation in youth gives sound character in middle-age is amply attested by research.' Consider this statement. Do you think it reasonable? Can you think of the way in which research might have led to this conclusion?
15. 'Research has shown that those university departments that select their undergraduate entry by interview would have done better if they had picked them out with a pin.' How do you think this result could have been reached? Explain the logical processes involved.
16. 'The essence of science consists in specifying the range of error of a prediction. The advance of science consists in reducing the error.' Consider these statements carefully.
17. To many philosophers the distinction between positive and normative economics made in this chapter is unacceptable. Can you think of reasons why the distinction might break down?
18. 'Spare the rod and spoil the child.' 'Corporal punishment should be retained in schools because, while there is evidence that schoolmasters and senior boys enjoy inflicting it there is no evidence that it does any harm to those who suffer it.' Are either of these arguments scientific?

SUGGESTED READING

J. Robinson, *Economic Philosophy* (Pelican, 1962) ch. i.
F. Zeuthen, *Economic Theory and Method* (Longmans, 1955) chs. i–v.
R. G. Lipsey, *An Introduction to Positive Economics*, 2nd ed. (Weidenfeld & Nicolson, 1967) introduction and ch. i.
M. Friedman,† *Essays in Positive Economics* (Chicago, 1953) ch. i.
T. W. Hutchinson,† *The Significance and Basic Postulates of Economic Theory* (Macmillan, 1938).
A. R. Louch,† *Explanation and Human Action* (Oxford, 1966) chs. iv, v.
† More advanced reference.

3 Definition of Concepts and Measurement of Output

IN this chapter we define some of the concepts which we shall need to employ in describing how the economy operates and developing a theory to explain why the economy operates as it does.

Our picture of the economy, which is very much simplified, is this. Resources, which we shall call *factors of production* are combined in various ways, by *firms* or *enterprises*, to produce an annual flow of *goods* and *services*. We define these terms as follows

   (i) The *factors of production* are defined to be *land, labour* and *capital*.

  (ii) *Land* consists of natural resources provided free by nature: examples are mineral deposits, forests and, surprisingly enough, water in the form of rivers and natural lakes.

 (iii) *Capital* consists of all those aids to production which have been made by man. Examples are machinery, roads, houses, railways, tools, canals and man-made lakes.

 (iv) *Labour* consists of human resources. These are partly mental and partly physical. They are also partly inherited and partly acquired.

  (v) *Production* is the process of making goods and services which is organised by *enterprises*.

 (vi) *Enterprises* are organisations (which may take various legal forms such as public companies, private companies, partnerships, nationalised corporations) which take economic decisions.

 (vii) Those enterprises which take decisions relating to production we call *productive enterprises*.

This system of classification is set out schematically in Fig. 3.i. Here we see the factors of production, i.e. services of land, labour and capital, being organised as *inputs* by enterprises so as to produce an *output* of goods and services.

This flow of goods and services (or output) is available for the satisfaction of human wants. The process of using these goods and services for the satisfaction of immediate wants is called *consumption*; and goods that are used for this purpose we assume to be used up (or consumed) either at the moment of purchase or a very short

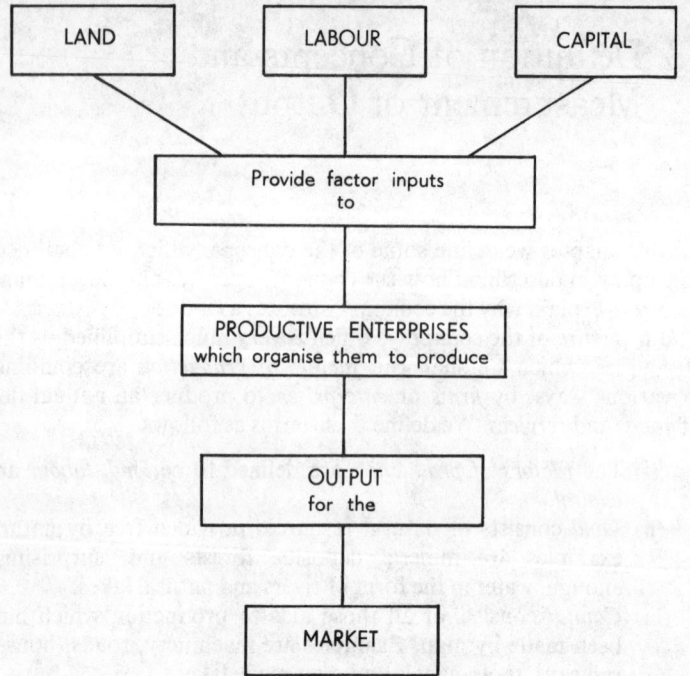

FIG. 3.i The organisation of production

while afterwards. Beer, for example, is an obvious type of consumption good and the purchase of beer an obvious form of *consumption expenditure*. In other cases such as expenditure on durable goods the distinction between *consumption* and *investment* is more difficult to draw.

Not all goods produced by the economy in any period are *consumed*. Some are added to the capital stock of the economy existing at the beginning of the period. *This process of adding to the capital stock is called investment*. Notice that this definition differs from popular usage.

Obviously, in any period, that part of output which is not *consumed* must be added to the capital stock existing at the beginning of the period. This increment in capital is, by definition, *investment*. Hence the total flow of output becoming available to the community in any period is, again by definition, equal to the sum of the flows of *expenditure* on *consumption* and *investment*. This equality, which is illustrated in Fig. 3.ii, can be simply expressed as follows:

$$pO \equiv pC + pI,$$

where

> pO is money value of the flow of goods and services in a given period;
> pC is money value of the flow of consumption expenditure in that period;
> pI is money value of the flow of investment expenditure in that period;
> p is the price level, i.e. the price of a unit of output.

So that

> O is the real flow of goods and services
> C is the real flow of consumption expenditure.
> I is the real flow of investment expenditure.

This equality is written with three horizontal lines instead of the usual two to indicate that it is an *identity which is always true* not an equation which is satisfied only for certain values of O, C and I.

The identity $pO \equiv pC + pI$ is illustrated in Fig. 3.ii where we have introduced the new concept *households*. A household is defined as an individual (or group of individuals) that receives income from the sale of factor services and engages in consumption expenditures. Though in practice the household sector of the economy does engage in investment expenditure also, we have assumed here, and in general shall continue to assume, that (i) all consumption expenditure is made by *households*; (ii) all investment expenditure is made by *productive enterprises*.

There is one difficulty here which needs to be faced if it is not to cause confusion. It relates to the meaning of investment expenditures.

As far as consumption expenditures are concerned, there is, in general, little difficulty in relating these expenditures to a money flow. By and large consumption goods are bought (by consumers) and sold (by enterprises) at identifiable market prices. As goods flow from enterprises to households, money flows from households to enterprises.

This analogy holds satisfactorily for investment where the investment of an enterprise consists in expenditure on some good (say a machine tool) which is produced and sold by some other enterprise. Again there is a money flow and an identifiable price.

Now consider the case (say of a farmer) where the investment by the farmer consists of the accumulation of inventories (stocks). Suppose, for example, the farmer grows a crop of which some part is sold to consumers. Again a money flow exists and there is an identifiable price. The remainder of the crop, that which is *unsold*, the farmer retains. It is thus an addition to his capital stock and, *by*

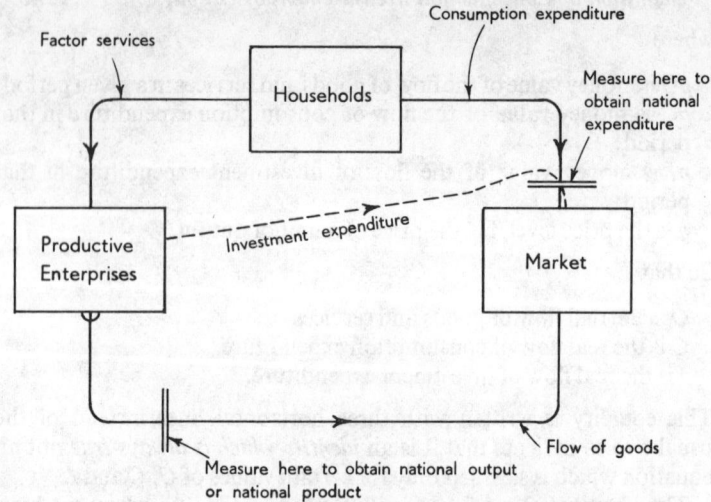

Factor services

Consumption expenditure

Households

Measure here to obtain national expenditure

Productive Enterprises

Investment expenditure

Market

Measure here to obtain national output or national product

Flow of goods

FIG. 3.ii National expenditure and national product

definition, constitutes investment. But there is no money flow. The farmer does not purchase this part of the crop for himself. Moreover there is *no* identifiable market price.

To deal with this situation we assume a *notional* expenditure by the farmer on the unsold part of his crop: that is an *investment* in the form of inventory accumulation. Moreover we value this investment at the price at which the remainder of the crop was sold in the market. On this basis the value of output in any period is, *by definition*, equal to the value of expenditure on output though not all expenditures now can be identified with *actual* money flows. Some consist in *notional* money flows.

Now $C+I$, if we measure it as a money flow, is simply the sum of the *expenditures*, valued at the prices ruling in the period, on output produced in the period and thus available for the satisfaction of human wants. Hence in any period the value of output, at the prices ruling in the period, is always by definition equal to the value of expenditure on that output. Thus for the economy of any country we may write:

the value of national output ≡ the value of national expenditure ≡ the value of consumption *plus* the value of investment.

The upshot of these simple considerations is that we have now developed a *set of rules* for measuring output. We add together the heterogeneous collection of goods and services becoming available in any period for the satisfaction of human wants by valuing each at its price. The resultant total is then expressible in terms of monetary units. It is simply the money value of national output or national product. For example suppose we picture a simple community which produces, in a given period, the following goods which become available for the satisfaction of human wants:

1000 loaves of bread
10 wheelbarrows
800 suits of clothes.

If the price of a loaf of bread is 5p, that of a wheelbarrow £2 and that of a suit £10 then the value of national output, at these prices, is

$$£[1000 \times \tfrac{1}{20}] + £[10 \times 2] + £[800 \times 10] = £8070.$$

We have thus established a method of adding together a heterogeneous collection of goods so as to produce a single readily comprehensible measure.

At this stage it is convenient to introduce four assumptions which are of considerable importance. In what follows we shall continue to assume (as we have in Fig. 3.ii) that

   (i) all *consumption* expenditure is made by *households*;
  (ii) all *investment* expenditure is made by *enterprises*;
 (iii) there is no government sector;
 (iv) that the economy does not engage in international trade.

On the basis of these assumptions we can now draw Fig. 3.iii. This shows a flow of *factor services* from *households* to *enterprises*. *Enterprises* use these services in *production*. The result is a flow of *goods* and *services* on to the *market*. The expenditure on goods and services is shown as a flow from *households* in the form of *consumption* plus a flow from *enterprises* in the form of *investment*.

If we measure the flow of goods and services from enterprises to the market, we obtain the value of *national output*. If we measure the flow of expenditure,† we obtain the value of *national expenditure*. These two totals are equal by definition. Or, as this proposition is usually stated and as we have stated it above,

national output ≡ national expenditure ≡ consumption + investment.

Fig. 3.iii is considerably more satisfactory than Fig. 3.ii for it shows where *households* obtain the incomes they spend on *consumption* and where *enterprises* obtain the resources they devote to *investment*. These two problems can now be explained more fully.

† Including the notional expenditure on stock accumulation.

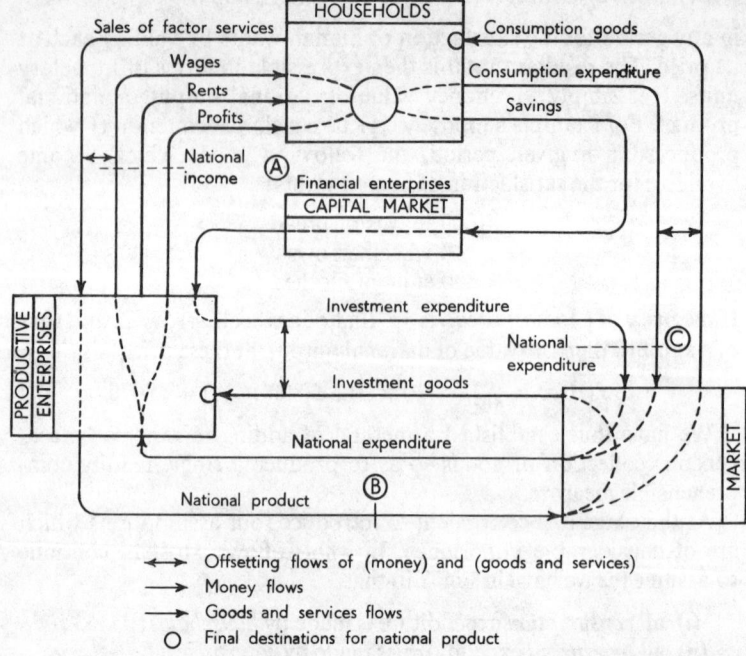

FIG. 3.iii The circular flow of income, output and expenditure

The factors of production used by enterprises are owned by the individuals who constitute households. In return for selling their factor services to enterprises these individuals receive rewards which constitute their *incomes*. For the sale of labour services, the reward is *wages*; for the sale of the services of land and buildings the reward is *rent*; for the sale of the services of capital (other than buildings) the reward is *profit*. These are definitions of *factor incomes* or, to the enterprise, *factor costs*. What is cost to one is income to another.

Two of these costs, *wages* and *rent*, are contractual. The third, *profit* is a *residual*. *Profit* is now *defined* as the difference between the value of output and the sum of *wages* plus *rents*, the contractual costs incurred in producing it. That is,

the value of output ≡ the values of wages + rent + profits.

National income may now be *defined* as the *sum of factor incomes generated by the process of production*. Hence:

$$\text{the value of national output} \equiv \text{wages} + \text{rent} + \text{profits} \equiv \text{national income}.$$

Combining this *identity* with those on earlier pages we have:

$$\frac{\text{national}}{\text{output}} \equiv \frac{\text{national}}{\text{income}} \equiv \frac{\text{wages}+\text{rent}}{+\text{profits}} \equiv \frac{\text{consumption}}{+\text{investment}} \equiv \frac{\text{national}}{\text{expenditure}} \cdot$$

This is the fundamental identity of what is called national income accounting. It is always true because we have defined our terms so that it must be. In short, the three aggregates national income, national output and national expenditure are simply three ways of looking at the same thing.

The simple extension of our conceptual scheme shows where households obtain the income they spend, in part, upon consumption. How do they dispose of the whole of it?

Households do not invest. Hence their income must either be *consumed* or *not consumed*. The act of abstaining from consumption we define as *saving*. Hence, from the income disposal side,

$$\frac{\text{national}}{\text{income}} \equiv \frac{\text{sum of wages}+\text{rent}}{+\text{profits}} \equiv \text{consumption } plus \text{ saving}.$$

However we already know that national income is identically equal to national expenditure which is identically equal to consumption *plus* investment. Hence:

$$\frac{\text{national}}{\text{income}} \equiv \frac{\text{consumption}}{+\text{saving}} \equiv \frac{\text{national}}{\text{expenditure}} \equiv \frac{\text{consumption}}{+\text{investment}} \cdot$$

So it is obvious that

$$\text{saving} \equiv \text{investment}.$$

We thus reach the conclusion that, *as far as our national income accounting framework is concerned, saving and investment are always identically equal. That is, they are equal by definition.*

The commonsense of this result should be obvious. If in some period a part of the national product is not consumed then, by definition, it is saved. It must therefore be added to the capital stock existing in the economy at the beginning of the period. But we have already defined the process of adding to the capital stock as investment. Hence saving and investment, *as we have here defined them*, are simply two different ways of looking at the same quantity of output.

Now this *identity* between the accounting concepts of savings and investment has, surprisingly enough, caused a lot of confusion. The student should remember (i) that it is an identity which is true by definition; (ii) that it refers to the *results* of past decisions and does not tell us whether those results were expected or unexpected, wanted or unwanted. These are important points, for in the accounting sense, precisely the same identity holds between demand and supply.

This can easily be seen as follows. The value of demand in any period can be defined as the value of purchases on the market for all that is purchased must be demanded. That is:

$$\text{value of demand} \equiv \text{value of purchases.}$$

The value of supply on the other hand must be equal to the value of sales for all that is sold must be supplied. Hence;

$$\text{value of supply} \equiv \text{value of sales.}$$

Now since sales $\equiv$ purchases (they are merely two aspects of the same set of transactions) demand must equal supply *by definition*. This means that, in accounting terms, demand and supply are always identically equal.

Though this last statement is correct, *on these definitions*, it does not prevent our arguing that demand and supply may be unequal, for when we do *we are using the terms in different senses. Analogously there are, as we shall see, senses in which saving and investment can be unequal.* In later chapters we shall refer to saving and investment in the accounting sense as actual saving and actual investment. Hence the identity above merely states that

$$\text{actual } or \text{ accounting saving} \equiv \text{actual } or \text{ accounting investment}$$

and does not preclude there being other important senses in which saving and investment *need not* be equal except in special circumstances.

We have now answered the question of where the *enterprises* obtain the real resources to devote to *investment*. The answer is, in our conceptual scheme, from the *saving* of *households*. The financial flows by which the saving of households is made available to enterprises does not at present concern us. We merely note that they usually occur through the medium of *financial enterprises* – such as banks, building societies and finance houses – which we define as constituting the *capital market*.

Thus Fig. 3.iii sets out the full conceptual framework which we have elaborated. This diagram depicts what is often called the circular flow of income, expenditure and output. If we enter the diagram at the point *A*, we measure the sum of wages *plus* profits *plus* rents – that is, national income. If we enter at *B* we measure the value of the flow of goods and services produced by enterprises – that is national output or national product. If we enter at *C* we measure the value of consumption *plus* investment – that is, national expenditure. Whichever point of entry we choose, the total we arrive at will be the same for, as we have seen,

$$\begin{matrix} \text{the value of} \\ \text{national output} \\ \text{(or national product)} \end{matrix} \equiv \begin{matrix} \text{the value of} \\ \text{national income} \end{matrix} \equiv \begin{matrix} \text{the value of} \\ \text{national expenditure} \end{matrix}.$$

QUESTIONS AND EXERCISES

1. 'It is evident that everything produced in an economy during a period such as a year must have been used up by someone during the period or added to what someone possessed at the beginning of the period. Therefore national output must be equal to national expenditure.' Explain.

2. What is the purpose of measuring national product and expenditure? How far do expenditure estimates represent money flows?

3. Can consumption exceed national income? If so what are the implications of such an excess for saving and investment? Illustrate your answer by reference to a situation in which

    national income $\equiv$ £10,000 m.
    consumption $\equiv$ £11,500 m.

4. 'Driving tests do not measure driving skill. They measure whatever qualities are necessary to pass driving tests. In the same way national income is whatever it is that the national income estimates measure.' Discuss critically.

5. 'The national income is a measure of the money value of goods and services becoming available to the nation from economic activity. It can be regarded in three ways: as a sum of incomes derived from economic activity . . . ; as a sum of expenditure . . . ; or as a sum of the products of the various industries of the nation.' *National Accounts Statistics. Sources and Methods.* Explain.

6. From *Economic Trends* table A, prepare a table showing quarterly estimates of gross domestic product at factor cost for 1962–72 (i) at current prices; (ii) at 1963 prices; (iii) unadjusted; (iv) seasonally adjusted.

    Why do you think the authorities provide four estimates in this way? What is the point of providing a 'seasonally adjusted' series?

7. Express consumers' expenditure, gross fixed capital formation at home and the value of physical increase in stocks and work in progress as proportions of gross domestic product. Which item shows the 'greater fluctuations'?

8. What is the meaning of the negative investment in stocks in the fourth quarter of 1962 and the first quarter of 1968? Can gross fixed capital formation ever be negative?

9. From *Economic Trends* show that gross domestic expenditure is gross expenditure on the domestic product and not gross expenditure by home nationals. What is the distinction? In what circumstances would the two concepts be identical?

SUGGESTED READING

R. Marris,† *Economic Arithmetic* (Macmillan, 1958) chs. i–iii.

J. R. Hicks,† *The Social Framework* (Oxford, 1971).

H. C. Edey and A. T. Peacock,† *National Income and Social Accounting* (Hutchinson, 1969).

C.S.O., *National Accounts Statistics: Sources and Methods* (H.M.S.O., 1968) chs. i–iv.

C.S.O., *National Income and Expenditure* (H.M.S.O. Annual publication).

E. Devons, *An Introduction to British Economic Statistics* (Cambridge, 1958) chs i, ix.

† Alternative reference.

4 National Income and National Product

IN the last chapter we erected a consistent set of definitions which provided us with a conceptual scheme in terms of which we can (and shall) describe economic behaviour. How do we measure the concepts we have defined? The easiest way of answering this question is to construct, and work through, a simple example.

1 NATIONAL OUTPUT OR NATIONAL PRODUCT

Suppose we assume an economy with only two firms and that, at the end of the period for which we wish to prepare accounts, the books of these concerns reveal the following information.

Table 4.1   *Hypothetical data: Firms A and B*

FIRM *A*

Allocations		Receipts	
Purchases from *B*	2,300	*Sales*	
Wages	15,000	to households	20,000
Rent	3,000	to firm *B*	14,000
Profit (residual)	13,700		
	34,000		34,000

FIRM *B*

Purchases from *A*	14,000	*Sales*	
Wages	15,300	to households	24,000
Rent	3,300	to firm *A*	2,300
Profit (residual)	5,700	Addition to stocks†	6,000
		Addition to fixed capital†	6,000
	38,300		38,300

† Notional sale.

We now wish to prepare an estimate of national product (or output). If we sum the sales of the two firms we obtain the figure £72,300. Is this a correct estimate of the national product?

Looking back to our conceptual framework we know that

national product ≡ national income ≡ wages + rents + profits.

If, however, we add the factor incomes we obtain:

$$\frac{\text{national}}{\text{income}} \equiv \text{wages} + \text{rent} + \text{profits}$$

$$\equiv £(15{,}000 + 15{,}300) + £(3000 + 3300) + £(13{,}700 + 5700)$$

$$\equiv £56{,}000.$$

This result is, *by definition*, impossible. What has gone wrong? The answer is simply that the total value of sales is *not* the same thing as the value of national product. The latter is correctly interpreted as the sum of the values produced by *each firm alone*. This we have not measured. For, as the table shows, in estimating the value of output of Firm A we have included the value of output it purchased from Firm B. And, demonstrating consistency in error, we have repeated this procedure with B. We have thus double counted.

We avoid this difficulty by defining

$$\frac{\text{national}}{\text{output}} \equiv \frac{\text{national}}{\text{product}} \equiv \frac{\text{sum of the value added}}{\text{by firms in the economy}}$$

and

$$\frac{\text{value added}}{\text{(of any firm)}} \equiv \text{sales of the firm} - \text{purchases from other firms}$$

$$\equiv \text{addition to the value of the product attributable to the firm in question alone.}$$

Applying these definitions to Table 4.1 we obtain:

$$\frac{\text{national}}{\text{product}} \equiv \text{value added by } A \text{ *plus* value added by } B$$

$$\equiv [\text{sales by } A - \text{purchases from } B]$$
$$\quad + [\text{sales by } B - \text{purchases from } A]$$

$$\equiv £[34{,}000 - 2300] + £[38{,}300 - 14{,}000]$$

$$\equiv £31{,}700 + £24{,}300$$

$$\equiv £56{,}000.$$

The reasoning behind this procedure is readily demonstrated by considering (say) a pint of beer selling at 12p. Tracing this back through the productive process we might have:

Table 4.2

Stages of productive process	Value of sales	Cost of materials	Value added
1. Farmer sells hops to dealer	0·5p	nil	0·5p
2. Dealer sells hops to brewer	0·7p	0·5p	0·2p
3. Brewer sells beer to publican	6·0p	0·7p	5·3p
4. Publican sells beer to consumer	12·0p	6·0p	6·0p
	19·2p	7·2p	12·0p

In this table the total value of all sales is 19·2p; the total value of intermediate sales is 7·2p. Hence the total *value added* by the farmer, dealer, brewer and publican is: the sum of sales – purchases from other firms = 12p. What this means is that we cannot count in the national product the value of the hops sold by the farmer *and* the whole value of the beer of which they become part. And this, as the reader can see, is precisely the error we made in summing the sales of Firms *A* and *B* to obtain national product. It was this error which resulted in arithmetic inequality of national product and national income: an inequality inadmissible by definition.

2 NATIONAL EXPENDITURE

National expenditure is the total expenditure on the national product. As we know national expenditure ≡ consumption *plus* investment. Consumption expenditure is recorded as sales to households by both firms. This amounts to £44,000. We know also that Firm *B* added to its stocks by £6000. There is thus a *notional* expenditure of £6000 on investment since, as we have defined investment, an addition to stocks constitutes investment. There is also a £6000 addition to the fixed capital of Firm *B*. Hence we have:

$$\text{national expenditure} \equiv \text{expenditure on the national product} \equiv$$
$$\text{consumption } \textit{plus} \text{ investment}$$
$$\equiv £44,000 + £12,000$$
$$\equiv £56,000.$$

3 NATIONAL INCOME AND DEPRECIATION

In the previous chapter we stated that

$$\text{national income} \equiv \text{national product} \equiv \text{national expenditure};$$
$$\text{national income} \equiv \text{wages} + \text{rents} + \text{profits}$$

We now need to examine this more closely.

The concept of national income is of interest because it measures the flow of factor incomes generated by the production of output in the current period available to satisfy human wants. What then do we mean by 'income'?

What we usually mean by income in any period is the amount which the income recipient *could* consume and leave himself as well off at the end of the period as he was at its beginning. There are, of course, immense difficulties in saying what is meant by 'as well-off as'. Nevertheless it is clear that, to obtain a measure of income, allowance must be made for that part of the output of the current period which is due *not* to economic activity in the current period but to economic activity *in past periods*. How does this arise?

In any period some part of the output produced is attributable to the using up of capital equipment existing at the beginning of the period. To arrive at income, therefore, it is necessary to subtract from output of the current period a sum which is sufficient to restore the capital at the end of the period to what it was at the beginning of the period. Failure to make such a subtraction results in an over-estimate of income and hence of the flow of goods and services which can be consumed without becoming worse off and, what is the same thing, the flow attributable to the economic activity of the current period.

To make this correction we set aside an annual sum to cover *depreciation*. Our identities now become:

$$\text{national income} \equiv \text{wages} + \text{rents} + [\text{profits} - \text{depreciation}]$$
$$\equiv \text{wages} + \text{rents} + net \text{ profits,}$$

where

$$net \text{ profits} \equiv \text{gross profits} - \text{depreciation.}$$

On the expenditure side we have

$$\frac{\text{gross national}}{\text{expenditure}} \equiv \text{consumption} + gross \text{ investment.}$$

$$\frac{\text{net national}}{\text{expenditure}} \equiv \text{consumption} + [gross \text{ investment} - \text{depreciation}]$$

$$\equiv \text{consumption} + [net \text{ investment}]$$
$$\equiv \text{gross national expenditure} - \text{depreciation.}$$

And on the output side we have:

$$\frac{\text{gross national}}{\text{product}} \equiv \text{gross values added;}$$

$$\frac{\text{net national}}{\text{product}} \equiv \text{gross national product} - \text{depreciation.}$$

So that:

$$\frac{\text{national}}{\text{income}} \equiv \frac{net \text{ national}}{\text{expenditure}} \equiv \frac{net \text{ national}}{\text{product}} .$$

Formally speaking these adjustments are simple enough. But this is because we have avoided the problem of saying *how the value of depreciation should be calculated*. This is a difficult question the discussion of which would take us too far afield. It is worth noting, however, that in the United Kingdom, because of the difficulty of calculating the proper annual allowance for depreciation, the estimates of national income and expenditure did not contain an estimate of *net investment* until 1956. Since that date the Central Statistical Office has been prepared to publish a figure based upon rather detailed calculations of 'capital consumption'.† The caution of the C.S.O. in this matter serves to remind us of the complex problems involved in the calculation of the appropriate adjustment.

4 The Introduction of Government

So far we have proceeded on the convenient assumption that our economic system contains no government. This assumption we shall now relax. As a result our conceptual system will become more realistic. The cost of this additional realism is additional complication.

In a modern 'mixed economy' the government (or, as we shall call it, the *public sector*) undertakes the following activities

(i) through the nationalised corporations the public sector produces a part of output which is sold on the market like the output of any private enterprise;

(ii) the public sector undertakes expenditure on the provision of common services such as defence, education, law and justice, which are, in general, not sold on any market;

(iii) in addition the public sector makes payments to individuals in the form of social service benefits. These payments as we shall presently explain are called *transfer payments*;

(iv) finally the public sector imposes taxes.

Our problem is how to integrate these activities into the system of national accounts.

Item (i) causes no difficulty. The ownership of an enterprise is clearly irrelevant in determining its contribution to national product. Public enterprises are thus to be dealt with precisely like private

† On this point the reader should consult *National Accounts Statistics: Sources and Methods*, and *National Income and Expenditure* – the latter published annually by H.M.S.O. and hereafter referred to as the Blue Book.

enterprises and their values added, calculated in the usual way, form part of national product. Hence the expenditure on their output forms part of national expenditure and the factor incomes generated by their activities form part of national income. This accords with commonsense since it would obviously be absurd to include the operations of (say) the coal industry in national product if it were privately owned and exclude them if it were publicly owned.

Item (ii) is more troublesome. The first problem is a conceptual one. Should the common services performed by the public sector be regarded as part of national product or not? Alternatively does it make more sense to regard, let us say, the provision of education, as an intermediate rather than a final product – an expense which must be incurred if output is to be produced at all? In practice the statisticians responsible for the U.K. National Income estimates solve this problem by *adopting the convention* of including *all* common services provided by the public sector as part of national product. This convention thus disposes in practice of the question of principle involved. But now a second problem arises. If we are to include these common services in national product how are we to value them?

This valuation problem arises because these services are not sold upon a market. They therefore have no identifiable price. *The solution adopted is to value such services at the cost of providing them.* This cost is, of course, the value of the factor incomes (wages and rents) paid to the persons who provide them. Hence the value of the common services provided by the public sector appears

(i) in national expenditure as   public sector expenditure on goods and services;

(ii) in national output as   the value of the output of common services;

(iii) in national income as   the factor incomes generated by their production.

In short once we have agreed to the convention that includes these services in output, we have *defined* expenditure on them as part of national expenditure and the factor costs of providing them as part of national income.

If we now incorporate these modifications into our basic identities we have:

$$
\begin{array}{l}
\text{gross national} \\
\text{product}
\end{array}
\equiv
\begin{array}{l}
\text{gross value of} \\
\text{output of} \\
\text{private sector}
\end{array}
+
\begin{array}{l}
\text{gross value of} \\
\text{output of} \\
\text{public sector}
\end{array}
$$

$$\equiv \begin{array}{c} \text{gross value of} \\ \text{output of} \\ \text{private sector} \end{array} + \begin{array}{c} \text{gross value} \\ \text{added by} \\ \text{public enterprises} \end{array} + \begin{array}{c} \text{value of} \\ \text{public sector's} \\ \text{common services.} \end{array}$$

On the expenditure side the adjustment is straightforward. We have:

$$\begin{array}{c} \text{gross national} \\ \text{expenditure} \end{array} \equiv \text{consumption} + \text{gross investment} + \begin{array}{c} \text{government} \\ \text{expenditure on} \\ \text{common services} \end{array}$$

In practice, however, some part of gross investment is undertaken by the public sector. Hence the national expenditure identity can be expanded to read:

$$\begin{array}{c} \text{gross} \\ \text{national} \\ \text{expenditure} \end{array} \equiv \text{consumption} + \left\{ \begin{array}{c} \textit{gross} \text{ investment by private sector} \\ + \\ \text{gross investment by public sector} \end{array} \right\}$$

$$+ \text{ government (public sector) expenditure on common services.}$$

On the income side

national income $\equiv$ wages + rents + (gross profits − depreciation)

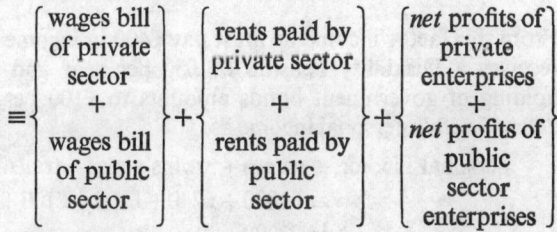

$$\equiv \left\{ \begin{array}{c} \text{wages bill} \\ \text{of private} \\ \text{sector} \\ + \\ \text{wages bill} \\ \text{of public} \\ \text{sector} \end{array} \right\} + \left\{ \begin{array}{c} \text{rents paid by} \\ \text{private sector} \\ + \\ \text{rents paid by} \\ \text{public} \\ \text{sector} \end{array} \right\} + \left\{ \begin{array}{c} \textit{net} \text{ profits of} \\ \text{private} \\ \text{enterprises} \\ + \\ \textit{net} \text{ profits of} \\ \text{public} \\ \text{sector} \\ \text{enterprises} \end{array} \right\}$$

As we have seen the problems so far raised by government economic activity are two. The basic conceptual problem is that of *defining* product. The subsidiary problem is that of *valuing* product. Once conventions are adopted to deal with these, the adjustment of our original identities presents no difficulties. The result is to make our main aggregate slightly more complicated. In return the information they provide is more comprehensive. That is all.

We now turn to consider items (iii) and (iv) and ask the question: What complications occur as the result of the raising of taxation by the public sector and the payment of transfers by the public sector?

We begin by classifying taxes into two groups: *direct* and *indirect*. *Direct taxes* are those imposed upon persons or enterprises. The most important example of them is *income tax*. *Indirect taxes* are levied not upon persons but on commodities. The most familiar example here is *purchase tax*.†

In addition to levying taxes the government also makes what are called *transfer payments*. These are defined as payments made to persons which are not classifiable as payments made for the provision of a productive service. *Old age pensions, unemployment benefits and disability pensions* are examples of such payments. So too is the *interest on the national debt*.

Transfer payments of this kind can be regarded as negative direct taxes. Neither type of transaction modifies any of the concepts we have so far defined. Taken together, however, direct taxes and transfer payments cause what are called *personal incomes* and *personal disposable incomes* to differ from the sum of net factor incomes ($\equiv$ national income). It is easy to see why this should be. Consider some (hypothetical) individual called Smith who receives the following *factor incomes* in a given year:

	£
Wages	1800
Profits	240
Rents	100
	£2140

From this factor income he must pay £400 in income tax. Smith also receives a Disability Pension of £50 per year and interest on his holding of government bonds amounts to £100 per year. We then define Smith's personal income as:

$$\text{personal income} \equiv \text{wages} + \text{profits} + \text{rent} + \text{transfer receipts}$$
$$\equiv £1800 + £240 + £100 + £100 + £50$$
$$\equiv £2290$$

and his personal disposable income as:

$$\left.\begin{array}{l}\text{personal disposable}\\\text{income}\end{array}\right\} \equiv \text{personal income} - \text{direct taxation}$$
$$\equiv \text{wages} + \text{rent} + \text{profits} + \text{transfer receipts}$$
$$- \text{direct taxation}$$
$$\equiv £2290 - £400$$
$$= £1890$$

We must now take account of indirect taxes and subsidies. The effect of an indirect tax is to raise the *market price* of a commodity

† Now replaced by V.A.T.

above its *factor cost*. A subsidy, which is, from this point of view, a negative indirect tax simply does the reverse. For example suppose the factor cost of a packet of 20 cigarettes is 30p made up as follows:

Wages	20p
Rent	7p
Profits	3p
	30p

If the government now imposes a tax of 10p per packet, the *market price* becomes $30p + 10p = 40p$.

The effect of indirect taxes (and subsidies) is therefore to complicate matters slightly by giving us two sets of prices at which output, expenditure and income may be valued, namely, *market prices* and *factor costs*. The two are related by the definition:

$$\text{market price} \equiv \text{factor cost} + (\text{indirect taxes} - \text{subsidies})$$
$$\equiv \text{factor cost} + \text{net indirect taxes}.$$

The adjustment defined by this identity may be applied to a single commodity (as we have applied it) or to any one of our aggregates. Thus:

$$\left\{ \begin{array}{c} \text{gross national product} \\ \text{(at market prices) } less \\ \text{net indirect taxes } equals \\ \text{gross national product} \\ \text{(at factor cost)} \end{array} \right\} \equiv \left\{ \begin{array}{c} \text{gross national expenditure} \\ \text{(at market prices) } less \\ \text{net indirect taxes } equals \\ \text{gross national expenditure} \\ \text{(at factor cost)} \end{array} \right\}$$

We have not shown the corresponding adjustment on the income side since, by convention, national income, which is simply the sum of net factor income, is always valued at *factor cost*.

These, in outline, are the principal modifications to our conceptual scheme made necessary by the introduction of public sector activity. None of the changes is unduly complicated in principle and, as the example at the end of this chapter makes clear, it is a simple matter to handle the modifications in practice.

5 The Introduction of International Trade

So far, simply as a matter of convenience, we have proceeded on the assumption that our hypothetical economy does not engage in international trade – that is, is a 'closed' economy. This assumption is unrealistic. Accordingly we must relax it. This requires that we adjust our system of accounts to allow for the influence of the sale of goods to foreigners, i.e. *visible* exports, the sale of services to foreigners, i.e. *invisible* exports; and the corresponding purchases from foreigners, i.e. *visible and invisible imports*.

To see what is necessary here, consider the expenditure side. Without international trade we have:

gross national expenditure (at market prices)

$$\equiv \text{consumption} + \begin{matrix}\text{gross}\\\text{investment}\end{matrix} + \begin{matrix}\text{public sector}\\\text{expenditure on}\\\text{final output}\\\text{(all at market prices)}\end{matrix}$$

$$\equiv \quad C \quad + \quad I \quad + \quad G$$

Now the expenditure of foreigners on our goods and services is, by definition, *exports* which we write as E. Clearly this forms part of the total expenditure on our national product. E must therefore be *added* to $C+I+G$.

Equally some part of $C+I+G$ will be spent on the goods and services produced by foreigners. By definition the sum of these expenditures is equal to the value of *imports* which we write as M. To arrive at the value of expenditure on our national product we must *subtract* M from $C+I+G+E$. Hence we have:

gross national expenditure $\equiv C+I+G+E-M$.

On the *output* side we now need to calculate *value added* for each firm as:

total sales (including exports) *less* purchases from other firms (including imports).

Obviously the sum of the value added by all firms, since intermediate purchases and sales cancel out, is then:

$$\begin{matrix}\text{Sales to}\end{matrix}\qquad\qquad\begin{matrix}\text{Purchases from}\end{matrix}$$

$$\left\{\begin{matrix}\text{households (consumption)}\\\text{enterprises (investment)}\\\text{government (government}\\\text{expenditure)}\\\text{foreigners (exports)}\end{matrix}\right\}\textit{less}\text{ foreigners (imports)}$$

which is identical with $C+I+G+E-M$ as it must be.

Finally national income can be obtained from the factor incomes generated in producing gross national product or output. To obtain these we first adjust G.N.P. to a net basis by subtracting depreciation or capital consumption. Next we subtract net indirect taxes to obtain N.N.P. at factor cost. This, as we have already seen, is equal to the sum of factor incomes which is, by definition, national income.

Table 4.3 *National Income Accounting: Principal Aggregates*

	consumers' expenditure		income from employment
plus	public authorities' current exp.	plus	income from self employment
plus	gross fixed capital formation at home	plus	gross trading profits of companies
plus	value of physical increase in stocks and work in progress	plus	gross trading surplus of public corporations
plus	Exports and income received from abroad	plus	gross profits of other public enterprises
minus	imports and income paid abroad	plus	rent
		plus	residual error
		minus	stock appreciation
equals	gross national exp. at market prices	equals	gross domestic product at factor cost
minus	taxes on expenditure	plus	income from abroad (net)
plus	subsidies		
		equals	gross national product at factor cost
equals	gross national exp. at factor cost	minus	capital consumption
minus	capital consumption		
		equals	national income
equals	net national exp. at factor cost	plus	transfers to persons
		minus	undistributed profits
		minus	surpluses of public enterprises and corporations
		equals	personal income
		minus	direct taxes on persons
		equals	personal disposable income

We can now summarise the relationships between the principal aggregates in tabular form. Before we do this, however, we need to make an adjustment due to the fact that in some countries, of which the United Kingdom is one, a part of the income received by households is derived from the ownership of property overseas. Analogously some property in the United Kingdom is owned by foreigners hence the income arising out of its productive services is paid to overseas residents. We thus have an item:

$$\text{net income} \atop \text{from abroad} \equiv \text{income receipts} \atop \text{from abroad} - \text{income payments} \atop \text{to abroad} \quad .$$

Clearly this item is part of national income. Equally clearly it does not arise out of production within the domestic economy. To meet this problem we distinguish between gross domestic product (the result of the productive process within the economy) and gross national product. These are related as follows:

G.N.P. $\equiv$ G.D.P. + net income from abroad.

national income $\equiv$ net domestic product + net income from abroad

gross national expenditure $\equiv C + I + G + E - M +$ net income from abroad

net domestic product $\equiv$ gross domestic product – depreciation.

The reader should now carefully examine Table 4.3 and compare it with the latest Blue Book.

6 THE SAVING–INVESTMENT IDENTITY

In our simple system of accounting identities we showed that

$$\left. {S \atop \text{Saving}} \right\} \equiv \left. {I \atop \text{Investment}} \right\}$$

where these two concepts were defined net (of depreciation) or gross. How must this identity be modified to take account of our introduction of government and international trade?

Let us begin by recalling that we now have three sources of *net* saving:

    (i) households;
   (ii) enterprises;
  (iii) public sector;

and three classifications of *net* investment:

   (iv) *net* investment of private enterprises } net investment at
    (v) *net* investment of public sector;   } home
  (vi) *net* investment overseas.

Our identity therefore expands to:

$$
\begin{array}{c}
\textit{net} \\
\text{household} \\
\text{saving}
\end{array}
+
\begin{array}{c}
\textit{net} \\
\text{saving of} \\
\text{enterprises}
\end{array}
+
\begin{array}{c}
\textit{net} \\
\text{saving of} \\
\text{public sector}
\end{array}
\equiv
\begin{array}{c}
\textit{net} \\
\text{investment} \\
\text{at home}
\end{array}
+
\begin{array}{c}
\textit{net} \\
\text{investment} \\
\text{overseas.}
\end{array}
$$

To show how this extension occurs consider first the net saving of households. This is given by:

$$
\begin{array}{c}
\textit{net} \\
\text{personal} \\
\text{saving}
\end{array}
\equiv
\begin{array}{c}
\text{personal} \\
\text{disposable} \\
\text{income}
\end{array}
-
\begin{array}{c}
\text{household} \\
\text{consumption}
\end{array}
$$

$$
\equiv
\begin{array}{c}
\text{national} \\
\text{income}
\end{array}
-
\begin{array}{c}
\text{undis-} \\
\text{tributed} \\
\text{profits}
\end{array}
+
\begin{array}{c}
\text{transfer} \\
\text{incomes}
\end{array}
-
\begin{array}{c}
\text{direct} \\
\text{taxes on} \\
\text{persons}
\end{array}
-
\begin{array}{c}
\text{household} \\
\text{consumption}
\end{array}
$$

Now

$$
\text{national income } (Y_n) \equiv \frac{\text{net national product}}{\text{at market prices } Y} - \text{net indirect taxes } (T_i)
$$

so, writing:

$$
\begin{aligned}
U &\equiv \text{undistributed profits} \\
R &\equiv \text{transfer incomes} \\
T_h &\equiv \text{direct taxes on households,}
\end{aligned}
$$

we have:

net personal saving $(S_h) \equiv$

$$
\begin{array}{c}
\text{national} \\
\text{income} \\
(Y - T_i)
\end{array}
-
\begin{array}{c}
\text{undis-} \\
\text{tributed} \\
\text{profits } (U)
\end{array}
+
\begin{array}{c}
\text{transfer} \\
\text{incomes } (R)
\end{array}
-
\begin{array}{c}
\text{direct} \\
\text{taxes on} \\
\text{h'holds } (T_h)
\end{array}
-
\begin{array}{c}
\text{consump-} \\
\text{tion of} \\
\text{h'holds } (C_h).
\end{array}
$$

The *net* saving of the public sector we define as S_g.

$$
S_g \equiv
\begin{array}{c}
\text{total tax} \\
\text{receipts } (T_i + T_h)
\end{array}
- \text{transfers } (R) -
\begin{array}{c}
\text{public sector current} \\
\text{expenditure on goods} \\
\text{and services } (C_g).
\end{array}
$$

The *net* saving of enterprises is a new concept to us for, so far, we have assumed enterprises not to save. However where profits are not distributed – and thus do not enter personal disposable income – enterprises whether public or private are saving.
Hence we define

net saving of enterprises $(S_e) \equiv$ undistributed profits (U).

Adding household, public sector and enterprises' saving we have:

$$S = S_h + S_g + S_e$$

$$
\underset{\substack{\text{net saving} \\ \equiv \text{of h'holds} \\ (Y - T_i - U + R - T_h - C_h)}}{} + \underset{\substack{\text{net saving} \\ \text{of public} \\ \text{sector} \\ (T_i + T_h - R - C_g)}}{} + \underset{\substack{\text{net} \\ \text{saving of} \\ \text{enterprises } (U)}}{}
$$

$$\equiv Y - (C_h + C_g),$$

which is obviously net national product (Y) – consumption (C) as before. In short we still have $S \equiv Y - C$ just as we did in our earliest set of accounts.

On the investment side we have:

$I_e \equiv$ *net* investment of enterprises

$I_g \equiv$ *net* investment by public sector

$I_f \equiv$ *net* investment overseas $\equiv$ exports (E) – imports (M)†

Our saving-investment identity therefore becomes:

$$
\left\{ \begin{array}{c} S \\ S_h + S_g + S_e \\ Y - C \end{array} \right\} \equiv \left\{ \begin{array}{c} I \\ I_e + I_g + I_f \\ I_e + I_g + (E - M) \end{array} \right\},
$$

or, rearranging the items slightly,

$$Y \equiv C + (I_e + I_g) + (E - M)$$
$$\equiv (C_h + C_g) + (I_e + I_g) + (E - M).$$

Now total public sector expenditure on goods and services (G) is obviously $G \equiv C_g + I_g$. Hence:

$$Y \equiv C_h + I_e + G + (E - M),$$

which is the net national expenditure identity we have already met.

All this may seem a trifle complicated but in practice all we have done is

(i) to expand the basic definition of *net* saving ($S = Y - C$) into three elements:

(a) $S_h \equiv$ *net* savings of households;

(b) $S_e \equiv$ *net* savings of enterprises;

(c) $S_g \equiv$ *net* savings of public sector;

† An excess of exports (receipts) over imports (payments) means that domestic nationals are accumulating assets overseas (usually in the form of foreign currency, bank balances or securities). These claims on foreigners form part of the capital of the country. Hence an increase in them constitutes investment.

(ii) to show that *net* investment now consists of three elements:

(a) I_e ≡ *net* investment by enterprises;
(b) I_g ≡ *net* investment by the public sector;
(c) I_f ≡ *net* investment overseas; and

(iii) to demonstrate, what should be obvious, that our fundamental identity of $S \equiv I$ still remains.

7 MONEY AND 'REAL' VALUES

We have now set out a conceptual framework in terms of which we can (i) describe how the economic system has behaved; and (ii) seek to develop a theory to explain *why* it behaved as it did. This conceptual system defines for us, and tells us how, in principle, we are to measure, the money value of certain flows in any given accounting period. This is helpful. But it does not give us all the information we want. For many purposes, particularly when we seek to compare different years (*or* quarters *or* months) it is not the *money value of output* which primarily interests us but its *real* value – the *quantity* of (different) goods and services to which the measured money value corresponds. For it is *real* output that satisfies human wants and it is to produce *real* output that enterprises must organise the input of *real* factor services. Accordingly we need a measure of real output or a method of converting our money value of output – and, of course, other associated aggregates – into real terms.

In practice there are four methods of obtaining such estimates.

The first is to revalue the quantities of goods and services *produced* in each year in terms of the prices of some particular base year – for example 1963. This is called the *output* or *production* method.

The second is to conduct a similar exercise from the *expenditure side*. In this case we revalue each item of expenditure in any year at the prices ruling in some base year.

The third, obviously enough, is to perform the same exercise from the *income side*.

Since income, expenditure and output are defined to be equal, whether measured in money or 'real' terms, if we had complete information the results of these methods would be identical. Each would provide an estimated value of output (expenditure) in any year valued at constant (base year) prices. In practice our information is not complete. The methods therefore provide slightly different results as they do for estimates in money terms. But, as the following table shows the results are in close conformity.

The fourth method is to estimate the extent to which *prices* have changed, from one period to another, by a *price index number*. This simply expresses the prices of any given year as a ratio of the prices

Table 4.4   *Indices of Gross Domestic Product at 1963 Factor Cost, U.K.*

Year	Expenditure method	Output method	Income method
1960	92	94	93
1961	95	96	95
1962	96	97	96
1963	100	100	100
1964	105	106	106
1965	108	109	109
1966	110	111	111
1967	113	113	113
1968	116	117	117
1969	119	120	119
1970	121	122	121
1971	122	124	121

Source: Blue Book.

in some chosen *base year* in which the price index is taken to be 100 (or unity).

Armed with this estimate we can then *deflate* the value estimates of any year by dividing them by the *index number* of prices in that year and multiplying by 100.

For example, gross domestic product at *current* factor cost in the United Kingdom was:

	£m.
1969	38,557
1970	42,229
1971	47,491

In the same years the index of *retail* prices was:

1969	127·2
1970	135·3
1971	148·1

We can now obtain estimates of *real* gross national product at constant (1963) *factor cost* by *deflating* the values of these years as follows:

Year	Value in £m. (1)	Index of retail prices (2)	Estimated 'real' value in 1963 prices Col. (1) ÷ Col. (2) £m.
1969	38,557	127·2/100	30,312
1970	42,229	135·3/100	31,211
1971	47,491	148·1/100	32,067

These estimated 'real' values can now be compared with those given in the Blue Book. They differ – which tells us that the *index of retail prices* has moved differently from the *index of factor costs*. The example, however, is simply offered to illustrate the process of *deflating* – that is, in this case, of *revaluing* gross national product at 1963 (base year) prices.

In principle all four methods are the same in that they involve revaluation and thus an *explicit*, or *implicit*, price index number. In the fourth case the index number of prices was calculated independently of the estimates of G.N.P. at *current factor prices* and then applied to them to obtain 'real' or constant price G.N.P. In the first and second cases 'real' or 'constant' G.N.P. was obtained by revaluing quantities of output (production method)† or expenditure (expenditure method) directly. The resultant 'real' values define an 'implicit price index' by the following relation:

$$\frac{\text{G.N.P. (current prices)}}{\text{G.N.P. (constant prices)}} \equiv \text{implicit index of final product prices.}$$

$$\equiv \text{implicit G.N.P. deflator.}$$

The following table, derived from the Blue Book, gives the value of this implicit *price index* as well as the values of other well known indexes of various types of prices. In general, as one might expect, price indexes tend to move together but the movements are not identical.

Table 4.5   *Price Indices U.K. 1964–1971*

	Average Annual Value (1963 = 100)							
	1964	1965	1966	1967	1968	1969	1970	1971
1. Implicit G.N.P. deflator	103	108	112	115	121	126	135	146
2. Consumers' goods and services	103	108	112	115	120	127	133	144
3. Food	102	104	107	110	115	119	128	140
4. Fuel	104	105	108	108	117	121	126	133
5. Housing	107	118	126	134	141	151	160	181
6. Wholesale prices of manufactures	103	107	110	111	115	120	128	138
7. Fixed assets	102	106	110	111	115	121	130	141

Sources: 1. *Economic Trends*; 2. *Monthly Digest of Statistics*: 3. Blue Book; 4. *The British Economy – Key Statistics*.

† In principle this method requires the revaluation, in constant prices, of all 'values added'. This requires the revaluation of all input and output prices.

The theory of index numbers cannot be discussed here. All we need to remember at this stage is that from our aggregate estimates in terms of current prices (market or factor) we can obtain, by deflating, estimates in terms of constant prices (or relative '*real*' values) and that, for many purposes, it is 'real' values which concern us.

QUESTIONS AND EXERCISES

1. Suppose you were interested in the change in 'economic welfare' in the United Kingdom between 1948 and 1970. How would you seek to define it? Which aggregate or aggregates would you use to estimate it? Why?

2. Assume that the authorities replace *all* direct taxation by indirect taxes producing an equivalent yield. What would be the consequences for the estimates of gross domestic product, national income and personal disposable income? Would your estimate of economic welfare be affected? If so, how and why?

3. 'If a householder repairs his own leaking roof national income is unaltered; if he hires a builder to do it, national income is increased.' Is this so? If it is does it imply any serious criticism of national income estimates? Can we increase economic welfare by doing each other's washing?

4. Suppose that an outbreak of lawlessness makes it necessary to put 250,000 additional men into the police force where they are paid (in total) precisely what they were paid in their previous occupations. What would happen to national income? What would be the effect on economic welfare? In the light of your answers discuss the limitations of the national income concept.

5. Interest on the national debt is treated as a transfer payment. Why is this? Where the expenditure financed by the government borrowing was used to build factories is the procedure sensible?

6. Net investment is defined as gross investment *minus* depreciation. Explain the theoretical relationship between net investment and the community's stock of real capital. Can net investment be negative? If so in what periods of British history would you expect to find negative net investment? Can gross investment ever be negative? Give your reasons.

7. In a particular period an economy consisting of two firms (*A* and *B*) and a public sector records the following data:

FIRM *A*

Allocations		Receipts	
Purchases from		Sales to	
Firm *B*	6,000	households	10,000
foreigners	5,000	Firm *B*	21,000
Wages	20,000	government	5,000
Rents	1,000	foreigners	8,000
Indirect taxes	1,000		
Taxes on profits	2,000	Additions to	
Depreciation	5,000	fixed capital	6,000
Dividends	7,000	stocks	4,000
Undistributed profits	7,000		
	54,000		54,000

FIRM *B*

Purchases from		Sales to	
Firm *A*	21,000	households	45,000
foreigners	19,000	Firm *A*	6,000
Wages	22,000	foreigners	21,000
Rents	500		
Indirect taxes	1,500	Additions to	
Taxes on profits	700	stocks	−1,000
Depreciation	3,300		
Dividends	1,000		
Undistributed profits	2,000		
	71,000		71,000

GOVERNMENT

		Taxes:	
Interest on national			
debt	1,000	direct taxes on	
Wages and salaries	6,000	companies	2,700
Purchases from *A*	5,000	direct taxes on	
Net decrease in		persons	7,000
indebtedness	200	indirect taxes	2,500
	12,200		12,200

(i) Prepare estimates of gross national product and gross national expenditure at both market prices and factor costs.

(ii) From your results in (i) prepare estimates of national income, personal income and personal disposable income.

(iii) Next prepare a capital account showing the saving and investment identity of Section 6, p. 66.
What is the saving of households, enterprises and government? Has the government a surplus or deficit? What is the value of *net* investment?

(iv) Finally prepare an account showing transactions with the rest of the world. Is the balance of trade favourable or unfavourable? What is the value of investment overseas?

8. Use Table 1 of the Blue Book to provide data for the national expenditure identity on p. 63 for the years 1950–70. What are the *average* ratios over the period of the following sub-aggregates to gross national expenditure.

(i) Consumers' expenditure.
(ii) Public authority's current expenditure.
(iii) Investment (gross and net)
(iv) Exports.
(v) Imports.

Do any of the ratios show fluctuations around their average? Can you suggest and defend a simple way of comparing the extent to which the different ratios fluctuate? Do you get a different picture if you distinguish between fixed capital formation and the increase in stocks? Which is the most 'volatile' series?

9. Distinguish carefully between (i) the increase in the value of stocks; (ii) the value of the increase in stocks.
Write

P_1 for the price of a unit of stocks in year 1

P_2 for the price of a unit of stocks in year 2

Q_1 for the quantity of stocks in year 1

Q_2 for the quantity of stocks in year 2,

and formulate expressions for (i) and (ii) above.
Use your answer to explain the significance of the item 'stock appreciation'. Compare your discussion with that in *National Accounts Statistics: Sources and Methods*, particularly ch. 13.

10. 'The concept of depreciation is difficult enough. Its measurement is more difficult still'. Explain. Compare your explanation with that given in *National Accounts Statistics*.

11. Use the latest Blue Book to extend Table 4.4. Graph the

relationship between the expenditure and production output indices. Do the differences between the two indices show any systematic pattern?

12. Which aggregate would you expect to be most closely related to domestic unemployment? Why? Test your conclusions by plotting G.N.P., G.D.P. and national income against the percentage of the work force unemployed for the years 1960–70.

13. 'Quarterly data on Gross Domestic Product will always tell us whether output is expanding or contracting.' Do you agree? Compare your answer with the G.D.P. estimates in *Economic Trends* for all three methods of calculation. Does each tell the same story?

SUGGESTED READING

R. Marris,† *Economic Arithmetic* (Macmillan, 1958) ch. iii.

J. R. Hicks,† *The Social Framework* (Oxford, 1971).

H. C. Edey and A. T. Peacock,† *National Income and Social Accounting* (Hutchinson, 1969).

E. Devons, *An Introduction to British Economic Statistics* (Cambridge, 1958) chs. i, ix.

C.S.O., *National Accounts Statistics: Sources and Methods* (H.M.S.O., 1968).

W. A. H. Godley and C. Gillon, 'Measuring National Product', *N.I.E.S.R. Review* no. 27 (1964).

† Alternative reference.

5 Output and Capacity

WE have now defined a set of accounting concepts in terms of which we can describe, in a systematic and unambiguous way, the behaviour of the United Kingdom economy. To do this we had to spend some time and effort in looking at purely accounting problems. There is therefore a risk that in concentrating on the development of a conceptual framework we have lost sight of our main objective. Accordingly this is a good point at which, before looking at the behaviour of the United Kingdom economy in Chapter 6, to take stock of what we have learned.

We began, in Chapter 3, by picturing the simplest possible economic system. In this there was no governmental economic activity and no international trade. Our sketch of the economy in operation was correspondingly simple. Households sold factor services to enterprises. Enterprises organised these services to produce a flow of goods and services. These passed, via the market, either to households (as consumption) or to enterprises (as investment). For convenience we reproduce our earlier Figure describing this below.

The whole of Chapters 3 and 4 were concerned to develop a consistent and unambiguous set of concepts in terms of which we could give a numerical description of economic activity in a model of this kind. Description, however, presupposes analysis. Our first aim was to measure the flow of goods and services becoming available, in any given period, to satisfy human wants while leaving the community as well off at the end of the period as it was in the beginning. Measurement of this flow – which we called real national income or real net national product – is obviously an important problem. For real national income is a measure of the potential economic welfare of society in any given period.

Our second aim, however, was rather more ambitious. We sought to answer the questions:

(i) What determines the magnitude of real national income in any period?

(ii) What determines the rate at which real national income grows from one period to another?

Logically this second aim was prior to our first. It was *because*

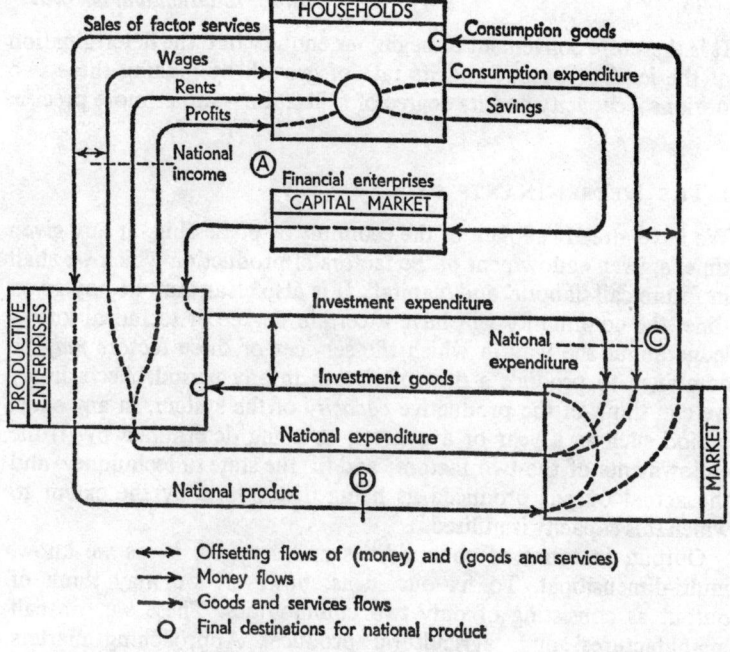

Offsetting flows of (money) and (goods and services)
⟶ Money flows
⟶ Goods and services flows
○ Final destinations for national product

FIG. 3.iii The circular flow of income, output and expenditure

we wanted to explain the level of potential economic welfare in any period and its rate of growth between periods that we embarked on the tasks of defining national income and its associated aggregates and sub-aggregates and elaborating a set of rules for measuring them. Asking our two questions – that is posing our two problems for analysis – told us what facts were likely to be relevant to our enquiry. Now we have defined our facts – which we shall shortly need to explain – we can take a more systematic look at the analytical problem from which we started.

Obviously enough the level of real output produced in the economy in any accounting period depends upon

(i) the *capacity* of the economic system to produce output; and
(ii) the *extent* to which the capacity in existence is utilised.

Equally clearly the growth in output between two accounting periods depends upon

(iii) the growth in *capacity* between the two periods; and
(iv) the change between the two periods in the *extent* to which capacity is utilised.

It is therefore convenient to begin our enquiry into the determination of the level of output and its rate of growth by making these two notions – capacity and its degree of utilisation – rather more precise.

1 THE DETERMINANTS OF CAPACITY

We have already spoken of the economy as possessing, at any given time, a given endowment of the factors of production which we shall in future call 'labour' and 'capital'. It is also clear that, at any given time, the community will have a certain degree of technical knowledge about the way in which the services of these factors *may* be combined to produce a flow of output in any period. Accordingly we can think of the productive *capacity* of the system, in any short period such as a year or a quarter, as being determined by (i) the endowments of the two factors; and (ii) the state of technique – and the actual output produced as being determined by the extent to which this capacity is utilised.

Output, in terms of commodities and services, is, as we know, multi-dimensional. To fix our ideas, however, we may think of output as consisting of only two commodities. These we can call 'manufactures' and 'agricultural produce'. Approaching matters along these lines we can then construct a simple diagram showing the various combinations of these two outputs which the economy can produce with its 'capacity' fully and optimally utilised. This is done in Fig. 5.i.

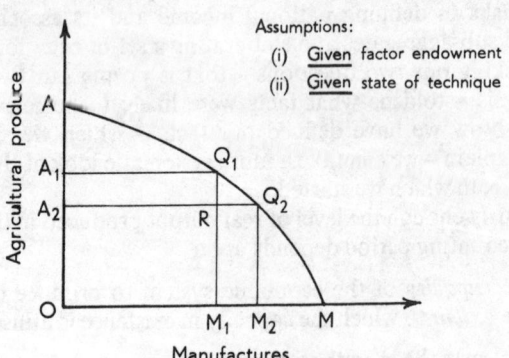

FIG. 5.i Production possibility curve. Assumptions: (i) *given* factor inducement, (ii) *given* state of technique

Interpreting this diagram is relatively straightforward. Suppose only agricultural produce is to be produced. If the whole of capacity is employed, output of agricultural produce is *OA* and output of manufactures is zero. Suppose now that the community's preferences change in favour of manufactures. Through the working of the market, enterprises redeploy factors so as to produce more manufactures and less agricultural produce. If this process continues we shall trace out a curve showing all the combinations of the two commodities which can be produced by the community on the assumptions that (i) both factors are fully employed; (ii) the production of each commodity is optimally organised; (iii) the state of technique is given. Of these three assumptions only (ii) has a meaning which is not self evident. What does 'optimal' organisation mean? The answer, which at this stage we ask the reader to take on trust, is that at all points on the curve *AM* (i) enterprises, in the search for profit, are using factors in such a way as to keep costs at a minimum and that, provided they do this, (ii) at no point on *AM* is it possible to have more of either commodity without giving up a *greater* value of the other. The curve *AM* is thus not defined simply by the technical conditions of production and the factor endowment. It also depends on the implicit assumption that the market processes, which underlie the curve, produce an 'optimal' allocation of resources in the sense defined above.

Given this assumption – which in future we shall continue to make – the shape and position of the curve *AM*, which we call *the production possibility curve*, depends upon (i) the state of technique; and (ii) the factor endowment. In formal terms it represents a first attempt at answering the question: What determines the capacity of the economy to produce output?

On this approach the *growth* of capacity over time takes the form of an outward shift in the curve. Clearly it can occur because the process of *net investment* increases the endowment of capital, because *technique is improving* or because the work-force is *growing*. To explain the rate of growth of capacity economists need to develop a theory which explains

   (i) the *rate* at which the factor endowments grow;
  (ii) the *rate* at which technique improves; and
 (iii) the way in which capacity output responds to these growth rates.

2 THE SLOPE OF THE PRODUCTION POSSIBILITY CURVE

Before we leave this production curve can we say anything about the meaning of its slope? A little reflection shows that we can.

Consider the points Q_1 and Q_2 on the curve. If we move from Q_1 to Q_2 we obtain an additional output of manufactures of M_1M_2 at the *cost* of giving up A_1A_2 of 'agricultural produce'. We then say that the *'opportunity cost'* of M_1M_2 of 'manufactures' is A_1A_2 of 'agricultural produce'. Their ratio, that is the 'opportunity cost' of M_1M_2 in terms of A_1A_2, is given by the *slope* of Q_1Q_2. Clearly if the distance M_1M_2 is made smaller and smaller, then A_1A_2 is also made smaller and, by the same token the line Q_1Q_2 is shortened. As this process is continued the slope of the line Q_1Q_2 becomes closer and closer to the slope of the production possibility curve. Where the distance Q_1 to Q_2 is indefinitely small, the 'opportunity cost' of manufactures in terms of agricultural produce is simply the slope of the production possibility curve at the point under consideration.

This concept of 'opportunity cost' is of considerable importance in economics. *It is a valid concept if, and only if, choice between alternatives is enforced by some limitation – in this case the capacity output of the system.* A precisely similar situation arises for a man who is acceptable in marriage to Joan and Jean and is strongly attracted to both. If it is not legally possible to marry both girls, Joan is the opportunity cost of Jean and Jean the opportunity cost of Joan. Where society permits polygamy the man can marry both and the concept of opportunity cost does not arise. The polygamous situation is depicted in economic terms by the point R in Figure 5.i. If the economic system is at a point like R *inside the production possibility curve* (as it was throughout the thirties) capacity is *not* fully utilised. Here 'agricultural produce' can be increased *without* reducing the output of manufactures. There is no opportunity cost of increasing either form of output simply because the whole of productive capacity is not being used.

In terms of Fig. 5.i, we can now rephrase our questions, which become

(i) what determines the position of the production possibility curve in any given period?

(ii) what determines whether the economy operates, in any given period, at a point (such as Q_1) *on* the production possibility curve or at a point (such as R) *inside* it?

(iii) what determines the rate at which, through time, the production *possibility curve* moves outwards (to the right)?

(iv) what determines the rate at which, through time, actual output grows?

Finally one last point about the *production possibility curve* itself. We have seen that at any point on it, (say Q_1) the *slope* of the curve is the opportunity cost ratio. As the curve in Fig. 5.i is drawn the opportunity cost of manufactures in terms of agricultural produce rises as the output of manufactures grows. Conversely, if we move *down* the curve the opportunity cost of agricultural produce in terms of manufactures also grows. Fig. 5.i thus depicts a situation of increasing opportunity cost.

Why should costs be increasing? In general this will follow even if the factors of production are homogeneous† and equally well adapted to the production of either agricultural produce or manufactures. A formal proof of this is a little complicated. But the following argument should serve to clarify the issue.

Suppose we are at some point (say *Q*) on the production possibility curve and we wish to give up a unit of agricultural produce to gain an extra unit of manufactures. Suppose also that, at *Q*, the factors labour and capital are used in the two forms of production as follows:

	Unit of agric. produce	Unit of manufactures
Units of labour	1	1
Units of capital	4	10

If we give up a unit of agricultural produce we release 1 unit of labour and 4 of capital. But to produce a unit of manufactures we require 1 unit of labour and 10 of capital. Too little capital is therefore released to maintain the same cost of manufactures. In producing manufactures the ratio of labour to capital must rise above the ratio of 1 : 10. Since this was, *because businessmen choose the least cost combination in order to earn maximum profit*, the cheapest method (optimal factor ratio) for producing manufactures, cost *must* rise. Hence there are increasing costs as we move *down* the production possibility curve *AM* towards *M* for what is true of point *Q* is true of any point on *AM*.

Now move the other way from *Q* – that is give up manufactures to obtain *more* agricultural produce. Now inputs are *required* in the ratio 1 labour : 4 capital and *released* in the ratio 1 labour : 10 capital. Too little labour is released. The ratio of labour to capital must *fall* in agricultural produce. Hence, by the argument above, the cost of agricultural produce must rise.

It follows that (i) *whichever* direction we move from *Q* we encounter increasing costs; provided only that (ii) factors are *not* used in the *same* proportion in producing *both* types of output. This second condition will be satisfied if both types of output do

† Homogeneity simply means that one unit of any factor is indistinguishable (economically) from any other unit of the same factor.

not possess the same production function – a reasonable enough assumption.

Since we have not yet met the concept of a production function a brief explanation of this statement is necessary.

Consider the output of 'agricultural produce'. This depends upon (i) the inputs of labour and capital; and (ii) the state of technique. Given (i) and (ii) there will be a single value of output of 'agricultural produce'. Thus we may write a *production function*† for agricultural produce as:

$$Y_{ag} = f(N_{ag}, K_{ag}),$$ (5.I)

where

$Y_{ag} \equiv$ the output of agricultural produce;

$N_{ag} \equiv$ the labour input to the industry;

$K_{ag} \equiv$ the capital employed in the industry.

This equation may be read as follows:

$$\text{output of agricultural produce} \quad \text{is} \left\{ \begin{array}{l} \text{a function of, i.e.} \\ \text{systematically} \\ \text{dependent upon} \end{array} \right\} \begin{array}{l} \text{the inputs of} \\ \text{labour} \\ \text{and capital} \end{array}$$

What about 'technique'? We could have included a symbol (say T) in this function to stand for the 'state of technique'. Indeed in later chapters – as a pedagogic device – we adopt this procedure. In the equation at (5.I) however we simply regard the functional relation – denoted by the letter f in front of the bracket – as reflecting a given state of technique. If technique changes so does the function. For manufacturing there will be a function of a similar type written formally:

$$Y_{man} = f(N_{man}, K_{man})$$ (5.II)

For our earlier argument to hold we simply require these two functions (systematic relationships) to be different in the sense that, given the prices of the factor inputs, the *ratios* in which they are employed in order to minimise costs differ in the two uses. As the reader will see this is not a strong assumption since agricultural output is likely, in general, to require very different factor inputs, at any given set of factor prices, from manufactured goods.

At this stage some readers may find this argument hard to follow. They should take courage for, in the Questions and Exercises which

† The notion of a 'production function' is more fully explained in Chapter 7.

follow Chapter 7, they will find themselves proving, with great ease, most of the propositions which we have here asserted.

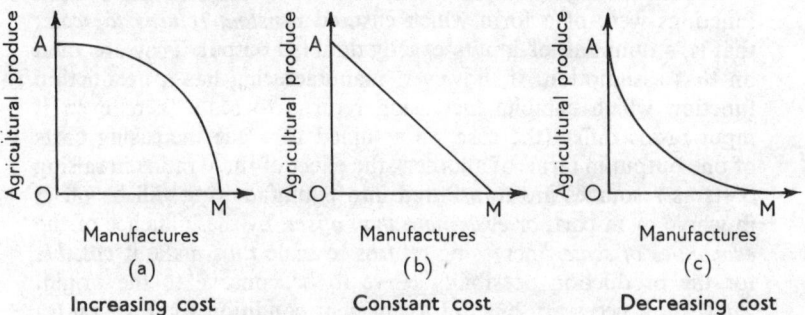

FIG. 5.ii Production possibility curves. Increasing, constant and decreasing cost

From this argument in terms of ratios it is easy to see that if, given the price of factor inputs, the ratios in which factors are employed in order to minimise costs *are the same in each use*, then the opportunity cost curve will be a straight line and costs will be constant. This is illustrated in Fig. 5.ii (b).

How can we have decreasing costs? At first sight our two ratio arguments seem to exclude this possibility. But suppose the production function for manufacturing is of the particular form:

$$Y_{\mathrm{man}} = A N_{\mathrm{man}} K_{\mathrm{man}},$$

where A is some constant. To fix ideas put $A = 1$, $N = 100$, $K = 1000$. Then

$$Y_{\mathrm{man}} = 1 \times 100 \times 1000$$
$$= 100,000.$$

Now suppose both N_{man} and K_{man} to double. We have:

$$Y_{\mathrm{man}} = 1 \times 200 \times 2000$$
$$= 1 \times 100 \times 1000 \times 2 \times 2$$
$$= 4[1 \times 100 \times 1000]$$
$$= 400,000.$$

Doubling factor inputs has *more* than doubled output – it has in fact quadrupled it. When this occurs, or more generally when a doubling of factor inputs leads to *more* than doubling output, we say that there are *economies of scale* or *increasing returns to scale*. Conversely when a doubling of inputs leads to *less* than doubling output we say that there are *decreasing returns to scale* or *disecono-mies of scale*.

Our earlier arguments assumed, implicitly, that both production functions were of a form which ensured *constant returns to scale*: that is, a doubling of inputs exactly doubled output. They are valid on that assumption. If, however, manufacturing has a production function which exhibits increasing returns to scale then, even if input ratios differ (the case we assumed to argue increasing costs of one output in terms of another), the effect of these ratios in raising costs as resources are transferred into manufacturing will be offset in whole or in part, *or even more than offset*, by the influence of the *economies of scale*. Increasing returns to scale thus make it *possible* for the production possibility curve to be concave to the origin. They are a necessary but not a sufficient condition for Fig. 5.ii (c) to be the appropriate one.

Thus each of the production possibility curves we have drawn is logically permissible. Which is appropriate is a question of fact. In general we shall proceed on the assumption that the production functions in our economy (i) exhibit constant returns to scale; and (ii) differ in the sense explained on pp. 79–80.

It thus follows that the reader may picture the production possibility curve – or, as it is sometimes called, 'the transformation curve' – as it is drawn in Fig. 5.i.

3 THE THREE PROBLEMS

Now that we have restated our three problems concerning the determination of output in terms of the production possibility curve we can develop a convenient method of approach to them. We shall begin by examining the question – what determines whether the economy operates *on* the production possibility curve (i.e. at full capacity) or at some point R inside it (i.e., at less than full capacity)?

In considering this problem we shall take the position of the production possibility curve as given and invariant. Since the position of this curve depends upon:

   (i) the real capital stock – which we know is increasing as the result of net investment;
  (ii) the work-force – which we know is also growing as the result of population growth and the increasing proportion of the population which seeks employment;
 (iii) the state of technique – which is also improving;

we are taking as constant and unchanged variables which we know in practice to be changing. To do this is obviously convenient for it enables us to leave the problem of the growth of capacity for later examination. But is it justified? Provided we restrict the time period involved, it is a reasonable procedure for though capacity does grow over time, in any period of (say) a year it grows relatively little – probably by about 3 per cent or even less. We proceed, in other words, like a man buying a new suit. He knows that, in fact, his measurements *are* changing. He is getting heavier. His stomach muscles are weakening. Nevertheless he proceeds on the assumption (sometimes shown to be unjustified) that over the expected life of the suit these changes can be ignored. In economic terms the man buying the suit undertakes a *short-run* analysis. That is, he obtains a garment which fits his existing contours on the assumption that in the short-run they are constant even though he knows that, in practice, they are changing.

Our analysis of question (ii) will be a *short-run* analysis in this sense. For we shall take, as given and invariant, the determinants of *the position of the production possibility curve* even though we know that, over time, these are changing: that is, *economic growth* in capacity is proceeding. This device simplifies matters but requires the reader to make the proper intellectual allowances for its limitations and the artificiality it inevitably introduces.

In much of what follows we shall make a further simplification in that we shall not in general explicitly introduce time into our analysis. To see what this means consider Fig. 5.iii.

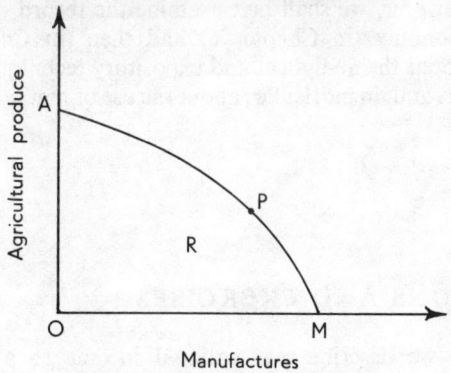

Fig. 5.iii Capacity and its utilisation

Suppose we succeed in developing a theory which explains why the economy operates at the point *R*. Let us suppose that this theory tells us that *if* some variable (let us call it x) takes the value x_1 we shall be at R while *if* it takes the value x_2 we shall be at P. On the basis of this theory we can work out that if x changes from x_1 to x_2 the economy will move from R to P. This information is obviously useful. But it is equally obviously incomplete for it does *not* tell us (i) *how long* the system takes to get from R to P; (ii) by *what path* it gets from R to P; (iii) whether, once at P, the system will stay there. Economic theories that only compare positions such as R and P we call *static* theories. Theories which also explain the path the system takes from R to P – and how long it takes to get there – we call *dynamic* theories since they involve time in an *explicit* way.

Dynamic theories, since they tell us more, are obviously likely to be (and in practice are) more complicated than static theories. For simplicity therefore we begin by developing a static theory. Once again the reader, who intuitively thinks in dynamic terms, must make the necessary intellectual adjustment. Above all he must avoid mixing statics with dynamics. Since static analysis is artificial this requires a continuous intellectual effort.

These warnings do not imply that this book contains no discussion of dynamic problems. It does. Those chapters, however, which develop a short-run macro-economic theory of the determination of output are largely *static* while those which discuss economic growth, economic fluctuations, and rising prices respectively are explicitly *dynamic*.

We are now almost ready to embark upon the development of our *short-run* and *static* theory of the determination of output. Before we do so, however, we shall first examine the record of the United Kingdom economy (in Chapter 6) and then (in Chapter 7) say something about the analytical and expository techniques employed by economists and, in particular, about the use of mathematics.

QUESTIONS AND EXERCISES

1. Why do we describe real national income as a measure of 'potential economic welfare' rather than 'economic welfare'? What limitations are there to the validity of either description?
2. From the following data plot the production possibility curves. Do they describe increasing, decreasing or constant costs?

Three Production Possibility Curves: Numerical Data

1		2		3	
Output of		Output of		Output of	
Agri-cultural products	Manu-factured products	Agri-cultural products	Manu-factured products	Agri-cultural products	Manu-factured products
(i)	(ii)	(iii)	(iv)	(v)	(vi)
1000	nil	1000	nil	1000	nil
950	24·5	950	34	950	15
900	49·0	900	67	900	31
850	73·5	850	99	850	48
800	98·0	800	130	800	66
750	122·5	750	160	750	85
700	147·0	700	189	700	105
650	171·5	650	217	650	126
600	196·0	600	244	600	148
550	220·5	550	270	550	171
500	245·0	500	295	500	195
450	269·5	450	319	450	220
400	294·0	400	342	400	246
350	318·5	350	364	350	273
300	343·0	300	385	300	301
250	367·5	250	405	250	330
200	392·0	200	424	200	360
150	416·5	150	442	150	391
100	441·0	100	459	100	423
50	465·5	50	475	50	456
nil	490·0	nil	490	nil	490

3. Construct a figure similar to 5.iii. Show, geometrically, how you would seek to measure the proportion of capacity employed at the point R. With what observable phenomena, for which statistical data are usually available, would you expect your measure to be related? Give your reasons.

4. 'As a nation we spend far too little on education. We should increase our expenditure on it by at least £100 m. a year.' Discuss this statement in the light of the concept of 'opportunity cost'.

5. 'In the short run, by definition, some variable or variables which are known to be changing over time are assumed to be constant. How misleading short-run analysis is, is therefore a question of fact.' Elucidate.

6. A tank is connected to a hose through a valve controlled by a ball cock. Initially the water in the tank is at a level of 3 inches. The hose is turned on at 11.0 a.m. Give (i) a static and (ii) a

dynamic analysis of the operation of this system. What is the new equilibrium level?

7. The following Table gives estimates of the rate of growth in real output in 11 countries over the period 1950–9. In terms of a production possibility analysis how would you seek to explain the relative position of the United Kingdom?

Percentage Growth in Output: Selected Countries 1950–9

Country	Growth rate	Country	Growth rate
Japan	8·6	Norway	3·4
U.S.A.	3·4	Germany	7·4
Canada	4·0	France	4·1
Sweden	3·3	Italy	5·7
Denmark	2·6	U.K.	2·2
Netherlands	4·6		

Source: *Economic Review* (July 1961).

8. Construct hypothetical production possibility curves, in terms of agricultural produce and manufactures for (i) the United Kingdom; (ii) New Zealand. Would you expect their shapes to differ? If so in what way? Justify your hypothetical curves.

9. Suppose the community, with a production possibility curve defined by cols. (i) and (ii) of the data in Question 2 is in equilibrium at the following point:

Output of

agricultural products	manufactured products
550	220·5

What is the price of agricultural output in terms of manufactures? Why? Interpret your answer in the light of the earlier discussion of the working of a market economy.

10. What statistical data would be relevant to any attempt to test your answer to Question 8? Why?

SUGGESTED READING

P. A. Samuelson, *Economics* (McGraw-Hill, 1973) ch. 2.

6 A Sketch of British Economic Experience

IN Chapter 5, in making use of the concept of the production possibility curve, we distinguished between two macro-economic problems.

The first of these, which we called a *short-run* problem, was to find an answer to the question

> *given* the capacity of the economic system to produce output what determines the extent to which the given capacity is utilised?

The second, which we called the *long-run* problem, was to find an answer to the question

> what determines the rate at which the capacity to produce output grows over time?

These problems were clearly distinguishable in terms of the production possibility curve. But this is simply a geometric device. We now need to enquire whether they are real problems capable in principle of investigation by positive economic analysis. If, for example, examination of the record of the British economy showed that the economy always operated at full capacity, our first problem would lose much of its interest. If alternatively there was no evidence that capacity ever grew, so would the second. Moreover, if the record shows them to be real problems, its examination may also suggest particular aspects of them which call for analysis.

The function of this chapter is, therefore, to sketch the economic experience of the U.K. economy in terms of macro-economic concepts we have already met (and some of those we shall soon meet) in order to see what are the facts which our theory needs to explain.

1 OUTPUT, CAPACITY AND EMPLOYMENT

Our first step is to examine what has happened to annual output – the flow of goods and services produced by the economy in each year. To do this we make use of a series for real gross domestic product. This, in the form of an index number (with 1963 = 100) is plotted on the figure below for two periods: 1920–38 (the inter-war years); and 1948–70 (the post-World War II period). The 'war'

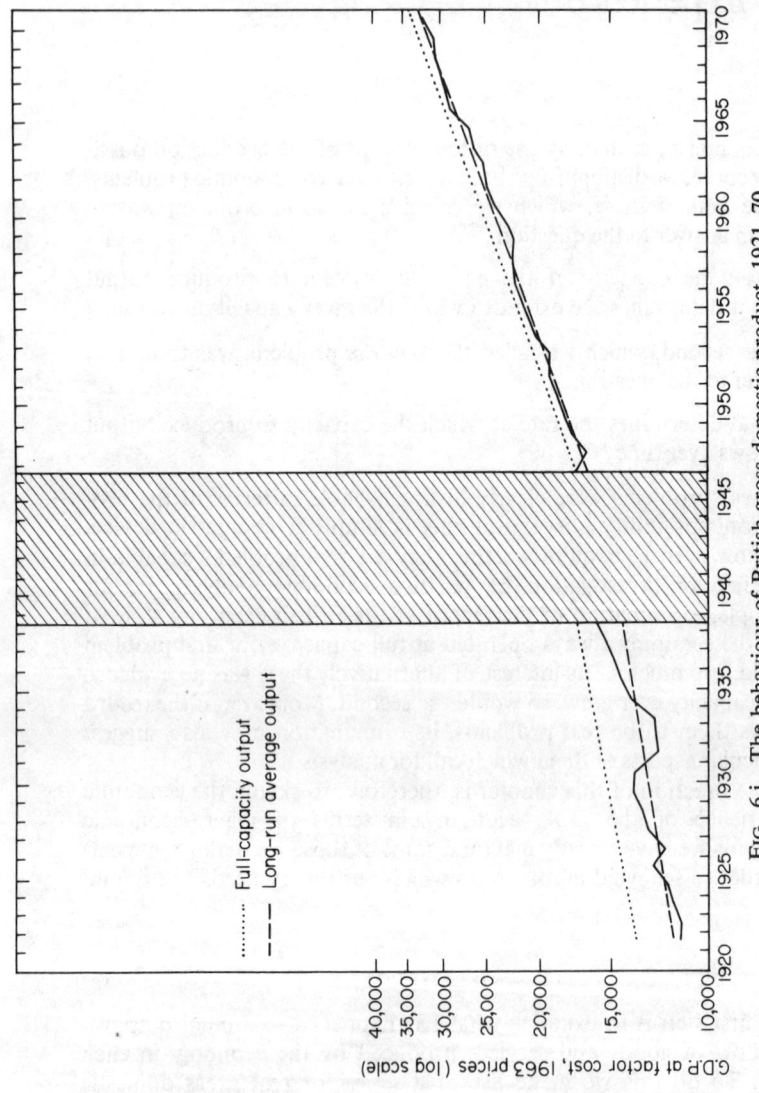

FIG. 6.i The behaviour of British gross domestic product, 1921–70

Sources: 1921–47, *The British Economy – Key Statistics 1900–1966* (published by Times Newspapers for London and Cambridge Economic Service); 1948–64, Blue Book (1970); 1965–70, *Monthly Digest* (July 1971)

Full-capacity output

Long-run average output

G.D.P. at factor cost, 1963 prices (log scale)

10,000

15,000

20,000

25,000

30,000

35,000

40,000

1920 1925 1930 1935 1940 1945 1950 1955 1960 1965 1970

years (1939–47) have been excluded simply because, in these, the performance of the economy was atypical. What does this Figure tell us?

In the first place it is clear that in both periods the general long-run tendency was for gross domestic product to grow.†

In the second place growth, in both periods, did not take place at a smooth rate. In some sub-periods, for example 1922–5, 1932–7, 1948–51 and 1958–61, growth took place at a rate faster than the average of the relevant long-period (shown by the *dashed* line). In others it was notably slower or even (as in 1925–6 and 1929–32) negative.

In the third place, it seems, since the *dashed* line for the period 1948–70 is more steeply sloped than that of the inter-war years, that the average rate of growth has been somewhat faster – around 2·8 per cent per annum as against 2·3 per cent. How much of this apparent 'long-run' growth was due to the growth of capacity?

To answer this we must ask how fast has capacity grown – that is, how fast has the production possibility curve moved outward to the right through time? We can make a rough estimate of this by finding, in each of our two main periods, two years in which it seems plausible to argue that the proportion of capacity employed was the same. Between two such years since, by assumption, the extent to which capacity employed is invariant, observed growth in gross domestic product must be entirely due to the growth of capacity itself. We can thus calculate, for the period in question, the rate of capacity growth. How can we identify years in which the degree to which capacity was employed was the same?

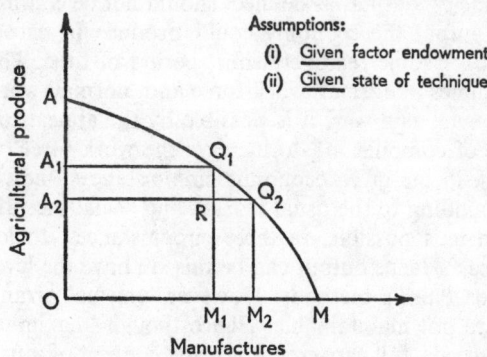

FIG. 5.i Production possibility curve. Assumptions: (i) *given* factor inducement, (ii) *given* state of technique

† Since the vertical scale is logarithmic the slope of any straight line on the Figure is a constant percentage rate of growth.

To see this consider again the production possibility curve of Fig. 5.i.

In the *short run*, since both the state of technique and the community's capital stock are constant, output can vary only if the employment of capital and labour varies. It is not easy to measure the extent to which capital is employed. On the other hand the extent to which the available work-force is employed seems certain to be reflected in the percentage of the work-force unemployed. The greater is the observed percentage of unemployment, the less is capacity being utilised. It thus seems plausible to argue that any two years in which the percentage of the work-force unemployed was the same were two years in which the percentage of capacity employed was the same.

Using this procedure, by comparing the outputs of any two years which satisfy the unemployment percentage condition, we can make an estimate – though only rather a crude one – of the rate at which capacity grew between the two observations: that is of the percentage rate of growth of capacity.

Notice that this procedure does not identify any particular level of unemployment with 'full capacity' working. This can be done but it requires a separate assumption. For example Prof. F. W. Paish has taken 'full capacity' to be defined by 1 per cent of the work-force unemployed. Applying this additional assumption (and a broadly similar one for the inter-war years) gives a line showing the rate of growth and level of full capacity output. This is shown by the *dotted* line in Fig. 6.i.

'Full capacity' output, as defined, should not be confused with the maximum output the economy could produce in exceptional circumstances for some relatively short period of time. This is so because it assumes a 'normal' work-force and 'normal' working hours. In a crisis, such as a war, it is possible by the appeal to patriotism (or the use of compulsion), to increase the work-force over what it would be if, in the given economic circumstances, individuals were simply responding to the usual market and social incentives. By the same token it is possible, in these circumstances, to lengthen the working week. Hence output can be raised above the level identified by Professor Paish's methods. However, unusual arrangements of this kind are not maintainable. Hence though 'maximum potential capacity' exceeds 'full capacity' it is not a concept of much relevance in this context. To put matters more concisely 'full capacity' output is defined with reference to the 'normal' work force: that is, individuals who in a wide range of economic circumstances will seek employment. By contrast 'maximum potential' output is defined with reference to a work-force which, by one means or another, has been temporarily augmented by an influx of (say) married women, pensioners and even the 'normally' unemployable.

In contrast to the rate of growth of capacity, as we defined it, we can think of the *actual* rate of growth of output over the two periods under review. We can think of this as being represented by a long-term 'trend' operating over time. Essentially the 'trend' is a statistical concept which requires statistical definition. To be precise it should be defined in this way. If, however, we simply think of it as the general tendency of output to rise with time and measure it approximately by the average percentage rate of growth, we find that actual output grew, in both our periods, at rates very similar to our own estimated rate of growth of 'capacity'. This is, in any case, strongly suggested by Fig. 6.i. Two conclusions thus seem reasonable:

(i) in the long run the growth in output is *primarily* to be explained by the growth in capacity; and

(ii) the *extent* to which capacity was employed has exhibited sharp fluctuations. For example from 1958 to 1960 output grew much faster than capacity. Hence the extent to which capacity was employed also grew. Thus over a period of 2–3 years growth in output is primarily to be explained by growth in the extent to which capacity is employed.

We can take this argument a little further. Since the extent to which capacity is employed fluctuates, so should the observed percentage of the work-force unemployed. Moreover the percentage should fall as capacity employed increases and increase as capacity employed falls.

In Fig. 6.ii we again plot the series for output, the *dotted* line showing the estimated rate of growth of capacity, together with the percentage of the work-force unemployed.

As the reader can easily see for himself the unemployment percentage exhibits fluctuations closely related to fluctuations in the extent to which capacity appears to be employed. This suggests a further conclusion:

(iii) Any theory which explains the level of output over a short period of time (say 1 or 2 years), may alternatively be viewed as a *theory of employment*.

We can now ask a question of some interest. To what extent was capacity *fully employed* in our two periods? Inspection of the unemployment percentages shows that, in the inter-war years, un-

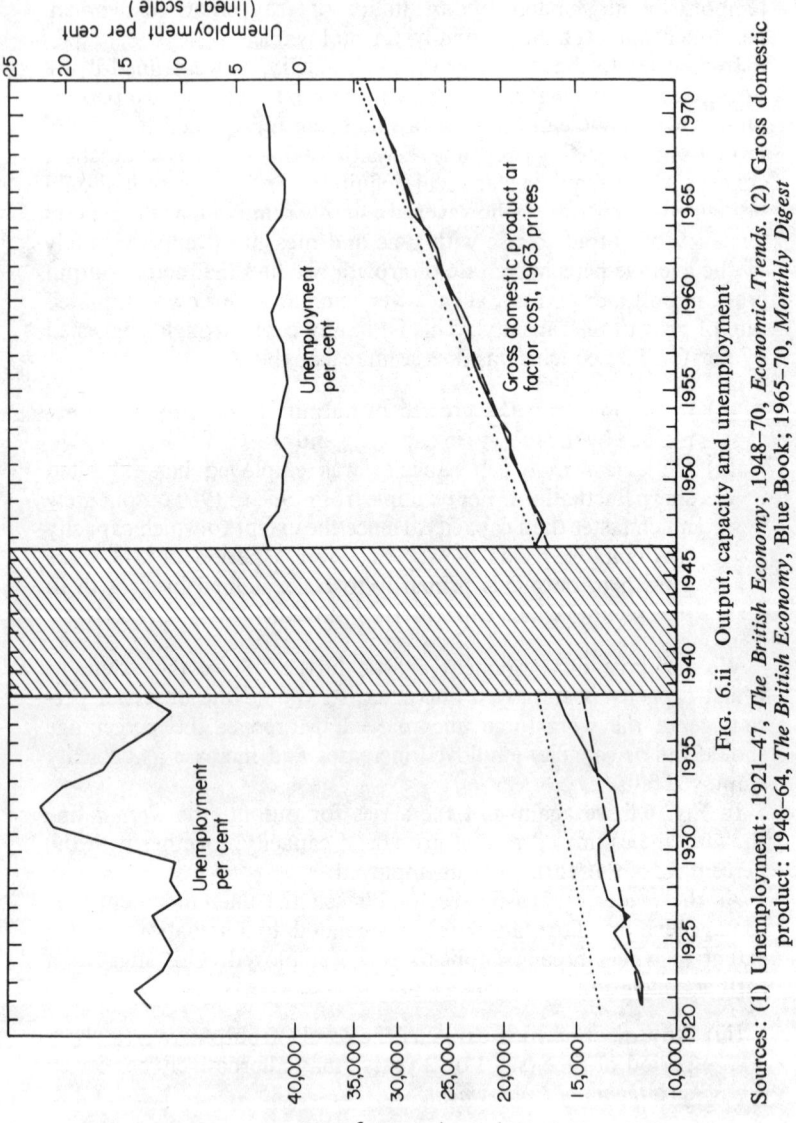

Unemployment per cent (linear scale)

25 — 20 — 15 — 10 — 5 — 0

Unemployment per cent

Unemployment per cent

Gross domestic product at factor cost, 1963 prices

40,000 — 35,000 — 30,000 — 25,000 — 20,000 — 15,000 — 10,000

G.D.P. at factor cost, 1963 prices (log scale)

1920   1925   1930   1935   1940   1945   1950   1955   1960   1965   1970

FIG. 6.ii   Output, capacity and unemployment

Sources: (1) Unemployment: 1921–47, *The British Economy*; 1948–70, *Economic Trends*. (2) Gross domestic product: 1948–64, *The British Economy*, Blue Book; 1965–70, *Monthly Digest*

employment was, on average, around 14 per cent of the work-force. In the post-war years it has been rather less than 2 per cent.

Obviously, since 1948, we have, in terms of the behaviour of gross domestic product, done far better than in the inter-war years, for (i) both output and the capacity to produce output have grown rather faster; (ii) unemployment has on average been far lower (and hence the extent to which capacity has been employed far greater); (iii) fluctuations in output and employment have been less severe.

We can now list the questions suggested by our figures for which we may reasonably require our theory to suggest explanations. These are:

  (i) what explains the rate at which capacity grows?

 (ii) what explains the level of output (and employment) in the short period?

(iii) what explains the wave-like fluctuations in output and employment?

(iv) why did these wave-like fluctuations in the inter-war years take place about a level of capacity utilisation substantially lower (and a percentage of unemployment substantially higher) than in the post-war years?

 (v) why were fluctuations more severe in the inter-war years?

Taken together these five questions imply a sixth:

(vi) why have we done so much 'better' in terms of output and employment since 1948 than we managed to do from 1920 to 1938?

This brief review of the inter-war years and the comparison of the behaviour of gross domestic product between the wars with its behaviour since 1948 unavoidably leaves many things out of account. In the inter-war years potential output was obviously wasted on a gigantic scale. Mass unemployment was tragically endemic. The statistical series give no adequate picture of the misery this mass unemployment brought. For an understanding of this the reader should consult the works of social historians or, better still, some of the novels and biographies of the time.

2 PRICES AND MONEY WAGES

Output and employment are not the only two macro-economic variables of interest to economists. Macro-economics is also concerned with such variables as the general level of prices and money wages. Moreover since the real wage is defined as the purchasing power, in terms of goods and services, of the money wage, i.e. real wage ≡ money wage/price level, a study of these two series easily yields information regarding the real wage. Accordingly Figure 6.iii brings together series for (i) prices; (ii) money wages; (iii) real wages; (iv) the percentage of unemployment, while Fig. 6.iv plots derived series for the annual percentage rate of change of

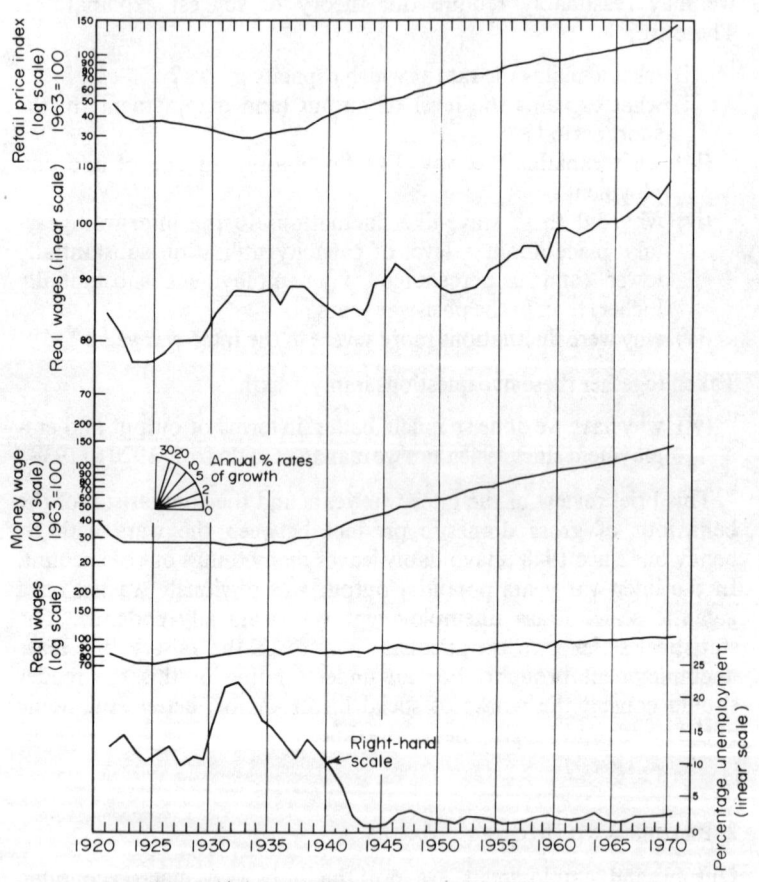

FIG. 6.iii   Prices, money wages and real wages

Sources: (1) Prices, (2) Money wages: 1921–66, *The British Economy*; 1966–70, *Monthly Digest*. (3) Real wages: computed from the ratio Money wages/Prices. (4) Unemployment: 1921–47, *The British Economy*; 1948–70, *Economic Trends*

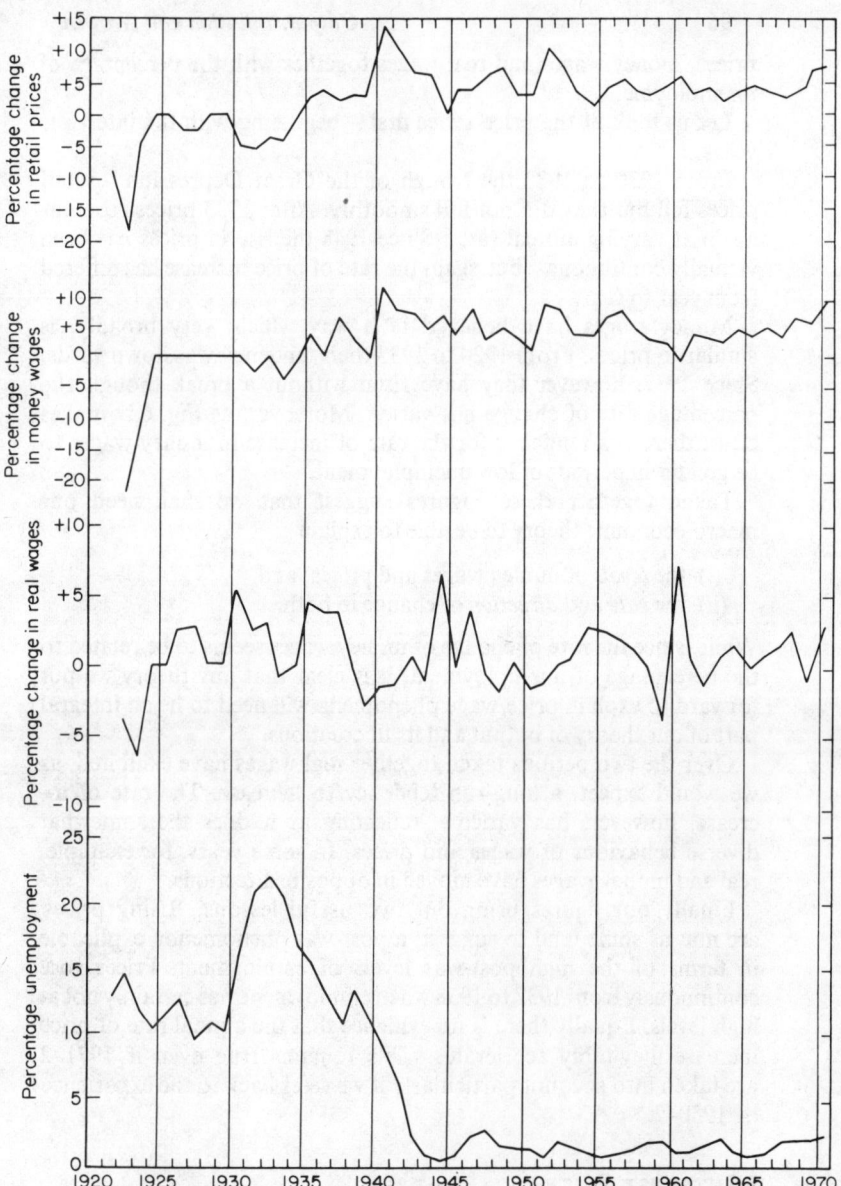

FIG. 6.iv Percentage rate of change in prices, money wages and real wages

Sources: (1) Prices, (2) Money wages: 1921–66, *The British Economy*; 1966–70, *Monthly Digest*. (3) Real wages: from Fig. 6.iii. (4) Unemployment: 1921–47, *The British Economy*; 1948–70, *Economic Trends*

prices, money wages and real wages together with the percentage of unemployment.

Let us look at the price series first – beginning with the inter-war years.

From 1920 to 1933 the trough of the Great Depression – retail prices fell but they did not fall smoothly. After 1933 prices rose but again at varying annual rates. Since 1948 the rise in prices has been virtually continuous – but again the rate of price increase has differed from year to year.

Money wages have behaved in a way which, very broadly, is similar to prices. From 1920 to 1933 their tendency was downwards. Since 1932, however, they have risen without a break though the percentage rate of change has varied. Moreover, as Fig. 6.iv makes clear, there is a tendency for the rate of increase in money wages to be greater in periods of low unemployment.

Taken together these Figures suggest that we shall need our macro-economic theory to be able to explain

(i) the *levels* of money wages and prices; and
(ii) the *rate* and *direction* of change in both.

While, since the rate of change of money wages seems to be related to the percentage of unemployment, it is clear that any theory we put forward to explain price/wage phenomena will need to be an integral part of our theory of output and its fluctuations.

Over the two periods taken together real wages have exhibited, as we would expect, a long-run tendency to increase. The rate of increase, however, has varied – reflecting as it does the somewhat diverse behaviour of wages and prices. In some years, for example, real and money wages have moved in opposite directions.

Finally our figures bring out two useful lessons. Rising prices are not, as some tend to suggest, a post-war phenomenon explicable in terms of the high post-war levels of employment. Prices rose continuously from 1932 to 1938 when employment was certainly not at high levels. Equally there is no evidence that the annual rate of price increase inevitably accelerates. This remains true even if 1971–2 are taken into account particularly if we refer back to the experience of 1950–2.

3 INTEREST RATES

A variable to which attention will frequently be directed as we develop our theory is 'the rate of interest'. There is, of course, no single interest rate any more than there is a single 'price' of output.

To measure 'the general level of prices' we make use of an index number which calculates the price of a defined 'basket' of goods or the implicit G.D.P. deflator. We could follow the same procedure in measuring 'the interest rate'. Instead we shall use the rate of return on irredeemable government bonds as a measure of 'the interest rate'. This is arbitrary and implicitly assumes that all interest rates tend to move together. The relevance of this procedure for our theory will become clearer in later chapters. Ultimately, of course, its appropriateness or otherwise turns on the question of fact as to whether, as a matter of experience, various interest rates do, or do not, tend to move together.

In Fig. 6.v (see p. 98) we plot

(i) the annual average yield of a 2½ per cent Consols (an irredeemable stock issued by the government):

(ii) the rate of interest on Treasury Bills (a short-term debt issued by the government); and

(iii) the percentage of the work-force unemployed.

In the inter-war years the interest rate (so defined) was high from 1920 to 1931. From 1932 to 1935 the rate declined sharply. Since 1932–5 were years of recovery from the trough of the Great Depression the inter-war years seem to suggest that *falling* unemployment (i.e. output rising faster than capacity) is associated with *falling* interest rates. This inference, however, is not supported by the observations for 1920–31. Nor is it easy to reconcile with post-war experience for since 1947 the tendency has been for the interest rate to rise while unemployment has been on average low and its fluctuations around the average level have been small.

We must conclude that though the rate of interest does exhibit fluctuations these do not seem to be simply related to fluctuations in employment. We shall need, therefore, as part of our macro-economic theory, to develop an explanation of the determination of the rate of interest capable of explaining very diverse experience.

4 THE ALLOCATION OF OUTPUT

In developing our national accounting concepts we defined gross national expenditure as:

gross national expenditure

$$\equiv \text{consumption} + \text{investment} + \frac{\text{government}}{\text{expenditure}} + \text{exports} - \text{imports}.$$

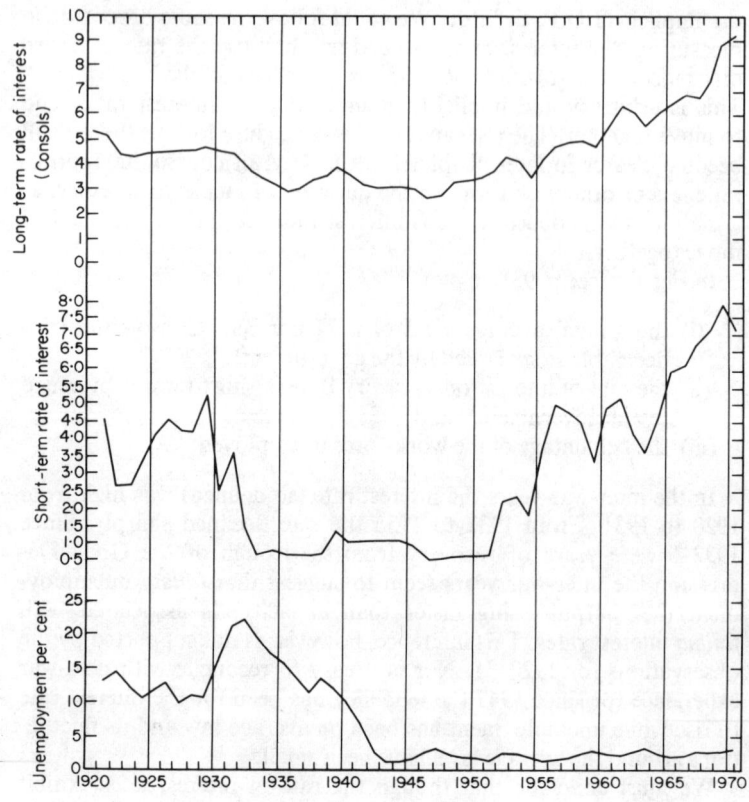

FIG. 6.v   The rates of interest

Sources: 1921–47, *The British Economy – Key Statistics 1900–1966*;
1948–70, *Economic Trends*

Of the five items on the right-hand side of this identity the first three consist of domestic expenditure† while the last two comprise what is called the current account balance of payments. Since, as we have seen, output can fluctuate and since, by definition, if output fluctuates so must expenditure, it is worthwhile seeing which expenditure items exhibit the greatest fluctuations. Moreover it is also worth seeing how output is allocated by society between alternative uses.

In Fig. 6.vi (p. 99) we present data for three of the main components

† Exports are now defined to include income received from abroad and imports to include income paid abroad.

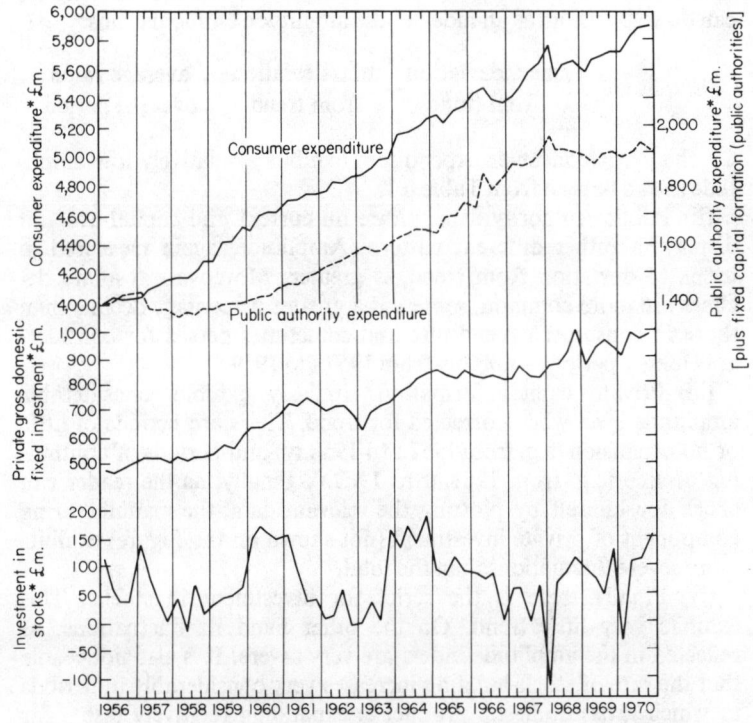

FIG. 6.vi The allocation of output

Source: *Economic Trends* (Oct 1967, July 1971)

* All at 1963 prices, seasonally adjusted. Quarterly rates.

of gross national expenditure, namely consumer expenditure, private investment and government expenditure.

Examination of the figure reveals the following main points.

(i) Consumer expenditure has risen almost continuously over the period. Significant absolute declines seem to have occurred only rather rarely.† The 'trend' – that is, the general tendency of the observations over the period under review – has therefore been a rising one. On the other hand the increase in consumer expenditure has by no means been smooth. There have, in short, been *deviations*

† The roman numerals occurring after the years refer to quarters. Thus 1965.ɪɪ indicates the second quarter (April–June) of 1965. Declines occurred in 1965.ɪɪ, 1966.ɪɪɪ, 1966.ɪᴠ, 1968.ɪɪ and 1969.ɪ.

from the trend. If we use these deviations to provide a rough measure of the extent to which the series has fluctuated around its trend we can do so by using, as an index of the amplitude of fluctuations:

$$\text{amplitude} \equiv \left(\begin{matrix}\text{max. deviation} \\ \text{from trend}\end{matrix} - \begin{matrix}\text{min. deviation} \\ \text{from trend}\end{matrix}\right) \Big/ \begin{matrix}\text{average value} \\ \text{over the period}\end{matrix}$$

On this basis consumer expenditure exhibits a relatively low amplitude as can be seen from Table 6.1.

(ii) Public Authority expenditure on current and capital account displays a rather different pattern. Amplitude, again measured in terms of deviation from trend, is greater. Moreover, absolute declines are more common, represent a greater percentage decline than those in consumer expenditure and sometimes persist for considerably longer periods – notably from 1957.ɪ to 1959.ɪ.

(iii) Private capital formation similarly exhibits considerable amplitude even when corrected for trend. There are periods of little or no expansion (e.g. from 1957.ɪ to 1958.ɪᴠ) and periods of continuing decline (e.g. from 1961.ɪɪɪ to 1963.ɪ). Finally, as the reader can check for himself by plotting the relevant data, the manufacturing component of private investment (not shown on the Figure) exhibits more severe fluctuations than the total.

(iv) Finally there is the series for investment in stocks. This exhibits very little trend. On the other hand its fluctuations, as reflected in the amplitude index, are very severe. It is also noticeable that the rate of stock-building increases very considerably in periods in which gross domestic product is expanding relatively fast – for example, from 1958.ɪᴠ to 1960.ɪɪ and from 1963.ɪ to 1964.ɪᴠ.

Finally a word of warning is in order. Though fluctuations in each of these series are important, the effect of a given percentage change in any one depends upon its relative importance in gross national expenditure. For example:

1 per cent change in	Value at 1963 prices (quarterly rates)
consumer expenditure	£49·7 m.
public authority expenditure	£16·2 m.
private gross investment	£7·3 m.
investment in stocks	£0·7 m.

These calculations, based upon the average values of Table 6.1, are simply illustrative. The point they illustrate, however, is important.

Table 6.1 *The Allocation of Output*

	Consumer expenditure	Public authority expenditure (current plus gross fixed capital formation)	Gross fixed capital formation (private sector)	Investment in stocks
				£ million.
Average value	4965	1619	733	73
Maximum deviations from linear trend {Positive	183	127	82	100
{Negative	−135	−62	−83	−196
Amplitude = $\dfrac{\text{max. positive} - \text{max. negative}}{\text{average}}$	0·064	0·117	0·23	4·055

Sources: *Economic Trends* (Oct 1967, July 1971)
The linear trend was estimated by least squares regression.
All data is quarterly seasonally adjusted at constant (1963) prices.

5 THE BALANCE OF PAYMENTS ON CURRENT ACCOUNT

Since World War II successive British governments have been increasingly obsessed by what is sometimes called 'the problem of the British balance of payments'. This has three elements; first, the balance of payments on *current account* arising out of international trade in goods – called the *visible* balance – and in services such as insurance, freight charges and tourist expenditure – called the *invisible* balance; second, the balance on *long-term* capital account arising out of capital transactions, for example, investment in the purchase of factories overseas or the financial obligation of foreigners; and third, the balance of *short-run* capital reflecting Britain's position as an international banker and the movement of short-term funds to or from London. In Figs. 6.vii (a) and (b) we present series chosen to illustrate the behaviour of the first component – the *current balance of payments*.

In Fig. 6.vii (a) we first show the behaviour of *visible trade* from 1948 to 1970. A certain amount can be learned from this figure.

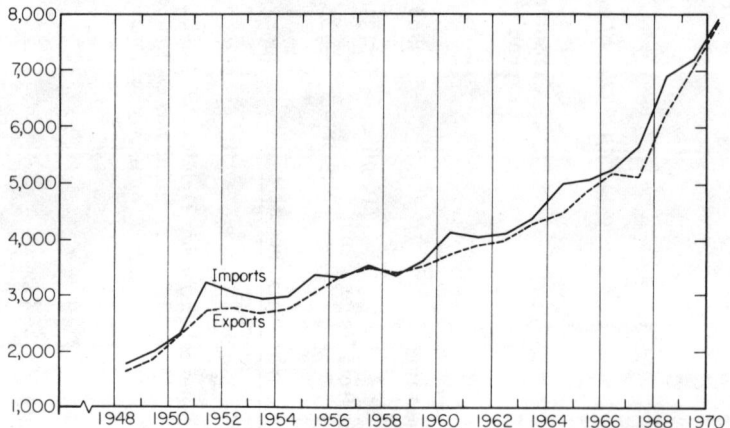

FIG. 6.vii(a)   The balance of payments on current account

Sources: Blue Book (1970) and *Economic Trends* (July 1971). Constructed series: Imports and exports both F.O.B. and seasonally adjusted

The first point is that the balance of visible trade is usually negative. Hence, for the balance on current account to be positive, since current account balance ≡ visible balance + invisible balance, the invisible balance must be favourable.

The second point is that though, over the whole period, exports rise relatively steadily, the import figure is much less stable. For example there was a very sharp increase in the import bill, and a less sharp one in exports, during the Korean War period (1950-2). Further relatively sharp increases in imports took place in 1958-60 and 1963-4 – significantly enough, as reference back to Fig. 6.i will confirm, periods of rapid expansion in output. If the increase in imports, which apparently accompanies an expansion, is not accompanied by an offsetting improvement in the *invisible balance* then the current account balance as a whole must deteriorate. Does this happen?

In Fig. 6.vii (b) we present *quarterly* data for the visible, invisible and current account balances for the years 1958-70. The deterioration in the visible balance in the expansion of 1958-60 is very marked. This was accompanied by a rather sharp deterioration in the invisible balance. As a result the current balance which was favourable (i.e. in surplus) to the extent of some £330 m. in 1958 was, by 1960, unfavourable (i.e. in deficit) to the extent of £275 m. – a total 'swing' of £600 m. Much the same story, though with an even larger current account deficit, occurred in the expansion of 1963-4.†

From these two figures it seems clear that the fluctuations in the U.K.'s current balance are dominated by those of the visible balance and that these, in their turn, are to be explained primarily by fluctuations in import demand.

There is also evidence that the behaviour of imports is closely related to the behaviour of U.K. output and employment. When both are rising fast (relative to their trend), so is the import bill. Conversely when output is rising relatively slowly, the visible balance and with it the current balance tends to improve. We shall therefore require any theory we develop to explain fluctuations in imports and the current balance as part of a single theory explaining fluctuations in output and employment and other relevant variables.

In this brief review we cannot deal with the vicissitudes of the capital accounts. It is worth noting, however, that the principal sterling crises, often reflecting the speculative movement of short-term funds *out* of London, took place in 1949, 1952, 1955, 1960-1, 1964 and 1967. Some at least of these difficulties *followed* the sharp

† The sharp deterioration in 1967.IV reflects the impact effect of the devaluation of sterling in that quarter.

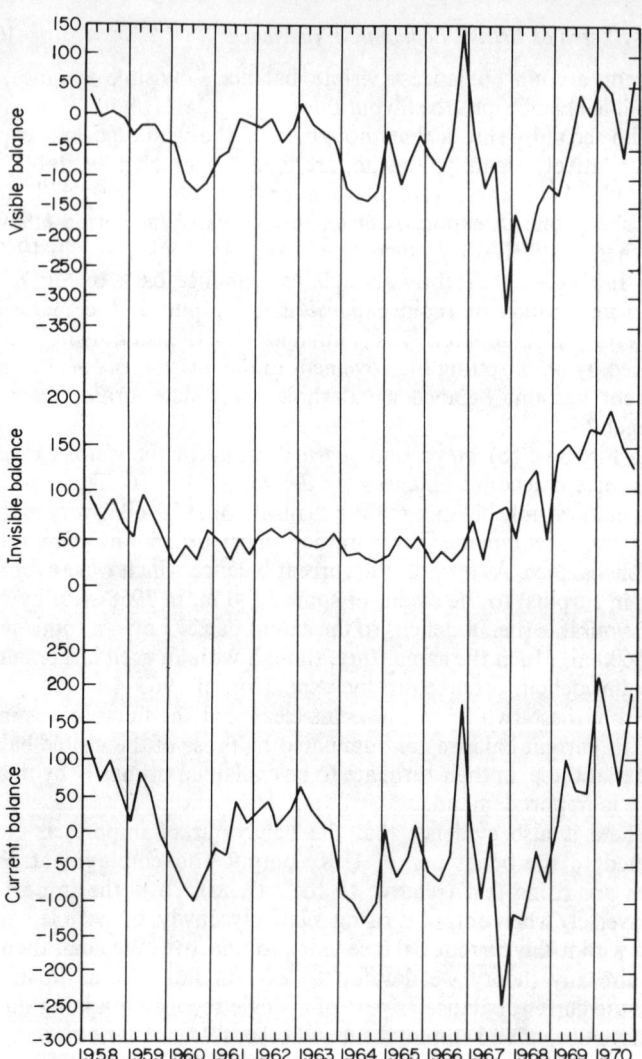

FIG. 6.vii(b)   The balance of payments on current account
Source: *Economic Trends* (Sep 1970, July 1971). All seasonally
adjusted and F.O.B.

deteriorations in the current balance which appear to be associated
with expansions. Hence, at least in part, short-term capital outflows,
and their associated exchange crises, may be part of a single mechanism properly to be explained by a single theory.

6 OBSERVATIONS AND THEORY

In the earlier sections of this Chapter we have sought to give a sketch of the behaviour of the principal macro-economic variables. In the following chapters – after a brief digression designed to discuss some analytical techniques – we seek to develop a macro-economic theory which will (i) provide a systematic explanation of the observations we have described; and (ii) provide us with the means of assessing policy recommendations designed to influence their behaviour in the future.

Though the description of these sections has been brief it is clear that the phenomena we have to explain are diverse. Moreover there are reasons, even at this stage, for believing them to be interrelated. The theory which follows is, for pedagogic reasons, presented in parts. It forms, however, a single integrated whole. Since this book is an introductory text, the theory presented has been somewhat simplified. The reader should, therefore, at the conclusion of Chapter 22, return to this chapter and ask himself: How far can the theory of later chapters explain the observations recorded in this one?

All that can be asked from an introductory text of this kind is that the theory it presents shall do four things:

(i) throw some light on the observations and give the reader some understanding of the analytical problems involved;
(ii) make the reader constructively sceptical of popular dogma and insistent on systematic evidence in support of arguments;
(iii) make it clear where the theory needs extension or modification; and
(iv) whet the reader's intellectual appetite for more advanced studies.

QUESTIONS AND EXERCISES

1. What criticisms can you make of our method of calculating the rate of growth of capacity?
2. According to Prof. F. W. Paish the proportion of productive capacity employed is, for 'small' percentages of employment, given by the relation:

$$\left(\begin{array}{c}\text{proportion of} \\ \text{capacity employed}\end{array}\right) = 105 - 5\left(\begin{array}{c}\text{percentage of the work-force} \\ \text{unemployed}\end{array}\right)$$

Hence 'full capacity' is defined by 1 per cent observed unemployment. Can you apply this formula to the inter-war years? If not, why not? Why do you think 1 per cent unemployment is equated to 'full capacity'?

3. According to another eminent economist *full employment* output in 1938 would have been 11 per cent higher than observed output. Accepting this estimate, can you suggest a way of calculating *full employment* output for each year from 1920 to 1938? Give an approximate estimate of (i) the total loss in output due to unemployment over the period; (ii) the average annual loss.

4. According to *National Income Statistics: Sources and Methods*, p. 36, the estimates of gross national product at *current prices* are subject to an error which is ± 3 per cent. In real terms the range of error probably lies between ± 3 per cent–10 per cent for relatively 'long' periods. How, in these circumstances, would you value the reliability of our calculated rates of growth in capacity? Between what upper and lower limits do the 'true' rates lie? Can we be confident that capacity really grew faster from 1948–70 than in the inter-war years? Give your reasons.

5. On the basis of Figs. 6.i and 6.vi, what value judgment is implied in the statement that we have done 'better' in the post-war years than we did in the inter-war years? Do you accept it?

6. A 'cycle' in an economic variable can be defined as a *repetitive wave-like motion over time*. The length of a cycle is measured from peak to peak in the series (A–A' below) or trough to trough (B–B'). Identify the peaks and troughs in the series for (i) gross domestic product; and (ii) unemployment. What are the lengths of the 'cycles' they suggest? Compare your dating with that given in *Economic Trends*.

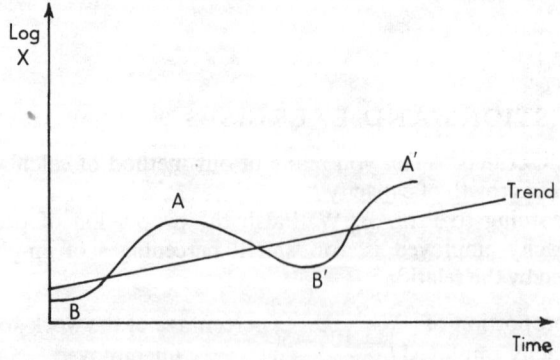

7. How would you seek to measure the 'amplitude' of the fluctuations in either G.D.P. or the percentage of unemployment? Use your measure to compare the experience of the inter-war and post-war years. Discuss your results.

8. Assemble the evidence for and against the statement that (i) the current balance of payments deteriorates sharply in periods in which output grows faster than capacity because of (ii) the resultant increase in imports.

9. Prices rose from 1932 to 1938. They rose also from 1948 to 1972. It is nowadays common to speak of the price increases in the second period as constituting 'inflation'. Did we have 'inflation' from 1932 to 1938? If not, why not? What does your view imply for the definition of inflation?

10. Fig. 6.ii suggests that 'capacity' grew steadily at about 3 per cent from 1948 to 1970. Make use of the concept of the production possibility curve, the determinants of its rate of movement and the data of Fig. 6.vi and Table 6.1 to criticise this hypothesis.

11. Between 1948 and 1970 real gross output seems to have grown at an average rate of about 3 per cent per annum. How fast has 'economic welfare' grown? How would you seek to define 'economic welfare' and measure its rate of growth?

12. From the charts given in *Economic Trends* examine critically the Figures and discussion given in this chapter. What amendments would you make and why?

13. Use the diagram of Question 6 to distinguish between the two concepts 'amplitude' and 'amplitude corrected for trend'. Which is the 'better' measure? Why?

14. Again using *Economic Trends*, examine critically our discussion of investment in stocks. Is there any reason to suppose a relationship between the rate of investment in stocks and the rate of imports? If so why do you think that such a relationship might exist?

15. According to the same source seasonally adjusted final expenditure in 1963 factor prices rose by £173 m. (at quarterly rates) between 1969.i and 1972.i Prepare a table showing how this increase came about. How important was 'capital formation' relative to consumption?

16. Extend Fig. 6.vi to include the latest available observations. Plot the unemployment percentage for the same period. Does the additional data modify your answer to Question 6?

17. It is sometimes said that the rate of change of prices is explained by the percentage of the work-force unemployed. Does the data in this chapter support this hypothesis?

18. Is the 'British balance of payments problem' exclusively or even primarily one of the current account? Discuss carefully.

19. Use *Economic Trends* to extend Fig. 6.iv to the latest available date. Do you agree that there is no evidence that the rate of price increase inevitably accelerates?

20. Which sterling crises did *not* occur after sharp expansions in U.K. output? How would you (i) describe and (ii) explain them.

SUGGESTED READING

D. C. Paige, 'Economic Growth in the Last Hundred Years', *N.I.E.S.R. Review* no. 16 (1961).

Sir Wm. Beveridge, *Full Employment in a Free Society* (Allen & Unwin, 1945) particularly pp. 40–88 and 242–58.

J. Knapp and K. Lomax, 'Britain's Growth Performance: the Enigma of the 1950s', *Lloyds Bank Review* (Oct 1964).

F. W. Paish, *Studies in an Inflationary Economy* (Macmillan, (1966) ch. xvii.

F. W. Paish, 'The Management of the British Economy', *Lloyds Bank Review* no. 76 (1965).

W. A. H. Godley and J. R. Shepherd, 'Long-Term Growth and Short-Term Policy', *N.I.E.S.R. Review* no. 29 (1964).

M. F. G. Scott, *A Study of United Kingdom Imports* (Cambridge, 1963) chs. i–ii.

J. C. R. Dow, *The Management of the British Economy* (Cambridge, 1964).

G. Orwell, *The Road to Wigan Pier* (Penguin, 1962).

W. Greenwood, *Love on the Dole* (Cape, 1934).

H. L. Beales and R. S. Lambert (Eds.), *Memoirs of the Unemployed* (Gollancz, 1934).

W. A. Lewis, *Economic Survey 1919–39* (Allen & Unwin, 1949) particularly chs i–v.

7 Analytical and Expository Devices

MANY students of economics find the analytical and expository devices used by economists forbidding or even frightening. This is particularly the case where the devices employ – or look as if they employ – mathematical modes of expression and mathematical methods of reasoning.

Those who read this book are therefore reassured at this stage that, in the pages which follow, no mathematical knowledge or manipulatory skill above that demanded at G.C.E. 'O' Level is assumed. If readers have reached this level, *and resolutely refuse to be upset by the use of symbols* – however terrifying they look – they have nothing to worry about at all. If they have passed this level and studied, let us say, 'A' Level Mathematics,† so much the better for them. But 'O' Level plus a little determination is all that is required.

After this reassurance readers are now asked to study carefully the following short notes on particular concepts and devices and to work through the Questions and Exercises at the end of the chapter.

1 THE CONCEPT OF A FUNCTION

In later chapters we shall frequently have to make assumptions about human behaviour which imply that some variable (call it X) depends systematically upon some other variable (call it Y). In this case we shall say that

$$X \text{ is a function of } Y$$

and write this:

$$X = f(Y) \tag{7.I}$$

where the notation f can be translated 'is a function of' or 'depends systematically upon'.

The notation $X = f(Y)$ is used because of its convenience. It is

† The advantage of mathematical knowledge in studying economics is immense. The fact that such knowledge is *not* necessary for this book should not obscure from the reader the immense gains to be derived from access to the principal technique of analytical thinking developed by man.

obviously nothing to worry about since it merely states a general dependence of X (the *dependent* variable) on Y the *independent* variable and this is not of itself a very difficult idea.

Now $X = f(Y)$ is a general statement. It tells us nothing about *the way* X depends upon Y. If we want to know this, we must know the *form* of the function. Three simple forms are as follows:

$$\left. \begin{array}{l} X = A + bY \\ X = F + cY^2 \\ X = H + dY^{-2} \end{array} \right\} \text{(7.II)} \qquad \left. \begin{array}{l} X = 100 + 0{\cdot}8\,Y \\ X = 80 + 2Y^2 \\ X = 50 + 11\,Y^{-2} \end{array} \right\} \text{(7.II}n\text{)}$$

where A, F and H are constants independent of Y and thus give the value of X where Y is zero.

All of these are special cases of the general statement $X = f(Y)$. They tell us *generally* that a particular value of Y implies a particular value of X and *specifically* how to *calculate* X given Y, the constant term (A, F, H) and the coefficient (b, c, d).

Obviously it is possible for one variable (X) to depend systematically upon (be a function of) more than one variable. Thus we could write;

$$X = f(Y, Z, Q, L, M) \qquad \text{(7.III)}$$

which is simply translated as:

X depends systematically upon the variables Y, Z, Q, L and M.

A particular and simple example is:

$$X = A + aY + bZ + cQ + dL + eM \qquad \text{(7.IV)}$$

or, to give a numerical version:

$$X = 0{\cdot}79 + 0{\cdot}2Y + 4{\cdot}7Z + 6{\cdot}23Q + 8L + 0{\cdot}0001M \qquad \text{(7.IV}n\text{)}$$

This tells us that, to calculate X, we now need to know the values of the constant A and of the five independent variables Y, Z, Q, L and M. Once we know these, and the values of the co-efficients a, b, c, d, e, it is a simple matter to calculate X.

In Chapter 2 we developed a rather crude behaviour hypothesis to explain the monthly consumption of beer. This was to the effect that the monthly consumption of beer (the dependent variable) depended systematically upon, *or* was a function of;

(i)   the weather (defined as the average monthly temperature);
(ii) the level of general prosperity (defined as the reciprocal of the percentage of unemployment); and
(iii) the ratio of the price of whisky to the price of beer.

Written in general functional form this would appear:

$$B_c = f(T, U, P_w/P_B) \qquad (7.\text{V})$$

where

$B_c \equiv$ monthly beer consumption

$T \equiv$ average monthly temperature

$U \equiv$ average percentage of the work force unemployed in each month

$P_w \equiv$ average price of whisky in each month

$P_B \equiv$ average price of beer in each month.

Let us take the 'beer' example a little further. In Chapter 2 we argued that *if*, with U and P_w/P_B constant, T increased *then B_c* would increase.

We now define a symbol to indicate this *marginal response* of the *dependent* variable (beer consumption) to a change in *one* of the *independent* variables, *the remaining independent variables being held constant as*:

$\dfrac{\partial B_c}{\partial T} \equiv$ marginal response of beer consumption to a change in

T (temperature) $- U$ and $\dfrac{P_w}{P_B}$ constant

$\dfrac{\partial B_c}{\partial U} \equiv$ marginal response of beer consumption to a change in

U (unemployment) $- T$ and $\dfrac{P_w}{P_B}$ constant

$\dfrac{\partial B_c}{\partial (P_w/P_B)} \equiv$ marginal response of beer consumption to a change in $\dfrac{P_w}{P_B}$

(the ratio of the price of whisky to the price of beer) $- T$ and U constant.

Our behaviour hypothesis did not specify numerical values for these *marginal response coefficients*. That is it did not set out either the *form* of the function or the *numerical value* of the *marginal response coefficient* as, for example, we did at (7.IIn). It did, however, specify the *sign* of the coefficients as the reader can easily see by looking back. We argued that

$$\frac{\partial B_c}{\partial T} > 0 \quad \frac{\partial B_c}{\partial U} < 0 \text{ and } \frac{\partial B_c}{\partial (P_w/P_B)} > 0.$$

To fix our ideas let us now give an (assumed) *form* and *set of numerical values* to (7.V) and write:

$$B_c = aT + b\frac{1}{U} + c\left(\frac{P_W}{P_B}\right); \qquad (7.\text{VI})$$

$$B_c = 0.7T + 6.71\,\frac{1}{U} + 32\left(\frac{P_W}{P_B}\right) \qquad (7.\text{VIn})$$

If we now assume values for T, U and (P_w/P_B) we can calculate the resulting values for B_c by (fairly) simple arithmetic. A few such calculations are given in Table 7.1.

Table 7.1 *The Monthly Consumption of Beer varying with the Weather, the Level of General Prosperity and the Price-Ratio of Whisky and Beer*

$$\left(\text{Hypothetical values of } T, U, \frac{P_W}{P_B}\right)$$

Month	$\dfrac{\partial B_c}{\partial 1}$	T	$\dfrac{\partial B_c}{\partial(1/U)}$	$\dfrac{1}{U}$	$\dfrac{\partial B_c}{\partial(P_W/P_B)}$	$\dfrac{P_W}{P_B}$	B_c
1	0·7	(40)	+6·71	(⅓)	+32	(1·2)	= 68·6
2	0·7	(44)	+6·71	(⅓)	+32	(1·2)	= 71·4
3	0·7	(48)	+6·71	(1/3·2)	+32	(1·5)	= 83·7
4	0·7	(52)	+6·71	(1/3·2)	+32	(1·5)	= 86·5
5	0·7	(56)	+6·71	(⅓)	+32	(1·9)	= 102·2
6	0·7	(60)	+6·71	(⅓)	+32	(1·9)	= 105·0
7	0·7	(64)	+6·71	(⅓)	+32	(2·0)	= 111·0
8	0·7	(70)	+6·71	(⅓)	+32	(1·9)	= 112·0
9	0·7	(64)	+6·71	(⅓)	+32	(1·9)	=
10	0·7	(55)	+6·71	(1/3·4)	+32	(1·3)	=
11	0·7	(45)	+6·71	(1/3·4)	+32	(1·3)	=
12	0·7	(40)	+6·71	(1/3·2)	+32	(1·3)	=

In this table a number of values of B_c have been left blank. These the reader should calculate for himself.

A lot can be learned from this table. For example, between months 4 and 5 all three independent variables changed. What was the resultant *change* in beer consumption? If we look carefully we see that it was:

$$15.7 = 0.7 \times (4.0) + 6.71 \times (0.021) + 32 \times (0.4), \qquad (7.\text{VIIn})$$

or, to forget our numbers for a moment,

$$\Delta B_c = \frac{\partial B_c}{\partial T} \cdot \Delta T + \frac{\partial B_c}{\partial (1/U)} \cdot \Delta\left(\frac{1}{U}\right) + \frac{\partial B_c}{\partial (P_w/P_B)} \cdot \Delta\left(\frac{P_w}{P_B}\right) \quad \text{(7.VIIn)†}$$

where the notation Δ indicates 'the change in' the variable to which it is applied. It all looks very complicated at first sight but a little patience – and a little practice – will soon convince the reader that it is not complicated at all.

Let us now take one more example of the use of functions. In the previous Chapter we argued that real output depended upon (or was a function of) (i) the quantity of capital employed; (ii) the input of labour services; and (iii) the state of technique. This hypothesis can be, and often is, written in the form of a *production function* which would appear thus:

$$Y = f(K, N, T)$$

where

$Y \equiv$ real output

$K \equiv$ real capital stock employed in production

$N \equiv$ labour employed

$T \equiv$ state of technique.

For this function we would expect $\partial Y/\partial K > 0, \partial Y/\partial N > 0, \partial Y/\partial T > 0$, since it is reasonable to suppose that an increase in any input (the quantity of the other input(s) and the state of technique remaining constant) would raise output as would an improvement in technique (with both inputs constant).

A particular production function, commonly met in macro-economics, is:

$$Y = TK^\alpha N^{1-\alpha}.$$

This too is an awkward looking expression at first sight but again there is really nothing to be afraid of. Suppose $\alpha = 0.5$ so that $1-\alpha$ also is 0·5. For simplicity assume $T=10$. Then since any number raised to the power of 0·5 is merely the square root of the number we can calculate Y from the values of the two independent variables K and N either by using logarithms or, simpler still, by employing a table of square roots. This is done for assumed values of K and N in Table 7.2. As before, the reader should complete the table for himself.

If we read *down* any column of Table 7.2 we find what happens to output when the input of *labour* increases with *capital* and *technique* constant. If we read *across* any row we find what happens to

† Those readers familiar with the calculus will be aware of the special nature of this case.

Table 7.2   *Production Function Relating Output to Varying Combinations of Inputs*

number of units of capital

		25	50	75	100	125	150	175	200	225	250	275
number of units of labour	5	112	158	194		250	274	296	317	336	354	371
	10	158	224	274	316	353		418	447	474	500	524
	15	194	274	336	387	432	474	512	547	581	612	642
	20	224	316	387	448	500	548	592	632	671	707	
	25		353	432	500	560	613	662	707		791	829
	30	274	387	474	548	613	672	725		822	866	909
	35	296	418		592	662	725	784	836	888	936	982
	40	317		547	632	707	775		896	948	1,000	1,049
	45	336	474	581	671		822	888	949	1,008	1,060	1,113
	50	354	500	612	707	791	866	936	1,000	1,060	1,120	1,173
	55	371	524	642	742	829	909	982	1,049	1,113	1,173	1,232

$$Y = TK^{\alpha}N^{1-\alpha} \quad \text{where}$$
$$\alpha = 0 \cdot 5$$
$$T = 10.$$

output when the input of *capital* increases with labour *input* and *technique* constant. If we read down a *diagonal* we discover what happens to output when both labour and capital inputs experience *equiproportional* increases.

We now give the names to the *marginal response coefficients* of the *production function* employed by economists. These are:

$\dfrac{\partial Y}{\partial K} \equiv$ marginal product of capital $\equiv$ the increase in output produced by a unit increase in K with N, T constant.

$\dfrac{\partial Y}{\partial N} \equiv$ marginal product of labour $\equiv$ the increase in output produced by a unit increase in N with K, T constant.

The reader should now check, from the table, that the following propositions are correct for this particular production function:

(i) doubling (trebling) both capital and labour always doubles (trebles) output;

(ii) the marginal product of both factors is always positive;

(iii) the marginal product of either factor tends to fall as more of it is employed with the other factor constant;

(iv) the marginal product of either factor is greater the smaller is the ratio of the quantity of it employed to the quantity employed of the other factor.

This particular function has a number of other important and interesting properties which we shall have to discuss in detail when we turn to consider economic growth. At this stage, however, they do not concern us for our aims are merely

  (i) to explain what is meant by a function;
 (ii) to show that the functional notation is nothing to worry about; and
(iii) to explain what is meant by *marginal response coefficients*.

2 Graphs

Economists make considerable use of graphs (or diagrams) to represent functional relations. A graph expresses a relationship between two variables, one of which is the dependent variable and the other the independent variable. Graphs are useful but, since they are limited to two dimensions, less powerful than the analytical methods discussed under the heading of *marginal response coefficients* which, obviously enough, can handle any number of 'systematic dependencies' we care to postulate. To illustrate we can draw a graph derived from our *production function*:

$$Y = f(K, N, T) \qquad \text{(7.VIII)}$$

This graph measures Y on the vertical axis and N on the horizontal. To construct the graph we then take K and T to be constant. The resulting relationship gives Y as a function of N (output as a function of labour input) with both the stock of capital (K) and the state of technique (T) given. It is thus a *short-run production function*. The slope of this curve relating Y and N is easily seen to be the *marginal response coefficient* $\partial Y/\partial N$ – that is, the marginal product of labour – or the increment in output brought about by a unit increase in labour (N) with both capital (K) and technique (T) constant.

We have drawn the curve to illustrate the propositions that

 (i) the marginal product of labour is always positive
(ii) the marginal product of labour diminishes as labour input increases.

If K and/or T changes the curve itself will shift. Suppose, for example, we were to draw a second curve on the basis of a greater capital stock. This curve would lie above the old.

The points to notice about graphs are:

(i) a graph only shows the relationship between a dependent

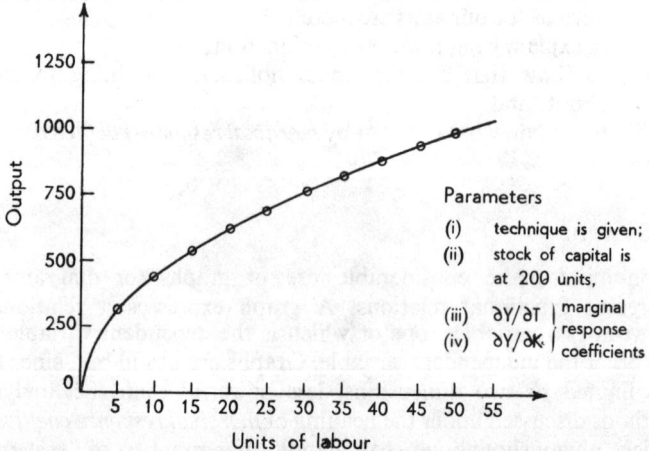

FIG. 7.i(a) The relationship between total product and varying units of labour output

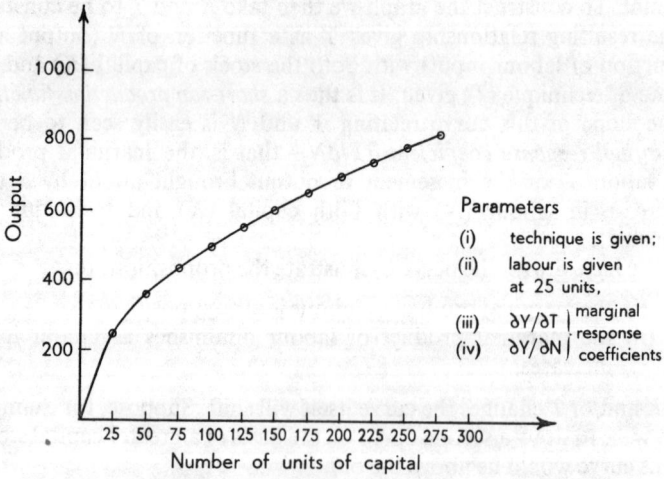

FIG. 7.i(b) The relationship between total product and varying units of capital input

variable and *one* independent variable of which the former is a function; given

(ii) the values of any other independent variables on which the dependent variable systematically depends (i.e. of which it is a function);

(iii) the slope of the graph is the *marginal response coefficient* relating the dependent variable to the independent variable.

The independent variables not measured on either axis and their marginal response coefficients, taken as given in drawing a graph (i.e. in our example K, $\partial Y/\partial K$, T and $\partial Y/\partial T$) are termed the *parameters* of the curve. Hence whenever the student is confronted with a curve relating two variables he should *always* ask himself two questions:

(i) what are the parameters of this curve?

(ii) which way would the curve shift if one of the parameters changed?

3 THE CONCEPT OF ELASTICITY

So far we have discussed the response of one (dependent) variable to a change in another (independent) variable in terms of the concept of a marginal response coefficient. Thus the marginal response of beer consumption to a change in temperature was defined as $\partial B_c/\partial T$ and given, in equation (7.VII) the hypothetical value of 0·7.

The marginal response coefficient is an important concept. Nevertheless it is not free from ambiguity for it depends crucially upon the units in which the dependent and independent variables are measured. To see this, assume beer to be measured in thousands of barrels (of standard size) and temperature in degrees of Fahrenheit. Then:

$$\frac{\partial B_c \text{ (in thousands of barrels)}}{\partial T \text{ (in degrees Fahrenheit)}} = 0·7.$$

So a *one* degree rise in temperature increases beer consumption by 700 barrels for, holding all other variables in equation (7.VII) constant,

$$\Delta B_c = \frac{\partial B_c}{\partial T} \cdot \Delta T$$

$$= 0·7 \text{ thousand barrels per degree} \times 1·0$$

$$= 700 \text{ barrels.}$$

If we now measured beer in units of 100 barrels we should have $\partial B_c/\partial T = 7\cdot 0$ and, if we measured in single barrels, $\partial B_c/\partial T = 700$. Behaviouristically speaking nothing has changed: only the units of measurement have altered and with them $\partial B_c/\partial T$.

This dependence of marginal response coefficients, the constants of human behaviour in linear functions like (7.VI), on the units in which the variables are measured is awkward for it makes it hard to estimate their importance – and thus compare two or more marginal response coefficients. Hence economists tend to use a measure which is independent of the units in which the variables are measured. This measure is known as *elasticity* and defined as:

$$\begin{array}{c}\text{the proportionate change} \\ \text{in the} \\ \text{dependent variable}\end{array} \equiv \frac{\Delta B_c}{B_c}$$

divided by

$$\begin{array}{c}\text{the proportionate change} \\ \text{in the} \\ \text{independent variable}\end{array} \equiv \frac{\Delta T}{T}.$$

bringing it about.

So that the elasticity of beer consumption with respect to temperature alone is:

$$\frac{\Delta B_c}{B_c} \div \frac{\Delta T}{T} \equiv \frac{\Delta B_c}{\Delta T} \cdot \frac{T}{B_c}$$

$$\equiv \frac{\dfrac{\partial B_c}{\partial T} \cdot \Delta T}{\Delta T} \cdot \frac{T}{B_c}$$

$$\equiv \frac{\partial B_c}{\partial T} \cdot \frac{T}{B_c} \cdot \equiv \frac{\partial B_c}{\partial T} \div \frac{B_c}{T}.$$

In short, the elasticity is the marginal response coefficient relating B_c to T *divided* by the ratio B_c/T. Since the latter expression is measured in the same units as the former, the choice of units has no influence on the elasticity which is a pure number. For example, using equation (7.VIIn) and taking two hypothetical values of T, we have:

$$B_c = 0\cdot 7 \times (40) + 6\cdot 71(\tfrac{1}{3}) \ + 32 \ (1\cdot 2) = 68\cdot 6 \qquad \text{(7.IXn(a))}$$
$$B_c = 0\cdot 7 \times (44) + 6\cdot 71(\tfrac{1}{3}) \ + 32 \ (1\cdot 2) = 71\cdot 4 \qquad \text{(7.IXn(b))}$$

$$\therefore \quad \Delta B_c = 0\cdot 7 \ \Delta T$$
$$= 0\cdot 7 \times 4\cdot 0$$
$$= 2\cdot 8.$$

and the elasticity is:

$$\text{elasticity}_{(1)} \equiv \frac{\partial B_c}{\partial T} \div \frac{B_c}{T} \simeq 0{\cdot}7 \div \frac{68{\cdot}6}{40} = 0{\cdot}7 \div 1{\cdot}715 = 0{\cdot}408.$$

Why do we use the sign $\simeq$ signifying *approximate* equality? Simply because we *could* have written, by using (7.IXn(b)) to give the values of B_c and T,

$$\text{elasticity}_{(2)} \equiv \frac{\partial B_c}{\partial T} \div \frac{B_c}{T} \simeq 0{\cdot}7 \div \frac{71{\cdot}4}{44{\cdot}0} = 0{\cdot}7 \div 1{\cdot}623 = 0{\cdot}431.$$

Hence the numerical value of the elasticity over a *range* of change in the independent variable is not unambiguous. If we began with (7.IXn(a)) and moved to (7.IXn(b)) we estimated the elasticity as 0·408. Reversing the procedure we found a different value. A diagram may make the point clearer.

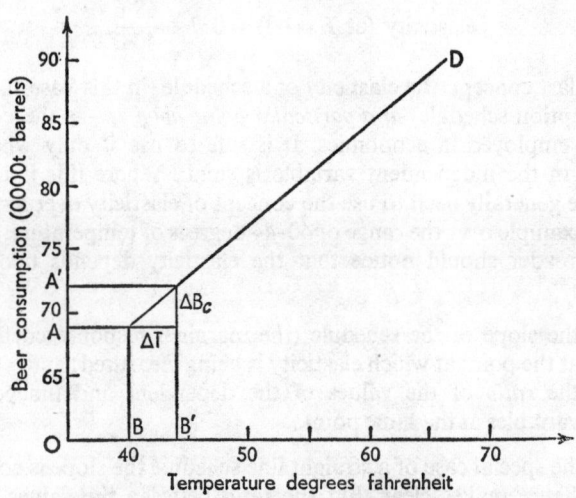

Fig. 7.ii   Beer consumption function

At 40° F the ratio $\dfrac{B_c}{T} = \dfrac{OA}{OB} = \dfrac{68{\cdot}6}{40{\cdot}0}$

At 44° F the ratio $\dfrac{B_c}{T} = \dfrac{OA'}{OB'} = \dfrac{71{\cdot}4}{44{\cdot}0}.$

The marginal response coefficient

$$= \frac{\partial B_c}{\partial T} = \frac{\dfrac{\partial B_c}{\partial T} \cdot \Delta T}{\Delta T} = \frac{\Delta B_c}{\Delta T}.$$

Suppose now we make the temperature change not four degrees but 0·004 degrees: that is one-thousandth part of our first example. We have for our two measures:

$$\text{elasticity}_{(1)} \simeq 0·7 \div 1·715 = 0·408163$$

and $$\text{elasticity}_{(2)} \simeq 0·7 \div 1·71505 = 0·408151.$$

Clearly the *smaller* we make the temperature change (and thus the resultant beer consumption change) the nearer our two elasticity measures approach. As the temperature change tends to zero – that is becomes smaller and smaller – the elasticity becomes closer to $0·7 \div 68·6/40·0$. In the limit – that is, when ΔT is indefinitely small – we can say that the elasticity *at temperature 40* is given by:

$$\text{elasticity (at } T = 40) = 0·7 \div \frac{68·6}{40·0}.$$

This last concept, the elasticity of a schedule (in this case the beer consumption schedule) *at a particular point upon it* – is the concept usually employed in economics. It is safe to use it only when the change in the independent variable is small. Where this is not the case, we generally need to use the concept of elasticity over a range – in our example over the range of 40–44 degrees of temperature.

The reader should notice that the elasticity depends upon two factors:

  (i) the slope of the schedule (the marginal response coefficient) at the point at which elasticity is being measured; and
  (ii) the *ratio* of the values of the dependent and independent variables at the same point.

For the special case of a straight line schedule the slope is constant as the figure makes clear. But the ratio between the values of the variables is not (in general) constant. Hence the elasticity will vary along the curve. The reader should make sure that he understands this point by working a few examples in addition to those given in the Questions and Exercises at the end of this Chapter.

Though in general straight line curves do *not* exhibit constant elasticity some straight line curves exhibit this property.

There are in fact two special straight line curves commonly used to illustrate elasticity. They are shown in the Figure on page 121.

The first of these curves has zero elasticity of demand for butter over the price range $p_A - p_B$. The second has infinite elasticity at

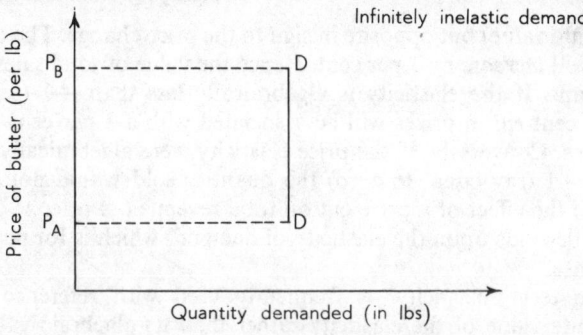

Infinitely inelastic demand

Zero elasticity of demand over the price range
$P_A - P_B$

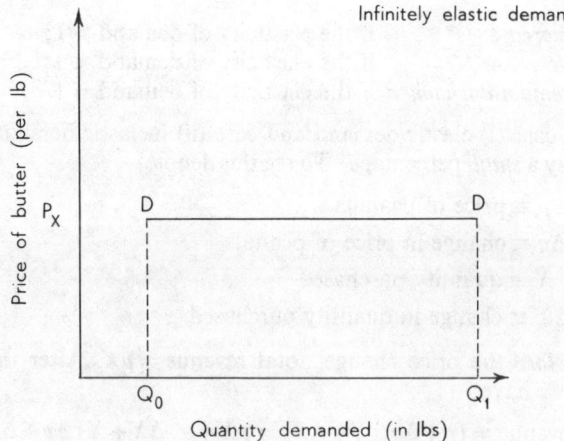

Infinitely elastic demand

Infinite elasticity at the price P_X over the range
$Q_0 - Q_1$

FIG. 7.iii Hypothetical demand curves for butter

the price p_x. The reader should satisfy himself that these statements are consistent with our earlier discussion of elasticity.

Apart from its freedom from the problem of units, the concept of elasticity has other uses. Suppose that the community's demand for peanuts (X) depends only on their price (p). Suppose now that producers lower price by (say) 1 per cent. If the elasticity of demand is -1, then the proportionate change in quantity will be equal (in absolute value) but opposite in sign to the price change. The quantity sold will *increase* by 1 per cent. Hence the value of total sales will be constant. If the elasticity is algebraically less than -1 (say -3) a 1 per cent *cut* in prices will be associated with a 3 per cent *increase* in sales. Conversely, if the price elasticity were algebraically greater than -1 (say equal to zero) the quantity sold would not change. Hence the effect of a price cut on total revenue ($\equiv$ price $\times$ quantity sold) depends upon the elasticity of demand, which is for peanuts in this case.

The term 'elasticity' is frequently used with reference to the absolute value of the elasticity rather than its algebraic value. The *sign* of the elasticity is usually clear from the context. Adopting this convention we may summarize the peanut example by saying that if the price of peanuts is reduced by a *small* percentage then the value of sales will

(i) *increase*   if the elasticity of demand > 1;
(ii) *decrease*   if the elasticity of demand < 1;
(iii) *remain unchanged* if the elasticity of demand $= 1$.

We call case (i) elastic demand and case (ii) inelastic demand. Why do we say a *small* percentage? To see this denote

$p \equiv$ price of peanuts

$\Delta p \equiv$ change in price of peanuts

$X \equiv$ quantity purchased

$\Delta X \equiv$ change in quantity purchased.

Then *before* the price change, total revenue $= pX$. After the price change we have:

total revenue $= (p+\Delta p)(X+\Delta X) = pX + p \cdot \Delta X + X \cdot \Delta p + \Delta p \cdot \Delta X.$

Hence the change in revenue is given by:

$$\Delta \text{ (total revenue)} = pX + p \cdot \Delta X + X \cdot \Delta p + \Delta X \cdot \Delta p - pX$$
$$= p \, \Delta X + X \cdot \Delta p + \Delta X \cdot \Delta p.$$

Now this expression can be rewritten as:

$$\Delta \text{ (total revenue)} = pX \left\{ \frac{\Delta X}{X} + \frac{\Delta p}{p} + \frac{\Delta X}{X} \cdot \frac{\Delta p}{p} \right\}$$

$$= pX \left\{ \begin{array}{c} \text{prop.} \\ \text{change} \\ \text{in} \\ \text{quantity} \end{array} + \begin{array}{c} \text{prop.} \\ \text{change} \\ \text{in} \\ \text{price} \end{array} + \begin{array}{c} \text{prop.} \\ \text{change} \\ \text{in} \\ \text{quantity} \end{array} \times \begin{array}{c} \text{prop.} \\ \text{change} \\ \text{in} \\ \text{price} \end{array} \right\}.$$

Suppose the last term is sufficiently small to be neglected. Then:

$$\Delta\left(\begin{array}{c} \text{total} \\ \text{revenue} \end{array}\right) \gtreqless 0 \quad pX\left\{\begin{array}{cc} \text{prop.} & \text{prop.} \\ \text{change} & \text{change} \\ \text{in} & + \text{in} \\ \text{quantity} & \text{price} \end{array}\right\} \gtreqless 0.$$

Clearly, since the proportionate change in price is *negative*, the right-hand inequality can be written:

$$pX\left\{\frac{\text{prop. change in quantity}}{\text{prop. change in price}} + 1\right\} \lesseqgtr 0.$$

i.e. $\qquad pX\{\text{elasticity of demand} + 1\} \lesseqgtr 0.$

Hence revenue will increase if the elasticity is < -1; which is the result which we reached verbally above. To reach this result we have, however, had to set $\Delta p/p \,.\, \Delta X/X$ (the product of the proportionate changes) to zero. This is permissible if Δp is close to zero. Hence our elasticity *result*, not very surprisingly in view of our *definition* of point elasticity, holds strictly only where Δp is indefinitely small. *In all other cases it is an approximation which involves an error dependent on $\Delta p/p \,.\, \Delta X/X$.* The reader should calculate for himself how good this approximation is by assuming a variety of values for $\Delta p/p$ and $\Delta X/X$.

4 FUNCTIONS AND SCHEDULES

In our beer consumption example we wrote quite generally;

$$B_c = f\left(T, U, \frac{P_w}{P_B}\right), \tag{7.V}$$

and specifically:

$$B_c = aT + b\left(\frac{1}{U}\right) + c\left(\frac{P_w}{P_B}\right) \tag{7.VI}$$

This specific function (7.VI) is said to be *linear* in the independent variables because it involves no powers of these variables other than unity. Had we written

$$B_c = a_1 T + aT^2 + b\left(\frac{1}{U}\right) + c\left(\frac{P_w}{P_B}\right)^2 + d\left(\frac{P_w}{P_B}\right)$$

the function would have been *quadratic* in T and (P_w/P_B) and *linear* in $(1/U)$.

In general, in economics, we must expect non linear relationships to occur. Nevertheless, in most of this book, we shall only use functions which are *linear* – that is, of the form:

$$Y = a + b.x + c.z + d.w$$

or *logarithmically linear* – that is, of the form:

$$\log Y = \log a' + b' \log x + c' \log z \qquad (7.\text{VI})$$

The latter function, since multiplying the logarithm of a variable means raising the variable to the power of its multiplier, can be written:

$$Y = a'x^{b'}z^{c'},$$

a form we have already met in the production function discussed earlier.

The justification for restricting ourselves to linear or log linear functions is two-fold. The first point is that these functions are algebraically convenient. Thus the linear function (7.VI) has the constant marginal response coefficients $\partial B_c/\partial T = a$, $\partial B_c/\partial(1/U) = b$ and $\partial B_c/\partial(P_w/P_B) = c$ while the log linear function also has the constant marginal response coefficients $\partial \log y/\partial \log x = b'$ and $\partial \log y/\partial \log z = c'$.

There is also the second point that any function, *over a sufficiently small range of values of the independent variable, can be approximated by a linear function*. This is illustrated in the figures below which show how two functions which are certainly not linear can be approximated in this way.

Thus in Fig. 7.iv (a) for values of the independent variable close to x_1 we can approximate the function by the line aa', for values around x_2 by the line bb' and so on. In the same way the function in Fig. 7.iv (b) can be approximated reasonably well by the four straight lines aa', bb', cc' and dd' each of which is applicable only over a range of values (or a particular value) of the independent variable.

To visualise the properties of the logarithmic function (7.VII) consider some variable Y which is growing through time as follows:

Time	0	1	2	3	4
Value of Y	10	15	22·5	33·75	50·625.

It is easy to see that the law of growth in this case is a 50 per cent increase in Y per period of time. If we graph this function using *a*

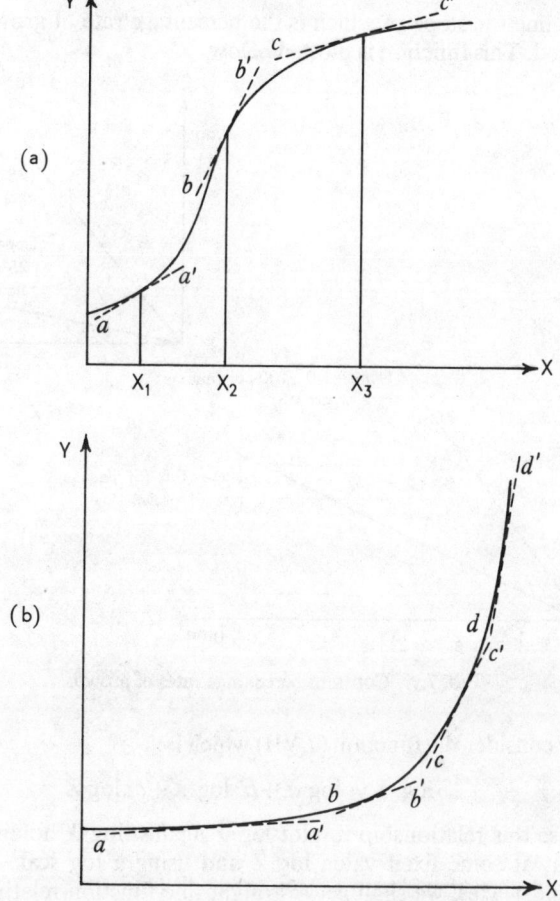

FIG. 7.iv Linear approximations to non-linear relations

logarithmic scale for Y and a natural scale for time we have the values:

Time	0	1	2	3	4
Log Y	1·0	1·1761	1·3522	1·5281	1·7042
Y	10·0	15	22·5	33·57	50·625.

From this table it is easy to see that constant *absolute* differences in the logarithm of a variable imply constant percentage increases in the variable itself. The graph of log Y against time will thus be a straight line the slope of which is the percentage rate of growth in Y per period. This function is plotted below.

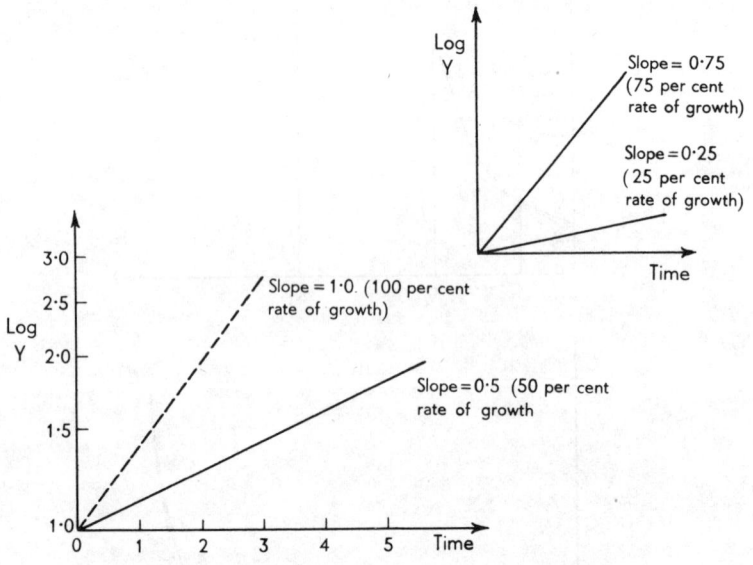

FIG. 7.v   Constant percentage rates of growth

Now consider the function (7.VII) which is:

$$\log Y = \log a' + b' \log X + c' \log Z$$

If we use this relationship to plot $\log Y$ against $\log X$ holding $\log Z$ constant at some fixed value $\log \bar{Z}$ and using a log scale for *both* the x and y axes, we shall get a straight line function relating $\log X$ and $\log Y$. The slope of this function will be the marginal response coefficient $\partial \log Y / \partial \log X = b'$. The constant will define the origin of the curve at the point $\log X = 0$ and $\log Z = \log \bar{Z}$. This curve is plotted in the figure below.

Suppose now that $\log X$ increases from x_1 to x_2. This distance defines a percentage increase in X. The resultant change in $\log Y$ from y_1 to y_2 defines a percentage increase in Y. The slope of the function is thus:

$$\frac{\Delta Y}{Y} \div \frac{\Delta X}{X} \equiv \text{elasticity of } Y \text{ with respect to } X.$$

Hence functions of the form of (7.VII) have constant marginal

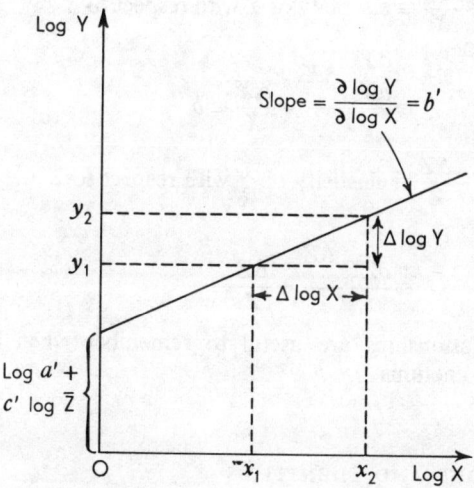

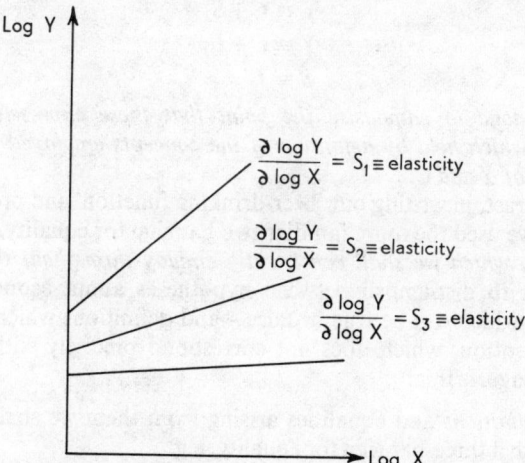

FIG. 7.vi   Elasticities and logarithmic relationships
Three different marginal response coefficients

response coefficients which are elasticities (slopes of straight lines in the logarithms). Thus the properties of (7.VII) are:

$$\frac{\Delta Y}{Y} \div \frac{\Delta X}{X} \equiv \text{elasticity of } Y \text{ with respect to } X$$

$$\equiv \frac{\frac{\partial Y}{\partial X} \cdot \Delta X}{Y} \div \frac{\Delta X}{X} \equiv b$$

$$\frac{\Delta Y}{Y} \div \frac{\Delta Z}{Z} \equiv \text{elasticity of } Y \text{ with respect to } Z$$

$$\equiv \frac{\frac{\partial Y}{\partial Z} \cdot \Delta Z}{Y} \div \frac{\Delta Z}{Z} \equiv c$$

These relationships are useful to remember when interpreting graphs and functions.

5 EQUATIONS AND IDENTITIES

In Chapters 3 and 4 we set out the framework of definitions which we use in national income accounting. In these chapters we always wrote equality with this sign $\equiv$ rather than the more familiar $=$. Thus we wrote:

$$Y \equiv C + S$$
$$Y \equiv C + I$$
$$\therefore \quad S \equiv I.$$

This was done to emphasise the point that these expressions were identities which held by definition of the concepts employed whatever the values of Y and C.

By contrast, in writing our 'beer-drinking function' and production function we used the more familiar two bar sign for equality. *This is a convention which we shall consistently employ throughout this book.* We use it to distinguish between hypotheses about economic behaviour – which can be true or false – and definitions which cannot. Our convention, which does not correspond precisely with mathematical usage, is this:

  (i) *Definitions* and equalities arising from them we shall express with a three-bar sign for equality, e.g.
$$Y \equiv C + I.$$
These will be referred to as *identities*.

(ii) *Hypotheses* about economic behaviour, including, of course, equilibrium conditions, we shall express with the two-bar sign for equality, e.g. our 'beer-drinking hypothesis' which we write:

$$B_c = f\left(T, U, \frac{P_w}{P_B}\right).$$

These we shall speak of as *equations*.

In short meaningful (because conceivably testable) propositions will always be expressed as *equations* simply because they may or may not be found to hold in the real world. Such relations are often called *behaviour equations*. Definitional relationships, which *always* hold irrespective of the values of the variables, we shall always express as *identities*.

This distinction we employ between identities and equations is of great importance and is commonly found in economic writing. The significant point is that identities, which hold whatever the values of the variables, tell us nothing about economic behaviour and cannot be tested by empirical observation. Equations, on the other hand, embody propositions about economic behaviour which can be tested by empirical observation either directly or via predictions derived from them.

6 STOCKS AND FLOWS

Economic variables fall into two groups which we shall call *stocks* and *flows*: a *stock* variable is one which has no time dimension but is described at a moment of time: a *flow* variable necessarily involves a time dimension.

To give an example of a flow variable we may take income. To say that a man's income is £1000 is meaningless *unless* we know the *time period of measurement*. An income of £1000 *per year* is very different from an income of £1000 *per decade* or £1000 *per week*. All flow variables are thus rates (of flow) over some defined time period. This applies, as a little reflection will make clear, to all the national income accounting concepts we discussed in Chapters 3 and 4.

Stock variables, on the other hand, do not require a time dimension to have meaning. It makes sense to say that on 1 January 1965 a man's height is 5 feet 11 inches or his wealth £10,027 without specifying a period of time. We may conclude that

(i) *flow* variables are necessarily defined with reference to a period of time, i.e. a year, month, decade or quarter, and can be measured and given meaning only in terms of this (or some other) period;

(ii) *stock* variables are measured at a moment of time and have meaning independently of any period.

It should also be clear that many flow variables are simply the change in some stock variable *over a given period*. For example if at the end of December 1970 real capital (a stock variable) is £10 millions and at the end of December 1971 it is £14 millions then the increment in real capital *over the year* is £4 millions. We have already defined the increase in real capital as real net *investment*. Hence the *rate* of real *net* investment (a flow variable) is £4 millions *a year* for the year 1970.

Much confusion arises from a failure to distinguish between *stocks* and *flows*. The reader is strongly recommended to ask himself, on meeting any economic variable for the first time, is this a *stock* variable or is it a *flow*?

7 THE CONCEPT OF EQUILIBRIUM

Economists constantly speak of the 'economic system' or the 'market for some commodity' as being in 'equilibrium'. By this they imply no more than that the system or market has reached a position from which it has no tendency to depart – in short a position of rest. Such a position will occur only if the forces making for movement in one direction are exactly counterbalanced by the forces making for movement in the opposite direction. The *equilibrium* value of any variable is thus simply the value of the variable which, if reached, will tend to persist unchanged.

Since, as we have seen, economics is a social science and thus concerned with human behaviour, we may now ask what this concept of equilibrium implies *in terms of human behaviour*. To see this let us take an example and enquire what is meant by, let us say, the market for peanuts being in *equilibrium* at a price of 10p per packet and a monthly volume of sales of 2 million packets. Clearly the market will only be in equilibrium if *both* buyers and sellers are 'satisfied' with the ruling price and quantity sold. If they are not one group or the other will, in future periods, modify its behaviour which will *change* the price and quantity sold. Thus we may enunciate the general proposition that, for *equilibrium* to exist in any period, people must be 'satisfied' with the actual price ruling in the market and the actual quantities sold in any period. When they are *not* 'satisfied' *disequilibrium* exists *and some persons will modify their behaviour.*

What is meant by being 'satisfied'? All we mean by this expression is that what people *plan* to do is in conformity with what *actually* occurs. For where this is not so, *those people whose plans are not satisfied, will, in the next period of time, modify their plans.* Equilibrium thus requires *all plans to be satisfied* which again requires all *plans to be consistent.*

A table depicting hypothetical situations in the market for peanuts will serve to illustrate the point.

Suppose that, in some period producers plan to make and sell 2 million packets of peanuts at a price of 10p per packet and that, in the same month, consumers plan to purchase 2 million packets at 10p per packet. In this case

  (i) all plans are consistent; and
 (ii) the actual price and quantity sold (and purchased) will correspond with the plans of both groups; hence
(iii) the market is in equilibrium.

Suppose now that in period two producers' plans are the same as period one but, because of a change in consumers' tastes, consumers now plan to purchase only 1·5 million packets at the price of 10p.
In this case

  (i) all plans are *not* consistent;
 (ii) the *actual* price and/or quantity sold (and purchased) can *not* and hence will *not* correspond with the *plans* of *both* groups; hence
(iii) the market is in *disequilibrium* and, in the next period, producers will obviously wish to modify their plans.

Table 7.3   *Equilibrium and the Peanut Market*

	Price (per packet)	Planned sales of producers (m)	Planned purchases of consumers (m)	Remarks
Position 1	10p	2·0	2·0	Consistent plans – equilibrium
2	10p	2·0	1·5	Inconsistent plans – disequilibrium
3	8p	1·75	1·75	Consistent plans – equilibrium

We may sum up the discussion so far by the following statements:

(i) to say that a system is in *equilibrium* means that it has reached a position of rest from which it has no tendency to depart;

(ii) where an economic system is in equilibrium then:

    (a) the *actual* values of the variables it contains must correspond with

    (b) the values of the same variables which people *planned* or *expected*;

(iii) this can only occur when *all plans* are consistent;

(iv) where plans are *not* consistent *disequilibrium* exists;

(v) the sign of the existence of disequilibrium is that, for some persons or groups, *planned* and *actual* values of variables do not coincide;

(vi) the outcome of *disequilibrium* is a *change* in *plans* by the persons or groups for whom *actual* and *planned* variables do not coincide.

It is obviously a simple matter to extend this argument one stage further. Suppose our peanut market reaches position 2 – a position of disequilibrium. Then producers will modify their *plans* until a new position (say position 3) is reached. At this position we have once again a situation in which

(i) *all* plans are consistent

(ii) the *actual* price and quantity sold (and purchased) corresponds with the plans of both producers and consumers so that

(iii) neither group has any need to modify its behaviour and

(iv) the peanut market is in *equilibrium* once again.

8 STATICS AND DYNAMICS

In Chapter 5 we drew a distinction between *static* and *dynamic* analysis. This distinction can now be illustrated in terms of our 'peanut' example.

In *static* analysis – commonly called *comparative statics* – we compare only positions of equilibrium: that is we compare positions 1 and 3 and note that, as a consequence of a change in consumers' tastes *both* the *equilibrium price* of a packet of peanuts and the *equilibrium quantity* sold (and purchased) is lower than it was in the initial equilibrium position.

We do not, however, seek to explain either *how long* (i.e. how many months) it takes to get from position 1 to position 3 or the *path* by which *price* and *quantity* adjust to the new *equilibrium* position, for these questions, though important, form part of *dynamic* analysis.

Comparative statics thus simplifies reality by ignoring the *process* of change. Hence in comparative statics the rates at which variables change are ignored. At one period we are at position 1. At another we are at position 3. Our sole aim is to compare these two positions. Perhaps the simplest way of moving in this somewhat unreal world is to regard all changes as taking place instantaneously.

QUESTIONS AND EXERCISES

1. The 'beer-consumption' hypothesis of (7.VIn) is:

$$B_c = 0 \cdot 7 \, T + 6 \cdot 71 \, \frac{1}{U} + 32 \Big(\frac{P_w}{P_B} \Big).$$

Assume U to be constant at 2 per cent (i.e. $\frac{1}{U} = \frac{1}{2}$)

$\frac{P_w}{P_B}$ to be constant at 1·5.

Then calculate the values of B_c for the following values of T

$$T = 40, 45, 50, 55, 60, 65, 70, 75, 80.$$

Draw a graph with B_c on the vertical axis and T on the horizontal. From this curve identify (i) the marginal response coefficient $\partial B_c / \partial T$. (ii) the quantity $6 \cdot 71(\frac{1}{2}) + 32(1 \cdot 5)$.

On what does the position of the curve depend? In what way would the curve shift if the public's taste for beer suddenly increased?

What is the (theoretical) value of beer consumption when T is zero?

2. From the following data, again using (7.VIn) plot a graph with B_c on the vertical axis and T on the horizontal.

T	U	P_w/P_B
40	2	1·5
45	2	1·5
50	3	1·8
55	3	1·8
60	2	1·8
65	4	2·0
70	1	1·1

   (i) What meaning, if any, can be given to the *slope* of this curve?

  (ii) What is the relation between the slope of this curve and the slope of the curve constructed in Question 1?

 (iii) In what circumstances, if any, could the slope of a curve which simply plots observed values of a dependent variable (in this case B_c) and one independent variable (in this case T) give a good estimate of the marginal response coefficient $\partial B_c / \partial T$?

3. Plot the following graphs putting X on the vertical axis and Y on the horizontal.

$$X = A + bY \qquad \text{where } A = 100; b = 0 \cdot 8$$

$$X = F + cY^2 \qquad \text{where } F = 100; c = 0 \cdot 2$$

and Y takes the following values:

$$Y = 0, 2, 10, 12, 20, 40, 50.$$

In each case find the value of $\partial X / \partial Y$ (the marginal response coefficient) when $Y = 2$ and $Y = 10$. What difficulties arise with the second function?

Show that, for one curve, $\partial X / \partial Y$ is a constant while for the other $\partial X / \partial Y$ depends upon (is a function of) Y.

At what value of Y do the two curves cut? What is the corresponding value of X?

4. In economics the elasticity of any dependent variable (X) with respect to some other independent variable (Y), of which it is a function, is defined as follows:

$$\text{elasticity} \equiv \frac{\text{proportionate change}}{\text{in } X} \div \frac{\text{proportionate change}}{\text{in } Y}$$

$$\equiv \frac{\Delta X}{X} \Big/ \frac{\Delta Y}{Y} = \frac{\frac{\partial X}{\partial Y} \cdot \Delta Y}{X} \Big/ \frac{\Delta Y}{Y}$$

Using this formula find the approximate elasticity of both curves in Question 3 when Y changes from 50 to 51 and 100 to 101.

Can you find the elasticity of output (Y) with respect to labour (N) from the production function $Y = TK^{\alpha}N^{1-\alpha}$? Put $T = 10$, $K = 10,000$, $N = 100$, $\alpha = 0 \cdot 5$. Is there a relationship between this elasticity and $1 - \alpha$? [Hint: use the logarithmic formulation.]

5. Fig. 7.i (a) is drawn on the assumption that the production function is:

$$Y = TK^{\alpha}N^{1-\alpha} \quad \text{where } T = 10, K = 200, \text{ and } \alpha = 0 \cdot 5.$$

What would happen to the curve if K became 100? Would the slope of the curve $\partial Y/\partial N$ be greater, less or the same at any given value of N? What does your answer mean in terms of economics? Suppose alternatively that with $K = 200$, T became 20. Plot the new curve and explain your result.

6. Using the same production function $Y = TK^\alpha N^{1-\alpha}$ put $T = 1$ and $\alpha = 0.5$ and show that the following table gives numerical values of K and N which produce a given constant output.

K Capital stock units	N Labour input units
8	1,250
10	1,000
20	500
25	400
40	250
50	200
100	100

(i) What is the constant value of Y?

(ii) What is the cheapest method of those shown of producing the given output when
   (a) labour costs £1 per unit per year; capital £25 per unit per year?
   (b) labour costs £1 per unit per year; capital £4 per unit per year?
   (c) labour costs £2 per unit per year; capital £50 per unit per year?

(iii) What can you learn by comparing (a) and (c)?

(iv) What can you learn by comparing (b) and (a)?

Explain your results and the lessons you draw from them.

7. Using the same function as Question 6, the marginal physical products of labour and capital respectively are:†

$$\frac{\partial Y}{\partial K} \equiv \frac{\text{marginal physical}}{\text{product of capital}} = T\alpha \left(\frac{N}{K}\right)^{1-\alpha} = 0.5 \left(\frac{N}{K}\right)^{\frac{1}{2}}$$

$$\frac{\partial Y}{\partial N} \equiv \frac{\text{marginal physical}}{\text{product of labour}} = T(1-\alpha)\left(\frac{K}{N}\right)^{\alpha} = 0.5 \left(\frac{K}{N}\right)^{\frac{1}{2}}.$$

Find numerical values for these marginal physical products

† Readers familiar with the calculus will readily accept these results. Those not so familiar are asked to take them on trust.

for your answer to Question 6 (ii) (a). What do you notice about the relationships of marginal physical products to factor prices? Can you find a simple formula expressing minimum cost conditions?

8. Re-read and reformulate in the light of your answers to these two questions the discussion of the shape of the production possibility curve in Chapter 6. What kinds of production possibility curve would you expect to derive from the following pairs of production functions? Give your reasons.

Situation *A*.

   agricultural output $= T_A K_A^{\alpha_A} N_A^{1-\alpha_A}$ where $\alpha_A = \alpha_M$

   manufacturing output $= T_M K_M^{\alpha_M} N_M^{1-\alpha_M}$ where $T_M \gtrless T_A$.

Situation *B*.

   agricultural output $= T_A K_A^{\alpha_A} N_A^{1-\alpha_A}$ where $\alpha_A \neq \alpha_M$

   manufacturing output $= T_M K_M^{\alpha_M} N_M^{1-\alpha_M}$ where $T_A \lessgtr T_M$.

9. Suppose the production function is:

$$Y = TK^\alpha N^{1-\alpha} \text{ where } T = 1; \ \alpha = \tfrac{1}{3}.$$

Show (as in Question 6) that the following Table gives numerical values of K and N which produce a given constant output.

K Capital stock	N labour input
1	1,000
4	500
6·25	400
16	250
25	200
100	100

Show that, of the possibilities depicted in this Table, the combination $K = 25$, $N = 200$ is the cheapest when labour costs £1 per unit per year and capital costs £4 per unit per year. Compare this result with that of Question 6. What is its relationship to the argument by which we justified the increasing cost production possibility curve of Chapter 5?

10. The elasticity of output with respect to labour asked for in Question 4 is given by:

$$\frac{\Delta Y}{Y} \bigg/ \frac{\Delta N}{N} \equiv \frac{\frac{\partial Y}{\partial N} \cdot \Delta N}{Y} \bigg/ \frac{\Delta N}{N} \equiv \frac{\frac{\partial Y}{\partial N} \cdot \Delta N}{\Delta N} \cdot \frac{Y}{N} \equiv \frac{\partial Y}{\partial N} \cdot \frac{Y}{N}$$

Using the information given in Question 7 express this in terms of α.

11. Suppose labour is paid its marginal product. Then

$$\frac{\text{wage bill}}{\text{output}} \equiv \text{share of wages}$$

$$\equiv \frac{\text{no. of workers} \times \text{marginal product of labour}}{\text{output}}$$

Calculate this for the production function of Question 4 using the information given in Question 7. What is its relation to α? What is the share of capital? Is capital paid its marginal product?

12. The production function $Y = TK^\alpha N^B$ has constant returns to scale if $B = 1 - \alpha$. Show that it has increasing returns if $\alpha + B > 1$ by two arithmetic examples. If either α or B are < 0 the function does not make economic sense. Why?

13. Suppose the production function is $Y = TK^\alpha N^B$ when $\alpha = 0 \cdot 5$; $B = 0 \cdot 6$.

    Find the share of labour. If labour receives this can capital also receive its marginal product? If not, why not? Can you give an economic interpretation to your results?

14. The demand for peanuts is written:

$$Q^D \equiv \begin{array}{l} \text{number of packets} \\ \text{demanded in millions} \end{array} = f(P_p, P_c, Y) = aP_c + bP_p + cY$$

where $P_p \equiv$ price of peanuts; $P_c \equiv$ price of potato crisps; $Y \equiv$ consumers' money income. The quantity supplied is:

$$Q^S = f(P_p, P_c) = A + dP_c + eP_p.$$

Equate Q^D and Q^S to find the equilibrium values of P_p in terms of a, b, c, d, e, A, P_c and Y.

Put

$$\begin{array}{ll} a = 10 & d = -10 \\ b = -2 & c = 13 \\ c = 0 \cdot 1 & A = 0 \\ Y = 100 & P_c = 1 \end{array}$$

and calculate the equilibrium values of P_p, Q^S and Q^D. How would you justify the signs of marginal response coefficients? Assume Y rises to 200. What are the new equilibrium values of P_p, Q^S and Q^D? Illustrate your calculations on a simple diagram.

15. The elasticity of any dependent variable (X) with respect to any independent variable (Y) of which it is a function is given by:

$$\frac{\Delta X}{X} \Big/ \frac{\Delta Y}{Y} \equiv \frac{\frac{\partial X}{\partial Y} \cdot \Delta Y}{X} \Big/ \frac{\Delta Y}{Y} \equiv \frac{\frac{\partial X}{\partial Y} \cdot \Delta Y}{\Delta Y} \cdot \frac{Y}{X} \equiv \frac{\partial X}{\partial Y} \cdot \frac{Y}{X}.$$

If $X = A + bY$, show that (i) the elasticity is not in general a constant; (ii) that it will be constant if $A = 0$.

Illustrate your conclusions by a graph identifying both $\partial X/\partial Y$ and Y/X. What general conclusion can you reach regarding the relationship between constant marginal response coefficients and constant elasticities? Show, by a numerical example of your own choice, that while the elasticity is independent of the *units* in which X and Y are measured, the marginal response coefficient is not.

16. Suppose the *observed* change in some dependent variable (X) is ΔX and the *observed* change in some independent variable (Y) on which X depends is ΔY. In what circumstances will the observed ratios $\frac{\Delta X}{X} \Big/ \frac{\Delta Y}{Y}$ be a good measure of the elasticity $\frac{\partial X}{\partial Y} \cdot \frac{Y}{X}$? Check your answer with the data at Question 7.

SUGGESTED REFERENCES

As a supplement to this chapter readers should consult:

R. G. D. Allen, *Mathematical Analysis for Economists* (Macmillan, 1953) chs i–iii, ix.

F. Zeuthen, *Economic Theory and Method* (Longmans, 1955) chs vi–ix.

Those who wish to proceed further with mathematics should continue with:

R. G. D. Allen, *Mathematical Analysis for Economists*.

W. J. Baumol, *Economic Dynamics* (Collier-Macmillan, 1959).

R. J. O'Brien and G. G. Garcia, *Mathematics for Economists and Social Scientists* (Macmillan, 1972).

8 The Determination of Equilibrium Output

In this chapter we begin our main job of constructing an economic theory which can be used to explain *why* the economic system behaves as we saw that it did in Chapter 6. We approach this task by developing *a model* of the economic system. Since the economic system is complicated, the model, to be useful, must necessarily also be complicated. We shall begin, however, by constructing a model of extreme simplicity and introduce complexities later only when the properties of the simple model have been thoroughly understood. Accordingly we start with a system in which (i) there is no government (i.e. no public sector) economic activity; and (ii) there is no international trade. We also make one additional assumption, namely that the price of a unit of output is constant. This enables us to identify changes in the money values of variables with changes in their 'real' values and postpone discussion of the determination of prices. Each of these assumptions is removed later.

1 Output, Employment and Business Decisions

In any period of time it is *enterprises* which determine how much output shall be produced. Since our theory is a *short-run* theory which takes as given both the real stock of capital (K) and the state of technique (T) then our production function tells us that $Y = f(N)$ with K and T given, or that the level of output (Y) per period depends only on the input of labour (N). Assuming hours per period per worker to be unchanged this tells us that a given level of output determines a given level of employment in terms of workers. Hence if we can explain the level of output which enterprises produce we can also explain, in the *short run*, the level of employment.

The full study of the behaviour of enterprises belongs to *microeconomics*. We can, however, make considerable progress by assuming, as a first approximation, that *the behaviour of enterprises* is, in general, *governed by the aim of maximising profits*. Since profits can only be earned by the sale of products, we can argue that (i) what enterprises will plan to produce in any period is what they think they can sell in that period; (ii) what they think they can sell depends upon their expectations regarding demands. We can indeed go a little further than this by arguing that the planned level of output not only depends upon *expected* demand but will adjust itself to *actual* demand so that, if actual demand in any period is *less* than expected, output will tend to be reduced, in later periods, to the level of actual demand. Only when *expected* and *actual demand*, and so *planned* and *actual sales*, coincide will the enterprise be in equilibrium.

The following arithmetical example should make the point clear:

Table 8.1

Example	Price per unit of output	Planned output ‖ actual output	Planned value of output	Wage cost	Planned profit	Actual sales	Unsold output added to stocks	Realised distribu- table profit	Result
(1)	(2)	(3)	(4)	(5)	(6)	(7)	(8)	(9)	(10)
1	£1	15,000	£15,000	£12,000	£3,000	£10,000	£5,000	£2,000	Contraction
2	£1	15,000	£15,000	£12,000	£3,000	£17,000	− £2,000	£3,400	Expansion
3	£1	15,000	£15,000	£12,000	£3,000	£15,000	nil	£3,000	Equilibrium

This statement tells us that, in some period, which we have called 1, the XYZ Co. expected demand for its products to be, at given prices, equal to £15,000. It therefore *planned* to produce, and did produce† this value of output. At the ruling level of money wages this involved a wage bill of £12,000. To this wage cost the firm added a 25 per cent 'mark-up' which gave it an *expected* profit of £3000. In the event, however, *actual* sales were only £10,000 as against the *planned* value of £15,000. As a result the XYZ Co. would certainly contract output (and employment) in future periods.

The position depicted is clearly one of *disequilibrium* in that we have:

planned sales ≠ actual sales, *but* planned sales > actual sales
planned profits ≠ actual profits, *but* planned profits > actual profits

and our argument tells us that, in a disequilibrium of this particular kind, the result would be *contraction* in output and employment.

How are the figures in Table 8.1 to be interpreted? The first eight columns give no trouble. The ninth, however, requires a word of explanation.

The realised distributable profit of an enterprise will be estimated by an accountant as:

$$\frac{\text{sales } plus \text{ value of}}{\text{increase in stocks}} - \text{costs} \equiv \frac{\text{realised distributable}}{\text{profit}}$$

† We shall assume that producers' plans are always realised in that planned output = actual output.

Accountants, however, will value the increase in stocks not at the price at which the enterprise would *sell* from stocks but at the cost it incurs in increasing its stocks. That is, the profit element is not included in the valuation of stock increases. Now in our example the planned profit margin is $\dfrac{£3000}{£15,000}$ which, in percentage terms, is 20 per cent. We thus have, in the first case:

$$\text{realised distributable profit} \equiv \frac{\text{sales} + \text{increase in stocks}}{\text{(valued at cost)}} - \text{total costs}$$

$$\equiv £10,000 + £5000[1 - \tfrac{20}{100}] - £12,000$$

$$\equiv £10,000 + £4000 - £12,000$$

$$\equiv £2000.$$

This is the figure shown in the ninth column of the Table.
Now take the second case. We have, since inventories *fall*:

$$\text{realised distributable profit} \equiv \frac{\text{sales} + \text{increase in stocks}}{\text{(valued at cost)}} - \text{total costs}$$

$$\equiv £17,000 + (- £2000[1 - \tfrac{20}{100}]) - £12,000$$

$$\equiv £17,000 - £1600 - £12,000$$

$$\equiv £3400.$$

Finally in case three we have:

$$\text{realised distributable profit} \equiv \frac{\text{sales} + \text{increase in stocks}}{\text{(value at cost)}} - \text{total costs}$$

$$\equiv £15,000 + \text{nil} - £12,000$$

$$\equiv £3000.$$

Obviously, as Table 8.1 shows,

in case 1   planned profit > realised distributable profit.

2   planned profit < realised distributable profit.

3   planned profit = realised distributable profit.

Notice that in cases 1 and 2 – the disequilibrium situations – the XYZ Co. experienced *unplanned* stock changes. Only in case 3 – the equilibrium situation – is there *no unplanned* change in stocks.

It follows from this example that only if *actual* sales turn out to be exactly £15,000 – as the XYZ Co. *planned*, is there *equilibrium*, for then planned sales = actual sales; planned profits = realised distributable profits and the firm has no reason to change its *plans*.

Let us now generalise this example to all firms and define

total value of planned output ≡ aggregate supply.

We may, on the demand side, also write:

total value of planned expenditure ≡ aggregate demand.

Then utilising the *assumption* that

$$\text{total value of planned expenditure} = \text{total value of actual expenditure,}$$

that is, the *assumption* that consumers' plans are always realised, we can argue that

(i) for *output* to be in equilibrium we required aggregate demand = aggregate supply

and predict that if

(ii) aggregate demand > aggregate supply, output will expand,

while if

(iii) aggregate demand < aggregate supply, output will contract.

These three possibilities are depicted in the table below.

In each situation enterprises pay out £150 m. in wages and rents. They *plan* a profit of £50 m. Aggregate supply is therefore £200 m.

In situation 3, planned expenditure (and hence by assumption actual expenditure) equals £180 m. The result is: planned profits > realised distributable profits and output *contracts*.

We thus have the following propositions:

(i) If agg. demand > agg. supply, *planned* profits will be less than realised distributable profits. Result: expansion of output.

(ii) If agg. demand < agg. supply, *planned* profits will be greater than realised distributable profits. Result: contraction of output.

(iii) If agg. demand = agg. supply, planned profits will equal realised distributable profits. Result: equilibrium.

We can now take our analysis a little further and show its relationship with our national income accounting concepts.

It will be remembered that we have assumed prices to be constant throughout the discussion. Hence *planned* output (which we have

Table 8.2 *Aggregate Demand and Supply*

Situation	Value of planned and actual output			Value of aggregate supply	Aggregate demand		Realised profits	Unsold output added to stocks	Result
	Wages	Rents	Planned profit		Planned expenditure	Actual expenditure			
	£m.	£m.	£m.	£m.	£m.	£m.	£m.	£m.	
1	100	50	50	200	200	200	50	nil	Equilibrium
2	100	50	50	200	220	220	55	−20	Expansion
3	100	50	50	200	180	180	45	20	Contraction

Table 8.3

Situation	Value of output	Wages	Rents	Planned distributable profits	Expenditure		Earnings Side		Profits	
					Consumption	Investment in inventories	Wages	Rents	Realised distributable profit	Unrealised profit
	(1)	(2)	(3)	(4)	(5)	(6)	(7)	(8)	(9)	(10)
1	£200m.	£100	£50	£50	£180	£20	£100	£50	£45	£5
2	£200m.	£100	£50	£50	£200	nil	£100	£50	£50	nil
3	£200m.	£100	£50	£50	£220	−£20	£100	£50	£55	−£5

assumed to be actually produced) is equal in value to the national product. This, *in each situation*, is equal to £200 m.

In situation 1 of Table 8.3 only £180 m. is sold on the market to consumers. It follows that the remaining £20 m. of output must be added to stocks. But this, by definition, *is investment whether firms planned to make the addition or not*. Accordingly we can rearrange the data of Table 8.3 as shown.

On looking at this table we have:

national product ≡ sum of cols. (2), (3) and (4) ≡ £200 m.

On the expenditure side we have:

national expenditure ≡ consumption + investment

≡ £180 m. + £20 m.

≡ £200 m.

Turning to the earnings side matters are a little more complicated. We know that

national income ≡ wages + rents + profits

≡ £100 m. + £50 m. + £50 m.

≡ £200 m.

This, however, appears to show that, at £50 m. actual profit equals planned profit – a situation we have learned to think of as one of equilibrium. This is awkward since we know that the situation we are depicting is one of disequilibrium. How do we reconcile this apparent contradiction? We have:

national income ≡ wages + rents + profits

                                              realised
≡ wages + rents + distributable + unrealised profits
                                              profits

≡ £100 m. + £50 m. + £45 m. + £5 m.

≡ £200 m.

Disequilibrium manifests itself in the discrepancy between actual profits, as measured by the national income statistician (£50 m.) and the realised distributable profits accruing to the enterprise (£45 m.). The difference arises from the mark-up hypothesis.

In situation 2 we have:

national product $\equiv$ £200 m.

national expenditure $\equiv$ consumption + investment

$\equiv$ £200 m. + nil

$\equiv$ £200 m.

national income $\equiv$ wages + rents + profits

$\equiv$ wages + rents + $\begin{array}{c}\text{realised}\\ \text{distributable}\\ \text{profits}\end{array}$ + $\begin{array}{c}\text{unrealised}\\ \text{profits}\end{array}$

$\equiv$ £100 m. + £50 m. + £50 m. + nil

$\equiv$ £200 m.

In situation 3:

national product $\equiv$ £200 m.

national expenditure $\equiv$ consumption + investment

$\equiv$ £220 m. − £20 m.

$\equiv$ £200 m.

national income $\equiv$ wages + rents + profits

$\equiv$ £100 m. + £50 m. + $\begin{array}{c}\text{realised}\\ \text{distri-}\\ \text{butable}\\ \text{profits}\end{array}$ + $\begin{array}{c}\text{unrealised}\\ \text{profits}\end{array}$

$\equiv$ £100 m. + £50 m. + £55 m. − £5 m.

$\equiv$ £200 m.

In short, we can say that unless the situation is one of equilibrium then (i) there will be *unplanned* increases/decreases in stocks; (ii) realised distributable profits will *not* be equal to planned profits. Only in equilibrium will there be *no unplanned* increase/decrease in stocks and no discrepancy between planned profits and realised distributable profits.

Notice that though in each situation we have our familiar identity of:

national product $\equiv$ national expenditure $\equiv$ national income,

each situation is, *from the point of view of behaviour*, a very different one.

To say that disequilibrium manifests itself in a discrepancy between actual profits as measured by the national income statisticians and realised distributable profits is, on our definitions and assumptions, correct. Some explanation of what this implies is nevertheless necessary.

In our table we have taken the value of output, as measured by the statistician, to be £200 m. Of this sum wages are £100 m.; rents £50 m.; and profits £50 m. If the national income statistician adopts this definition he must value the increase in stocks at £20 m. to preserve the definitional relationship: output ≡ consumption *plus* investment. This means that he values the increase in stocks *inclusive* of the profit element. On this basis the income accruing to households in the form of wages, rents and profits is £200 m. but the statistician is including, in the profits of the current period, an element which will not be *realised* until the goods added to inventory are actually sold.

As we have seen, in situation 1, the realised distributable profit of firms, as calculated by their accountants, will be £45 m. and not the £50 m. taken (on this contention) by the national income statistician. If the whole of this £45 m. is paid out to households, the income received by households, £195 m., will be *less* than the income which the statisticians attribute to them. Conversely in situation 3 it will be more.

If on the other hand the statistician adopts the accountants definition of realised profit he must value the change in stocks at cost. In which case each of our hypothetical situations yields a different total for national income thus:

$$\text{situation 1} \quad \text{national income} \equiv \text{wage} + \text{rents} + \frac{\text{realised distributable profits}}{}$$

$$\equiv £100 \text{ m.} + £50 \text{ m.} + £45 \text{ m.}$$

$$\equiv £195 \text{ m.}$$

$$3 \quad \text{national income} \equiv \text{wages} + \text{rents} + \frac{\text{realised distributable profits}}{}$$

$$\equiv £100 \text{ m.} + £50 \text{ m.} + £55 \text{ m.}$$

$$\equiv £205 \text{ m.}$$

$$2 \quad \text{national income} \equiv £100 \text{ m.} + £50 \text{ m.} + £50 \text{ m.}$$

$$\equiv £200 \text{ m.}$$

In each case, by assumption, the flow of output is the same. The second way of defining profit therefore leads to a contradiction worse than the first for the main purpose of national income accounting is to measure the flow of goods and services produced in the current period. A system of definitions which describes an identical flow by three different totals is obviously awkward. Accordingly the first definition of profit – arrived at by valuing the increase in stocks at market prices – seems preferable.†

Notice that, in all this, there is no dispute as to what has occurred. This was assumed at the start. What matters is to find a consistent and convenient way of *describing what has occurred*.

The fundamental lessons of this example are, however, clear enough:

(i) Though actual *expenditure and* actual *output as defined in national income accounting are always* identically *equal it makes sense to speak of* planned *expenditure being equal to, greater or less than,* planned output.

(ii) *The national income accounting concepts can tell us nothing about economic behaviour for though each of our three situations is, from the behaviour aspect, entirely different, from the national income accounting point of view they exhibit no essential differences.*

The general point is a simple one:

(i) *national income* accounting is concerned with *actual* magnitudes;

(ii) *economic behaviour* is determined by the relationship between *planned* magnitudes about which national income accounting, *of itself*, has nothing whatsoever to say.

This reflects the important points we made in discussing the concept of equilibrium in Chapter 6. *Plans to purchase, sell and produce may not be realised.* They will, in fact, only be realised when they are consistent: that is when equilibrium exists. In this situation, and only in this situation, will *all actual* magnitudes correspond with planned magnitudes.

Of course, in any given period there will only be one set of actual magnitudes in terms of national accounting definitions and these are what the statisticians will record. But in disequilibrium situations these *actual* magnitudes *result* from the interaction of *inconsistent plans*. The statisticians' estimates do not record the existence of inconsistent plans although, as we have shown, plans may well be inconsistent. They merely record *what happens whether it is planned or unplanned*. This is why they are identities and not equations and,

† Cf. *National Accounts Statistics: Sources and Methods*, ch. 13.

by the same token, why they can tell us nothing about economic behaviour except its results. It is, indeed, precisely because they give a measure of these results that the statistician's estimates are important.

This section contains propositions of such fundamental importance that a summary of them is essential. The propositions are as follows:

(i) Output and employment are only in equilibrium when aggregate (planned) demand = aggregate (planned) supply.

(ii) Where aggregate demand > aggregate supply the resultant disequilibrium will manifest itself as

    (a) an *unintended* decumulation in inventories: i.e. *unplanned* disinvestment in stocks;

    (b) an excess of realised distributable profits over *planned* profits.

The *result* will be an expansion in output and employment.

(iii) These propositions are simply reversed for the situation where aggregate demand < aggregate supply.

(iv) Despite the fact that, in national income accounting,

$$\text{actual expenditure} \equiv \text{actual output}$$

it is perfectly possible, provided *plans* are inconsistent, for

$$\text{aggregate demand} \neq \text{aggregate supply.}$$

(v) Without additional assumptions relating *planned* to *actual* magnitudes, national income concepts can tell us nothing about *plans* and therefore do not register any inconsistency in them.

2 THE SAVING AND INVESTMENT ANALYSIS

We now know that output is in equilibrium only when aggregate demand = aggregate supply. In our present simple model we can divide aggregate demand into two components thus:

$$\begin{matrix} \text{aggregate} \\ \text{demand} \end{matrix} = planned \text{ consumption } plus \text{ } planned \text{ net investment.}$$

If we assume, as we have so far, that producers' *plans* for output are always realised, then

$$\begin{matrix} \text{aggregate} \\ \text{supply} \end{matrix} \equiv \text{planned value of output} \equiv \begin{matrix} \text{national} \\ \text{product} \end{matrix} \equiv \begin{matrix} \text{national} \\ \text{income} \end{matrix}.$$

Hence our *equilibrium* condition can be rewritten:

national income = *planned* consumption + *planned* net investment,

or, using the notation which is now fashionable,

$$Y = C_p + I_p, \qquad (8.\text{I})$$

where the suffix p denotes *planned* magnitudes and Y denotes national income. *Planned* net saving is now defined as income *minus planned* consumption, i.e.

$$S_p \equiv Y - C_p. \qquad (8.\text{II})$$

Hence, combining (8.I) and (8.II), our equilibrium condition becomes:

$$S_p = I_p \qquad (8.\text{III})$$
$$\textit{planned} \text{ saving} = \textit{planned} \text{ investment}$$

Thus the propositions:

aggregate demand $\gtrless$ aggregate supply

and

planned investment $\gtrless$ *planned* saving

are simply alternative ways of saying the same thing.

We have already shown that, despite the fact that, by definition, national expenditure is always equal to national product, it makes sense to speak of aggregate demand being equal to, greater or less than aggregate supply. We now show that despite the fact that, by definition, *actual* saving is always identically equal with *actual* investment, it makes sense to speak of *planned* saving being equal to, greater or less than, *planned* investment.

Obviously when we write:

$$S_p \gtrless I_p$$
$$S \equiv I$$

we are using the terms in different senses. This is the crucial point and must be understood. It looks and is simple. But in the past failure to understand the distinction has caused great trouble not only to students but also to professional economists.

The former *equation* refers to *planned* saving and investment and the expression is a genuine equation which may or may not be satisfied: the latter *identity* refers to *actual* saving and investment which *by definition are always equal* since they are, in fact, alternative ways of describing the same thing.

Since economic terminology is not uniform, the student is certain to meet in his reading many expressions which are, broadly speaking, synonyms for our terms 'planned' and 'actual'. For convenience they may be tabulated as follows:

$$S_p \gtrless I_p$$

$$\left\{\begin{array}{l}\text{planned} \\ \textit{ex ante} \\ \text{scheduled} \\ \text{intended}\end{array}\right\} \quad \text{saving} \gtrless \quad \left\{\begin{array}{l}\text{planned} \\ \textit{ex ante} \\ \text{scheduled} \\ \text{intended}\end{array}\right\} \quad \text{investment}$$

while,

$$S \equiv I$$

$$\left\{\begin{array}{l}\text{actual} \\ \textit{ex post} \\ \text{observable} \\ \text{realised}\end{array}\right\} \quad \text{saving} \equiv \quad \left\{\begin{array}{l}\text{actual} \\ \textit{ex post} \\ \text{observable} \\ \text{realised}\end{array}\right\} \quad \text{investment}$$

Although we may now be satisfied that, since we are using the terms 'saving' and 'investment' in two senses, we are not involved in a logical contradiction, it is nevertheless interesting to enquire how it is that actual saving and investment can be equal when planned saving and investment are not equal; that is when the system is in disequilibrium. This may be made clear by taking a further look at our earlier examples.

Table 8.4

Case	Aggregate supply Y_p	Planned consumption C_p	Actual consumption C	Planned saving S_p	Actual saving S	Planned investment I_p	Actual investment I	Unplanned investment I_u	Overall situation
1	£200m.	£180m.	£180m.	£20m.	£20m.	zero	£20m.	£20m.	$S_p > I_p$
2	£200m.	£220m.	£220m.	– £20m.	– £20m.	zero	– £20m.	– £20m.	$I_p > S_p$
3	£200m.	£200m.	£200m.	nil	nil	zero	zero	zero	$S_p = I_p$

Consider case 1. The value of output is £200 m. But aggregate demand $(C_p + I_p)$ is equal to only £180 m. It follows therefore that output unsold during this period will be £200 m. – £180 m. = £20 m. This unsold output (saving) must be added to stocks existing at the beginning of the period. It therefore constitutes *actual* investment. But it *does not constitute planned investment* which, by assumption, is zero. In case 1, therefore, actual saving (output which is not consumed) is, as it must be, equal to actual investment. Actual investment, however, exceeds planned investment by an amount we shall speak of as *unplanned investment*. It follows therefore that when planned saving exceeds planned investment, actual investment also exceeds planned investment by the value of unplanned investment. This unplanned investment, taking the form of an unexpected (and unwelcome) accumulation of stocks, is a signal to firms to *contract* output. Nevertheless, despite the assumed discrepancy between planned saving and investment and the resultant disequilibrium it is clear that actual saving and investment, as measured by the national income statistician, are necessarily equal.

Case 2 illustrates the alternative form of disequilibrium. In that case planned investment exceeds planned saving which means that aggregate demand $(C_p + I_p)$ exceeds aggregate supply. Clearly this is so for the table shows aggregate demand of £220 m. and the aggregate supply of £200 m. To meet this excess demand of £20 m. producers must decumulate stocks. Now the decumulation of stocks constitutes *disinvestment*. Hence actual investment, which we know to be equal to planned investment *plus* unplanned investment, is given by:

$$I \equiv I_p + I_u$$
$$\equiv \text{nil} - £20 \text{ m.}$$
$$\equiv -£20 \text{ m.}$$

In this case an unexpected *decumulation* of stocks is a signal to producers to *expand* production and thus employment and incomes.

In case 3 we have assumed equilibrium. In this situation planned and actual investment coincide at zero. Unplanned investment is therefore also zero. Hence producers' expectations are realised. They therefore have no incentive to expand or contract production, employment and incomes.

From this account of matters we may draw the following conclusions:

(i) there is no contradiction in the statements
   (a) planned saving and investment are equal only when incomes are in equilibrium; and
   (b) actual (accounting) saving and investment are always equal by definition:
(ii) where planned saving is not equal to planned investment the resulting disequilibrium will show itself in the form of a discrepancy between planned and actual investment;
(iii) we define:

unplanned investment		actual investment	planned investment
I_u	$\equiv$	I $-$	I_p

(iv) where $S_p > I_p$ then $I_u > 0$, i.e. there is unintended inventory
accumulation;

where $I_p > S_p$ then $I_u < 0$, i.e. there is unintended inventory
decumulation;

where $I_p = S_p$ then $I_u = 0$, i.e. no unintended change in inventories;

(v) it is the presence of unintended investment (positive or
negative) which provides the signal to firms to contract or
expand output. This is merely another aspect of the
discrepancy between planned and actual (sales) and planned
and realised distributable profits illustrated earlier.

3 THE BASIC POSTULATE OF THE SAVING AND INVESTMENT ANALYSIS

The analysis of the earlier sections of this chapter has made it
plain that

(i) any inconsistency between the rates at which the community
plans to invest and to save will involve discrepancies between:
  (a) firms' *expected* and *realised* distributable profits; and
  (b) firms' *planned* and *actual* investment;
(ii) such discrepancies will cause firms to modify their production
plans in the light of experience thus bringing about changes
in output (income) and employment;
(iii) there is no contradiction between speaking about the possible
inequality of *planned* saving and *planned* investment while at
the same time insisting upon the definitional identity of actual
savings and investment as measured in national income
accounts.

So far so good. But this analysis, though logically consistent,
would be of little interest if, as a matter of experience, planned saving
and investment tended automatically (in the sense of without any
need for changes in the level of output) to achieve and maintain
equality. In that case the saving and investment analysis and the
theory of income determination which we develop in later chapters
would be a theoretical curiosity of no empirical significance whatsoever. Clearly, if a theory based upon the saving/investment analysis
is to have any practical importance it can only be because, as a matter
of fact, there is no mechanism tending to ensure that any plan to

save (or invest) will automatically be matched by a corresponding plan to invest (or save).

Now there are two important facts concerning saving and investment decisions in the modern developed 'mixed economy' which make it reasonable to accept the view that there is no 'automatic' correspondence between the amount per period that the community plans to save and invest. They are that

(i) saving and investment plans tend to be made by different groups in the community; i.e. broadly speaking households save, firms invest; and

(ii) decisions to save and invest are undertaken for very different reasons.

Admittedly enterprises (firms) do undertake saving in the form of depreciation allowances and undistributed profits. But a considerable part of saving is still performed by persons. Again it is true that households and persons do undertake investment expenditure.

Nevertheless the overwhelming share of private investment is undertaken by firms. It is thus in accordance with experience and acceptable to commonsense to admit that saving and investment decisions are carried out to a significant extent by different groups. As a first approximation we might assume that *only* households save and *only* enterprises invest. This indeed will be a convenient assumption on which to build the model from Chapter 9 onwards. The reader should remember its limited correspondence with facts.

The second assertion, that saving and investment decisions are undertaken for different reasons, is also in accordance with common observation once the precise economic meaning of the term investment is recalled. Men save, after all, for a bewildering variety of reasons. The more obvious are: to provide for old age; to provide a contingency fund against any sudden loss in earning power; because they were brought up to believe that to save was a 'proper' mode of behaviour; because they were in the past unable to resist the appeals of life assurance salesmen; because they are compelled to do so through a legal obligation to join a superannuation scheme; or merely because of habit. None of these have much (if anything) to do with the wish to undertake investment which, as we know, is defined as making an addition to the *real* stock of capital. Most of the things savers do with their saving, and therefore which presumably provide much of the motive for saving do *not* constitute investment. Many savers for example buy government bonds. If Brown buys a bond and Smith sells it Brown's 'investment' is cancelled by Smith's 'disinvestment'. In any case the transaction does not directly increase the real capital stock and so, by definition, is not investment. This argument can be extended to cover nearly all the transactions undertaken by persons who save, most of whom use their saving to carry out what economists call *capital transfers. Once it is realised that purchases of bonds, shares, life policies, mortgages, debentures, old houses and so on though commonly called* investment *do not constitute investment as economists define the term but are merely transfers*, the very remote relation between personal planned saving and planned investment becomes clear.

If we accept that plans to save and plans to invest are made independently of each other then the economic system must contain some mechanism to bring the different plans into equality. The central tenet of modern macro-economics, derived from the work of Lord Keynes, is that the price mechanism does not effectively perform this task and in particular that the rate of interest does not do so. Consequently adjustment requires a change in the level of income (output). To put the same point rather differently we can, given the independence of the plans to save and invest, develop a model of the economy which uses the saving and investment analysis to explain the determination of output (income) and employment.

It is important, however, for the student to notice that, while it is reasonable to accept the postulated dichotomy between savers and investors in a modern developed 'mixed economy', it is not a reasonable assumption in all economies or in the same economy at all times. This is obvious even if we neglect the special case so thoughtfully provided by Defoe. Robinson Crusoe clearly saved (refrained from consumption) *only in order to invest* (add to his real capital stock). Neglecting Robinson, however, broadly similar conditions prevail in the subsistence economies of some underdeveloped territories in which peasant farmers, in general, save only in order to invest: indeed, to put the matter more concisely, a plan to save *is* a plan to invest. Hence, though the dichotomy certainly holds with respect to (say) Britain, America and Australia today, it would probably not have held in Britain during the eighteenth century and it may not hold in any of the three countries during the twenty-first.

This is an important point. A theory which seeks to explain the level of output by requiring it to adjust in order to bring the community's plans to save and invest into equality will always be logically consistent. It may not, however, be a useful theory in the sense that the community may have another mechanism for adjusting saving and investment plans or, alternatively, may be organised institutionally in such a way that automatic correspondence between saving and investment plans is assured. The importance of Keynes' theory arises because under modern social conditions and institutional arrangements it is both logically consistent and useful.

4 SUMMARY

This is an important chapter outlining a number of ideas fundamental to the whole theory of income determination. The *basic* ideas underlying the theory and sketched in the earlier sections are summarised below.

(i) A firm will adjust output in accordance with its experience of demand. This proposition which is, of course, empirical and not logical in nature may be regarded as either
   (a) derived from the study of business behaviour or
   (b) deduced from the assumption that firms seek to maximise profits – which is itself an assumption derived from observing business behaviour. This assumption about business behaviour, when generalised for all firms, enables us to derive the equilibrium condition for output as a whole ($S_p = I_p$) and the conditions in which output will tend to expand ($I_p > S_p$) or contract ($S_p > I_p$).

(ii) In a modern 'mixed' capitalist economy saving and investment decisions are taken by different groups for dissimilar reasons. This fact enables us to argue that the consequences which must logically follow if, in any period, $S_p \neq I_p$ are of great practical interest since there is no reason to suppose that S_p will automatically tend to equal I_p.

(iii) In the short run, the quantity of employment is uniquely related to the quantity of output firms plan to produce.

These three propositions form the basis for the whole of the analysis contained in the rest of this part of the book. The remaining assumptions, namely the absence of government activity, the absence of international trade, and the constancy of the price level are made for expositional convenience only and are relaxed later. Beyond stating and examining the implications of the ideas listed above, the chapter is also concerned to explain and emphasise the distinction between *planned* saving (investment) on the one hand and *actual* saving (investment) on the other. The comprehension of this distinction is fundamental and the student is recommended to read Section 2 very carefully and to work out some arithmetic examples for himself.

QUESTIONS AND EXERCISES

1. 'The aim of the Government's policy is to equate saving and investment at a level of output corresponding to full employment. Their success is demonstrated by this year's national income estimates which show saving equal to investment.' Discuss.
2. 'If saving increases then, since saving equals investment, investment increases. It follows that aggregate demand and supply always increase together and are always equal.' Discuss.
3. Assuming

$$C_P = C_A = £1000 \text{ m. per period};$$

$$I_P = £500 \text{ m. per period},$$

what is the *equilibrium* level of output?

   If planned output is £1700 m. per period and planned output = actual output find (i) gross national product; (ii) gross national expenditure; (iii) actual investment; (iv) unintended investment.

   In future periods would you expect output to expand or contract? Why?

   In what forms does the disequilibrium in the system show itself?
4. 'People spend with that part of their income that they save just as surely as with that part of their income they consume.' Do you agree? If so, why? If not, why not? What, in terms of this chapter, is the assumption implicit in the statement?
5. The national income estimates of a hypothetical economy reveal the following data for the first half of 1965:

G.N.P.	£4000 m.
Consumption	£3000 m.
Gross investment in:	
(i) fixed capital	£900 m.
(ii) inventories	£100 m.

   Do these figures throw any light upon whether the economy was in equilibrium or not? If so, how?
6. Suppose that, contrary to our assumptions, an act of saving was undertaken only in order to make investment. How would the level of output in an economy of this kind be determined? Would 'full capacity' output be automatic? If so where would the equilibrium of the economy appear on the 'production possibility curve'?

7. According to a Liberal M.P. the £600 m. the 1967 (Labour) government expended on the purchase of steel companies (as part of nationalisation) would have been better spent on the construction of roads. Is his statement sense or nonsense? Does the purchase of steel companies increase aggregate demand?

8. Assume

$$C_p = C_A = £2000 \text{ m. per period};$$
$$I_p \equiv I_{fp} + I_{sp}$$

   planned investment   planned investment
   $\equiv$ in fixed capital + in inventories.

If $I_{fp} = £250$ m. per period; $I_{sp} = £400$ m. per period;
What is the equilibrium level of output?
If planned output = actual output is £3000 m. then

   (i) how much is actual investment in inventories?
   (ii) how much is unplanned investment in inventories?
   (iii) how much are actual saving and investment?

9. Reconstruct the example of Table 8.1 and the subsequent discussion on the assumption that the 'mark-up' of firms is $\frac{5}{12}$ *not* $\frac{3}{12}$. Show that the basic analysis is unaffected by this change.

10. Reformulate the discussion of Table 8.1 *et seq* on the assumption that firms adjust their 'mark-up' percentage to the level of output. Assume that planned profit $\equiv P^*$ is given by: $P^* = A + bY$ where $b = 0.1$ and $Y \equiv$ actual = planned output. What is the value of A assumed in Table 8.1? Does the new assumption *significantly* affect the analysis? What do you mean by *significantly*?

11. 'The function of what is called the capital market – that is the Stock Exchange and related financial institutions – is to facilitate capital transfers.' Discuss.

12. Use the Blue Book to construct a table of personal and business savings for the years 1960–70. What is the average share of each source in total private saving?

SUGGESTED READING

P. A. Samuelson, *Economics: An Introductory Analysis* (McGraw-Hill, 1973) chs. xi–xii.

F. S. Brooman, *Macro-Economics* (Allen & Unwin, 1962) chs i, iii.

P. Davidson and E. Smolensky, *Aggregate Supply and Demand Analysis* (Harper & Row, 1965) ch. i.

9 The Consumption Function and the Multiplier

IN the last chapter we argued that enterprises would adjust their output per period until *planned* sales and *actual* sales were equal. At this level of output enterprises would be in equilibrium: that is, have no reason to adjust their output *plans* in any way.

Examining this condition a little further we discovered that output (income) would be in equilibrium when aggregate supply = aggregate demand, or, what is the same thing, $S_p = I_p$. Where this condition prevailed all planned and actual magnitudes would coincide: both sectors of the economy – that is enterprises and households – would then have no reason to modify their behaviour.

Retaining our assumption that production plans are always realised so that actual and planned production coincide and the notation of Chapter 8 we can write our equilibrium condition as:

$$Y \quad = \quad C_p + I_p$$

aggregate supply = aggregate demand.

Hence, to explain the equilibrium value of Y, we need to develop theories which explain the determination of C_p and I_p. These theories will, obviously enough, contain hypotheses about human behaviour for what we are trying to explain is first the rate at which households (in general) will plan to spend upon consumption and second the rate at which enterprises (in general) will plan to spend upon investment.

In this chapter we concentrate on the first problem and seek to develop a theory of consumption. Accordingly we shall assume, without either explanation or justification, that enterprises plan to spend upon investment at some fixed rate. This assumption, which is obviously artificial and made merely for convenience, will be relaxed in the next chapter. It amounts to treating planned investment expenditure as an *exogenous* variable – that is one determined (like the weather) outside our model. Formally it may be expressed as follows:

$$I_p = \bar{I} \tag{9.I}$$

$$I_p = £500 \text{ m. per year} \tag{9.In}$$

This leaves us free to concentrate on the determination of planned consumption.

1 THE AGGREGATE CONSUMPTION FUNCTION

The aim of our consumption hypothesis is to explain the determination of 'real' *aggregate* planned consumption expenditure – that is the total 'real' expenditure of all households together. On what variables is it reasonable to argue that aggregate 'real' planned consumption would depend?

The first (and most important variable) is clearly *the level of real income*. Statistical studies of household expenditure confirm that the simple hypothesis that the real expenditure of households is related to their real income levels is well grounded. Moreover the same studies show that households with 'high' real incomes (say those in the top 10 per cent) save more, proportionately to income as well as absolutely, than those in 'low' real income groups (say the bottom 10 per cent). Since any given total of *household* incomes may be distributed more (or less) equally and since the *more equally* any given total household income is distributed the *greater* will be the level of planned consumption associated with it, we know, from these studies, *two* variables that influence real planned consumption. They are:

(i) the level of real income: (Y) and
(ii) the distribution of real income (α).†

Of these the first, the level of real income, is of primary importance in the sense that variations in planned consumption are due largely to changes in income.

It also seems plausible to argue, and there is empirical evidence to support the hypothesis, that in general any individual with a given real income will plan to consume *more* the greater is his real *wealth*. We thus have a third variable to consider: the real value of assets.

The real value of assets is a *stock* concept which relates to the capital account or balance sheet of the household and not its income account. Our hypothesis states that, in general, if we look at two households which are otherwise identical and which each enjoy an income of (say) £2000 per year one of which holds (say) bank deposits, government bonds, equity shares and real property to the value of £10,000 and the other which holds only bank deposits to the value of £100, the former type of household will in general plan

† We use the term α to describe the distribution of income so that the *greater* is α the *more equally* income is distributed. The parameter α thus refers to income distribution in this sense and *not* to the *functional* distribution between Wages and Profits.

the higher rate of consumption. Extending this hypothesis to the community as a whole gives us a third variable influencing the value of real planned consumption namely:

(iii) the real value of household asset holdings (A).

A fourth variable which *may* influence consumption expenditure is the rate of interest which we now *define* as

the rate of return (per cent per annum) obtainable in the market on long-term government securities.

As everyone knows the act of saving – that is of abstaining from consumption – does not, of itself, entitle the saver to receive interest. If, for example, accumulated savings (wealth) are held in the form of bank notes no interest accrues. Nevertheless accumulated savings (wealth) *can* be held in a form which provides their owner with an income in the form of interest (for example as bonds or building society deposits). Hence it is reasonable to believe that some people would plan to save more out of their incomes if the rate of interest were (say) 20 per cent rather than 5 per cent. Moreover, some people who now tend to consume more than their incomes (that is, to *dis-save*) by making use of hire purchase finance, would probably be less willing to do so if the rate charged by hire purchase companies (which is related to the rate of interest) was 40 rather than 16 per cent.

In short there are some reasons to suppose that, the *higher* the rate of interest, the *more* willing some people will be to save and the *less* willing some other people will be to dis-save.

As against this some people save, in the main, to provide an income on retirement. The higher is the rate of interest the smaller the accumulated savings necessary to provide any *given* income on retirement. Those who save primarily to provide for retirement and who aim at a fixed income at a certain age (say 60) may thus save *less* if the rate of interest is (say) 20 per cent than they would if it were (say) 5 per cent. It follows that though there are some reasons for thinking that the rate of interest is a variable which influences consumption out of any given income we cannot, on *a priori* grounds, be any too confident about either the *direction* or *magnitude* of its influence. Nevertheless it is clearly a variable which needs to be included in any hypothesis designed to explain aggregate consumption. Hence our fourth variable is

(iv) the rate of interest (r).

A fifth variable is the psychological attitude of members of households (consumers) as conditioned by the 'accepted' behaviour of the society in which they live and have their upbringing. Some people are brought up to believe that to save is a virtue which, if not rewarded in this world, will be in the next. Others believe that income is for spending. Hence these psychological attitudes – which we shall call preferences – are an important determinant of aggregate consumption.

There are a whole host of other variables which have some claim to be considered as factors influencing consumption plans. The age composition of society, for example, might well be an influence. So might expectations with regard to future incomes and expectations with regard to future prices. The problem in economics is not, however, to find the *longest* possible list of independent variables which might, in general, be thought to exert some influence on the dependent variable, aggregate consumption, but to find the *smallest* number of variables which permits us to make useful predictions of the dependent variable. *Which these variables are is a question of fact.* It is thus always wise to begin with a simple hypothesis and modify it only when tests show it to be inadequate. Accordingly we shall put forward the following hypothesis to explain real aggregate planned consumption:

aggregate real planned consumption   depends upon $\left\{ \begin{array}{l} \text{real income} \\ \text{real value of assets} \\ \text{rate of interest} \\ \text{distribution of income} \\ \text{preferences.} \end{array} \right\}$

In our functional notation this may be conveniently written as a *consumption function* thus:

$$C_p = f(Y, A, r, \alpha) \qquad (9.\text{II})$$

where the last influence, households' preferences, is expressed in the form of the functional relationship (systematic dependence) between C_p (the dependent variable) and Y, A, r and α (the independent variables).

At this point the reader should notice the obvious analogy between the *consumption function* of (9.II) and our 'beer drinking' function of earlier chapters. This new function, like the earlier one, expresses an hypothesis about economic behaviour which may be true or false. Moreover since Y, A, r, α and (assuming that consumption plans are always realised) C_p are all conceptually measurable, our consumption function hypothesis is meaningful: that is, it can be tested.

What properties is this consumption function likely to have? If we refer back to Chapter 7 we see that this question first requires us to say what *signs* we expect the marginal response coefficients to possess. Our discussion has already given us expectations about these so we can immediately write down the signs of the marginal response coefficients as follows:

$$\frac{\partial C_p}{\partial Y} \equiv \text{the increase in real planned consumption result-ing from a unit increase in real income } \textit{alone} > 0$$

$$\frac{\partial C_p}{\partial A} \equiv \text{the increase in real planned consumption result-ing from a unit increase in the real value of assets } \textit{alone} > 0$$

$$\frac{\partial C_p}{\partial \alpha} \equiv \text{the increase in real planned consumption result-ing from a unit increase in the equality of in-come distribution } \textit{alone} > 0 \qquad (9.\text{III})$$

$$\frac{\partial C_p}{\partial r} \equiv \text{the increase in real planned consumption result-ing from a unit increase in the rate of interest } \textit{alone} \quad ?$$

Notice that these marginal response coefficients are descriptive of human behaviour.

This information, which simply restates the results of our earlier discussion, tells us something about the consumption function. We now ask what is the *form* of the function?

On empirical grounds there are good reasons for writing the function in the following form:

$$C_p = Q + cY + dA + e\alpha + fr, \qquad (9.\text{IV})$$

which is the form illustrated in Chapter 7. In this notation Q is *autonomous* consumption – that is consumption which is independent of Y, A, α and r. The form chosen in addition to being plausible on empirical grounds is also convenient for with it each of the marginal response coefficients is a constant. Thus:

$$\frac{\partial C_p}{\partial Y} \equiv c > 0, \quad \frac{\partial C_p}{\partial A} \equiv d > 0, \quad \frac{\partial C_p}{\partial \alpha} \equiv e > 0, \quad \frac{\partial C_p}{\partial r} \equiv f \gtrless 0.$$

These are the properties which, in what follows, we shall assume our consumption function to possess. We now proceed to illustrate by means of a numerical example.

2 THE PROPENSITY TO CONSUME AND ITS FORMAL PROPERTIES

Our consumption hypothesis is that real planned consumption is a function of four variables. Of these real income Y is by far the most important. Hence, if we take the values of Q, A, α, and r as given

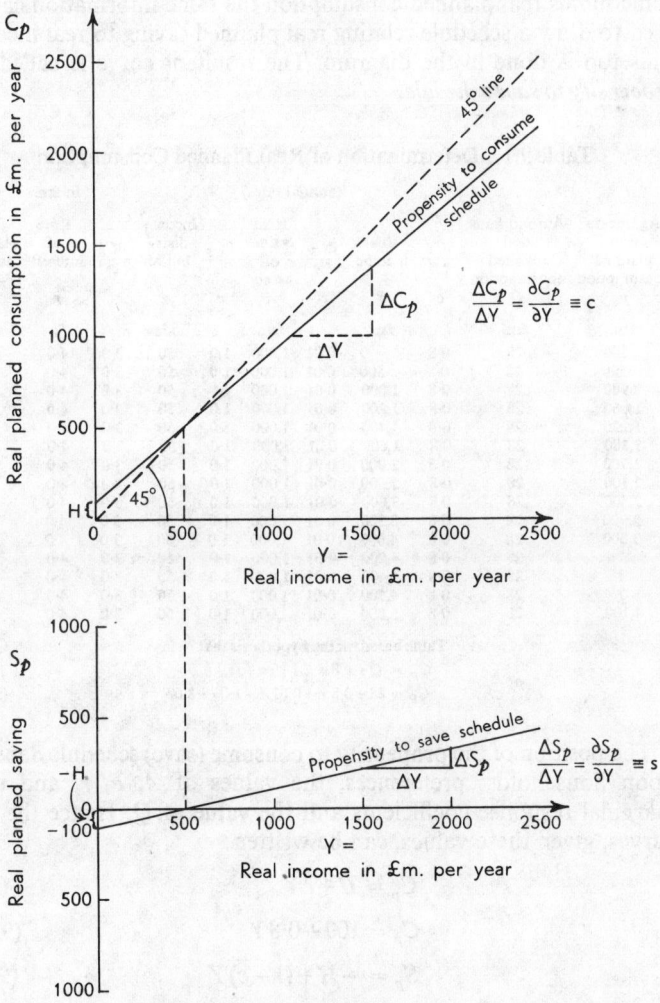

FIG. 9.i   **Propensity to consume and save schedules**

together with the values of their marginal response coefficients, we can draw, on a graph, the relation between C_p and the remaining independent variable Y. This is done in the Figure above using data set out in the Table. The resultant curve or schedule is called the *propensity to consume schedule*. It shows (for given values of Q, A, α, r, d, e and f) the rate of real planned consumption at each real income level. Since real planned saving is equal, by definition, to real income minus real planned consumption the same information can be used to draw a schedule relating real planned saving to real income. This too is done in the diagram. The resultant curve is called the *propensity to save schedule*.

Table 9.1   Determination of Real Planned Consumption

(annual rates)   in £m.

Aggregate real planned consumption p	Autonomous real planned consumption Q	$\frac{\partial C_p}{\partial Y}$ c	Real income Y	$\frac{\partial C_p}{\partial A}$ d	Real value of assets A	$\frac{\partial C_p}{\partial \alpha}$ e	Income distri- bution α	$\frac{\partial C_p}{\partial r}$	Rate of interest r	Real planned saving $Y_s - C_p$ p
£m.	£m.		£m.		£m.	Index			%	£m.
100	28	0·8	0	0.01	1,000	1·0	50	3·0	4·0	– 100
500	28	0·8	500	0·01	1,000	1·0	50	3·0	4·0	0
900	28	0·8	1,000	0·01	1,000	1·0	50	3·0	4·0	100
1,060	28	0·8	1,200	0·01	1,000	1·0	50	3·0	4·0	140
1,220	28	0·8	1,400	0·01	1,000	1·0	50	3·0	4·0	180
1,380	28	0·8	1,600	0·01	1,000	1·0	50	3·0	4·0	220
1,700	28	0·8	2,000	0·01	1,000	1·0	50	3·0	4·0	300
2,100	28	0·8	2,500	0·01	1,000	1·0	50	3·0	4·0	400
2,500	28	0·8	3,000	0·01	1,000	1·0	50	3·0	4·0	500
2,900	28	0·8	3,500	0·01	1,000	1·0	50	3·0	4·0	600
3,300	28	0·8	4,000	0·01	1,000	1·0	50	3·0	4·0	700
?	28	0·8	4,200	0·01	1,000	1·0	50	3·0	4·0	?
?	28	0·8	4,400	0·01	1,000	1·0	50	3·0	4·0	?
?	28	0·8	4,700	0·01	1,000	1·0	50	3·0	4·0	?
4,100	28	0·8	5,000	0·01	1,000	1·0	50	3·0	4·0	900

Table based on the hypothesis that

$$C_p = Q + cY + dA + e\alpha + fr \tag{9.IV}$$
$$C_p = 28 + 0\cdot8Y + 0\cdot01A + 1\cdot0\alpha + 3\cdot0r \tag{9.IVn}$$

The position of the propensity to consume (save) schedule depends upon households' preferences, the values of A, α, r, and their marginal response coefficients and the value of Q. Hence the two curves, given these values, can be written:

$$C_p = H + cY \tag{9.V}$$

$$C_p = 100 + 0\cdot8Y \tag{9.Vn}$$

$$S_p = -H + (1-c)Y \tag{9.VI}$$

$$S_p = -100 + 0\cdot2Y \tag{9.VIn}$$

The *slope* of the propensity to consume schedule is $\partial C_p/\partial Y \equiv c$: the marginal response of real planned consumption to real income. This has a special name in economics which is the *marginal propensity to consume*. It is the increment in real planned consumption resulting from a unit increase in real income alone. Analogously the *slope* of the propensity to save schedule is known as the *marginal propensity to save* $\partial S_p/\partial Y \equiv s$. Since, by definition, households must plan to save (or consume) the whole of any increase in income then:

$$\frac{\partial C_p}{\partial Y} + \frac{\partial S_p}{\partial Y} \equiv 1 \quad \text{or} \quad c + s \equiv 1$$

so that
$$\frac{\partial S_p}{\partial Y} \equiv 1 - \frac{\partial C_p}{\partial Y} \quad \text{or} \quad s = 1 - c.$$

The consumption schedule, as plotted, shows that, when real income is zero, real planned consumption is H or, in numerical terms, £100 m. per annum. *This is the value of consumption which is autonomous with respect to income.* Notice that it depends on Q, A, α, r as well as d, e and f. Analogously autonomous saving is $-£100$ m. – which, of course, is simply *dis-saving*, for when $Y =$ zero,

$$S_p \equiv Y - C_p \equiv 0 - £100 \text{ m.} \equiv -£100 \text{ m.}$$

Finally we define the *average propensity to consume* as:

$$\frac{C_p}{Y} \equiv \frac{\text{real planned consumption}}{\text{real income}}$$

and the *average propensity to save* as S_p/Y. Clearly since all income must be consumed or saved we have:

$$C_p + S_p \equiv Y$$

or
$$\frac{C_p}{Y} + \frac{S_p}{Y} \equiv 1$$

that is, the average propensities to save and consume add to unity. Notice that, if autonomous consumption (H) is positive, the average propensity to consume exceeds the marginal. If autonomous consumption is zero, the two are equal. If autonomous consumption is negative, the marginal propensity exceeds the average.

This is easily established from (9.V) where we wrote:

$$C_p = H + cY$$

so:
$$\frac{C_p}{Y} = \frac{H}{Y} + c,$$

which tells us that the average propensity to consume C_p/Y is equal to the marginal propensity (c) *plus* the term H/Y. Clearly if H is negative $c > C_p/Y$ and conversely H is positive.

We have now listed the formal properties of the propensity to consume schedule. But formal properties are not of themselves economics. We now look at the economics.

The *position* of the schedule depends upon

(i) households' preferences;
(ii) the values of Q, and A, α, r – the three independent variables not shown in the Figure;
(iii) the marginal response coefficients d, e and f.

A change in any one of these will shift the whole schedule – upwards or downwards – leaving its slope unaltered. Suppose, for example, α increases (income becomes more equally distributed). The schedule shifts upwards and we say that the propensity to consume has increased for now, at *each* level of real income real planned consumption is greater.

The *slope* of the schedule – the marginal propensity to consume – describes the reaction of real planned consumption to an increase in real income, *everything else held constant. It is an important proposition of economics that, when real income increases real consumption also increases but by less than the increase in real income.* That is, the marginal propensity to consume $\partial C_p/\partial Y$ is greater than zero but less than unity – a proposition which also applies to the marginal propensity to save. Thus we have the hypothesis:

$$0 < c \equiv \frac{\partial C_p}{\partial Y} < 1$$

$$0 < s \equiv \frac{\partial S_p}{\partial Y} < 1.$$

An increase in the propensity to consume must be sharply distinguished from an increase in consumption. The former as we have seen means an upward shift of the whole schedule indicating that, *because of a change in one of the parameters of the schedule,* households now plan a higher rate of real consumption at *each* level of real income. This is called an autonomous increase in consumption since it is autonomous with respect to income.

By contrast an increase in real planned consumption may occur simply because real income rises and, as a result, we move *along* an *unchanged* propensity to consume schedule. Consumption then rises because, as we have already seen, the marginal propensity to consume is positive. This is called an *induced* increase in consumption because it is brought about (induced) by an increase in real income.

It is extremely important for the reader to bear these distinctions clearly in mind. Words are often used loosely in the belief that their precise meaning can be distinguished in the context. Thus 'an increase in consumption' is a potentially misleading phrase since, of itself, it does not make it clear whether there has been a *shift* in the consumption function (propensity to consume schedule), or movement along it, or some combination of the two. The same confusion can occur with the phrase 'an increase in demand' referred to some commodity – say peanuts. Does this mean a shift in the demand schedule, a movement along it or some combination of the two?

In practice, though for pedagogic reasons we discuss shifts in the consumption function (and hence the propensity to consume schedule), this function is believed to be relatively stable: that is, to shift rather rarely. Hence most increases in consumption which are observed are probably induced: that is, due to movements along an unchanged function.

3 THE DETERMINATION OF THE EQUILIBRIUM LEVEL OF OUTPUT

At the beginning of this chapter we wrote our equilibrium condition in two equivalent ways: $Y = C_p + I_p$, and $S_p = I_p$. We also assumed that $I_p = \bar{I}$ and took, as a numerical illustration, the value of $\bar{I}$ to be £500 m. a year. This value we treated as *exogenous* – that is determined outside our model – and hence independent of income (output). We shall continue to treat r, A and α also as *exogenous* and assume them to take the special values $\bar{r}$, $\bar{A}$, $\bar{\alpha}$, shown in Table 9.1. Obviously from Table 9.1, simply by adding the rate of planned investment (I_p) to the rate of planned consumption we can draw up a new table showing aggregate demand ($C_p + I_p$) *at each level of real income*. This is done in the Table below. Plainly the equilibrium level of income, defined by the condition $Y = C_p + I_p$, is £3000 m.

By the same token we can use Table 9.1 to give the rates of real planned saving at each level of real income. Our second version of the equilibrium condition tells us that income will be in equilibrium when real planned saving is £500 m. – i.e. equal to the fixed rate of real planned investment. The reader can easily verify that this gives the same result.

Precisely the same result can be arrived at by elementary algebra.

Table 9.2   *Aggregate Demand at each Level of Real Income in £m.*

Real income (aggregate supply)	Real planned consumption C_p	Real planned investment I_p	Real aggregate demand (C_p+I_p)
0	100	500	600
500	500	500	1,000
1,000	900	500	1,400
1,200	1,060	500	1,560
1,400	1,220	500	1,720
1,600	1,380	500	1,880
2,000	1,700	500	2,200
2,500	2,100	500	2,600
3,000	2,500	500	3,000
3,500	2,900	500	3,400
4,000	3,300	500	3,800
4,200	?	500	?
4,400	?	500	?
4,700	?	500	?
5,000	?	500	4,600

Assumptions:

(1) $I_p = \bar{I} = £500m.$

(2) $C_p = Q + cY + dA + e\alpha + fr$ with the value of the parameters as in Table 9.1.

We have, in fact a simple problem which can be set out and solved as follows: First we write the equilibrium condition:

$$Y = C_p + I_p$$

Our consumption hypothesis tells us that:

$$C_p = Q + cY + d\bar{A} + e\bar{\alpha} + f\bar{r} \qquad (9.\text{VII})$$

$$C_p = 28 + 0\cdot8Y + 0\cdot01\bar{A} + 1\cdot0\bar{\alpha} + 3\cdot0\bar{r} \qquad (9.\text{VIIn})$$

Our investment assumption gives:

$$I_p = \bar{I} \qquad (9.\text{VIII})$$

$$I_p = £500 \text{ m.} \qquad (9.\text{VIIIn})$$

If we now substitute (9.VII) and (9.VIII) into the equilibrium condition we obtain a single equation in Y – which is equilibrium income – which can easily be solved in terms of $\bar{I}$, the given rate of investment, and the parameters of the consumption function. The manipulation is extremely simple. We have, on substitution,

$$Y = Q + cY + d\bar{A} + e\bar{\alpha} + f\bar{r} + \bar{I} \qquad (9.\text{IX})$$

$$Y = 28 + 0\cdot8Y + [0\cdot01 \times 1000] + [1\cdot0 \times 50] + [3\cdot0 \times 4] + 500 \quad (9.\text{IXn})$$

therefore:

$$Y - cY = Q + d\bar{A} + e\bar{\alpha} + f\bar{r} + \bar{I}$$

$$Y - 0{\cdot}8Y = 28 + [0{\cdot}01 \times 1000] + [1{\cdot}0 \times 50] + [3{\cdot}0 \times 4] + 500$$

so that

$$Y = [\{Q + d\bar{A} + e\bar{\alpha} + f\bar{r}\} + \bar{I}]\frac{1}{1-c} \qquad (9.X)$$

$$Y = [\{28 + 10 + 50 + 12\} + 500]\frac{1}{1-0{\cdot}8} \qquad (9.Xn)$$

The elementary algebra yields, as it must, the same result as elementary arithmetic. Equilibrium real income is £3000 m. per year. The algebraic formulation of (9.X) however, brings out explicitly three points which the arithmetic formulation obscures.

First, the expression in the *curly* brackets is that rate of consumption which is independent of (autonomous with respect to) income. It is, in fact, the constant (H) of equation (9.V). Equation (9.X) therefore confirms *explicitly* that H depends on the values of A, α, r and their marginal response coefficients as well as on Q. It, in short, depends on *all* the parameters of the propensity to consume schedule – a point which we earlier stated without full demonstration. Second, the result for equilibrium Y takes the form of one expression (in the square brackets) *multiplied* by a second expression which is $1/1-c$. What is the expression in the square brackets? A moment's thought shows that it is the sum of all those planned expenditures – whether consumption or investment – which are independent of income. This tells us that the equilibrium level of income is given by the sum of those expenditures which are independent of income multiplied by the expression $1/1-c$. Third, what can we say about the expression $1/1-c$? This is simply $1/1-$marginal propensity to consume. Since the marginal propensity to consume is positive – but less than unity – the denominator of this expression must be less than 1. Hence $1/1-c$ must be greater than 1. Indeed in our example it is 5. We should also remind ourselves that, since $1-c \equiv s$, this 'multiplier' can also be written as $1/s$. The precise significance of this 'multiplier' will be explained later. It is, however, obvious that the 'multiplier' will be greater the greater is c – that is the more nearly c approaches unity.

We have now shown that either via arithmetic or algebra we can, if we are given (i) the consumption function; and (ii) the rate of planned investment, determine the equilibrium level of income (output) and hence the equilibrium level of employment.

This is the crucial result of the modern theory of the short-run determination of output and employment. Its meaning is simply that, given the rate of planned investment, income will adjust (upwards or downwards) until it reaches a level at which households will plan to save at the same rate at which enterprises plan to invest. In short, income (and hence employment) is the variable which moves to equate the saving and investment plans of the community.

These important results which we have reached by arithmetic and algebra are commonly presented geometrically. Since arithmetic is tedious while some people dislike algebra we now perform the same exercise, using the same data, geometrically.

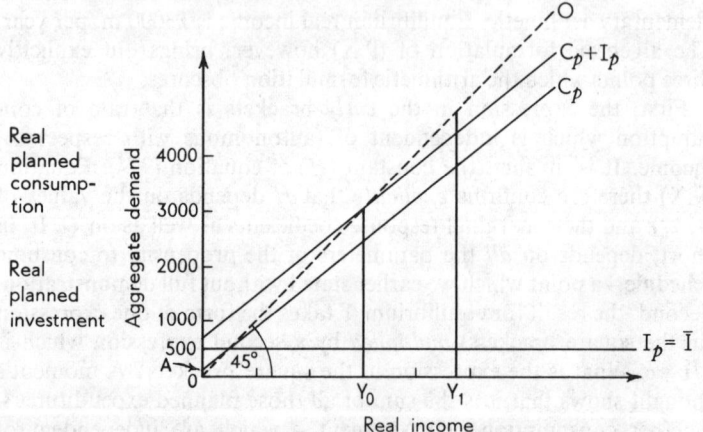

FIG. 9.ii(a)   Income determined by the aggregate demand schedule

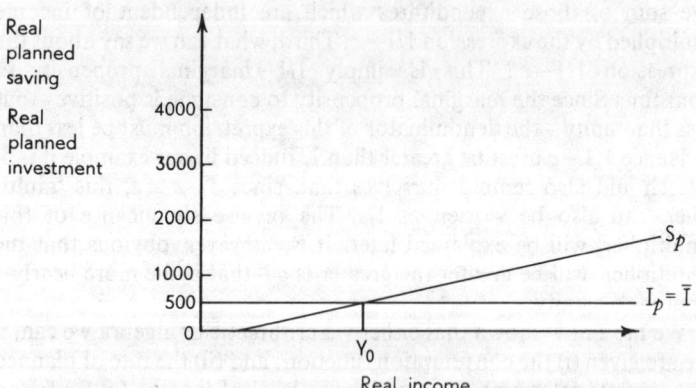

FIG. 9.ii(b)   Income determined by saving and investment schedules

On the vertical axis of Fig. 9.ii(a) we measure real planned expenditures (C_p and I_p). On the horizontal axis real income. The line marked C_p is thus the propensity to consume schedule of Fig. 9.i. Its *slope*, as before, is the marginal propensity to consume. Its *position* is determined by OA—the rate of planned consumption which is independent of income. The distance OA is therefore given by:

$$OA \equiv Q + d\overline{A} + e\overline{a} + f\overline{r} \equiv H$$

$$\equiv £100 \text{ m. per year.}$$

From the origin of the diagram we draw a line 00 at an angle of 45°. Geometrically this line has the property that any point on it subtends equal distances along the horizontal and vertical axes. It follows that at any point on 00

aggregate real planned expenditure = aggregate real income (output)

that is $C_p + I_p = Y$

or $I_p = S_p$

The line 00 thus defines all possible positions of equilibrium.

To this diagram we now add a third line showing the rate of real planned investment (I_p). Since this is independent of income ($I_p = \overline{I}$) the line is horizontal and drawn showing a rate of £500 m. per year. We now add this rate of planned investment to the rates of consumption shown by the consumption schedule. This gives us the $C_p + I_p$ schedule or *the schedule of aggregate demand.* The schedule cuts 00 at the point X. At X income is Y_0. Y_0 is the equilibrium level of income for since X lies on 00 it is a point at which aggregate demand is equal to aggregate supply (income). It is indeed the only point at which, with our given consumption and investment schedules, aggregate demand does equal aggregate supply.

The same result is depicted on Fig. 9.ii(b) where we have drawn, instead of the consumption schedule, the saving schedule. On this we have superimposed the investment schedule. Where these two curves cut – that is, where $I_p = S_p$ – determines the equilibrium level of income. Again this is $Y_0 = £3000$ m. per year.

Both diagrams thus depict the determination of equilibrium output (income) either (as in Fig. 9.ii(a)) by the condition that $Y = C_p + I_p$ or (as in Fig. 9.ii(b)) by the equivalent condition that $S_p = I_p$.

Suppose income is not at Y_0 but at some higher level Y_1. Will it tend to move towards Y_0? At Y_1 we can see from Fig. 9.ii(a) that

$C_p + I_p$ (aggregate demand) is less than Y (aggregate supply). Hence some part of output will be unsold so that there will be *unintended* investment in inventories. In short, *actual* investment ($Y_1 - C_p$) will exceed *planned* investment (I_p). In this situation, as we have already shown, enterprises will *reduce* output and employment. Hence income will move *towards* Y_0. This argument is readily reversible for income levels less than that of Y_0. It follows that Y_0 is not only the *equilibrium level of income* but is a *stable*† equilibrium in the sense that, if income departs from it, forces will be set up which tend to compel it to return to Y_0.

We have now shown, by arithmetic, algebra and geometry, that if we know (i) the consumption function; and (ii) the rate of planned investment, we can determine the equilibrium level of income (output) and employment. We have also shown that, provided the marginal propensity to consume is less than unity, the equilibrium level of income is *stable*.

The meaning of this analysis can be summed up as follows: Assuming

    (i) constant prices; and
    (ii) a given level of the interest rate; then,
         (a) the variable which adjusts to equate aggregate demand with aggregate supply – that is to reconcile the saving plans of households with the investment plans of enterprises – is income; and
         (b) the equilibrium level of income which reconciles these plans need not be – and in general will not be – a level of income corresponding to full employment.

4 THE MULTIPLIER AND THE MARGINAL PROPENSITY TO CONSUME

Our analysis so far tells us that, given the rate of real planned consumption which is independent of income (H in equation 9.V) and the rate of real planned investment, we can determine the equilibrium level of real income. It follows that if either of these determinants changes so will the equilibrium level of income. What determines the extent of the change?

Originally we assumed I_p to be £500 m. per year. Suppose this rises to £900 m. What will be the new equilibrium level of income?

A glance back at Table 9.1 tells us that, to generate a rate of

† Strictly, stability is a dynamic concept.

planned saving of £900 m. a year, incomes will need to be £5000 m. Hence:

$$\Delta Y \equiv \text{the change in equilibrium real income}$$
$$= £5000 \text{ m.} - £3000 \text{ m.} = £2000 \text{ m.}$$

while $\Delta I_p \equiv$ the change in real planned investment
$$= £900 \text{ m.} - £500 \text{ m.} = £400 \text{ m.}$$

Hence

$$\frac{\Delta Y}{\Delta I_p} = \frac{£2000 \text{ m.}}{£400 \text{ m.}} = 5$$

We now define $\Delta Y / \Delta I_p$ as the 'multiplier': that is, *the coefficient relating the change in real income to the change in real autonomous expenditure bringing it about.* We use 'real autonomous expenditure' rather than 'real investment' because *the same multiplier applies to changes in autonomous consumption.* If we refer back to equation 9.X or Fig. 9.ii(a) this is obvious enough. Using this equation we have, for the initial equilibrium level which we now call Y_0:

$$Y_0 = [H + \bar{I}]\frac{1}{1-c} \qquad \text{where } H = Q + d\bar{A} + e\bar{a} + f\bar{r} \quad (9.\text{XI})$$

If $\bar{I}$ increases by $\Delta\bar{I}$ the new equilibrium level Y_1 is given by:

$$Y_1 = [H + \bar{I} + \Delta\bar{I}]\frac{1}{1-c} \qquad\qquad (9.\text{XII})$$

so that

$$\Delta Y = Y_1 - Y_0 = \Delta\bar{I}\frac{1}{1-c} \quad \text{and} \quad \frac{\Delta Y}{\Delta\bar{I}} = \frac{1}{1-c} = \frac{1}{1-0\cdot8} = 5.$$

Obviously had the change been in the propensity to consume so that H increased by ΔH we should have had:

$$\frac{\Delta Y}{\Delta H} = \frac{1}{1-c} = \frac{1}{1-0\cdot8} = 5 \qquad\qquad (9.\text{XIII})$$

In the short run, therefore, *any* change in autonomous real expenditure has a multiplied effect on income whether (in terms of Fig. 9.ii(a)) it shifts the consumption schedule upwards or the investment schedule.

The multiplier is given by the formula:

$$\frac{1}{1-c} \equiv \frac{1}{s} \qquad \text{where } c \equiv \text{marginal propensity to consume;}$$

$$\text{and } s \equiv 1 - c \equiv \text{marginal propensity to save.}$$

So far this, though obvious enough, is merely algebra. What does it mean in economic terms?

Suppose autonomous consumption increases by £100 m. per year, i.e. $\Delta H = £100$ m. Additional income is thus created for those who produce the additional output. From this income they spend $c£100$ m. $= 0 \cdot 8£100$ m. $= £80$ m. This generates further output and incomes which cause a further induced increase in consumption. This in turn generates further income for those who produce the additional consumption goods and so the process continues.

We have, indeed, the following series for the increase in income:

$$\Delta Y = £100 \text{ m.} + c£100 \text{ m.} + c^2£100 \text{ m.} + c^3£100 \text{ m.} + \ldots +$$
$$c^n£100 \text{ m.}$$

or $\quad \Delta Y = £100 \text{ m.} + 0 \cdot 8£100 \text{ m.} + (0 \cdot 8)^2£100 \text{ m.} + (0 \cdot 8)^3£100 \text{ m.} + \ldots$
$$+ (0 \cdot 8)^n£100 \text{ m.}$$

This series is easily summed to give:

$$\Delta Y = £100 \text{ m.} \times \frac{1 - c^{n+1}}{1 - c} = £100 \text{ m.} \times \frac{1 - (0 \cdot 8)^{n+1}}{1 - 0 \cdot 8} \qquad (9.\text{XIV})$$

As n, the number of income 'rounds', approaches infinity, c^{n+1}, since c is less than unity, approaches zero. Hence the *limit* of (9.XIV) as $n \rightarrow$ infinity is:

$$\Delta Y = £100 \text{ m.} \, \frac{1}{1 - c}$$

which is, clearly enough, our formula at (9.XIII), for we have simply taken ΔH to be £100 m.

In other words the new equilibrium level of income, reached after an infinitely large number of income 'rounds', is greater than the original level by:

$$\Delta Y = £100 \text{ m.} \, \frac{1}{1 - c}$$
$$= £100 \text{ m.} \times 5$$
$$= £500 \text{ m.}$$

The change in income is greater than the change in autonomous expenditure which causes it because, as long as $c > 0$ the multiplier, $1/1 - c$ must be > 1. Notice that if $c = 0$ the multiplier is unity. This, however, is economically quite implausible.

The common-sense proposition underlying this result is that one man's income is another man's expenditure – which is obviously correct – and, as a result, the more the latter spends the more the former will receive and spend in his turn.

The multiplier is thus a *leverage coefficient* and, as such, works in either direction. To see this suppose ΔH to be negative and equal to $-£100$ m. We should then have:

$$\Delta Y = -£100 \text{ m.} \frac{1}{1-c}$$

$$= -£500 \text{ m.}$$

so that, in this case, equilibrium income would *fall* by £500 m.

To know that, after an infinite passage of time ($n\to$ infinity) equilibrium income will rise (or fall) by an amount determined by the multiplier and the increase (decrease) in the rate of autonomous expenditure is interesting. We are, however, not primarily concerned with what will *eventually* occur but only with *what will occur after the lapse of a finite period of time*. To see this we must engage in some elementary dynamics. Accordingly in the Table which follows we (i) *express* all flows at quarterly and *not* annual rates; (ii) *divide* time into periods of 3 calendar months' duration; (iii) *assume* that output takes one period (3 months) to adjust to a change in demand. On these assumptions, making use of the consumption function specified in Table 9.1 – that is, holding the variables A, α and r constant – we can set out the following multiplier process.

We begin in period 0 with income in equilibrium at £750 m. In period 1, I_p increases to £225 m. Output however does not increase until period 2, since, by assumption, it takes one period to adjust. Hence in period 1 aggregate demand $(C_p + I_p)$ exceeds aggregate supply and there is involuntary decumulation of stocks to the extent of £100 m.

In period 2 output adjusts upwards by £100 m. Since the marginal propensity to consume is 0·8 this raises consumption by £80 m. Again aggregate demand exceeds supply – this time by £80 m. and there is a second involuntary decumulation of stocks.

In period 3 output expands again – this time by £80 m. Hence consumption rises by (0·8) × £80 m = £64 m. and in this way the process continues with enterprises always adjusting output upwards in an endeavour to catch up with expanding aggregate demand.

This Table, which gives a somewhat oversimplified account of a dynamic multiplier process, conveys some interesting information. This can be summarised as follows:

Table 9.3 The Multiplier Process
£m. at quarterly rates

Period (1)	Income (1)	Planned consumption (2)	Actual consumption (3)	Planned saving (4)	Actual saving (5)	Planned investment (6)	Actual investment (7)	Unintended investment (8)
0	750	625	625	125	125	125	125	nil
1	750	625	625	125	125	225	125	−100
2	850	705	705	145	145	225	145	−80
3	930	769	769	161	161	225	161	−64
4	994	820·2	820·2	173·8	173·8	225	173·8	−51·2
5						225		
6						225		
·								
·								
n	1,250	1,025	1,025	225	225	225	225	nil

Note: (1) Based on the consumption function of Table 9.1.

(i) The *ultimate* change in the *quarterly* rate of income is given by:

$$\Delta Y = \Delta I_p \times \frac{1}{1-c}$$

$$= \text{£100 m.} \times 5$$

$$= \text{£500 m.}$$

By the fourth period – that is, after one year – 48·8 per cent of this change has occurred.

(ii) From period 1 to period $(n-1)$ the system is in disequilibrium. Hence:

$$Y < C_p + I_p$$

and $\qquad I_p > I$

and so periods 1 to $(n-1)$ are characterised by unintended disinvestment in stocks which diminishes as the system moves towards its new equilibrium.

(iii) In *all* periods – that is whether equilibrium exists or not

$$S \equiv I$$

and $\qquad Y \equiv C + I$

where S, I and C denote saving, investment and consumption in their national accounting sense.

These points the reader should check for himself. He should also calculate the values for columns (1) (2) (3) (4) (5) (7) and (8) for periods 5 and 6.

QUESTIONS AND EXERCISES

1. The following observations are generated by a consumption function of the form: $C_p = Q + cY + dA + e\alpha + fr$.

Year	C_p	Y	A	α	r
1	662·4	1000	1000	0·5	4
2	762·4	1200	1000	0·5	4
3	767·4	1200	1500	0·5	4
4	817·4	1200	1500	1·0	4
5	766·2	1200	1500	0·5	2

Calculate the numerical values of the marginal response coefficients c, d, e, f and the constant Q. Next, taking $A = 1000$, $\alpha = 0.5$ and $r = 4.0$ per cent, plot the propensity to consume schedule. What is the value of consumption when income is zero? Draw a second schedule for the value $A = 1000$; $\alpha = 1.0$; $r = 4$ per cent.

2. The elasticity of consumption with respect to income is defined as:

$$\frac{\Delta C_p}{C_p} \bigg/ \frac{\Delta Y}{Y},$$

when Y is the only independent variable to change. This can be rewritten:

$$\frac{\Delta C_p}{\Delta Y} \cdot \frac{Y}{C_p}.$$

Since $\Delta C_p = (\partial C_p / \partial Y) . \Delta Y$ calculate from *both* the propensity to consume schedules the elasticity of consumption with respect to income. Show that the elasticity will be unity only if autonomous consumption is zero. Why is this? What general relationship does it reflect between the average and marginal propensities and the elasticity? In what circumstances will the elasticity be independent of the level of income?

3. Use the U.K. national income estimates to obtain figures for real consumption and real income on a quarterly basis for the years 1957–71. Draw (freehand) a straight line through these observations when plotted on a graph. Measure consumption on the vertical axis and income on the horizontal axis.

   (i) Explain and justify your choice of data.
   (ii) What is the slope of your straight line?
   (iii) In what circumstances, if any, would the slope of your line be a 'reasonable' estimate of the marginal propensity to consume?
   (iv) Assuming that it is a 'reasonable' estimate, what is the value of the multiplier?
   (v) What do you think is meant by 'reasonable'?

4. Using the data of Question 1 plot C_p and Y as for Question 3. Again draw (freehand) a straight line through the observed points. Why is the slope of this line not a good estimate of $\partial C_p / \partial Y$?

5. *Ceteris paribus* according to Table 9.1 a 10-unit increase in income 'induces' an 8 unit increase in consumption. Give a precise statement of what is meant by *ceteris paribus*. Explain the meaning of 'induced'.

6. For the multiplier of Table 9.3 what proportion of the ultimate change in income is completed after (i) two quarters; (ii) four quarters; (iii) eight quarters.

7. Discuss critically the assumptions about human behaviour underlying the consumption function of Question 1. Are all the variables measurable (i) in principle (ii) in practice? How would you attempt to measure A, α and r?

8. The multiplier model of Table 9.3 can be written formally as follows:

$$C_p(t) = H + cY(t) \qquad \text{with } H = 25, c = 0.8$$

$$I_p(t) = \bar{I} \qquad\qquad \bar{I} = 125,$$

$$Y(t) = C_p(t-1) + I_p(t-1)$$

where the suffixes in brackets indicate the period (t, $t-1$, etc.) of the variable and the last equation indicates that it takes one period for output to adjust to demand.

An alternative model can be written:

$$C_p(t) = H + cY(t-1)$$

$$I_p(t) = \bar{I}$$

$$Y(t) = C_p(t) + I_p(t),$$

where the lag of output behind demand no longer exists and, in its place, we have put the hypothesis that this period's consumption depends upon last period's income.

Construct a table similar to 9.3 showing the multiplier process for this model. How does disequilibrium manifest itself? Why are there no unplanned stock changes? Is the equilibrium result of the two processes the same? Which model do you consider the more realistic?

9. Plot the following data on an appropriate graph:

Per cent of income recipients	Per cent of income received
10	3
20	7
30	11
40	16
50	22
60	29
70	36
80	47
90	59
100	100

What would a graph showing equal distribution of income look like? Construct one and compare it with the graph of the data. From your comparison suggest a way of measuring α (the parameter of income distribution). What would graphs of $\alpha = 0$ (perfect inequality of income distribution) and $\alpha = 1$ look like?

10. The multiplier model of Table 9.3 yields the following equilibrium results.

Period	Y	$C_p = C_A$	I_A	I_p	S_p	S_A
t	750	625	125	125	125	125
$t+n$	875	750	125	125	125	125

How much of the increase in consumption is due to: (i) a shift in the consumption function; and (ii) a movement along it?

11. The multiplier process of Table 9.3 can be written as follows:

Period	Change in income
2	ΔI_p
3	$c\Delta I_p$
4	$c^2\Delta I_p$
5	$c^3\Delta I_p$
.	
.	
$n+2$	$c^n\Delta I_p$

So the total change in income is:

$$\Delta Y = \Delta I_p \,[1+c+c^2+\ldots\ldots+c^n]$$
$$= \Delta I_p \left[\frac{1-c^{n+1}}{1-c}\right].$$

Use this formula to calculate the proportion of the total change which will have occurred by the end of (i) period 2; (ii) period 4; (iii) period 10. Would your results have been different if c had been 0·5 and not 0·8? Do your results imply that the greater the multiplier the greater the number of periods required to achieve any given proportion (say 50 per cent) of its equilibrium result?

12. How would you characterise the business behaviour assumed in Table 9.3?

13. From the National Income Estimates obtain figures for the quarterly expenditure on (i) consumption of non-durables; (ii) consumption of durables, for the years 1957–70. Graph them against income. Compare these graphs with that you pre-

pared for Question 3. What does the comparison suggest to you? What additional variables (if any) would you introduce into the consumption function hypothesis to obtain a better explanation of expenditure on durables? How would you seek to measure them?

14. The function $C_p = Q + cY + dA + e\alpha + fr$ used in this chapter has, in our numerical examples, $Q = 28$. Has Q any economic meaning? Is $Q \neq$ zero possible? Discuss carefully in the light of (i) your answer to Question 3 and (i) the fact that the equation of a straight line is $Y = A + bX$.

SUGGESTED READING

T. F. Dernburg and D. M. McDougall, *Macro-Economics* (McGraw-Hill, 1963) ch. v.

M. Evans,† *Macroeconomic Activity* (Harper & Row, 1969) chs 2, 3.

G. Ackley,† *Macro-Economic Theory* (Macmillan, 1961) chs x–xi.

J. M. Keynes, *The General Theory of Employment, Interest and Money* (Macmillan, 1936) chs viii–x.

L. Metzler in *Incomes, Employment and Public Policy* (Norton, 1948).

L. R. Klein and A. S. Goldberger,† *An Econometric Model of the United States, 1929–52* (Amsterdam, 1955) chs. ii, iv.

J. C. R. Dow, *The Management of the British Economy, 1945–60* (Cambridge, 1964) ch. xi.

† More advanced reference.

10 The Investment Function

IN Chapter 9 we showed that if we knew

    (i) the propensity-to-consume schedule; and

    (ii) the rate of real planned investment

we could determine the equilibrium level of output and hence, via the production function, the equilibrium level of employment. We also demonstrated that the equilibrium level of output (= income) was stable.†

These are important conditions. We established them, however, on the pedagogically convenient assumption that the rate of real planned investment was exogenously determined by (say) some hypothetical 'planning authority'. In a market economy there is no such authority. It follows that, to develop our theory, we must now put forward an explanation of how real planned investment is determined.

The purpose of this chapter is therefore to develop a theory of how investment is determined: or, as we shall call it, by analogy with the consumption function already discussed, the theory of the investment function.

At this stage the reader should recall our definition of the term 'investment'. This must be carefully distinguished from colloquial usage in which it is common to speak of 'investment' in financial assets such as bonds, shares or deposits. There are three fundamental points:

    (i) real net investment is the process of increasing the real capital stock of the community;

    (ii) an investment decision is a decision to bring about such an increase; and

    (iii) real gross investment is defined as real net investment *plus* real depreciation.

In practice, net investment expenditure by the private sector takes three forms which it is useful to distinguish

$I_f \equiv$ real planned net investment in fixed capital (other than dwellings)

† We return to this issue – in a dynamic context – in Chapter 20.

$I_d \equiv$ real planned net investment in dwellings;
$I_s \equiv$ real planned net investment in inventories

so that

$$I_p \equiv \text{real planned net investment} \equiv I_f + I_d + I_s.$$

There are certain features of investment in inventories which need special consideration. Accordingly discussion of I_s is postponed until Chapter 20. Hence the theory of this chapter should be regarded as primarily applicable to investment in fixed capital and dwellings.

We begin by asking: who takes investment decisions and why?

1 INVESTMENT DECISIONS

In our simple model, by assumption, all investment decisions are taken by enterprises or, more strictly, by the businessmen who run them. We have assumed that the aim of businessmen is to maximise profits; our problem is therefore to explain in what circumstances a profit-maximising businessman will plan to invest.

In outline, the explanation is not far to seek nor difficult to comprehend. It states that a profit-maximising businessman will purchase an additional real capital asset (i.e. invest) if:

the rate of return (per cent per period) he expects to derive from the asset over its life $>$ the rate of cost (per cent per period) he must pay for borrowing the funds with which to finance the investment

The remainder of this chapter is concerned to make this simple proposition rather more precise and derive from it a theory of aggregate real planned investment.

The easiest approach to this problem is to consider a simple hypothetical example. Let us assume, therefore, that some businessman is considering whether (or not) to invest by adding a new machine costing £10,000 to his shoe-manufacturing factory. He *knows* the cost of the machine? Is it worth his while to purchase it?

In buying the machine the businessman can be thought of as purchasing the right to the net returns produced by the machine over its *useful economic life*. Since these returns lie in the future, he cannot *know* them. He must *forecast* them. Equally he cannot *know* the economic life of the machine since this too depends on future events – for example, the development of economically superior machines. This too must be *forecast*. However, making such forecasts and taking decisions under uncertainty is precisely the job of the creative businessman. How, then, does he go about it?

His first step is to *forecast* the economic life of the machine. This is *not* the same as its technical life. The machine may be operating efficiently, from a *technical* point of view, long after it has become economically inefficient because of the development of superior machines. This is one consideration. A second is that, since he cannot know the future, he may feel unable to make forecasts for more than a few years ahead simply because the future is economically – and perhaps politically – uncertain. Let us suppose that after weighing (what he believes are) the relevant factors, he forecasts the economic life of the machine as five years.

We shall assume that no second-hand market in capital assets exists. The machine, once purchased, must be held for five years and then sold as scrap. Our businessman forecasts the scrap value as £1,900. This gives our businessman the following data:

(i) he *knows* the cost of the machine to be £10,000;
(ii) he *estimates* its useful economic life at five years;
(iii) he *estimates* its scrap value at £1,900.

He must now make estimates of the net returns from the asset in each year of its useful life. This is not simple – for to obtain estimates he must calculate:

(i) the output of shoes in each year and the prices in each year at which the output can be sold;
(ii) the raw materials required in each year and their prices in each year;
(iii) the labour required to work the machine in each year and its wage cost in each year.

To do this he has information on the technical capacity of the machine to produce shoes, its technical requirement for raw materials, the present and past costs of raw materials and labour and present and past shoe prices. He can only do the best he can with the information he has. Let us suppose that he does this and produces the following *estimates* of returns net of raw material and labour costs:

Year 1	£2,500	Year 4	£2,000
Year 2	£2,500	Year 5	£2,000
Year 3	£2,500		

Given these (obviously uncertain) estimates, how can the business-man decide whether to invest or not? There are two possible methods of proceeding.

In the first method he asks: what is the *present value* of this stream of prospective returns: that is, what sum, if held in a form which yielded the current interest rate, would provide an equivalent income stream? If this calculated present value *exceeds* £10,000 – the known cost of the capital asset – the investment is worth while: if it is less, it is not worth while.

An elementary example may make this clearer. Suppose a man is asked: what sum would you pay *today* for £105 receivable in *one year's time*? He can answer this question by asking himself:

> What sum accumulated for one year at the existing rate of interest would provide £105 in one year's time?

This sum is the *present value* of £105 in one year's time.

If we call the present value ($\equiv$ P.V.)x we have the equation

$$x(1+r) = £105,$$

where r is the market rate of interest. Obviously if $r = 5$ per cent (that is 0·05) we have

$$x(1·05) = £105$$

so that
$$x = £100,$$

that is, the P.V. of £105 in one year's time is £100 if $r = 5$ per cent.

Suppose instead the man had been offered £105 in *two* years' time. Interest would then have accumulated twice and the expression for the P.V. would be

$$x(1·05)^2 = £105,$$

which gives
$$x = £95·45.$$

In general, the P.V. of a stream of prospective returns over the life of an asset can be written:

$$\text{P.V.} = \frac{Q_1}{1+r} + \frac{Q_2}{(1+r)^2} + \dots + \frac{Q_n}{(1+r)^n}, \qquad (10.\text{I})$$

where $Q_1 \dots Q_n$ are the returns expected in each year

n is the number of years
r is, as before, the rate of interest.

Notice that this formula somewhat simplifies matters by assuming a constant value of r over the life of the asset.

Applying this formula to our example we have

$$P.V. = \frac{£2,500}{(1+r)} + \frac{£2,500}{(1+r)^2} + \frac{£2,500}{(1+r)^3} + \frac{£2,000}{(1+r)^4}$$

$$+ \frac{£2,000 + £1,900}{(1+r)^5}, \tag{10.II}$$

which for three assumed values of r yields, to a close approximation:

	$r = 0.05$	$r = 0.10$	$r = 0.15$
P.V.	£11,511	£10,000	£8,791.

Notice that if $r < 0.10$ (10 per cent) the present value exceeds the cost: conversely if $r > 0.10$ the cost exceeds the present value. In the former case the investment is profitable since the businessman expects a higher return on the project than the interest cost: in the latter it is not.

An alternative approach is not to use the present value method but to calculate directly the rate of return which the businessman expects to obtain by purchasing the asset. In this case we replace P.V. (the unknown) in Equation (10.II) by the *known* cost of the asset (£10,000). The unknown is now the rate of return which we shall call i. We thus obtain:

$$£10,000 = \frac{£2,500}{1+i} + \frac{£2,500}{(1+i)^2} + \frac{£2,500}{(1+i)^3} + \frac{£2,000}{(1+i)^4} +$$

$$+ \frac{£2,000 + £1,900}{(1+i)^5}, \tag{10.III}$$

which we solve for i.

Clearly i is the rate of return which makes the present value of the stream of prospective returns expected over the life of the asset exactly equal to its supply price (cost). This rate is known as the *marginal efficiency of the capital asset*.† As one of our P.V. calculations has already shown, it is equal to 0·10 (10 per cent). The decision rule is now: if $i > r$, the project is worthwhile: if $i < r$ it is not. Obviously this is a nasty-looking problem since the unknown (i) appears in the equation raised to the power of 5. How then do we find it? The practical answer is by successive approximations.

† This is substantially identical to the definition given by Keynes. J. M. Keynes, *The General Theory of Employment, Interest and Money* (Macmillan, 1936) p. 135.

This is illustrated below:

Table 10.1 *Hypothetical Estimation of the Marginal Efficiency of Capital Trial with* i = 9 *per cent*

(1)	(2)	(3)	(4)	(5)
			$i \times$	
	Capital		Capital	
Year	employed	Return	employed	Depreciation
	£	£	£	£
1	10,000	2,500	900	1,600
2	8,400	2,500	756	1,744
3	6,656	2,500	599	1,901
4	4,755	2,000	428	1,572
5	3,183	$\left\{\begin{array}{l}2,000\\1,900\end{array}\right\}$	286	3,614

Accumulated depreciation = £10,431.

In cols. (2) and (3) of Table 10.1 we set out the data of our example and try the experiment of putting i = 9 per cent. On this basis we require to earn 9 per cent on the capital employed in each year. For example in year 1 the capital employed is £10,000. Hence, given i = 9 per cent, we require to earn £900. This figure is shown in col. (4) of the table.

In year 1, however, the estimated return is £2,500. Hence £1,600 (i.e. £2,500 *minus* £900) is available for depreciation. Alternatively we may write:

$$\text{depreciation} \equiv \text{return} - i \times \text{capital employed}$$

which gives us the figure of £1,600 entered in col. (5).

In year 2 capital employed is £8,400 – the original £10,000 *minus* the depreciation in year 1. Hence, with i = 9 per cent the required return is £756 and the depreciation (£2,500 – £756) is £1,744.

This process is continued for each year until the fifth, when the receipts are:

$$\text{return (£2,000) } plus \text{ scrap value (£1,900).}$$

Given the value of the capital employed in year 5 and i = 9 per cent this gives a final depreciation figure of £3,614.

If we now add col. (5), which is the depreciation including the accumulated scrap value, we find that this comes to £10,431. We require, of course, that it should come to £10,000 for if we calculate our available income ($i \times$ capital employed) correctly the accumulated depreciation including the scrap value should just suffice to maintain our capital intact. In short we have depreciated too fast or, what is clearly the same thing, *underestimated* the marginal efficiency of capital.

Accordingly we try a higher value – say $i = 11$ per cent. This gives us Table 10.2.

Table 10.2 *Hypothetical Estimation of the Marginal Efficiency of Capital Trial with* i $= 11$ *per cent*

Year	Capital employed £	Return £	$i \times$ Capital employed £	Depreciation £
1	10,000	2,500	1,100	1,400
2	8,600	2,500	946	1,554
3	7,046	2,500	775	1,725
4	5,321	2,000	585	1,415
5	3,906	2,000⎱ 1,900⎰	430	3,470

Accumulated depreciation = £9,564.

Here the sum of the depreciation allowances – plus the scrap value – is *less* than the original investment. We have not recovered the whole of our investment because we have depreciated too *slowly*. In short $i = 11$ per cent is *too large*.

We now know that: 9 per cent $< i <$ 11 per cent. Accordingly we try 10 per cent and obtain Table 10.3.

Table 10.3 *Hypothetical Estimation of the Marginal Efficiency of Capital Trial with* i $= 10$ *per cent*

Year	Capital employed £	Return £	$i \times$ Capital employed £	Depreciation £
1	10,000	2,500	1,000	1,500
2	8,500	2,500	850	1,650
3	6,850	2,500	685	1,815
4	5,035	2,000	504	1,496
5	3,539	2,000⎱ 1,900⎰	354	3,546

Accumulated depreciation = £10,007.

Here the sum of depreciation allowances – plus the scrap value – is £10,007. This is close enough to £10,000 for our purpose for, since all the figures in the table – apart from the initial £10,000 – are *estimates* of the future – which are obviously *uncertain* – there is no point in straining after arithmetic precision. To a quite satisfactory degree of approximation we have found that:

marginal efficiency of the capital asset $\equiv i = 10$ per cent.

We now know, in principle and in practice, how to calculate the marginal efficiency of a capital asset. *We also know, since the calculation depends upon estimates of the future, what a subjective and uncertain quantity the marginal efficiency of a capital asset is.*

2 THE DEMAND FOR CAPITAL AND THE MARGINAL EFFICIENCY OF INVESTMENT SCHEDULES

We have now seen how our hypothetical businessman can calculate the marginal efficiency of a particular capital asset and, by comparing the estimated M.E.C. with the rate of interest, make a rational (profit-maximising) decision to purchase the asset or not.

At any time the typical businessman will be faced with a number of possible capital asset purchases. Since the estimation of the M.E.C. can be applied to any type of capital asset, the M.E.C. can be calculated for each and the projects ranked in descending order. This is done in Fig. 10.i with K', defined as the real quantity of additional capital, measured along the horizontal axis, and the marginal efficiency of capital (i) and the interest rate (r) measured on the vertical axis. Because of our ranking the resultant schedule is downward-sloping from left to right.†

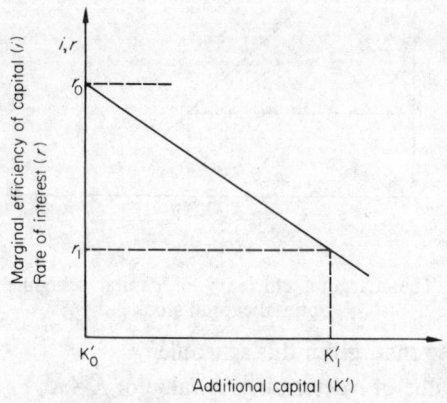

FIG. 10.i The marginal efficiency of capital schedule

† In long-run equilibrium this slope can be explained by the fall in the marginal product of capital as K increases.

If we now superimpose the rate of interest (assumed to be constant) on the figure it is easy to see that this determines an optimum value for K' – in the sense of that value of K' which the businessman estimates will maximise his profits at the given value of r. For example, if $r = r_1$ then $K' = K'_1$, and so on. We see at once that the value of K' will be greater the *lower* is r.

Suppose $r = r_0$. Then according to our figure $K' = K'_0 =$ zero. Does this mean that the optimal capital stock is zero? Certainly not. It simply means that at r_0 it is not worth the businessman's while to purchase any of the *additional* capital assets he has in contemplation. But if this is so then, at r_0, the capital he actually possesses, which we denote by $\overline{K}$, must coincide with the optimal† value. This enables us to re-label the horizontal axis of Fig. 10.i in a way which makes clear precisely what we meant when we defined it earlier as additional capital. We now define

$$\hat{K} \equiv \text{optimal real capital stock;}$$
$$\overline{K} \equiv \text{the existing real capital stock.}$$

Hence the horizontal axis of Fig. 10.i can now be labelled $\hat{K} - \overline{K}$ where we earlier used the notation K'.

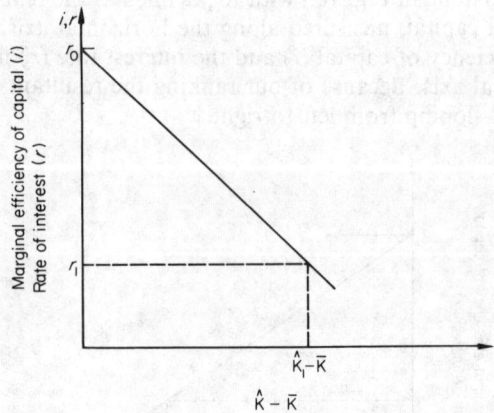

FIG. 10.ii   The marginal efficiency of capital schedule and the optimal capital stock

We now see that, given this schedule,

(i) any value of r determines a value of $\hat{K} - \overline{K}$;

(ii) this value will be greater the *lower* is r; while

(iii) $\hat{K} - \overline{K} = 0$ for $r = r_0$.

† In the sense of profit maximising.

These conditions may be written formally as

$$\left.\begin{array}{l} \hat{K} - \bar{K} = f(r) \\[6pt] \dfrac{\partial(\hat{K} - \bar{K})}{\partial r} < 0 \\[6pt] \hat{K} - \bar{K} = 0 \quad \text{for} \quad r = r_0. \end{array}\right\} \qquad (10.\text{IV})$$

What would happen if $r > r_0$? Theoretically we should have $\hat{K} - \bar{K} < 0$ – which simply states that, if $r > r_0$, our businessman's optimal capital stock is *less* than he presently possesses. Hence it would be optimal to *decumulate* capital whereas if $\hat{K} - K > 0$ it is optimal to *accumulate* capital. We shall confine ourselves to situations in which $\hat{K} - K \geqslant 0$: that is, situations depicted in the figure.

What determines the position of this schedule? Clearly all the elements which we have already found to enter into the estimation of the marginal efficiency of capital. In particular these are:

(i) the cost of capital assets;
(ii) the wage rate;
(iii) the state of technique;
(iv) the existing capital stock $(\bar{K})$;
(v) the state of expectations;
(vi) the degree of uncertainty attaching to (v);

How changes in these parameters of the schedule will shift it to the left or right should be clear from our earlier calculations. In the long run, of course, all are variables. It seeme likely, however, that, over relatively short periods of time, shifts in the position of the schedule, if they occur, will be due mainly to changes in expectations and the uncertainty attaching to them. An increase in business optimism will shift the curve to the right: a leftward shift would occur if optimism declined. The reader should work out further possibilities for himself.

Conceptually, we can construct such a curve for each and every businessman and, by adding the individual values of $\hat{K} - \bar{K}$ for any given interest rate, obtain an aggregate curve for the private sector as a whole.

The resultant curve we define as the Marginal Efficiency of Investment schedule. For formal completeness we redefine the marginal efficiency of capital as the marginal efficiency of investment (M.E.I.), Why do we do this? Simply because the quantity $\hat{K} - \bar{K}$ is the optimal amount of capital accumulation at any given interest rate. Since additions to the real capital stock are, by definition, real net investment, $\hat{K} - \bar{K}$ defines the optimum *quantity* of real net investment at any given value of r. For this reason the aggregate schedule, depicted in Fig. 10.iii can properly be called the marginal efficiency of investment schedule.

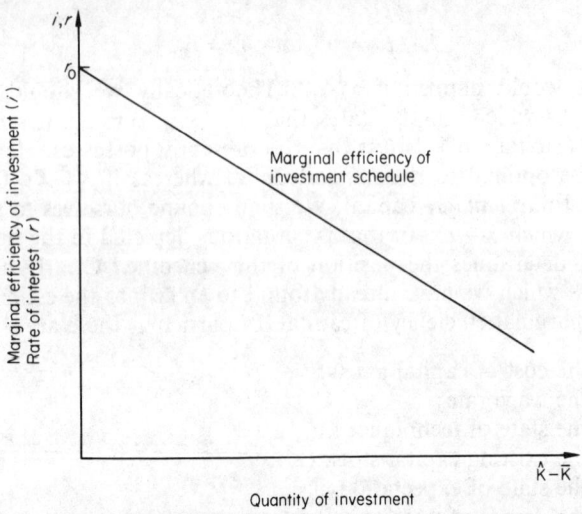

Fig. 10.iii   The marginal efficiency of investment schedule

In the opening section of this chapter we were careful to define $I_p \equiv$ real planned investment as a rate per period of time. The quantity $\hat{K} - \bar{K}$ does not enable us to determine the *rate* of real planned investment for this depends on how *quickly* businessmen undertake expenditure to eliminate the gap between $\hat{K}$ and $\bar{K}$. For example, if they planned to eliminate it within one quarter, the quarterly rate of net investment would be $\hat{K} - \bar{K}$. Alternatively, if they planned to eliminate it within a year the (average) quarterly rate would be

$$\frac{\hat{K} - \bar{K}}{4}.$$

In short, additional analysis is required to move from

(*a*) the existence of a positive value of $\hat{K} - \bar{K}$ to
(*b*) a *rate* of real planned net investment (I_p).

All we can say at this moment is that I_p will be functionally related to $\hat{K} - \bar{K}$ and thus to r. We now seek, by analysis of the problems involved, to develop a relationship between I_p and r –

given the values of certain other variables. The resultant schedule we shall call the Investment Demand schedule.

3 INVESTMENT DEMAND SCHEDULE

Simply to fix our problem precisely, let us begin by supposing that businessmen always undertake real net investment at a rate per period proportional to $\hat{K} - \overline{K}$. We should then have a theory which stated

$$I_p = [\hat{K} - \overline{K}] \qquad 0 < \lambda \leqslant 1, \qquad (10.\text{V})$$

which, since, given a number of other variables, $\hat{K} - \overline{K}$ is a function of r, could be written

$$I_p = \lambda f(r), \qquad (10.\text{VI})$$

where λ is the constant proportionality factor which is always positive but cannot exceed unity. We can now gain a better understanding of the problem by examining why λ is, in practice, unlikely to be constant.

In the first place, undertaking net investment involves the typical firm in internal costs which are likely to rise as the rate of investment increases. For example, the higher the rate of investment, the more time the firm's executives will have to devote to the organisation and planning connected with it. To do this they have to be diverted from more and more important work connected with the firm's existing operations – a process which is certain to result in rising internal costs. Hence, unless $\hat{K} - \overline{K}$ is very small, we may reasonably expect λ to be less than 1. Moreover, as $\hat{K} - \overline{K}$ increases, we may, on this account, expect λ to decline.

So far, we have assumed that, whatever the rate at which net investment is undertaken, that is, whatever the rate at which the capital goods industries are required to produce, the price of such goods (in terms of the output they will generate) is constant. This assumption, though convenient, is unrealistic. As the rate of net investment increases, we must expect the supply price of capital goods (relative to the price of their output) to rise. Hence, if we refer back to our formula for calculating the marginal efficiency of capital, we must expect the estimated rate of return per pound of investment to decline. Hence the return per pound on investment will tend to fall as the rate of investment increases for reasons which are external to the firm.

If we now incorporate these modifications into our marginal efficiency of investment schedule and (recalling that profit maximisation implies that businessmen will equate the M.E.I. with r)ʹ plot r on the vertical axis and I_p on the horizontal, we obtain a curve we shall call the investment demand schedule.

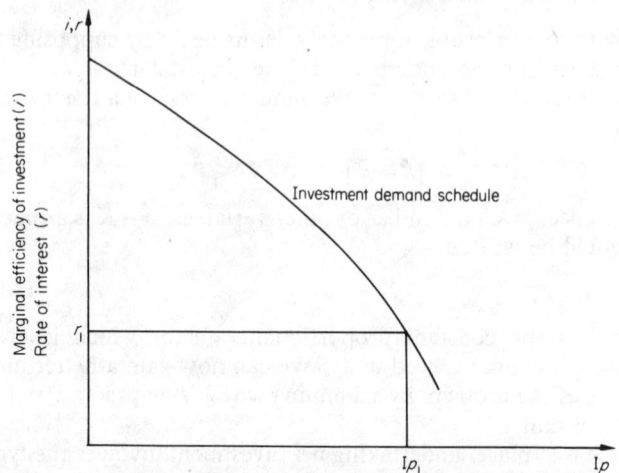

FIG. 10.iv   The investment demand schedule

. Note that because of the internal and external factors this curve is more steeply sloped than our original M.E.I. schedule. Note also that it expresses the rate of real net investment (I_p) as a function of r and suggests that the slope of the schedule becomes steeper as r declines.

As we have constructed it the curve reflects the following hypotheses:

   (i) $\hat{K} - \overline{K}$ is a function of r with $\dfrac{\partial(\hat{K} - \overline{K})}{\partial r} < 0$;

  (ii) at r_0, $\hat{K} - \overline{K} = 0$; hence, at r_0, I_p will be zero;

 (iii) the supply price of capital assets (in terms of the prices of their output) rises as I_p increases;

 (iv) the internal costs associated with I_p rise with I_p so that λ will be unity only if $\hat{K} - \overline{K}$ is small and will decline after $\hat{K} - \overline{K}$ reaches some critical value.

Given this investment demand schedule we can now determine I_p for any given value of r. For example, at r_1 the rate of net investment is I_{p_1}.

It may now be helpful if we bring together the elements of our theory. These are as follows:

(i) the optimum capital *stock* ($\hat{K}$) is determined by the condition that the rate of interest is equal to the marginal efficiency of capital;

(ii) the optimum *quantity* of real net investment is determined by $\hat{K}$ and the existing quantity of real capital ($\bar{K}$);

(iii) the *rate* at which businessmen will plan to undertake net investment – eliminate the gap between $\hat{K}$ and $\bar{K}$ – depends upon:

(a) the internal costs of net investment;
(b) the supply conditions of capital goods.

It follows that if we take as given the items 3 (*a*) and 3 (*b*) *and* the parameters of our marginal efficiency of investment schedule, we may write

$$I_p = f(r) \quad \text{with} \quad \frac{\partial I_p}{\partial r} < 0. \qquad (10.\text{VI})$$

This theory is commonly simplified by saying that the rate of real planned net investment is determined by the rate of interest and the marginal efficiency of investment schedule.

Since the investment demand schedule depends upon all the parameters of the marginal efficiency of investment, it clearly incorporates the assumption of a given capital stock ($\bar{K}$). But net investment is simply the rate of increase of the capital stock. It appears therefore that we are seeking to determine the rate of increase in K on the assumption that K is constant at $\bar{K}$. This looks like an internal contradiction. Can we rationalise it?

There are two ways of doing this. The first, which is imprecise, consists in saying that, in the period of time in which we are interested, the rate of net investment makes so small an addition to the capital stock that we can neglect it – at least as a first approximation.

The second, which is precise, is to relate our procedure to that of the differential calculus. Suppose, for example, we describe K, the real capital stock, as a function of time as depicted in Fig. 10.v, which plots $K = f(t)$ where t is time.

Now, by definition, dK/dt is the rate of increase of the capital stock: that is, the rate of net investment. Graphically, it is also the slope of the curve. If we evaluate this slope at a point on the curve, say point A, we obtain the rate of net investment at a particular point in time (t_A) or, alternatively, at a particular value of $K = K_A$.

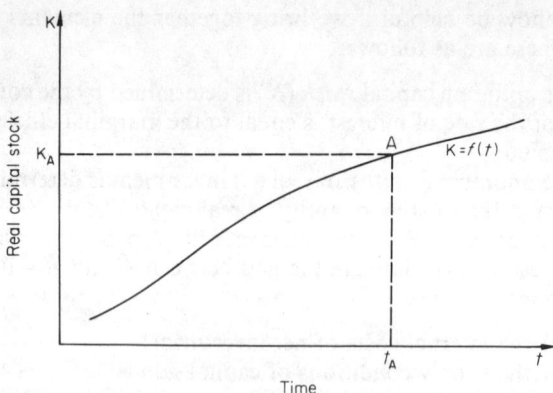

FIG. 10.v   Real capital and time

Thus, for those who are familiar with the differential calculus –
which is generally not necessary for comprehension of this book – I_p
need only be identified with dK/dt for a rationalisation of our
assumption that K is held constant at $\bar{K}$.

A final difficulty relates to the objection that, given r, sooner or
later continuing net investment must eliminate the gap $\hat{K} - \bar{K}$.
When this occurs, provided r is unaltered, net investment must
cease. As a matter of observation, however, net investment is
typically positive. Is there, then, some contradiction between our
theory and observation?

There is no contradiction once we recall that, in the dynamic
real world, the M.E.I. schedule will typically be moving to the
right because of expected increases in the demand for output and
technical innovations. Thus, though our theory is essentially a
capital *stock* adjustment theory, there is no presumption that we
shall ever observe a situation in which, for all firms, $\hat{K} = \bar{K}$ and
hence I_p is zero: that is, a situation in which the actual capital stock
is precisely adjusted to the optimal capital stock for all firms in the
economy.

4   THE INVESTMENT FUNCTION

Our investment demand schedule is essentially a *two*-dimensional
representation of a function which involves *more* independent
variables than r. These variables are treated as parameters in
constructing the M.E.I. schedule. Can we now develop, from our

earlier analysis, an investment function analogous to our consumption function?

An important parameter of the M.E.I. schedule (and thus the investment demand schedule) was the state of business expectations. Essentially this refers to the demand for output which businessmen expect in the future. Since demand depends upon income, we might make our notion of expectations more precise by relating it to the income expected when the new capital goods begin to produce output. Let us call this Y^*.

Clearly a wide variety of factors will influence Y^*. Perhaps the most important, however, will be the present level of income (Y). On this assumption we might write our investment function provisionally as

$$I_p = f_1[r, Y^*, u_{y^*}, \overline{K}], \tag{10.VII}$$

where u_{y^*} is an index of the uncertainty attaching to the expectation Y^*.

Then, introducing the assumption that Y^* is a function of Y, we obtain

$$I_p = f_2[r, Y, u_{y^*}, \overline{K}] \tag{10.VIII}$$

with $\quad \dfrac{\partial I_p}{\partial r} < 0 \quad \dfrac{\partial I_p}{\partial Y} > 0 \quad \dfrac{\partial I_p}{\partial u_{y^*}} < 0 \quad \dfrac{\partial I_p}{\partial \overline{K}} < 0.$

In this relation the state of technique, the supply conditions for capital goods and the internal investment cost schedules of the individual firms are subsumed in the function itself.

The expression in (10.VIII) relates only to the rate of net investment. If we wish – as we usually do – to explain the rate of gross investment we recall

$$I_{pg} \equiv \text{rate of real planned gross investment}$$
$$\equiv I_p + D = f_2(r, Y, u_{y^*}, \overline{K}) + D, \tag{10.IX}$$

where D is real depreciation.

What explains depreciation? A simple hypothesis is that $D = \delta \overline{K}$ with $0 < \delta < 1$: that is, depreciation is a constant proportion of the existing capital stock. Since (10.VII) already contains $\overline{K}$, we may now write

$$I_{pg} = f_3[r, Y, \overline{K}, u_{y^*}]. \tag{10.X}$$

Unfortunately, we can now say nothing definite regarding the sign of $dI_{pg}/\partial \overline{K}$ since it consists in two elements: the negative marginal response coefficient $\partial I_p/\partial \overline{K}$ and the positive marginal response coefficient $\partial D/\partial \overline{K}(\equiv \delta)$. Clearly, their sum could be positive, negative or zero.

If we now set out a linear version of (10.VIII) – which in view of our earlier analysis of the investment demand schedule is not very plausible – we obtain

$$I_{pg} = a_1 r + a_2 Y + (a_3 + \delta)\overline{K} + a_4 u_y. \qquad (10.XI)$$

with the theoretical expectation that a_2, a_3, $a_4 < 0$ and a_2, $\delta > 0$.

This is a simple formal representation of our basic theory of the rate of real planned gross investment.

5 THE RATE OF INTEREST AND THE COST OF FUNDS

Thus far we have identified the cost of borrowed funds to the firm with the rate of interest which we have already defined as the rate of return on government bonds. This approximation obviously requires reconsideration since typically firms cannot borrow as cheaply as the U.K. Government.

In addition we have implicitly assumed that each firm can borrow as much as it likes at the going rate of interest that is, that the cost of funds to the firm does *not* rise as the amount borrowed increases. If this is not correct, the marginal cost of funds will exceed the average cost and this needs to be allowed for in our formulation.

Lending to the U.K. Government is riskless in the sense that the nominal capital and interest are fully secured. Lending to any business, however, involves *some* risk. Any business may fail – through incompetence, dishonesty, or the occurrence of events which no reasonable degree of competence could have foreseen. Hence lenders will typically require from firms a premium over the interest rate to compensate them for assuming these risks. We may call this the lenders' risk premium. Thus the cost of borrowing may be thought of as

rate of interest *plus* a lenders' risk premium.

In general it is also likely to be the case that individual firms cannot borrow as much as they like at a constant cost. As firms borrow – and the debt/equity ratio rises – bond holders tend to feel increasingly vulnerable in the face of any short-fall in profits. Hence they will supply additional funds only at higher rates. Thus the marginal cost of borrowing to the firm will differ from the average cost and must be regarded as the relevant concept in determining investment.

Accordingly, in so far as firms invest with borrowed funds, the rising average cost of borrowing will consist of the rate of interest (as defined) plus a rising lenders' premium.

In practice, of course, some net investment is undertaken from firms' own savings in the form of undistributed profits. If the alternative to employing this net cash flow to finance net investment is for the firm to hold government bonds, then for the rate of net investment which this flow could finance, the rate of interest is the opportunity cost and is constant over the relevant range.

Taking all these considerations into account the determination of real planned net investment is shown on Fig. 10.vi, which superimposes the investment demand schedule on a schedule showing the marginal cost of borrowing.

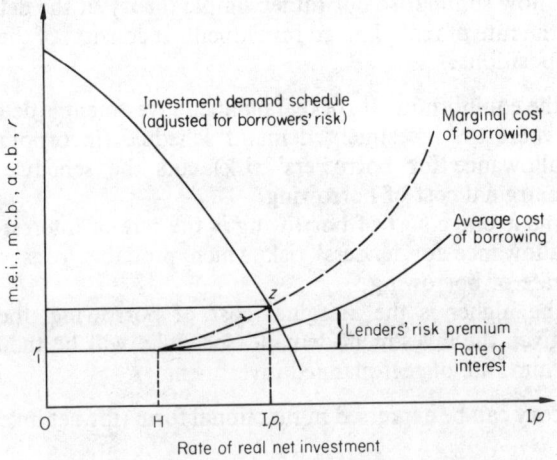

FIG. 10.vi   Real net investment and cost of borrowing

    m.e.i. $\equiv$ marginal efficiency of real net investment
    m.c.b. $\equiv$ marginal cost of borrowing
    a.c.b. $\equiv$ average cost of borrowing
       $r \equiv$ interest rate
    OH $\equiv$ rate of undistributed profit

On this slightly more complete formulation the rate of real planned investment is now determined by the condition:

$$\frac{\text{marginal efficiency}}{\text{of investment}} = \text{marginal borrowing cost}$$

where the average cost of borrowing is equal to the rate of interest *plus* a lenders' risk premium. That is, the rate of investment is I_{p1} determined by the intersection of the investment demand schedule and marginal cost of borrowing schedules at Z.

Since borrowers also assume risks while we have made no mention of a borrowers' risk premium (which clearly reduces the M.E.I. associated with any given value of I_p) we have in Fig. 10.vi emphasised that the investment demand schedule, as we have defined it, already allows for the risk arising from uncertainty of expectations. In our formal presentation in (10.IX) we symbolised this adjustment by the inclusion of the variable u_{y^*} – defined as an index of uncertainty.

6 SOME FINAL PROBLEMS

We can now summarise our rather simple theory of the determination of the rate of real planned investment. It consists of the following propositions:

    (i) the equilibrium rate of real planned investment is determined where the investment demand schedule (incorporating an allowance for borrowers' risk) cuts the schedule of the marginal cost of borrowing;

   (ii) the average cost of borrowing is the rate of interest *plus* an allowance for lenders' risk which probably rises with the rate of borrowing;

  (iii) the higher is the marginal cost of borrowing, the lower, given the investment demand schedule, will be the equilibrium rate of real planned investment.

This theory can be expressed in functional form (for net investment) as

$$I_p = f_2[Y, \tilde{r}, u_{y^*}, \bar{K}], \qquad (10.\text{VIII})$$

where $\tilde{r}$ is now defined as the marginal cost of borrowing.

Is this function likely to be stable in the sense in which we have referred to the consumption function as stable? This is a difficult question to answer despite the fact that, since expectations obviously have a crucial role in it, the scope for instability seems greater. Unfortunately there is no generally accepted test by which we could assert the relative instability of an investment function of this form. We thus leave this question unanswered. Though we expect investment functions to be typically less stable, we cannot, in the present state of knowledge, assert this to be so for the United Kingdom since the Second World War.

On the other hand if the function does shift, say in response to a change in the expectational relation connecting Y^* with Y, it is unlikely, for reasons that will become clearer later, that any such shifts would be offset by changes in r. Hence shifts in the function would generate sharp changes in the rate of real planned investment which, as we know from our previous examination of the consumption function, bring about 'multiplied' changes in real income.

Moreover, as we shall see, dynamic versions of the same rather general investment hypothesis, that is, versions which explicitly involve dating the variables entering the function, are compatible with considerable fluctuations in real net investment even if the dynamic function is relatively stable.

Can we make our investment function operational in the way we made our earlier consumption hypothesis operational? In its linear version, for gross investment, we wrote

$$I_{pg} = a_1 r + a_2 Y + (a_3 + \delta)\bar{K} + a_4 u_{y^*}. \tag{10.XI}$$

Y is directly observable and we can use estimates of K (which exist) at the beginning of any period as a measure of $\bar{K}$. Difficulty arises, however, with u_{y^*} and with $\tilde{r}$ which we now know should replace r. No obvious measure of u_{y^*} can be defined or approximated. We therefore truncate our theory, replace r by $\tilde{r}$, and concentrate upon

$$I_{pg} = a_1 \tilde{r} + a_2 Y + (a_3 + \delta)K_{-1},$$

where $K_{-1} \equiv$ the real capital stock at the end of the previous period, and, in particular, concentrate upon the meaning of $\tilde{r}$.

Strictly $\tilde{r}$ is the marginal cost of borrowing. Typically we have no means of measuring this, so we are generally content to use the average cost of borrowing and measure this by (say) the rate of return on firms' debentures.

This use of the average rate as a proxy for the marginal will involve an error: but a more important source of error may arise from the use of a *nominal* rate rather than a *real* rate. To see the distinction – and its importance – consider the following example:

Suppose today (at time t) we lend £100 for one year on the promise of £106 at the end of the period. The nominal rate of interest (r) is 6 per cent. In real terms, however, the gain from the transaction appears thus:

$$\frac{£106}{p(t+1)} - \frac{£100}{p(t)} = £100\left[\frac{1+r}{p(t+1)} - \frac{1}{p(t)}\right],$$

where $p(t) \equiv$ price level ruling now
$p(t+1) \equiv$ price level *expected* to rule at the time of repayment.
Assume

$$p(t+1) = p(t)[1+\alpha],$$

where $\alpha \equiv$ *expected* percentage price change.
Therefore the real rate of return (r_r) is – putting $p(t) = 1$ – given by

$$r_r = \frac{1+r}{1+\alpha} - 1 = \frac{r-\alpha}{1+\alpha}$$

Hence: $r_r - r = \dfrac{r-\alpha}{1+\alpha} - r = \dfrac{-\alpha - \alpha r}{1+\alpha}$, which is a measure of the

difference between the real rate (r_r) and the nominal rate (r) valued at the prices of period $t+1$. Revaluing in terms of prices at time t gives

$$r_r - r = -\alpha - \alpha r,$$
whence: $$r_r \quad = r - \alpha - \alpha r$$

Typically the term in αr is neglected since for plausible values of α and r it is small compared with either.† Hence the usual approximation is

$$r_r \approx r - \alpha \qquad \text{where } \alpha \equiv \text{ expected percentage change} \atop \text{in prices.}$$

The obvious conclusion is that we must distinguish between nominal and real rates whenever, as is currently the case, there is a general expectation of price changes.

We have no theory to explain satisfactorily how people form their expectations concerning $1/p \, dp/dt$ – that is, select α. This being so, we cannot exclude the possibility that r and r_r may not always move together in the relatively short run. Hence it may matter very much whether we interpret $\tilde{r}$ in equation (10.XI) as appropriately measured by:

   (i) the debenture rate (a nominal rate);
   (ii) the dividend yield on equities (a rough proxy for r_r); or
   (iii) a weighted average of the two (which is an increasingly common proceeding).

† In our example, $r = 0.06$. Suppose $\alpha \equiv$ the expected rate of inflation is 5 per cent, i.e. $\alpha = 0.05$. Then $\alpha r = 0.06 \times 0.05 = 0.003$, which is small compared with r or α.

Though we would expect the real rather than the nominal rate to be relevant, most empirical work until recently has employed a nominal rate. But clearly this is an important issue requiring further investigation.

Given a definition of $\bar{r}$, equation (10.XI) is now operational and we may – by appropriate econometric means – hope to estimate a_1, a_2 and $(a_3+\delta)$. From our estimate of a_2 ($\equiv \partial I_p/\partial\bar{r}$) we can obtain an estimate of

$$\frac{\partial I_p}{\partial\bar{r}}\frac{\bar{r}}{I_p} \equiv \text{the borrowing cost elasticity of gross investment.}$$

Considerable controversy has been waged over this partial elasticity and much early work yielded very low estimates. More recent studies suggest, however, a value in the neighbourhood of $-0\cdot4$. This is certainly not a negligible elasticity and clearly has important implications, if it is correct, regarding the possibility of influencing I_p through variations in the cost of borrowing.

Finally, a word of warning to the reader. In many formal expositions later in this book we shall continue, in the interests of pedagogic simplicity, to make use of investment functions written

$$I_p = f[r]$$

or in more explicit linear form

$$I_p = Z+hr, \qquad h<0,$$

where r denotes the cost of borrowing. Since our original function, in linear form, would have been written

$$I_p = a_1r+a_2Y^*+a_3\bar{K}+a_4u_{y^*}$$

we must have

$$Z = a_2Y^*+a_3\bar{K}+a_4u_{y^*}$$
$$h = a_1.$$

Hence, for simplicity, treating Z as constant involves treating Y^* as constant. This means, in models in which we seek to determine Y, that we are ignoring the (empirically plausible) link between Y and Y^* – otherwise changes in Y by changing Y^* would change Z.

This procedure is followed *only* to simplify exposition. It would readily be possible to work with

$$I_p = Z'+a_1r+a_2'Y$$

with
$$Z' \equiv a_3\bar{K}+a_4u_{y^*}.$$

but the gain in generality does not seem sufficient compensation, in elementary comparative statics, to justify the resulting complication.

Additionally, for most purposes, we shall continue to interpret r as the *nominal* interest rate on long-term government bonds. The logical justification for this is that until Chapter 21 we present no account of the theory of inflation as an essentially dynamic process – and confine ourselves in the main to constructing a *static* model of the macro-economic system. This is, of course, a simplification for pedagogic purposes which imposes a limitation upon our analysis. This limitation, however, may not be too serious if we can assume that changes in the nominal interest rate brought about by government action (as explained in Chapters 11, 15 and 16) do not, over a period such as (say) one year, significantly change α. For if this is so, changes in the nominal rate ($\equiv r$) will involve equivalent changes in the real rate (r_r).

QUESTIONS AND EXERCISES

1. If the market rate of interest is 5 per cent what is the present value of the following two prospects?

	Return at end of Year 1	Return at end of Year 2
Prospect 1	£105	£110·25
2	110·25	105

   Which would you prefer? Would you purchase either at £200? Give your reasons. Why are the present values not identical?

2. From the following data calculate, by trial and error, the marginal efficiency of capital.

   Would you invest if the market rate of interest (= cost of borrowing) was 7 per cent?

Year	Capital cost £	Estimated return £
1	10,000	2800
2		2800
3		2800
4		2800

   At the end of Year 4 the asset is expected to have a disposal value of £990.

3. What do you think would happen to the marginal efficiency of investment schedule if a threat of war arose in Europe? Why?

4. You are asked to construct an investment hypothesis which gives the rate of real planned investment in fixed capital as a function of observable quantities. What function would you propose and why? What variables, other than those discussed in the text, would you include in the function?

5. From the national income estimates of the U.K. obtain quarterly figures for real gross private investment in manufacturing for the years 1957–70 and plot them on a graph measuring (i) the quarterly rate of investment on the vertical axis; (ii) time on the horizontal axis.

   Do these observations tend to support our judgment that the marginal efficiency of investment schedule is likely to be volatile? How would you explain the observed fluctuations in investment in fixed capital?

6. Perform the same exercise for investment in stocks. Are there any special theoretical difficulties in interpreting this series?

7. Using the data of Question 2 assume that a company tax of £0·1 in the pound is levied on the net annual return *after* charging depreciation. Recalculate the marginal efficiency of capital. Is the investment still worth while if the cost of borrowing is 7 per cent? Use your answer to show the effect on the marginal efficiency of investment schedule of (i) raising the rate (per pound) of taxation on company profits; and (ii) increasing the tax allowance for depreciation.

8. Suppose that the relationship between planned investment and the rate of interest is given by:

$$I_p = Z - g.r \qquad \text{where } Z = 1000 \text{ and } -g = \frac{\partial I_p}{\partial r} = -10.$$

Plot the resulting Investment function for all integral values of r up to 20 per cent.

If the propensity to consume schedule is given by;

$$C_p = A + bY \qquad \text{where } A = 100 \text{ and } b \equiv \frac{\partial C_p}{\partial Y} = 0\cdot8$$

then   aggregate demand $\equiv C_p + I_p = A + bY + Z - g.r$.

In equilibrium we require, assuming planned and actual output to be equal,

$$Y = A + bY + Z - g.r.$$

Find

(i) all the pairs of values of Y, r which satisfy this equation:
(ii) plot the resulting values on a graph with r on the vertical axis and Y on the horizontal;
(iii) interpret the curve traced out by these pairs of values.

Show

(iv) which way the curve would move if

(a) business expectations became more optimistic;
(b) incomes were redistributed from 'rich' to 'poor'; and

(v) interpret these changes in terms of the equations describing the investment and consumption hypotheses.

9. Using the investment function of Question 8 find the *interest elasticity of investment* when $r = 10$ per cent and $r = 4$ per cent. At what rate of interest will the elasticity be -1?
Why is the elasticity not a constant? Is the marginal response coefficient $\partial I_p / \partial r$ a constant? What can you recall about the elasticity of any straight line schedule?

10. In the text we proceed on the assumption of constant prices. What sense (if any) do you therefore find in the explanation of the downward slope of the investment demand schedule? What is meant by a 'rise in the price of capital goods'?

11. Superimpose on your graph for Question 5 a second graph plotting quarterly values for the rate of interest (represented by the rate of return on Consols). Can you reconcile your observations with the theory of this Chapter? What are your difficulties?

12. An alternative simple investment hypothesis could be written

$$I_p = Z + g\pi + h\mu,$$

where $\pi \equiv$ ruling percentage rate of profits
$\mu \equiv$ rate of interest on debentures
$Z \equiv$ autonomous real net investment

putting

$$g \equiv \frac{\partial I_p}{\partial \pi} = 100 \quad \text{and} \quad h \equiv \frac{\partial I_p}{\partial \mu} = -200$$

Complete the following table and explain the values of I_p.

How far is the behaviour of I_p explained by movements *along* the function and how far by *shifts* in its position?

Period	Observed values		
	I_p	π	μ
1	1000	12	4
2	1000	12	4
3	1200	14	5
4	1400	16	8
5	1900	20	8
6	1500	18	8
7	1100	15	8
8	1100	12	6
9	1100	12	6
10	1200	10	4

Clearly π enters the function as a proxy for the expected rate of profits. Is this, in your view, compatible with the data?

13. Consider the view that the theory of investment put forward in this chapter fails because its central hypothesis is that businessmen's investment behaviour is rational – that is dictated by the aim to maximise profits.
14. Examine critically the suggestion that the dividend yield on equities is a good proxy for the 'real' rate of interest.
15. Construct a graph of: (i) the dividend yield on equities and (ii) the rate of return on Consols using annual data for 1955–72. How do you explain the changing relations between the yields?

Suggested Reading

M. Evans,† *Macroeconomic Activity* (Harper & Row, 1969) chs iv, v.

J. M. Keynes, *The General Theory of Employment, Interest and Money* (Macmillan, 1936) chs xi, xii.

J. C. R. Dow, *The Management of the British Economy, 1945–1960* (Cambridge, 1964) ch. xi.

C. J. Hawkins and D. W. Pearce, *Capital Investment Appraisal* (Macmillan, 1971).

H. D. Henderson in *Oxford Studies in the Price Mechanism*, ed. T. Wilson and P. Andrews (Oxford, 1951).

J. C. R. Dow in *Radcliffe Committee: Memoranda of Evidence*, vol. 3 (H.M.S.O., 1960).

P. N. Junankar,† *Investment: Theories and Evidence* (Macmillan, 1972).

J. R. Meyer and E. Kuh,† *The Investment Decision* (Harvard, 1959) ch. ii.

   † Advanced reference.

11 Liquidity Preference and the Theory of Interest

IN Chapter 10 we developed a theory of investment and found that, given (i) the marginal efficiency of capital schedule adjusted for borrowers' risk; and (ii) the cost of borrowing, we could determine the equilibrium rate of real planned investment. Given the rate of real planned investment (determined in this way) we could then, from the schedule of the propensity to consume (itself derived from the consumption function) determine the equilibrium level of output and employment from the condition that, in equilibrium, planned saving must be equal to planned investment.

Moreover our analysis of the determinants of investment – in particular of the marginal efficiency of capital schedule – showed that the rate of real planned investment depended crucially upon (i) business expectations; and (ii) business uncertainty. Hence, even in the short run, investment seemed likely to fluctuate sharply (thus bringing about fluctuations in the equilibrium levels of output and employment) since both business expectations and uncertainty were liable to change in response to the 'state of the news'.

Our theory has thus become closer to completion for we are now able to abandon the artificial assumption that the rate of real planned investment is determined by some hypothetical (and mythical) planning authority.

In formal terms our theory now stands as follows:

$$Y = C_p + I_p \tag{11.I}$$
$$C_p = f(Y, r) \tag{11.II}$$
$$I_p = f(r) \tag{11.III}$$

We thus have three equations to determine the four unknown variables Y, C_p, I_p and r. Such a system cannot give us a solution. This reflects the fact that, so far, we have no theory to explain the determination of the rate of interest. To provide a theory of interest determination is the task of this chapter.

1 ASSUMPTIONS AND DEFINITIONS

To simplify our exposition we need to speak of 'the rate of interest'. A glance at the financial page of any reputable paper, however, makes it clear that there is not one rate of interest but many. Accordingly our first assumption is that

> all rates of interest in the market move together, so that any one rate can stand as an index of all rates.

On this assumption we then continue to define *the* rate of interest as

> the rate of return per cent per annum obtainable in the market on long-term government securities.

Defined in this way the rate of interest must be carefully distinguished from the *coupon rate* on long-term government securities. An example should make this distinction clear.

In 1966, looking in the *Financial Times*, we find the following information:

	Price	Rate of interest per cent
3½ per cent Electricity Stock 1979	£80	5·45

This tells us that

(i) the market price of £100 nominal value of 3½ per cent Electricity Stock is £80; and
(ii) at this price the rate of interest obtainable until 1979 – when the government will repay us £100 is 5·45 per cent;
(iii) the *coupon rate* is 3½ per cent.

The method of calculation is essentially the same as that we have already employed to find the 'marginal efficiency of real capital assets'. Each year that we hold £100 *nominal* of this security we receive as income the *coupon rate* on the *nominal* value of the security:

$$3\tfrac{1}{2}\% \times £100 = £3\cdot50$$

In 1979 we shall be repaid in full: that is the government will redeem its bond by paying us £100 in cash. We thus have (in 1966) an asset with

(i) a price of £80;
(ii) a life of 13 years;
(iii) twelve annual returns of £3·50;
(iv) one return (the last) of £103·50.

We find the rate of interest *r* from the formula: †

$$S = \frac{Q_1}{(1+r)} + \frac{Q_2}{(1+r)^2} + \dots + \frac{Q_n}{(1+r)^n}$$

† In practice, since interest is paid half-yearly, this formula is only an approximation.

or:

$$£80 = \frac{£3\cdot50}{(1+r)} + \frac{£3\cdot50}{(1+r)^2} + \ldots + \frac{£3\cdot50}{(1+r)^{12}} + \frac{£103\cdot50}{(1+r)^{13}}$$

We do not need to go to the trouble of calculating r since the *Financial Times* has already done so. The formula reminds us, however, that (i) the *coupon rate* ($3\frac{1}{2}$ per cent) is *not* the rate of interest; and (ii) the rate of interest (on any bond) is *lower* the *higher* is the *market price* of the bond.

In short, the rate of interest depends upon three factors:

  (i) the price of the bond;
 (ii) the coupon yield;
(iii) the length of time which must elapse before the bond is redeemed

and the rate of interest will be *lower* the *higher* is the price of bonds.

In the discussion which follows we shall take the last two factors as given. Hence the rate of interest will be determined simply by the price of bonds and is inversely related to it.

We now know not only what we *mean* by the rate of interest but also *how to calculate it.* In the theory we shall shortly develop to explain the determination of the rate of interest (i.e. bond prices) we need to make use of a second concept. This is the *quantity* of *money.* We *define* this to be

the quantity (measured in pounds and pence) of *legal tender notes and coin* and *demand deposits with the commercial banks* in the possession of the *non-bank public.*

Precisely *why* we use this definition, and *how* the *quantity of money* so defined, gets determined we shall explain later. Throughout this chapter we shall assume, for simplicity, that the *quantity of money* – which is often called the *money supply* – is fixed and invariant with respect to all other variables in the system. Readers are also asked to notice that, *unlike* consumption, saving and investment, the money supply is a *stock* variable. On our present assumption it is also an *exogenous* variable independent of every other variable in the system.

2 AN OUTLINE OF THE LIQUIDITY PREFERENCE THEORY OF INTEREST

The first problem which arises in developing any interest theory is why is interest paid at all? At first sight it seems natural to answer that interest is the reward for saving. A moment's reflection shows

that this view is untenable. Saving is the act of refraining from consumption. If an individual saves (i.e. refrains from consumption) *and holds his accumulated savings in the form of money* (say as notes and coin) he receives no interest. Interest is only received if the saver is prepared *to hold his accumulated savings in the form of bonds.*†
This tells us two things: first, interest is paid to induce wealth owners to hold their accumulated wealth in the form of bonds rather than money; hence, second, the determination of the rate of interest is intimately connected with the decisions of wealth owners as to how to hold their wealth: or, more precisely, how they should allocate their wealth between money (which provides no interest) and bonds (which do).

Why is an inducement necessary to persuade wealth owners to hold their assets in the form of bonds rather than money?

As an asset money has a number of obvious attractions. These are:

   (i) it is *perfectly liquid* in the sense that it can readily be converted into anything (good or service) which is sold on a market;
  (ii) it can be held, either as legal tender or better still as demand deposits, without incurring either

      (a) significant storage costs *or*
      (b) risks of loss;

 (iii) *if the price level is constant* (as we are at present assuming) money is an asset which does not deteriorate over time.

Hence to hold accumulated wealth in the form of money is to obtain a subjective *convenience yield* [due to (i) and (iii) above] at virtually zero costs [due to (ii)].

To sacrifice this convenience yield wealth owners must be offered an inducement. This inducement is the rate of interest.

Approaching the problem in this way we can think of the rate of interest as the price of money: for (i) *interest* is what wealth owners must *forgo* if they wish to hold *wealth* in the form of *money* rather than bonds; (ii) *interest* is what an individual who wishes to hold money must *pay* to some other individual to induce him to *part with it.*

If the rate of interest is the price of money how is it determined? Economists are accustomed to argue that equilibrium prices are determined by the equality of demand and supply. There is a simple analogy here with our theory of income determination. In this we argued that the equilibrium level of income was determined by the equality of aggregate demand and aggregate supply. In a commodity

---

† Bonds stand here for all interest bearing financial assets.

market we argue that the equilibrium *price* is determined by the equality of planned purchases (demand) and planned sales (supply). Putting the interest problem in these terms we may say that:

> *the rate of interest is the price which equates the community's planned money holdings (demand for money) with the quantity of money (supply of money) in existence.*

To illustrate this argument consider the following example.

Suppose we construct a schedule showing the quantity of money the community will *plan* to hold at any given rate of interest. We assume (what we shall later defend and elaborate) that the quantity of *planned* money holdings *is less the higher is the rate of interest.* Formally we have the general proposition:

$$M_p^D = f(r) \quad \text{and} \quad \frac{\partial M_p^D}{\partial r} < 0 \tag{11.IV}$$

and the *specific* proposition:

$$M_p^D = R + q.r \qquad M_p^D = \pounds 1000 \text{ m.} - \pounds 100 \text{ m. } r, \tag{11.V}$$

where

$$M_p^D \equiv \text{planned money holdings}$$

$$r \equiv \text{rate of interest}$$

$$q \equiv \frac{\partial M_p^D}{\partial r} \equiv -\pounds 100 \text{ m.}$$

We plot the curve defined by (11.V) as the *LL* schedule of Fig. 11.i.

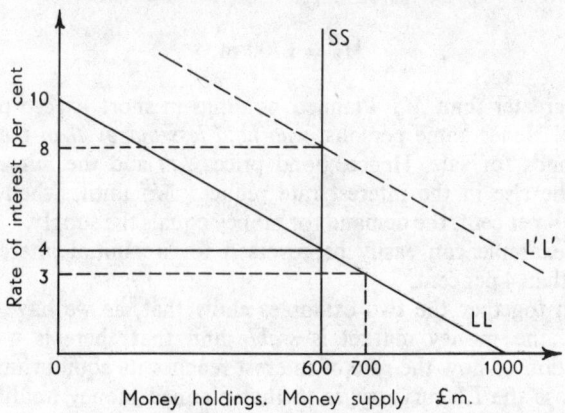

FIG. 11.i The rate of interest and the demand for and supply of money

For equilibrium in the money market – that is, for the rate of interest to be in equilibrium – we require:

$$M_P^D = M_P^S \qquad (11.\text{VI})$$

which is simply the statement that *planned* holdings must equal *planned* supplies.

We assume that *actual* supplies $(M_A^S) = M_P^S$. That is, whoever, (which we have yet to explain) *plans* the supply of money always carries out his plans. Since we have aleady assumed that the quantity supplied is fixed (say equal to M_0) we have:

$$M_P^S = M_A^S \qquad (11.\text{VII})$$

$$M_A^S = M_0 \qquad M_0 = £600 \text{ m.} \qquad (11.\text{VIII})$$

Hence equilibrium requires:

$$M_P^D = M_0.$$

To illustrate this we construct a line (SS) on Fig. 11.i at a distance along the horizontal axis equal to £600 m. This line is vertical reflecting the assumption that M_P^S is *independent of r*.

Equilibrium is determined where the LL curve cuts the SS curve. At this point the rate of interest is 4 per cent and the planned money holdings are £600 m. exactly equal to actual money supplies. All actual and planned magnitudes coincide.

Suppose the rate of interest was not 4 per cent but 3 per cent. Then, from (11.I) we should have:

$$M_P^D = £700 \text{ m.}$$

This is greater than M_P^S. Planned holdings in short *exceed* planned supplies. Hence some persons, *who hold less money than they plan*, offer bonds for sale. Hence, bond prices *fall* and the *interest rate rises*. The rise in the interest rate reduces M_P^D until, when it has reached 4 per cent, the demand for money equals the supply.

This example can easily be reversed for an initial interest rate greater than 4 per cent.

Taken together the two examples show that, as we have drawn Fig.11.i, the money market is *stable* and that there is a simple explanation of how the rate of interest reaches its equilibrium level.

Suppose the *LL* curve *shifts* so that planned money holdings *are greater at each interest rate* (i.e. the demand for money increases).

We have a new curve $L'L'$ and a new equilibrium rate of interest, 8 per cent. How do we get it? An increased demand for money means that some persons who at 4 per cent *were* happy to hold bonds *now* wish to hold money. They offer bonds for sale. Bond prices *fall*. The rate of interest *rises* until, at the new rate of 8 per cent, we have once again:

$$M_P^D = M_A^S$$

planned money holdings = actual (= planned) money supplies.

Notice that, unless M_A^S *changes*, the community *cannot* hold more (or less) money than £600 m. *All that it can determine is the price at which it will hold the given supply.*

The demand for money (represented by LL and $L'L'$) depends, amongst other things, on wealth owners' preferences for holding accumulated wealth in the form of money. This, for reasons which should be obvious, we call 'liquidity preference'. Hence the essentials of what is called the liquidity preference theory of interest can be summarised as follows:

(i) interest is paid to induce persons to sacrifice the convenience of holding wealth in liquid form: i.e. to overcome liquidity preference;

(ii) the determination of the rate of interest is thus bound up with decisions of wealth owners as to how to distribute their assets between money and bonds;

(iii) the rate of interest is the price or opportunity cost of holding money;

(iv) it is determined by the relationship between the demand for money (planned money holdings) and the supply of money (planned quantity of money supplied);

(v) the greater (smaller) is the demand for money then, with a given money supply, the higher (lower) is the equilibrium rate of interest;

(vi) the greater (smaller) is the money supply then, with any given demand for money, the lower (higher) is the rate of interest;

(vii) the higher (lower) is the price of bonds the lower (higher) is the rate of interest.

These propositions should be carefully studied. We now seek to develop this skeletal interest theory by examining, in greater detail, the determinants of the demand for money – that is the LL curve of Fig. 11.i.

3 THE FOUR DEMANDS FOR MONEY

To analyse the demand for money we break it down into four components:

    (i) The Transactions Demand
    (ii) The Precautionary Demand
    (iii) The Asset Demand
    (iv) The Speculative Demand

Aggregated together these constitute the total demand for money. We begin with the *transactions demand*.

i. Transactions Demand

Households and enterprises are continually receiving money and making money payments. A certain money holding is, on average, required over any period of time, to avoid the difficulties which can arise from running completely out of money and thus being unable to make necessary payments. How much is required depends upon (i) the value of receipts and payments in the period; (ii) the time correspondence between receipts and payments. To see this, picture an individual whose annual income is £365 and who spends it all at the regular rate of £1 per day.

If this income is received at the rate of £1 per day his average balance over the year would be 50 pence. If, alternatively, his income was received as a single payment on 1 January his average balance would be £182·50. In practice some incomes are received daily, some weekly, some monthly, some quarterly, some half-yearly and some at varying intervals throughout the year. However, in modern financially developed communities the ways in which most people receive their incomes change only very slowly. *There is, in short, an institutional pattern of income receipts which, though it does change, can in a short-run analysis such as ours, be taken as given and invariant.*

In the same way conventions exist regarding a whole host of payments from rent, building society repayments and car licence fees to tradesmen's accounts.

We may thus argue that where the time correspondence pattern of receipts and expenditures is determined by a developed institutional environment, households and enterprises will need a certain minimum average amount of transaction balances to finance any given level of *foreseeable* expenditures.

The value of these expenditures depends upon two quantities. The first is the planned level of *real* expenditure. The second is the price level. Since real expenditure depends upon real income it follows that the demand for transactions balances depends upon real income and the price level. Formally:

$$M_p^D \text{ (transactions)} = f(Y, p) \tag{11.IX}$$

where

$M_p^D \equiv$ planned holdings of transactions balances

$Y \ \equiv$ real income (= output)

$p \ \equiv$ price of a unit of output,

and both marginal response coefficients are positive that is,

$$\frac{\partial M^D}{\partial Y} \text{ and } \frac{\partial M^D}{\partial p} > 0.$$

What form is this function likely to take? If money income is zero it is reasonable, as a first approximation, to expect the transactions demand to be zero. In addition we have, at this stage, developed no theory to suggest that as income increases, the transactions demand will increase other than proportionately. A plausible first approximation would thus be a linear and proportional relationship between transactions demand and money income of the form:

$$M_p^D \text{ (transactions)} = KYp \tag{11.X}$$

or, in numerical form,

$$M_p^D \text{ (transactions)} = 0 \cdot 15 \ Yp \tag{11.Xn}$$

with $K = 0 \cdot 15$.

At the moment we are taking the price level p as given, and invariant. Hence any change in Y will bring about an equal proportionate change in Yp – which is money income. Moreover, since p is constant, money income can change only if Y – real income – changes. Hence we can, for the time being, simplify (11.X) by writing:

$$M_p^D \text{ (transactions)} = KY \text{ (with } p \text{ given and taken equal to unity)} \tag{11.X*}$$

where K is the planned ratio of transactions balances to real income at the given constant price level $p = 1$. To give a numerical illustration we write:

$$M_p^D \text{ (transactions)} = 0 \cdot 15 Y \text{ (with } p = 1) \tag{11.Xn*}$$

The demand curve for transactions balances is now depicted in Fig. 11.ii as the L_T function.

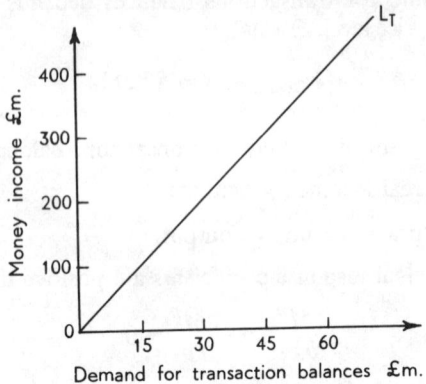

FIG. 11.ii   The transaction demand for money holdings

Its parameters are:

(i) institutional arrangements regarding receipts and payments;
(ii) the given level of prices.

ii. Precautionary Demands

Not all income receipts or payments can be *foreseen with certainty*. Hence, in practice, households and enterprises will need to hold rather more than the minimum amount of transaction balances to guard against the risks arising out of the uncertainty of future receipts and payments. Consider for example a businessman setting out to drive from London to Glasgow to negotiate an important contract. He calculates his expenditure on petrol, oil, food, drink and accommodation and, in accordance with (11.X), sets off with the minimum amount of transaction balances necessary to finance these foreseeable expenditures. En route his car breaks down and he has to pay a garage £20 for repairs. He must now either (i) go without food, drink or accommodation and/or (ii) incur the expense and delay of telephoning his London bank for funds. If he does (i) he will suffer discomfort. If he does (ii) he may lose his contract and suffer serious loss. Had he started on his journey with sufficient *precautionary* balances over and above his *minimum transaction* requirements he could have avoided both.

It is easy to see that this illustration applies with particular force to enterprises who may suffer severe losses due to an *unforeseen* shortage of money holdings arising from the need to make an unforeseen payment or the unforeseen postponement of an expected receipt.

The demand for *precautionary* balances is thus readily explicable in terms of uncertainty about the timing of future expenditures and receipts and their expected values. We thus regard this demand as a function of real income, the price level and uncertainty of this particular type. Formally, again taking p as given:

$$M_p^D \text{ (precautionary)} = f(Y, u_y) \tag{11.XI}$$

where u_y is an index of uncertainty regarding future receipts and payments.

This demand is now added to the transaction demand to get what is called the *demand for active balances*. Thus:

$$M_{p(\text{active})}^D \equiv M_{p(\text{trans.})}^D + M_{p(\text{precautionary})}^D = f(Y, u_y) \tag{11.XII}$$

which, *for a given value of u_y*, we can assume to take the specific form:

$$M_{p(\text{active})}^D = k'Y \quad or \quad M_{p(\text{active})}^D = 0 \cdot 20\,Y \tag{11.XIII}$$

again taking $p \equiv$ price level $= 1$, and to be represented diagrammatically as in Fig. 11.iii as the L_1 function.

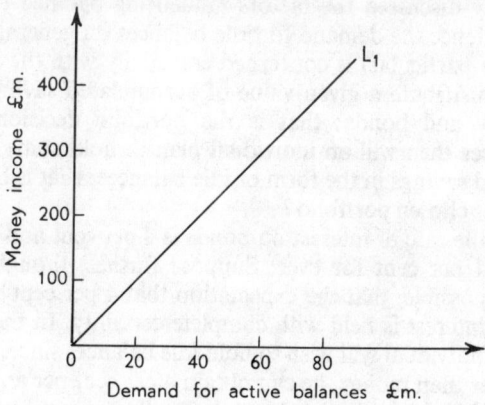

Fig. 11.iii   The demand curve for active balances

This curve, the demand curve for active balances, we call the L_1 function. Its position depends upon (i) institutional arrangements for receiving income and making payments; (ii) uncertainty regarding future income payments and receipts; (iii) the given level of prices.

iii. The Demand for Idle Balances: Asset Demand

Some households and enterprises will plan to hold money in excess of their planned holdings of active balances. These additional balances we call *idle*. Hence in addition to the demand for active balances (analysed above) there is a demand for idle balances which requires analysis. To facilitate this analysis we divide idle balances into two classes: *asset* balances and *speculative* balances. The three concepts are related by the identity:

$$M^D_{\text{idle}} \equiv M^D_{\text{asset}} + M^D_{\text{speculative}}.$$

Consider now the demand for asset balances. This is related to money's ability to act as a store of wealth. Money, to put the same point rather differently, *is one form of asset in which an individual may hold his accumulated savings* (*wealth*). The demand for asset balances is thus related to an individual's capital account and reflects what is called a *portfolio decision*: that is a decision regarding the assets over which an individual chooses to distribute his accumulated savings.

In the simple macro-economic model we are constructing there are, by assumption, only three forms of asset: money, bonds and goods. In our examination of the consumption and investment functions we have already discussed the factors influencing planned expenditure on goods. Hence the demand for idle balances (in general) and asset balances (in particular) is concerned essentially with the decision as to how to distribute a given value of accumulated savings (wealth) over money and bonds: that is the portfolio decision. In what circumstances then will an individual plan to hold some part of his accumulated savings in the form of idle balances: that is hold money as part of his chosen portfolio?

Suppose the rate of interest on bonds is 4 per cent and is expected to remain 4 per cent for ever. Suppose further, though this is in practice impossible, that the expectation that 4 per cent will remain the rate of interest is held with complete certainty. In these circumstances no individual will wish to hold idle balances since, by holding bonds rather than money, he can obtain 4 per cent per annum on his accumulated savings *without risk*. Admittedly converting money into bonds or bonds into money costs something in time, trouble and brokerage fees. It is possible therefore that some persons whose accumulated savings are small or who plan to dissave in the near future may consider it not worthwhile to purchase bonds. But if we neglect these cases, which are probably rather rare and quantitatively unimportant, our general proposition holds. In the postulated circumstances no individual wealth owner would wish to hold any part of his wealth in money for money earns no interest and bonds, by assumption, earn 4 per cent. Thus the portfolio of (say) John Smith who has (say) accumulated savings of £10,000 would look like this:

Accumulated savings	10,000	Money (asset balances)	nil
		Bonds	10,000
Total wealth	10,000	Total assets	10,000

This example, though unrealistic, is nevertheless instructive for in demonstrating that, in our assumed conditions, John Smith will *not* plan to hold any asset balances, we have provided ourselves with a clue to the explanation of why, in general, people will choose to hold such balances. This is so because the implausibility of our hypothetical example lies in the assumption that John Smith's expectations were held with perfect certainty. In such a situation Smith clearly, because the future rate of interest was expected with complete certainty, ran no risk of a fall in bond prices (rise in interest rates) or rise in bond prices (fall in interest rates). The portfolio of 'bonds only' thus emerges in a situation in which there is *no uncertainty* about the future interest rate and thus *no risk* of changes in the value of the bond holding. As we know complete certainty about the future of the interest rate or anything else is impossible. However confident Smith may feel about his expectation of an unchanged rate, the rate *may* change. Hence, in practice, uncertainty (and thus risk) will always be present in some degree. What happens to the portfolio choice when the existence of uncertainty is admitted? Before examining this problem let us see first the consequence of interest rate changes.

Suppose Smith holds his whole wealth in bonds purchased when the ruling rate of interest is 4 per cent; then if the rate rises to 5 per cent each £100 worth of bonds he holds will be valued in the market at £80. He will have incurred a £2000 capital loss – a capital loss sufficient to reduce the market value of his wealth by 20 per cent. Conversely, if the rate *falls* to (say) 2 per cent, the market value of his bond holding, and thus his accumulated savings, will have doubled for each £100 of bonds purchased at 4 per cent which he holds will now be worth £200. We may thus conclude that where there is, as there always will be, uncertainty about the rate of interest ruling in the future, to hold accumulated savings in the form of bonds (i) provides a money income; but (ii) involves the acceptance of uncertainty and hence the risk of capital gain or loss.

Most individuals seek money income but try to avoid risk. It is therefore likely that Smith will distribute his portfolio between money (asset balances) and bonds in such a way as to give him his preferred combination of interest income and risk. This means that he will tend to hold a *mixed portfolio* – reducing his risk (at the cost of sacrificing some interest income) by holding some of his wealth in the form of money. In short he will heed the ancient adage on the unwisdom of 'putting all his eggs in one basket' and distribute them over two: bonds *and* money.

We can perhaps make the argument slightly clearer by a table illustrating three possible portfolio positions.

PORTFOLIO I

	£		£	Portfolio characteristics
Accumulated savings	10,000	Money	nil	Maximum money income
		Bonds	10,000	Maximum risk

PORTFOLIO II

Accumulated savings	10,000	Money	10,000	Zero income
		Bonds	nil	Zero risk

PORTFOLIO III

Accumulated savings	10,000	Money	2,000	*Less* than maximum income
		Bonds	8,000	*Less* than maximum risk

Portfolio I provides maximum income *and* maximum risk. It will be selected only by those who are either indifferent to risk or who positively relish it. Portfolio II provides zero income and zero risk. It is unlikely to be selected. Portfolio III represents a mixed portfolio strategy – an attempt to find the optimal income/risk combination.

We may thus argue that where individuals seek, as we have assumed John Smith to do, to avoid risk (i) they will in general hold mixed portfolios of assets and thus (ii) hold some of their wealth in the form of idle (asset) balances.

Hence the demand for asset balances arises because

(i) the future rate of interest cannot be known with certainty; and
(ii) individuals are, in general, risk avoiders; although
(iii) they have no reason to expect the rate of interest to be higher or lower in the future.

Assumption (iii) is worth spelling out in slightly greater detail. It is, clearly enough, an alternative way of expressing an assumption that the rate of interest is expected to remain unchanged at 4 per cent. Where expectations are of this form – sometimes called neutral – the demand for idle balances is, by definition, purely an asset demand. Money is held as an asset simply to reduce risk.

Suppose, however, that with the rate of interest at 4 per cent some individual, say Henry Snodgrass, though uncertain of the future rate of interest (as he must be) expects *not that it will remain un-changed but that it will fall to 3 per cent*. Then, by buying bonds now (at 4 per cent) and holding them until the rate falls to 3 per cent, Snodgrass can obtain not only his interest income but also a capital gain equal to $33\frac{1}{3}$ per cent of his bond holding. In short Snodgrass can make a speculative gain from 'knowing better than the market what the future will bring forth'. As we shall see shortly it is from considerations of this kind that the *speculative* demand for idle balances arises. In such a case we say that expectations are non-neutral.

The demand for *asset balances* thus gives rise to planned money holdings in excess of planned active balances and arises fundamentally because the future of the rate of interest is uncertain. *It contains no speculative element whatever*. Its basic assumption is that whatever the ruling rate of interest happens to be, so it is expected to remain.

Now for a given degree of risk, that is a given amount of uncertainty, it is reasonable to argue that the higher is the rate of interest – and thus the stronger the reason for accepting risk – the greater the proportion of accumulated wealth which will be held in the form of bonds and, what is the same thing, the smaller the proportion of accumulated wealth which will be held in the form of money. Hence the planned holdings of asset balances will depend upon

(i) the value of wealth (W) or accumulated savings;
(ii) the rate of interest (r);
(iii) uncertainty regarding the future value of r (u_r);
(iv) people's attitudes towards risk and income.

In our usual functional notation we may write:

$$M^D_{p(\text{asset})} = L'_2\,(r, u_r . W) \qquad\qquad (11.\text{XIV})$$

and expect the marginal response coefficients to have the following signs:

$$\frac{\partial M^D_{p(\text{asset})}}{\partial r} < 0 \qquad \frac{\partial M^D_{p(\text{asset})}}{\partial u_r} > 0 \qquad \frac{\partial M^D_{p(\text{asset})}}{\partial W} > 0$$

This, of course, is a very general statement. Since our theory is short-run we may regard wealth as a constant. Then, given the (constant) value of wealth, we might postulate a familiar linear function thus:

$$M^D_{p(\text{asset})} = T + n . r + o . u_r \qquad\qquad (11.\text{XV})$$

$$M^D_{p(\text{asset})} = \text{£100 m.} - \text{£6 m.}\, r + \text{£1 m.}\, u_r \qquad (11.\text{XVn})$$

This formulation presupposes that we can define, and measure, an appropriate index of uncertainty (u_r). Taking a given value for this index (say $u_r = 20$) we can plot the resultant demand curve in Fig 11.iv.

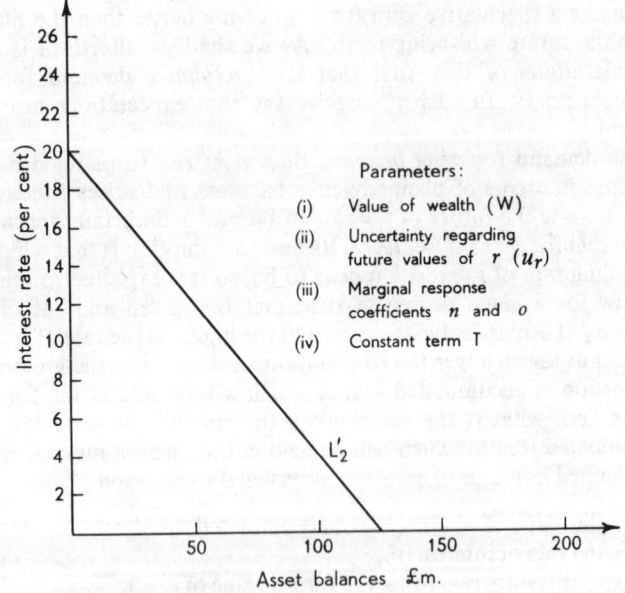

FIG. 11.iv   The asset demand for money (from 11.XVn)

Notice that, at rates of interest above 20 per cent, this function makes no economic sense. This is a limitation not of theory but of the functional form which is only an approximation and a very simple one at that.

What are the parameters of the function? Apart from wealth which we have suppressed, they are as usual the value of the constant (T), the value of the marginal response coefficients n and o and the value of u_r (the uncertainty index). T, n and o reflect the public's preference for holding wealth in money rather than bonds: they thus reflect its preference for liquidity or its liquidity preference. Hence *demand schedules* of this type are frequently referred to as *liquidity preference schedules*.

Suppose the public becomes more anxious to avoid risk. The curve will move to the right. Alternatively suppose, with unchanged preference on the part of the public, the index of risk u_r increases: the curve will move to the right. Similarly if wealth were greater the curve would lie further to the right.

In interpreting this curve it is important to remember that it reflects the assumption that, whatever the rate of interest is, it is expected to remain unchanged. Put another way the curve shows the demand for idle balances when the expected capital gain or loss from holding bonds is zero: that is gains and losses are equally probable. It supposes a zero speculative demand for idle balances. Hence the L'_2 schedule as we have called it is *not* the demand for idle balances but simply a component of it. It is identical with the total demand for idle balances only in the special case in which the public expects no gains from speculation. If it was empirically the case, as the L'_2 curve assumes, that whatever the rate of interest ruling the expected capital gain or loss was zero, then the L'_2 curve would be identical with the total demand for idle balances. However, as we shall now demonstrate, this is not likely to be the case and the demand for idle balances, when account is taken of the speculative element, differs very significantly from the asset demand which assumes neutral expectations.

iv. The Demand for Idle Balances: Speculative Demand
As we have seen, the asset demand for idle balances arises because

(i) future interest rates (bond prices) are not known with certainty; and
(ii) wealth owners in seeking to reduce the risk of capital losses which then arise will, in general, adopt a mixed portfolio, selecting it so that,

(iii) the quantity of idle balances demanded for asset reasons will be greater the smaller is the interest rate.

The fundamental assumption of the asset demand as we have defined it is that whatever the rate of interest ruling in the market is, it is expected to remain unchanged in the future. Expectations in this case are neutral.

The *speculative demand* arises where future interest rates are uncertain, as is always the case, and some people think they know better than the market what the future will bring forth. Thus, for some people at least, *expectations are not neutral*. Accordingly they will buy bonds, if they expect rates to fall (and thus anticipate a capital gain) and sell bonds if they expect interest rates to rise (thus avoiding an anticipated capital loss).

In short, where the ruling market rate is above (below) the rate of interest expected to rule in the future people will *for speculative reasons*, wish to hold more bonds (money) than the analysis of the asset demand would suggest. Or, to put the same point another way, when the rate of interest is expected to rise (bond prices to fall) wealth owners have a *positive* demand for idle money balances on speculative account; when the rate of interest is expected to fall (bond prices to rise) wealth owners have a *negative* demand for idle money balances on speculative account.

This second proposition does not imply a negative demand for idle balances as a whole. This demand cannot be less than zero. Recalling our basic identity, which was

$$M^D_{\text{idle}} \equiv M^D_{\text{asset}} + M^D_{\text{speculative}},$$

shows that all it implies is that $M^D_{\text{idle}} < M^D_{\text{asset}}$.

We may thus argue that the speculative demand for money depends upon

(i)   the market rate of interest (r);
(ii) uncertainty about the rate of interest (u_r); and
(iii) the rate of interest which is expected to rule in the future $(\hat{r})$; as well as
(iv) the general attitude of wealth owners towards speculation.

The reader can now see that, in formulating the asset demand, we made the special assumption that, whatever the value of r, the general expectation was that $r = \hat{r}$: that is expectations were neutral. The speculative demand arises once this assumption is relaxed so that $r \lessgtr \hat{r}$: that is expectations can be non-neutral.

Suppose now wealth owners possess a unanimous and firmly held expectation that the 'safe' or 'normal' rate of interest at long term is 5 per cent. The expectation can be regarded as being based on historical experience of interest rates and the current state of the news. Two conclusions emerge immediately:

(i) If the ruling rate in the market is 5 per cent, the speculative demand for money will be zero. Hence:

$$M^D_{\text{idle}} = M^D_{\text{asset}}.$$

(ii) If the ruling rate is 6 per cent, capital gains will be expected from bond holding and the speculative demand for money will be *negative*. Hence:

$$M^D_{\text{idle}} < M^D_{\text{asset}}.$$

The Fig. 11.v depicts the demand curve for speculative balances in such a case.

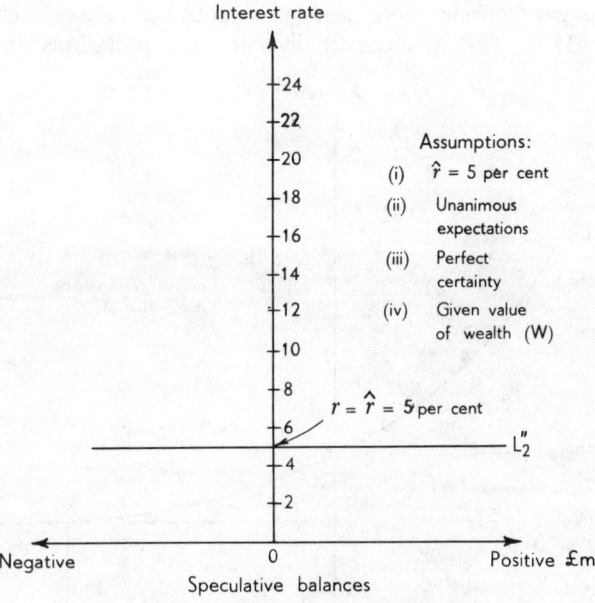

FIG. 11.v The speculative demand for money

How is this Figure to be interpreted? At $r = 5$ per cent we have $r = \hat{r}$ and $M^D_{\text{speculative}}$ is consequently zero. Immediately the rate of interest rises *above* 5 per cent we have $r > \hat{r}$. Since we have assumed that expectations are unanimous and firmly held speculators will move out of asset balances into bonds in order to make a capital gain when r returns to $\hat{r}$. Conversely if r is *below* 5 per cent we have $r < \hat{r}$ and the prospect of a capital loss, speculators would move out of bonds and into idle (speculative) balances.

Clearly if expectations were unanimous (as we have assumed) and held with perfect certainty (as in practice they cannot be) we should have the curve shown in Fig. 11.v – simply a straight line with $r = \hat{r}$. The demand for speculative balances would be infinitely elastic at the rate $r = 5$ per cent and the rate of interest could never depart from this value for if r rose *above* $\hat{r}$ (i.e. above 5 per cent) speculators would rush to buy bonds and drive up their price until r fell to 5 per cent. Conversely if r was *below* $\hat{r}$ speculators would rush to sell bonds and their price would fall until r rose to 5 per cent.

The case depicted in Fig. 11.v, though useful expositionally, is extremely artificial for (i) expectations are not likely to be unanimous; and (ii) expectations cannot be held with complete certainty.

These two considerations lead us to construct a new curve as in Fig. 11.vi. This assumes (i) diversity in expectations and (ii)

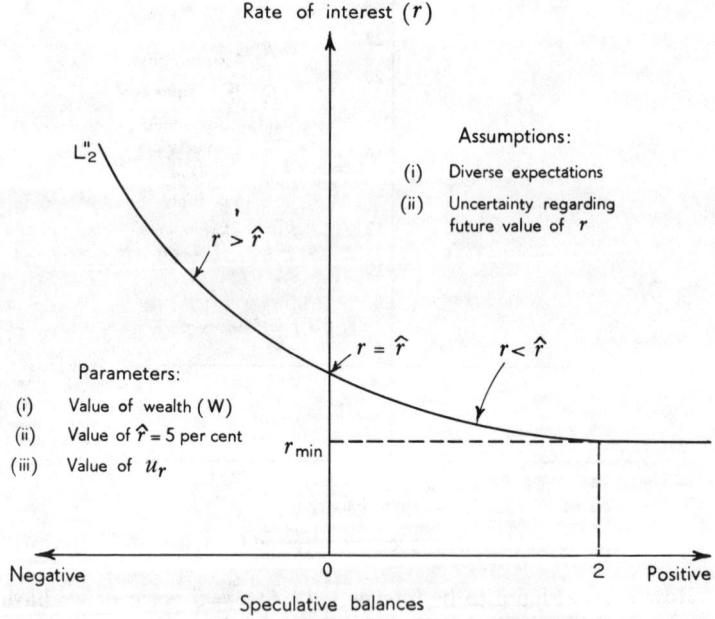

FIG. 11.vi The speculative demand for money assumptions; (i) diverse expectations, (ii) uncertainty regarding future value of r

incomplete certainty. As a result it shows the speculative demand increasing (negatively) as r rises *above* $\hat{r}$ (which must now be interpreted as an average of the diverse expectations of wealth owners) and increasing (positively) as r falls *below* $\hat{r}$.

This curve also incorporates a further hypothesis to the effect that at some interest rate, which we have called r_{min}, the L_2'' curve becomes completely horizontal. This is the lowest rate of interest acceptable to the community. At this rate, provided speculative balance holdings are greater than or equal to OZ, the community is indifferent between money and bonds. In short, because expectations are diverse, the horizontal part of the L_2'' function indicates a range along which even the most sanguine speculators expect the capital losses from bond holding to offset so much of the income derived from interest that, allowing for the uncertainty which always attaches to holding bonds, the marginal advantages of holding bonds and money are equal.

Reverting to our usual functional presentation, we may write the demand for speculative balances (given wealth) as:

$$M^D_{\text{speculative}} = L_2''(r, \hat{r}, u_r), \qquad (11.\text{XVI})$$

with $\qquad \dfrac{\partial M^D_{\text{speculative}}}{\partial r} < 0 \quad \dfrac{\partial M^D_{\text{speculative}}}{\partial \hat{r}} > 0 \quad \dfrac{\partial M^D_{\text{speculative}}}{\partial u_r} > 0.$

From this analysis we may also argue that the L_2'' curve is likely to be volatile. Expectations concerning r (i.e. the value of $\hat{r}$) may easily change in response to the news and changes in $\hat{r}$ will shift the curve. Moreover, the more important, quantitatively, speculators are in the market, the more likely is it that the L_2'' function will be volatile since individual speculators make profits on capital account essentially by guessing (correctly) how speculators in general will respond to changes in the news. An unexpected announcement of a general election, an international crisis or, in some cases, even a change in the weather, may cause the L_2'' function to shift though any such shift is unlikely to change the value of r_{min}.

We can now add the asset and speculative demands for money to obtain the total demand for idle balances. To do this we make use of the L_2' and L_2'' curves and the identity:

$$M^D_{\text{idle}} \equiv M^D_{\text{(asset)}} + M^D_{\text{speculative}}$$
$$= L_2'(r, u_r) + L_2''(r, \hat{r}, u_r)$$
$$= L_2(r, \hat{r}, u_r).$$

Thus our hypotheses are that the demand for idle balances is dependent upon liquidity preference (reflected in the L_2 function itself) and the values of the rate of interest (r), the expected 'safe' rate of interest ($\hat{r}$) and the uncertainty of the expectation (u_r). This formulation is, of course, essentially short-run in that it takes as given and constant the value of wealth.

The addition of the asset and speculative demands to obtain the total demand for idle balances is carried out geometrically in Fig. 11.vii. Interpretation of the figure is simple enough, for it is constructed to reflect the hypothesis that

(i) with $r > \hat{r}$ $M^D_{speculative}$ is negative;

(ii) with $r = \hat{r}$ $M^D_{speculative}$ is zero;

(iii) with $r < \hat{r}$ $M^D_{speculative}$ is positive;

and the constraint that $M^D_{p(idle)}$ cannot be less than zero.

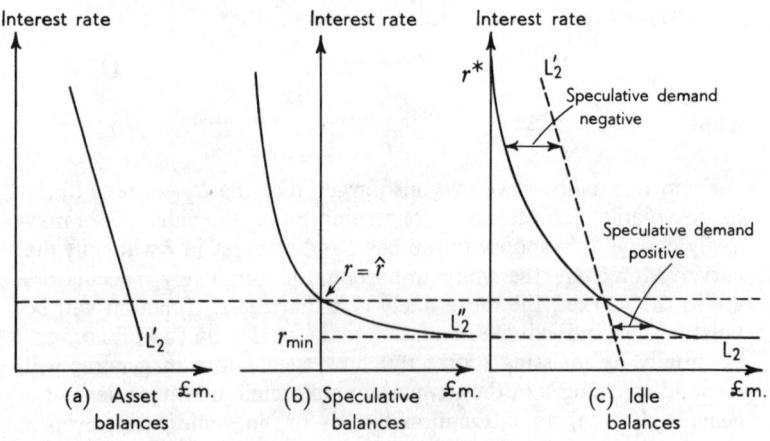

FIG. 11.vii The demand for idle balances

Obviously, from the shape of the L_2 curve, no simple linear function can be used to represent it though if the speculative motive were absent a linear relationship might be a plausible approximation (as we have assumed).

Consider now the L_2 curve shown in Fig. 11.vii. At some interest rate r^*, the sum of the asset and speculative demands is zero: that is the public would plan to hold no idle balances whatever. As the rate (r) falls below r^*, the demand for idle balances increases until at

$r = \hat{r}$ it is equal to the demand shown by the L_2' function. As r falls below $\hat{r}$ the planned holdings of idle balances increase and with $r = r_{min}$ the L_2 curve (like the L_2'' curve and for the same reason) becomes horizontal – that is infinitely interest elastic.

What are the parameters of the L_2 function? Since the L_2 function depends upon both the L_2' and L_2'' functions, the reader may work the answer to this problem himself and use his answer to explain the circumstances in which an increase or decrease in liquidity preference might be expected. Both changes are illustrated in Fig. 11.viii.

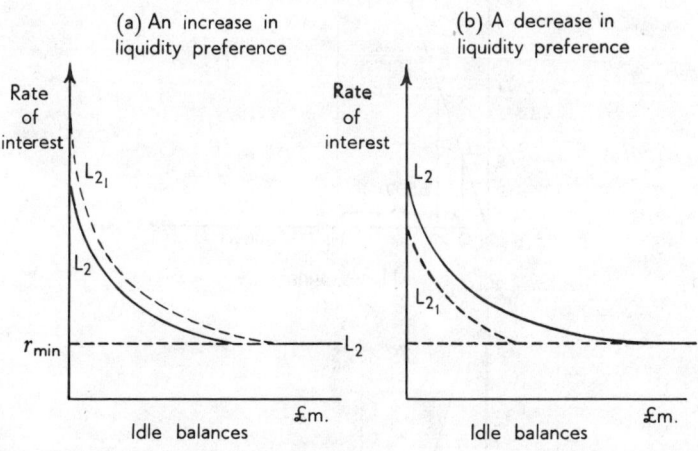

Fig. 11.viii The demand for idle balances

4 THE DEMAND FOR MONEY AND THE INTEREST RATE

We can now write the total demand for money, given the price level, as:

$$M_p^D \equiv M_{p(\text{active})}^D + M_{p(\text{idle})}^D$$

$$\equiv L_1(Y, u_y) + L_2(r, \hat{r}, u_r)$$

which, taking u_y, $\hat{r}$ and u_r as given, is more commonly written as:

$$M_p^D = L_1(Y) + L_2(r) \qquad (11.XVII)$$

We know that, in equilibrium,

$$M_p^D = M_p^S \quad \text{and assume that} \quad M_a^S = M_p^S = M_0.$$

Hence if we are given (i) the level of Y; (ii) the L_1 and L_2 functions; (iii) the money supply; and (iv) the price level, we can find the equilibrium value of r – the rate of interest.

To see this look at Figs 11.ix(a) and 11.ix(b).

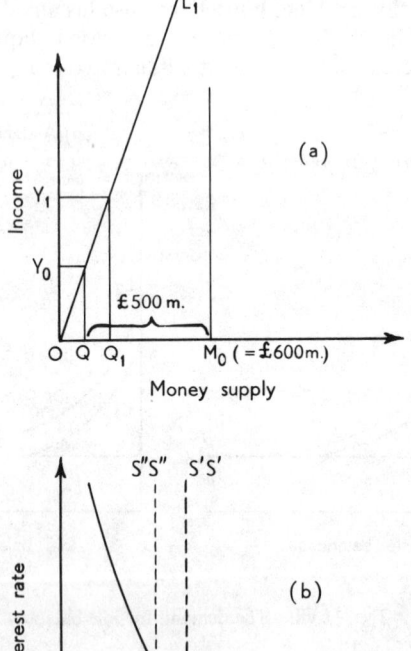

FIG. 11.ix   The determination of the equilibrium rate of interest

From Fig. 11.ix(a) if $Y = Y_0$ the $M^D_{p(\text{active})} = OQ = £100$ m. It follows that the supply of idle balances is:

$$M_0 - M^D_{p(\text{active})} = £600 \text{ m.} - £100 \text{ m.} = £500 \text{ m.}$$

This supply of idle balances can now be inserted into Fig. 11.ix(b) as the dotted line $S'S'$. Where this line cuts the L_2 curve determines the rate of interest at r_0. This is easy to see since when income is Y_0 and the rate of interest r_0 we have:

$$M_p^D \equiv M_{p(\text{active})}^D + M_{p(\text{idle})}^D = M_0 = £600 \text{ m.}$$

Notice that levels of income higher than Y_0 involve (i) *greater* demands for active balances and so with a fixed money supply (ii) a *smaller* supply of idle balances and (iii) a *higher* equilibrium rate of interest. How does this come about? Suppose income rises to Y_1. As a result the demand for active balances rises from OQ to OQ'. As a consequence firms and households find their active money holdings too small. Accordingly they try to increase their money holdings by selling bonds. This drives bond prices down and interest rates up until the interest rate reaches r_1. At this rate the demand for money is again equal to the supply.

What happens if the community revises its estimate of $\hat{r}$ upwards? The L_2 curve shifts upwards: that is to the right. At the ruling interest rate people are now holding less as idle balances than they wish. They offer bonds for sale and hence bond prices fall and the interest rate rises.

We can now give a short summary of our interest theory as follows:

(i) the rate of interest is determined by the supply and demand for money;

(ii) the demand for money can be written:
$M_p^D = L_1(Y) + L_2(r)$ taking u_y, $\hat{r}$, p, u_r as given and the value of wealth as given;

(iii) an increase in liquidity preference (upward shift in L_2 function), given the money supply, raises r: a decrease lowers r;

(iv) an increase in Y raises r: a decrease lowers r;

(v) an increase in the money supply (given L_1, L_2) lowers r;

(vi) the L_2 function is likely to be volatile and respond quickly to changes in the 'state of the news'.

The reader should now verify that all these propositions are compatible with our introduction to the theory of interest in Section 2 of this chapter.

QUESTIONS AND EXERCISES

1. 'The essence of the liquidity preference theory of interest is that the rate of interest is the price which brings about equality between the demand for and supply of money'. Explain.
2. If the quotation in Question 1 is correct, what relationship would you expect to observe between the ratio of gross national product/money supply and the rate of interest? Give your reasons and construct a rough graph of the relationship you predict.
3. Construct, from data given in the *Monthly Digest of Statistics* (C.S.O.) a series for the average money supply for each year from 1950 to 1971. Selecting other series for the annual interest rate and gross national product, construct a scatter diagram with (i) the interest rate on the vertical axis; (ii) the ratio G.N.P./ money supply on the horizontal axis, by plotting a point to represent each year's observation.

   Draw freehand a curve to represent the observations. Does its shape conform with your answer to Question 2? If not is the theory refuted? If so is the theory proved?
4. Assume that the demand for active (M_1) balances is given by:

$$M^D_1 = KYp \quad \text{where } K = 0.25 \text{ and } p = 1$$

Approximate the demand for idle balances by assuming that $r_{min} = 2$ per cent, and that with $r > 2$ per cent the following linear relationship is acceptable:

$$M^D_2 = T + n.r \quad \text{with } T = 1375 \text{ and } \frac{\partial M^D_2}{\partial r} = n = -50.0.$$

Take the money supply as exogenously given, i.e.

$$M^S = M_0 \quad \text{with } M_0 = 2500,$$

remember that equilibrium in the money market requires:

$$\left\{ \begin{matrix} M^D \\ \text{demand for money} \end{matrix} \right\} = \left\{ \begin{matrix} M^S \\ \text{supply of money} \end{matrix} \right\}.$$

Applying this condition,

   (i) find all the pairs of values of Y and r compatible with money market equilibrium;
   (ii) plot these on a graph with r on the vertical axis and Y on the horizontal;
   (iii) interpret the curve defined by these points;

(iv) explain the relationship between this curve and the curve you constructed from observed data in Question 3;
(v) what is the rate of interest when $Y < 4900$?;
(vi) what is the rate of interest when $Y = 6500$?;
(vii) what is the maximum level of Y that the money supply can finance?

5. Using the model of Question 4 show the consequences of (i) an increase of 100 in the money supply; (ii) an increase of 100 in the demand for idle balances; (iii) a rise in p from 1 to 2. Treat each problem separately and specify clearly the conditions under which your prediction holds.

6. 'It is possible to control *either* the money supply *or* the rate of interest but not both.' Use the analysis of Chapter 11 to discuss this contention.

7. 'It is well known that the prospect of a Socialist government can only raise interest rates.' 'The Labour Party is, because of its detestation of rentiers, traditionally the party of low interest rates and cheap money.' Are these statements compatible? How do they relate to our theory?

8. Using the data of Question 4, what is the interest elasticity of the demand for money when

   (i) $r = 2 \cdot 0$ per cent;
   (ii) $r = 5 \cdot 0$ per cent;
   (iii) $r = 27 \cdot 5$ per cent?

9. If the rate of interest is 5 per cent and expected to fall to 4 per cent a man stands to make a capital gain by holding bonds rather than money. Would he hold *all* his wealth in the form of bonds rather than money? Or would he hold some bonds and some money – a mixed portfolio? Give your reasons.

10. 'As long as a wealth owner holds some bonds, the value of his wealth must be inversely related to the rate of interest.' Explain. Does this complication modify significantly or even invalidate the analysis of Sections 3 and 4 of this chapter? Give your reasons.

11. The accounts of John Hawgood on two dates gave the following information:

Date: 31 Dec 1970		Date: 31 Dec 1971	
Assets		Assets	
Money	1,500	Money	4,000
Bonds	4,000	Bonds	1,500
House	15,000	House	15,000

    (i) Did Hawgood save or dis-save in 1971? By how much?
   (ii) Did he invest in 1971? If so how much?
  (iii) Did his liquidity preference increase/decrease in 1971?
   (iv) What was his demand for money on 31 December 1970 and 31 December 1971?
    (v) On what assumptions and definitions are your answers based?

12. 'If there were no speculation, there would be no demand for idle balances.' Do you agree? If not why not?

13. A week in advance of their publication you find on Wimbledon Common a copy of the July trade returns for the United Kingdom. These show a 10 per cent *increase* in exports and a 2 per cent decrease in imports. Your existing portfolio of assets is:

	£
Money	14,000
Bonds	16,000

You have no inhibitions about using the information you find. Do you rearrange your portfolio? If so in what direction? Give your new portfolio and your reasons for selecting it.

14. How far are the reasons for selecting your new portfolio (in Question 13) compatible with the analysis of Chapter 11 and what light do they throw upon it?

15. 'In the short run, wealth is constant.' Elucidate. Does this simply reflect the definition of the short run? If it does not is it correct?

16. 'Ultimately it is a question of fact whether it is the speculative or asset motives which dominates the demand curve for idle balances.' Elucidate. In what institutional environments would you expect the asset motive to be dominant? Can you suggest a way of testing whether the speculative motive is present?

17. The discussion of the speculative motive runs in terms of *both* diverse expectations and uncertainty. What would the speculative demand curve look like if expectations were diverse and uncertainty *absent*? Give your reasoning fully.

18. What do you think would be the consequences for (i) the L_2 function; and (ii) the rate of interest, of a statement by the Prime Minister that 'Her Majesty's Government are actively considering ways and means of reducing the rate of interest'? Why?

19. 'Even with the liquidity preference theory an increase in the propensity to save will reduce the interest rate – through its

effect upon income.' Elucidate. Are there any limitations to this proposition?

20. In the text we have assumed a constant price level so that real and nominal interest rates coincide. How would the expectation of a rise in prices modify the analysis?

21. Can you suggest a method of defining and constructing a measurable index of 'uncertainty regarding interest rates (u_r)'?

22. The following hypothetical data relates to John Smith's expectations regarding the future interest rate on two different dates.

31 Dec 1966		31 Dec 1967	
Interest rate %	Expected with probability of	Interest rate %	Expected with probability of
3·0	0·10	3·0	0·00
4·0	0·20	4·0	0·10
5·0	0·40	5·0	0·80
6·0	0·20	6·0	0·10
7·0	0·10	7·0	0·00

At each date the ruling rate in the market is 5 per cent.

(i) At each date what is the value of $\hat{r}$?

(ii) At either date will Smith have a speculative demand for money?

(iii) Which set of expectations implies the greater value of u_r?

(iv) Assuming no change in Smith's wealth between the two dates, in which situation will Smith have the greater demand for idle balances? Why?

(v) Can you *now* define a measurable index of u_r?

23. Use the current *Financial Times* to obtain the ruling rate of interest on U.K. government 2½ per cent Consols. Then

(i) write down the highest rate which you think might rule in a year's time;

(ii) the lowest rate you think might rule in a year's time; and

(iii) the rate you think most likely to rule in a year's time.

Identify $\hat{r}$. Have you a speculative demand for money? How would you estimate the value of u_r attaching to your expectations?

SUGGESTED READING

Miles Fleming, *Monetary Theory* (Macmillan, 1971).

D. W. Laidler,† *The Demand for Money* (Scranton, 1969).

H. G. Johnson (ed.),† *Readings in British Monetary Economics* (Oxford, 1972) pp. 138–50.

W. T. Newlyn, *The Theory of Money* (Oxford, 1962) chs iv–v.

J. M. Keynes, *The General Theory of Employment, Interest and Money* (Macmillan, 1936) ch. xv.

A. M. Khusro, 'An Investigation of Liquidity Preference', *Yorkshire Bulletin of Economic & Social Research* (Jan 1952).

J. C. R. Dow in *Memoranda of Evidence*, vol. 3 (H.M.S.O., 1960), particularly paras 59–75 and p. 102.

F. W. Paish, ibid., pp. 183–8.

† Advanced reference.

12 The Theory of Income Determination

As a result of our work in Chapter 11 we now have a theory of the determination of the equilibrium rate of interest. Our elementary model is thus complete. It is, therefore, convenient at this point to summarise our argument: that is to display in full the characteristics of the model at this stage. Once this is done we can proceed (i) to see where the model needs further extensions; and (ii) to see what predictions it yields.

How then can we conveniently summarise the model we have developed?

1 CHARACTERISTICS OF THE MODEL: GOODS MARKET

As we have developed it our model consists of *two* markets: one for goods and services (the *goods market*) and one for money (the *money market*). For the *whole system* to be in equilibrium, *both* these markets must *simultaneously* be in equilibrium. What does this imply?

Consider the market for goods and services. Equilibrium here requires that aggregate demand is equal to aggregate supply. In short that $C_p + I_p = Y$. To explain C_p and I_p we have a theory of aggregate consumption (developed in Chapter 9) and a theory of investment (developed in Chapter 10). These two theories may be written:

$$C_p = f(Y, r, A, \alpha)$$
$$I_p = f(\lambda, r).$$

We take the values of $A \equiv$ real value of households' assets, $\alpha \equiv$ the distribution of income, and $\lambda \equiv$ schedule of marginal efficiency of investment as *given*. This enables us to write:

$$C_p = f(Y, r)$$
$$I_p = f(r)$$

From this it follows that for any given value of r we can determine the rate of real planned investment I_p. Once we know this, since we know the schedule of the propensity to consume, we can determine the equilibrium level of real income (Y). In other words, for any given rate of interest there will be (i) a determinate rate of real planned investment which, *given* (ii) the schedule of the propensity to consume, *determines* (iii) an equilibrium level of real output.

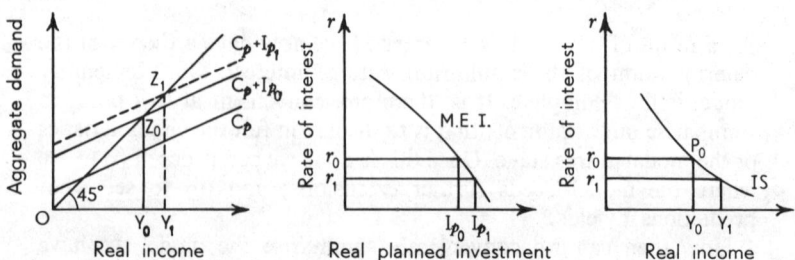

FIG. 12.i The determination of the equilibrium level of income, given the rate of interest, the marginal efficiency of investment schedule and the consumption function

To see this consider Fig. 12.i. On the left we have the familiar 45° diagram of Chapter 9. In the centre the theory of investment of Chapter 10. On the right we have a new graph with the rate of interest plotted on the vertical axis and the level of real income on the horizontal.

Take any rate of interest r_0. This determines, *from the M.E.I. Schedule*, a rate of real planned investment I_{p_0}. This rate can now be transferred to the 45° diagram yielding an aggregate demand schedule $C_p + I_{p_0}$. This cuts the 45° line at Z_0 and determines the equilibrium level of income Y_0. The pair of values r_0, Y_0 now define a point (P_0) on the third diagram.

Repeat the process with rate of interest r_1 and rate of planned investment I_{p_1} to obtain the equilibrium income Y_1. This yields a second point (r_1, Y_1) in the third figure. Obviously for *any* value of r we can find *that* level of Y at which the *goods market is in equilibrium* and these pairs of values, plotted on the third diagram will trace out a curve – called the *IS* curve – *which shows all the pairs of values of r and Y at which the goods market is in equilibrium.*

The slope of this IS curve is downwards because the higher is r the lower is I_p and the lower is I_p the lower is the value of Y at which the goods market is in equilibrium.

The position of the IS curve depends upon (i) the marginal efficiency of investment schedule; and (ii) the schedule of the propensity to consume.

The reader is invited to work out for himself the direction in which the *IS* curve will shift in response to shifts in either the propensity to consume schedule or the M.E.I. schedule and to refresh his memory as to why either of these schedules may shift.

2 CHARACTERISTICS OF THE MODEL: THE MONEY MARKET

The *IS* curve is not, by itself, sufficient to tell us the equilibrium level of income. All it can say is that *if* the rate of interest is (say) r_0 *then* the level of income at which aggregate demand equals aggregate supply will be Y_0. To find *the* equilibrium level of income we must find the value of r. To do this we turn to the money market.

The equilibrium condition in the money market is

$$M_p^D = M_p^S$$

demand for money = supply of money.

As in Chapter 11 we assume a fixed and invariant supply of money M_0. Hence we require $M_p^D = M_0$. The demand for money, M_p^D, we already know can be written: $M_p^D = L_1(Yp) + L_2(r)$.

Our model takes the value of p ($\equiv$ the price level) as given and constant. Hence real income (Y) and money income (Yp) move together in the sense that any given value of Y implies a single value of Yp. This being so we can think of the demand for money as

$$M_p^D = L_1(Y) + L_2(r) \; given \; p.$$

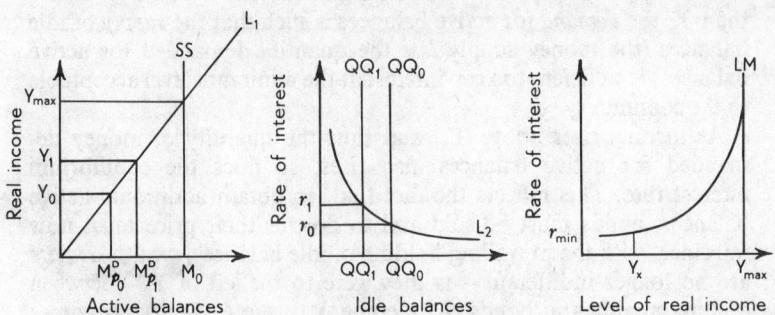

FIG. 12.ii The *LM* schedule establishing a relation between real income and the rate of interest, given the liquidity preference function, the money supply and the price level

Now look at Fig. 12.ii. As before this is divided into three sections.

On the left we have the demand curve for *active balances* (the L_1 function). In the centre we have the demand curve for *idle balances* (the L_2 function). On the right we have a diagram with the same axes as we had on the right of Fig. 12.i. On the left-hand figure the vertical line SS is drawn at a distance along the horizontal axis equal to the given money supply M_0.

Suppose income is Y_0. Then the demand for *active* balances is $M^D_{p(\text{active})_0}$. Hence the supply of the idle balances is $M_0 - M^D_{p(\text{active})_0}$. This is shown by the curve QQ_0. The equilibrium rate of interest is r_0. Thus (Y_0, r_0) are a pair of values which equate the community's planned holdings of money balances with the money supply.

Now assume income to be Y_1. The new supply curve of *idle* balances is QQ_1. The new equilibrium rate of interest is r_1. Hence (Y_1, r_1) is a second pair of values at which the demand for money equals the supply. Clearly by running through all possible levels of Y – and finding the associated equilibrium values of r, we can trace out a curve – which we call the *LM* curve – showing *all the pairs of values of r and Y at which the money market is in equilibrium.*

The *position* of the *LM* curve depends upon:

   (i) the L_1 and L_2 functions: the two liquidity functions as they are often called;
   (ii) the quantity of money (M_0);
   (iii) the assumed level of prices (p).

The *shape* of the curve is dominated, as the diagram shows, by the L_2 function. Over a range this curve is horizontal at the rate of interest $r_{\min}$. This tells us that so long as income is equal to or less than Y_x the *demand* for active balances is such that the *supply* of idle balances (the money supply *less* the quantity demanded for active balances) is sufficient to keep interest at the minimum level acceptable to the community.

As income rises above Y_x, and thus the quantity of money demanded for active balances also rises, so does the equilibrium interest rate. This reflects the fact that, to obtain additional active balances, bonds must be sold and to do this their price must now fall since, with the prevailing holding of idle balances, wealth owners are no longer indifferent – as they were to the left of Y_x – between holding money and bonds. At income $Y_{\max}$ the *LM* curve becomes vertical. At this income level the whole of the existing money supply is required as active balances. Hence, so long as the L_1 function is unaltered, $Y_{\max}$ (given the value of p) is the highest level of *real income* which the community can finance with the given money supply. Attempts to obtain additional active balances, by offering bonds for sale, cannot succeed. They can only drive up interest rates by lowering bond prices.

3 THE COMPLETE MODEL

Now that we have constructed both the *IS* and *LM* curves we can put them on a single diagram. This is done in Fig. 12.iii.

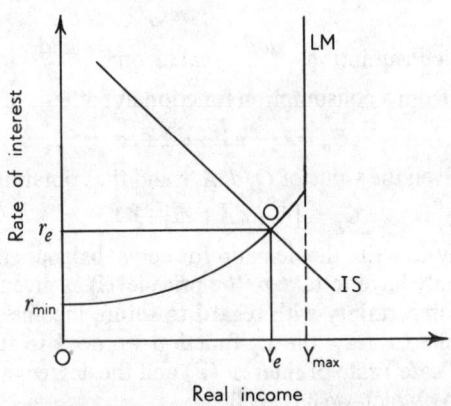

FIG. 12.iii The determination of the equilibrium income and the equilibrium rate of interest, given the *LM* and the *IS* schedule

The curves cut at the point *O* which has co-ordinates Y_e and r_e. The significance of this point is clear from the definition of *IS* and *LM*. Because (i) *O* lies on *IS* then Y_e and r_e are a pair of values at which

$$C_p + I_p = Y$$

and the *goods market is in equilibrium*. Because (ii) *O* lies on *LM* then Y_e and r_e are a pair of values at which

$$M_p^D = M_p^S$$

and the *money market is in equilibrium*.

It follows that Fig. 12.iii describes the full equilibrium of the system, in short it shows how the equilibrium values of the *two* dependent variables, income and the rate of interest, are simultaneously determined by the independent variables which are, *as a first approximation*,

(i) the propensity to consume schedule;
(ii) the marginal efficiency of investment schedule;

(iii) the liquidity preference (L_1 and L_2) functions;
(iv) the money supply; and, in the simple version of the model,
 (v) the given level of prices.

Why do we say 'as a first approximation'? Simply because in depicting our system in these terms we need to remember that the first three independent variables – as we are here defining them – are themselves simplifications. For example, our propensity to consume schedule is a relationship between

$$\underset{\text{real planned consumption}}{C_p} \quad \textit{and} \quad \underset{\text{real income}}{Y} \quad \textit{and} \quad \underset{\text{interest rate}}{r} \cdot$$

We derived it from a consumption function hypothesis of the form:†

$$C_p = Q + cY + dA + e\alpha$$

by taking as given the value of Q, d, A, c and thus obtaining

$$C_p = [\bar{Q} + d\bar{A} + e\bar{\alpha}] + cY.$$

Analogously to write the demand for active balances as a function of Y we not only have to take p (the price level) as given, but also u_y, the degree of uncertainty with regard to future income receipts and payments, while to draw the L_2 function we need to take as given the expected ('safe') rate of interest ($\hat{r}$) and the degree of uncertainty with respect to r which we have called u_r.

In short, in interpreting Fig. 12.iii, the reader needs to keep constantly in mind not only that the IS and LM curves depend on the four independent variables listed above but that these themselves are but convenient simplifications of relatively complicated theories. Provided this is done Fig. 12.iii is a convenient and useful device for thinking about problems in the theory of income determination.

In Fig. 12.iii we do not show *directly* the determination of employment. However since we can from the figure determine Y_e – the equilibrium level of real output (income) – we need only to refer back to our short-run production function (Chapter 7) to find the equilibrium level of employment.

4 WHAT THE MODEL PREDICTS

Now that we have got our model, what predictions does it yield? A prediction, we must recall, is a statement of the form:

if X occurs in context *Y then Z* will occur.

† In this form we have omitted the rate of interest for reasons given earlier.

Our model is not specified quantitatively. Hence our predictions can only be qualitative. Let us generate a few to show how the model operates.

i. An Increase in the Marginal Efficiency of Capital

This means a *rightward* shift of the M.E.I. schedule. From Fig. 12.i we see that this shifts the *IS* curve to the *right*. In *general* the new equilibrium will give (i) a higher level of income and (ii) a higher rate of interest than the initial level. The precise result, however, will depend upon the nature of the initial equilibrium. The geometry of this is shown in Fig. 12.iv where *IS'* is the position of the *IS* curve after the M.E.I. has increased.

What lies behind the geometry?

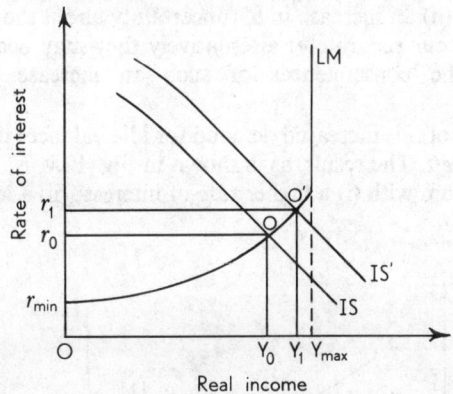

FIG. 12.iv   A shift in the *IS* curve and the changes in the level of income and the rate of interest

The rightward shift in the M.E.I. raises the level of planned investment at each interest rate. Hence the multiplier comes into operation to raise income. However, as income rises the quantity of active balances demanded increases. To satisfy this demand, bonds are offered for sale and bond prices fall (the interest rate rises). This rise in the interest rate brings about an *induced* decline in investment which thus increases by less than the *autonomous* increase brought about by the shift in the M.E.I. schedule. Our prediction is, therefore, than an increase in the M.E.I. schedule will in general raise *income* and *the rate of interest*.

The conditions we assume for this result are:

(i) *given* and *invariant* nominal money supply and price level;
(ii) *given* and *invariant* propensity to consume schedule;
(iii) *given* and *invariant* liquidity functions.

ii. An Increase in Liquidity Preference

This is usually interpreted, as a matter of geometry, as an upward shift in the L_2 function which leaves unchanged the level of the minimum acceptable interest rate and, of course, the maximum money income which, given the price level, the given money supply can finance.

How can such a shift come about? The reader can refer back to Chapter 11 for the full range of possibilities but two obvious reasons for such a shift are (i) an upward revision in $\hat{r}$ (the expected rate of interest) and (ii) an increase in u_r (uncertainty about the future of r). Either can occur separately: alternatively they may occur together. What are the consequences of such an increase in liquidity preference?

As a result of this increased demand for idle balances the *LM* curve shifts to the *left*. The result, as is shown in Fig. 12.v, is, in general, a new equilibrium with (i) a higher rate of interest; (ii) a lower level of income.

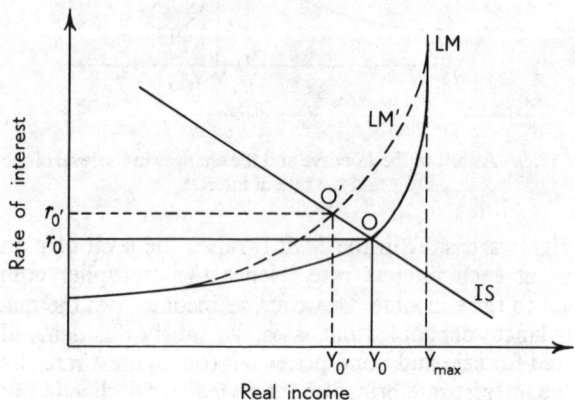

FIG. 12.v   An increase in liquidity preference

What is the economic mechanism underlying this result?

The increase in the demand for *idle* balances means that, at the initial rate of interest and income the community's actual holding of idle balances is now less than their planned holding. Accordingly bonds are offered on the market as some people seek to move out of bonds and into money. As a result bond prices fall (interest rates rise). This rise in the rate of interest reduces real planned investment. Hence the multiplier comes into operation and incomes fall. This reduces the quantity of active balances demanded and so increases the supply of idle balances. This rise in the supply of idle balances somewhat reduces the extent to which the rate of interest increases. This is now less than it would have been had income remained constant.

What conditions are we assuming to reach this result? They are:

(i)   given and invariant propensity to consume schedule;
(ii) given and invariant M.E.I. schedule;
(iii) given and invariant money supply and price level.

iii. *An Increase in the Nominal Money Supply*

Suppose the money supply increases because of, let us say, the purchase of bonds from the general public by the government. In this case the additional money (created by the central bank by methods explained more fully in Chapter 16) enters the system as a result of a capital account transaction. The new money does not enter the system as anyone's income but simply as an asset received for the transfer of another asset (bonds). What happens?

In terms of our diagram the *LM* curve moves to the *right*. Hence the new equilibrium is characterised by (i) a higher level of income; and (ii) a lower rate of interest than the old. This is shown in Fig. 12.vi.

What is the mechanism?

By hypothesis the government is purchasing bonds from the public and giving money in exchange. At the initial equilibrium the public was holding its preferred ratio of money/bonds. To persuade it to *raise* this ratio, the interest rate must fall. Hence as the government seeks to purchase bonds, bond prices rise to persuade those who, at the initial prices preferred bonds to money, to move *out of* bonds and *into* money. A rise in bond prices is a fall in interest rates. The mechanism is thus straightforward.

The fall in the rate of interest induces an increase in investment. This brings the multiplier into operation and raises income. The rise in income increases the quantity of active balances demanded. Hence

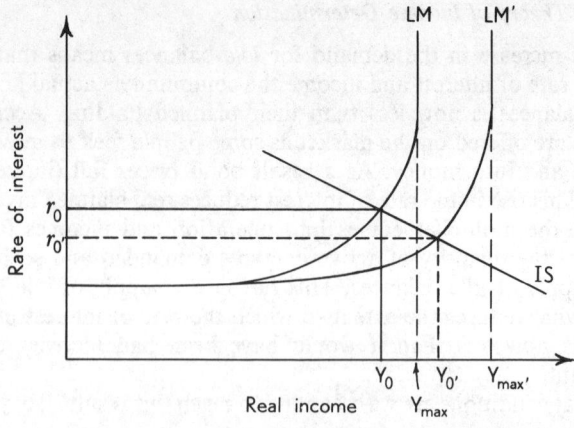

FIG. 12.vi An increase in the money supply

the final increase in the supply of idle balances is *less* than the increase in the money supply and the fall in the rate of interest *less* than it would have been if income had not changed.

The conditions we assume to reach this result should be worked out by the reader.

The qualitative predictions set out above have been reached by a highly formal process of reasoning in which the assumed conditions under which they will be valid are stated in some detail. This is a necessary step in economic analysis. But it is very far from being the whole of economics. We must always remember that a shift in one schedule may itself induce changes in others. According to our model such induced changes need not occur. Whether they do so or not is a question of fact. It follows that, after making a prediction from the model and specifying the conditions under which it is valid, it is essential to consider whether, in practice, these conditions are likely to hold or not and, if they are not, in what way we should modify our initial prediction.

To give an example: we predicted that *if* the M.E.I. schedule shifted upwards then *both* income *and* the rate of interest would tend to rise. We reached this result by assuming, amongst other things, unchanged L_1 and L_2 functions.

Suppose that the M.E.I. schedule shifted upwards because of a decline in business uncertainty. Might the factors which brought this about not also lead to a decline in the uncertainty regarding future income payments and receipts (thus shifting the L_1 function) or the uncertainty regarding the future expected interest rate (thus shifting the L_2 function)? If so can we be very confident in our prediction that the rate of interest would rise?

This sort of consideration is important. Formal theoretical analysis is the first step in economic analysis. And it is essential. Failure to specify our model, and its properties, carefully and precisely, is simply to invite confusion. The second step, however, must always be to review the assumptions underlying any given prediction. Failure to do this is to risk irrelevance.

5 WEAKNESS OF THE MODEL

In its present form the model has four principal weaknesses which we must try to remove in later chapters.

In the first place it is entirely static. This means that we can use it only to compare positions of (short period) equilibrium and *not* to discuss how the system *moves* from one equilibrium position to another. For many problems, for example, the *stability* of the model and for the theory of investment, *dynamics* are of crucial importance. In short we need at least some elementary dynamic developments.

In the second place the model admits no government activity and assumes that there is no international trade. This reduces its usefulness for the study of policy problems. We need extensions here.

In the third place the model treats the price level as given and invariant: that is, as an *exogenous* variable. This is convenient but no more than that. We need a theory of prices.

Finally we need to explain the workings of the monetary system.

All these weaknesses are removed in later chapters.

QUESTIONS AND EXERCISES

1. 'If the rate of investment is greater the *lower* is the rate of interest, why is it that, as a matter of observation, the rate of interest is high when investment is high?' Explain.
2. From the following information construct the *IS* and *LM* curves and graph them. Then find the equilibrium value of (i) income (Y); (ii) the rate of interest (r).

$$C_p = A + cY \qquad \text{when } A = 100 \quad c = 0.8$$

$$I_p = Z - gr \qquad \text{when } Z = 1000 \quad g = 10$$
$$M_1^D = kYp \qquad \text{when } k = 0.25 \quad p = 1$$
$$M_2^D = R - hr \qquad \text{when } R = 1375 \quad h = 50$$
$$M^S = M_0 \qquad \text{when } M_0 = 2500$$
$$r_{min} = 2.0 \text{ per cent.}$$

One way of increasing the equilibrium level of Y is to reduce r to its minimum level. Suppose this is done.

    (i) What is the new equilibrium level of Y?

    (ii) What is the minimum value of the money supply necessary to equate r to r_{min} at the new equilibrium level of Y?

    (iii) What are the consequences of a shift in the consumption schedule raising A to 200?

3. Using the model of Question 2 assume the investment function to shift upwards so that, in the new situation,

$$I_p = Z + \Delta Z - gr \quad \text{where } Z \text{ and } g \text{ are as before but}$$
$$\Delta Z = 100$$

Calculate the new equilibrium level of: (i) income (Y); (ii) interest (r); (iii) planned investment (I_p).

What is (i) the value of the multiplier? (ii) the *induced* change in I_p?

4. Write down as fully as possible the assumptions underlying the consumption and investment functions of Question 2: What are

    (i) the interest elasticity of M_2^D when $r = 4$ per cent;

    (ii) the income elasticity of C_p when income is 5300;

    (iii) the interest elasticity of investment when $r = 4$ per cent.

5. Using the data of Question 2 suppose the price level to double so that $p = 2$. Which curve (*IS* or *LM*) is affected? Why? Calculate the new equilibrium values of income and interest.

6. 'An increase in the propensity to save does not lower the rate of interest. On the contrary it lowers income.'

'An increase in the propensity to save always lowers the rate of interest. In some cases it may also lower income.'

Discuss these two statements in the light of the analysis of this chapter.

7. In Question 3 the autonomous change in $I_p \equiv \Delta Z = 100$.

According to the simple multiplier theory the change in equilibrium income should be given by:

$$\Delta Y = \Delta Z \frac{1}{1-c} \quad \text{where } c \equiv \frac{\partial C_p}{\partial Y}$$

From Question 2 the value of c is 0·8. Hence we should find

$$\Delta Y = \Delta Z \frac{1}{1-0·8} = 5\Delta Z.$$

Reconcile this result with your answer to Question 3. What are the *ceteris paribus* assumptions of the simple multiplier which are not satisfied in the more general model? Illustrate the simple multiplier on the *IS/LM* diagram. Is there any part of the diagram to which simple multiplier theory is applicable?

8. Suppose the money supply were increased not by purchases of bonds from the general public but by a single payment to all persons reaching their twenty-first birthday in a given year. How would your analysis differ from the analysis in the text? Why would it differ? Can you predict the change in the interest rate?

9. If the M.E.I. schedule is volatile how will income and the rate of interest behave? Do your conclusions throw any light on Question 1?

10. On what behaviour hypotheses would the *IS* curve be a horizontal straight line? Do they seem plausible to you? On what hypotheses would it be vertical.

11. Analyse the consequences for income, employment and the interest rate of an increase in the equality of income distribution. Illustrate your analysis on the *IS/LM* diagram.

12. 'A movement *along* one function may in practice cause a *shift* in another function.' Do you agree? Suggest plausible examples.

SUGGESTED READING

T. Dernburg and D. M. McDougall, *Macro-Economics* (McGraw-Hill, 1963) ch. ix.

Miles Fleming, *Monetary Theory* (Macmillan, 1971).

D. W. Laidler, *The Demand for Money* (Scranton, 1969).

W. T. Newlyn, *The Theory of Money* (Oxford, 1971) ch. viii.

R. G. D. Allen,† *Macro-Economic Theory* (Macmillan, 1968) ch. 7.

J. M. Keynes, *The General Theory of Employment, Interest and Money* (Macmillan, 1936) ch. xviii.

J. R. Hicks,† 'Mr. Keynes and the Classics' in *Readings in the Theory of Income Distribution*, ed. W. Fellner and B. Haley (Allen & Unwin, 1950).

† More advanced reference.

13 The Public Sector and the International Sector

Now that we have developed our static theory of the determination of income and interest in an economy *without* either government economic activity or international trade we need to extend our model to take account of these elements of the problem.

We begin by introducing government economic activity.

1 THE PUBLIC SECTOR

Where the system contains a government sector, aggregate demand must be redefined to include the real planned spending of government on goods and services. This we divide into two components, government investment and government consumption, writing:

$$G_p \equiv I_g + C_g. \tag{13.I}$$

Using this notation our equilibrium condition is:

$$Y = C_p + I_p + G_p. \tag{13.II}$$

This modification takes account of government spending. We now take account of the *direct taxes* imposed by government by reframing our consumption hypothesis in terms of personal disposable income rather than national income.

Reference to Chapter 4 tells us that, if we neglect the complication of undistributed profits,

$$\text{personal disposable income} \equiv Y - T + R \tag{13.III}$$

where $T \equiv$ direct taxes on persons

$R \equiv$ income transfers to households.

We now introduce the consumption function hypothesis by writing:

$$C_p = Q + c(Y - T + R), \tag{13.IV}$$

which relates planned expenditure on consumption to real personal disposable income.

For convenience let us write real planned investment as a function of the rate of interest.

$$I_p = H - br \qquad (13.\text{V})$$

We now assume that the real planned expenditure of government ($\equiv G_p$) is *exogenous*: that is, is unaffected by the value of any other variable in the system. Formally:

$$G_p = \bar{G}$$

Substituting yields:

$$\left. \begin{aligned} Y &= C_p + I_p + G_p \\ &= Q + c(Y - T + R) + H - br + \bar{G} \\ &= [Q + H + \bar{G} - br + c(R - T)]\frac{1}{1 - c} \end{aligned} \right\} \qquad (13.\text{VI})$$

which is an expression for the equilibrium value of output (income) in terms of

(i) the *autonomous* expenditures, $Q, H, \bar{G}, -br, c(R-T)$;

(ii) the *rate of interest* (r); and

(iii) the *multiplier* $\dfrac{1}{1-c}$.

By examining this expression it is easy to see the effect on the equilibrium value of income of governmental economic decisions.

Suppose, for example, that the government sector increases its expenditure on goods and services (G_p) by an amount $\Delta\bar{G}$ per period. Clearly the resultant increase in income will be:

$$\Delta Y = \Delta\bar{G}\,\frac{\partial Y}{\partial \bar{G}} = \Delta\bar{G}\,\frac{1}{1-c}$$

so that the multiplier for government expenditure on goods and services *financed by borrowing* – or the 'marginal response coefficient' – is:

$$\frac{\partial Y}{\partial \bar{G}} = \frac{1}{1-c}, \qquad (13.\text{VII})$$

the familiar multiplier of Chapter 9.

Why do we say *financed by borrowing*? Expenditure must always be financed in the sense that the money required to undertake it must be made available. The government derives its receipts from two sources: *taxation* and *borrowing*. In our example we have postulated an increase in $\bar{G}$ *without* any increase in T ($\equiv$ tax receipts). Hence the increased expenditure *must be financed by borrowing*.

Notice that $\partial Y/\partial \bar{G}$ is the 'marginal response coefficient' relating the increase in income to an increase in G_p with *everything else held constant*. In practice, as we have already shown, an increase in Y raises the quantity of active (M_1) balances demanded and this, with a given money supply, will raise the rate of interest (r). Since a higher level of the rate of interest is associated with a reduced rate of real planned investment by the private sector the *total change* in income will be *less* than indicated by the simple multiplier of (13.VII). We shall illustrate this proposition in a moment by reference to our *IS/LM* diagram.

What is the 'simple' (interest rate constant) multiplier for an increase in direct taxation?

Suppose T is increased. A glance at (13.VI) shows that the simple multiplier is

$$\frac{\partial Y}{\partial T} = -\frac{c}{1-c}. \qquad (13.\text{VIII})$$

This tells us that an increase in taxation *reduces* income (i.e. the multiplier operates in reverse). It also tells us that an increase in taxation does not have the full 'simple' multiplier but a smaller one: $c/1-c$.

We can now show a result known as 'the balanced budget' theorem. Suppose the authorities increase government expenditure on goods and services by an amount $\Delta\bar{G}$. From (13.VII) the resulting *increase* in income (assuming the rate of interest is held constant) is:

$$\Delta Y_1 = \Delta\bar{G}\frac{\partial Y}{\partial \bar{G}} = \Delta\bar{G}\frac{1}{1-c}.$$

Assume further that the additional expenditure is financed entirely by taxation. The increase in taxation ΔT *reduces* income. We have:

$$\Delta Y_2 = \Delta T\frac{-c}{1-c}.$$

The net effect of the *two* transactions is:

$$\Delta Y_1 + \Delta Y_2 = \Delta\bar{G}\frac{1}{1-c} - \Delta T\frac{c}{1-c}.$$

Assume that $\Delta\bar{G} = \Delta T$, i.e. that the whole of the additional expenditure on goods and services is financed by additional taxation.

Hence the effect of an increase in government expenditure financed by taxation is:

$$\Delta Y = \Delta \bar{G} \left[\frac{1}{1-c} - \frac{c}{1-c} \right]$$

$$= \Delta \bar{G} \left[\frac{1-c}{1-c} \right]$$

$$= \Delta \bar{G}. \tag{13.IX}$$

This tells us that the multiplier effect of an increase in government expenditure financed by taxation is unity.

At first sight this is a somewhat surprising result. A little reflection, however, shows that there is really nothing surprising about it at all. Let us write out the multiplier series of an increase in government expenditure using the method of Chapter 9. We have

$$\Delta Y_1 = \Delta \bar{G} + c\Delta \bar{G} + c^2 \Delta \bar{G} + ... c^n \Delta \bar{G}$$

$$= \Delta \bar{G}(1 + c + c^2 + c^3 + ... + c^n) \tag{13.X}$$

The corresponding series for the increase in taxation is:

$$\Delta Y_2 = -\Delta T(c + c^2 + c^3 + ... + c^n) \tag{13.Xa}$$

The latter series, it should be noted, *lacks the first term found in the government expenditure series. This reflects the fact that an increase in taxation does not reduce household consumption by its full amount but only by that part of the additional tax which would have been spent on consumption.* This is the increase in tax multiplied by the marginal propensity to consume i.e. $-c\Delta T$. Subsequent reductions in consumption occur because the initial fall in consumption $-c\Delta T$ reduces incomes by this amount and thus consumption by $-c^2\Delta T$ and so on.

Obviously if we now add ΔY_1 and ΔY_2 and equate $\Delta \bar{G}$ and ΔT all the terms in the two series drop out apart from the first term in the government expenditure series. To show this perform the operation thus:

$$\Delta Y_1 + \Delta Y_2 \equiv \Delta Y$$

$$= \Delta \bar{G}[1 + (c - c) + (c^2 - c^2) + (c^3 - c^3) + ... + (c^n - c^n)]$$

$$= \Delta \bar{G}$$

so that we have

$$\Delta Y = \Delta \bar{G}, \tag{13.Xb}$$

the result we obtained above.

For simplicity we can tabulate these results as follows:

Action	Method of finance	ΔY	Interest Rate constant Simple multiplier	Full or total multiplier
Increase in govt exp. on goods and services	Borrowing	$\Delta\bar{G}\dfrac{1}{1-c}$	$\dfrac{1}{1-c}$	$\leqslant\dfrac{1}{1-c}$
	Taxation	ΔG	unity	$\leqslant 1$
	Reduction in transfer payments	ΔG	unity	$\leqslant 1$
Increase in taxation	—	$\Delta T\dfrac{-c}{1-c}$	$\dfrac{-c}{1-c}$	$\geqslant\dfrac{-c}{1-c}$
Increase in transfer payments	Borrowing	$\Delta R\dfrac{c}{1-c}$	$\dfrac{c}{1-c}$	$\leqslant\dfrac{c}{1-c}$

In this Table the 'full multiplier' is the value of the multiplier allowing for

   (i) the effect of the increase in income on the rate of interest;
  (ii) the effect of the increase in the rate of interest on the rate of real planned investment by the private sector;
 (iii) the effect of the change in real planned investment on income.

To illustrate the action of the 'simple' and 'full' multipliers let us go back to our *IS/LM* diagram.

We have, from equation (13.VI), the following equilibrium condition in the goods market:

$$Y = [Q+\bar{G}+H-br+c(R-T)]\,\frac{1}{1-c}. \qquad (13.XI)$$

From this, just as we did previously, we can find all *pairs* of values of r and Y which equate aggregate demand and supply. This gives us a new *IS* curve the position of which now depends on $\bar{G}$, R and T: that is, upon the fiscal decisions of government.

The *LM* curve we find in the same way as in Chapter 7. The resulting diagram is set out below. The initial equilibrium is at Y_0, r_0.

Suppose now the $\bar{G}$ is increased. The *IS* curve shifts to the right.

If the rate of interest remains **unaltered the** new equilibrium of income is Y_1. The change in income $(\Delta Y \equiv Y_1 - Y_0)$ is the result of the 'simple' multiplier operating on $\Delta \bar{G}$. That is,

$$\Delta Y = \Delta \bar{G} \frac{1}{1-c}.$$

In practice, assuming a constant money supply, the rate of interest will *not* in general remain unaltered. Hence we shall move not to Y_1 but to Y_2. Thus

$$\Delta Y' \equiv Y_2 - Y_0$$

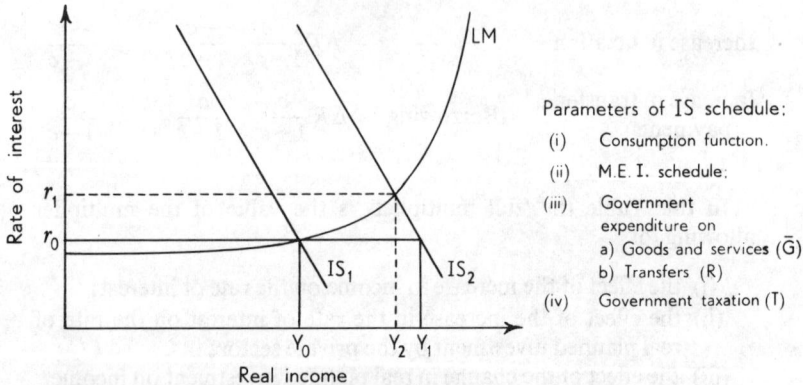

Parameters of IS schedule:

  (i)   Consumption function.

  (ii)   M.E. I. schedule:

  (iii) Government expenditure on
        a) Goods and services ($\bar{G}$)
        b) Transfers (R)

  (iv)   Government taxation (T)

FIG. 13·i   The effect of increased government expenditure on goods and services ($\bar{G}$)

is a diagrammatic representation of the change in income resulting from the operation of the 'full multiplier'. Except in the special case in which the *IS* curve (before *and* after its shift) cuts the *LM* curve at the minimum rate of interest,† we shall always have $\Delta Y' < \Delta Y$.

In short, the change $(\Delta Y')$ allows for the effects of the higher level of income on the demand for money; the increased demand for money on the rate of interest; the higher rate of interest on the rate of real planned investment by the private sector and the lower rate of real planned investment on income.

† Or the *IS* curve is vertical. Note that if the *LM* curve is vertical, income will not change.

2 ELEMENTS OF FISCAL POLICY

Now that we know how the government's decisions regarding expenditure on goods and services, taxation and transfer payments influence income and employment we can see something of their importance. Suppose, for example, it is the objective of the authorities to maintain the percentage of the work-force unemployed within the range of $1-2\frac{1}{2}$. This objective given the production function defines a range of output (income) $Y_f - Y'_f$ which is shaded in Fig. 13.ii. Suppose further that income is at Y_0 with unemployment at (say) 5 per cent.

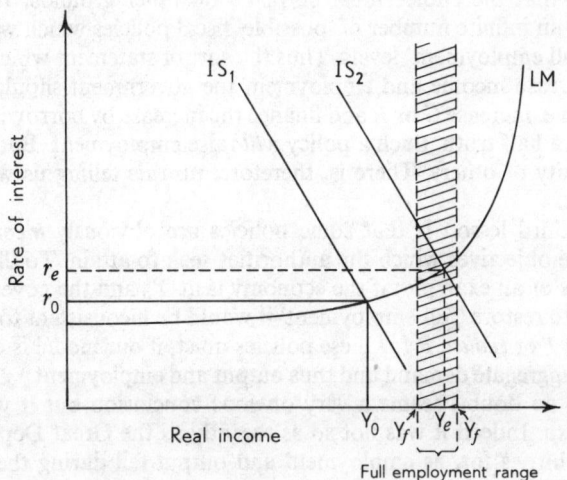

FIG. 13.ii   Fiscal policy and full employment

Clearly, by changing $\bar{G}$, R or T, the authorities can raise the equilibrium level of income to a value Y_e which falls within the range $Y_f - Y'_f$ and thus restore 'full employment'.

Fiscal policy – defined as the manipulation of government expenditure, transfers and taxation – is thus a powerful device for controlling the level of output and employment. This is the first lesson to be derived from the formal discussion of the preceding section.

There is, however, a second lesson. This is that there are no simple rules by which, merely by reference to the employment target, we can calculate the 'proper' fiscal policy. For example to raise income from Y_0 to a level within the range $Y_f - Y'_f$ the government could

   (i)   increase $\bar{G}$ and finance the increase by borrowing;
   (ii) increase $\bar{G}$ and finance the increase by raising taxation or reducing transfers;
   (iii) reduce taxation;
   (iv) increase transfers financing the increase by borrowing; or
   (v)   make use of some combination of (i)–(iv).

The point is that *each* of these courses of action will raise Y. Each therefore *can* be used to reach 'full employment'. The employment objective cannot therefore tell us *which* is the one to choose. It follows that the choice must be made on other grounds. In short there is an infinite number of 'possible' fiscal policies which will raise Y to 'full employment' levels. Thus the sort of statement which runs: 'To increase income and employment the government should run a deficit (i.e. increase $\bar{G}$ or R and finance the increase by borrowing)', is, at best, a half truth. Such a policy *will* raise employment. But so will an infinity of others. There is, therefore, no *rule* telling us we must adopt it.

The third lesson is that some policies are obviously *inconsistent* with the objectives which the authorities seek to attain. To illustrate in terms of an example: if the economy is at Y_0 and the government wishes to restore 'full employment' it would be inconsistent to *reduce* $\bar{G}$, *raise* T or *reduce* R for these policies must, if our model is correct, *reduce* aggregate demand and thus output and employment.

This, no doubt, seems a very obvious conclusion but it was not always so. Indeed it was not so as recently as the Great Depression of the thirties for, as employment and output fell during the Great Depression, governments in many countries sought to *avoid* deficits, to *cut* expenditure and even, on occasions, to *raise* taxes. As a result they *reduced* aggregate demand and made the depression, quite unnecessarily, a great deal worse than it need have been. This was usually done on the argument that since an individual family faced by a fall in its income must, to avoid bankruptcy, reduce its expenditure so too must a nation faced with a fall in national income. The fallacy in this, often called the fallacy of composition, consists in assuming that what is true for an individual is necessarily true for the sum of individuals.

The fourth lesson, which is in reality a special case of the third, is simply that there is no particular virtue in a 'balanced budget'; that is, a situation in which $\bar{G} + R = T$. Here again the argument is often derived from the consideration of an individual household and then, via the fallacy of composition, applied to the community as a whole. 'No family can, for long, spend more than its income: that is, run a deficit. A nation is a family. Hence what is true for the family must be true for the nation.' It is easy to see that this 'rule' too is nonsense. This does not mean that there are no arguments in favour of a balanced budget: there are many. But the question of whether to maintain a balanced budget, run a deficit or a surplus, is an open one which has to be considered in relation to the economic objectives of the authorities and the properties of the economic system. It cannot be settled by appeal to some 'rule' – and certainly not by appeal to a 'rule' which involves a particularly glaring example of the fallacy of composition.

The fifth lesson which we can obtain from our discussion is this. In considering a Budget introduced by a particular Chancellor we must always ask:

> will this Budget influence aggregate demand in a way consistent with the Chancellor's employment objectives?

3 THE INTERNATIONAL SECTOR

We now consider the effect on our theory of introducing international transactions.

Clearly, as we have already learned from national income accounting, some part of the demand for domestic output arises out of the expenditure by foreigners. To a manufacturer it is a matter of indifference whether his output is purchased by a Scotsman, a Scandinavian, a Chinese or the man next door. A purchase by a foreigner is a purchase which generates income just like any other.

We call the demand for domestic goods by foreigners 'planned purchases of exports' (E_p), and assume that foreigners' plans are always carried out. Hence planned exports (E_p) equal actual exports (E) and these constitute an *addition* to domestic demands for domestic output.

Planned expenditure by home nationals on goods and services is, as we have already seen, the sum of planned consumption, planned private investment and planned government expenditure on goods and services. Some part of this expenditure will, however, not be devoted to the purchase of domestic output but to the purchase of output produced by foreigners. This we call imports (Z). Again we shall assume that planned purchases of imports (Z_p) equal actual purchases of imports (Z).

Clearly the purchase of imports does not generate domestic incomes but incomes abroad. Hence, from the point of view of the aggregate demand for domestic output, imports constitute a 'leakage' from expenditure of the same type as planned saving. Hence Z, the total of imports, must be *subtracted* from domestic expenditure to arrive at the domestic expenditure on domestic output.

Accordingly our equilibrium condition in the goods market becomes:

$$Y = C_p + I_p + G_p + E - Z. \tag{13.XII}$$

This shows that our expression for aggregate demand now includes a term for exports (E) and imports (Z). This is helpful but we need now a theory to explain the value of exports (E) and the value of imports (Z).

Consider exports first. The exports of the U.K. are part of the imports of the rest of the world. As a first approximation we may think of the rest of the world's expenditures on our products as depending on two variables:

  (i) the level of real incomes in the rest of the world (Y_w)
  (ii) the price of British goods (and services) in relation to the prices of similar goods and services.

Formally we can write this simple hypothesis thus:

$$E = f\left(Y_w, \frac{P_w}{P_{UK}}\right) \tag{13.XIII}$$

where

  $E \equiv$ actual $=$ planned, purchases of exports

  $P_w \equiv$ prices of rest of the world's goods and services in their own currencies

  $P_{UK} \equiv$ prices of British goods and services in pounds sterling.

The prices of British goods are expressed in pounds. Other countries use other units of account such as the dollar, franc, mark, pengo, rupee, and rouble. These prices can only be compared if we know the rate of exchange between the pound and other currencies. Hence the ratio P_w/P_{UK} depends upon the rate of exchange. As we have written it it is meaningless.

Let us call q the rate of exchange and interpret it to mean the price (in terms of foreign currency) of £1 sterling. A rise in q thus means that the pound is worth *more* in terms of foreign currency and, therefore that, for any given level of P_{UK}, British goods and services are relatively *dearer* than they were (to foreigners) and foreign goods and services relatively *cheaper* than they were (to U.K. residents).

Our exports hypothesis is now:

$$E = f\left(Y_w, \frac{P_w}{P_{UK}}, q\right). \tag{13.XIV}$$

What general form do we expect this function to take? If real incomes rise in the rest of the world then, with no change in P_w, P_{UK} or q, our expectation is that E will rise. In other words we expect the 'marginal response coefficient' $\partial E/\partial Y_w$ to be positive but less than unity.

An increase in q makes British goods and services *dearer* to foreigners. With Y_w and P_w/P_{UK} unchanged we would expect this to *reduce E*. Thus we expect the 'marginal response coefficient' $\partial E/\partial q$ to be negative.

An increase in the ratio P_w/P_{UK} makes British goods *relatively cheaper* to foreigners. We would thus expect $\partial E/\partial(P_w/P_{UK})$ to be positive.

The function (13.XIV) provides a very simple hypothesis with which to try to explain the rate of British exports. Obviously many variables (foreign tariffs, trade regulations and so on) are omitted. For our present purposes it is nevertheless helpful, for of the four variables on which we expect E to depend *two*, namely Y_w and P_w, are determined in the rest of the world and are thus reasonably regarded as exogenous.

So far we are taking domestic prices to be constant. Hence P_{UK} is invariant by assumption. It follows that, as far as the domestic economy is concerned, E can only be varied by alteration in the exchange rate (q). If we assume the exchange rate (q) to be invariant we may then reasonably regard E as an exogenous variable. This we shall do and write:

$$E = \bar{E}. \tag{13.XIV*}$$

What of imports? We have already argued that our exports (part of foreigners' imports) are likely to be dependent upon the real income of foreigners. By the same reasoning our imports (part of foreigners' exports) are likely to depend upon *our* real income.

Which is the appropriate income concept? If imports consisted entirely in consumption goods it might be plausible to regard imports, like consumption expenditure itself, as dependent on personal disposable income. But British imports consist in large measure of raw materials. The demand for these is much more plausibly related to national income or even gross national product. Accordingly we shall write our import hypothesis:

$$Z = f\left(Y, \frac{P_{UK}}{P_w}, q\right) \tag{13.XV}$$

and expect

$$0 < \partial Z/\partial Y < 1; \qquad \partial Z/\partial(P_{UK}/P_w) > 0 \quad \text{and} \quad \partial Z/\partial q > 0.$$

We are taking P_{UK} and q as given and invariant. Let us make the same assumption about P_w. We can then write a linear import function analogous to the linear consumption function

$$Z = F + zY,$$

where $Z \equiv$ real imports

$F \equiv$ autonomous real imports

$z \equiv$ marginal propensity to import out of real national income $\equiv \partial Z/\partial Y$

$Y \equiv$ real national income.

This is illustrated in the Figure.

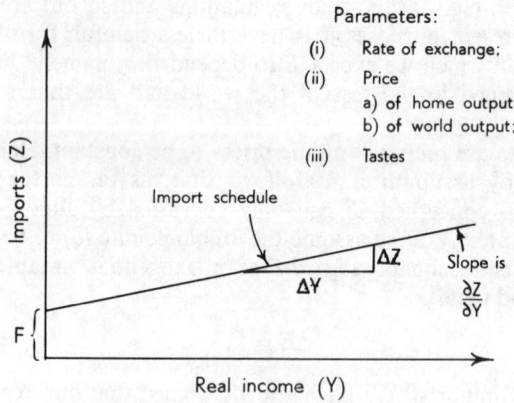

Fig. 13.iii   The propensity to import

Substituting these relations into the equilibrium condition for aggregate demand we have:

$$Y = C_p + I_p + G_p + E - Z$$
$$= Q + c(Y - T + R) + H - br + \bar{G} + \bar{E} - F - zY,$$

so that

$$Y = [Q + c(R-T) + H - br + \bar{G} + \bar{E} - F] \frac{1}{1-c+z} \quad \text{(13.XVI)}$$

Now this expression (13.XVI) is analogous to our earlier expression (13.XI) in that it gives the equilibrium level of income in terms of (i) the *autonomous* items in expenditure; (ii) the rate of interest; and (iii) the multiplier. The difference between (13.XVI) and (13.XI) occurs because

(i) the *autonomous* items now include exports (E) and that part of expenditure on imports which is independent of income (F); while

(ii) the multiplier now depends upon the marginal propensity to import (z) as well as the marginal propensity to save ($1-c$).

Now, as we have remarked, $1 - c \equiv s \equiv$ the marginal propensity to save. Thus where our earlier multiplier was

$$\frac{1}{1-c} \equiv \frac{1}{s}$$

our new multiplier is

$$\frac{1}{1-c+z} \equiv \frac{1}{s+z}.$$

In short the appearance of the marginal propensity to import (z) in the multiplier reflects (and justifies) our earlier assertion that, *from the point of view of income determination*, expenditure on imports constitutes a 'leakage' from expenditure on domestic output just as does saving. To put the same point slightly differently the new form of the multiplier arises because the equilibrium condition which, in the simplest model is

planned saving = planned investment

is now

planned saving = planned investment *plus* (exports − imports)

or, explicitly recognising the existence of the government sector,†

$$\left\{ \begin{array}{c} \text{planned saving of households} \\ \text{plus} \\ \text{planned saving of government} \end{array} \right\} = \left\{ \begin{array}{l} \text{planned investment of} \\ \text{private sector } plus \\ \text{planned investment of} \\ \text{government sector } plus \\ \text{(exports − imports).} \end{array} \right\}$$

† The reader should refer back to the national accounting identity of Chapter 4 which was $S \equiv I$

$$\equiv I_c + I_g + I_f.$$

The multiplier $\dfrac{1}{1-c+z} \equiv \dfrac{1}{s+z}$ is often called the 'international trade' multiplier. It is the multiplier appropriate to an economy engaging in international trade and maintaining constant interest rates. Thus, for example, the multipliers we have hitherto found become, when the international sector is introduced,

$$\frac{\partial Y}{\partial I_p} = \frac{1}{1-c+z} \quad \text{investment multiplier}$$

$$\frac{\partial Y}{\partial Q} = \frac{1}{1-c+z} \quad \text{(autonomous) consumption multiplier}$$

$$\frac{\partial Y}{\partial G} = \frac{1}{1-c+z} \quad \text{government expenditure multiplier}$$

$$\frac{\partial Y}{\partial T} = \frac{-c}{1-c+z} \quad \text{taxation multiplier.}$$

These propositions the reader may readily verify for himself by carrying out the appropriate operations on (13.XVI).

We can now ask two questions. First, what effects do changes in international transactions have on the level of income and the balance of payments? Second what effects do changes in the propensity to consume, private investment or fiscal decisions have on the balance of payments?

Suppose there is an increase in exports by $\Delta \bar{E}$. Then, from (13.XVI), the increase in income is given by:

$$\Delta Y = \Delta \bar{E}\, \frac{1}{1-c+z}.$$

In other words, given constant interest rates, incomes rise by the multiplier times the increase in exports.

What happens to the balance of payments? Exports increase, by assumption, by $\Delta \bar{E}$. This however raises income which, since imports are a function of income, brings about an *induced* increase in imports. The amount that imports increase depends upon

(i) the rise in income $\Delta \bar{E}\, \dfrac{1}{1-c+z}$; and

(ii) the marginal propensity to import (z).

Hence, the *change* in the balance of payments is given by:

increase in exports − increase in imports

$$\Delta \bar{E} \qquad - \qquad z[\Delta \bar{E}]\, \frac{1}{1-c+z}$$

$$= \Delta E\, \frac{1-c}{1-c+z} = \Delta E\, \frac{s}{s+z}.$$

Since s is greater than zero this tells us that the balance of payments must improve but will never improve by as much as the increases in exports unless $z = 0$: that is, imports are *independent* of income.

We cannot speak unambiguously of an increase in imports but only of a *shift* (upwards or downwards) in the *import function*. Suppose the import function shifts upwards (the propensity to import increases): what happens? First let us see what this means from the Figure 13.iv.

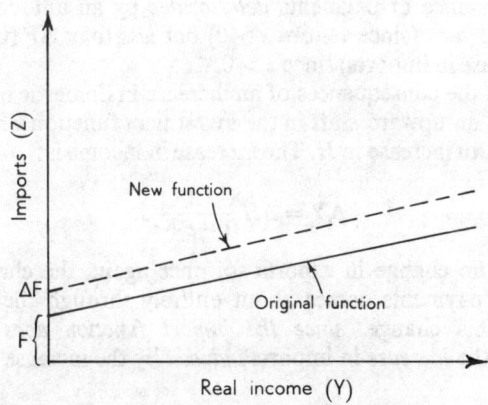

FIG. 13.iv   An upward shift in the propensity to import

In this Figure we have assumed, as we did when discussing an increase in the propensity to consume, that the shift in the function leaves its slope (z) unaltered. Formally then an increase in the propensity to import is an increase in F—the 'constant' term in the import function. A glance at (13.XVI) tells us immediately that the change in income is

$$\Delta Y = -\Delta F \frac{1}{1-c+z}.$$

In short, as we would expect, an increase in the propensity to import, like an increase in the propensity to save, *lowers* income.

What happens to the balance of payments? Exports, which are exogenous, do not change. We have, however, two types of change in imports. First the *autonomous increase* (ΔF). Second the *induced decrease* due to the decline in income operating via the marginal propensity to import $(z\Delta Y)$. The change in the balance of payments is therefore:

increase in exports *minus* increase in imports

$$0 \quad - \quad [\Delta F + z\Delta Y]$$

$$- \left[\Delta F - z\Delta F \frac{1}{1-c+z}\right]$$

$$- \left[\Delta F \frac{1-c}{1-c+z}\right].$$

Thus the balance of payments *deteriorates* by an amount which is greater than zero (since $1-c \equiv s > 0$) but *less* than ΔF (the autonomous increase in imports) since $z > 0$.

What are the consequences of an increase in domestic investment? This means an upward shift in the investment function which, in our notation, is an increase in H. The increase in income is:

$$\Delta Y = \Delta H \frac{1}{1-c+z}.$$

There is no change in exports so, once again, the change in the balance of payments comes about entirely through the change in imports. This change, *since the import function does not shift*, consists of the *increase* in imports *induced* by the increase in income. This is:

$$z\Delta Y = \frac{z}{1-c+z} \Delta H,$$

which is the amount by which the balance of payments deteriorates.

It would be tedious, and pointless, to work out the consequences of increases in the propensity to consume, government expenditure on goods and services, taxation or transfer payments. These the reader is invited to establish for himself. Our results can easily be summarised in a few simple propositions of great practical importance.

   (i) Any change in one (or more) of the *domestic* determinants of income will change income through the multiplier and thus bring about an *induced* change in imports and the state of the balance of payments.
  (ii) Any change in exports will change income and bring about an induced change in imports.
 (iii) Any change in the import function will change income and bring about both an *autonomous* and an *induced* change in imports.

Two points need now to be noticed. The first is that the multiplier $\dfrac{1}{1-c+z}$ is the 'simple' multiplier which is strictly applicable only when the rate of interest is constant. The 'full' or 'total' multiplier, assuming an invariant quantity of money, will be less than this because of the effect of the change in the rate of interest on real planned private investment.†

The second, and more important point, is that the *equilibrium of income* does not imply the equality of exports and imports: that is, *external equilibrium*. To illustrate this suppose the economy is operating at (say) 5 per cent unemployment and exports = imports so that external equilibrium exists. If the government, in an endeavour to reach 'full employment', increases expenditure on goods and services, incomes will rise by an amount, assuming the interest rate to be constant, given by:

$$\Delta Y = \Delta \bar{G} \, \frac{1}{1-c+z}.$$

The increase in income, however, will increase imports by an amount:

$$\Delta Z = \Delta Y = z\Delta G \, \frac{1}{1-c+z}.$$

Hence the balance of payments will move into *deficit*. Since no country can, for long, import more than it can pay for by means of its exports, the authorities, in solving the 'employment problem', find that they have created a 'balance of payments problem'.

We can put the same point in a number of different ways two of which are particularly useful.

The first is to say that the equilibrium level of income and the state of the balance of payments are interdependent *not* independent. Any change in one entails a change in the other.

The second is to say that the *full* equilibrium of the system requires, once international trade takes place, the simultaneous satisfaction of three conditions:

   (i) $Y = C_p + I_p + G_p + (E-Z)$
         i.e., aggregate demand = aggregate supply;
   (ii) $M^D = M^S$
         i.e., demand for money = supply of money;
   (iii) $E = Z$
         i.e., external receipts = external payments.

† And, if planned consumption is a function of the interest rate, on consumption.

The importance of the interdependence between income and the state of the balance of payments differs in different countries. For example in the U.S.A. international trade is relatively unimportant as a component in G.N.P. Both the average and marginal propensities to import are small – probably of the order of 0·05. In the U.K. international trade is of far greater significance and both the average and marginal propensities to import are far greater, the latter probably being of the order of 0·2. This means that while quite a large (absolute) increase in U.S. G.N.P. produces only a small (absolute) increase in imports this is not so for the U.K. As a result the British authorities, in endeavouring to implement a 'full employment' policy, have constantly to divert their attention to the state of the balance of payments. Indeed the interdependence of income and the state of the balance of payments as analysed above, lies at the heart of many of the difficulties which have beset the British economy since the end of the Second World War.

QUESTIONS AND EXERCISES

1. How important are public sector expenditures in total demand? Prepare a table, using data from the latest Blue Book, showing (i) the ratio of $\bar{G}/Y$ in each year; (ii) the ratio $\Delta\bar{G}/\Delta Y$ in each year.
2. Suppose the government changes its tax system so that, for a given value of gross national product, direct taxes on income are reduced by £100 m. and indirect taxes increased by £100 m. thus leaving the total tax yield unaltered. What will be the consequences for (i) consumption; (ii) aggregate demand; (iii) the rate of interest; and (iv) output?
3. 'To control the economy Chancellors manipulate tax rates and government spending.' Explain. Which do you think is the easier to adjust and why?
4. 'The maintenance of "full employment" does not define the "optimal" fiscal policy. It simply gives us one condition which the "optimal" fiscal policy must satisfy.' Explain. What other criteria would you wish to take into account in specifying the 'optimal' fiscal policy? Why?
5. Analyse the consequences of an increase in child allowances financed by increased taxation on those with incomes of over £5000 per annum. Why does the formal analysis of Chapter 13,

Section 2 appear to suggest an answer at variance with the analysis of Chapter 9?

6. From the Blue Book obtain annual data for U.K. imports and G.N.P. for each year from 1956 to 1970. Plot each year's observations on a scatter diagram with imports on the vertical axis and G.N.P. on the horizontal axis. Does a linear function usefully describe the observations? If not why not? If so, fit such a function freehand and measure its slope. On what assumptions is this slope a good estimate of the marginal propensity to import?

7. Suppose import restrictions are imposed and reduce imports by 10 per cent. Analyse the consequences for aggregate demand and employment.

8. Examine critically the assumption that the demand for British exports is independent of the level of British imports.

9. 'If we were to devalue now (in 1967) we should need to impose large increases in taxation.' Why? In the light of your answer comment on the budgets of 1968, 1969 and 1970.

10. 'The invariable response of the British authorities to external deficits is to reduce demand and employment. The aim is to achieve strength through misery.' Discuss with an examination of the relevant statistical data.

11. The model used to analyse fiscal decisions assumes that both the total revenue from direct taxes (T) and the total of transfer payments (R) are independent of the level of income. This is implausible. Replace these assumptions by the hypotheses

$$T = \hat{T} + tY \quad \text{where } t \equiv \frac{\partial T}{\partial Y} > 0 < 1;$$

$$R = \hat{R} + rY \qquad r \equiv \frac{\partial R}{\partial Y} < 0 > -1.$$

Rework the analysis of Section 1 of this chapter. How do the new hypotheses modify the analysis?

12. A system such as that defined by Question 11 is said to have a measure of 'built-in fiscal stabilization'. Elucidate this statement and propose an appropriate way of measuring the 'stabilization' provided. (Hint: compare the simple multipliers of Question 11 and the text.)

13. Does the 'balanced budget theorem' hold for the system of Question 11? Assume an increase of ΔG in government expenditure which is to be financed by (i) reducing taxation; and (ii) reducing transfer payments. How much of the additional

revenue must be provided by a *shift* in the tax (and/or transfer function) and how much must be *induced* by the change in income for the balanced budget theorem to hold?

14. The model used in Section 1, even when modified along the lines of Question 11, is over-simplified. What are its main limitations? How would you seek to develop it?

15. In practice the marginal rate of tax rises with income. Since this is so is the hypothesis $T = \hat{T} + tY$ reasonable? Can you suggest a more plausible function? If so can you incorporate it in your answer to Question 11?

16. From the Blue Book obtain estimates for the annual receipts of the government from direct taxation for each year from 1960 to 1972. Construct a 'scatter diagram' with receipts from direct taxation on the vertical axis and national income on the horizontal axis. Use this scatter to reconsider your answer to Question 15. Is a linear function a reasonable approximation? If so, fit it to the observed points by eye and estimate (i) the marginal response coefficient $\partial T / \partial Y$; and (ii) the income elasticity of direct tax receipts for the year 1970.

17. Assume that the U.K. needs to improve its current account balance of payments by £300 m. a year. If exports are exogenously determined and the marginal propensity to import is 0·25 what is the annual cost of doing this by reducing incomes?

18. Suppose a 1 per cent devaluation would improve the current balance by £30 m. a year. What is your estimate of the relative merits of achieving the £300 m. improvement mentioned in Question 17 by a 10 per cent devaluation rather than the method of Question 17?

19. Retaining the quantitative assumptions of Question 18 what fiscal policy would you recommend should accompany a 10 per cent devaluation? Give your reasons.

20. Is management of an economy simplified or otherwise by the existence of a numerically small marginal propensity to import? Why?

SUGGESTED READING

G. K. Shaw, *Fiscal Policy* (Macmillan, 1972).

J. C. R. Dow, *The Management of the British Economy 1945–1960* (Cambridge, 1964) chs vii–viii.

J. E. Meade, 'The International Monetary Mechanism', *The Three Banks Review* (Sep 1964).

Radcliffe Report (H.M.S.O., 1959) ch. viii.

O. Eckstein, *Public Finance* (Prentice-Hall, 1964), particularly ch. vii.

I. M. D. Little in *The British Economy in the Nineteen-Fifties* (Oxford, 1962).

W. A. H. Godley and J. R. Shepherd, 'Forecasting Imports', *N.I.E.S.R. Review* no. 33 (1965).

M. FG. Scott in *Economic Growth in Britain*, ed. P. D. Henderson (Weidenfeld & Nicolson, 1966) ch. iv.

C. D. Foster, ibid. ch. vi.

F. R. Brechling and J. M. Wolfe, 'The End of Stop-Go', *Lloyds Bank Review* (Jan 1965).

J. C. R. Dow, 'Fiscal Policy and Monetary Policy as Instruments of Control', *Westminster Bank Review* (May, Aug and Nov 1960).

M. FG. Scott, 'Should the Pound be Devalued?' *The Bankers' Magazine* (Apr 1967).

14 Money, Debt and Liquidity

In our outline of the liquidity preference theory of interest we have already put forward a definition of the money supply. This definition, however, was stated dogmatically and the principles underlying it were never discussed. At the same time we made reference to the concept of liquidity. Our task in this chapter is to examine the concepts of money and liquidity in more detail and thus explain and justify the brief references made in the course of our earlier analysis.

1 THE FUNCTIONS OF MONEY

Modern economic organisation is based upon a highly complex division of productive function. This in turn depends upon the process of exchange. *The supreme importance of money is that it facilitates exchange.* It thus makes possible the extreme division of productive function upon which our material well-being rests. Money, accordingly, must be regarded as one of man's most useful and revolutionary inventions.

Every purchase involves the creation, expression and settlement of a debt. Consider, for example, the purchase of a tennis racquet. Once the racquet has been chosen by the purchaser and received by him, a debt is created which is owed by the purchaser to the seller of the racquet. The value of this debt must be expressed in terms of some unit comprehensible to both parties. The unit in which debts (prices) are expressed is known as the *unit of account*. In Britain the unit of account is the pound sterling; in India the rupee; in the U.S.A. the dollar; in the U.S.S.R. the rouble.

Historically the pound, as its name implies, was related to a certain weight of metal. Modern units of account are, however, essentially abstract concepts. There is no 'pound', 'dollar' or 'rouble'. The abstract unit of account is also found in primitive monetary systems for, even where the unit of account was a 'slave', a 'goat', or a 'bottle of gin', it remained an abstract concept of a 'standard' or 'normal' slave, goat or bottle of gin to which any given slave, goat or bottle of gin might, or might not, correspond.

Once the debt has been expressed in terms of the unit of account, the next problem is that of settlement. If the money of the society is purely a money-of-account, settlement proceeds by barter. In this case money's single function is to provide a unit in which prices may be expressed. Modern moneys, however, do more than this. They furnish *a means of settling indebtedness*. For settlement of debt something must pass from the debtor to the creditor which, either by law or custom, the latter is compelled or prepared to accept in settlement. The *things* which pass must, of course, have values expressed in terms of the unit of account or directly related to it. Those *things* which are acceptable by law in settlement of debt are known as *legal tender money*; those *things* which are generally acceptable as a matter of custom we call *customary money*.

The third function of money is to act as *an asset or store of value*. Once society develops a *thing* (or *things*) which acts both as a means of settling indebtedness and unit of account (two attributes which together constitute a *medium of exchange*) then those *things* can be held by individuals as assets or stores of value. *To hold money thus becomes one way of holding wealth.* As earlier analysis has made clear this function of money in acting as an asset is the fundamental one for monetary theory.

It is convenient to summarise our brief discussion of money's functions by a simple diagram.

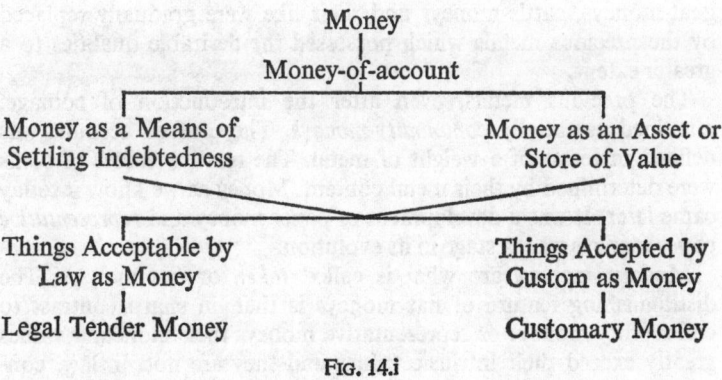

FIG. 14.i

On the basis of this analysis how best can money be defined? Essentially money is as money does. Hence we may define *money* as: *anything legally or customarily acceptable in settlement of debt*.

Our next step must be to consider what are the 'things' which, in developed economies, perform the functions of money.

2 THE CHARACTERISTICS OF MODERN MONEY

In the early stages of monetary development the things which served as money were commonly familiar and widely used commodities. As one example of a *commodity-money* we may take slaves which, as recently as the first decade of the present century, still performed monetary functions in parts of West Africa.

An efficient money needs to possess, in as high a measure as possible, the attributes of (i) portability, (ii) divisibility, (iii) durability, (iv) homogeneity, and (v) stability in value. Slave money was deficient in most of these. Admittedly, slaves, in view of their ability to walk, were portable. On the other hand they were not divisible; moreover, being subject to the hazards of accident, disease, escape, and suicide they were not always very durable. Again, slaves were scarcely homogeneous, a state of affairs which gave unlimited opportunities for disputing whether a particular slave was, or was not, a 'standard' slave in terms of the unit of account. Finally, slave moneys were additionally defective in that a successful slave raiding war, or outbreak of disease, could cause sharp fluctuations in their supply and thus their value. Many of the early commodity moneys shared these defects in greater or lesser degree. Hence slave-moneys, goat-moneys, cattle-moneys and their like were gradually replaced by the precious metals which possessed the desirable qualities to a greater extent.

The precious metals, even after the introduction of coinage, remained essentially *commodity-moneys*. The unit of account was defined in terms of a weight of metal. The relative values of coins were determined by their metal content. Money as we know it today came later. It was a development of paper money and *representative* paper moneys were a stage in its evolution.

Modern moneys are what is called *token* or *fiat* moneys. The distinguishing feature of fiat moneys is that, in sharp contrast to commodity-moneys or representative moneys their monetary values greatly exceed their intrinsic values and they are not, in law, convertible into anything other than themselves. An admirable example of such money is provided by the pound note. The cost of printing such a note is considerably less than a penny. Its value, as a commodity, is virtually zero. Indeed, apart from its possible use as a rather unattractive wallpaper, it is difficult to see any non-monetary employment for a note at all. Legally, the pound note is convertible only into other notes or coins though, as a matter of fact, the Bank of England will in certain circumstances exchange such notes for other currencies at a rate of exchange which the British authorities choose and may alter. The value of the pound note, in its monetary function, thus depends upon its scarcity and this is preserved by legal and institutional arrangements which we shall examine later. On the other hand, notes are legal tender throughout the United Kingdom. And, together with *token* coin, despite their intrinsic worthlessness, they provide a currency which possesses, in high measure, those attributes of portability, divisibility, durability, and homogeneity which our earlier discussion has shown to be desirable. Thus, as money has developed, the *things* which serve as money have become specialised to their monetary functions and are now virtually valueless apart from them.

What are the things which serve as money in the United Kingdom? First there are the notes issued by the Bank of England and declared to be legal tender by the state. Second there are token coins issued by the state and declared to be limited legal tender. These, under law, must be accepted in full and final settlement of debts. It is, however, a matter of common experience that debts may also be settled by means of cheques. A cheque is an order to a banker, signed by the drawer, ordering the banker to transfer a stated sum, standing to the credit of the drawer in the bank's books, into the possession of the payee. *A cheque is not in itself money.* What performs the monetary function when a payment is made by cheque is the *bank deposit* which the cheque is merely an order to transfer. Bank deposits are not, of course, legal tender. Anyone can refuse to accept a cheque offered to him and demand payment in legal tender notes and coin. Nevertheless, in many developed societies, cheques are very widely accepted and bank deposits form the principal means of payment. Bank deposits are, in fact, the outstanding example of *customary money*. Plainly, only those deposits subject to transfer by cheque can be regarded as money. Hence time deposits and savings bank deposits, though in many respects similar to money, are *not* money while *demand* or *current account* deposits most certainly are money. Indeed, in the United Kingdom, they are the most important type of money.

The line of reasoning so far followed in this section can be set out very briefly in the form of a skeleton diagram.

The reasoning underlying Fig. 14.ii leads us, of course, back to the definition of the money supply given earlier. For the things which are money in Britain are *coin*, *notes* and *demand deposits* with the banking system. More than this, however, it suggests a further question: granted that coin, notes, and demand deposits are money, what precisely are they? What, in other words, is the essential nature of the *things* which serve as money?

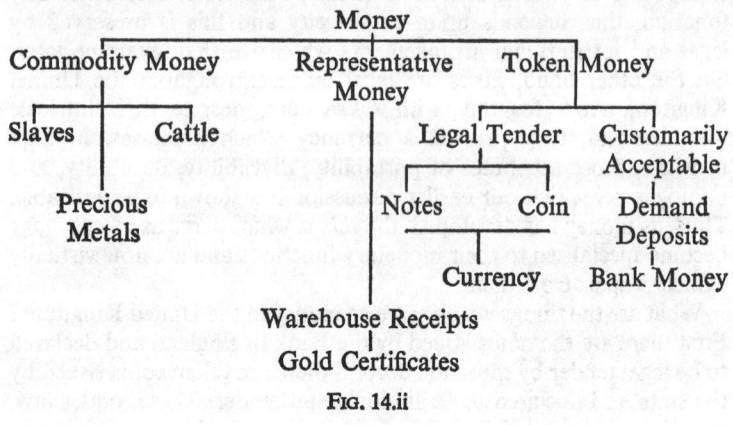

FIG. 14.ii

3 MONEY AS DEBT

It is convenient to begin an examination of modern money with notes which are, of course, the principal form of legal tender. What then is a British pound note?

British notes are issued by the Bank of England whose *liabilities* they are. They are, in fact, paper tokens of indebtedness which represent claims against the Bank. These claims (or titles to wealth) mean that the Bank *owes* the *bearer* of the note the sum stated on its face. Notes are therefore no more than IOU's made payable to bearer on demand which, as a matter of convenience, are issued in certain fixed values and printed upon paper. They differ, of course, from the IOU's of private persons, which are claims against the issuer, in that the Bank is under no legal obligation to convert *its* IOU's into anything other than different types of its own obligations; a private individual's IOU must, if payable on demand, be converted into legal tender money.

The fact that Bank notes are merely tokens of the Bank's indebtedness to the bearer is immediately apparent from contemplation of the notes themselves for Bank of England pound notes still carry the inscription: 'I promise to pay the Bearer on Demand the sum of One Pound' and this promise is signed: 'For the Gov.ʳ and Comp.ᵃ of the Bank of England' by the Chief Cashier of the Bank. Bank of England notes are not legally convertible into anything other than the notes or deposits of the Bank of England. The promise is, in consequence, completely meaningless. It is, in practice, no more than an anachronistic survival of the days when Bank of England notes were legally convertible into gold; that is when the pound note was *representative* rather than *fiat* money. Nevertheless, although the promise is specious, it has the merit of making plain the essential nature of a note which is, as we have already said, the token of a debt owed by the Bank to the bearer of the note, payable on demand, and not legally convertible into anything other than a similar note or notes of identical origin, though possibly of different denomination.

If a note is an inconvertible token of indebtedness payable to bearer on demand, what is a coin? Token coins may best be regarded as notes which are, purely as a matter of convenience, printed upon metal. Some countries do, in fact, make little use of coin and provide small change by issuing notes of very low denomination. In general, however, coins are preferred since small denomination notes, as a consequence of repeated use, become torn and dirty and ultimately present an appearance which is at once unlovely and unhygienic. If coins are tokens of indebtedness printed on metal whose obligations are they? In Britain, token coins are manufactured by the Mint. They are issued to the banks and the public through the Bank of England. In principle, therefore, they are the obligations of the state. In law, somewhat paradoxically, there is no obligation upon the state to convert coin into notes. In practice, however, the full convertibility of coin into notes is maintained by various administrative devices. The difference between the cost of producing coin, including the cost of the metal, and its monetary value is known as 'seignorage' and is treated as part of the income of the state.

We have thus reached the position that *legal tender money* in Britain (currency) consists of acknowledgements of indebtedness issued either by the State or the Bank of England. What then is *customary* money?

Demand deposits are acknowledgements of indebtedness in precisely the same way as are notes and coins. If John Smith has a demand (current account) deposit standing to his credit in the ledgers of Lloyds Bank, this means that Lloyds Bank is in debt to John Smith for this sum which the Bank has borrowed from him. A bank deposit of this type differs from a note in a number of significant ways. First, it is the debt, not of the state or a state-owned institution, but of a private banking company. Second, it is not inconvertible since Lloyds Bank is obliged, if John Smith demands it, to convert the deposit into legal tender. Third, a deposit, which is merely a book entry in the Bank's ledger, has no 'bearer'. Its transfer from one person to another is made by the Bank only on the instructions of the holder. Fourth, a deposit is less vulnerable to loss, theft, or

Table 14.1   *The Statistics of the Components of Money Supply in the U.K., U.S.A., Switzerland and Australia in the years 1959, 1960, 1961, 1962, 1971*

	U.K. (millions of pound sterling: approximate end of period)				
	1959	1960	1961	1962	1971
1. Legal tender	2,046	2,126	2,215	2,197	3,589
2. Demand deposits	4,151	3,924	3,852	4,033	6,053
3. Total money supply (1 + 2)	6,197	6,050	6,067	6,230	9,642
4. Demand deposits (2) as % of the total money supply (3)	67·0	64·9	63·5	64·7	62·8

	U.S.A. (billions of U.S. dollars: end of period)				
	1959	1960	1961	1962	1971
1. Legal tender	28·3	28·6	28·5	29·5	53·4
2. Demand deposits	109·0	108·4	109·8	115·7	182·2
3. Total money supply (1 + 2)	137·3	137·0	138·3	145·2	235·6
4. Demand deposits (2) as % of the total money supply (3)	79·4	79·1	79·4	79·7	77·3

	Switzerland (billions of francs: end of period)				
	1959	1960	1961	1962	1971
1. Legal tender	6·81	7·34	8·16	9·03	15·6
2. Sight (= demand) deposits	8·60	9·65	11·38	12·49	31·87
3. Total money supply (1 + 2)	15·41	16·99	19·54	21·52	47·47
4. Sight deposits as % of the total money supply (3)	55·8	56·8	58·2	58·0	67·1

	Australia (millions of Australian dollars: average of weekly figures for last month of period)				
	1959	1960	1961	1962	1971
1. Legal tender	812	848	838	852	1,477
2. Demand deposits	2,712	2,700	2,610	2,668	4,266
3. Total money supply (1 + 2)	3,524	3,524	3,448	3,520	5,743
4. Demand deposits as % of the total money supply (3)	77·0	76·1	75·7	75·8	74·3

Source: *International Financial Statistics*, International Monetary Fund (supplement to 1963/64 issues).

damage than legal tender money, though it is exposed to the hazards (negligible in developed economies) of banking failure. From these attributes we can see that a bank deposit (current account) though not legal tender, is a very convenient form of money which can easily be transferred in settlement of indebtedness. This accounts for its widespread popularity. In essentials it is, of course, like legal tender money, no more than an acknowledgement of indebtedness and a promise to pay legal tender to the (deposit) holder on demand.

What is the relative popularity of these two types of debt as money in developed countries? Recalling our earlier definition of the money supply in the hands of the public, Table 14.1 presents statistics of the three components in recent years. The Table makes plain the overwhelming importance of bank-money.

4 DEBTS AND LIQUIDITY

All token money, it seems, is debt but not all debt is money. What is the relationship between the debts which are money and the debts which are not?

Money, as we know, serves as an asset or store of value. So too do a variety of other acknowledgements of debt such as Savings Bank deposits, bonds, debentures and shares. It is obvious, therefore, that as assets these claims are all, in differing degrees, substitutes for money. Money, however, alone possesses the property of being generally acceptable in settlement of debt. Hence the holder of money may, at any time, convert his holding into any other type of asset he wants. In doing so, he *shifts* his money holding to someone else in exchange for, let us say, a bond. In a market economy money is therefore the most readily *shiftable* of assets and one which, in view of its general acceptability, enjoys, from the point of view of any individual, a perfect market. Moreover, if the price level in general is stable (or relatively so) money can be converted into other assets without loss: that is money enjoys *capital certainty*. These two attributes, *shiftability* and *capital certainty* are the determinants of *liquidity*. Because money possesses them in greater measure than other claims on real goods it is the *most liquid of all assets* and an object of *liquidity preference* on the part of the public. These ideas are familiar to us since we have already sketched them briefly in our outline of the liquidity preference theory of interest.

Now it is easy to see that *all assets*, from secondhand running shoes to British government bonds, possess *some* measure of shiftability and price certainty. The liquidity of any asset is therefore a matter of degree. The greater the measure of shiftability and price certainty possessed by an asset, the greater its substitutability for money, or, to put the same point rather differently, the greater its 'moneyness'. All assets are liquid; but some are more liquid than others. In general, claims of various kinds are relatively liquid assets when compared with goods.

If shiftability is a necessary condition for liquidity, what confers it upon an asset? This question can best be answered by taking a look at a particular asset as an example, let us say a government bond.

The holder of a bond who wishes to sell it experiences few difficulties. There are well organised markets for dealing in claims including bonds. These are the stock exchanges. Disposal of a bond therefore entails little more than a telephone call to a broker. Since bond prices are quoted daily, dealings in bonds frequent, while bond markets contain many participants, any individual wishing to sell his bond holding will know the price he will obtain within very narrow limits for, unless he is a Rockefeller or a Getty, sale of his holdings is unlikely to influence market prices. Bonds are clearly very readily shiftable because they enjoy an active, highly organised and near perfect market. We may conclude that *marketability* confers *shiftability*.

Marketability is, as we have seen, a sufficient condition for shiftability. This, however, does not make it a necessary condition. Some assets, because of *special institutional arrangements*, are also highly shiftable though they are non-marketable. A good example of such an asset is provided by Post Office Savings Bank deposits. These are wholly without a market. Nevertheless, their conditions of issue are such that any holder of them can demand their conversion into legal tender by the State. They can, in other words, be shifted since, provided the depositor gives the necessary notice, the Post Office will convert them into legal tender. Fixed (or time) deposits with the commercial banks are further examples of the same type of shiftability though they are not marketable. Assets of this kind are shiftable because they are encashable.

As regards the first attribute of liquidity, namely shiftability, we reach the general conclusion that it can be conferred either by the existence of a market or by special institutional arrangements. What of the second attribute, *capital certainty*? The prices of marketable assets are subject to fluctuation, though those of encashable assets are not. Savings Bank deposits and fixed deposits with the commercial banks are examples of encashable assets whose money values are invariant. Marketable assets, however, do fluctuate in price though some, such as bonds, fluctuate relatively less than most.

Shares and debentures which, provided they are *quoted* on the Stock Exchange, enjoy a good measure of marketability, experience wider price fluctuations than bonds while commodities, the markets for which are usually imperfect, are particularly subject to price changes.

From this discussion, despite its brevity, we are sufficiently familiar with the meaning of liquidity to attempt a rough liquidity ranking of assets, a ranking in order of their money-ness. We set it out, in diagrammatical form in Fig. 14.iii.

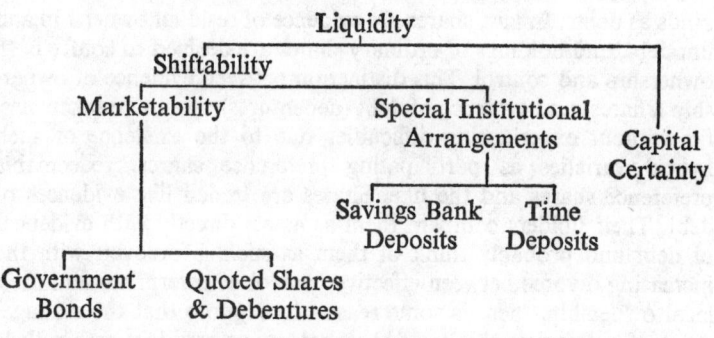

FIG. 14.iii

Now, keeping in the forefront of our minds the reasoning underlying Fig. 14.iii, we may attempt a purely ordinal ranking. This is set out

Table 14.2 *The Liquidity Ranking of Claims*

Type of asset	Liability of:	Classification	General grouping
Coin	State		
Notes	Central Bank	Money	
Demand Deposits	Commercial Banks		
Savings Bank Deposits	Post Office Savings Bank	Near-Moneys	Liquid Assets
Time Deposits	Commercial Banks		
Bonds	State	Marketable Government securities	
Local Government Bonds	Local Government		
Debentures (quoted)	Corporate Enterprises	Marketable securities	
Preference Shares (quoted)	,,　　　,,		
Ordinary Shares (quoted)	,,　　　,,		
Debentures (unquoted)	,,　　　,,	Non-marketable securities	
Preference Shares (unquoted)	,,　　　,,		
Ordinary Shares (unquoted)	,,　　　,,		

in Table 14.2. This Table is confined to claims (or acknowledgements of debt) since real assets are, in general, less liquid than claims.

A few comments on this Table may assist the reader. The first three items, that is, money, near-moneys, and marketable government securities, are sometimes called the *liquid assets of the public*. In discussions of the role of liquid assets in promoting inflation it is these three groups which are being considered. This is the first point to note.

The reader will also perceive that we have treated shares of all kinds as debts. In law, shares are evidence of residual ownership and not debt, and holdings of ordinary shares are deemed to confer both ownership and control. This distinction between evidence of ownership (shares) and evidence of debt (debentures) cannot be taken very far without experiencing difficulties due to the existence of such hybrid varieties as participating preference shares, redeemable preference shares and the like. Shares are traded like evidences of debt. Their holders compare them as assets directly with evidences of debt and probably think of them as such. Moreover, with the increasing divorce between effective control of enterprises and their legal ownership, there is some reason to suppose that the management of enterprises thinks of shareholders as creditors rather than owners. For all these reasons, as well as convenience, we have treated shares of all types as debts.

Finally, the reader will notice that although our Table lists thirteen categories of claim, it is far from comprehensive. Two points are worth noting in this respect. First the reader may derive much benefit from considering, in the light of our discussion, where claims which we have not listed would be placed in the Table. Second, the Table suggests that, in developed economies, there exists a highly complex network of claims arising from the fact that the liabilities of one group are the assets of another. This second point emphasises the level of abstraction at which we discussed interest theory in Chapter 11.

5 SUMMARY

In this chapter we have been concerned to justify the definition of the money supply we put forward in Chapter 11. To provide such a justification we had first to examine the function of money in a modern developed economy and then indicate which *things* performed these functions. The answer we found was consistent with our earlier definition.

Next we asked what *were* the things which constituted the money supply? Our examination showed that modern money consists of debt issued either by the central bank (in Britain the Bank of England) or the commercial banks (in Britain such banks as Lloyds, National Westminster and so on). In short modern money, which is an asset to its holder, is the liability of some banking institution on which it is a claim.

After this we considered the characteristics of money as an asset and found that, *given reasonable price stability,* money was the most 'liquid' of all assets. This justified our earlier argument that, in a model assuming constant prices money was *perfectly liquid* and, as an asset, provided a way of holding wealth, which, at zero or negligible storage costs, possessed also a convenience yield. This sustained our earlier argument that to induce them to sacrifice this convenience (overcome this liquidity preference) and hold wealth in the form of claims which were *not* money, wealth owners would require to receive a reward in the form of a rate of interest.

Finally we showed that though, in our highly simplified model, there is by assumption only *one* type of interest bearing claim (bonds) in reality there is a whole range of claims. This complication we shall continue to ignore basing our theory, as in Chapter 11, on the assumption that only three forms of asset exist: namely money, bonds and goods.

QUESTIONS AND EXERCISES

1. Rank the following assets in order as to 'shiftability' and 'capital certainty'. Give your reasons. Then insert them into their appropriate place in Table 14.2:

   (i) building society deposits;
   (ii) shares in British Leyland;
   (iii) an I.O.U. from the most honest man you know;
   (iv) a traveller's cheque issued to you by Barclays Bank;
   (v) a 1970 model Triumph Herald;
   (vi) a portrait of one of your ancestors by an unknown artist (believed 'in the family' to be Gainsborough);
   (vii) a Norman Castle on Romney Marsh.

2. It is sometimes hard to change notes into coin. In what circumstances, if any, would a pound note exchange for less than one

hundred p in coin? Why do these circumstances rarely, if ever, arise?

3. Can a millionaire ever be short of money? If so, how?

4. 'The introduction of a decimal currency – as expected – raised all prices and made us all worse off.' Discuss.

5. Suppose prices are expected to rise by 2 per cent during the year. On this assumption reconsider the ranking of assets given in Table 14.2. Is money's ranking affected? If so why?

6. Is a credit card money? Does the issue of Barclay cards increase the money supply?

7. 'Price certainty' is said to exist when an asset can be sold on a large organised market with frequent quotations. Is 'price certainty' related to 'capital certainty'? Give your reasons.

8. Can you describe an asset which has complete 'capital certainty' but virtually no 'liquidity'?

9. 'To hold long-term bonds confers "income certainty": to hold short-term bonds or Treasury bills confers "capital certainty".' Elucidate. Use your explanation to estimate the way in which (i) the childless widow of a retired senior civil servant and (ii) a bank, would distribute a portfolio of £100,000 over (a) money; (b) Treasury bills; (c) long-term bonds. Would it matter if this widow was not childless?

10. 'A banker is a man who is in the fortunate position of having his I.O.U.'s acceptable as money.' Explain.

SUGGESTED READING

W. T. Newlyn, *The Theory of Money* (Oxford, 1971) ch. i.
R. S. Sayers, *Modern Banking*, 7th ed. (Oxford, 1967) chs i, ii, vii, viii.
B. Tew, *Wealth and Income*, 4th ed. (Cambridge, 1964) chs i–vii.

15 Commercial Banks and the Money Supply

IN the previous chapter we saw that modern money consists of two components: (i) demand deposits with the commercial banks; (ii) notes. Of these the first, and most important component, consists of liabilities of the *commercial banks*, the second of liabilities of the *central bank*. Since we have defined the money supply as:

the nominal value of demand deposits and notes held by the non-bank public

it follows that, to explain its determination, we must examine the behaviour of the commercial banks and the central bank for, just as an individual controls the nominal value of the I.O.U.s he issues, so do banks and, in doing so, the latter control the money supply.

1 COMMERCIAL BANKS: DEFINITION AND FUNCTIONS

A bank may be defined as an institution which

(i) accepts deposits which are subject to transfer by cheque; and
(ii) makes loans and advances.

Since deposits are tokens of indebtedness *by* banks while advances are tokens of indebtedness *to* banks it is clear that, like other financial institutions which borrow from the public in order to acquire a portfolio of financial assets, banks are dealers in debts. Commercial banks are, broadly speaking, those which perform the two functions above by dealing mainly with households and enterprises. The special significance of commercial banks, which distinguishes them from other financial institutions such as life assurance offices, lies in the fact that the principal type of liability which they issue to the public, demand deposits, is customary money and in developed societies is the most important kind of money. By increasing or reducing their borrowing from the public, that is by expanding or contracting their deposit liabilities, commercial banks can plainly exert an important influence on the money supply: or, to put the matter another way, they can act as either manufacturers (or destroyers) of money.

Commercial banks, like other privately owned enterprises, are concerned to earn profits for their shareholders. In explaining their behaviour, therefore, the first question we need to ask is how do their profits arise?

Commercial banks have three main sources of revenue. These are:

    (i) the interest *received* on their asset portfolio;

    (ii) charges made for the operation of current accounts; and

    (iii) the commissions earned by them on the provision of particular services.

Against the sum of these must be set two main items of expenditure:

    (iv) the interest *paid* by banks to induce persons to hold their deposits; and

    (v) their operating expenses, i.e. salaries of managers and clerks, stationery, rent, and so on.

If we look at the revenue items it is easy to see that the income received from interest on the asset portfolio must be of major importance.

We are already familiar with the fact that different types of claim carry different rates of return. This is true of bank assets. Notes and coin, for example, provide no money return to their holder. Treasury bills usually offer a low return. Securities (government bonds) are typically† more remunerative returning perhaps, from 3–5 per cent while advances, the most remunerative of all bank assets, might provide 5–7 per cent. Plainly, given the magnitude of its asset portfolio, any commercial bank will enjoy a higher average rate of return the greater is the proportion of the higher yielding assets in its portfolio. Hence, bearing it in mind that they aim to maximise profits, commercial banks might be expected to aim at holding a large part of their portfolios as advances and securities.

Commercial banks, however, must, when selecting their asset distributions, take full account of their obligations to depositors. Holders of a bank's deposits are its creditors to the extent of their balances in its books. It is the obligation of the bank to pay its creditors, that is, encash its deposits if asked to do so by giving legal tender money (notes) on demand (to holders of demand deposits) or at the end of a stated period (to holders of time deposits). Any bank's ability to do this depends upon the liquidity of its asset portfolio. The greater the liquidity of the asset portfolio the greater the bank's ability to encash its deposits if called upon to do so: that is the greater its ability to meet the fundamental obligation of deposit banking.

† Rates are currently far higher than those quoted.

In modern developed economies the rates of return on financial assets tend to be inversely related to their liquidity. Hence, while the need to earn profits pulls commercial banks towards high-yielding (illiquid) asset portfolios, the need to keep liquid pulls them in the reverse direction. The distribution of assets actually chosen by banks thus represents a compromise between the *conflicting claims of profitability and liquidity*. This argument is illustrated in Table 15.A1 which, on the basis of assumed rates of return on the various categories of asset presents a clear contrast between liquid and illiquid asset portfolios.

Table 15.A1   *Alternative Asset Distributions of Bank X†, ‡*

Liabilities		(1)			Asset distributions Return in per cent per annum (2)	A (3)	B (4)
1. Shareholders' funds	} 100	Liquid Assets	Cash {	Coin	0	50	500
				Notes	0	25	400
				Dep. at central bank	0	85	100
Capital reserves }				Treasury bills	1	200	400
2. Deposits							
Demand	1,000	Risk Assets	Earning Assets {	Government securities	3	520	120
Time	500			Advances	5	720	80
TOTAL LIABILITIES	1,600			TOTAL ASSETS		1,600	1,600

† Certain assets such as bank premises have been neglected.
‡ The rates of return assumed in col. (2) have been chosen arbitrarily. However, they are not unreasonable historically,

	Distribution	
	A	B
1. Average rate of return on asset portfolio	$2\frac{11}{16}\%$	1%
2. Ratio of cash to total liabilities	10%	$62\frac{1}{2}\%$
3. Ratio of liquid assets to total	$22\frac{1}{2}\%$	$87\frac{1}{2}\%$

It is easy to see, from this table, that distribution A offers the bank concerned a higher average return ($2\frac{11}{16}$ per cent) than distribution B (approximately 1 per cent). On the other hand A is markedly less liquid a portfolio than B.

Notes, coin, and demand deposits at the central bank may be regarded as constituting the *cash holding* of the bank. Deposits at the central bank are included since, like notes, they are central bank liabilities and the central bank will convert them into legal tender on demand. The ratio of cash to total liabilities (the cash ratio) is one rather crude index of the liquidity of an asset portfolio. With distribution A this ratio is 10 per cent; with B 62½ per cent. A second rough measure of liquidity is the ratio of cash plus Treasury bills† to total liabilities. This is sometimes called the 'liquid assets' ratio. The table shows this ratio to be 22½ per cent in A and 87½ per cent in B. Both ratios, of course, are greater in the lower yielding portfolio B. It is also clear that there are, in principle, an infinite number of differing asset portfolios possible. The selection of bank portfolios is thus, though it always requires a compromise between profitability and liquidity, a highly complicated matter. Can we be more precise regarding the likely ratios?

Each business day the customers of any bank are drawing out and paying in legal tender money. Since receipts and payments do not match precisely the bank will need, as till money, certain minimum working balances. Moreover, beyond these minimum working balances, banks will require a secondary precautionary reserve to cover unexpected demands on deposits. Since cash provides no income the bank will economise in cash to the limit of its ability and, where possible, hold its *secondary reserves* in the form of readily shiftable interest bearing assets of high capital certainty such as Treasury bills. In making its decisions regarding the cash and liquid asset ratios a bank will rely heavily upon past experience. Past experience will give a good guide to the minimum of till money required. And past experience will provide a fair guide to the probable fluctuation in deposits. Thus, on the basis of its accumulated experience over the years any bank is likely to develop fairly fixed notions regarding its desired cash and liquid asset ratios. In some cases, particularly in the United Kingdom, the conventional cash and liquid asset ratios have, over the years, become – at least in the case of the cash ratios – very close to unwritten laws. In most countries with highly developed financial systems there is a considerable degree of stability in these ratios.

Once the bank has assured itself of sufficient cash and liquid assets the remainder of its portfolio can be allocated between government securities and advances. These are sometimes called 'illiquid' or 'risk' assets.

This brief discussion of the principles underlying banks' choice of assets leads to the following conclusions:

(i) banks' asset portfolios represent a compromise between the claims of profitability and liquidity;

† Or other assets of equivalent 'liquidity'.

(ii) in developed financial systems banks commonly establish conventions regarding:
  (a) the desired ratio of cash to total (or deposit) liabilities;
  (b) the desired ratio of liquid assets to total (or deposit) liabilities;
(iii) these conventions are based on the accumulated experience of the past and usually change only rather slowly.

2 DEPOSIT CREATION IN WHICH THE COMMERCIAL BANKS ARE ACTIVE

We have already spoken of the commercial banks' ability to vary the money supply by the creation or destruction of deposits. How and why are deposits created and destroyed?

In examining these questions it is convenient to begin with the assumption that the commercial banking system consists of a single bank. Suppose this is so; how can that bank's deposits increase? We may distinguish two general cases: that in which the bank is the active or initiating agent and that in which it is passive. Let us consider the former category first.

Commercial bankers in general are in the happy position that their I.O.U.s are accepted as money by the community. To purchase an asset from a member of the public and thus increase its earnings, our bank has merely to draw a cheque upon itself. Since the recipient of the cheque must bank with it, the consequence of such a purchase is to increase its deposit liabilities by the amount of the cheque paid to whoever is selling the asset to the bank, and increase the bank's assets by the value of the asset purchase, plainly an equal amount. Such a transaction can be illustrated very simply.

We assume our single bank to begin operations with its liabilities and assets in the following position.

Bank *X*; Position 1
(£ m.)

Liabilities		Assets	
Deposits	1,000	Cash	100
		Securities	400
		Advances	500
	1,000		1,000

Bank X now decides to purchase £10 millions of government securities. It does so by sending an order to its broker who purchases these securities in the market from John Smith and Peter Robinson each of whom receive cheques for £5 millions drawn by Bank X on itself. Both these individuals will have accounts with Bank X into which they will pay the cheques. Their deposits, Bank Xs liabilities, will accordingly rise by £10 millions. At the same time Bank Xs security portfolio will expand by £10 millions. Thus we reach Position 2.

Bank X; Position 2
(£ m.)

Liabilities		Assets		
Deposits (Pos. 1)	1,000	Cash		100
plus J. Smith	5	Securities (Pos. 1)	400	
plus P. Robinson	5	plus purchases from		
		J. Smith	5	
	1,010	P. Robinson	5	410
		Advances		500
Total liabilities	1,010	Total assets		1,010

This simple transaction has had the following obvious consequences:

    (i) Bank Xs deposit liabilities *and hence the money supply* have increased by £10 millions;

   (ii) the public is now holding an additional £10 millions of money;

  (iii) Bank X is now holding an additional £10 millions of *earning assets*.

Moreover, it has had the additional consequence, which is not too obvious, of *reducing Bank Xs cash ratio from 10 per cent in position 1 to 9·9 per cent in position 2*.

Now it can be objected to this example that Messrs Smith and Robinson would probably not be willing to hold the whole of their additional money balances in the form of bank deposits but would keep a portion of them in notes and coin. Let us suppose that this is the case and Smith and Robinson decide to hold $\frac{1}{5}$ of their increased money balances in the form of legal tender. With this assumption we reach position 2a.

Bank X; Position 2a
(£ m.)

Liabilities		Assets		
Deposits (Pos. 1)	1,000	Cash (Pos. 1)	100	
		less withdrawals by		
plus J. Smith	4	J. Smith	1	
plus P. Robinson	4	P. Robinson	1	98
Total deposits		Securities (as Pos. 2)		410
(Pos. 2a)	1,008			
		Advances		500
	1,008			1,008

Corresponding with Position 2a the additional money holdings of Robinson and Smith would be:

	J. Smith	P. Robinson	Total
Bank deposits	4	4	8
Notes or coin	1	1	2
	5	5	10

In this case (2a) we have the additional consequences that:

(i) Bank Xs *cash holding* has been reduced;

(ii) its cash ratio has fallen rather more sharply to approximately 9·7 per cent. Hence, on the basis of this simple example we are justified in reaching the following tentative conclusions:

    (a) A bank may increase its deposits and hence the money supply by purchasing any asset from the public.

    (b) Such an increase in its deposits will involve a fall in its cash to deposits ratio.

    (c) The fall in this ratio will be greater the greater the proportion of the increase in the money supply which the public wishes to hold in the form of legal tender notes and coin.

Let us now see what would happen if Bank X grants additional advances for, say, £10 millions. Let us suppose such advances are granted first of all as a loan to the XYZ Manufacturing Co. Ltd. Since the advance is made as a *loan* the balance of the XYZ Co.

rises by £10 millions. Hence deposit liabilities increase by £10 millions while there is an equal increase in advances. We move, therefore, from Position 1 to Position 3.

Bank *X*; Position 3
(£ m.)

Liabilities			Assets		
Deposits (Pos. 1)	1,000		Cash		100
plus new deposits			Securities		400
of XYZ Manf.			Advances (Pos. 1)	500	
Co. Ltd.	10	1,010	plus new advance		
			of XYZ Manf. Co.	10	510
Total liabilities	1,010		Total assets		1,010

If the advance is granted as an overdraft the matter is a little more complicated since the *granting* of the overdraft does not in itself alter the Bank's balance sheet. Indeed, all that is likely to occur is the receipt by the XYZ Co. of a letter from Bank *X* authorising it to overdraw its existing balance up to £10 million if it wishes to do so. Only as the XYZ Co. makes use of this facility by drawing cheques in favour of, say, Robinson and Smith is there any change in deposits and the amount of advances. For example, let us suppose the XYZ Co. pays £8 million to Smith and £2 million to Robinson. Then we have a new Position 3a.

Bank *X* Position 3a
(£ m).

Liabilities			Assets		
Deposits (Pos. 1)	1,000		Cash		100
plus J. Smith	8		Securities		400
plus P. Robinson	2	1,010	Advances (Pos. 1)	500	
			plus overdraft		
			XYZ Co.	10	510
		1,010			1,010

It is clear from comparison of Positions 2, 3 and 3a that granting an advance, whether in the form of a loan or an overdraft, has the same effect on the balance sheet position of Bank X as the purchase of an equivalent amount of securities, though, in the case of an overdraft, the balance sheet is not altered until the overdraft facilities are actually used. Our tentative conclusions are thus perfectly general. If Bank X sets out to increase its earning assets the consequences are first an increase in its deposit liabilities, and hence in the money supply, and second a fall in its cash ratio.

What are the limits upon bank expansion of this type? We have already noticed that banks tend to maintain a conventional (or legally imposed) cash ratio. As long as this is the case, the planned cash ratio, *given the extent* of the bank's existing cash holding, is sufficient to define a maximum of deposit liabilities and to place a limit upon *active* deposit creation by banks. To see this, we need only to look back to Position 1. At that stage Bank Xs cash ratio was 10 per cent. If 10 per cent had been the Bank's planned ratio, the expansions in our examples would never have taken place since each involved *a fall in the actual cash ratio*. The effect of adopting a rigid cash ratio convention is thus to remove final control of the volume of its deposits from Bank X. Whatever its cash holding Bank X will now buy (or sell) securities and grant (or recall) advances until its cash holdings represent 10 per cent of its deposits. This means that the money supply is determined by (i) the cash ratio, which determines the volume of bank deposits which can be based upon a given cash holding; and (ii) whatever influences determine the magnitude of the Bank's cash holdings.

3 DEPOSIT CREATION IN WHICH THE COMMERCIAL BANKS ARE PASSIVE

Now that we have seen how a bank may create deposits actively let us examine how deposits may alter when the bank is passive.

There are certain assets which a commercial bank will always purchase if offered to it by any individual (or enterprise) and thus create a deposit in his (its) favour. These assets are (i) legal tender notes and coin; (ii) the obligations of other banks; (iii) foreign exchange. To illustrate these possibilities let us start again from Position 1 and assume that the public now decides that it would rather hold £10 million of its existing money holdings as bank deposits than as notes. Accordingly it pays £10 millions to the credit of its accounts with Bank X. Thus we reach Position 4.

Bank *X*; Position 4
(£ m.)

Liabilities			Assets		
Deposits (Pos. 1)	1,000		Cash (Pos. 1)	100	
			plus new cash	10	110
New deposits	10	1,010			
			Securities		400
			Advances		500
		1,010			1,010

The consequences of this decision on the part of the public are:

(i) to increase their deposits with Bank *X* by £10 millions;
(ii) to increase Bank *X*s cash holdings by £10 million;
(iii) to leave the public's money holdings (the money supply) unaltered. The public are now holding an additional £10 million of deposits (bank money) but £10 million less of legal tender money (notes);
(iv) to increase Bank *X*s cash ratio from 10 per cent to 10·9 per cent.

Bank *X* if it wishes can now set about restoring its cash ratio to 10 per cent by undertaking an *active* expansion of deposits through, for example, the purchase of £90 millions worth of additional securities. With the Bank's cash ratio restored to equilibrium we reach this position:

Bank *X*; Position 5
(£ m.)

Liabilities			Assets		
Deposits (Pos. 1)	1,000		Cash (Pos. 1)	100	
plus passively			plus new cash	10	110
created	10		Securities (Pos.		
plus actively			1)	400	
created	90	1,100	plus new		
			purchases	90	490
			Advances		500
		1,100			1,100

In Position 5 we can see that Bank *X*, by purchasing an additional £90 millions of securities, has expanded its deposits sufficiently to restore its desired cash ratio of 10 per cent. This final position is reached, it is worth noticing, by an expansion in which the bank was first passive and then active.

The second type of asset which a bank will always purchase is a claim upon another bank. We have assumed Bank X to be the only commercial bank in the system. The only other bank on which claims may be issued is therefore the central bank. Let us assume that John Smith has a cheque drawn on the central bank for £10 millions. This he pays into his account at Bank X. We reach Position 6.

Bank X; Position 6
(£ m.)

Liabilities			Assets	
Deposits (Pos. 1)	1,000		Cash	100
			Claim on central	
plus J. Smith	10	1,010	bank	10
			Securities	400
			Advances	500
		1,010		1,010

At the conclusion of the day's business Bank X will present its claim upon the central bank and the central bank will credit Bank Xs account with itself. Accordingly we reach Position 7.

Bank X; Position 7
(£ m.)

Liabilities		Assets		
Deposits (Pos. 6)	1,010	Cash (Pos. 6)	100	
		plus new deposit		
		at c.b.	10	110
		Securities		400
		Advances		500
	1,010			1,010

Again we see that Bank Xs cash holding has increased by £10 millions. This is because Bank X holds part of its cash in the form of deposits at the central bank. Such deposits from its point of view are cash. Hence its cash holdings have increased and its cash ratio risen once more, as in Position 4, to 10·9 per cent. Once again it can undertake an active expansion to Position 5.

If John Smith had received his deposit at Bank X not because of a £10 millions cheque on the central bank but because he had sold £10 millions of foreign exchange we should have had a similar process. This is shown below at Positions 6a and 7a.

Bank X; Position 6a
(£m.)

Liabilities			Assets	
Deposits (Pos. 1)	1,000		Cash	100
J. Smith	10	1,010	Foreign exchange	10
			Securities	400
			Advances	500
		1,010		1,010

At the close of business Bank X will sell the foreign exchange to the central bank. This is usually done since commercial banks hold only small working balances of foreign exchange and sell any surplus to the central bank. Thus we reach Position 7a which is identical with Position 7.

Bank X; Position 7a
(£m.)

Liabilities		Assets		
Deposits (Pos. 6a)	1,010	Cash (Pos. 6)	100	
		plus new deposits		
		at c.b.	10	110
		Securities		400
		Advances		500
	1,010			1,010

This last case is very important since when any country's balance of payments is in surplus, that is, its inhabitants are receiving more foreign exchange than they are paying out, there will be net sales of foreign exchange to the commercial bank(s). It is therefore essential to notice that not only does the country concerned gain foreign exchange in such circumstances but that there is: (i) an equal rise in both the deposits and cash holdings of the commercial banks; and (ii) a rise in the cash ratio.

We may thus conclude that a passive expansion of commercial bank deposits, commercial bank cash holdings, and a rise in the cash ratio of commercial banks may be brought about by

  (i) an increase in the public's preference for holding their money as bank deposits rather than notes and coin (Position 4).†
 (ii) deposit by the public at the commercial banks of cheques drawn upon the central bank (Positions 6 and 7);
(iii) net sales by the public to the commercial banks of foreign exchange resulting from a surplus on the balance of payments (Positions 6a and 7a).

Any one of these will make possible an active (secondary) expansion by the commercial banks (Position 5).

In practice the public's preferences regarding the form in which they wish to hold their stocks of money are fairly stable in the short run. Hence the principal short-run determinants of the cash holdings of the commercial banks and, in consequence, of the money supply are: first, the behaviour of the central bank; second, the state of the balance of payments.

4 SEVERAL COMMERCIAL BANKS

Our analysis so far has been based upon the simplifying assumption of a commercial banking system consisting of a single bank – Bank X. Do our conclusions hold if more than one bank is introduced? This is an important question for, as a matter of fact, there are no countries where the commercial banking system consists of only one bank. In order to answer it we therefore present a single example involving not only Bank X but also Banks Y and Z. Our single assumption is that each bank maintains a 10 per cent cash ratio.

We begin our example by assuming (Position 1) that Banks Y and Z each have a cash ratio of 10 per cent. Bank X, however, has recently experienced a £10 millions increase in both deposits and cash giving it a ratio of 10·9 per cent. What happens when Bank X expands its advances portfolio by, say, £30 millions in order to restore its cash ratio?

As these advances are spent it is plain that not all the deposits created will be with Bank X. Since the banks are of roughly equal size it is reasonable to assume that $\frac{1}{3}$ of the advances are paid to customers of Y and Z. Each of these banks will therefore experience

† This is *not* a change in liquidity preference which relates to the public's plans to hold money rather than bonds.

Table 15.2

Position 1

	Bank X				Bank Y				Bank Z	
Dep. 1,010	Cash	110	Dep. 1,000	Cash	100	Dep. 1,000	Cash	100
	Securities	400		Securities	600		Securities	200
	Advances	500		Advances	300		Advances	700
1,010		1,010	1,000		1,000	1,000		1,000

Cash ratio: 10·9%   Cash ratio: 10%   Cash ratio: 10%

Position 2
(After Bank X has expanded advances by £30 millions)

	Bank X				Bank Y				Bank Z	
Dep. 1,020	Cash	90	Dep. 1,010	Cash	110	Dep. 1,010	Cash	110
	Securities	400		Securities	600		Securities	200
	Advances	530		Advances	300		Advances	700
1,020		1,020	1,010		1,010	1,010		1,010

Cash ratio: 8·8%   Cash ratio: 10·9%   Cash ratio: 10·9%

Position 3
(After Banks Y and Z have expanded their security portfolios by £15 millions)

	Bank X				Bank Y				Bank Z	
Dep. 1,030	Cash	100	Dep. 1,020	Cash	105	Dep. 1,020	Cash	105
	Securities	400		Securities	615		Securities	215
	Advances	530		Advances	300		Advances	700
1,030		1,030	1,020		1,020	1,020		1,020

Cash ratio: 9·7%   Cash ratio: 10·3%   Cash ratio: 10·3%

Position 4
(After all adjustments have been completed)

	Bank X				Bank Y				Bank Z	
Dep. 1,040	Cash	104	Dep. 1,030	Cash	103	Dep. 1,030	Cash	103
	Securities	400		Securities	627		Securities	227
	Advances	536		Advances	300		Advances	700
1,040		1,040	1,030		1,030	1,030		1,030

Cash ratio: 10%   Cash ratio: 10%   Cash ratio: 10%

Increase in bank deposits (Position 4–Position 1)
Bank X (1,040–1,010) = £30 millions
Bank Y (1,030–1,000) = £30 millions
Bank Z (1,030–1,000) = £30 millions
Total commercial banking system = £90 millions.

a £10 millions increment in deposits against which they will hold £10 millions of cheques drawn on X. At the end of the day's business these cheques will be presented to X for payment. X will settle in cash and will thus find its cash reserves reduced by £20 millions. *This cash, is, however, not lost to the commercial banks as a whole.* It merely passes from X to Y and Z, who now find both their cash holdings and cash ratios increased. This brings us to Position 2.

In Position 2 both Y and Z are under some incentive to expand their earning assets. Let us assume that each decides to expand their earning assets by purchasing £15 millions of securities. Each will now lose cash to the other two. *Y*s losses to *Z* will be exactly offset by *Z*s losses to *Y*. Each, however, will lose $\frac{1}{3}$ of £15 millions to *X*. In other words *X* will gain deposits and cash to the value of £10 millions. In this way we reach Position 3. Finally, by further adjustments we reach Position 4 in which each bank has restored its cash ratio to 10 per cent and *the commercial banking system* as a whole is fully adjusted to the £10 millions increment in its cash base which was the cause of the expansion.

It is easy to see that the expansion of deposits (and hence the money supply) has been precisely £90 millions. This, of course, is identical with the result obtained in an earlier example which was based upon a single bank. This suggests that our 'three bank' analysis allows us to draw the following conclusions.

(i) A system of deposit banks, *provided all expand* together, may increase deposits in response to an increment in their cash holdings to the full limit imposed by their cash ratio.

(ii) Hence, if in our earlier examples, Bank *X* is considered to stand for the commercial banking system, the conclusions reached in these examples may perfectly properly be applied to a 'commercial banking system' comprising several banks.

Our three bank analysis, however, also tells us rather more, for it is an obvious inference from the losses in cash experienced by Bank *X* (Position 2) that, in a multi-bank system, a single bank cannot, unless the other banks also participate, go very far in expanding deposits. With this lesson in mind the reader may safely apply all the conclusions, reached in our earlier analysis merely on the basis of Bank *X*, to a commercial banking system as a whole.

QUESTIONS AND EXERCISES

1. 'The principal function of commercial banks is to bring borrower and lender together'. Discuss.
2. Use the *Bank of England Bulletin* to prepare a table giving the rates of interest on (i) Treasury bills; (ii) trade bills; (iii) short-term bonds; (iv) medium term bonds; (v) long-term bonds; (vi) company debentures; (vii) industrial ordinary shares.

Are the lower rates to be obtained on the more 'liquid' assets?

Can you explain why ordinary shares yield *less* than bonds? To explain this, which assumption of our model have you to abandon?

3. 'A banker's business is founded on confidence'. Explain.
4. Why do some countries have a comparatively small proportion of bank deposits in their money supply?
5. 'An individual bank has little ability to expand the money supply unless all the other banks expand in step.' Elucidate.
6. Use the *Bank of England Bulletin* to compare the liabilities and assets of the London Clearing Banks with the hypothetical structure of Table 15.A1. Would our arguments need substantial revision before they could be applied to the Clearing Banks? If so what revisions would you propose?
7. Write short notes on: (i) Treasury bills; (ii) government bonds; (iii) advances.

What are the principal characteristics of each asset from the point of view of the banker? Base your notes on chapter vi of the Radcliffe Report.
8. 'A banker can lend no more than he can borrow'. 'A banker can create money and lend it where he will.' Comment. Are these two statements reconcilable?
9. In what circumstances would money lose its liquidity premium? Why?
10. Use the *Bank of England Bulletin* to examine the proposition that commercial banks tend to maintain stable asset/deposit ratios.

SUGGESTED READING

R. S. Sayers, *Modern Banking*, 7th ed. (Oxford, 1967) chs i–iii, viii.
W. T. Newlyn, *The Theory of Money* (Oxford, 1971) chs i–iii.
W. Manning Dacey, *The British Banking Mechanism* (Hutchinson, 1954) chs i–iii.
Radcliffe Report (H.M.S.O., 1959) chs i–iii.

16 Central Banking and the Money Supply

In the previous chapter we found that there were three determinants of the money supply:

(i) the *asset preferences* (cash/deposit ratio) of the commercial banks;

(ii) the *preferences of the non-bank public* regarding the *form* in which they wish to hold their *money* (i.e. as deposits or notes);

(iii) the *cash reserves* of the commercial banks.

Of these (i) and (ii) can as a first approximation be regarded as invariant in the short run. Hence the money supply is determined by the *cash reserves* of the commercial banks.

The importance of the central bank in developed monetary systems arises from the fact that it can control the cash reserves of the commercial banks. It follows that, in the short run, it is the policy of the central bank with regard to these reserves which determines the money supply.

We must now see how the power of the central bank to control the cash reserves of the commercial banks arises.

1 THE CENTRAL BANK AND ITS FUNCTIONS

The central bank is an institution, often but not always owned by the State, which has the overriding duty of conducting the monetary policy of the government. It is, in terms of our model, the duty of the central bank to control the money supply (and thus the rate of interest) in a manner which has an effect on aggregate demand which the government deems to be appropriate. *The general and overriding function of the central bank is thus discretionary monetary control.* Its particular functions, from which its capacity to perform its main function derive, are the following:

(i) it is the sole source of *legal tender money* (notes) which are central bank liabilities;

(ii) it acts as *bankers' bank* in that commercial banks keep accounts with the central bank just as individuals and enterprises keep accounts with commercial banks;

    (iii) it is the *government's banker* and keeps the main government accounts and provides the government with economic and financial advice;

    (iv) it *holds the gold and foreign exchange reserves* of the country;†

    (v) it acts, if the need arises, as *lender of last resort*;

    (vi) it *determines* (under the government) the *rate of exchange* between the domestic and foreign currencies;

    (vii) it manages the *government debt* (usually known as the national debt).

Just as the borrowing and lending activities of the commercial banks were reflected in their balance sheets, so too are the functions of a central bank. To see this consider the (highly simplified) central banking balance sheet set out in Table 16.B.1

Table 16.B1 *Balance Sheet of Central Bank of Erehwon*

Liabilities			Assets	
Notes			Gold and foreign exchange	100
with public	50		Securities	100
with banks	50	100		
Deposits				
of bankers	50			
of government	50	100		
Total liabilities		200		200

Note: This balance sheet neglects the following items which appear on central bank balance sheets:
    Liabilities: Capital and reserves; Other liabilities.
    Assets: Premises and equipment; Other assets.

On the *liabilities* side we have first *notes*, a part of which is in the tills of the commercial banks; a part of which is held by the *non-bank public* and thus, by definition, forms part of the money supply [function (i)].

The second liability consists of *deposits* – partly owned by the *commercial banks* and partly by the *government* [functions (ii) and (iii)].

As *assets* it holds first *gold and foreign exchange* [function (iv)] and, second, *government securities* which reflect past lending to the State [functions (i) and (iii)].

† This is not true of the United Kingdom where reserves are held by the Exchange Equalisation Account.

Table 16.B2 *Position I*

Central bank

Liabilities		Assets	
Notes		Gold and foreign exchange	100
with public	50	Securities	100
with banks	50		
Deposits			
of bankers	50		
of govt	50		
	200		200

Commercial banks

Liabilities		Assets	
Demand deposits	1,000	Cash: notes	50
		deposit at central bank	50 } 100
		Securities	500
		Advances	400
	1,000		1,000

Non-bank public

Holdings of notes	50
of deposits	1,000
Total money supply	1,050
Securities	5,000

Behaviour assumptions:

(i) Banks preferred cash ratio $= \dfrac{\text{Cash}}{\text{Deposits}} = 10\% = q$.

(ii) Non-bank public's preferred ratio of legal tender to customary money $= \dfrac{\text{Notes}}{\text{Deposits}} = 5\% = \alpha_1$

Other assumption:

total gross debt outstanding $=$ central bank holding $+$ commercial bank holdings $+$ non-bank public holdings

$= 100 + 500 + 5,000$

$= 5,600.$

Retaining this balance sheet let us now assume that (i) commercial banks have demand deposits equal to their total deposits; and (ii) have a planned cash/deposits ratio of 10 per cent. Then, since the commercial banks' *cash* (≡ note holdings *plus* deposits at the central bank) are 100, total commercial bank deposits are 1000 and demand deposits 1000. Since the non-bank public holds 50 units of notes, the money supply (≡ demand deposits *plus* notes held by the non-bank public) is 1050 units.

We have, in short, the position shown in Table 16.B2, p. 305.

We shall use this table, in the whole of what follows, to explain the consequences of central banking operations. From the table it is plain that if the central bank can vary the cash holding of the commercial banks it can vary the money supply. Let us see how this can be done.

2 THE CONTROL OF COMMERCIAL BANK CASH: OPEN MARKET OPERATIONS

Suppose the central bank purchases, in the open market, 10 units of bonds from members of the public. To pay for these it draws cheques on itself. These are paid into the commercial banks who present them to the central bank for payment. The central bank in response then credits the commercial banks with 10 units in its books. As a result, starting from Position 1 (Table 16.B2) we reach Position 2 (Table 16.B3, p. 307).

What has happened is this:

    (i) in the central banks balance sheet assets (securities) have increased by 10 units: so have liabilities (bankers' deposits);

   (ii) in the commercial banks' balance sheet assets (cash) have increased by 9·5 units: so have liabilities (demand deposits);

  (iii) in the non-bank public's balance sheets assets are unchanged *but* money holdings are *up* by 10 units, bond holdings *down* by a similar amount.

We thus see that, as a result of an *open-market purchase* of 10 units, there has been a *primary increase* in the money supply of 10 units.

Adjustment, however, cannot stop at the position depicted by 16.B3 for the *actual* cash/deposits ratio now exceeds the *planned* cash/deposits ratio of 10 per cent. Moreover the non-bank public is now holding too high a ratio of notes/deposits.

If the banks try to restore the cash/deposit ratio to its planned value they will expand their assets (by buying securities and/or making advances) and thus their deposits until the cash/ratio is

Table 16.B3 Position 2

Central bank

Liabilities		Assets	
Notes with public	50·5	Gold and foreign exchange	100
with banks	49·5	Securities	110
Deposits of bankers	60		
of govt	50		
	210		210

Commercial bank

Liabilities	Assets	
Deposits 1,009·5	Cash: notes	49·5
	deposit at central bank 60	109·5
	Securities	500
	Advances	400
1,009·5		1,009·5

Non-bank public

Holdings of notes 50·5
of deposits 1,009·5
Money supply 1,060
Securities 4,990

Table 16.B4 Position 3

Central bank

Liabilities		Assets	
Notes with public	53·33	Gold and foreign exchange	100
with banks	53·17 106·5	Securities	110
Deposits of bankers	53·5		
of govt	50 103·5		
	210		210

Commercial bank

Liabilities	Assets	
Deposits 1,066·67	Cash:	106·67
	Securities	550
	Advances	410
1,066·67		1,066·67

Non-bank public

Holdings of notes 53·33
of deposits 1,066·67
Money supply 1,120·0
Securities 4,990·0

restored to its planned value. This is known as the *secondary* increase in the money supply.

After the secondary expansion, the final Position 3 is reached. This is shown in Table 16.B4, p. 307.

It follows that our open market operation (purchase) has produced an increase in the money supply which is a multiple of itself. We have:

$$\text{total increase in money supply} \equiv \Delta M^S = 70$$

of which

$$\text{primary increase} \equiv X_1 = 10 \text{ units}$$

$$\text{secondary increase} \equiv X_2 \equiv 60 \text{ units}$$

There is, in short, a credit multiplier at work which we can define as:

$$\text{credit multiplier} \equiv \lambda \equiv \frac{\Delta M^S}{X_1} \equiv \frac{\text{total increase in money supply}}{\text{open market purchase}}$$

We can easily set up a *model* of this credit multiplier as follows:
By definition we have

$$M^S \equiv D + C_h \qquad (16.\text{B I})$$

where $D \equiv$ commercial bank deposits; $C_h \equiv$ non-bank public's holding of notes.

Assume the public's preferred ratio of $\dfrac{C_h}{D} = \alpha_1$ $\qquad (16.\text{B II})$

Then $\qquad\qquad\qquad M^S = D(1 + \alpha_1) \qquad (16.\text{B III})$

Now $\qquad\qquad\qquad D = \dfrac{C_b}{q} \qquad (16.\text{B IV})$

where $C_b \equiv$ commercial bank cash holdings; $q \equiv$ commercial bank planned cash ratio,
so that

$$M^S = (1 + \alpha_1)\frac{C_b}{q} \qquad (16.\text{B V})$$

But $\qquad\qquad\qquad C_b \equiv N + B_d - C_h \qquad (16.\text{B VI})$

where $N \equiv$ notes issued by central bank; $B_d \equiv$ bankers' deposits at the central bank; $C_h \equiv$ notes held by non-bank public, so that, if we substitute in (16.B VI) from (16.B II) we get

$$C_b = N + B_d - \alpha_1 \frac{C_b}{q}$$

$$C_b = (N + B_d) \frac{q}{q + \alpha_1} \qquad (16.\text{B VII})$$

Hence we have, on substituting again into (16.B V),

$$M^S = (N + B_d) \left(\frac{q}{q + \alpha_1} \right) \left(\frac{1 + \alpha_1}{q} \right)$$

$$= (N + B_d) \left(\frac{1 + \alpha_1}{q + \alpha_1} \right). \qquad (16.\text{B VIII})$$

An open market purchase of X_1 increases $N + B_d$ by X_1. Hence the credit multiplier is given by:

$$\frac{\Delta M^S}{X_1} \equiv \lambda = \left(\frac{1 + \alpha_1}{q + \alpha_1} \right) \qquad (16.\text{B IX})$$

In our example

$$\alpha_1 = \tfrac{1}{20} = 0 \cdot 05$$

$$q = \tfrac{1}{10} = 0 \cdot 10$$

therefore
$$\lambda = \frac{1 \cdot 05}{0 \cdot 15} = 7. \qquad (16.\text{B IXn})$$

Hence, as Table 16.B4 shows,

(i) the total increase in the money supply is 70 units of which, rounding up the figures,

the increase in deposits is   66·67 units

the increase in notes held by the non-bank public is

3·33 units

while

(ii) the increase in the banks' cash is   6·67 units

This model, it should be noticed, contains *two* behaviour assumptions (Equations 16.B II and 16.B IV), the former relating to the non-bank public, the latter to the commercial banks. Assuming these to hold we can generalise our conclusion by saying that

(i) *any* purchase (sale) of an asset by the central bank from (to) a member of the non-bank public brings about

    (a) a primary increase (decrease) in the money supply equal
to the value of the purchase (sale);

    (b) a secondary increase (decrease) in the money supply which
is a multiple of the primary increase (decrease);

  (ii) the magnitude of the total change in the money supply
depends upon

    (a) the value of the open market operation;

    (b) the commercial banks' preferred cash ratio;

    (c) the (marginal) ratio in which the non-bank public prefers
to hold deposits and notes.

As presented here the argument is formally symmetrical: an
open-market purchase of X_1 increases the money supply by λX_1;
an open market sale of X_1 reduces the money supply by λX_1. In
practice this may not be so. In general a central bank can always
compel a contraction: it cannot, however, *compel* an expansion. In
some circumstances the commercial banks may prefer – perhaps
because of uncertainty – to hold a cash/deposit ratio *above* the 10
per cent they usually prefer. Hence it is possible that the secondary
expansion resulting from a given open market *purchase may* be less
than the contraction resulting from a corresponding open market
sale. This qualification is worth noting.

What assets does the central bank buy and sell? Primarily, as our
example suggests, it buys and sells government securities. Purchases
(sales) of this kind, conducted on the market by the central bank's
broker, are called open market purchases (sales). They are the most
important single device which the central bank can use to control
the money supply.

In addition the central bank buys (sells) foreign exchange at whatever rate of exchange it wishes to maintain. Net purchases (sales) of
foreign exchange from the non-bank public have an influence on the
money supply of the type we have already discussed. However
where there is a fixed rate of exchange which the central bank (on
government instructions) seeks to maintain, the bank has no option
but to act as residual buyer or seller. If, for example, at the ruling
rate of exchange the demand for foreign exchange in terms of the
domestic currency exceeds the supply, *either* the rate of exchange
will move *against* the domestic currency to equate supply and demand
or the central bank must sell whatever foreign exchange is necessary
to satisfy demand. In conducting such residual net purchases (or
sales) the central bank is *passive*. It provides to (sells) or takes off
(purchases from) the market whatever is necessary to maintain the
price (rate of exchange). By contrast in open market operations the

Table 16.B5 Position 2a

Central bank

Liabilities			Assets	
Notes			Gold and foreign exchange	110
with public	50·5		Securities	100
with banks	49·5			
Deposits				
of bankers	60			
of govt	50			
		210		210

Commercial bank

Liabilities		Assets		
Deposits	1,009·5	Cash:		
		notes	49·5	
		deposit at central bank	60	109·5
		Securities		500
		Advances		400
	1,009·5			1,009·5

Non-bank public

Holdings	
of notes	50·5
of deposits	1,009·5
Money supply	1,060
Securities	5,000

Table 16.B6 Restriction of Money Supply by Means of Variation in Required Reserve Ratio

Central bank

Liabilities			Assets	
Notes			Gold and foreign exchange	100
with public	37·4		Securities	100
with banks	56·3	93·7		
Deposits				
of banks	56·3			
of govt	50	106·3		
		200		200

Commercial bank

Liabilities		Assets		
Deposits	750·1	Cash:		
		notes	56·3	
		deposits	56·3	112·6
		Securities		280·4
		Advances		357·1
	750·1			750·1

Commercial bank's cash ratio $= \dfrac{112·6}{750·1} \simeq 15\%$.

Non-bank public

Holdings	
of notes	37·4
of deposits	750·1
Money supply	787·5
Securities	5,219·6

central bank is *active* in the sense that, unless it is compelled to maintain an invariant rate of interest (fixed price for bonds) it chooses *when* open market operations are necessary and the scale on and direction in which they should be conducted.

To illustrate: suppose that, to maintain the rate of exchange at its existing level, the central bank has to purchase 10 units (in terms of domestic currency) of foreign exchange. Starting, as before, from Position 1 (Table 16.B2, p. 305) we reach Position 2a (Table 16.B5, p. 311).

Comparison of this table with Table 16.B3 (Position 2 of the earlier example) shows only one variation namely that, in this case, it is the central bank's holdings of *gold and foreign exchange* which have risen by 10 units *not* its holdings of government securities. Apart from this Positions 2 and 2a are identical. Hence since Position 2, via a *secondary* expansion, led to Position 3 so will Position 2a. This illustrates proposition (i) above, namely that *any* purchase (sale) of assets by the central bank from the non-bank public has the same consequences for the money supply.

Table 16.B5 shows that the central bank is holding, on behalf of the community, increased foreign reserves. An increase in reserves occurs whenever a country receives more foreign exchange (as export proceeds) than it pays out (in import costs). Hence, since this is simply a situation in which exports – imports > zero, the balance of payments is in surplus. We may add to our two previous propositions:

(iii) a balance of payments surplus (deficit) causes the central bank to purchase (sell) foreign exchange equal to the value of the surplus (deficit) in domestic currency.

(iv) this brings about

    (a) a primary increase (decrease) in the money supply equal to the surplus (deficit); and

    (b) a secondary increase (decrease) in the money supply determined in the usual way.

(v) as long as the balance of payments is in surplus (deficit) there will be a tendency for the money supply to undergo an expansion (contraction) which is a multiple of the surplus (deficit).

Finally it is worth noting that, if there is a *surplus* on the balance of payments of 10 units per period, the central bank can offset the impact of its consequential *passive* purchases of foreign exchange on the money supply by undertaking *active* open market *sales* of 10 units per period. This keeps its total assets, and hence the money

supply, constant. Such a policy is sometimes called *neutralisation*.†
Its distinguishing characteristic is that the central bank's domestic
assets (in our model securities) change in the opposite direction to its
external assets (gold and foreign exchange). In short, disequilibrium
on the balance of payments does not prevent the central bank from
determining the money supply though it may make it harder for it to
do so.

3 CONTROLLING BANK CASH: OTHER DEVICES

In some countries, Australia is a notable example, the central bank,
in its task of controlling the money supply, is faced by (i) very
large surpluses (deficits) on external account due primarily to sharp
fluctuations in the price of exports; and (ii) a market in securities
which is too small to permit the massive open market operations
necessary to achieve a reasonable measure of neutralisation. In
these circumstances central banks are usually given special legal
powers which enable them to control the commercial banks. Two
types are particularly well known. They are:

(i) powers to *vary* the ratio which commercial banks are *required*
to maintain between cash and deposits: known as the power
to employ 'variable reserve ratios';
(ii) powers to *freeze* a part of commercial bank deposits at the
central bank thus removing them, *by definition*, from the
commercial bank's *cash*; the frozen deposits are then defined
as 'Special Deposits' or 'Special Account Deposits', or some
such classification.

Essentially what happens in these cases is that the central bank,
finding itself unable to control the money supply by dealings with
the non-bank public, obtains legal powers to exert direct control
over the cash holdings of the commercial banks.

In our model, Equation (16.B VIII) gave an expression for the
equilibrium money supply in terms of:

$(N+B_d) \equiv$ notes issued by the central bank *plus* bankers' deposits
at the central bank

$q \equiv$ the preferred cash/deposits ratio of the commercial
banks

$\alpha_1 \equiv$ the ratio of the public holding of notes to deposits.

† The Exchange Equalisation Account automatically provides for
neutralisation in this sense.

Variation in the reserve ratio illustrated formally in terms of the model consists of an *enforced* variation in q. In such a case there is no *primary* change in the money supply. The total change is the *secondary* expansion or contraction forced upon the banks. Clearly if q is *raised* a *contraction* must result. If q is reduced an expansion may (if the banks wish) take place. This asymmetry simply reflects our earlier argument concerning open market operations. We can use Equation (16.B VIII) to illustrate. This is:

$$M^S = (N + B_d)\left(\frac{1+\alpha_1}{q+\alpha_1}\right)$$

or using Position 1,

$$M^S = (150) \times 7 = 1050$$

where

$$q = 0.10$$
$$\alpha_1 = 0.05$$
$$N = 100$$
$$B_d = 50$$

Suppose q is now said to become 0·15. In numerical terms the money supply becomes, as a result of a *secondary* contraction,

$$M_1^S = 150\left(\frac{1.05}{0.20}\right) = 787.5 \quad \text{or} \quad \lambda = 5.25$$

Clearly the variable reserve ratio device is potentially at least one of great power though, in practice, reserve ratios are unlikely to be varied as drastically as this example would suggest.

The alternative device, which we will call that of *special deposits*, simply freezes a part of commercial deposits (B_d). Suppose 10 units are so frozen. B_d now becomes 40 and our model yields for the new equilibrium money supply:

$$M_2^S = (100 + 40) \times 7 = 980$$

In short the *variable reserve ratio* device changes the *multiplier* leaving the quantity of bank cash initially unaltered. The *special deposit* device changes *bank cash* (by freezing what before was a part of it) leaving the *multiplier unaltered*. Neither device has any *primary* effect on the money supply and both make it unnecessary for the central bank to conduct open market operations.

Table 16.B7 Effect of a Call to Special Accounts of 10 Units

Position 2b

Central bank

Liabilities		Assets	
Notes		Gold and foreign exchange	100
with public	50	Securities	100
with banks	50		
Deposits			
Bankers			
(i) free	40		
(ii) special	10		
government	50		
	200		200

Commercial banks

Liabilities		Assets	
Deposits	1,000	Cash: Notes	50
		Deposit at CB	40
		Special deposits	10
		Securities	500
		Advances	400
	1,000		1,000

Holdings of Non-bank public

Notes	50
Deposits	1,000
Money supply	1,050
Securities	5,000

$$\text{Cash ratio} = \frac{90}{1000} < 10\%$$

Table 16.B8 Final Position

Commercial banks

Liabilities		Assets	
Deposits	933·3	Cash: Notes	53·3
		Deposit at CB	40
		Special deposits	10
		Securities	450
		Advances	380
	933·3		933·3

Holdings of Non-bank public

Notes	46·7
Deposits	933·3
Money supply	980
Securities	5,050

As for Position 2b

$$\text{Cash ratio} = 10\%$$

These procedures, for a given change in the money supply from Position 1 (Table 16.B2, p. 305) are illustrated in Tables 16.B6 and 7, pp. 311 and 315.

4 Lender of Last Resort

The central bank's function as lender of last resort is, in the United Kingdom, primarily of historical interest for, strictly speaking, this function refers to the obligation on the central bank to lend, virtually without limit, if the stability of the financial system is ever called into question. A hypothetical example may serve to illustrate what is implied.

Suppose we begin, as usual, in Position 1 as set out in Table 16.B1. In this situation we assume that the non-bank public becomes doubtful of the capacity of the commercial banking system to encash deposits on demand: that is to meet its obligations. There is, in short, a crisis of confidence.

Now the public will hold bank deposits (customary money) only so long as it is confident of the banks' capacity to encash deposits on demand. If the public thinks that the banks may *not* be able to encash deposits, it will rush to cash them. In terms of our model, there will be a catastrophic shift in α_1 i.e. the ratio in which the public wishes to hold notes and deposits.

Now the banks have deposit liabilities of 1000 units and hold cash of only 100 units. Hence when the public has encashed 100 units of deposits we reach Position 2c shown in Table 16.B9, p. 317. In this position, the banks' cash is zero. Deposits, however, are still 900 units. If the public insists on trying to encash further deposits then, *unless the banking system can find additional cash*, the banks must suspend payment. In this event the banking system and with it the monetary system will collapse. Deposits will no longer serve as customary money save possibly at a discount in terms of notes. Such a financial collapse would, beyond all doubt, have immense economic and social consequences. In a situation of this kind it is the duty of the central bank to act as lender of last resort and, by doing so, to ensure the liquidity and hence stability of the banking and monetary systems.

To illustrate what acting as *lender of last resort* means, assume that, after encashing 100 units of deposits, the public insists on cashing a further 300 units. To meet this demand, which the banks cannot meet, the central bank lends to the banks (say) 400 units. The banks take these loans in the form of Notes and pass 300 units to the public. Thus we reach Position 3c (Table 16.B10, p. 317). Here we see that the central bank's liabilities (Notes) have risen by

Table 16.B9 Operation as Lender of Last Resort: Position 2c – The Crisis

Central bank

Liabilities			Assets	
Notes			Gold and foreign reserves	100
with public	150			
with banks	nil	150	Securities	100
Deposits				
of bankers	nil			
of govt	50	50		
		200		200

Commercial banks

Liabilities		Assets	
Deposits	900	Cash:	
		notes	nil
		deposit at cen. bank	nil
		Securities	500
		Advances	400
	900		900

Holdings of public

Notes	150
Deposits	900
Money supply	1,050
Securities	5,000

Table 16.B10 The Lender of Last Resort: Position 3c

Central bank

Liabilities			Assets	
Notes			Gold and foreign reserves	100
with public	450			
with banks	100	550	Securities	100
Deposits			Advances to commercial banks	400
of bankers	nil			
of govt	50	50		
		600		600

Commercial bank

Liabilities		Assets	
Deposits	600	Cash:	
Loan from cen. bank	400	notes	100
		deposits at cen. bank	nil
		Securities	500
		Advances	400
	1,000		1,000

Holdings of public

Notes	450
Deposits	600
Money supply	1,050
Securities	5,000

400 units above the figure at Position 2b. Against this they have a corresponding asset 'Advances to commercial banks' of 400 units.

The commercial bank liabilities have risen by 100 units, the net result of a 400 unit increase in liabilities *to* the central bank and a 300 unit decrease in their liabilities to the non-bank public.

The money supply is unaltered in total. However, the public now holds only 600 units of deposits (as against its original 1000, and, as a result, has 450 units of notes (as against its original 50).

As long as the 'crisis of confidence' persists, the central bank must continue to act as lender of last resort. Once the non-bank public is sure that it *can*, if it wishes, always convert deposits into notes on demand, it will no longer wish to do so. Notes will be deposited at the commercial banks. As a result they will pay off their loans from the central bank and the system will revert to Position 1 – the position which existed *before* the crisis of confidence occurred.

This example illustrates, in simple terms, the 'classic' case of a central bank acting as lender of last resort in a financial panic. Such situations are nowadays rare – at least in developed economies. Essentially the example illustrates a situation in which the central bank is compelled, in order to preserve the financial and monetary system, to act as *residual lender*. This it commonly still does though not usually in a situation in which confidence has collapsed. *It now acts as residual lender in situations in which it has, deliberately, compelled the commercial banks to borrow from it.* This sounds perverse. How can it occur?

Suppose we are in Position 1 and the central bank wishes to contract the money supply. We assume that it cannot undertake open-market sales so it 'freezes' in special deposits, say, 10 units of what was bank cash.

In this situation the banks have a cash ratio *below* their preferred ratio. The result must be a secondary contraction. But this cannot be carried out instantly for, if the central bank cannot sell 10 units of securities on the open market nor can the commercial banks, while to reduce advances necessarily takes time. Hence to maintain their cash ratio the commercial banks borrow from the central bank. It *must*, to meet its obligations as lender of last resort, act as a *residual lender*. Hence it lends. But though it will never refuse to lend, *it can charge whatever rate it likes on its loans*. In the postulated circumstances it will charge a rate sufficiently high to compel the banks to get out of debt to it (carry out their secondary contraction) as quickly as they can. Such a rate is sometimes called a *penal* or *penalty* rate. Its object is twofold: (i) to compel contraction; and (ii) to raise interest rates.

The general conclusion is that whenever a central bank acts as residual lender it can, if it wishes, raise interest rates and compel contraction by charging the banks a penalty rate for their advances. For in such circumstances the banks, compelled to borrow at a rate higher than that at which they *can* currently lend, will, (i) raise their own lending (and borrowing) rates and (ii) embark on a secondary contraction. In our formal discussion of the rate of interest we saw that it was a price equating the demand to hold money with the supply of money. A contraction in the money supply *ceteris paribus* raises the rate of interest. This analysis is quite consistent with the above example. Indeed the example can best be viewed by the reader as an illustration, in institutional terms, of the formal analysis of Chapter 11.

The rate at which the central bank will lend is known by various names in various countries. In Britain, for example, it was called 'Bank Rate'† and, for historical reasons, was charged not on loans made *directly* to the banks but on advances made *indirectly* through the *discount houses*. In Australia the rate is known as the 'central bank rate'. Unlike Bank Rate, it is not published. Often it is called 'the central bank discount rate' because the *method of lending* takes the form of the purchase *by* the central bank *from* the commercial banks of a particular government debt known as a *Treasury bill*. Since the initial purchase of the Treasury bill from the Treasury by the commercial bank is called 'discounting' its sale to the central bank is called 'rediscounting'. In short, each financial system has its own individual institutional arrangements and its own nomenclature. These details, though fascinating and important, do not concern us in this context. What matters is the essential nature of the operation and this is, at our present level of abstraction, very much the same in all systems.

We may conclude by saying that

   (i) *historically* the role of the central bank as *lender of last resort* arose because of the need to protect the financial and monetary system from 'crises of confidence';

  (ii) *contemporaneously* central banks rarely have to act as lender of last resort in this sense though they often act, frequently as a matter of deliberate choice, as *residual lender*;

 (iii) the central bank must *always* be prepared to act in this way;

 (iv) whenever it does it *can charge whatever rate it thinks fit*;

  (v) this power gives it a measure of direct control over interest rates which is quite compatible with the theory set out in Chapter 11.

    † Now replaced by 'Minimum Lending Rate'.

Table 16.B11 The Impact of a Surplus of 10 Units: Position 2d

Central bank

Liabilities			Assets	
Notes			Gold and foreign exchange	100
with public	50		Securities	100
with banks	50			
Deposits				
of bankers	40			
of govt	60			
		200		200

Commercial bank

Liabilities		Assets		
Deposits	990	Cash:		
		notes	50	
		deposit at cen. bank	40	90
		Securities		500
		Advances		400
	990			990

Non-bank public

Holdings	
of notes	50
of deposits	990
Money supply	1,040
Securities	5,000

Table 16.B12 Repayment of Debt held by the Central Bank: Position 3d

Central bank

Liabilities			Assets	
Notes			Gold and foreign exchange	100
with public	50	100	Securities	90
with banker	50			
Deposits				
of bankers	40	90		
of govt	50			
		190		190

Commercial banks

Liabilities		Assets		
Deposits	990	Cash:		
		notes	50	
		deposit at cen. bank	40	90
		Securities		500
		Advances		400
	990			990

Non-bank public

Holdings	
of notes	50
of deposits	990
Money supply	1,040
Securities	5,000

5 GOVERNMENT FISCAL OPERATIONS AND DEBT MANAGEMENT

Suppose, in any period, we have a situation in which

$$T \quad - \quad (G+R) \quad = 10$$

tax receipts $-$ (government expenditure) $= 10$

Then the government is running a *surplus* at the rate of 10 units per period. It follows that the public is paying into the government account (at the central bank) a net sum of 10 units. Starting, as usual, from Position 1 we reach Position 2d (Table 16.B11, p. 320).

As a result of the surplus

(i) government deposits are up by 10 units: bankers' deposits are down by 10;

(ii) the money supply is down by 10 units;

(iii) commercial bankers' cash ratio is *below* their preferred ratio.

Clearly a secondary contraction will tend to follow from Position 2d. What does the government do with its surplus? It has two choices: first, it can continue to hold higher balances idle or, second, it can use these balances to repay some of its debt by buying up some of its outstanding obligations in the market.

Obviously by acting on the second choice the government can lower its annual interest bill (reduce R). It will therefore repay debt (by purchase) and the central bank will advise it as to which debt to repay. Strictly this is not one question but two. For the government has two types of choice:

(i) shall it repay debt held by the central bank or debt held outside the central bank?

(ii) what type of debt (short-term or long-term) shall it repay?

Our model contains only one kind of government debt – long-term bonds. We cannot therefore deal with question (ii) although, in practice, government debt in many differing maturities is outstanding and the choice of which to repay may influence the relative interest rates on the debts of different maturities. We can, however, ask question (i) in terms of our model.

Suppose the 10 units is used to repay debt held by the central bank. We reach Position 3d (Table 16.B12, p. 320).

From this position a secondary contraction must follow.

Table 16.B13 Repayment of Debt held by Non-Bank Public: Position 4d

Central bank		Commercial banks		Non-bank public	
Liabilities	**Assets**	**Liabilities**	**Assets**		
Notes	Gold and	Deposits 1,000	Cash:	Holdings	
with public 50	foreign exchange 100		notes 50	of notes	50
with bank 50 100	Securities 100		deposit at	of deposits	1,000
			cen. bank 50 100		
Deposits	Securities 200		Securities 500	Money supply	1,050
of bankers 50			Advances 400	Securities	4,990
of govt 50 100					
200	200	1,000	1,000		

Alternatively, suppose the 10 units is used to repay debt held by the non-bank public. We reach Position 4d which, from the monetary point of view, must lead to a restoration of Position 1 (Table 16.B13, p. 322).

Generalising this result we may say that

(i) a government surplus in any period brings about a primary decrease in the money supply equal to the surplus;

(ii) if the surplus is used to repay debt held by the central bank the primary decrease will be followed by a secondary decrease;

(iii) if the surplus is used to repay debt held by the general public (or the commercial banks) there will be no change in the money supply which will return to its original values.

It is a simple matter for the reader to work out the corresponding propositions with regard to a *deficit*. Here the result turns on whether the *deficit* is financed by *borrowing* from the central bank or the public.

This analysis shows that, in advising the government on debt operations, even of the limited kind permitted by our model, the central bank can exert an important influence on the money supply and the rate of interest.

6 SUMMARY

In this chapter we have attempted to show what a central bank is: how a central bank can control the nominal money supply; and some of the devices it employs to do so.

Our method has been to erect a *model* of the central bank and its associated commercial banking system. No monetary system is precisely like this model. Nevertheless the model displays many of the essential features of developed monetary systems sufficiently well to be useful in gaining a *general* understanding of the principal central banking techniques and operations. Typically, however, each national monetary system possesses individual characteristics and complexities. A full understanding of any system therefore requires a detailed knowledge of the institutions which comprise it. The reader is thus urged to study the references given at the end of this chapter and, in particular, the report of the Radcliffe Committee, for a fuller account of the United Kingdom system.

We may now ask whether we were justified, for example in Chapters 11 and 12, in treating the nominal money supply as a variable determined independently of all other variables in the model and thus *exogenous*. Undoubtedly this is a convenient pedagogic device – akin to assuming that the consumption function is such that real planned consumption depends on real income alone. Unfortunately convenient expository assumptions can be misleading. Now that we know that the principal proximate determinant of the money supply is central banking policy we must ask how misleading it is to write

$$M^S = \overline{M} \equiv \text{some exogenously determined quantity.}$$

The short answer to this question is that it may well be very misleading indeed and is certain to be misleading in some degree. The principal reason why this is so is that the central bank, in managing the nominal money supply, typically does so with certain objectives in mind. One of these, which in practice seems to be of considerable importance, is preserving the orderly operation of money and capital markets ($\equiv$ market for long-term funds). Hence central banks commonly seek to prevent large fluctuations in r. Thus if r is above what they think it ought to be, or is rising faster than they think is desirable, they tend to carry out open market purchases. Since r responds to changes in money income, this means that the nominal money supply, via central bank actions, is to some extent functionally related to other variables within the system. Thus it might be more realistic to write, instead of our usual hypothesis, a nominal money supply function of the form (say)

$$M^S = M_0 + \alpha_1 p Y + \alpha_2(r - r^*) \qquad \alpha_1, \alpha_2 > 0,$$

where $r^* = $ the central bank's target long-term interest rate
 $M_0 = $ autonomous element in M^S.

Typically, in the chapters which follow, we shall *not* do this. We shall retain, in the interests of simplicity, the assumption that the nominal money supply is exogenous. The reader is therefore warned, at this stage, that this is done for expository purposes only and that, in practice, the money supply has a substantial endogenous element. As we shall see, the importance of this element has a considerable bearing on the relevance of the recent revival of the quantity theory of money, which is briefly discussed in Chapter 17*.

QUESTIONS AND EXERCISES

1. Use the model of this and earlier chapters to explain the consequence for the money supply and interest rate of a government

deficit of 10 units financed by borrowing from the non-bank public. What happens to the public's holdings of government securities?

2. Suppose the central bank wishes to reduce the money supply by 140 units. Use the model of Section 1 to calculate (i) the size of the necessary open market sales and (ii) the size of the increase in the cash ratio necessary to obtain the same result.

   In what circumstances would bond sales by the *banking system* as a whole be greater under method (ii) than method (i)?

3. Study chapter iii of the Radcliffe Report. How applicable is the model of Chapter 16 to the conditions it describes?

4. Between December 1960 and December 1964 the security holdings (investments) of the London Clearing Banks fell by £109 m. Which assets increased? What are the consequences of a bank selling securities and making advances?

5. When the Exchange Equalisation Account buys foreign exchange it borrows the sterling in the market by issuing Treasury bills. Conversely when it sells foreign exchange it uses the proceeds to buy Treasury bills. Add the Exchange Equalisation Account to the model of Chapter 16 and analyse the consequences of a balance of payments surplus of 10 units.

6. 'It is, broadly speaking, true to say that private individuals cannot put into a modern banking system anything which is not there already'. Do you agree? If not, why not? If so, why?

7. 'An increase in saving raises bank deposits.' 'The notion that an increase in saving will raise bank deposits rests upon a crude and elementary confusion of *stock* and *flow* concepts.' Discuss.

8. 'In recent years the banks have lost deposits to both building societies and hire purchase companies.' Are such deposit losses possible? If so, how? If not, why not?

9. In what circumstances would you advise the Bank of England to conduct open market sales? Why?

10. Analyse the consequences for income, employment, the rate of interest and the balance of payments of open market purchases by the central bank.

SUGGESTED READING

R. S. Sayers, *Modern Banking*, 7th ed. (Oxford, 1967) chs iv–vii, ix.
W. T. Newlyn, *The Theory of Money* (Oxford, 1971) ch. iii.
W. Manning Dacey, *The British Banking Mechanism* (Hutchinson, 1954) chs iv–vi.

D. C. Rowan, 'The Evolution of British Monetary Policy 1951–1972', *Manchester School* (Feb 1973).

Bank of England and H.M. Treasury, *Money in Britain: 1959–1969* (Oxford, 1970).

— 'Official Transactions in the Gilt-Edged Market', *Bank of England Quarterly Bulletin* (June 1966).

Radcliffe Report (H.M.S.O., 1959) ch. iv.

Radcliffe Committee: Memoranda of Evidence, vol. 1 (H.M.S.O., 1960) pp. 35–42.

R. Crouch, 'The Futility of Funding', *The Bankers' Magazine* (Jul 1965).

G. Maynard, 'The Futility of Funding: A Comment', ibid. (Sep 1965).

A. B. Cramp, 'The Control of Bank Deposits', *Lloyds Bank Review*. (Oct 1967).

R. Crouch,† 'The Inadequacy of "New-Orthodox" Methods of Monetary Control', *Economic Journal* (Dec 1964).

† More advanced reference.

17 The Theory of the Price Level

So far the whole of our analysis has proceeded on the simplifying assumption that the price level is given and invariant. This does not mean that the level of prices exerts no influence in our model. Indeed if we look back at Chapter 11 we see that the price level is a determinant of the demand for active (M_1) balances and thus of the rate of interest. Since the rate of interest, given the M.E.I. schedule, determines (as explained in Chapter 10) the rate of real planned investment which, in its turn, determines, via the multiplier, the equilibrium level of real income and, via the production function, the level of employment, it is clear that the level of prices exerts a considerable influence in our system. It is plain, therefore, that to complete our theory we need to consider how the price level itself gets determined. To explain this is the job of this chapter.

1 PRICE DETERMINATION AND PROFIT MAXIMISATION

Our basic hypothesis concerning business behaviour is that businessmen seek to maximise profits. From this hypothesis we derive the *supply side* of our theory of prices.

Consider a businessman contemplating the production of an additional unit of output. If he produces it – and sells it at the price already established in the market – he will obtain additional revenue equal to the additional output multiplied by the price of a unit of output. The revenue so obtained we call the *marginal revenue* simply because it is the *additional revenue* derived from producing the additional unit. Call the additional units of output ΔO and write the price of a unit of output as p. Then if the marginal units can be sold *without* reducing prices† we have

$$\text{Additional revenue} = p.\Delta O.$$

Obviously the businessman will only produce this output if it increases his profits. Since profits are the excess of revenue over

† This implies that the goods market is one of 'pure' competition in which no single producer is sufficiently large for variation in his output to influence price.

costs if we call the costs of producing the marginal units *marginal costs*, then the hypothesis of profit maximisation tells us that

(i) if m. revenue > m. costs the businessman will *expand* output;
(ii) if m. revenue < m. costs the businessman will *contract* output;
(iii) if m. revenue = m. cost the businessman will be in equilibrium,

that is, he will have no incentive either to expand or contract his level of output.

If we now think of a closed economy, and of businessmen as a whole and not simply one individual businessman, and use a short-run analysis, then the cost of producing an additional unit of output, marginal cost, is the cost of employing the additional labour necessary to produce it. Write the money wage rate as W and the increase in employment, necessary to produce ΔO increase in output, as ΔN. Then

$$\text{Marginal cost of } \Delta O \text{ output} = W.\Delta N.$$

We have already found that, for businessmen to be in equilibrium, we require marginal revenue = marginal cost,

that is, $$p.\Delta O = W.\Delta N, \tag{17.I}$$

or $$p = W.\frac{\Delta N}{\Delta O}. \tag{17.II}$$

This tells us that p, the price at which the profit-maximising businessman would *plan* to produce ΔO additional unit of output, is determined by

$$W \equiv \text{the money wage rate}$$

and $\Delta N/\Delta O \equiv$ the amount of labour necessary to produce the additional units of output.

For the moment let us assume that W (the money wage rate) is given and constant: that is, it takes some special value W_h. Equation (17.II) then tells us that, if we know $\Delta N/\Delta O$, since we know that $W = W_h$, we can readily determine p. What then is the quantity $\Delta N/\Delta O$?

2 THE PRODUCTION FUNCTION AND THE MARGINAL PRODUCT OF LABOUR

The meaning of $\Delta N/\Delta O$ is plain enough. It is the (marginal) labour input required to produce the increase in output. We have not met this concept before. We are, however, familiar with its reciprocal form

$$\frac{1}{(\Delta N/\Delta O)} \equiv \frac{\Delta O}{\Delta N} \equiv \text{marginal physical product of labour.}$$

To see what this means divide both sides of (17.II) by $\Delta N/\Delta O$. We get

$$p \cdot \frac{\Delta O}{\Delta N} = W. \tag{17.III}$$

This tells us that businessmen will employ additional labour up to the point at which the marginal revenue product of labour ($\equiv$ marginal physical product $\times$ price of product) is equal to the marginal cost of doing so, i.e. the money wage rate. To give an example. Suppose we produce cricket balls which sell at £1 each and that, by employing an additional man, we can make another 40 cricket balls per week. Then $p = £1$; $\Delta O = 40$; $\Delta N = 1$, so that

$$p\frac{\Delta O}{\Delta N} = £40 \text{ per week.}$$

If $W < £40$ we shall gain by hiring an additional man. If $W > £40$ we shall lose. Only if $W = £40$ per week shall we have no incentive to hire (or fire) an additional man.

It follows that, given that $W = W_h$, *we can explain at what prices businessmen will be prepared to produce given levels of output, provided we can relate the marginal product of labour (and thus its reciprocal) to the level of output.*

Very early on in this book, in Chapter 7 to be precise, we introduced the notion of a *production function*. This stated quite generally that we could write a production function of the form: $Y = f(T, K, N)$, showing that total output (Y) depended upon $T \equiv$ the state of technique; $K \equiv$ the quantity of real capital; $N \equiv$ the quantity of employment.

The particular function we made use of was $Y = TK^{\alpha}N^{1-\alpha}$. This function, and its properties, we discussed in some detail in Chapter 7 and the reader is now referred back to that earlier discussion. In the *short run* we take T and K as *given*. We can therefore plot the function on a diagram as a relationsip between N and Y with K and T given. This is done in Fig. 17.i.

Now the *slope* of the curve relating Y to N in this figure is the marginal response coefficient $\partial Y/\partial N$. This is the marginal physical product of labour. The curve thus tells us – and this is confirmed by Fig 7.1(a) in Chapter 7 – that

  (i) the marginal physical product of labour $\partial Y/\partial N$ is always positive;
 (ii) the marginal physical product of labour $\partial Y/\partial N$ falls as Y (or N) increases;
(iii) for any level of Y (or N) there is a given value of $\partial Y/\partial N$, i.e. of the marginal physical product of labour.

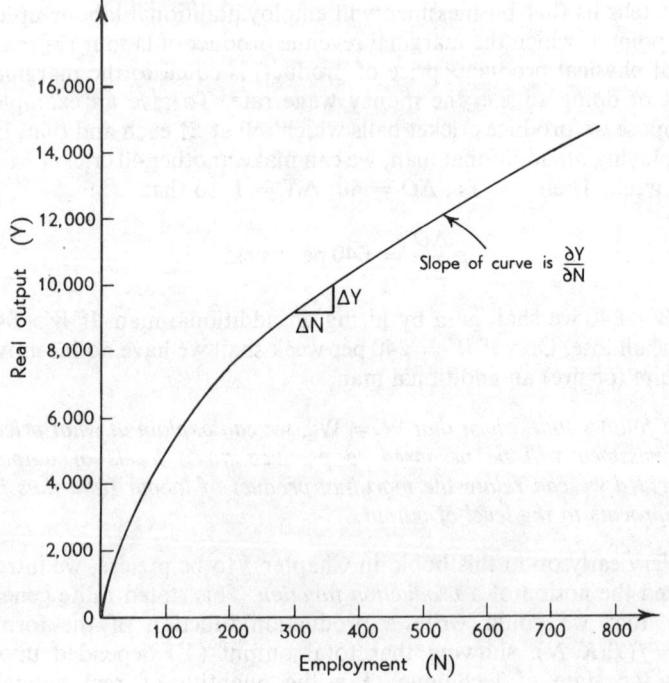

FIG. 17.i Short-run production function

It follows that, for any given value of Y, *there is a given value of* $\partial N/\partial Y$ – *the marginal labour cost of a unit of output*† *and also that* $\partial N/\partial Y$ *increases as* Y *increases. This arises because of the operation of the principle of diminishing marginal physical productivity.*

† That is, the additional labour input required, given the production function, the state of technique and the capital stock, to produce an additional unit of output.

We can now say that (i) for any level of real output there is a given marginal labour cost of a unit of output, hence, since $W = W_h$ by assumption, (ii) for any level of real output there will be a single determinate price level while, since the marginal labour cost is higher, the higher the level of output (iii) the higher the level of real output the higher the price level associated with it.

3 THE AGGREGATE SUPPLY FUNCTION

We now know that, with a given money wage rate, businessmen will require, in order to maximise profits, a higher level of prices the higher the level of output simply because the *marginal labour cost of producing output* is higher the higher is the level of output. To see what this implies let us construct two curves.

The first of these curves relates the level of output (Y) to the price level (p) which will just induce businessmen to produce it. The second curve relates the level of output (Y) to the level of money proceeds (pY) which will just induce businessmen to produce it. The two curves are simply related. Any point on the first curve, say the point O, defines both a price level (p_0) and an output level (Y_0). It thus defines a rectangle $(p_0 Y_0)$ which is a point on our second curve. The two curves are thus alternative ways of presenting the same information. They are illustrated in Fig. 17.ii.

Both these curves can be regarded *as forms* of the *aggregate supply function*. Usually the aggregate supply function is defined as

A function relating the quantity of employment (N) which businessmen would be prepared to offer to each level of expected total proceeds (Yp).

However, from the short-run production function we know that any level of employment (N) determines a given level of output (Y). Hence the usual definition can easily be converted into the form which we use here. Alternatively the reader can construct the traditional curve from our curve relating output (Y) and expected proceeds (Yp).

Let us look at these two curves rather carefully taking first the range from zero output to the point of discontinuity $Y = Y_{FE}$. Each curve takes as given (i) the production function; (ii) the stock of capital (K); (iii) the state of technique (T); (iv) the money wage rate (W_h); and (v) *assumes* that businessmen seek to maximise profits. The curves both slope upwards because, as output (Y)

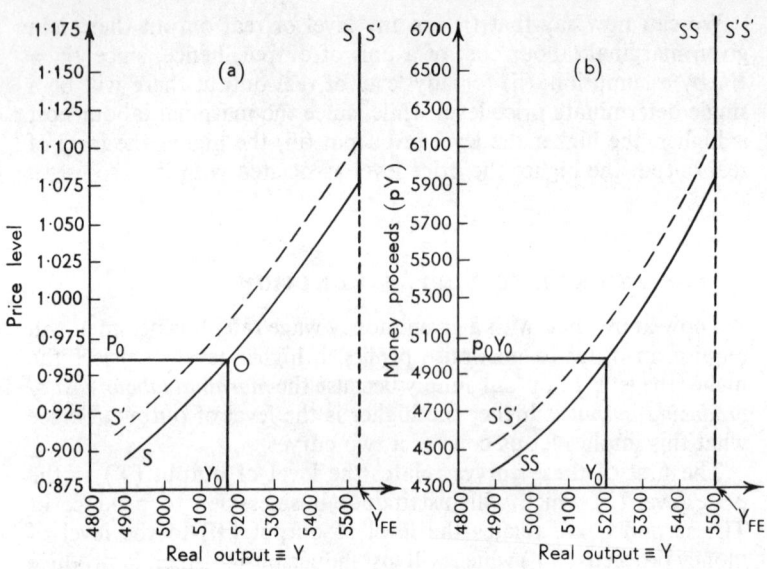

FIG. 17.ii   The aggregate supply function

rises, so does the labour input required to produce an additional unit of output. Hence with a given money wage the price level (p) and the value of money proceeds (pY), which will just induce businessmen to produce any given level of output rise as the level of output rises.

What is the meaning of the point of discontinuity? At some level of output, which we have called Y_{FE}, labour will be fully employed. In the short run, therefore, Y cannot exceed Y_{FE} whatever the expected level of prices (p) or money proceeds (Yp). Hence at this point of discontinuity the curves become vertical.

In what circumstances will the aggregate supply curve shift and in what way? The parameters of the curve are listed at (i) to (iv) above and the behaviour hypothesis it reflects is listed at (v). Of these parameters (i) to (iii) are constant in a short-run analysis. Hence only the money wage rate is available as a source of shifts unless we permit, as we shall *not* do, the business behaviour hypothesis to change. What then is the effect on the curve of (say) an increase in the money wage rate (W_h) to some new higher value W'_h?

We know from an earlier analysis that, given the production function, the state of technique and the capital stock, any level of real output will entail a particular marginal labour cost (input requirement) for additional output. Hence the price level which will just induce businessmen to produce the given level of output will, from the relation $p = W(\partial N/\partial Y)$, rise if W increases. It follows that any level of output will be associated with a higher value of money proceeds (pY) if the money wage rate is W'_h rather than W_h. Hence the SS curve of Fig. 17.ii (b) shifts *upwards* in the manner shown by the dashed line $S'S'$. This line will, of course, coincide with the original curve for all values of money proceeds greater than a certain figure (6,100 on our figure) at the point of discontinuity given by Y_{FE}. For a cut in money wages from W'_h to W_h the argument, at this formal level, is simply reversed. The $S'S'$ curve becomes the SS curve.

The reader, relaxing one of the assumptions of the short-run analysis, should now work out the consequences for the SS curve of a greater value for K ($\equiv$ the real stock of capital). He should also work out for this example – and the change in the money wage rate already discussed – the effect on the aggregate supply curve of Fig. 17.ii (a).

Of course the SS curve by itself cannot determine the price level. To show the simultaneous determination of prices (p), output (Y) and thus money proceeds (Yp) we must superimpose upon it an aggregate demand curve. How can this be done?

4 The Aggregate Demand Function

We know, from our earlier analysis, that aggregate demand, relating now to our simplest model, and ignoring government economic activity and international trade, is given by

$$\text{aggregate demand} \equiv C_p + I_p \equiv D.$$

Now I_p (real planned investment) depends upon the rate of interest. For a given money supply, following the analysis of Chapter 11, the rate of interest depends upon the two liquidity functions (L_1 and L_2) and the level of *money income*. The higher is money income, the higher in general is the rate of interest.

Suppose, for example, we choose the level of real output Y_0 in Fig. 17.ii. Then the equilibrium price level (to satisfy businessmen) will be p_0 and the equilibrium value of money proceeds is $p_0 Y_0$ which is the money income received. This assumes, of course, that production plans are always realised. With a given money supply this immediately determines a rate of interest (r_0) which, via the investment function, gives us the value of real planned investment

(I_{p0}). From the consumption function, since we know output (Y_0) we know real planned consumption (C_{p0}). We thus know

$$C_{p0} + I_{p0} \equiv \text{aggregate demand in real terms} \equiv D$$

at the price level p_0. This enables us to plot, by repeated experiment in this way, a curve relating $C_p + I_p \equiv$ real planned expenditure to the price level (p). Such a curve is depicted in Fig. 17.iii (a). Equally, simply by multiplying real planned expenditure by the price level to which it refers we can obtain: $p(C_p + I_p) \equiv$ money value of real planned expenditure at any level of output (Y). This curve is plotted on Fig. 17.iii (b).

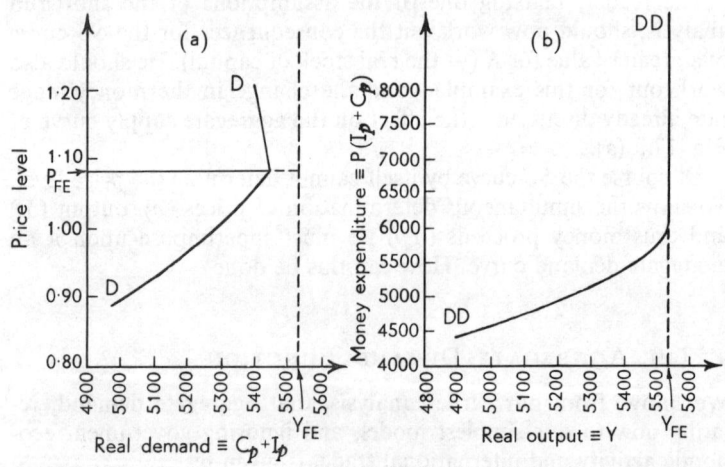

FIG. 17.iii   Aggregate demand functions

Both these curves (which are obviously simply related) are forms of the aggregate demand function. This function, like the aggregate supply function, is more usually expressed in terms of employment (N) than output (Y). The transformation, if it is required, can however very easily be made through the production function which, in its short-run version, gives a unique relation between Y and N as Fig. 17.i reminds us.

What do we take as given in drawing these curves? Obviously they reflect the influence of

(i) a given consumption function;
(ii) a given marginal efficiency of investment schedule;

(iii) a given money supply;
(iv) given L_1 and L_2 (liquidity preference) functions;
 (v) a given production function;
(vi) a given state of technique and capital stock;
(vii) a given money wage rate.

This is a lengthy list and the fact that it is so reflects the complicated chain of reasoning which we used to construct the curves. Examination of this list also reveals that the items (v), (vi) and (vii) on which the aggregate demand curve depends are also determinants of the aggregate supply curve. It follows therefore that, in some cases, changes which shift the former curve will also shift the latter. These two curves thus have a degree of interdependence – a point which must be kept very carefully in mind. This interdependence arises from the definition of the functions which the reader needs to keep constantly in the forefront of his mind. To put matters concisely:

 (i) the aggregate supply function tells us how much output businessmen will plan to supply at any given price level; and
 (ii) the aggregate demand function tells us how much businessmen will *sell* if they produce their planned output at a given price level.

Finally we should add that though the construction of these aggregate demand functions is complicated, we have in fact constructed them on an implicit simplifying assumption which must now be brought into the open. This implicit assumption is that the distribution of income, which, as the reader will recall, is a parameter of our consumption function, is constant. In certain cases, as we shall see later, this is a very strong assumption. Nevertheless in the *formal parts of our analysis* we shall retain it.

Because the aggregate demand functions are complicated concepts, we need to interpret them with considerable care. To see how to interpret them consider Fig. 17.iv (b). In this we have superimposed the aggregate demand function which relates $p(C_p + I_p)$ to Y on the aggregate supply function of Fig. 17.ii (b).

Suppose now that businessmen expect money proceeds to be OA. From the aggregate supply function they will produce output of Y_A. Money income will therefore be $p_A Y_A = OA$. Given this level of money income, the value of the money supply and the two liquidity preference functions (L_1 and L_2) this will, in the money market determine a rate of interest r_A which, via the given M.E.I. schedule, tells us the rate of real planned investment (I_{pA}). Real planned consumption (C_{pA}) depends, by hypothesis, only on real income (Y_A). Hence this too is known. Thus we have determined $D_A \equiv C_{pA} + I_{pA}$. Multiplying this by the price level (P_A) gives us the value of money expenditure. As we have drawn the curves we have

$$P_A D_A > P_A Y_A$$

money expenditure > expected proceeds.

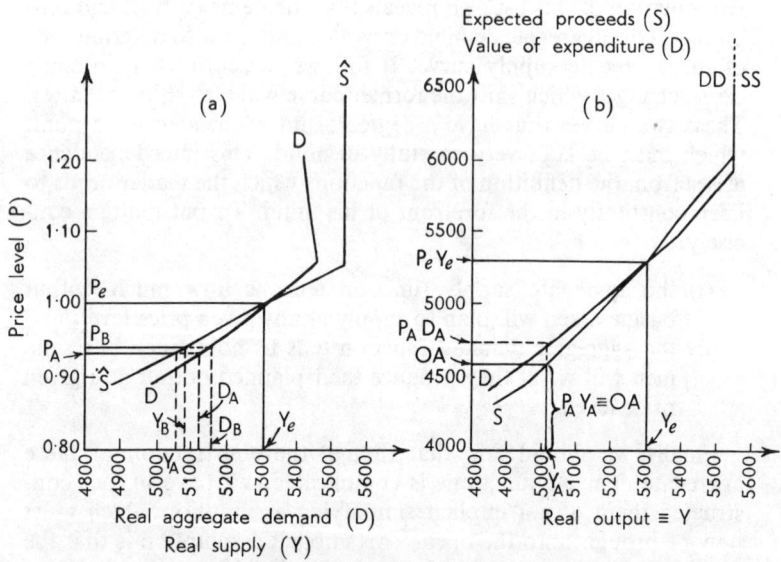

FIG. 17.iv Aggregate demand and supply

In such a situation competition will induce businessmen to expand output until the curves intersect at Y_e. At Y_e (the equilibrium level) aggregate demand is equal to aggregate supply. Expected proceeds and actual proceeds coincide and businessmen have no incentive to expand or contract output. This argument, as the reader can see, is readily reversed for a hypothetical level of output in *excess* of Y_e.

Now in Fig. 17.iv (b) both the *DD* and *SS* curves are upward-sloping to the right. The validity of the analysis therefore depends upon *two* conditions being met:

(i) the *DD* curve must lie *above* the *SS* curve for all $Y < Y_e$; and
(ii) the *DD* curve must be *less* steeply sloped than the *SS* curve.

The first condition is met by our model. Assume a very low (but not zero) planned real output. Then, if the consumption function is linear and autonomous consumption positive, planned real consumption will exceed output. Since the price level is low the interest rate (*ceteris paribus*) will also be low and planned real investment correspondingly high. Hence the value of planned expenditure $p(C_p + I_p)$ will exceed the value of expected proceeds (pY). But what of the second condition?

By construction $pD \equiv p(C_p + I_p)$. Assume, to simplify matters, that I_p does not react to the rate of interest. Then, as output rises, pD rises for two reasons: (i) because the price level (p) rises; (ii) because as Y rises so does C_p. Similarly aggregate supply $(S) \equiv pY$ and increases as Y increases (i) because p (the price level) rises and (ii) because Y rises. Obviously since C_p rises by *less* than Y, then pD rises by *less* than S as Y increases. This is simply another way of saying that the slope of DD is flatter than the slope of SS.

Hence both our conditions are satisfied: pD does lie *above* S for low values of Y *and* the slope of DD is *flatter* than that of SS even if investment does *not* fall as the rate of interest rises. If we now allow for this latter effect our conclusion is simply strengthened. Now look at the curves on Fig. 17.iv (a). The aggregate supply curve $\hat{S}$ needs no further explanation. What of the aggregate demand curve? Again assume businessmen to expect a low price level (say p_A) and thus produce output Y_A. As we have shown above, real planned expenditure (D_A) will exceed Y_A. Thus at a low price level (p_A) the D curve must be to the right of the aggregate supply curve $\hat{S}$.

Now suppose businessmen expect a price level higher than p_A (say p_B). Accordingly they produce output Y_B. If the rate of interest was at its minimum at p_A and remains at its minimum level at p_B (i.e. we are on the flat part of the L_2 function) $C_p + I_p$ will rise by an amount determined by the increase in Y and the marginal propensity to consume. Hence at the *higher* price level (p_B) the value of $C_p + I_p$ will be *greater*. The D curve slopes *upwards to the right*. Hence to cut the $\hat{S}$ curve it must slope upwards, as p rises, at a *faster* rate than the $\hat{S}$ curve. This can be shown to be the case by an argument analogous to that used above in relation to the curves of Fig. 17.iv (b).

Where the D and S curves cut we determine the equilibrium values of the price level (p_e) and real output (Y_e). This point, obviously enough, gives the value $p_e Y_e$ which we found in Fig. 17.iv (b). In short, Fig. 17.iv (a) gives no *more* information than Fig. 17.iv (b). Its advantage is simply that it gives, explicitly rather than implicitly, the equilibrium value of the price level.

It should be noticed that, at some point, the D curve of Figs. 17.iii (a) and iv (a) *reverses* its direction of slope. Why is this? The explanation is not hard to seek. At p_{FE} the $\hat{S}$ curve becomes vertical for reasons we have already explained and output (Y) is at its full-employment ceiling. Hence real planned consumption is also at its ceiling for the given consumption function. Now as p rises above p_{FE}, the rate of interest rises and I_p falls. Hence $C_p + I_p$ *falls* and the D curve bends backwards to the left.

The introduction of aggregate demand and supply curves of the kind dealt with here clearly involves some unavoidably intricate argument. The reader is therefore exhorted to go very carefully over this analysis and that of Section 5 below. Then, after completing the chapter, he (or she) should construct the numerical model given in the Questions and Exercises. In this way it is relatively simple to understand the central lessons of aggregate demand and supply analysis which are that

  (i) *The equilibrium level of prices is simultaneously determined with the equilibrium levels of output, employment and the rate of interest.*
 (ii) *The aggregate demand and supply functions depend on many of the same determinants.*
(iii) *An increase in aggregate supply increases aggregate demand but typically by less than the increase in supply.*

5 A Numerical Example of the Construction of Aggregate Demand and Supply Schedules

The purpose of this section is to give a precise illustration of the construction of the model of Section 4.

To do this, it is convenient to begin with the Aggregate Supply schedule. We thus require a simple approximation to an aggregate production function. Let us write this as

$$Y = F + eN - fN^2, \tag{1}$$

where $Y \equiv$ real output and $N \equiv$ labour input and we are assuming that the stock of capital (K) is invariant as is the state of technique.

Now if both goods and factor markets are purely competitive and employers seek to maximise profits, labour will be demanded until the real marginal product of labour ($\partial Y / \partial N$) is equal to the real wage (W_h / p), i.e. until

$$\frac{\partial Y}{\partial N} = \frac{W_h}{p}, \tag{2}$$

where $W_h \equiv$ the historically given money wage rate.

If we now differentiate the production function (1) we obtain

$$\frac{\partial Y}{\partial N} = e - 2fN \tag{3}$$

which, provided $f > 0$, falls as N increases as we must expect. Combining (2) and (3) yields

$$p = \frac{W_h}{e - 2fN} \tag{4}$$

and thus yields a functional relation between p ($\equiv$ the price level) and N ($\equiv$ employment) which, since, from (1), any given value of N implies a unique level of Y, could also be written as a functional relation between p and Y: that is, as an aggregate supply schedule.

This is illustrated in Table 17.1, taking the following assumed numerical values for the coefficients of (1) and for the historically given money wage rate (W_h).

$$F = 4{,}400 \qquad f = 0{\cdot}01$$
$$e = 10 \qquad W_h = 8{\cdot}0$$

Table 17.1 *Illustrative Calculation of Aggregate Supply Schedules*

(1)	(2)	(3)	(4)
			Money proceeds
		Aggregate	(to 4 significant
Price level	Labour input	real supply	figs)
p	N	Y	pY
0·89	50	4,873	4,332
0·91	60	4,964	4,513
0·93	70	5,051	4,699
0·95	80	5,136	4,898
0·98	90	5,219	5,091
1·0	100	5,300	5,300
1·03	110	5,379	5,517
1·05	120	5,456	5,744
1·08	130	5,531	5,994
1·11	130	5,531	6,110

Note: Figures have been rounded and $N = 130$ defines full employment.

Sources: Col. (2): derived from labour demand function:

$$N^D = 500 - 50 \frac{W_h}{p}.$$

Col. (3): derived from production function.
Col. (4): col. (1) × col. (3).

Notice that from this table we can easily construct aggregate supply schedules relating p to Y or pY to Y. The former type of function is illustrated in Fig. 17.v, the latter the reader can readily construct for himself. Notice also that at each point on the aggregate supply schedule businessmen are assumed to be maximising profit.

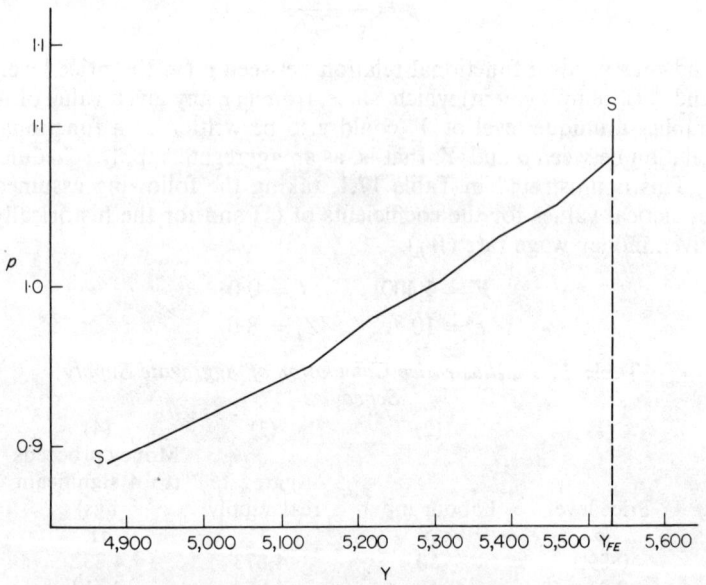

FIG. 17.v   Aggregate supply curve

We now turn to construct the aggregate demand schedule. To do this we first define

$$\text{real aggregate demand} \equiv D \equiv C_p + I_p. \tag{5}$$

Retaining our simple consumption hypothesis, we may write

$$C_p = A + cY, \tag{6}$$

which gives us the familiar linear propensity-to-consume schedule. If we use a similar linear approximation to the investment hypothesis – such as, for example,

$$I_p = H - br \tag{7}$$

we can construct a schedule relating I_p to r. Since H is a positive constant, I_p will have some maximum value associated with the minimum interest rate which the community will accept: that is, the value of $r_{\min}$. To fix our ideas, let us assume that, numerically, we have

$$A = 100 \qquad H = 1{,}000 \qquad r_{\min} = 2{\cdot}0 \text{ per cent.}$$
$$c = 0{\cdot}8 \qquad b = 10$$

Given this information we can construct Fig. 17.vi, which, in its two panels, depicts the consumption and investment hypotheses.

From (6) and (7) by making use of the identity (5) we can obtain

$$D \equiv C_p + I_p = (A+H) + cY - br, \tag{8}$$

which reminds us that real aggregate demand depends upon *both* real income (Y) and the interest rate (r). Thus to find D for any given Y we must also know r.

To find r we make use of the equations describing the money market. These are

$$M^S = M_0 = \text{the supply hypothesis} \tag{9}$$

$$M^D = KpY + Z - dr = \text{the demand hypothesis} \tag{10}$$

$$M^S = M^D \qquad = \text{the equilibrium condition.} \tag{11}$$

As the reader can readily check substitution of (9) and (10) into (11) yields the following solution for r:

$$r = [KpY + Z - M_0]\frac{1}{d} \tag{12}$$

Inserting this into (8) yields the following rather formidable-looking expression for D:

$$D = (A+H) + cY - \frac{b}{d}[KpY + Z - M_0]$$
$$= \left[A + H - \frac{b}{d}(z - M_0)\right] + cY - \frac{b}{d}KpY. \tag{13}$$

Again assuming numerical values for the demand and supply of money functions, we can now calculate D for any value of Y and pY. Unfortunately Y and pY remain to be determined.

From the aggregate supply function, however, we already know that a given value of p implies a given value of Y and thus pY. Thus if Y in (13) is replaced by the aggregate supply function

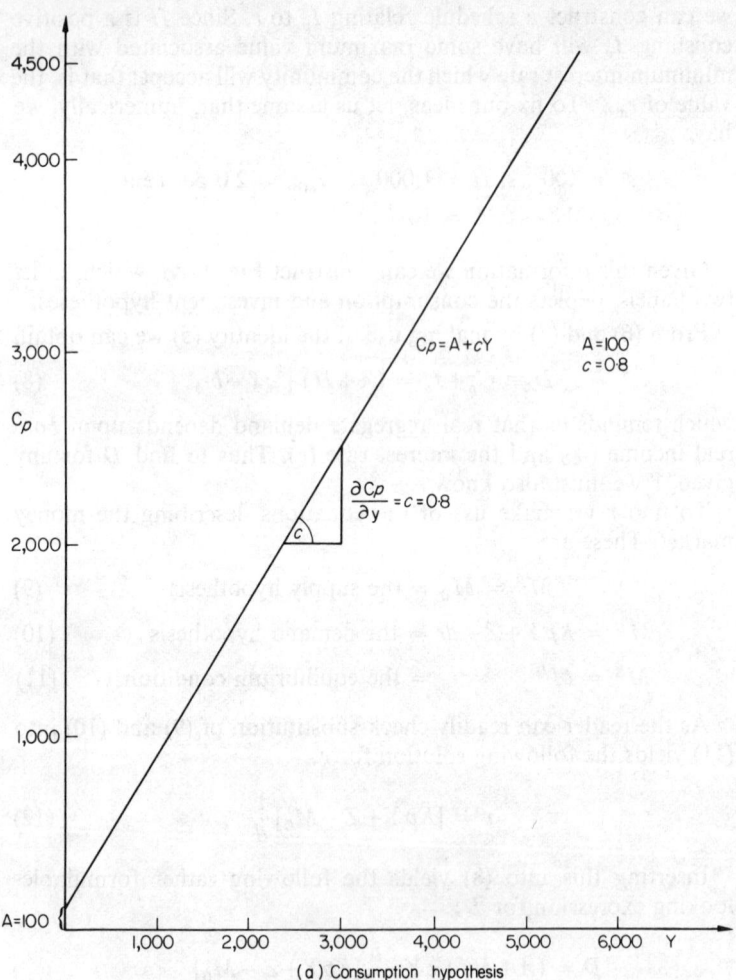

FIG. 17.vi Consumption and investment hypotheses

relating Y to p – written purely for convenience as $Y = s(p)$ – then (13) becomes

$$D = \left[A + H - \frac{b}{d}(Z - M_0)\right] + cs(p) - \frac{b}{d}Kps(p), \qquad (14)$$

which clearly gives D as a function of p while yet emphasising that aggregate demand depends upon aggregate supply (via both the

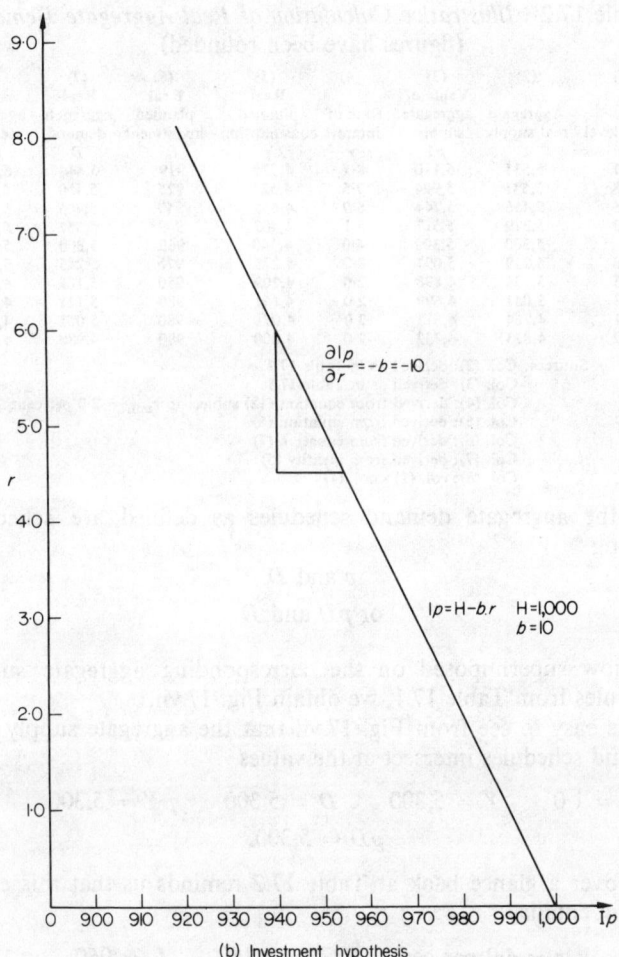

FIG. 17.vi Consumption and investment hypotheses

consumption and investment functions) and on the characteristics of the demand and supply functions for money.

Taking the following numerical values for the money market equations

$$M_0 = 2{,}500 \qquad K = 0{\cdot}25$$
$$Z = 1{,}375 \qquad d = 50$$

we can calculate D as is shown in Table 17.2.

Table 17.2   *Illustrative Calculation of Real Aggregate Demand*
(figures have been rounded)

(1)	(2)	(3)	(4)	(5)	(6)	(7)	(8)
		Value of		Real	Real	Real	Value of
	Aggregate	aggregate	Rate of	planned	planned	aggregate	aggregate
Price level	real supply	supply	interest	consumption	investment	demand	demand
p	Y	pY	r	C_p	I_p	D	pD
1·11	5,531	6,110	8·1	4,525	919	5,444	6,043
1·08	5,531	5,994	7·5	4,525	925	5,450	5,886
1·05	5,456	5,744	6·0	4,465	940	5,405	5,675
1·03	5,379	5,517	5·1	4,403	949	5,352	5,513
1·0	5,300	5,300	4·0	4,340	960	5,300	5,300
0·98	5,219	5,091	3·0	4,275	970	5,245	5,140
0·95	5,136	4,898	2·0	4,209	980	5,189	4,930
0·93	5,051	4,699	2·0	4,141	980	5,121	4,763
0·91	4,964	4,513	2·0	4,071	980	5,051	4,596
0·89	4,873	4,332	2·0	4,000	980	4,980	4,432

Sources: Col. (2): derived as in Table 17.1
Col. (3): derived as in Table 17.1
Col. (4): derived from equation (12) subject to r_{min} = 2·0 per cent
Col. (5): derived from equation (6)
Col. (6): derived from equation (7)
Col. (7): derived from identity (5)
Col. (8): col. (1) × col. (7)

If the aggregate demand schedules as defined are schedules relating

$$p \text{ and } D$$

$$\text{or } pD \text{ and } D$$

are now superimposed on the corresponding aggregate supply schedules from Table 17.1, we obtain Fig. 17.vii.

It is easy to see from Fig. 17.vii that the aggregate supply and demand schedules intersect at the values

$$p = 1\cdot0 \qquad Y = 5,300 \qquad D = 5,300 \qquad pY = 5,300$$

$$pD = 5,300.$$

Moreover a glance back at Table 17.2 reminds us that this equilibrium entails

$$r = 4\cdot0 \text{ per cent} \qquad C_p = 4,340 \qquad I_p = 960.$$

Now consider a price level other than $p = 1\cdot0$ – say $p^* = 0\cdot91$. From Fig. 17.vii (a), or alternatively from Table 17.1, we find

$$\text{aggregate supply} \equiv Y^* = 4,964.$$

Similarly from Fig. 17.vii, or alternatively from Table 17.2, we find

$$\text{aggregate demand} \equiv D^* = 5,051;$$

hence the *excess* demand at the *disequilibrium* price p^* is $D^* - Y^* =$ 87 or, in value terms, $p^*[D^* - Y^*] = 4,596 - 4,513 = 83$. Clearly,

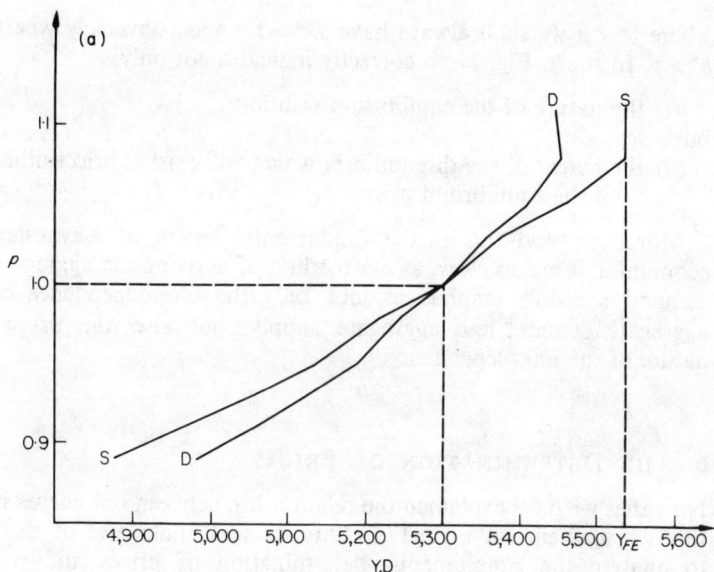

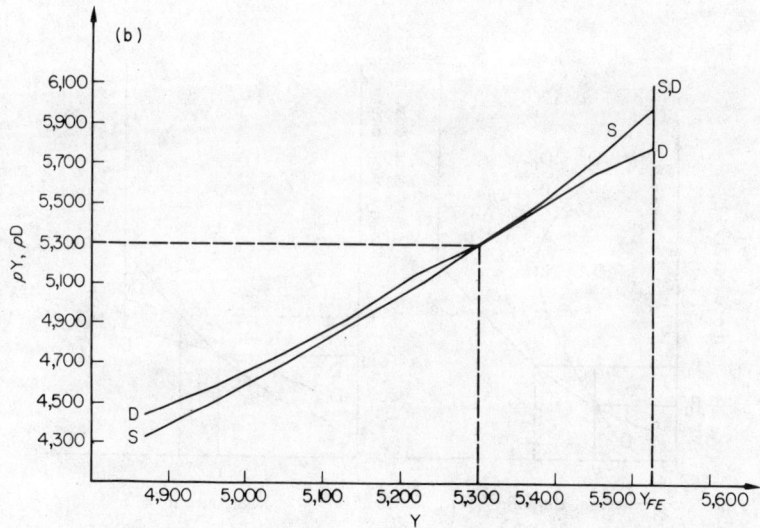

FIG. 17.vii Aggregate demand and supply schedules

where $p^* < p$ we shall always have $D^* > Y^*$ and conversely where $p^* > p$. In short, Fig. 17.vii correctly indicates not only

(i) the nature of the equilibrium solution

but also

(ii) the *extent* of the disequilibria which will exist at prices other than the equilibrium price.

Moreover, and this is the fundamental lesson of Keynesian economics, it makes clear, as our method of deriving the aggregate demand schedule emphasises, not only the interdependence of aggregate demand and aggregate supply, but also the precise nature of the interdependence.

6 THE DETERMINATION OF PRICES

Now that we have explained the relationship between our curves in the two segments of Figs. 17.ii–17.iv we shall make use of them to analyse the simultaneous determination of prices and real income. Suppose, for example, we are in a position depicted by Fig. 17.viii (b). Assume now that because of (say) an increase in optimism the M.E.I. schedule shifts to the right. What happens?

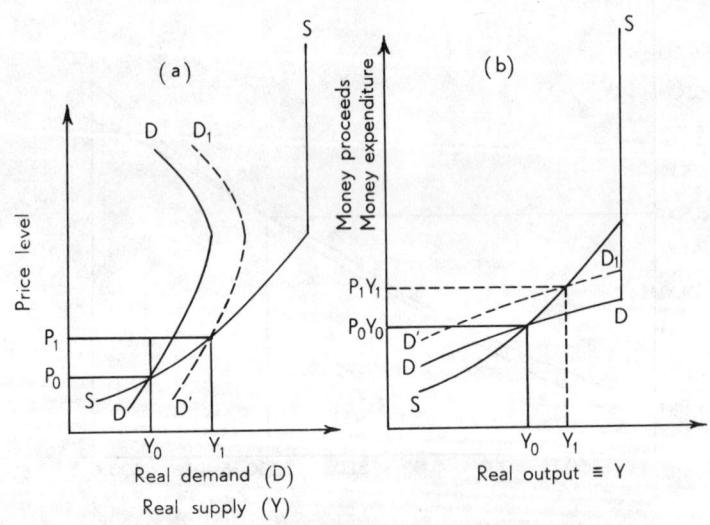

FIG. 17.viii   An increase in the M.E.I. schedule

Clearly the aggregate demand functions in both sections of Fig. 17.viii shift. Output rises from Y_0 to Y_1 and prices from p_0 to p_1. Employment, of course, also rises by an amount determined by the production function.

There is, however, *no simple relationship between the increase in aggregate demand and in the increase in prices.* What happens to prices (assuming an invariant money wage rate) depends upon the *slope* of the aggregate supply schedule. And this, as we have seen, depends upon the *extent* to which the marginal product of labour falls as output expands. If employment was initially rather low, capital might not be fully utilised. Machines, for example, might all be in use but be running at reduced speeds. In such a situation the marginal productivity of labour might fall very little and thus prices rise by very little, as output and employment expand. If this is so the increase in aggregate demand will go, in the main, to increasing output and employment. Conversely, if the initial equilibrium was close to full employment the fall in the marginal product of labour might be marked. In such a situation the increase in prices might be relatively large; the increase in output and employment relatively small.

7 INFLATION AND MONEY WAGE CHANGES

A special problem arises if aggregate demand increases from a position of equilibrium *at* full employment. This is illustrated in Fig. 17.ix (b) where the D curve, initially at DD moves to $D'D'$. Here output, in the short run, *cannot* increase. Yet at the initial (i.e. old equilibrium) price level the quantity of output demanded now exceeds that supplied. There is, in short, a situation of *excess demand.* Such a situation is a disequilibrium one characterised by inflationary pressure. We are, at present, assuming a perfectly competitive system in the goods market. Hence we shall expect the price level to rise. Since this, with a given money wage rate (W_h) implies a fall in real wages, an excess demand for labour will emerge.

So far we have, by regarding W_h as given, not specified how the labour market responds to excess demand for labour at full employment. The simplest assumption is that money wage rates are bid up by excess demand and thus tend to rise *pari passu* with prices so that the real wage is invariant as long as

$$N^D \equiv \text{demand for labour} \geqslant N_f \equiv \text{full employment.}$$

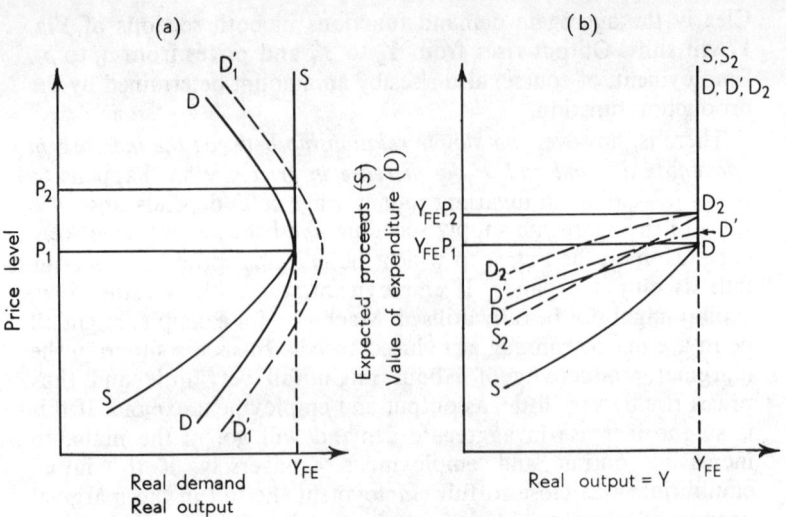

FIG. 17.ix   A shift in the aggregate demand function at full
employment

Given this assumption, the distribution of income between wage-
earners and profit-recipients is also invariant. Hence prices will
rise until the interest-rate mechanism has reduced aggregate
demand to the level of full-employment aggregate supply. De-
scriptively we may say that prices and wages rise proportionately,
thus *shifting both* aggregate demand and supply schedules. The
rise in prices increases the demand for money and this, given the
nominal money supply, raises the rate of interest, bringing about an
induced fall in planned investment. Since C_p is constant at the level
determined by Y_{FE}, aggregate real demand ($D \equiv C_p + I_p$) falls.
At the new equilibrium price level (p_2) the interest rate will have
increased sufficiently to equate D with Y_{FE} and hence $p_2 D$ ($\equiv$ money
expenditures) with $p_2 Y_{FE}$ ($\equiv$ the value of aggregate supply). Hence
the new equilibrium will be characterised by

a higher price level (p_2)
a higher money wage rate (W_{h2})

with real output and the real wage ($\equiv W_{h2}/p_2$) unaltered.
    It is now important to notice what is implied by our earlier
statement that both schedules *shift*. Since the original aggregate
demand and supply curves were constructed on the basis of W_h,

both now have as a parameter the new money wage rate W_{h2}. Thus the final equilibrium is characterised by new DD and SS curves labelled D_2D_2 and S_2S_2 in Fig. 17.vi (b). The curve $D'D'$ is thus no longer relevant. Nor is the initial aggregate supply curve. The reader should construct for himself the appropriate new curve for Fig. 17.vi (a) in which the curve $D_1'D_1'$ corresponds to $D'D'$ in Fig. 17.vi (b) and thus indicates the aggregate demand schedule *after* the initial shift but *before* money wages and prices have risen and hence before the new equilibrium has been attained.

In addition the reader should not be misled into thinking that the analysis is reversible: that is, if D_2D_2 shifted back to DD (because of a decline in business optimism) we should revert to the original price level (p_1), the original money wage rate (W_h) and the original aggregate supply curve (SS). This is because though, at the present level of abstraction, it is not unreasonable to assume that both prices and money wages are flexible *upwards* at full employment, it is almost certainly unreasonable to assume that wages are flexible *downwards*. Hence if demand falls so that $N^D < N_f \equiv$ full employment the new money wage rate W_{h2} must be regarded – at least as a first approximation – as invariant: in short the money wage rate exhibits downward rigidity in the short run.

Finally it should be noted that this analysis assumes not only that there is a determinate price level (p_2) at which aggregate demand is once again equal to aggregate supply (which depends on the analysis already discussed) but *also that the system will remain at this price level*. This second assumption is implicit: it is equivalent to assuming that the system is *dynamically stable*. The precise meaning of this will become clearer in later chapters. The reader, however, may for the moment simply assume that although the DD curve cuts the SS curve from above it is still easy to invest the system with dynamic properties which ensure that, once disturbed from equilibrium, the system will *not* return to it. That is that it will not remain at p_2. This implies, in the context of the present example, that an inflationary price rise once started never stops. Our method of analysis, though verbally it may appear dynamic, is comparative statics. Logically, however, we cannot compare equilibrium positions, as we have been doing, unless the system under study is *dynamically stable* for, if it is not, no equilibrium will be established. A basic assumption of our method is thus dynamic stability which implies, in this particular case, that prices will (at p_2) cease to rise: in short that the inflationary price rise is finite.

Starting again from equilibrium we may ask: What happens if the money wage rate is increased to a new constant level? The money wage rate is a parameter of *both* the aggregate demand and aggregate supply curves. Hence *both* curves must shift.

Consider first the *SS* curve. Given the profit-maximising behaviour of businessmen and the unchanged production function, the *SS* curve must shift upwards, for any level of output will now be associated with a higher price level and thus a higher level of expected proceeds. Since the price level is higher the money income generated by any level of output is now correspondingly higher. The nominal money supply is constant by assumption. Hence given the two liquidity functions (L_1 and L_2) the rate of interest associated with any level of output will be higher. Hence, at any level of Y, aggregate demand in real terms ($D \equiv C_p + I_p$) will be *smaller*. On the other hand the price level has *risen*. Has the value of money expenditure pD associated with any given Y risen or fallen? The answer to this question is not immediately obvious for, though the price level has risen, real planned investment (and thus real aggregate demand) has fallen. Fortunately it is not difficult to establish that money expenditure must have risen. To see this assume the contrary. Then $pD \equiv p(C_p + I_p)$ has fallen at any level of Y though p has risen. Since C_p depends only on Y (through the consumption hypothesis) the fall in $C_p + I_p$ must be due to a fall in I_p. But for I_p to fall *either* the M.E.I. schedule must have shifted (while we have assumed it to be constant) *or* the rate of interest must have risen. The rate of interest, however, will only rise if, with given L_1 and L_2 functions, money expenditure rises and thus increases the demand for active balances. Hence we have a contradiction: for $p(C_p + I_p)$ to *fall* requires $p(C_p + I_p)$ to *rise*. Hence $p(C_p + I_p)$ *cannot fall* for the very mechanism which brings about a fall in one of its components (I_p) – and thus raises the problem of its direction of change – depends upon the change being positive. Hence the aggregate demand curve *DD* shifts upwards.

If $p(C_p + I_p)$ cannot *fall* can it remain unchanged for any level of output (Y)? The argument which excludes a fall excludes this possibility also.

Since *both* the aggregate demand and aggregate supply curves are shifting upwards what is the nature of the final equilibrium? In general the new equilibrium will be characterised by

(i) a higher price level;
(ii) a higher level of money income;
(iii) a higher level of the rate of interest;
(iv) a lower rate of real planned investment;
(v) a lower level of real output; and
(vi) a lower level of employment.

In short the new DD and SS curves will intersect to the *left* of the initial equilibrium value of Y and at a *higher* value of money income.

Are there any circumstances in which predictions (v) and (vi) above would be inappropriate? There are two possibilities. If the initial equilibrium in the money market was at the minimum interest rate (r_{min}) and remained at that level *after* the change in the money wage rate, then I_p would not fall and $C_p + I_p$ would be unchanged at any level of Y. The same result would follow if the rate of interest changed in the manner discussed earlier but the marginal efficiency of investment schedule was completely interest inelastic. In both these cases (which could occur together) the aggregate demand and supply functions would shift upwards by an equal amount. Hence, though predictions (i) and (ii) remain generally appropriate, (iii) to (vi) in some special circumstances might be inappropriate.

Does it follow from this that a cut in money wages – even if it could be arranged – would *necessarily* increase output and employment? The answer is: no. Admittedly a lower level of the money wage rate implies a shift to a lower SS curve and a shift to a lower DD curve. But we must be careful not to be misled by our formal analysis. What is the mechanism involved? If the money wage rate is reduced then, at *any* level of real output, the price level consistent with profit maximisation will fall proportionately. Any level of real output will thus entail a lower level of money income than before. This will lower the demand for transaction balances. So much is certain. But the rate of interest will fall only if it is not already at its minimum. Hence the rate of interest may *not* fall. If it does not there will be no increase in real planned investment and thus in output. Admittedly this is essentially one of the special cases already discussed under money wage increases. In general a cut in the money wage rate, if that could be arranged without an outbreak of industrial strife or a wave of bankruptcies would, given the assumptions of our model, tend to increase output and employment.† There is, however, nothing in the model which guarantees that even the most severe money wage cut would enable the system to reach full employment. To see this let us revert temporarily to our earlier IS/LM analysis.

Suppose initially we are in equilibrium at Y_0 – a level of output substantially below Y_{FE}. The rate of interest is r_0. If we now cut

† Our formal model is slightly biased in favour of money wage cuts since it assumes income distribution constant. If a wage cut shifts distribution in such a way as to bring about a fall in the consumption function (which is quite possible) this would offset the interest effect.

the money wage rate the effect is to reduce the equilibrium interest rate at each level of output and raise the maximum level of output which can be financed with a given money supply. As a result the *LM* curve shifts to a new position LM_1. Output is now Y_1 and the rate of interest r_1. Employment has increased but it is still considerably below full employment.

As we have constructed the figure, r_1 is equal to r_{min}. *Hence any further cut in the money wage rate cannot reduce it.* Hence output cannot rise above Y_1. This difficulty occurs whenever the rate of interest which *would* equate planned saving out of full-employment income with planned investment (called r_{FE} on Fig. 17.x) is *less* than r_{min}. A special case of this occurs when r_{FE} is negative.

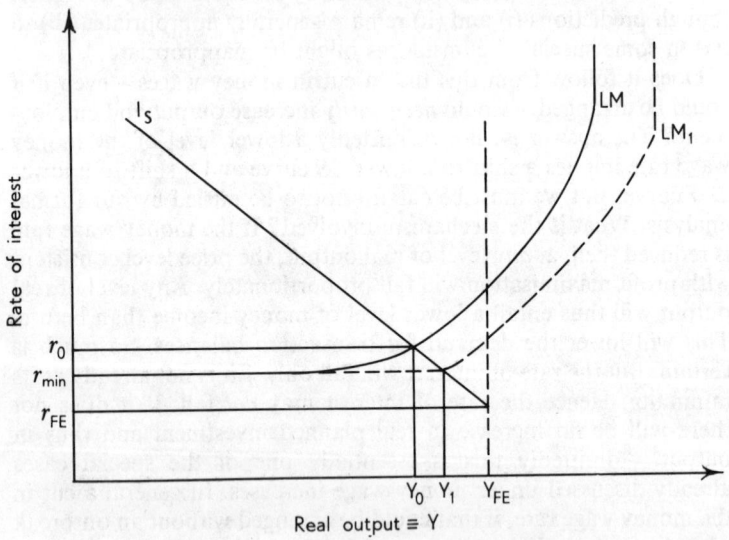

FIG. 17.x   Money wage cuts and employment

This is a point of considerable importance. In depressions businessmen tend to be pessimistic. The *IS* curve, therefore, because the M.E.I. schedule is low, is located far to the left. The rate of interest is in consequence likely to be at, or near to, its minimum.† It follows that cuts in the money wage rate will, in these circumstances, bring little or no fall in the rate of interest and thus little or no increase in employment. This point is significant because it has

† In post-Second World War recessions this statement is doubtful, particularly since also we are interpreting the interest rate to mean the *nominal* interest rate. It was approximately correct after 1932.

in the past often been argued that, to eliminate unemployment, it is essential to reduce money wage rates. At its crudest this argument is based upon a fallacy of composition. A *single* businessman, if he can reduce his wage rate, can reduce his prices and sell more output thus hiring more workers. This is true because if a *single* business-man reduces the wage rate he pays, the reduction in workers' money incomes will not affect significantly the demand for *his* product. If all businessmen do it, however, workers' incomes, and hence their demand for all products, must fall. Hence once again, what is true for the one is not true for all taken together – as our more formal analysis demonstrates. In contrast to this argument our model tells us that

(i) a cut in the money wage rate *may* increase employment but will not necessarily do so; and

(ii) however far this money wage cut is taken, it *may* not prove possible, by this method, to reach 'full employment'.

In this analysis we have implicitly proceeded on the basis of a consumption function which omits the real value of households' assets as a determinant of C_p. This was done for simplicity. Suppose, however, we replace our implicit function

$$C_p = H + cY$$

by $\qquad C_p = H' + cY + dA \qquad d > 0,$

where A is defined – as in Chapter 9 – as the real value of house-holds' assets. Our analysis will now be correct only if A is unaffected by changes in the price level (p): and this will be correct only if the nominal value of the assets entering A varies precisely with the price level.

In practice, households hold many assets (e.g. currency, bank deposits, building society deposits) which have values fixed in nominal terms. They also hold bonds whose market value, given the nominal money supply, is either invariant or increasing as p falls (since the lower p the lower, *ceteris paribus*, is the rate of interest). Incorporating this into our discussion means that we must expect the consumption function (as implicitly defined) to *shift* as p changes, for a fall in p must, to some extent, make households better off and a rise in p make them worse off. This is the basis for what is sometimes called in the literature 'the Pigou effect'.

Suppose we write the nominal value of such assets as L. Then our more complete consumption hypothesis becomes:

$$C_p = H' + cY + d\frac{L}{p} \qquad d > 0$$

and L/p is the 'Pigou effect' term.

Now if such a term exists and $d > 0$ then, logically, a cut in money wages (which reduces p) will raise L/p and hence C_p. Since there is, in logic, no limit to the extent of the cut in money wages and hence the fall in p, there is no limit to the rightward shift in the consumption schedule which can be brought about by money wage cuts. Hence there must be some cut in the money wage rate which will restore full employment by shifting the *IS* curve of Fig. 17.x sufficiently far to the right. Formally, then, our earlier argument and, in particular, our conclusion (ii) is destroyed.

In practice, however, as a matter of policy, it may not be destroyed in the sense that it may be correct to argue that money wage cuts are an *inefficient* method of restoring full employment since:

    (i) they are, to put it mildly, difficult to carry out
while
    (ii) their efficacy depends upon the value of the parameter d, which may well be small, and the other possible consequences of a rise in L/p.

Consider for a moment the meaning of L as those financial assets, held by households, whose values are fixed in nominal terms. Any such asset is the liability of some institution (e.g. a bank, building society, or the state). A rise in the real values of households' assets is thus a rise in the real value of some bodies' liabilities. If these bodies respond to a rise in their real liabilities by reducing their real expenditure, the rise in C_p will be partly offset. Indeed if debtors and creditors react symmetrically to variations in L/p the effect on real aggregate demand must be zero.

It is thus arguable that, for policy purposes, though not in logic, the case against money wage cuts remains. It must, however, be emphasised that this conclusion, in so far as it rests upon the implicit assumption that $D \equiv C_p + I_p$ is relatively insensitive to changes in L/p, implies empirical judgements about the magnitude of the parameter d and the extent to which its influence is offset by the reactions of debtors.

8   PRELIMINARY SUMMARY

The analysis of the preceding sections may be set out formally as follows.

First by assuming

    (i) that businessmen seek to maximise profits; and
    (ii) are operating in a purely competitive system

we showed that, given the money wage rate (W_h), businessmen would adjust output (and hence employment) until

$$p \frac{\partial Y}{\partial N} = W_h$$

which, since $\partial Y/\partial N$ is, via the short-run production function, uniquely related to Y, enables us to write

$$Y = S_1[p]$$

or

$$pY = S_2[p]$$

given W_h

as alternative forms of the aggregate supply function.

We next defined aggregate demand as

$$D \equiv C_p + I_p$$

and hypothesised the behaviour relations

$$C_p = f_c(Y)$$
$$I_p = f_i(r).$$

Assuming the nominal money supply to be given ($\equiv M^S$) we then adopted the money demand hypothesis

$$M^D = L(pY, r).$$

Equating M^D and M^S, that is requiring equilibrium in the money market, we now obtain an expression for r as a function of pY, M^S say

$$r = L'(pY, M^S).$$

Thus the aggregate demand function, on substitution, can be written

$$D = f_c(Y) + f_i L'(pY, M^S).$$

As we have already seen, Y (or pY) can be obtained as a function of p from the aggregate supply hypothesis. Hence

$$D = f_c S_1(p) + f_i L'[S_2(p), M^S],$$

which is the form of the aggregate demand function employed in Figs. 17.iv (a), 17.v (a) and 17.vi (a). Notice that

(i) this function *explicitly* depends on the aggregate supply hypothesis: it thus not only emphasises the interdependence of aggregate supply but specifies the *precise nature of the interdependence*;

(ii) D is now expressed, given M^S, as a function of p alone – albeit a complicated one since it depends upon p in two ways; and

(iii) since Y (provided employment is less than full) rises with p, then because of the consumption function hypothesis, D also will rise with p: that is, the D curve will be upward-sloping as we have drawn it.

This last point (iii) is worth some emphasis since in some expositions schedules called 'aggregate demand' are depicted sloping downwards with respect to the price level. Reasons for thinking that these curves are misleadingly named when called 'aggregate demand' curves are given in the Appendix to this chapter, which explains their derivation. At this point we merely note that they are *not* aggregate demand functions as we have defined them.

When, as in the earlier figures, the relevant aggregate demand and aggregate supply schedules are superimposed, we then see, in a slight paraphrase of Keynes's own words, that 'the volume of output is given by the intersection between the aggregate demand function and the aggregate supply function'. Simultaneously determined are the equilibrium values of the price level, the interest rate, the real wage rate, consumption, investment and the demand for money. Moreover at any price level *other* than the equilibrium price level, the discrepancy between the relevant points on the two schedules gives a measure of excess demand (or excess supply) in the goods market either in real terms ($D-Y$) or in value terms ($pD-pY$).

As we have seen, our theory implies a precise relationship between aggregate demand and aggregate supply such that given p ($\equiv$ price level) there will be a given value of Y ($\equiv$ real aggregate supply) and a given value of D ($\equiv C_p + I_p \equiv$ aggregate demand). The specification of the nature of this interdependence is the crucial lesson of the whole analysis since Keynes's aims were twofold: that is, he sought to show:

(i) the nature of the interdependence between D and Y; and

(ii) that this interdependence was *not* of a form commonly described by Say's Law.

Say's Law, which is usually paraphrased as stating that 'Supply creates its own demand', is ambiguous and can be interpreted in two very different ways.

The first of these, which we shall call Say's Identity, interprets it as saying that aggregate demand is equal to aggregate supply for all positive values of p. In this case the aggregate demand and supply schedules would coincide and p ($\equiv$ the price level) would be indeterminate.

The second proposition, which we shall call Say's Law, interprets it as saying that the economic system is so constructed, in institutional and behaviouristic terms, that the aggregate demand and supply schedules always intersect at a value of p ($\equiv$ price level) which implies $Y = Y_{FE}$: that is, that if output departs from the full-employment level, forces are automatically set to work which, if allowed to operate freely, will restore full employment. What kind of system this implies is discussed more fully in Chapter 18 where we present a brief sketch of Keynes and his predecessors. At the moment we are only concerned to make clear that the Keynesian theory which we have presented is a denial of both Say's Identity and Say's Law.

We must now re-emphasise that both the aggregate demand and supply functions which we have constructed depend upon the money wage rate which we have taken as given. Unless we can give an account of how this gets determined our theory must remain rather empty since its predictions depend upon the value of a variable for which we have, so far, given no explanation.

In Keynesian analysis, from which our model is derived, it is assumed that *the money wage rate is an exogenous variable (determined outside the model) by a process of industrial bargaining between employees (organised in trade unions) and employers (sometimes but not always organised in associations).* What is envisaged in this assumption, shorn of its institutional complexities, is that unions bargain for a rate of *money wages.* This does *not* mean that unions do not take prices into account at all: that is, possess a *money illusion.* It means that they bargain for money wages simply because the economic and institutional system is such that they cannot easily bargain for a real wage.

Once a level of money wages has been determined by bargaining, W in our model takes a particular value which we have called W_h. At this negotiated level of the money wage rate the whole of the work-force then offers itself for employment and the supply curve of labour is a horizontal straight line up to 'full employment' and a vertical straight line *at* 'full employment'. This supply curve is depicted in Fig. 17.xi.

The demand for *labour* curve can then be superimposed upon the supply curve. The derivation of this curve we leave as an interesting and difficult exercise for the reader. The excess of full-employment labour supply (N_f) over the quantity of labour actually employed (N_0) is then *involuntary unemployment*; that is, it is an index of the

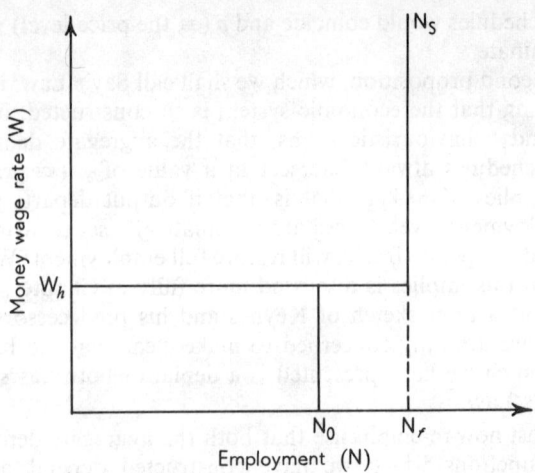

FIG. 17.xi The labour supply function

number of persons prepared to work at the existing money (and real) wage who cannot obtain employment.

There are, of course, other forms of unemployment. For example some unemployment is *seasonal* – such as that in the catering and holiday industries. In addition some unemployment is *structural*: that is, due to long-run changes in the commodity composition of demand involving (say) the transfer of workers from declining industries (such as mining) to expanding industries (such as chemicals). Observed unemployment will therefore tend to exceed the N_f-N_0 of our figure because of the presence of structural and seasonal elements.

9 THE QUANTITY OF MONEY AND THE PRICE LEVEL

Now that we have a theory of the price level let us see how it works – that is, what predictions it generates, by asking one of the oldest question in economics, namely: what are the consequences of an increase in the money supply?

We look first at aggregate demand; next at aggregate supply.

Suppose the central bank conducts open market purchases. Then, by the arguments of Chapter 16, we shall have a primary increase in the money supply equal to the value of the open market purchases and a secondary expansion undertaken by the commercial banks in order to restore their preferred asset ratios. In terms of our *LM–IS* curve analysis, the *LM* curve moves to the right. There is, in general, an expectation that (i) the equilibrium rate of interest will decline; and (ii) the level of output will increase. In terms of our *DD/SS* analysis, the *DD* curve tends to shift upwards, for any level of prices will now, for a given level of real income, imply a lower rate of interest and thus greater real aggregate demand.† Hence the new aggregate demand curve will in general lie to the right of our original curve.

How big will the increase in demand be? The answer must depend upon

  (i) the extent to which the rate of interest falls as a result of the increase in M^S, which depends upon
    (*a*) the slope of the L_2 function;
    (*b*) *where* we originally were on the function.

  Obviously if the rate of interest was initially close to $r_{\min}$ it might fall very little. If it were *at* $r_{\min}$ it could not fall at all;

  (ii) the extent to which the fall in the rate of interest increases real planned investment:‡ that is, the slope of the M.E.I. schedule;

  (iii) the response of output to the increase in real planned investment which depends upon the slope of the propensity-to-consume schedule: that is the marginal propensity to consume which determines the multiplier;

  (iv) the response of the demand for active balances to increases in output (= real income) determined by the L_1 function and the extent to which prices rise as output increases.

Obviously, in view of all this, there is no simple and invariant relationship between increases in the money supply (M^S) and increases in aggregate demand. There may be no response (if r does not fall or I_p does not respond to the fall in r). Or there may be a large response (if r falls considerably and I_p responds largely to reductions in r). To make a useful prediction we must know the *slopes* of the functions over the relevant ranges which are, of course, questions of fact.

† This, as the reader will be aware, assumes (i) that the demand for idle balances is not infinitely interest elastic; and (ii) that the investment schedule is not completely interest inelastic.

‡ Notice that if the consumption function contains a 'Pigou' term which incorporates the value of bond holdings, then a fall in the interest rate by increasing bond values will raise consumption.

Suppose we *do* know the relevant functions. Then we can work out the response of aggregate demand and thus the shift in the *DD* schedule. We already know that what happens when aggregate demand increases (the *DD* curve shifts) is in general (i) an increase in output and employment, and (ii) an increase in the price level.

The precise results now depend upon the nature of the *SS* function the slope of which depends on the production function and where we were originally on it. Clearly we may have either†

(i) a large increase in output (and hence) employment with a small price increase; or

(ii) a small increase in output (and hence) employment with a large price increase.

Thus, though there is a relation between the money supply (M^S) and the level of prices (p), there is no simple relationship between increases in the former and increases in the latter. In particular, unless the increase in the money supply takes place at 'full employment', prices will *not* rise in the same proportion as the money supply and they will not necessarily do so even at full employment. This is an important conclusion because one popular theory of the price level, *the quantity theory of money*, in its simplest form at least, asserts this proportionality proposition.

10 FINAL SUMMARY

In this chapter we have extended our model slightly in order to show that the price level, hitherto regarded as exogenously given, is more properly regarded as an endogenous variable, determined, along with other endogenous variables, in a general equilibrium model.

In order to explain the determination of the price level, we constructed aggregate demand and supply schedules. The intersection of these then depicted the determination of the equilibrium value of p ($\equiv$ the price level) and Y ($\equiv$ real output). The assumptions underlying these curves have already been discussed in some detail. The essential point to note is that the schedules are interdependent in the sense that the aggregate demand schedule depends on the aggregate supply schedule but that the latter does *not* depend upon

† Or, if r initially equals r_{min}, no change in either output or prices. The same result will also follow if planned investment is completely interest inelastic.

the former. Indeed this method of presenting an essentially Keynesian macro-static model is undertaken principally to make clear:

(i) the precise nature of the interdependence entailed in Keynesian theory; and

(ii) that this interdependence does not take a form compatible with either:

    (a) Say's Identity; or

    (b) Say's Law

as we have defined them.

These are crucial points since they are the very core of Keynes's analysis and the central message of Keynesian economics.

We then used the aggregate demand/supply analysis, albeit on a number of restrictive assumptions, to work out the consequences of

(i) an increase in business optimism;

(ii) a cut in the money wage rate; and

(iii) an increase in the nominal money supply.

Our analysis of (ii) – but not necessarily our policy conclusion – we qualified by extending our simple consumption hypothesis so as to include a 'Pigou effect' term. Our analysis of (ii) we shall, in the next chapter, compare with an alternative analysis arising out of what is called 'the Quantity Theory of Money'.

QUESTIONS AND EXERCISES

1. The following relations describe the complete Keynesian model used in Chapter 17 to provide a numerical example.

Goods market

$S_p = -A + (1-c)Y$	saving function	(17.I)
$I_p = H - br$	investment function	(17.II)
$S_p = I_p$	equilibrium condition	(17.III)

Money market

$M^S = M_0$	money supply	(17.IV)
$M^D = K(Yp) + Z - dr$†	demand for money	(17.V)
$M^D = M^S$	equilibrium condition	(17.VI)

† Assume that $r_{min} = 2 \cdot 0\%$.

Labour market

$$N^D = X - g\left(\frac{W}{p}\right) \qquad \text{demand for labour} \qquad (17.\text{VII})$$

$$N^S = f_n(W)\dagger \qquad \text{supply of labour} \qquad (17.\text{VIII})$$

$$W = W_h \qquad \text{money wage rate} \qquad (17.\text{IX})$$

$$Y = F + eN - fN^2 \qquad \text{production function} \qquad (17.\text{X})$$

$$\frac{\partial Y}{\partial N} = e - 2fN \qquad \text{marginal product of labour} \quad (17.\text{XI})$$

$$U \equiv N_f - N \qquad \text{definition of involuntary} \qquad (17.\text{XII})$$
$$\qquad\qquad\qquad\qquad\qquad \text{unemployment}$$

Given the numerical values of the constants and coefficients of the functions (set out below)

$A = 100$ $X = 500$
$c = 0\cdot8$ $g = 50$
$H = 1000$ $W_h = 8$
$b = 10$ $F = 4400$
$K = 0\cdot25$ $e = 10$
$Z = 1375$ $f = 0\cdot01$
$d = 50$ $r_{\text{minimum}} = 2\cdot0$ per cent
$M_0 = 2500$ $N_f = 130$

(i) construct and graph aggregate supply schedules relating Y to Yp and N to Yp; (ii) construct and graph aggregate demand curves relating Y to Yp and N to Yp for the following values of N: $N = 50, 60, 70, 80, 90, 100, 110, 120, 130$. Use these schedules to verify the equilibrium values of

$Y \equiv$ real income
$Yp \equiv$ money income
$N \equiv$ employment   given in the text.

2. Verify also the equilibrium values of

$C_p \equiv$ real planned consumption
$I_p =$ real planned investment
$r \equiv$ the rate of interest
$\dfrac{W}{p} \equiv$ real wage rate.
$U \equiv$ involuntary unemployment
$p \equiv$ the price level

† Interpret to mean the supply of labour infinitely elastic at the ruling money wage rate up to full employment and infinitely inelastic at full employment.

What is the maximum money income (Yp) which can be financed with the given money supply?

3. Suppose the money wage rate (W_h) is cut to reduce involuntary unemployment (U).

    (i) Will full employment ($N_f = N$) be restored?

    (ii) If not, what will be the value of U?

    (iii) What rate of interest (r) is necessary to reach full employment?

4. What is the relationship between equations (17.VII), (17.X) and (17.XI)? Explain in economic terms and show how (17.VII) can be derived from (17.X).

5. Use the model of Question 1 to find N (employment) for all integral values of W (money wage rate) from 6 to 10. Graph and interpret the resulting curve. Is this a demand curve for labour in terms of the *money wage rate*? What is its approximate elasticity at $W_h = 8$? Can it be superimposed on the supply curve of Fig. 17.xi.

6. Use the model to analyse the consequences of an increase in the money supply from 2,500 to 2,700. What reduction in the given money wage rate W_h would achieve the same result? Use your answer to discuss the relative advantages of increases in the money supply and cuts in the money wage rate as methods of reducing involuntary unemployment. Would fiscal policy be a more effective weapon than either?

7. Define the share of wages in the total product as:

$$\frac{N \times W}{Y \times p} \equiv \frac{\text{wage bill}}{\text{money income}}.$$

Find the share of wages when (i) $W_h = 8$; (ii) $W_h = 6$.

8. In terms of our model has involuntary unemployment any single cause? Comment on the view that it can exist only if the money wage rate is 'too high' or the consumption function is 'too low'.

9. 'Unemployment equilibrium can occur if, and only if, money wage rates are inflexible'. Discuss. On what assumptions would this statement be correct?

10. 'In so far as the central bank controls the money supply it is the *nominal* money supply which it controls. It is the public which determines the *real* money supply.' Elucidate and appraise.

11. In Fig. 17.iv (b) the aggregate supply and aggregate demand curves appear to coincide at values of expected proceeds in

excess of $Y_{FE}p_{FE}$. If this was so expected proceeds would be indeterminate over the relevant range. From the numerical model

(i) evaluate pY_{FE} and $p(C_p+I_p)$ at full-employment output for prices in excess of P_{FE};
(ii) show that with output at full employment (Y_{FE}) and $p \geqslant p_{FE}$, aggregate supply pY exceeds aggregate demand $[p(C_p+I_p)]$;
(iii) on the basis of these results reinterpret the relevant portions of Fig. 17.iv (b).

12. Suppose the money wage rate was higher the lower the level of unemployment. Redraw Fig. 17.xi on this assumption. Analyse its implications.

13. Modify the saving hypothesis of Question 1 to read $S_p = -A+(1-c)Y+b\left(\dfrac{Ms}{p}\right)$ with $b = -0.1$. How would you interpret the modification? What kind of behaviour hypothesis is implied? Does the introduction of the new term change the conclusions of our analysis with regard to the effect of money wage cuts on involuntary unemployment? Why?

14. A businessman of your acquaintance tells you: 'If I could cut my wage rate I could lower prices and sell more. If I sold more I could employ more people. All businessmen are in my position. It is obvious that a cut in money wages reduces unemployment.' Write him a reasoned explanation of his error.

15. What does it mean to say that an individual suffers from a 'money illusion'? Give a precise definition.

16. Which, if any, of the following consumption hypotheses implies a 'money illusion'? Explain carefully.

$$C_p = A+cY+b(M^S/p).$$
$$C_p = A+c(Yp)+b(M^S/p).$$
$$p(C_p) = pA+c(Yp)+bM^S.$$
$$p(C_p) = B+c(Yp)+bM^S.$$

17. A cut in money wages distributes real income away from wage-earners and profit-recipients and to those persons whose incomes are fixed in money terms. Why? How would this modify your analysis of money wage cuts?

18. 'A 10 per cent cut in money wages means a 10 per cent cut in prices. . . . In real terms therefore everything is as it was. There is no effect on output or employment.' Discuss critically.

19. What predictions would you suggest for a cut in money wages in an economy engaging in international trade? Why?
20. Discuss the recent (mid-1971) assertion that the rise in unemployment is the result of excessive wage claims.
21. Replace equation (17.v) of Question 1 by:

$$M^D = K(pD) + Z - dr$$

and rework Question 1. Interpret the new hypothesis and show that the equilibrium results are unaffected. Comment on the disequilibrium positions.

SUGGESTED READING

P. Davidson and E. Smolensky, *Aggregate Supply and Demand Analysis* (Harper & Row, 1965) chs i, ix–x.
Ibid. † chs xi–xiii.
J. M. Keynes, *The General Theory of Employment, Interest and Money* (Macmillan, 1936) ch. xviii.

† More advanced reference.

Appendix: On Alternative Aggregate Demand Curves

THE aggregate demand schedule employed in the text gives D ($\equiv$ real aggregate demand) as a function of p ($\equiv$ the price level). It is obtained as follows:

$$D \equiv C_p + I_p \tag{1}$$

$$C_p = c(Y) \qquad 0 < \frac{\partial C}{\partial Y} \leqslant 1 \tag{2}$$

$$I_p = i(r) \qquad \frac{\partial I}{\partial r} < 0 \tag{3}$$

$$M^D = L(r, pY) \qquad \frac{\partial M^D}{\partial r} < 0 \quad \frac{\partial M^D}{\partial(pY)} > 0 \tag{4}$$

$$M^S = \overline{M} \tag{5}$$

$$M^D = M^S. \tag{6}$$

Using (4)–(6) to solve for r we obtain

$$r = L'[pY, \overline{M}]. \tag{7}$$

Hence

$$D \equiv C_p + I_p$$
$$\equiv c(Y) + iL'[pY, \overline{M}]. \tag{8}$$

Now apart from D, equation (8) contains two endogenous variables, namely p and Y. We cannot, therefore, relate D to p, as the aggregate demand schedule conceptually requires, unless either

(i) Y is known; or
(ii) Y is eliminated.

Clearly route (i) is inappropriate since we should then have a curve relating D to p for a given value of Y, when our aim is to treat Y as an endogenous variable to be determined, along with p, by the intersection of the aggregate demand and supply schedules. We therefore choose alternative (ii) and eliminate Y by inserting the aggregate supply hypothesis which relates Y to p. This entails the further assumptions that

$$Y = f(K, N) \quad \frac{\partial Y}{\partial K}, \frac{\partial Y}{\partial N} > 0 \quad \frac{\partial^2 Y}{\partial K^2} < 0 \quad \frac{\partial^2 Y}{\partial N^2} < 0 \tag{9}$$

$$p\frac{\partial Y}{\partial N} = W_h \tag{10}$$

$$K = \bar{K}. \tag{11}$$

Equation (10) reflects two assumptions. The first is institutional in that it implies that the goods market is purely competitive: the second is behaviouristic in that it hypothesises that businessmen seek to maximise profits.

Equation (11) states that, in the short run, the capital stock is invariant. Equation (9) is the production function. Inserting (11) into (9) enables us to write

$$Y = f(\bar{K}, N)$$

and since, for any given K, $\partial Y/\partial N$ is a function of N (or Y) we may now rewrite (10) as

$$pf(Y) = W_h$$

or

$$Y = f(p, W_h). \tag{12}$$

This in turn, taking the value of W_h as given, yields

$$Y = S_1(p) \tag{13}$$

or

$$pY = S_2(p), \tag{13*}$$

which are our forms of the aggregate supply function. Inserting (13) into (8) now gives the aggregate demand functions

$$D = cS_1(p) + iL'[pS_1(p), \bar{M}] \tag{14}$$

or

$$pD = pcS_1(p) + piL'[pS_1(p), \bar{M}], \tag{14*}$$

which gives D (or pD) as a function of p given W_h and $\bar{M}$ ($\equiv$ the nominal money supply).

The two schedules (13) and (14) are drawn in Fig. 17.App.i. Notice that, at any price level which does not equate D and Y, say P_0, the horizontal distance between D_0 and Y_0 provides a measure of excess demand (or supply) in the goods market: that is, involuntary stock accumulation or decumulation.

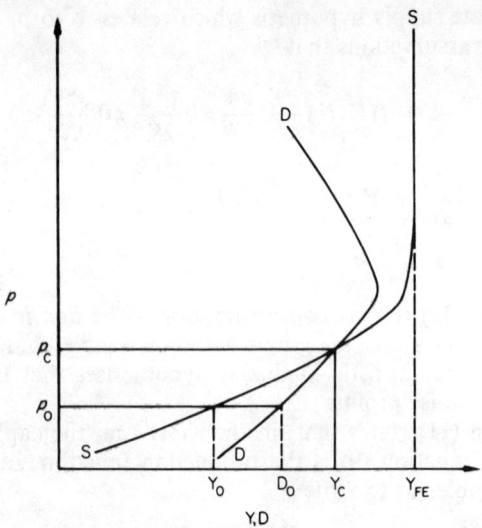

FIG. 17.App.i   Aggregate demand and supply schedules

The aggregate demand schedule constructed in this way has the following pedagogic advantages:

(i) it corresponds, save for the use of Y rather than N on the horizontal axis and the unstarred rather than starred versions, with Keynes's own formulation;

(ii) it makes explicit the dependence of aggregate demand on aggregate supply; and

(iii) it correctly identifies situations of disequilibrium in the goods market.

II

The alternative schedule found in the literature and identified as an 'aggregate demand curve' follows the same procedure as far as (8). That is, it obtains

$$D = c(Y) + iL'[pY, \overline{M}]. \tag{8}$$

However, confronted with the necessity of eliminating Y it does so, not by making use of the aggregate supply function as we have done, but by inserting the condition $D = Y$: that is, that the goods market is *always* in equilibrium. Thus it obtains

$$Y = c(Y) + iL'[pY, \overline{M}]$$

and eliminates not Y but D. The resultant curve relates Y to p on the assumption that *both* the money *and* goods markets are in equilibrium.†

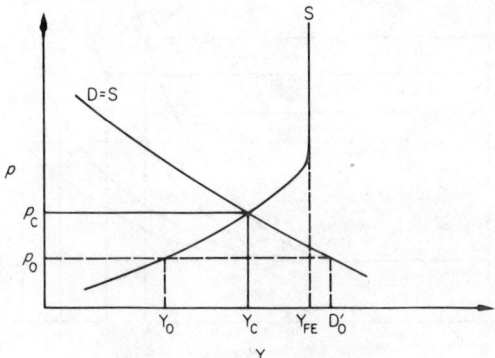

Fig. 17.App.ii   The $D = S$ schedule

The reader will have no difficulty in seeing that the resultant curve *must* slope downwards from left to right for the higher is p then, since M^S is constant ($= \overline{M}$) the higher is p the higher is r and the lower is I_p and the level of Y which equilibrates the goods market. This curve, which we have labelled the $D = S$ (demand equals supply) curve, is, of course, the locus of all the pairs of values of p and Y which are compatible with equilibrium in the familiar *IS–LM* diagram. This can easily be seen from Fig. 17.App. iii.

In this figure, recalling that p is a parameter of the *LM* curve, we have drawn *LM* schedules for $p = p_0, p_1, p_2, p_3$, where $p_0 < p_1 < p_2 < p_3$. Since the greater the value of p the greater for any Y is the demand for money, the higher will be the associated interest rate in the money market. Given the *IS* curve, this has the usual consequences for the equilibrium value of Y. Clearly the locus of pairs of r and Y can be used to trace out a curve relating Y to p, which is the $D = S$ curve already described.

Now return to Fig. 17.App.ii. It is trivial that the equilibrium position $p = p_e Y = Y_e$ depicted in Fig. 17.App.ii must be identical with the equilibrium position depicted in Fig. 17.App.i since, in

† In terms of behaviour this implies assuming that output is independent of p: that is, that producers simply supply whatever is demanded at any price level. The retention of the aggregate supply schedule in the diagram, however, shows that this behaviour is not being assumed.

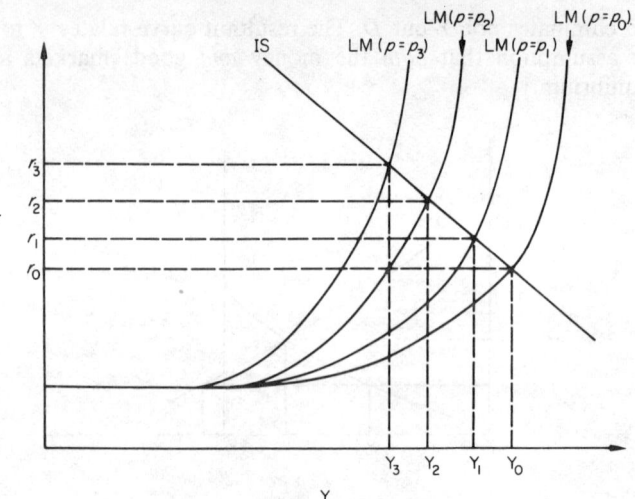

FIG. 17.App.iii   Constructing the $D = S$ schedule

equilibrium $D = S$ in both cases and the models are otherwise identical. Consider, however, a non-equilibrium price level, say p_0. The $D = S$ curve tells us that, in this situation

  (i) the quantity of output demanded is D'_0; and
 (ii) that excess demand is apparently therefore $D'_0 - Y_0$ even though
(iii) excess demand is assumed to be identically zero at all points on $D = S$.

Obviously $D'_0 - Y_0$ in Fig. 17.App.ii is *not* a correct measure of the excess demand in the goods market which will exist if $p = p_0$. For if $p = p_0$ and supply plans are carried out, this will generate a level of money income $p_0 Y_0$ which is *not* the level of money income implied by the $D = S$ curve at p_0. This is, of course, $p_0 D'_0$, which implies

  (i) a level of r other than that which will actually rule; and
 (ii) a level of Y which is not equal to Y_0.

Hence the $D = S$ curve incorrectly describes all positions of disequilibrium in the goods market and is correct only in the case of equilibrium.

The $D = S$ curve when defined as an 'aggregate demand' curve suffers also from the disadvantages

(i) that it encourages the notion that aggregate demand and supply are independent; and thus

(ii) assigns an incorrect sign to the derivative dD/dp ($\equiv$ the change in demand resulting from a change in the (expected) price).

Since the purpose of Keynes's analysis was to clarify the form of the interdependence between D and S, (i) is a serious defect from the pedagogic point of view. Moreover, since in partial equilibrium analysis, demand curves are treated as independent of supply curves and the quantity demanded as independent of the quantity supplied, a student may be too easily led into treating general equilibrium analysis in the same way as partial equilibrium analysis.

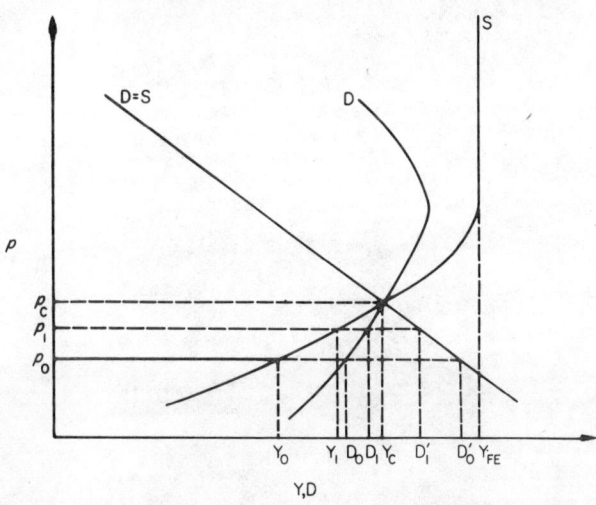

Fig. 17.App.iv   Aggregate demand and supply and $D = S$ schedule

Disadvantage (ii) may also be serious. For suppose businessmen expect a higher price than p_0 – say p_1 – they will expand output to Y_1 on Fig. 17.App.iv. However, according to the $D = S$ curve, demand *falls* from D_0' to D_1'. Since consumption is dependent on Y, which has risen, readers may find this puzzling. They may even be misled into thinking that demand falls because the rise in r consequent upon the higher level of money income, now $p_1 Y_1$, reduces investment sufficiently to offset the increase in consumption. Nothing of the kind is being asserted. Indeed all that the $D = S$ curve tells us is that if p and r are higher I_p will be lower and hence, via the multiplier, the *equilibrium* value of income, defined by $D = Y$, must also be lower.

This, of course, is not to say that the $D = S$ curve may not, for some purposes, be a useful teaching device. It is, on the contrary, simply to suggest that, even though definitions are matters of choice, it is not helpful to define, as the aggregate demand curve, a schedule which assumes that aggregate demand is equal to aggregate supply and which obscures the relationship between the quantity of output produced and the quantity demanded.

17* The Quantity Theory of Money

In the previous chapter we analysed the consequences for the endogenous variables of our model, and in particular for the price level, of an assumed exogenous change in the nominal money supply. We now seek to compare the predictions of our theory with an older theory known as the Quantity Theory of Money. What is the nature of this theory?

1 THE ELEMENTS OF THE QUANTITY THEORY

The Quantity Theory begins with the identity

$$\text{value of total purchases} \equiv \text{value of sales of} \quad (17^*.\text{Q.I})$$
$$\text{of final output} \qquad \text{total output}$$

which states that, in any period, the value of sales and purchases are equal – as they must be since they are alternative descriptions of the same transactions.

Now in a monetary economy, total purchases involve transfers of money from buyers to sellers. If the nominal money supply, on average over the relevant period, is M^S then we define

$$\frac{\text{value of total purchases of final output}}{M^S}$$
$$\equiv V_y \equiv \text{income velocity of money.} \quad (17^*.\text{Q.II})$$

Total sales (in value) can now be divided into two components: the quantity of real final output sold (Y) and the price of a unit of output (p). We thus have:

$$\text{value of total sales} \atop \text{of final output} \equiv pY \qquad (17^*.\text{Q.III})$$

and hence

$$M^S V_y \equiv pY. \qquad (17^*.\text{Q.IV})$$

Notice that thus far no testable *theory* (as opposed to conceptual framework) has been developed since (17^*.Q.IV) is an identity which contains no hypothesis regarding human behaviour.

We now develop what may be called the naïve Quantity Theory by introducing the postulate that people behave in such a way as to make V_y equal to some constant $\hat{V}_y$.

Thus we have

$$V_y = \hat{V}_y \qquad\qquad (17*.\text{Q.V})$$

so that

$$M^S \hat{V}_y = pY. \qquad\qquad (17*.\text{Q.VI})$$

If we now identify the left-hand side of $(17*.\text{Q.VI})$ with demand, the naïve Quantity Theory predicts

(i) that there is a constant relationship between the value of aggregate demand and the nominal money supply; and hence

(ii) a given proportionate increase in M^S brings about a corresponding proportionate increase in aggregate demand.

Notice that, in putting matters in this way, we are implicitly assuming that M^S is an exogenous variable: that is, causation runs *from M^S to pY.*

We now need to explain pY. There are, speaking generally, no particular hypotheses relating to pY which can be identified specifically with the Quantity Theory. It is, however, possible to construct an even more naïve version of the theory by

(a) assuming $Y = Y_{FE} = $ constant $\qquad\qquad (17*.\text{Q.VII})$

so that

(b) $\hat{V}_y / Y_{FE}$

is itself a constant.

We then have

$$M^S \frac{\hat{V}_y}{Y_{FE}} = p, \qquad\qquad (17*.\text{Q.VIII})$$

which, recalling that we have assumed M^S to be the exogenous variable, simply predicts that the price level will be proportional to M^S – the quantity of money in nominal terms – and also that the real variables of the system such as r, Y, C_p, I_p are independent of the nominal money supply. The proposition is sometimes paraphrased by the expression that 'money is a veil' in the sense that variations in M^S affect only money prices and money wage rates and have no influence on real phenomena. An alternative expression of the same idea is that 'money is neutral'. This problem – and the model necessary to support it – are discussed more fully in Chapter 18.

There is no need to saddle the Quantity Theory with the excessively rigid assumption that $Y = Y_{FE}$. If this is relaxed, and the theory of aggregate supply treated independently, then the Quantity Theory can either be interpreted as

(i) a theory which predicts that aggregate demand is always proportionate to the money supply; or
(ii) a theory which relates the demand for nominal money to money income.

To see (ii) let us write the demand function for money as follows:

$$M^D = LYp, \qquad (17^*.Q.IX)$$

where $L \equiv$ some constant proportion of Yp.†

Equating M^D and M^S – that is, assuming equilibrium in the money market – now gives

$$M^S = LYp \qquad (17^*.Q.X)$$

so that

$$L \equiv \frac{1}{\hat{V}_y} \quad \text{or} \quad \hat{V}_y \equiv \frac{1}{L}$$

On the basis of $(17^*.Q.X)$ assume an exogenous increase in M^S. The community is now holding excess money balances. Accordingly, individuals and enterprises increase their expenditures. The value of output (pY) increases as we move along the aggregate supply function. How far this is explained by a rise in p rather than Y (or vice versa) must depend on the nature of the aggregate supply function and where we initially were upon it. The essential point is that, in this simple version of the Quantity Theory, the *mechanism* of adjustment is the substitution of excess cash balances for goods and services, a process which must continue until the new values of p and Y again satisfy $(17^*.Q.X)$: that is, until aggregate demand is again proportional to M^S and equal to aggregate supply.

Now the theory that $\hat{V}_y$ (or L) was approximately constant was a useful approximation to what actually was observed until roughly the onset of the Great Depression in 1929. Since that date, however, $\hat{V}_y$ (and hence L) have exhibited considerable variation. Hence the principal prediction of the naïve Quantity Theory was found to be faulty and accordingly in this (over)-simple form at least, the theory became discredited.

† We use L rather than the more usual K, since the latter symbol has been employed for real capital. In practice L is identical with the Marshallian K. Notice that if we divide $(17^*.Q.IX)$ by p we obtain $M^D/p = LY$, which emphasises, as monetarists typically do, that the public demands real balances.

In recent years the Quantity Theory of the demand for money has been reformulated by a group of distinguished U.S. economists of whom Professor Milton Friedman is the best-known. This revival has taken the form of arguing that, when correctly understood, the Quantity Theory does not predict that L (or $\hat{V}_y$) is a constant *number* but a stable function of a relatively small number of variables. That is, the theory has been rewritten by asserting

$$M^D = Lp\,Y \qquad\qquad (17^*\text{.Q.XI})$$

where $L = f(\qquad\quad)$
so that $M^D = f(\qquad\quad)p\,Y$

and if, as usual, we put $M^S = M^D$ then

$$M^S = f(\qquad\quad)p\,Y. \qquad\qquad (17^*\text{.Q.XII})$$

The empirical form of (17*.Q.XII) is, not very surprisingly, a matter of some disagreement. The typical approach, however, has been to emphasise money's function as an asset and argue that L will, accordingly, be a function of the rate of return on alternative assets. A much simplified version of Friedman's reformulation would give

$$L = f\left(r, \hat{g}_r, r_e, \hat{g}_e, \frac{\hat{dp}}{p}\right) \qquad\qquad (17^*\text{.Q.XIII})$$

where $r_e \equiv$ rate of return on equities

$\dfrac{\hat{dp}}{p} \equiv$ expected rate of change of prices (i.e. rate of return on goods)

$\hat{g}_r, \hat{g}_e \equiv$ expected percentage and rate of capital gain on bonds $(\hat{g}_r)$ and equities $(\hat{g}_e)$.

Clearly this formulation is, in approach, similar to the Keynesian analysis of Chapter 11. It is, however, rather more general in that it introduces r_e, $\hat{g}_e$ and $\hat{dp}/p$.

Inserting (17.Q.XIII) now gives the reformulated Quantity Theory as

$$M^S = f\left(r, \hat{g}_r, r_e, \hat{g}_e, \frac{\hat{dp}}{p}\right)p\,Y. \qquad\qquad (17^*\text{.Q.XIV})$$

It is at once obvious that the theory can no longer be used to predict aggregate demand $(p\,Y)$ from M^S since five other variables, for which no theory is stated, must also be predicted. It follows that the Quantity Theory in this form, or even in the simpler approximations usually employed in empirical work, provides an alternative theory of the demand for money and no more. How does this theory differ from the 'Keynesian'?

If we neglect some subtleties the principal differences appear to be:

(i) it contains no theory of interest-rate expectations: that is, no hypothesis of a 'safe' or 'normal' rate;
(ii) it does not imply a liquidity trap;
(iii) in its empirical forms it places little emphasis on interest-rate expectations and thus on speculation but more emphasis on price expectations:
(iv) it emphasises the stability of the demand function compared with 'Keynesian' analysis;
(v) it does not separate money holdings into 'active' and 'idle' balances.

Additionally, some versions of the theory do not employ observed money income (pY) in the demand relation but some concept of 'expected' or 'permanent' income or alternatively wealth. Thus one well-known form of the function can be written

$$M^D = Ap^{\delta_1}W^{\delta_2}r^{\delta_3}, \qquad (17^*.Q.XV)$$

where $W \equiv$ real wealth and the theoretical expectations are that the relevant elasticities ($\delta_1, \delta_2, \delta_3$) are

$$\delta_1 = \delta_2 = 1{\cdot}0$$
$$\delta_3 < 0.$$

Whether functions of this form (derived from a Quantity Theory approach) perform better (that is, explain the observed facts better) than Keynesian-type functions is a question of fact. Any attempt to review the array of applied work in this field would take us far beyond the scope of this book. At this stage, the reader should simply note

(i) that this question has not yet been satisfactorily settled; but
(ii) for the United States at least there is a strong body of applied work tending to support hypotheses broadly similar to (17*.Q.XV).

We may thus conclude that the modern Quantity Theory

(a) denies the hypothesis of the naïve theory that M^D depends only on pY and not at all on interest rates; and
(b) contains elements similar to the Keynesian analysis.

In particular it accepts, as does Keynesian analysis, that pY/M^S $\equiv V_y$ is related to interest rates. Neglecting some subtleties the principal differences, in practice, between the two schools of thought can be said to be

1. the quantity theorists' greater emphasis on the stability of the demand function for money; and
2. the insistence of some quantity theorists on a major role for exogenous *changes* in the nominal money supply as an explanation of observed fluctuations in income.

These two points form the basis of what is now known as the 'monetarist' position.

2 THE 'MONETARIST' POSITION: SHORT-RUN IMPLICATIONS

In recent years a group of economists, many of them followers in some degree of the views of Professor Milton Friedman, have developed an account of macro-economic theory which has become known as 'monetarism' in contrast to so-called 'Keynesian' theory. As the name implies, 'monetarists' emphasise the role of money in explaining short-term changes in money income, real income and employment. Moreover, they argue that the importance of money has been overlooked, if not by Keynes himself, then certainly by many economists who would be classified as 'Keynesian'. At this point we cannot do more than give a brief sketch of the 'monetarist' position. Since the influence of 'monetarism' is probably still growing, the reader should supplement this by a careful look at the relevant references at the end of this chapter.

Though the model presented in this text is 'Keynesian', it is clear, however, that the nominal money supply (M^S) is, in principle, an important variable in it. For example, as Fig. 17*.i reminds us, an exogenous increase in M^S lowers r and raises Y, p and N.

On the other hand 'Keynesian' analysis does not predict any stable value for the money and real income multipliers

$$\frac{\Delta(pY)}{\Delta M^S} \quad \text{and} \quad \frac{\Delta Y}{\Delta M^S}.$$

As we have seen, aggregate demand, in money terms, may respond a lot, a little, or in theory not at all (if liquidity preference is absolute), to exogenous changes in M^S. Moreover, Keynesian analysis, in explaining income changes, tends to emphasise shifts in the marginal efficiency of investment function or demand for money

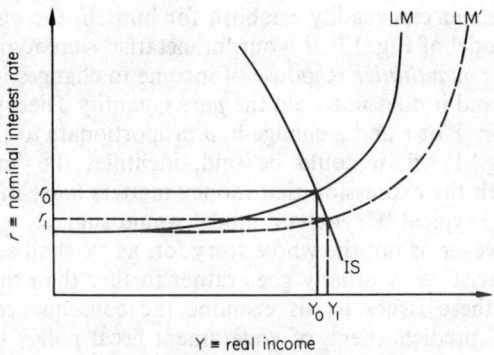

FIG. 17*.i The effect of a change in the nominal money supply

functions rather than exogenous changes in the nominal money supply. In addition, probably because Keynes originally was concerned to explain the existence of chronic depression, typical 'Keynesian' assumptions are a relatively interest-elastic demand-for-money function (though not infinitely elastic) and relatively interest-inelastic (though not of zero elasticity) consumption and investment functions.

In contrast, the 'monetarists' tend to assume a small (but not zero) interest elasticity of the demand for money function and relatively high (but not necessarily infinite) interest elasticities of the investment and consumption functions. In terms of the same familiar diagram, the short-run 'monetarist' position might be as set out in Fig. 17*.ii.

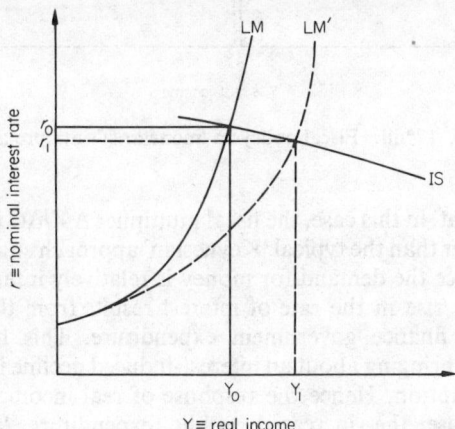

FIG. 17*.ii The effect of a change in the nominal money supply

As the reader can readily establish for himself, the *qualitatively* identical model of Fig. 17*.ii – our 'monetarist' stereotype – shows a far greater *quantitative* response of income to changes in M^S. On the other hand it does not yield the *pure* Quantity Theory result of no change in Y or r and a change in p proportionate to the change in M^S. Fig. 17*.ii, it could be said, identifies the 'monetarist' position with the expression that money matters *more* in the short run than the typical 'Keynesian' model would suggest.

This, however, is not the whole story for, as we shall see shortly, the 'monetarist' view usually goes rather further than this. Before examining these issues let us examine the consequences, as the 'monetarist' predicts them, of government fiscal policy taking the form (say) of an exogenous increase in real government expenditure (G). This shifts the IS curve to the right, to IS', and raises income to Y' and the interest rate to r' as depicted in Fig. 17*.iii.

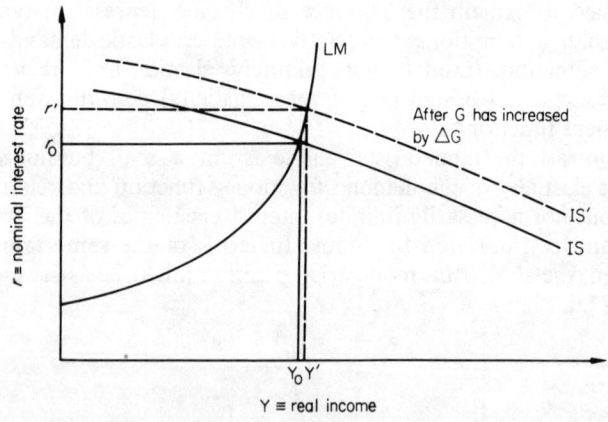

FIG. 17*.iii   Fiscal policy: a 'monetarist' interpretation

Notice that, in this case, the fiscal multiplier $\Delta Y / \Delta G$ is very small: much smaller than the typical 'Keynesian' approach suggests. This is because, since the demand for money is relatively interest inelastic, a very large rise in the rate of interest results from the additional demand to finance government expenditure. This has the consequence of bringing about an interest-induced decline in investment and consumption. Hence the response of real income is relatively small because the increased public expenditure 'crowds out' private expenditure which would otherwise have occurred. Formally this is because of the steepness of the *LM* schedule which reflects the twin assumptions of an exogenously given nominal money supply and a relatively interest-inelastic money-demand schedule. The 'monetarist' conclusion is therefore that fiscal policy (i.e. discretionary changes in government expenditure or taxes) is a relatively powerless device *unless accompanied by appropriate changes in the nominal money supply*.

As the reader can see, this argument can be generalised to *any* influence which operates through shifts in the *IS* curve. A *ceteris paribus* shift in the M.E.I. schedule, for example, tends to raise interest rates rather than real income and the rise in rates 'crowds out' other forms of public or private expenditure. Thus the 'monetarist' usually regards such explanations for income change, which 'Keynesians' tend to stress, either as unimportant or alternatively as being shifts which *reflect* business and household adjustments to exogenous changes in the nominal money supply – for example, because of revisions of expectations occurring as a result of changes in M^S.

Finally, the 'monetarists' regard the nominal money supply as a *predominantly* exogenous variable and, for this reason, regard causation as running *predominantly from* the money supply *to* real and money income. Modern 'Keynesians' are considerably less confident on this issue. Indeed, precisely because of the responsibility central bankers feel for managing the economy and preserving the stability of financial institutions, they regard the nominal money supply as having a considerable endogenous element. This has an important bearing on some recent empirical work and, at the same time, suggests that the causal link may be *from* money income *to* the money supply – a proposition which, if correct, would tend to imply an interest-elastic *LM* curve of the kind often assumed implicitly in 'Keynesian' discussion of fiscal policy.

At this stage it may be helpful to the reader to contrast, in tabular form, the 'Keynesian' position (as depicted in our model), and the 'monetarist' position (as specified in our stereotype). This is done in Table 17*.1 below.

As this table makes plain, the short-run versions of the theories differ because of differing empirical estimates of the magnitude of crucial elasticities; a dispute over the relative stability of the demand for money function; and a further dispute over the nature of the money supply function. Not very surprisingly, the literature investigating these issues is immense and continues to exhibit a very high rate of growth. Moreover, a good deal of it is rather technical. This is therefore not the place to review it. At this point,

Table 17*.1   *Comparison of 'Keynesian' and 'Monetarist'*
                                   Positions

Variable function or prediction	'Keynesian' position	'Monetarist' position
M^S ($\equiv$ nominal money supply)	Primarily endogenous	Primarily exogenous
Demand function for money	Relatively interest elastic; Interest elasticity a function of r; Unstable	Relatively interest inelastic; Interest elasticity not a function of r; Stable
Investment function	Relatively interest inelastic; Unstable	Relatively interest elastic; Cash-balance effect; Relatively stable
Consumption function	Relatively interest inelastic; Some wealth effect; Stable	Relatively interest elastic (via wealth); Cash-balance effect; Relatively stable
Predictions	Variation in Y primarily to be explained by shifts in investment functions Fiscal policy relatively powerful	Variation in Y primarily to be explained by changes in M^S Fiscal policy relatively weak

at least for the United Kingdom, we can only record a (controversial) assessment that the 'monetarist' case, as specified above,
remains rather weak since

   (i) what is known about the behaviour of the Bank of England
      suggests that M^S is *not* properly regarded as an exogenous
      variable;
  (ii) the U.K. demand function for money is relatively unstable;
      even though
 (iii) the interest elasticities of the demand functions estimated
      seem to be typically both rather small and constant as the
      'monetarists' predict.

In addition, attempts to distinguish between the capacity of the
nominal money stock (M^S) or autonomous expenditures to explain
the variation of income, while they strongly favour the latter
(Keynesian) variable in the inter-war years, produce no worthwhile results after the Second World War.

It is emphasised, however, that these are issues on which new information is steadily becoming available and the reader will do well to regard this particular controversy as far from settled.

3 THE 'MONETARIST' POSITION: LONG-RUN IMPLICATIONS

As we have seen, the pure Quantity Theory result is that an exogenous increase in M^S raises prices and money wages proportionately, leaving the equilibrium values of real income, employment and the interest rate unaltered.

Many 'monetarists' regard this result as typically holding in the longer run. Hence the results discussed in Section 2 are simply short-run or transitory. Moreover – and this is an area of dispute with 'Keynesians' – they do not regard the long run (in this context) as of any considerable length in terms of calendar time. Indeed they might identify the long run with a period as short as two to three years or even less. This is because many 'monetarists' regard the economic system, *if left to itself*, as essentially self-correcting and tending automatically and rapidly to an equilibrium at full employment.

We can, therefore, assert that many 'monetarists' broadly accept what we discuss, in the following chapter, as a 'classical' system. Hence the short-run results attributed to 'monetarism' in Section 2 arise because 'monetarists' are fully aware that the price/money wage flexibility (which as we shall see is a characteristic of so-called 'classical' models) takes some time to operate.

The analysis will become clearer to the reader after he has examined Chapter 18.

4 SUMMARY

The revival of the Quantity Theory in a more sophisticated form has led to the emergence of a 'monetarist' school of macro-economic analysis. This has gained considerable influence in the United States and is not without adherents in the United Kingdom.

In short-run analysis this school

(i) emphasises the role of changes in the nominal money supply (M^S) in explaining the behaviour of money (and real†) income;
(ii) regards fiscal policy as relatively ineffective.

† In the short run.

In longer-run analysis 'monetarists' tend to regard the macro-economic system as essentially stable and tending automatically to an equilibrium at full employment. In the long run, therefore – which may, in calendar time, be quite short – they expect the Quantity Theory results to follow. Additionally, since they regard the economy as stable, they tend to explain fluctuations in money and real incomes as due to destabilising changes in M^S arising from faulty discretionary monetary policies.

The relevance of the 'monetarist' approach turns on issues of fact which remain the subject of intensive professional debate.

QUESTIONS AND EXERCISES

1. 'The elementary quantity theory sweeps the whole of the theories of consumption, investment and liquidity preference into the single ragbag of income velocity. It thus explains virtually nothing and obscures virtually everything.' Elucidate and discuss.

2. From the *Monthly Digest of Statistics* construct data for quarterly changes in

   (1) the money supply
   (2) G.N.P. at current prices

   for the period 1960–70.

   How far are the observed changes in G.N.P. explained by (1) and how far are they explained by changes in observed income velocity? Comment on your results.

3. From the *Monthly Digest of Statistics* for the years 1956–70 use annual data for G.N.P. and M^S to calculate annual observations for V_y ($\equiv$ income velocity). Plot the resultant observations against a similar series for the rate of interest on long-term government securities. Is V_y a function of r? If so is the observed relation compatible with (i) the liquidity preference theory of Chapter 11, (ii) the revised Quantity Theory? How stable is V_y?

4. Assume the money-demand function of the naïve Quantity Theory, i.e.

$$M^D = kpY \qquad \text{where } k = \text{constant.}$$

   On this basis construct the usual *IS–LM* diagram. How does the *LM* curve differ from the usual construct? State your assumptions carefully and generate predictions for

(1) an increase in business optimism.

(2) an increase in government expenditure.

How do the predictions differ from those of the model of Chapter 12? Why?

5. 'The quantity theory predicts that an increase in the money suppy brings about a proportional increase in prices and leaves the rate of interest unaltered'. Explain. On what assumptions is the statement correct?

6. 'Reputable quantity theorists never regarded income velocity as a constant. On the contrary they regarded it as a function of a number of variables.' Elucidate. Develop a 'velocity function' and explain your choice of independent variables. How far, if at all, does your 'new quantity theory' differ from the Keynesian?

7. 'The quantity theory assumed that aggregate demand depended only on the money supply and was thus independent of the money wage rate. Keynes denied this.' Explain. Use aggregate demand and supply analysis to show how aggregate demand depends on the money wage rate.

8. Typically the Quantity Theory regards causation as running *from* changes in the nominal money supply *to* changes in G.N.P. How far do you think this is reasonable? What reasons are there for arguing the reverse direction of causation – that is, the nominal money supply responds to changes in G.N.P.? What evidence would you cite in favour of either view?

9. 'The Quantity Theory of Money emphasises the substitution of money for goods. The Keynesian approach, by contrast, emphasises the substitution of money for bonds or, more generally, interest earning financial assets.' Discuss.

10. Re-examine the data you have constructed to answer Question 3. Does your graph suggest a stable demand function for money or not?

11. 'Keynesian theory predicts that the (absolute value of the) interest elasticity of the demand for money *increases* as r *declines*. The Quantity Theory does not entail this prediction.' Explain and appraise.

12. 'For an exogenous change in the nominal money supply to have a predictable effect on G.N.P. we require *more* than a stable demand function for money.' Discuss.

13. The following macro-static model incorporates a money-supply function.

$$Y = C_p + I_p \qquad (13.1)$$

$$C_p = c_0 + c_1 Y + c_2 r \qquad\qquad 0 < c_1 < 1 \quad c_2 \leqslant 0 \qquad (13.2)$$

$$I_p = i_0 + i_1 Y + i_2 r \qquad\qquad i_1 > 0 \quad i_2 < 0 \qquad\qquad (13.3)$$

$$M^S = M_0 + \alpha_1 p Y + \alpha_2 (r - r^*) \qquad \alpha_1 \alpha_2 \geqslant 0 \qquad (13.4)$$

$$M^D = m_0 + m_1 p Y + m_2 r \qquad\quad m_1 > 0 \quad m_2 < 0 \qquad (13.5)$$

$$M^D = M^S \qquad\qquad\qquad\qquad\qquad\qquad\qquad\qquad (13.6)$$

$$p = \bar{p} \qquad\qquad\qquad\qquad\qquad\qquad\qquad\qquad\qquad (13.7)$$

$$r^* = \bar{r}^*. \qquad\qquad\qquad\qquad\qquad\qquad\qquad\qquad (13.8)$$

Solve the model for Y, treating $p = \bar{p} =$ constant, and from your solution obtain expressions for

$$\frac{dY}{dM_0} \equiv \text{an autonomous increase in the nominal money supply;}$$

$$\frac{dY}{dm_0} \equiv \text{an autonomous increase in liquidity preference.}$$

Analyse your results and discuss, in particular, the influence of the parameters $m_1, m_2, \alpha_1, \alpha_2$. In your discussion identify the result for

(i) the liquidity-trap assumption; and
(ii) the naïve Quantity Theory assumption.

What difference does the introduction of a money-supply function make?

14. In the light of your results in Question 13 re-examine your answer to Question 12.

15. Discuss the assumptions regarding central bank and commercial bank behaviour which might lie behind the money-supply function of equation 13.4 of Question 13. Can you think of any? Are they sensible?

16. From the model of Question 13 obtain an expression for

$$\frac{dM^S}{di_0} \equiv \text{change in money supply resulting from an increase in autonomous investment.}$$

Interpret your result in the light of your discussion in Question 8.

17. 'A *ceteris paribus* increase in Government spending has virtually no effect on real or money incomes. It simply raises

the interest rate.' (Monetarist.) 'A *ceteris paribus* increase in Government spending raises income by the full multiplier.' (Keynesian.) What is meant by *ceteris paribus* in these statements? Can you reconcile them? What, if any, are the issues of substance?

18. Write an essay setting out the main area of disagreement between Professors Friedman and Kaldor. Are the disagreements due to issues of fact, matters of interpretation or disputes over analysis?

19. Review your answer to Question 8 in the light of the papers by A. B. Cramp and F. de Leeuw and J. Kalchenbrenner in the list of recommended Readings.

20. Set out a reasoned defence of the use of fiscal policy attempting, at the same time, to meet the arguments of L. C. Andersen and J. L. Jordan.

SUGGESTED READING

J. M. Keynes, *The General Theory of Employment, Interest and Money* (Macmillan, 1936) ch. 21.

M. Friedman,† 'The Role of Monetary Policy', *American Economic Review* (May 1968).

N. Kaldor,* 'The New Monetarism', *Lloyds Bank Review* (July 1970).

M. Friedman,* 'Comment', ibid. (Oct 1970).

N. Kaldor,* 'Rejoinder', ibid. (Oct 1970).

A. B. Cramp, 'Does Money Matter?', ibid. (Oct 1970).

D. Fand, 'Some Issues in Monetary Economics', *Banca Nazionale del Lavoro Quarterly Review* (Sep 1969).

D. W. Laidler, *The Demand for Money* (International Textbooks, 1969) chs 1–5.

H. G. Johnson (ed.), *Readings in British Monetary Economics* (Oxford, 1972) pp. 3–109.

M. Friedman,† in *Studies in the Quantity Theory of Money* (Chicago, 1956).

M. J. Artis and A. R. Nobay,†‡ 'Two Aspects of the Monetary Debate', N.I.E.S.R. *Review* (Aug 1969).

L. C. Andersen and J. L. Jordan,† 'Monetary and Fiscal Actions: a Test of their Relative Importance in Economic Stabilization', *Federal Reserve Bank of St Louis Review* (Nov 1968).

F. de Leeuw and J. Kalchenbrenner,† 'Monetary and Fiscal Actions – Comment', ibid. (April 1969).

L. C. Andersen and J. L. Jordan,† 'Reply', ibid. (April 1969).

C. R. Barrett and A. A. Walters,†‡ 'The Stability of Keynesian and Monetary Multipliers in the United Kingdom', *Review of Economics and Statistics* (Nov 1966).

* Reprinted in *Money and Banking* (Penguin, 1973).

† Advanced reference.

‡ Partially reprinted in *Readings in British Monetary Economics*.

18 Keynes and His Predecessors

In Chapters 7–17 we have gradually developed a macro-economic model which is, in all essentials, derived from the work of Keynes. In developing this model there is a risk that, in our detailed examination of its component parts, we have lost sight of its overall characteristics. To guard against this, in this chapter we take, as it were, a step back and attempt to set out the principal characteristics of the model as a whole. We begin by looking at its structure.

1 THE STRUCTURE OF THE MODEL

In considering the structure of any theory the first step is to ask two questions:

(i) which variables does the model explain or determine? These we call the *endogenous* variables; and
(ii) which variables does the model take as given – that is determined outside the system? These we call the *exogenous* variables.

Let us now look at the first of these questions remembering that any model of this type is constructed not only of a set of *hypotheses* about behaviour but also of a set of assumptions about the institutional environment.

As we already know from our manipulation of the model, it contains *nine endogenous* variables. These are:

$Y \equiv$ real output

$C_p \equiv$ real planned consumption

$I_p \equiv$ real planned investment

$r \equiv$ rate of interest

$p \equiv$ price of a unit of output

$N^D \equiv$ quantity of employment demanded (employed)

$U \equiv$ the quantity of involuntary unemployment

$M_p^D \equiv$ quantity of money demanded

$\dfrac{W}{p} \equiv$ real wage rate.

To determine the equilibrium values of these variables we need to know (i) the values of the *exogenous* variables; (ii) the functional relationships which constitute the behaviouristic hypotheses of the theory; and (iii) any relationships between the variables which exist by definition.

In the short-run model, the variables which we take to be given – that is, determined outside the system and hence by definition *exogenous* – are:

M^S ≡ the nominal quantity of money – determined by central banking policy

W_h ≡ the value of the money wage rate – determined by an institutionalised process of bargaining between employers and employees

K ≡ the real capital stock

T ≡ the state of technique

A ≡ the real value of households' assets

α ≡ the distribution of income.

Notice here that, in purely formal terms, the variables we take to be *exogenous* are at choice. It would, for example, be a simple matter to regard the money supply (M^S) as *endogenous*. To do this we would need to formulate a behaviour hypothesis for the central bank which, given the institutional structure of the banking system, would permit us to write the money supply as a function of some endogenous variables on which the central bank bases its policy. A simple, but not necessarily plausible hypothesis, might regard the central bank as providing a greater nominal quantity of money the higher is the market rate of interest. This would give us a behaviour function of the form: $M^S = f(r)$, with $\partial M^S / \partial r > 0$, to replace our more familiar formulation $M^S = M_0$. Equally we could develop a hypothesis about the labour market which would make W_h an endogenous variable. This, at this stage of our analysis, we do not choose to do.

Though we shall proceed retaining our classification of M^S and W_h as *exogenous*, it should be clear to the reader that since we need not do so, part of the skill in building models is concerned precisely with deciding *which* variables are to be taken as exogenous. A sensible decision depends partly on knowledge of the institutional and social environment in which our model is to operate and partly upon the type of problem on which we wish our model to throw light. To put matters concisely, what is involved is 'judgment'; there are therefore no rules – simple or complex – which can be set out to ensure that any model constructed will be relevant.

Once we have taken our decision on this matter, in addition to the values of the *exogenous variables* we require certain behaviour assumptions. These are:

(i) a consumption hypothesis which explains consumption behaviour;

(ii) an investment hypothesis which explains investment behaviour;

(iii) a liquidity preference hypothesis which explains behaviour with respect to the demand for money;

(iv) a profit maximisation hypothesis which explains the demand for labour in terms of the real wage rate and also underlies some versions of (ii);

(v) a labour supply hypothesis which explains the supply of labour; and

(vi) the 'technical' relation, specified by the production function, which relates the inputs of labour (N) to quantities of real output (Y).

Our model, despite its heroic level of simplification, thus contains *fifteen* variables of which nine are endogenous and six exogenous. An elementary knowledge of mathematics tells us that, to determine the value of any variable, a single equation is required; for two variables we need two independent equations; for fifteen variables fifteen independent equations. Hence, if we wish, and it is often convenient to do so, we can write down our model in terms of 15 equations. These equations, which the reader will readily recognise from previous chapters, are set out in Table 18.1.

Though this mathematical method of expressing a model is undoubtedly convenient and useful, it may also help to set out the model in terms of a diagram. This is done in the figure. (Notice that though the figure does not explicitly show the interdependence of the three markets, certain variables are shown as affecting more than one market. This reflects the interdependence which is a feature of the model.

Taken together, the table and the figure make it clear what the structure of our system is. They also make it plain that by (i) taking as given the values of *six* exogenous variables; (ii) assuming *six* functional relations which reflect behaviour; (iii) adding the *two* equilibrium conditions for the goods and money markets; and

Table 18.1   *The Keynesian Model*

Equation	Meaning	Chapter references
1. $Y = C_p + I_p$	equilibrium in goods market	8
2. $C_p = f_1(Y, A, \alpha, r)$	consumption hypothesis	9
3. $I_p = f_2(K, r)$	investment hypothesis	10
4. $M_p^D = L_1(Yp) + L_2(r)$	demand for money hypothesis	11
5. $M^S = M_0$	supply of money assumption	11
6. $M_p^D = M^S$	equilibrium in money market	11
7. $N^D = f_3(W/p)$	demand for labour depends upon the real wage	17
8. $N^S = f_4(W)$	supply of labour depends upon money wage	17
9. $Y = f_5(T, K, N)$	production function hypothesis	7 and 17
10. $W = W_h$	money wage rate determined by 'historical' bargaining process	17
11. $T = T_0$	state of technique given	10 and 17
12. $K = K_0$	stock of capital given	10 and 17
13. $A = A_0$	real value of household assets given	9
14. $\alpha = \alpha_0$	income distribution given	9
15. $U \equiv N^S - N^D$	definition of involuntary unemployment	17

Note: The subscripts after the function signs inserted in equations
       2, 3, 7, 8 and 9 are used merely to remind the reader that
       the functions are not the same in each equation.

(iv) *one* definitional identity, we can determine the equilibrium
values of each of the fifteen variables and hence of the nine *endogenous* variables. Suppose we operate the model in this way and
the resulting equilibrium levels of output and employment are Y_0
and N_0. Suppose further that $N_0 < N_f$ so that involuntary unemployment (U) exists. Is it natural to ask: what 'causes' this involuntary
unemployment?

If we look at our system we immediately notice two important
characteristics. First, *the equilibrium values of all the endogenous
variables are simultaneously determined.* Hence, *in a system of this
type, crude notions of causation are obviously inappropriate simply
because the value of any endogenous variable depends upon the value
of all the exogenous variables and all the assumed functional relations.*

For example to 'explain' the existence of involuntary unemployment (U) we can point to (i) too small a money supply; (ii) too high a
money wage rate; (iii) too low a propensity to consume schedule;
(iv) too low a marginal efficiency of capital schedule; (v) too high a
liquidity preference schedule; or (vi) some combination of all these.

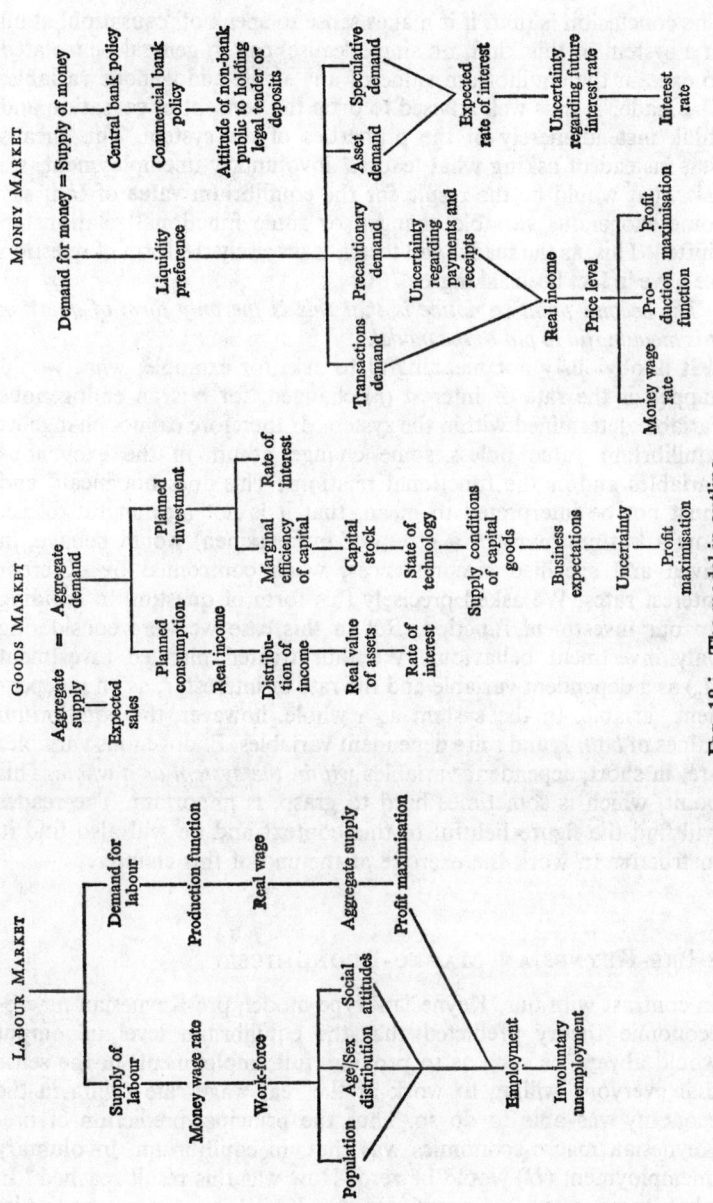

Fig. 18.i The model in outline

LABOUR MARKET

Supply of labour — Money wage rate — Work-force — Population / Age/Sex distribution / Social attitudes — Employment — Involuntary unemployment

Demand for labour — Production function — Real wage — Aggregate supply — Profit maximisation

GOODS MARKET

Aggregate supply = Aggregate demand

Aggregate supply — Expected sales

Aggregate demand — Planned consumption / Planned investment

Planned consumption — Real income / Distribution of income — Real value of assets — Rate of interest

Planned investment — Rate of interest / Marginal efficiency of capital — Capital stock / State of technology — Supply conditions of capital goods — Business expectations — Uncertainty — Profit maximisation

MONEY MARKET

Demand for money = Supply of money

Supply of money — Central bank policy / Commercial bank policy — Attitude of non-bank public to holding legal tender or deposits

Demand for money — Liquidity preference — Transactions demand / Precautionary demand / Asset demand / Speculative demand

Transactions demand / Precautionary demand — Uncertainty regarding payments and receipts — Real income — Price level — Money wage rate / Production function — Profit maximisation

Asset demand / Speculative demand — Expected rate of interest — Uncertainty regarding future interest rate — Interest rate

The conclusion is that, if it makes sense to speak of 'causation' at all in a system of this kind, no single 'cause' can in general be isolated to explain the equilibrium value of any single endogenous variable. The reader is thus well advised to drop the concept of causation and think instead merely of the properties of the system. This means that instead of asking what 'causes' involuntary unemployment, we ask what would be the result, for the equilibrium value of U, if say some exogenous variable changed or some functional relationship shifted. This, as the reader will recall, is precisely the form of question we have in fact been asking.

The second point to notice is that this is the only form of question it is meaningful to put to the model.

It is obviously not meaningful to ask, for example, what would happen if the rate of interest (r) changed, for r is an endogenous variable determined within the system. It therefore cannot change its equilibrium value unless some change occurs in the exogenous variables and/or the functional relations. This does not mean, and must not be interpreted to mean, that it is not meaningful to ask how a businessman (or a group of businessmen) would behave, in given and specified circumstances, when confronted by different interest rates. We asked precisely this form of question in building up our investment function. But in this case we were considering only investment behaviour. We thus treated planned investment (I_p) as a dependent variable and the rate of interest, r, as an independent variable. In the system as a whole, however, the equilibrium values of *both I_p and r are dependent variables. Endogenous variables are, in short, dependent variables *within the system as a whole*. This point, which is sometimes hard to grasp, is important. The reader will find the figure helpful in this context and he will also find it instructive to work the exercise at the end of this chapter.

2 PRE-KEYNESIAN MACRO-ECONOMICS

In contrast with our 'Keynesian' type model, pre-Keynesian macro-economic theory predicted that the equilibrium level of output would always be such as to provide 'full employment' in the sense that everyone willing to work at the real wage rate ruling in the economy was able to do so. Thus the principal prediction of pre-Keynesian macro-economics was that, in equilibrium, involuntary unemployment (U) would be zero. How was this result reached? In what main way, or ways, did pre-Keynesian macro-economics differ from Keynesian?

According to pre-Keynesian theory in its simplest form, the economy consisted of three markets: those for labour, goods and money. To show the nature of pre-Keynesian theory we consider each in turn.

In the labour market the quantity of labour *demanded* by businessmen is taken to be a *decreasing* function of the real wage. This proposition, which we have already discussed in Chapter 17, assumes that businessmen maximise profits and that there is a given short-run production function exhibiting diminishing marginal physical productivity of labour. Hence,

$$N^D = f^D\left(\frac{W}{p}\right). \tag{18.pK I}$$

On the supply side of the market individuals are assumed to offer their labour until the real wage exactly offsets the marginal disutility of working. If, as seems plausible, the marginal disutility of work rises as the amount of work done increases, then the quantity of labour offered by a given work-force will be an *increasing* function of the real wage. Hence

$$N^S = f^S\left(\frac{W}{p}\right) \tag{18.pK II}$$

For equilibrium in the labour market we require

$$N^S = N^D \tag{18.pK III}$$

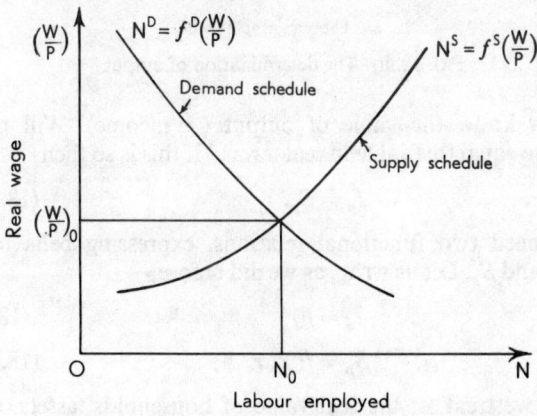

FIG. 18.ii   The equilibrium in the labour market

Hence when the labour market is in equilibrium we have a determinate (and equal) quantity of labour supplied and demanded and a determinate real wage. This is illustrated in Figure 18.ii, above, where

N_0 is the equilibrium quantity of employment

$\left(\dfrac{W}{p}\right)_0$ is the equilibrium quantity of real wage.

Note that since, at N_0, *all those who wish to work at the real wage* $(W/p)_0$ *are doing so, there is no involuntary unemployment.* N_0 thus corresponds to *full employment.* Given our production function and taking, as we must in short-run analysis, K and T as given, it is easy to see that the equilibrium level of real output (Y_0) is determined once N_0 is known. This is demonstrated in Fig. 18.iii.

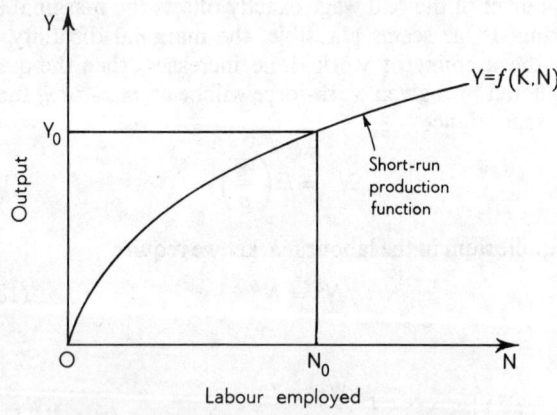

FIG. 18.iii   The determination of output

We now know the value of output ($\equiv$ income). Will planned expenditure equal this value in real terms? If this is so then

$$I_p = S_p. \tag{18.pK IV}$$

We now need two functional relations, expressing behaviour, to explain I_p and S_p. Let us write, as we did before,

$$I_p = f(r) \tag{18.pK V}$$

$$S_p = f(Y, r, A) \tag{18.pK VI}$$

As before we treat A, the real value of households' assets, as *exogenous.* From 18.iii we already know $Y = Y_0$. Hence, given A and Y_0, we can draw, on Fig. 18.iv, both planned investment and planned saving as functions of r (the rate of interest). We thus find r_0, the equilibrium value of r, and S_{p_0}, I_{p_0} the equilibrium values of S_P and I_P.

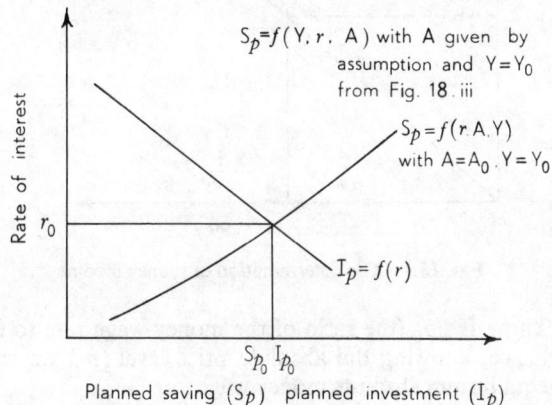

FIG. 18.iv Equilibrium in the goods market

In the money market, as before, we take the nominal money supply to be exogenous.

$$M^S = M_0. \qquad \text{(18.pK VII)}$$

To explain the demand for money we make use of the elementary quantity theory and write:

$$M_p^D = LpY, \qquad \text{(18.pK VIII)}$$

where L is the proportion, assumed to be constant, of their money incomes (pY) that people wish to hold command over in the form of money. Notice that (18.pK VIII) entails a *behaviour* assumption – namely that people *do* hold L constant.

Finally we impose the equilibrium condition

$$M^S = M_p^D \qquad \text{(18.pK IX)}$$

These three equations enable us to determine M^S, M^D and equilibrium money income $(pY)_0$ which, since we already know Y_0, immediately gives the equilibrium price level p_0. This is shown in Fig. 18.v.

Clearly once we know p_0 – the equilibrium price level – we also know W_0 – the equilibrium money wage rate – for, from 18.ii, we

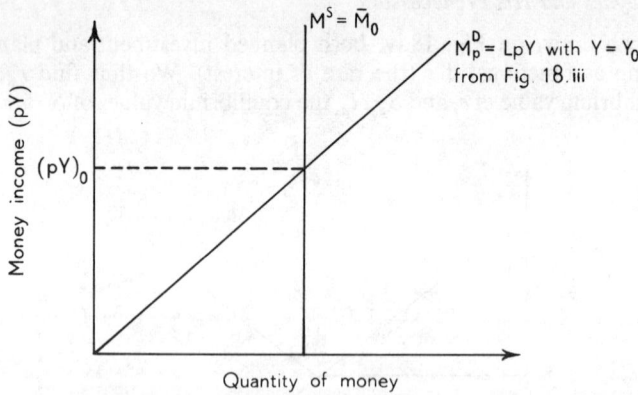

FIG. 18.v   The determination of money income

already know W_0/p_0 (the ratio of the money wage rate to the price level) whence, knowing the absolute price level (p_0) we can easily find the equilibrium absolute money wage rate (W_0).

It is not our purpose to give a detailed analysis of this pre-Keynesian system. Certain of its properties are, however, of great interest. For example,

(i) if the labour market is permitted to operate freely – on the usual competitive assumptions – equilibrium in this market will *always* be at full employment in the sense that all those who wish to work at the ruling real wage are able to do so. In short there can in equilibrium be no involuntary unemployment.

(ii) this suggests that involuntary unemployment, if it occurs, reflects some intervention in the working of the labour market.

This possibility is illustrated in Fig. 18.vi which again depicts the labour market. If the real wage, say because of governmental or union intervention, is fixed at $\overline{W}/p$ then the quantity of labour demanded is N_1^D and that offered is N_1^S. Involuntary unemployment is then $N_1^S - N_1^D \equiv U$.

It is easy to see that a policy *implication* of pre-Keynesian theory was that, to eliminate involuntary unemployment, the appropriate action was to *eliminate intervention* in the labour market so allowing the forces of competition to push real wages down to $(W/p)_0$ and thus restore full employment. Again when the wage rate was not flexible the implication of pre-Keynesian macro-economics was that a cut in money wages – by reducing the real wage rate – would

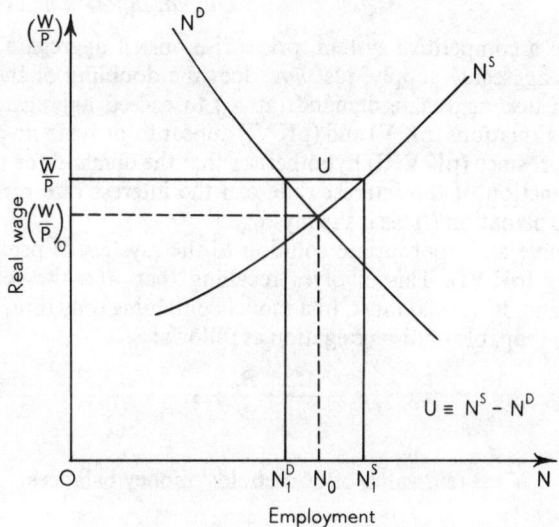

FIG. 18.vi Involuntary unemployment

restore full employment which, as we have seen, is not necessarily so in our (Keynesian) model. In addition it is worth noting that, in pre-Keynesian macro-economics, the quantity theory of money holds. Suppose, for example, the money supply is doubled. Then, from (pK VIII) or Fig. 18.iv, equilibrium money income $(pY)_0$ also doubles. Since equilibrium real income (Y_0) is determined by the level of employment which depends only on the real wage, then if both p_0 and W_0 also double, the system will once again be in equilibrium with prices and money wages twice their previous level but with employment, output, the real wage and the rate of interest unaffected. It follows that the *equilibrium* values of these variables, and of S_p and I_p, do not depend upon the money supply, which influences only the equilibrium value of p and W – *absolute* prices and money wages. For this reason it is sometimes said that in pre-Keynesian macro-economics 'money was a veil'. The pre-Keynesian system also carried the implication that rising prices (inflation) were to be explained by an increasing money supply.

Though our formal analysis shows the Quantity Theory of Money to hold when the nominal money supply is doubled, at least one mystery remains. Plainly, in the new equilibrium we must have

$$M_p^D = 2p_0 Y_0,$$

but this simple deduction leaves unexplained the *mechanism* which raises prices from p_0 to $2p_0$. To put the same point rather differently:

since, in a competitive system, prices rise only if aggregate demand exceeds aggregate supply, just *how* does the doubling of the money supply cause aggregate demand (at p_0) to exceed aggregate supply (at p_0)? Equations (pK V) and (pK VI) appear to provide no explanation. Nor, since (pK VIII) hypothesises that the demand for money is *not* a function of the interest rate, can the interest rate mechanism be the explanation? This is the mystery.

A simple and appropriate solution to the mystery is provided by rewriting (pK VI). This involves recalling that $A(\equiv$ the real value of households' assets) must, in a model containing only three types of assets, be capable of disaggregation as follows:

$$A \equiv \frac{M^S}{p} + \frac{B_0}{p} + K,$$

where

$\dfrac{M^S}{p} \equiv$ real value of households' money balances

$\dfrac{B_0}{p} \equiv$ real value of households' bonds

$K \equiv$ households' holdings of real assets.

Then, with B_0/p and K held constant, a doubling of M^S from M_0 to $2M_0$, must raise A by doubling M^S/p. This shifts the savings (consumption) schedule. We expect the marginal response coefficient relating planned consumption (C_p) to real assets (A) to be positive. Hence $\partial S_p/\partial A$ will be negative. Hence because of the 'cash balance' effect subsumed in (pK VI) there *is* a mechanism which will cause excess demand at the initial price level p_0 – though the existence of such a mechanism is not obvious at first glance.

In short, the 'classical pre-Keynesian' model's central hypothesis was that an increase in real money (real cash) balances caused households to substitute money for goods. By contrast the Keynesian model implies that an increase in real cash balances M/p leads households to substitute money for bonds.

The remaining properties of pre-Keynesian macro-economics the reader can readily establish himself by manipulating the model set out in the Questions and Exercises at the end of this Chapter.

What is the structure of pre-Keynesian macro-economics? The *exogenous* variables are:

$M^S \equiv$ the nominal quantity of money

$K \equiv$ real capital stock

$T \equiv$ state of technique

$A \equiv$ real value of households' assets.

The *endogenous* variables are:

$Y \equiv$ real output

$C_p \equiv$ real planned consumption

$I_p \equiv$ real planned investment

$r \equiv$ rate of interest

$p \equiv$ price of a unit of output

$N^D \equiv$ quantity of labour demanded

$N^S \equiv$ quantity of labour supplied

$W/p \equiv$ real wage rate

$M_p^D \equiv$ nominal quantity of money demanded;

$U \equiv$ the quantity of involuntary unemployment.

There are thus *fourteen* variables, *ten* endogenous and *four* exogenous. To determine them we have the nine equations (18.pK I–18.pK IX) *plus*

$$K = \overline{K} \tag{18.pK X}$$
$$T = \overline{T} \tag{18.pK XI}$$
$$A = \overline{A} \tag{18.pK XII}$$

the production function and the definitional identity $N^S - N^D \equiv U$. This gives us the fourteen equations we need.

3 KEYNESIAN AND PRE-KEYNESIAN MACRO-ECONOMICS: THE 'KEYNESIAN REVOLUTION'

In the broadest of comparisons both our 'Keynesian' model – and the model we have called 'pre-Keynesian' – are alike in that given: (i) the values of certain *exogenous* variables; (ii) a number of behaviour assumptions – including a production function; and (iii) any necessary definitions, each determines the equilibrium values of the *endogenous* variables. However the models differ sharply in their *predictions*. As a result they differ sharply in their *policy implications*. Because of this it is not uncommon to describe the development of modern macro-economics as originating in or amounting to a 'Keynesian revolution'. To see why this is so, let us look at the principal results of the two systems.

According to our (Keynesian) model

the equilibrium of the system may occur at any level of employment within the upper limit imposed by the size of the work-force. There is *no* mechanism which makes the system automatically tend towards a full-employment equilibrium.

This result, which it was obviously easy to reconcile with the severe involuntary unemployment of the inter-war years, carried the general policy implication that

to attain full employment, conscious intervention in the working of the economic system was necessary.

By implication, therefore, Keynesian macro-economics justified intervention for it not only showed that appropriate forms of intervention *could* raise the equilibrium of level of employment but also insisted that full employment – as simply one of a number of equally probable equilibria – would otherwise occur only as a fluke. In direct contrast pre-Keynesian macro-economics asserted that

(i) the economic system tended *always* towards a full-employment equilibrium; and hence implied that
(ii) intervention in the working of the system to attain full employment was *unnecessary* – indeed possibly harmful.

In short, Keynesian macro-economics was by implication in favour of governmental action to control aggregate demand: pre-Keynesian economics by implication in favour of 'laissez-faire'.

In the inter-war years it was, of course, not easy to reconcile the principal assertion of the pre-Keynesian model with the chronic persistence of involuntary unemployment on a massive scale. But where such unemployment was observed, pre-Keynesian macro-economics inevitably tended to focus attention on the failure of the labour market to behave competitively. As a result the pre-Keynesian macro-economics emphasised *wage-flexibility* and implied, though this was not so often advocated, that a reduction in the money wage, leading to a reduction in the real wage, would restore full employment. Hence the pre-Keynesian approach was to argue that since involuntary unemployment was (cf. Fig. 18.vi) incompatible with a *competitive* labour market, the labour market should be *made* competitive. In formal terms it predicted that

flexible money wages, which fell if $N^S > N^D$, would always restore full employment

while the Keynesian model predicted that

flexible money wages would restore full employment *if*, and only *if*, the rate of interest necessary to attain full employment (r_{FE}) was greater than the minimum rate of interest acceptable to the community (r_{min}).

It followed that, as a means of eliminating involuntary unemployment the Keynesian approach tended to emphasise the manipulation of government expenditure and tax rates (fiscal policy) and the manipulation of the money supply and hence interest rates (monetary policy) while the pre-Keynesian approach tended to emphasise wage policy. The 'revolution' in theory brought about a 'revolution' in policy.

In sum, the development of Keynesian macro-economics had important consequences not only for social attitudes towards economic policy but also for the forms of policy. Nowadays we all, irrespective of political allegiance, expect the government to manage aggregate demand so as to maintain 'full employment'. That we do so is, at least, in part the result of the 'Keynesian Revolution'.

It is not possible to say to what degree our relative success in maintaining 'full employment' after World War II (as compared with the period after World War I) is due to the Keynesian Revolution. It seems safe, however, to say that some part of it is. If this is so, two conclusions follow. First, the Keynesian Revolution has made a significant impact on all of our lives. Second, few men can, by their work, have given greater benefits to the world, particularly the developed Western World, than Lord Keynes.

4 SUMMARY

In this chapter we have presented a comparison between 'Keynesian' and 'pre-Keynesian' macro-economics. In two important senses this comparison has been unfair to pre-Keynesian economists. In the first place our comparison gives no hint of the very considerable debt Keynes owed to his predecessors upon whose work he necessarily built. In the second place while we have devoted many chapters to building the Keynesian model, pre-Keynesian theory has been expounded in a few pages. Inevitably, this has done it less than justice. As a result the pre-Keynesian theory has been over-simplified and the contrast between the two theories made not only too stark but too one-sided.

The reader should take careful account of these limitations of our treatment. Simplification is a legitimate device of exposition provided it does not involve distortion. Our comparison is designed to bring out the essential features of – and thus the significant differences between – the two systems. It does *not* seek to show how pre-Keynesian economics developed into Keynesian economics. Nor does it seek to give a comprehensive account of pre-Keynesian macro-theory. Readers who require a more comprehensive account of Keynes's great predecessors must look elsewhere.

As we have presented them, both theories are logically consistent: each contains sufficient independent equations to determine the variables it contains. Nevertheless, as the reader may easily verify, the two theories generate different predictions. These differences can arise only because the two theories contain different behaviour hypotheses. Which of these is the more relevant – and hence which theory is the more useful – is a question of fact. And the answer to this question, since both human behaviour and the institutional framework in which it operates change, may not always be the same. Pre-Keynesian macro-theory was relevant at one period in the history of capitalist economies. It may conceivably become relevant again. Until it does we shall act wisely if we make use of a Keynesian type model. But our allegiance to this model must never be unconditional. A theory must not become a dogma. For the relevance of a model is not a matter of its neatness, the elegance of its formulation or its familiarity but simply and solely its ability to explain why the economy operates as it does and not in some other way. This is the essential point.

Finally the reader should note that the two models discussed in this chapter imply sharply differing policy conclusions. However abstract and oversimplified an economic model may appear, it nevertheless entails policy implications. This is an important conclusion. Its converse is that every policy recommendation which has any claim to be regarded as rational must be derived from a theory or model plus, of course, some value judgment which defines the policy objective. Confronted by any policy recommendation the reader will find it instructive – though frequently dispiriting – to construct the model from which it is derived.

QUESTIONS AND EXERCISES

1. 'In pre-Keynesian economics the rate of interest was the variable which equated planned saving with planned investment. In Keynesian economics the variable which does this is income.' Explain.
2. In the pre-Keynesian model of Section 2, what would be the consequences of a government deficit? Does pre-Keynesian theory tend to support the notion of a balanced budget? If so why?

3. 'In *both* Keynesian and pre-Keynesian macro-economics a cut in money wages will raise employment if and only if it reduces the real wage.' Explain. Why does a cut in money wages always reduce the real wage in pre-Keynesian economics?

4. 'Variables are properly classified as exogenous or endogenous only in relation to an economic *model* containing a number of equations. The classification dependent and independent by contrast refers to a single equation.' Do you agree? Illustrate your answer by reference to Keynesian and pre-Keynesian theories.

5. Use the pre-Keynesian model below to find the equilibrium values of

$$Y; \frac{W}{p}; \quad W; \quad p; \quad S_p; \quad I_p.$$

From it develop predictions of the consequences of

    (i) an increase in autonomous consumption of 100 per period;

    (ii) an increase in the desired ratio of money to money income to $0 \cdot 5$;

    (iii) a shift in the investment function amounting to 100 per period.

Compare your predictions with those you would derive from a Keynesian model.

Pre-Keynesian Model

$$\left. \begin{aligned} S_p &= -A + (1-c)Y \\ I_p &= H - br \\ S_p &= I_p \end{aligned} \right\} \text{ goods market} \qquad \begin{aligned} &A = 100, (1-c) = 0 \cdot 2 \\ &H = 1000, b = 10 \end{aligned}$$

$$\left. \begin{aligned} M^S &= M_0 \\ M^D &= kYp \\ M^D &= M^S \end{aligned} \right\} \text{ money market} \qquad \begin{aligned} &M_0 = 2650 \\ &K = 0 \cdot 25 \end{aligned}$$

$$\left. \begin{aligned} N^D &= X - l\left(\frac{W}{p}\right) \\ N^S &= Q + n\left(\frac{W}{p}\right) \\ N^S &= N^D \end{aligned} \right\} \text{ labour market} \qquad \begin{aligned} &X = 500, l = 50 \\ &Q = 20, n = 10 \end{aligned}$$

$$Y = F + eN - fN^2 \qquad \text{production function } F = 4400, e = 10 \\ f = 0 \cdot 01$$

6. 'In pre-Keynesian economics the function of the rate of interest was to determine how a given output should be distributed between consumption and capital accumulation'. Explain.

7. In what sense, if any, is it true to say that pre-Keynesian macro-economics *assumed* full employment or a 'natural' level of unemployment?

8. 'Saving is spending just as much as consumption is. Moreover since saving entails capital accumulation – which in the *long run* makes us all better off – we should encourage saving at the expense of consumption'. What sort of theory is implied by these statements?

9. Which hypotheses of pre-Keynesian macro-economics seem to you most open to objection? Can you devise tests for them?

10. 'Say's Law stated that supply created its own demand. It was fundamental to pre-Keynesian theory'. Where – if anywhere – do you find such an assumption in the model of Section 2? Examine the view that Say's Law is not a single assumption but a statement about the workings of a price system.

11. If A (the real value of households' assets) is interpreted as $A \equiv M/p + B_0/p + K$, is it still correct to say that, in a Keynesian model, flexible wages will restore full employment if and only if $r_{FE} > r_{min}$? If not, why not?

12. Rewrite the pre-Keynesian model of Section 2 by replacing equation (pK VIII) with:

$$M_p^D = L_1(pY, r), \qquad\qquad \text{(pK VIII*)}$$

where L_1 is now a liquidity function such that $\partial M^D/\partial r < 0$. Show that the quantity theory of money still holds and re-interpret the mechanism whereby a doubling of the money supply produces excess demand in the goods market.

13. 'In a Keynesian system with no cash balance effect, an increase in the money supply leads households to substitute money for bonds. In the "pre-Keynesian system" the substitution was in favour of goods'. Explain. Construct a more general model containing both forms of substitution. In such a model will money wage cuts eliminate involuntary unemployment?

14. In Question 11 B_0/p denotes the real value of bond holdings and B_0 the nominal values. Hence B_0 depends upon B, the *quantity* of irredeemable bonds in the system and r, the rate of interest such that:

$$B_0 \equiv \frac{\bar{B}}{r},$$

where $\bar{B}$ is the quantity of irredeemable bonds each paying a coupon income of £1 per year in perpetuity. Explain the identity above. What assumption is entailed in the statement in Section 2 that B_0/p is constant? What difficulties would arise if it were not made?

15. Many pre-Keynesian economists emphasised the role of discretionary monetary policy in controlling the economy. Using the model of Section 2 as amended by Question 12, discuss the relevance of discretionary monetary policy.

16. ' "Monetarism" is nothing new. It is simply pre-Keynesian macro-economics in clothes sufficiently unfamiliar and ill fitting to look new.' Discuss critically.

SUGGESTED READING

J. Robinson, *Economic Philosophy* (Pelican, 1964) chs iv–vi.

G. Ackley, *Macro-Economic Theory* (Macmillan, 1961) chs v–viii, xiv, xv.

L. R. Klein,† *The Keynesian Revolution* (Macmillan, 1967) chs ii, vi, vii.

R. F. Harrod, *The Life of John Maynard Keynes* (Macmillan, 1951) particularly ch. xi.

R. L. Meek, *Economics and Ideology and Other Essays* (Chapman & Hall, 1967) pp. 179–95.

R. F. Harrod,† *Economic Essays* (Macmillan, 1952) ch. xii.

† More advanced reference.

19 Economic Growth

IN developing the analysis of earlier parts of this book we made use of the assumption that the *capacity* of the economic system to produce output was given.

We justified this convenient simplification by explicitly confining our analysis to a 'short run' – defined as a period over which capacity was invariant – and arguing that this assumption, over a time span of (say) one or two years, though it obviously introduced an error, did not introduce an error so great as to vitiate the analysis. The empirical justification for this position was, of course, that though capacity does grow continuously it grows only very slowly.

The theory of the third part of this book is thus, in essentials, a theory of aggregate demand. It explains how much of the (given) productive capacity will be utilised. In the short-run theory, output can be increased – up to the limit imposed by 'full capacity' – only by increasing the extent to which the given capacity is utilised – that is by increasing employment. An alternative way of describing the theory is thus to call it a theory of employment; or a theory of capacity utilisation.

In the long run, by contrast, capacity itself must be treated as a variable simply because, though it grows only slowly, slow growth over a long period is significant. It is, indeed, not much of an over-simplification to say that

    (i) in the short run output grows only when the extent to which capacity is utilised *increases*;

    (ii) in the *long run* it grows because capacity itself increases.

In the figure below we have plotted the behaviour of the gross domestic product of the United Kingdom in real terms between 1950 and 1970. On the same figure we have plotted the inverted percentage of the work-force unemployed.

If we use this percentage of unemployment inverted as a rough index of the percentage of capacity employed, we can, by comparing periods of equal 'capacity utilisation' (percentage unemployment) obtain a correspondingly rough measure of the rate of growth in capacity. For example, between 1951.II and 1955.III – two periods of identical percentage unemployment – real gross output rose by a

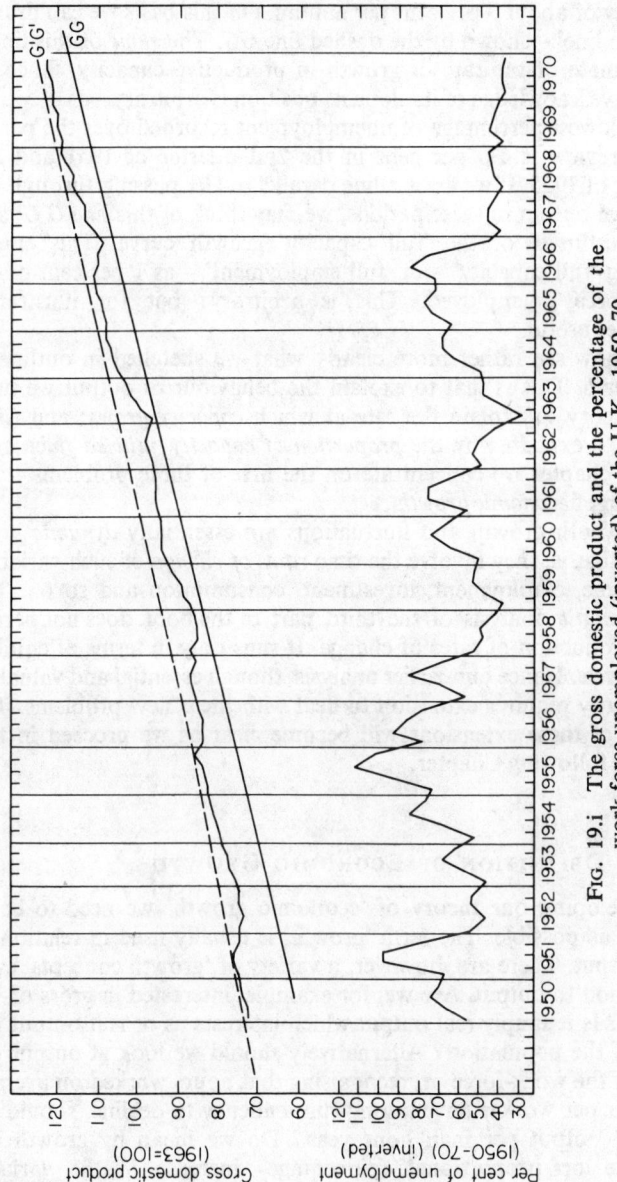

FIG. 19.i The gross domestic product and the percentage of the work-force unemployed (inverted) of the U.K., 1950–70

Sources: *London and Cambridge Economic Bulletin, Monthly Digest and National Institute Economic Review*

little over 12 per cent. This gives a compound rate of growth in
capacity of about 3 per cent per annum. On this basis we can draw a
'growth line' – shown by the dashed line *GG*. The *slope* of this line is
an estimate of the rate of growth in productive capacity. Since we
only have knowledge of its slope its position is arbitrary.

The lowest percentage of unemployment recorded over the period
under review is 1·0 per cent in the 2nd quarter of 1951 and 3rd
quarter of 1955. If we draw a line parallel to *GG* passing through the
values of output in these periods, we may think of this line *G'G'* as a
crude estimate of the 'full capacity' growth curve. This entails
defining 'full capacity' – or 'full employment' – as 1 per cent of the
work-force unemployed. This is arbitrary: but for illustrative
purposes useful.

We now see rather more clearly what we sketched in outline in
Chapter 6. This is that to explain the behaviour of output we need
(i) a theory to explain the rate at which *capacity grows*; and (ii) a
theory to explain why the *proportion of capacity utilised fluctuates*.
In this chapter we concentrate on the first of these problems – the
problem of *economic growth*.

Now both growth and fluctuations are essentially *dynamic problems* – that is, they involve the time *rates of change* of such variables
as income, employment, investment, consumption and so on. The
purely *static* analysis of the third part of the book does not permit
the introduction of rates of change. It runs only in terms of equilibrium levels. Hence our earlier analysis, though essential and valuable,
necessarily requires extension to deal with these new problems. The
nature of these extensions will become clear as we proceed in this
and the following Chapter.

1 THE DEFINITION OF ECONOMIC GROWTH

In developing our theory of 'economic growth' we need to be as
precise as possible. The term 'growth' is usually used in relation to
real output. There are, however, a variety of 'growth concepts' even
in relation to output. Are we, for example, interested in gross or net
output? Is it simply real output which interests us or is it output per
head of the population? Alternatively should we look at output per
head of the work-force or, recognising that hours worked on average
per year per worker have a long-run tendency to decline, should we
look at output per man hour year? Do we mean by growth the
absolute or proportional (percentage) increase in the variable
which interests us?

There is no single correct answer to these questions for the excellent reason that the concept which is relevant depends, as always, upon the question we are asking. For example if our concern is with *economic welfare*, net output per head is probably the appropriate variable while if we are interested in productivity we may prefer gross output per man hour year.

In the present context our concern is with the broad aspects of 'economic growth'. We shall therefore discuss the determinants of the proportional (percentage) rate of growth in the capacity of the economy to produce real net output. To see the relationship between this concept and the others mentioned in this Section, the reader should look carefully at Fig. 19.i. In terms of this figure our aim is to explain the *slope* of the dotted line $G'G'$.

2 The Growth of Productive Capacity

As far back as Chapter 7 we introduced, and in some degree explored the meaning of, the concept of a production function. The notion behind this function, it will be recalled, was that, assuming businessmen to employ labour and capital optimally – that is, to obtain maximum output from any given inputs – there was a stable relationship between real net output (Y), the real capital stock (K), the quantity of labour employed (N) and the state of technique or productive know-how (T). In formal terms this hypothesis was expressed in functional notation by writing:

$$Y = f(K, N, T) \tag{19.I}$$

In Chapter 17 we made use of this hypothesis – though, since our analysis was *short run* we took both the capital stock (K) and the state of technique (T) to be given and constant. Now, working in the *long run* context we treat all three as variables. Hence, thinking now of 'full capacity' output and writing this as Y_c we can state that:

where $$Y_c = f_1(K, N_f, T), \tag{19.Ia}$$

$N_f \equiv$ quantity of labour input corresponding to 'full employment'.

It is intuitively obvious that *if* (19.I) is a meaningful way of expressing a relation between capital, labour and net output – and we shall assume that it is – then the proportionate rate of growth in full capacity output must depend in some way upon the proportionate rates of growth in capital, the work-force and the state of technique. Formally, using lower case letters for proportionate rates of growth in the variables, we may say that

$$y_c = f_2(k, n_f, t) \tag{19.II}$$

This conclusion, which we stated much earlier in Chapter 7, is, as we noted above, intuitively obvious. Nevertheless, since we have, admittedly very crudely, estimated that, between 1948 and 1960 capacity grew at about 3 per cent per annum it immediately suggests a question: just how much did k (the rate of capital accumulation), n_f (the rate of growth of the work-force) and t (the rate of improvement in technique) contribute to our estimated 3 per cent growth in capacity? This question clearly has important implications for policy – particularly if we want – as at the moment of writing it seems that we do – to accelerate economic growth. It is also important because it is an issue on which economists are by no means unanimous. In explaining the rate of capacity growth some economists emphasise the role of capital accumulation; others emphasise technical improvement. Plainly both these factors – and the rate of growth of the work-force – play *some* part in explaining growth. The issues are their relative importance and the degree to which they are independent of each other.

3 A PRODUCTION FUNCTION HYPOTHESIS

The question of the relative importance of technical change, capital accumulation and growth in the work-force in determining the rate of growth in capacity is an empirical one. We must therefore look at our observations of what *has* happened and, from them, try to discover the contributions to past growth of each factor. To do this effectively we must approach the data with a theory formulated precisely enough to permit us to measure the parameters of the production function itself. There is, as the reader will doubtless notice, a precise analogy here with our theory of consumption. In developing this theory we began first with a very general notion of a consumption function. Next we postulated a *particular form* of consumption function which permitted us to estimate the value of the 'marginal response coefficients' relating real planned consumption to such variables as real income, the real value of households' assets and the rate of interest. How can we proceed from the general notions of the previous section to a particular production function hypothesis?

In order to develop the notion of the consumption function we placed *restrictions* upon it which seemed to us, for various reasons, to be plausible. Thus we argued that $\partial C/\partial Y$ ($\equiv$ marginal propensity to consume) would be positive but less than unity. What restrictions can we place on the form of the production function of (19.I)?

Economic theory tells us that, if businessmen maximise profits, they will employ labour until the marginal physical product of labour is equal to the real wage. It follows that – at least over the observed range – the marginal product of labour ($\equiv \partial Y/\partial N$) must always be positive.

We also expect, and indeed assumed throughout Chapter 17, that the marginal product of labour will fall if, with the capital stock and technique constant, additional labour is employed.

Symmetrically we are entitled to argue that, if businessmen try to maximise profits, they will employ capital up to the point at which *its* marginal product ($\equiv \partial Y/\partial K$) is equal to *its* cost to the businessman. Since the latter is positive so too will be the former. Moreover we may expect the marginal product of capital to fall if, with a given work-force and state of technique, additional capital is employed.

These considerations give us *four* conditions which we can immediately require any new – and less general – production hypothesis to satisfy.

In Chapter 7 we introduced – and indeed in some degree discussed – a *particular* production function of the form:

$$Y = TK^{\alpha}N^{1-\alpha}, \quad \text{where} \quad 0 < \alpha < 1. \tag{19.III}$$

This function, as we showed in Chapter 7, satisfied each of the four requirements we have set out above. Are there any other conditions we can impose?

As a matter of empirical observation the share of the national income accruing to wage earners seems to be relatively constant over long periods of time. This means that, since with only two factors of production what does *not* go to labour *must* go to capital, we can plausibly require the additional condition that (i) our function must be such that the shares of labour and capital are constant; if (ii) each factor is paid its marginal product.

In Chapter 17 we saw that a businessman who aimed at maximising profit would employ labour until the marginal product of labour (in real terms) was equal to the real wage. If each worker is paid this real wage, then the total receipts of labour (wage bill) are given by:

wage bill ≡ no. of employed workers × real wage

= no. of employed workers × marginal product of labour

$$= N \times \frac{\partial Y}{\partial N}.$$

Analogously the *share* of wages is given by:

$$\frac{\text{wage bill}}{\text{real income}} = \frac{N \times \partial Y/\partial N}{Y}.$$

Now *if* the function (19.III) entails, on this reasoning, a *constant share of wages* (and profits) in the national income, it will, on assumptions which, at this level of generality, are quite plausible, satisfy *five* restraints which empirical observation and economic theory suggest that we should impose. It would therefore seem a reasonable function in terms of which to seek to explain growth – at least as a first approximation. In practice it is easy to show that, on our assumptions about factor rewards, the function at (19.III) *does* entail constant shares of wages and profits. Indeed as an arithmetic example easily illustrates, the following conditions always hold:

$$\frac{\text{wages bill}}{\text{income}} = 1 - \alpha \qquad \frac{\text{profit bill}}{Y} = \alpha. \qquad (19.\text{IV})$$

For a numerical illustration put $\alpha = 0.5$, $T = 10$, $K = 100$ and $N = 10,000$. Then

$$Y = TK^{\alpha}N^{1-\alpha} = 10 \times (100)^{(\frac{1}{2})} \times (10,000)^{(\frac{1}{2})}$$

$$= 10 \times 10 \times 100$$

$$= 10,000.$$

The marginal product of labour is given by the expression

$$\frac{\partial Y}{\partial N} = (1-\alpha)TK^{\alpha}N^{-\alpha}\dagger = 0.5 \times 10 \times 100^{(\frac{1}{2})} \times 10,000^{-(\frac{1}{2})}$$

$$= 5(\tfrac{10}{100})$$

$$= 0.5,$$

whence   the wage bill $\equiv N \times \dfrac{\partial Y}{\partial N}$

$$\equiv 10,000 \times 0.5$$

$$= 5000.$$

† This formula is obtained by differentiating the production function partially with respect to N.

The *share* of wages is given by:

$$\frac{\text{wage bill}}{Y} \equiv \frac{N \times (\partial Y/\partial N)}{Y} = \frac{5,000}{10,000} = 0.5 = 1 - \alpha$$

which is the proposition set out at (19.IV).

It follows that the function $Y = TK^{\alpha}N^{1-\alpha}$ satisfies the *five* important conditions which we can reasonably require of it. To what 'growth hypothesis' [analogous to (19.II)] does this function lead? By making use of fairly elementary mathematics this is easily found to be:†

$$y_c = t + \alpha k + (1-\alpha)n_f. \tag{19.V}$$

To check (19.V) as before put $\alpha = 0.5$, $T = 10$, $K = 100$, $N = 10,000$. Then $Y_0 = 10,000$, as we showed in the paragraph above.

Now put $T = 10.001$, $K = 121$, $N = 12,100$. We have

$$Y_1 = 10.001 \times (121)^{\frac{1}{2}} \times (12,100)^{\frac{1}{2}}$$

$$= 10.001 \times 11 \times 110$$

$$= 12,101.210.$$

According to (19.V) we have

$$y_c = t + \alpha k + (1-\alpha)n_f \tag{19.V}$$

$$= \frac{.001}{10.0} + \alpha\left(\frac{21}{100}\right) + (1-\alpha)\frac{2,100}{10,000}$$

$$= 0.01 \text{ per cent} + 0.5 (21 \text{ per cent}) + 0.5 (21 \text{ per cent})$$

$$= 21.01 \text{ per cent.}$$

Now the percentage increase in Y is given by:

$$\frac{Y_1 - Y_0}{Y_0} = \frac{12,101.210 - 10,000}{10,000} = \frac{2,101.210}{10,000} = 21.0121 \text{ per cent,}$$

which, taken correct to two decimal places, is the result obtained from (19.V).‡

It follows that the function (19.III) first introduced in Chapter 7 is not only plausible (since it meets the *five* requirements we put upon

† This formula holds precisely only for indefinitely small values of the independent variables. It is obtained by logarithmic differentiation of the production function.

‡ Which, we recall, does not hold precisely for other than indefinitely small changes.

it) but also leads to a simple 'growth hypothesis'. This simple growth hypothesis tells us that

$$\frac{\partial y}{\partial k} \equiv \begin{array}{c} \text{marginal response coefficient} \\ \text{relating the rate of growth} \\ \text{in output to the rate of} \\ \text{capital accumulation} \end{array} = \begin{array}{c} \text{share of profits in the} \\ \text{national income} \end{array}$$

$$\frac{\partial y}{\partial n} \equiv \begin{array}{c} \text{marginal response coefficient} \\ \text{relating the rate of growth} \\ \text{in output to the rate of} \\ \text{increase in the work-force} \end{array} = \begin{array}{c} \text{share of wages in the} \\ \text{national income.} \end{array}$$

This means, since these shares are easily measured, that it is not difficult to estimate the marginal response coefficients – a result which puts us well on the way to calculating the relative importance of k, n and t in explaining the rate of growth in actual output and thus, adding the full employment assumption, the rate of growth of *full capacity* output.

4 THE GROWTH IN OUTPUT AND CAPACITY OUTPUT

The previous Section of this Chapter, though rather difficult, is an essential preliminary to an attempt to assess the relative importance of t, k and n in explaining growth. If we accept the rather heavy load of assumptions entailed in this Section we can now write our growth hypothesis:

$$y = t + \text{share of profits} \times k + \text{share of wages} \times n. \qquad (19.\text{V})$$

The two shares can readily be obtained from national income estimates.

$y \equiv$ the rate of growth of actual output – is conceptually measurable and, indeed, data exist in most countries which enable us to estimate it.

$k \equiv$ the rate of growth of the real capital stock is also conceptually measurable and in some countries – notably the U.S.A. – data exist which enable us to estimate it.

$n \equiv$ the rate of growth of labour input – is similarly capable of estimation.

Hence in (19.V), of the *six* terms – five are susceptible to measurement (in principle) and estimation (in practice). It follows that t – the rate of change of technique – can be estimated as a residual: that is as the difference between the *observed* rate of increase in output and the contributions explained by the *observed* rate of increase in capital (multiplied by its marginal response coefficient) and the *observed* rate of increase in labour (multiplied by its marginal response coefficient).

There are now several studies of the growth in output which are based on production functions of the form of (19.III) and growth hypotheses of the form (19.V). Many of them are rather technical. In what follows we set out some of their results adjusted so as to fit our model. Because of the need for adjustment the results are illustrative only.

According to recent U.S. data the share of wages (the marginal response coefficient of the growth in employment) is about 0·77. The corresponding marginal response coefficient for the growth of capital is therefore 0·23. Between 1929 and 1957, real national product in the U.S.A. grew at the compound rate of 2·93 per cent per annum. During the same period employment grew at an estimated 1·31 per cent. However the average hours worked per employee fell. Hence the input of labour (corrected for the change in hours) grew at only 1·08 per cent. Over the same period capital accumulated at the rate of 1·88 per cent. Hence, rewriting (16.V) we have:

$$t = y - \text{share of profits} \times k - \text{share of wages} \times n$$

$$= 2·93 - (0·23 \times 1·88) - (0·77 \times 1·08)$$

$$= 2·93 - 0·4324 - 0·8316$$

$$= 1·666.$$

Thus, on this calculation it seems that something like 57 per cent (i.e. 1·67/2·93 × 100/1) of the growth in the U.S. national product between 1929 and 1957 is to be explained by the process of technical improvement. Capital accumulation accounts for only a little more than 14 per cent while the growth of labour input accounts for about 28 per cent.

The calculation set out above, though it has the appearance of precision, is in reality extremely crude. If these figures are meaningful at all – and the reader should by now be aware that the method involves a heavy load of assumptions by which it stands or falls – they do no more than indicate orders of magnitude. Nevertheless *if* these orders of magnitude are even approximately correct, they are interesting for they suggest that the role of capital accumulation in promoting growth may be less significant than is commonly supposed. Suppose we assume that they are both meaningful and accurate as far as orders of magnitude are concerned. Then, plainly, provided we can calculate the rate of growth of the full employment labour input we can readily calculate the rate at which full capacity grew in the period. It follows that, in explaining the rate at which actual output grew we have developed – in operational terms – a method of explaining the rate of growth in 'full capacity' output.

It is, of course, arguable that the method we have used is erroneous: and, in consequence, the conclusions drawn are also erroneous. At this stage the reader is simply asked to take note of two points:

(i) the estimated contribution of technical progress to observed growth reflects the assumptions involved and, in particular, the assumption that the rate of technical progress is independent of the rate of capital accumulation and work-force expansion; and

(ii) that the method we have employed has been subjected to very considerable criticism on this and other grounds in the professional literature.

Unfortunately many of the criticisms of the method are technically difficult and thus beyond the scope of this book. The reader, therefore, is asked to consider our results *not* as generally accepted estimates of what are agreed to be the relevant coefficients, but rather as an illustration of *one way among many* in which the production function concept can be made operational and the results which follow from adopting it. It is certainly *not* claimed that the method used is the best way of approaching the problem. Nor are we arguing that economists as a whole are agreed that it is the best way or that the best way of approaching the problem is presently the subject of a professional consensus.

5 ACCELERATING GROWTH: CAPITAL ACCUMULATION

In recent years there has been growing dissatisfaction with the rate of growth of output in the United Kingdom. As a result considerable thought has been given – and is still being given – to how the rate of growth might best be increased. What light does our earlier analysis throw upon this problem?

According to our data for the U.S. economy we have our expression for the rate of growth of output in which the relevant orders of magnitude appear to be broadly as follows:

$$y_c = t + \alpha k + (1 - \alpha)n_f$$
$$= 1 \cdot 7 + 0 \cdot 25k + 0 \cdot 75n_f$$

Can we make use of this approximation to interpret U.K. experience?

If the concept of a production function is applicable and *if* the form of the production function is appropriate – both of which are open to considerable doubt – there remains the problem of whether parameter values derived from U.S. data are useful approximations in the U.K. case. Simply as an illustration we shall assume that they are. It follows that a 1 per cent increase in k (from (say) 2 to 3 per cent) would add only one-quarter of 1 per cent to the growth rate y_c.

Now k, by definition, is the proportional rate of capital accumulation per year. This is annual net investment (I) divided by the capital stock (K). In a closed economy, *ex post*, $I \equiv S$ where $S \equiv$ net savings. In general saving plans are carried out. Hence,

$I = sY$ where $s \equiv$ the proportion of income the community plans to save.

It follows that

$$k \equiv \frac{I}{K} = s\frac{Y}{K}.$$

In short, the rate of capital accumulation depends upon two factors:

(i) the average (which for convenience is now put equal to the marginal) propensity to save $= s$; and

(ii) the output/capital ratio (Y/K).

We may now take the output/capital ratio – in terms of annual output – to be about $\frac{1}{3}$. Hence if the average net propensity to save is around 0·09 the percentage rate of capital accumulation will be 3 and, to raise it to 4, the proportion of income saved must be raised to 0·12. And this, since the marginal response coefficient $(\partial y_c/\partial k)$ is assumed to be a quarter, will add only one-quarter of 1 per cent to the rate of growth in output. Alternatively we may say that, on these figures, to raise the growth rate in output by 1 per cent – from (say) 3 per cent to 4 per cent – by raising the rate of capital accumulation would, *ceteris paribus*, require an increase in s from 0·09 to about 0·21 – a very large increase indeed. This is an important and suggestive result as a simple diagram makes plain.

Suppose the economy is growing with continuous 'full employment' at 3 per cent per annum (in terms of real net output) with a given s. Then consumption will be growing at the same rate of 3 per cent since it is, *ex hypothesis*, a constant proportion $(1-s)$ of output. On the figure below we plot time on the horizontal axis and the logarithm of real consumption on the vertical. The dotted line CC

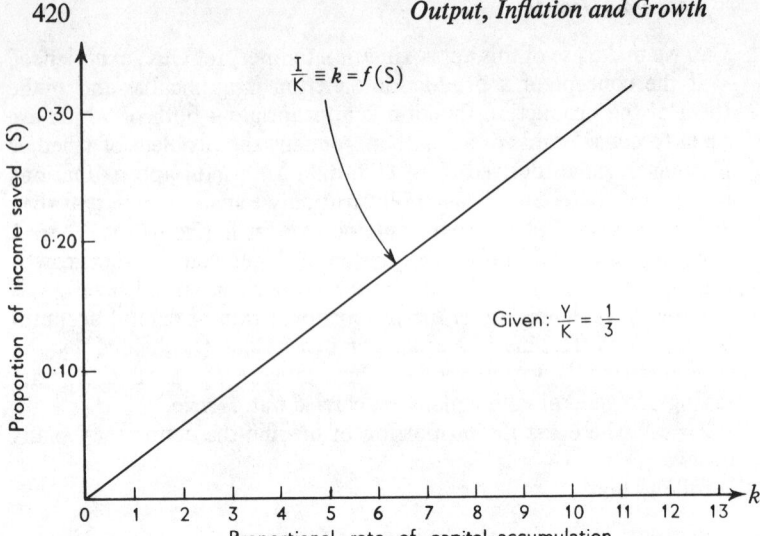

FIG. 19.ii   The rate of capital accumulation and the saving ratio

thus gives the path of consumption when income is growing at 3 per
cent per annum. Obviously in 1965 consumption is OA.

In 1965 suppose we decide to accelerate growth by increasing k –
the rate of capital accumulation. To do this we raise s. This immediately *reduces* consumption to OA'. The growth path of
consumption will now be steeper than before, since with a higher
rate of capital accumulation income must grow faster. And at some
point in the future we shall begin to enjoy a greater *level* of consumption as well as a greater *rate of growth* in consumption. How
soon this occurs will depend upon the response of y_c to the change in
s and this clearly depends upon (i) the output/capital ratio Y/K; and
(ii) the marginal response coefficient $\partial y_c/\partial k$. Where both are small,
the new growth path will be little steeper than the old so that it will
take many years for growth to 'offset' the initial reduction in the
proportion of income consumed.

In the figure the hard line $C'C'$ drawn through A' shows the new
path of consumption resulting from an increase in the proportion of
net saving from 0·09 to 0·21 on the assumptions – which are not
implausible – that (i) $Y/K = \frac{1}{3}$; and (ii) $\partial y_c/\partial k = \frac{1}{4}$, so that the 3 per
cent growth rate becomes 4 per cent. On these assumptions it takes
approximately: (i) $3\frac{1}{2}$ years to restore consumption to its original
1965 level (OA); (ii) $13\frac{1}{2}$ years before consumption on the *new* growth
line becomes equal to what it would have been on the *old* at the

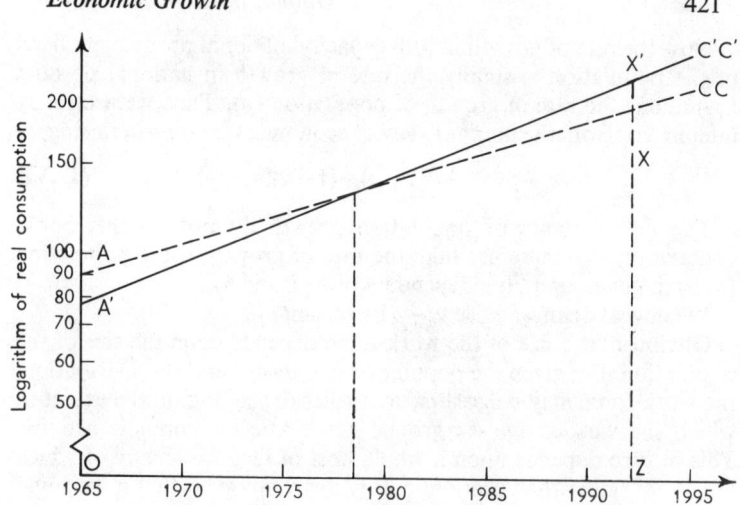

FIG. 19.iii   Capital accumulation and the rate of growth of
consumption

point where *CC* and *C'C'* cut; while (iii) not until 1992 does total
consumption for the years 1965-92 become equal under the two
systems.

From this analysis two conclusions follow. First, any attempt to
accelerate growth in Britain primarily by raising the rate of capital
accumulation seems likely to bring rather poor returns. Second, such
a policy has considerable costs in terms of consumption foregone.

6 ACCELERATING GROWTH: LABOUR INPUT

From (19.V) it is obvious that one way of increasing y_c (the rate of
growth of full capacity output) is to increase n_f (the rate of growth of
the 'fully employed' work-force). In general, of course, we are not
much interested in the growth of net national product as such.
Suppose for example net national product in real terms *quadrupled*
while the population *quintupled*. National product *per capita* – an
index of *potential* economic welfare – would have *fallen* despite the
immense growth in output. Apart, therefore, from the area of
international power politics where the total of output – as well as
output per head – seems to be a relevant consideration – growth in
the national product *per se* is not of major interest. What is of far
greater interest is the growth of national product *per head*.

Now the rate of growth in 'full capacity' national product per head of the population is simply the rate of growth in national product (y_c) minus the rate of growth of population (p). Thus we are really interested – from the point of view of economic welfare – in raising

$$y_c - p = t + \alpha(k-p) + (1-\alpha)(n_f - p). \qquad (19.\text{VI})$$

The determinants of population growth do not, in this book, concern us. We therefore take the rate of growth of the population (p) as (i) given; and (ii) independent of y_c, k and n_f.

We now ask can we raise $y_c - p$ by raising n_f?

Obviously the size of the work-force depends upon the size of the population. But given the population and its age and sex distribution, the work-force may be greater or smaller depending on the extent to which the various age/sex groups *participate* in economic activity. This in turn depends upon a whole host of factors – many of which are social rather than economic. It is clear, however, that if we could raise the rate of *participation* – that is the proportion of the population in the work-force – then while the participation rate is rising n_f can rise independently of p. Equally obviously this process must have a limit if only because not more than 100 per cent of the population can, as a matter of logic, enter the work-force. In practice, of course, nothing like the whole population *is* or *can be* in the work-force. Moreover though participation rates do change quite markedly for particular age/sex groups the overall percentage changes rather little. This is because while participation rates for some groups, notably females, have tended to rise – the participation rates for males over 64 and for boys and girls below 20 have tended to fall. In general we no longer work until we die and we require, and increasingly receive, a good deal more, and longer, education before we go to work.

It seems, therefore, that though, as a matter of theory, we could hope to raise $y_c - p$ by raising n_f – by policies designed to increase participation rates – this is likely to be very difficult in practice if not impossible. Indeed the increasing demands for education allied to the trend towards earlier retirement may well, on balance, reduce the overall participation rate. This conclusion is strengthened by the reflection that, in thinking of n_f simply as 'persons' we are neglecting the obvious point that n_f is really a measure of labour input which is 'persons' multiplied by the *average hours worked per period per person*. Secularly average hours worked are tending to fall. Hence for any given p the rate of growth of labour input seems if anything likely to decline. This is doubly unfortunate for as we have already shown $\partial y_c / \partial n_f$ (the marginal response coefficient relating the growth of output to the growth in labour input) is probably quite large – of the order of 0·75. Hence not only are we denied an opportunity of raising $y_c - p$ by raising n_f but we must, in practice, look forward to a fall in n_f in relation to p which will tend to reduce the rate of growth in output per head. It follows, therefore, that the principal hope of raising $y_c - p$ must rest in bringing about an increase in t (the rate of improvement in productive technique).

7 ACCELERATING GROWTH: INNOVATION

Improving productive technique – 'know-how' – consists in bringing about a change in productive methods such that for any given input of labour and capital services a larger output can be obtained. This process is continuous for the economy as a whole and as our earlier discussion suggests is probably the most important source of growth in real net output per head.

At this stage a qualification is essential. In Section 5 we estimated t (the rate of improvement in 'know-how') as a residual. Our estimate therefore attracts any errors in our estimates of the remaining five elements in Equation (19.V). Two conclusions follow. First, we should not be too dogmatic in asserting that our estimate of t is of the right order of magnitude. Second, t – as we have estimated it – is a 'catch all'. *It is in fact that part of the observed growth in output which cannot be explained, on our theory, by the growth in capital and labour inputs.* It may, therefore, contain a great deal more than is usually implied in the phrase 'technical change'. Despite these qualifications, until a more refined analysis shows our conclusion to be in error, we can, with proper caution, retain it.

The process of improving 'know-how' – which gives us a positive value for t – consists of a number of related activities. These can be classified into three processes:

(i) the *development* of knowledge which, if used in production, would permit a greater output from a given input of labour and capital;

(ii) the *application* of this new knowledge to the actual process of production;

(iii) the *reduction* of the *spread* in actual production methods between those employed by the most efficient and least efficient firms.

It follows that, to increase t, we need to increase the rates at which these three processes are taking place.

How we may hope to raise t needs an extensive examination beyond the scope of this book. At this stage it is sufficient for the reader to note that, contrary to what is often believed, *invention*, (process (i) above) is only a part – and possibly not the most important part – of improving 'know-how'. From which it follows that increasing the rate of invention may not be the most useful way of increasing t – that is, of raising the rate of improvement in technique.

8 SUMMARY

In this chapter we began by noticing (Fig. 19.i) that the 'productive capacity' of the U.K. economy has been expanding, since 1950, at a rate possibly a little above 3 per cent per annum. We then tried to develop a meaningful theory to explain the observed rate of growth. The centre-piece of this theory is the concept (introduced in Chapter 7) of an aggregate production function relating the rate of output per period to the inputs of capital and labour services per period and the state of productive technique. We then developed this theory in the form of a *particular* production function. We chose this function because it satisfied (cf. Chapter 7) a number of conditions which economic theory and empirical observation suggested to be important. Using this theory, and the assumption that both labour and capital were paid (as wages or profits) their marginal products, we then attempted to estimate the relative contributions of

$k \equiv$ the annual rate of capital accumulation;

$n \equiv$ the annual rate of growth in labour input;

$t \equiv$ the annual rate of improvement in technique,

to the observed rate of growth in real net output. From the estimates yielded by this exercise we then set out some observations on past growth and discussed, in a brief and general way, some of the problems of seeking to raise, from its apparent 3 per cent per annum, the rate of expansion in 'full capacity' output in the United Kingdom.

QUESTIONS AND EXERCISES

1. According to the N.E.D.C. the work-force would rise by about 0·8 per cent per annum from 1961–6 and by only around 0·2 per

cent after 1966. To achieve a 4 per cent rate of growth in output would thus have required an annual rate of increase in productivity per employed person of 3·2 per cent from 1961–6 and 3·8 per cent after 1966. What action do you think would be necessary to attain these rates? Compare your analysis with that given by the N.E.D.C. in *Growth of the United Kingdom Economy to 1966; Conditions Favourable to Faster Growth.*

2. 'The production function $Y = TK^{\alpha}N^{1-\alpha}$ assumes that the rate of technical progress is independent of the rate of capital accumulation. This is absurd.' Discuss these statements.

3. In a group of firms which employed business consultants the average increase in net productivity achieved, as a result of their advice, was of the order of 50 per cent. Does this surprise you? What light, if any, does it throw upon the production function used in the text?

4. One reason for using the production function $Y = TK^{\alpha}N^{1-\alpha}$ is that, if each factor is paid its marginal product, the shares of the factors are invariant at α and $1-\alpha$. Is this marginal productivity assumption reasonable?

5. How 'stable' *is* the share of labour? Use the Blue Book to calculate the share of labour for each year from 1950 to 1970. Plot your results on a graph. Is there a trend? Is the share 'stable'. What is the estimated value of $(1-\alpha)$?

6. In discussing the sources of growth in capacity we have *assumed* a production function of the form $Y = TK^{\alpha}N^{1-\alpha}$. Obviously this assumption could be wrong. How could it be tested?

7. The following hypothetical data is observed for the economy of Erewhon. What is the production function? What results would we get if we assumed it was of the form $Y = TK^{\alpha}N^{1-\alpha}$?

Year	Y	Capital stock (K)	Employed persons (N)	Wage bill	Profits
t	350	500	100	175	175
$t+1$	356	520	96	178	178
$t+2$	355	530	90	177·5	177·5
$t+3$	357	534	90	178·5	178·5
$t+4$	365	540	95	182·5	182·5
$t+5$	375	550	100	187·5	187·5
$t+6$	390	560	110	195	195

In the light of your answer reconsider Question 6.

8. In the exercise of Question 7 which assumption in our earlier analysis must be abandoned? Why? What is your estimate of the average propensity to save? How do you obtain it?

9. 'The present preoccupation with economic growth is simply a fashion. If people were aware of the economic and social costs of growing faster the fashion would be very short lived indeed.' Discuss in the light of (i) our earlier analysis; (ii) the costs of pollution; (iii) your own social preferences.

10. 'The so-called "technical progress coefficient" we derive from assuming a production function and applying it to observed data is really nothing more than a measure of our ignorance.' Elucidate and appraise.

11. 'The Soviet Union is a major industrial power to-day only because its planners imposed immense privations on its people during the inter-war years.' Explain.

12. 'Faster growth will require greater "mobility" of labour. Hence if we are serious about trying to grow faster, far from *reducing* immigration from the Commonwealth we should be trying to increase it.' Discuss with particular reference to the meaning of 'mobility'.

13. In Fig. 19.i we have used the straight line *GG* to represent the constant percentage rate of growth of capacity. This is only correct if national product is measured on a logarithmic scale. How big is the error involved? Show that the error is a function of the time span of the graph. Does the error invalidate the analysis?

14. 'The rate of growth of *capacity* output, since it depends on net investment, must depend upon the rate of growth of *actual* output. It therefore depends upon demand as well as supply considerations.' Elucidate and appraise.

15. Critically examine the assumptions underlying our method of estimating the rate of growth of capacity output.

16. Extend Fig. 19.i to include the latest data available. Use your data to re-estimate the rate of growth of capacity. How far does your estimate differ from the average rate of growth in output over the whole period?

17. Given the possible range of errors in national product estimates (from *National Accounts Statistics: Sources and Methods*), between what maximum and minimum values must your answer to Question 16 lie?

18. 'If businessmen expected the U.K. economy to grow faster, they would act in such a way as to ensure that it did.' Elucidate. Do you agree?

19. 'Whatever one does with the figures, the U.K. comes close to the bottom of the international growth league.' Is this so? If it is, how would you seek to explain it (i) in terms of the analysis of Chapter 19; (ii) in other terms? Are your explanations testable?

20. 'In most U.K. industries the least efficient firm is only about one-quarter as efficient as the most efficient.' If this is correct what does it suggest about the process and rate of innovation and what policy measures might bring about an increase in it?

Suggested Reading

D. C. Paige, 'Economic Growth: the Last Hundred Years', *N.I.E.S.R. Review* no. 16 (1961).

A. Maddison, *Economic Growth in the West* (Allen & Unwin, 1964).

A. Maddison, 'How Fast can Britain Grow?', *Lloyds Bank Review* no. 79 (Jan 1966).

J. C. R. Dow, *The Management of the British Economy* (Cambridge, 1964) particularly chs xiv–xvi.

N.E.D.C., *Conditions Favourable to Faster Growth* (H.M.S.O., 1963).

'Policies for Faster Growth', *N.I.E.S.R. Review* (Feb 1962).

W. A. H. Godley and J. R. Shepherd, 'Long-Term Growth and Short-Term Policy', *N.I.E.S.R. Review* (Aug 1964).

W. Beckerman and associates,† *The British Economy in 1975* (Cambridge, 1965) chs i, ii.

W. Beckerman in *Economic Growth in Britain*, ed. P. D. Henderson (Weidenfeld & Nicolson, 1966).

E. F. Dennison,† *The Sources of Economic Growth in the United States and the Alternatives Before Us* (Washington, 1962).

T. Balogh and P. Streeten,† 'The Coefficient of Ignorance', *Oxford Institute of Statistics Bulletin* (May 1963).

† More advanced reference.

20 Fluctuations in Economic Activity

IN Chapter 19 we developed an account of the process whereby, over the long run, the capacity of the economy to produce output grows. In this chapter we consider why, as a matter of observation, the growth path followed by the economy involves *fluctuations* in the extent to which, in any given year, *the available capacity* is utilised. The problem of economic *fluctuations* is often discussed under the heading of the theory of economic *cycles*. What then is a cycle?

A cycle may be defined as a repeated wave-like movement in the value of any economic variable over time. Most economic series when plotted against time exhibit such movements. The cycles, however, are not regular, that is their *periodicity* – the length of time over which they repeat themselves – is not constant. Nor do the individual series move in step. Nevertheless the wave-like movements exhibit a sufficient degree of regularity to make it reasonable to speak of 'cycles'.

In this chapter we shall be concerned only with cycles in *macro-economic variables*. Micro-economic variables such as the output of new houses, pigs, machine tools and many others also display cyclical fluctuations and these variables sometimes display a pattern of fluctuations dissimilar to that of the macro-economic concepts.

In Fig. 20.i below are plotted quarterly estimates of real gross domestic product in the United Kingdom. Through the resultant curve is drawn a dotted line *gg* representing the long-term rate of growth in gross domestic product. This we call the 'trend'. Passing through the observation for the II quarter of 1951 we draw a line *FF* parallel to *gg*. This represents the trend rate of growth in 'full capacity' output. Clearly output exhibits considerable fluctuations around its 'trend' *gg*. In short, there is a cycle in gross domestic product. This in some periods, for example the year 1959, rises *faster* than the trend while in others, for example 1956–8, it either rises more *slowly* or even, as in 1951–2 or the early part of 1956 actually *falls*. Obviously whenever output grows *faster* than the trend rate of increase in capacity, the proportion of capacity employed *rises*. It follows, therefore, as indeed was noted in Chapter 19, that fluctuations in the output of the U.K. economy *around its rising trend* can be viewed as fluctuations in the proportion of productive

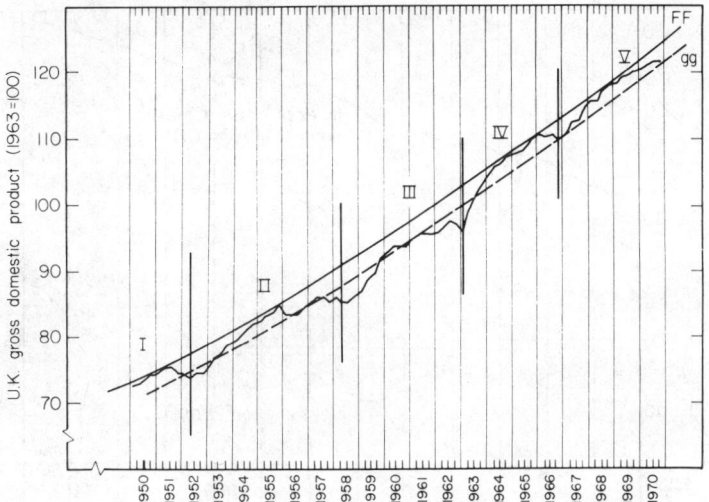

FIG. 20.i   Quarterly estimates of real gross domestic product of the
U.K., 1950–70

Source: *National Institute Economic Review* (Nov 1967, July 1971)

capacity employed. Since the theory which we developed in Chapters
8–12 argued that aggregate output would adjust, up to the limit of
'full capacity', to aggregate demand, it is clear that, to explain why
cycles of this kind occur, we need to explain why aggregate demand
fluctuates over time. In short, we have to try to explain the determinants of *the time rates of change* of such variables as consumption,
investment, exports, imports and government expenditure. Our
earlier analysis was *static* and *timeless* and sought to explain only
the equilibrium levels of these variables. Hence in this Chapter we
need to develop our theory in a *dynamic* way – that is a way which
essentially and explicitly involves time.

In Fig. 20.ii we have plotted the behaviour of employment,
consumption, gross investment in fixed capital, investment in
inventories, exports and imports. The reader should notice that
though these series too exhibit fluctuations, the timing and form of
these does not correspond at all precisely to the fluctuations in gross
domestic product. In some cases the fluctuations are more marked.
In others they are less. Fluctuation, however, is general.

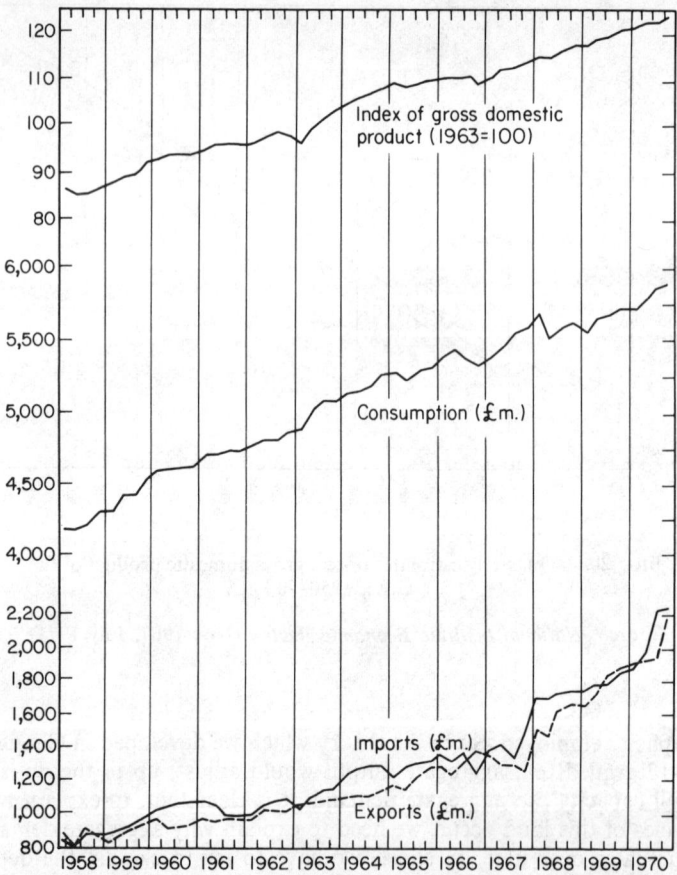

FIG. 20.ii(a)   Gross domestic product, consumption, imports and exports

Sources: (1) Gross domestic product, seasonally adjusted – 1963 = 100: *National Institute Economic Review*. (2) Consumption seasonally adjusted: *Economic Trends*. (3) Imports and exports (F.O.B.) seasonally adjusted: *Economic Trends*

1 THE TERMINOLOGY OF FLUCTUATIONS

In order to discuss cycles in economic activity we need a terminology in which to do so. This terminology is a matter of choice. But if we do not adopt one we run the risk of confused description from which can come only a confused and confusing analysis.

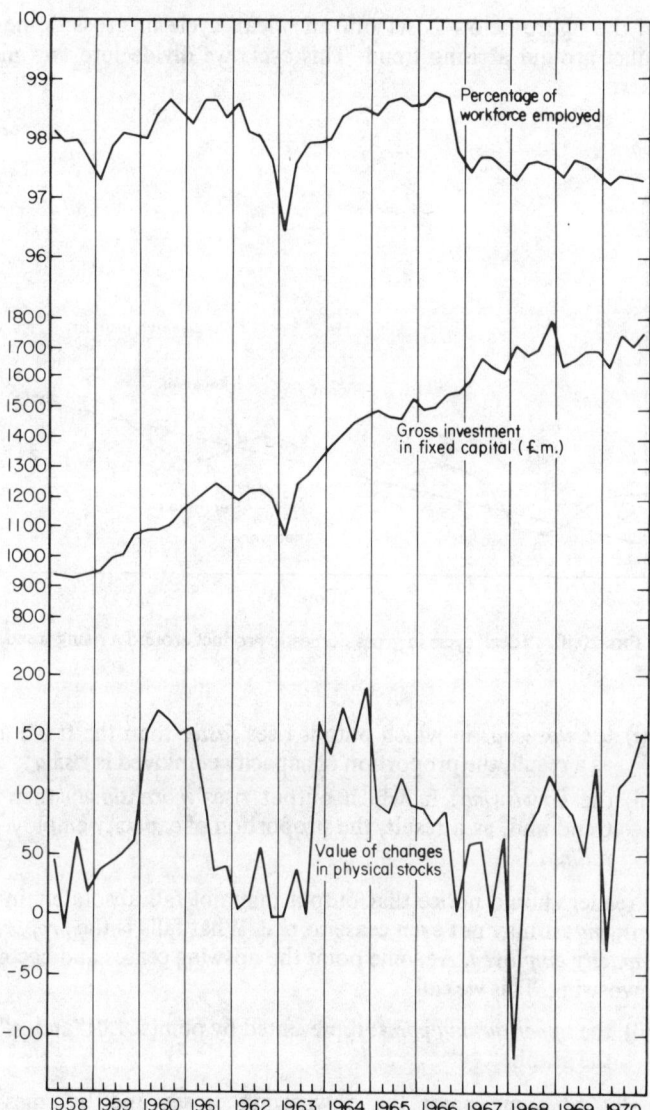

FIG. 20.ii(b)   Employment, gross investment in fixed capital, value
of changes in physical stocks, U.K., 1958–70

Sources: (1) Percentage of work-force employed: *Monthly Digest.*
(2) and (3) Gross investment in fixed capital and value of changes in
physical stock: *Economic Trends* (Oct 1967, 1969, July 1971)

In the figure below is set out an 'ideal' cycle in gross domestic product around a rising trend. This cycle we divide into two main *phases*:

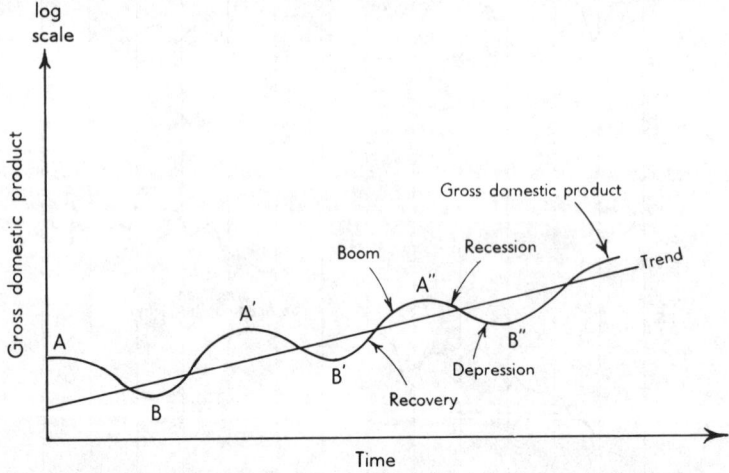

FIG. 20.iii   'Ideal' cycle in gross domestic product around a rising trend

    (i) the *upswing*: in which output rises *faster* than the trend and, as a result, the proportion of capacity employed is *rising*;

    (ii) the *downswing*: in which output rises *more slowly* than the trend and, as a result, the proportion of capacity employed is *falling*.

The reader should notice that output may not fall absolutely in the *downswing*: it may not even cease to rise. What falls is the *proportion of capacity employed*. At some point the upswing ceases and becomes a downswing. This we call

    (iii) the *upper turning point*: represented by points A, A' and A'' on the graph.

Equally, at some point the downswing ceases and becomes an upswing. This we call

    (iv) the *lower turning point*: represented by points B, B' and B'' on the graph.

A single cycle runs from upper turning point to upper turning point (or lower to lower). The time taken for this cycle we call

(v) the *length or periodicity of the cycle*: this is represented by the distances AA', $A'A''$, BB', $B'B''$ on the graph.

Notice that, as we have constructed our Fig. 20.iii, the periodicity of the cycle is constant. In practice, as Fig. 20.i and 20.ii make clear, the periodicity of economic fluctuations is *not* regular.

There are a number of other terms commonly used to describe economic fluctuations which are not always given precise meanings. Such terms are: recovery, boom, recession, depression. In terms of Fig. 20.iii we define these as follows:

(vi) *recovery*: that part of the upswing below the trend;
(vii) *boom*: that part of the upswing above the trend;
(viii) *recession*: that part of the downswing above the trend;
(ix) *depression*: that part of the downswing below the trend.

Finally we need a concept to enable us to compare the extent to which different economic variables fluctuate during the cycle. We call the extent of the fluctuation in any time series its *amplitude*. This we shall measure by

(x) the percentage increase in the variable (expressed as an annual rate) during the upswing minus the percentage change in the variable (expressed as an annual rate) during the downswing divided by the trend rate of growth (expressed as an annual rate).

To illustrate the use of this terminology let us return to Fig. 20.i.

The observations in Fig. 20.i are nothing like as well behaved as those of our 'ideal' cycle. Turning points cannot be unambiguously identified. In some degree, therefore, we must take arbitrary decisions about the turning points of the individual cycles in real gross domestic product. Accordingly we shall classify U.K. post-war experience as follows:†

No. of cycle	Upswing Lower turning point		Upper turning point		Downswing Lower turning point		Approx. length of cycle
	Year	*Quarter*	*Year*	*Quarter*	*Year*	*Quarter*	
1	1948	I	1951	III	1952	III	4 yrs 2 qtrs
2	1952	III	1955	IV	1958	II	5 yrs 3 qtrs
3	1958	II	1961	II	1963	I	4 yrs 3 qtrs
4	1963	I	1966	I	1966	IV	3 yrs 3 qtrs
5	1966	IV	1969	II	?		

† The reader is invited to identify the lower turning point of cycle no. 5 and the upper turning point of cycle 6 and to compare his datings of earlier cycles with Table 4.

On the basis of this classification it seems that the United Kingdom economy in the post-war period has (i) completed four cycles and is now in its fifth, while (ii) the periodicity of the completed cycles varies between 15 and 25 quarters: that is, roughly 4–6 years.

It is worth noticing that while the upper turning points of cycles 1 and 2 lay on the 'full capacity' growth line *FF*, that of cycle 3 did not. Moreover in terms of the proportion of the unused (or excess) capacity they represent, the lower turning points in cycle 2 and possibly 3 are lower than the corresponding turning point of cycle 1.† There may be, it seems, some reason to believe that booms are not proceeding as far as they did and depressions rather further. Finally it seems, as the reader can confirm for himself, that the *amplitude* of the U.K. cycles, as we have defined it, has been tending to increase.

These post-war cycles in U.K. economic activity are, of course, a great deal less severe than those experienced in the inter-war years. The cycle, however, has obviously not disappeared. It therefore requires explanation. What does a theory of cyclical fluctuations need to provide?

First, any such theory must explain why, at some point, a cumulative upward movement begins. Second, it must explain why, at some point, the cumulative upward movement ceases and in some cases (e.g. 1951 and 1955) reverses itself.

2 ELEMENTS OF CYCLE THEORY

According to our static theory of aggregate demand, the principal elements in demand independent of the level of income (output) are (i) investment; (ii) exports; (iii) government expenditure. It is these elements which, given stable propensities to consume and import, the money supply, the two liquidity functions, the money wage rate and the production function determine the equilibrium level of output. This suggests that it is likely to be *fluctuations* in these elements – or some of them – to which we must look to explain fluctuations in output.

According to our analysis, the rate of real planned investment depends upon the rate of interest and the schedule of the marginal efficiency of investment. As a matter of observation (cf. Chapter 10) the *amplitude* of investment fluctuations is very severe. Since interest rates change comparatively little in the cycle while the response of planned investment to changes in the rate of interest is probably

† This is, as the reader should check, even more marked with the lower turning point of cycle 5.

rather small (and slow) severe fluctuations in investment can only be explained, in terms of our theory, by cyclical shifts in the schedule of the marginal efficiency of investment – to the right in upswings, to the left in downswings. Why should such shifts occur?

In developing our theory of investment we emphasised the subjective nature of the schedule of the marginal efficiency of investment. In particular we pointed out that the position of the schedule depended upon (i) businessmen's *expectations* (which could be optimistic or pessimistic); and (ii) businessmen's *uncertainty* regarding their expectations. One possible explanation of fluctuations in planned investment over the cycle thus runs in terms of expectations and uncertainty. Suppose, for example, the economy starts upwards from its lower turning point as a result, let us say, of an expansionary Budget. Since, by assumption, there is plenty of spare capacity, output and employment expand. The multiplier operates and a cumulative recovery begins. This tends to raise profits, to make businessmen more optimistic and to reduce their uncertainty regarding prospects over (say) the next two or three years. In these circumstances it seems entirely plausible that the M.E.I. schedule should shift to the right. If it does, investment increases thus adding the effect of the investment multiplier to the Budget multiplier. And this may further increase investment by producing greater optimism and reducing uncertainty.

In upswings, output expands faster than capacity. In the early stages, when excess capacity is present, the additional output can be produced from the capacity already in existence. As expansion proceeds, and excess capacity is reduced, businessmen need to increase their capacity by undertaking investment. This takes two forms. First, there is investment in fixed capital such as factory buildings, plant and equipment. Second there is investment in inventories which must be increased, as output rises, if the process of production is to proceed smoothly.

Thus to our *expectational* (or psychological) explanation of fluctuations in investment we can add a second or *capacity* element which is primarily technical in character. These two elements provide a plausible explanation of why, once a recovery has started, it will be fed and sustained by an expansion of investment in fixed capital and in stocks. The result is a cumulative process of expansion – the upswing – which proceeds from recovery to boom.

The pattern of investment behaviour explains the cumulative process of expansion. It does not, however, explain why expansion ceases and possibly gives way to contraction. Why should expectations reverse themselves? Why should businessmen suddenly plan to reduce the rate at which they add to capacity? A theory which seeks to answer these questions is set out in later sections. In the meantime, however, we need simply note that if investment behaves as we suggest, the cumulative upswing, and the cumulative downswing, are not hard to understand. The awkward problems are the turning points.

What part do exports play in explaining the cycle? Our exports are part of other countries' imports and, as we saw in Chapter 13, these depend on the incomes of other countries. Hence if the incomes of *other countries fluctuate*, so will their demand for our exports. This will bring our export multiplier into operation (cf. Chapter 13). It follows that the existence of international trade is a means of transmitting the cyclical fluctuations of the rest of the world to Britain and, via our demand for imports (the exports of the rest of the world), our cyclical fluctuations to the rest of the world.

During the latter half of the nineteenth century, and during the first four decades of the twentieth, there is evidence to suggest that cyclical movements in exports were probably the major element in generating cycles in British economic activity. In the post-war period this evidence is much less marked. Domestic investment is now the dominant element in the cyclical process though, since investment usually starts to rise *after* the upswing has begun, it is clear that the cyclical fluctuation of investment cannot easily explain the lower turning point.

This brief sketch of the generation of cyclical fluctuations leaves us with three problems to explain

    (i) why an upswing halts;
    (ii) why it reverses itself;
    (iii) why recoveries begin.

3 THE DYNAMIC THEORY OF INVESTMENT: THE ACCELERATOR HYPOTHESIS

In this section we develop with more precision, and in more formal terms, the *capacity* element in the dynamic theory of investment sketched in the previous section.

Consider a businessman who produces, and has produced for many years, 10,000 pairs of shoes. To produce these shoes he requires 10 machines. One machine wears out each year and each year is replaced by an identical machine. In tabular form we have

Year	Total output (pairs of shoes)	Total no. of machines req.	Annual capital depreciation (in terms of machines)	Gross investment (in terms of machines)	Net investment (in terms of machines)
I	10,000	10	1	1	0
IV	10,000	10	1	1	0
VII	11,000	11	1	2	1
VIII	11,000	11	1	1	0

Suppose now that in year VII the demand for shoes rises to 11,000 pairs. In the very short run the businessman may satisfy this demand by using his existing 10 machines more intensively – say by working double shifts. By assumption, however, to maximise profits at an output of 10,000 pairs he requires 10 machines. Hence to maximise profits with an output of 11,000 pairs he requires 11 machines.

If he adds the new machine he undertakes *net investment* of one machine. As a result we have (i) a doubling of *gross* investment; and (ii) an increase in *net* investment from zero to one machine. Suppose now demand remains at 11,000. The businessman has adjusted his stock of machines completely to this output. He has no need for further machines. Hence net investment falls to zero: gross investment falls to the one machine required for replacement. It follows from this simple example that the level of *net* investment depends upon the *change in output*. When output is rising net investment is positive. When output is constant net investment is zero.

Let us now generalise this argument to the economy as a whole. We begin with the assumption that the desired (because most profitable) stock of fixed capital bears a fixed relation to output. Formally:

$$K^* = \alpha Y, \tag{20.I}$$

where

K^* is the desired stock of fixed capital

Y is annual output

α is the (average) ratio of K^* to Y and the marginal ratio of $\Delta K^*/\Delta Y$.

Now let Y_t and Y_{t-1} stand for output in years t and $t-1$ and K^*_t and K^*_{t-1} stand for desired capital at the end of years t and $t-1$.

We have:

$$K^*_{t-1} = \alpha Y_{t-1} \qquad (20.\text{II})$$

$$K^*_t = \alpha Y_t \qquad (20.\text{II})$$

whence

$$K^*_t - K^*_{t-1} = \alpha(Y_t - Y_{t-1}). \qquad (20.\text{II.ii})$$

We assume (as we did in our numerical example) that the capital stock actually in existence at the end of year $t-1$ (which we call K_{t-1}) was optimally adjusted to the output of that period. It follows that

$$K_{t-1} = K^*_{t-1} \qquad (20.\text{II.iii})$$

and

$$K^*_t - K_{t-1} = \alpha(Y_t - Y_{t-1}). \qquad (20.\text{II.iv})$$

This tells us that the desired capital stock for year t will exceed the capital stock in existence at the end of the previous year by an amount which depends upon (i) the capital/output ratio (α); and (ii) the change in output between the two years.

Now to bring the actual capital stock to the desired level – raise K_{t-1} to K^*_t – businessmen will undertake net investment. How much will they undertake in the year? This depends upon the *speed* at which they adjust the capital stock. Hence we can write, more generally,

$$I_t = \lambda\alpha(Y_t - Y_{t-1}), \qquad (20.\text{II.v})$$

where

$I_t \equiv$ net investment in year t

$\lambda \equiv$ a coefficient measuring the *speed of response* with $0 < \lambda \leqslant 1$

and $\lambda\alpha \equiv$ the accelerator coefficient which we shall call V.

In our numerical example $K_{t-1} = 10$ and $K^*_t = 11$ for $Y_t = 11,000$,

$$Y_{t-1} = 10,000 \text{ and } \alpha \equiv \frac{K}{Y} = \tfrac{1}{1000} \text{ so that}$$

$$I_t = \lambda \tfrac{1}{1000}(11,000 - 10,000) \qquad (20.\text{II.v.n})$$

$$= \lambda.$$

Since we argued that net investment would be *one* machine, we made, in our numerical example, the special assumption that λ was unity.

That is, that the shoe manufacturer's speed of response was such that he adjusted his capital stock *completely* during a single year. This may – or may not – be the case. It is commonly assumed,† with the result that the accelerator theory is often written:

$$I_t = \alpha(Y_t - Y_{t-1})$$

which gives it a rather narrow technical interpretation and obscures the element of time response completely. We shall write it,

$$I_t = V(Y_t - Y_{t-1}), \qquad (20.\text{II.vi})$$

where

$$V \equiv \lambda\alpha$$

so that V, our accelerator coefficient, depends upon two elements:

$\alpha \equiv$ the optimum (most profitable) capital/annual output ratio;

$\lambda \equiv$ the speed with which businessmen seek to adjust actual capital to the optimum.

The implications of this version of the *capacity* theory of investment are important. First, *net* investment determined by the accelerator will be positive if, and only if, output is *rising*. Second, *net* investment will *fall* if *the rate at which output is rising* declines. Third, *net* investment (due to the accelerator) will be *zero* if output is *constant*. Fourth, *net* investment will be negative if output is *falling*.

So far we have interpreted this *accelerator* theory only in relation to investment in fixed capital. It can, however, readily be adapted to the task of explaining investment in inventories. To do this we introduce the assumption that businessmen seek to maintain stocks in a fixed ratio to output. Thus we have:

$$S^*_t = \alpha'(Y) \qquad (20.\text{II.vii})$$

where

$S^*_t \equiv$ the desired (optimal) level of stocks

$\alpha' \equiv$ the desired (optimal) ratio of stocks to output

$Y \equiv$ output.

The formal structure of the argument is then identical with that already put forward. It yields:

$$I_{st} = V'[Y_t - Y_{t-1}] \qquad (20.\text{II.viii})$$

† For ease of exposition we shall adopt this assumption in our formal examples.

where

$I_{st} \equiv$ net investment in inventories

$V' \equiv$ the (inventory) accelerator coefficient.

In the United Kingdom the ratio of stocks to gross domestic product (at annual rates) is about 0·4. Since businessmen probably plan to adjust stocks fairly quickly, the speed of response coefficient is probably close to unity. Hence V' may, with some degree of plausibility, be thought of as being about 0·4.

Adding the two components of accelerator net investment we obtain:

$$I_t + I_{st} = (V + V')[Y_t - Y_{t-1}] \qquad (20.\text{II.ix})$$

for the sum of accelerator investment. This, simply because it is investment *induced* by the change in output, is often called *induced investment*. Naturally enough *some* net investment is only very loosely related to changes in output. This is the case with very long range investment. It is also likely to be the case with investment aimed at the production of new products. Net investment which is not induced in this way we call *autonomous*. This we shall write as H.

Our complete investment hypothesis may now be written as:

$$\left.\begin{aligned} \text{gross investment}_t &\equiv \text{net investment}_t + \text{replacement}_t \\ &\equiv H_t + I_t + I_{st} + R_t \\ &\equiv H_t + (V + V')(Y_t - Y_{t-1}) + R_t, \end{aligned}\right\} (20.\text{II.x})$$

where R_t depends upon the proportion of the capital stock requiring replacement in any year. Since R_t probably changes only slowly it follows that it is the induced component plus any changes in autonomous investment due to changes in business expectations which, on our hypothesis, explains the cyclical fluctuations in gross investment.

The impact of the *accelerator* may best be seen by combining it with the simple multiplier. To do this we take autonomous investment and replacement as constant and specify the following model:

$R_t = \bar{R}$ for all periods $\bar{R} = 20$

$H_t = \bar{H}$ for periods $t, t-1$, and $t-2$ $\bar{H} = 30$

$H_t = \hat{H}$ for periods $t+1$ and thereafter $\hat{H} = 40$

$I_t = V(Y_{t-1} - Y_{t-2}) + H_t + R_t$ $V = 0·8$

$C_t = A + cY_{t-1}$† $A = 100 \quad c = 0·5$.

† Notice that this model contains a *consumption lag* and no output lag.

Two points are worth noticing about this model. First we have made *induced investment* (I_t) depend upon the *past* change in output rather than the current change. This is probably more realistic. Second we have assumed that households base their current expenditure on consumption on the *last* period's income.

We can now write down the equation for gross output as:

$$Y_t = A + cY_{t-1} + V(Y_{t-1} - Y_{t-2}) + R_t + H_t. \quad \text{(20.II.xi)}$$

In equilibrium, by definition, output is constant. Hence $Y_t = Y_{t-1} = Y_{t-2}$. Call the *initial* equilibrium level $\overline{Y}_1$. We obtain, on substituting this into (20.II.xi),

$$\overline{Y}_1 = A + c\,\overline{Y}_1 + V(\overline{Y}_1 - \overline{Y}_1) + \overline{R} + \overline{H} \quad \text{(20.II.xi(a))}$$

$$\overline{Y}_1 = [A + \overline{R} + \overline{H}]\,\frac{1}{1-c}$$

$$= [100 + 20 + 30]\,\frac{1}{1 - 0 \cdot 5}$$

$$= 300.$$

In the new equilibrium ($\overline{Y}_2$) we have:

$$\overline{Y}_2 = A + c\,\overline{Y}_2 + V(\overline{Y}_2 - \overline{Y}_2) + \overline{R} + \hat{H} \quad \text{(20.II.xi(b))}$$

$$= [A + \overline{R} + \hat{H}]\,\frac{1}{1-c}$$

$$= [100 + 20 + 40]\,\frac{1}{1 - 0 \cdot 5}$$

$$= 320.$$

Two points emerge from this elementary substitution. They are:

(i) the *equilibrium* levels of output are unaffected by the accelerator; and

(ii) the *change* in equilibrium levels is given by the simple static multiplier with which we became fully familiar in Chapter 9.

To illustrate the *dynamic* behaviour of the system – how it moves over time – the simplest procedure is to construct a table. See page 442.

Examination of this table brings out a number of points.

(i) On our assumptions the system moves to its new equilibrium by a series of fluctuations.

(ii) The movement begins with an upswing which lasts until period $t+4$. But as the rate at which output rises during this upswing falls away, as it does by period $t+3$, the rate of induced investment begins to fall as it does in period $t+4$.

Table 20.1   *Dynamic Multiplier and Accelerator*

Period t	Income Y	Planned consumption C_p	Replacement R	Gross investment Autonomous H	Accelerator induced $I = V(Y_{t-1} - Y_{t-2})$	Planned saving S_p	Actual saving S_A
t	300	250	20	30	nil	50	50
$t+1$	310	250	20	40	nil	50	60
$t+2$	323	255	20	40	8	55	68
$t+3$	331·9	261·5	20	40	10·4	61·5	70·4
$t+4$	333·07	265·95	20	40	7·12	65·95	67·12
$t+5$	327·47	266·585	20	40	0·936	66·435	60·936
$t+6$			20	40			
$t+7$			20	40			
$t+8$			20	40			
$t+9$							
$t+10$							
.							
.							
.							
$t+n$	320	260	20	40	nil	60	60

Data: $\dfrac{\partial C_p}{\partial Y} \equiv C = 0·5$

$V = 0·8$

Assumptions: (i) constant prices; (ii) constant interest rates.
Note: The reader is invited to work out period $t+6$, $t+7$, $t+8$ for himself from the equation:

$$Y_{t+6} = A + cY_{t+5} + \bar{R} + \hat{H} + V[Y_{t+5} - Y_{t+4}].$$

(iii) This fall in induced investment itself slows the rise in output, and, by period $t+5$, causes output actually to fall.
(iv) By period? the fall has been checked and output has once again started upwards.†

The reader should also notice that though net investment depends upon output via the accelerator relation, its induced component nevertheless begins to fall *before* output. This is, of course, because it depends not on the *level* of output but *its rate of change*.

This table demonstrates, which is certainly interesting, that a model which contains *both* the multiplier and the accelerator may generate quite realistic cycles. Thus the accelerator-multiplier model *can* explain why, if output starts on an upswing, it will reach an upper turning point and why, if it starts on a downswing, it will eventually turn up – that is reach a lower turning point.

† The reader should calculate the period for himself.

The results in Table 20.1, however, depend upon the particular values we have selected for the marginal propensity to consume ($c = 0.5$) and the accelerator coefficient ($V = 0.8$). Both these values are probably on the low side. Suppose we take a more realistic value for V. What would happen?

V is, as we have shown, the (marginal) capital/output ratio. If this is equal to the average ratio, a plausible guess would put its numerical value between 3·0 and 4·0 say 3·0. Retaining all our other assumptions unchanged how does the model behave now? We can easily construct a table to show (Table 20.2, p. 444).

A glance at this table shows that the system now behaves very differently. The system starts upwards, as before, in period $t+1$. But it never turns down. In short it rises without limit or, as the same point is usually put, it *explodes. Notice also that the two models differ only in their dynamic behaviour for the static equilibria described by both are identical.*

In fact, with our basic equation (20.II) there are a number of possible dynamic paths of output. Which is relevant depends on the values of c (the marginal propensity to consume) and V (the accelerator coefficient). The possibilities can be classified as follows:

Type I. Damped fluctuations ultimately converging to new equilibrium (Table 20.1).

II. Explosion without fluctuations *never* converging to new equilibrium (Table 20.2).

III. Constant fluctuations around new equilibrium *never* converging to new equilibrium (Fig. 20.iv).

IV. No fluctuations: smooth convergence ultimately reaching new equilibrium (Fig. 20.iv).

V. Explosive fluctuations *never* reaching new equilibrium (Fig. 20.iv).

This is decidedly awkward for we can hardly suppose that the values of c and V are likely to be precisely those required to produce path Type III – the only path generating cycles of constant amplitude such as, in broad terms, we tend to observe. This makes the accelerator-multiplier model a much less satisfying explanation of the cyclical fluctuations in output though it has its place in any full explanation. For we obviously cannot exclude values of V of the order of 3·0. And such values, when inserted into our model, make it *dynamically unstable.* It does not fluctuate (as we would like it to). Nor does it ever reach its new static equilibrium of 320. Since an *explosive*

Table 20.2   *Dynamic Multiplier and Accelerator*

Period	Income Y	Planned consumption C_p	Replacement R	Gross investment Autonomous H	Gross investment Accelerator induced $V(Y_{t-1} - Y_{t-2})$	I_p	Planned saving S_p	Actual saving S_A
t	300	250	20	30	nil	50	50	50
$t+1$	310	250	20	40	nil	60	50	60
$t+2$	345	255	20	40	30	90	55	90
$t+3$	437·5	272·5	20	40	105	165	72·5	165
$t+4$	652·25	318·75	20	40	277·5	333·5	118·75	333·5
$t+5$								
$t+6$								
$t+7$								
$t+8$								

Data: $\dfrac{\partial C_p}{\partial Y} \equiv C = 0·5$ $V = 3·0$

Note: The reader is invited to work out periods $t+5$, $t+6$, $t+7$ for himself from the equation:
$$Y_{t+5} = A + cY_{t+4} + \bar{R} + \hat{H} + V[Y_{t+4} - Y_{t+3}].$$

system seems, empirically, absurd while it equally seems that empirically plausible values of V imply an explosive system, it is clear that we need to find some way of (i) putting a *ceiling* to the upswings of a *potentially* explosive system and explaining why it should ever turn down, and/or (ii) putting a *floor* to the system's downswings and explaining why it should ever turn upwards. This we shall attempt in the next section.

Before we discuss the problem of *ceilings* and *floors* we need to make one or two points about the accelerator itself.

Both in our Tables and in our exposition we have given a formal and mechanical interpretation of the accelerator. Pedagogically this is permissible. The accelerator hypothesis, however, seeks to describe human behaviour. Purely mechanical interpretations should therefore be avoided. In particular the following points, glossed over in our discussion, should be kept in mind.

(i) The accelerator theory is a *capacity* theory of investment. The accelerator coefficient may therefore take a lower value in recovery (where there is *ex hypothesis* considerable excess capacity in the economy) than in booms (when excess capacity is far less and still diminishing). Our model in treating V as constant may therefore seriously oversimplify matters.

(ii) The accelerator theory also contains room for the influence of *expectations* and *uncertainty*. In the early stages of recovery though businessmen may *observe* a given change in output

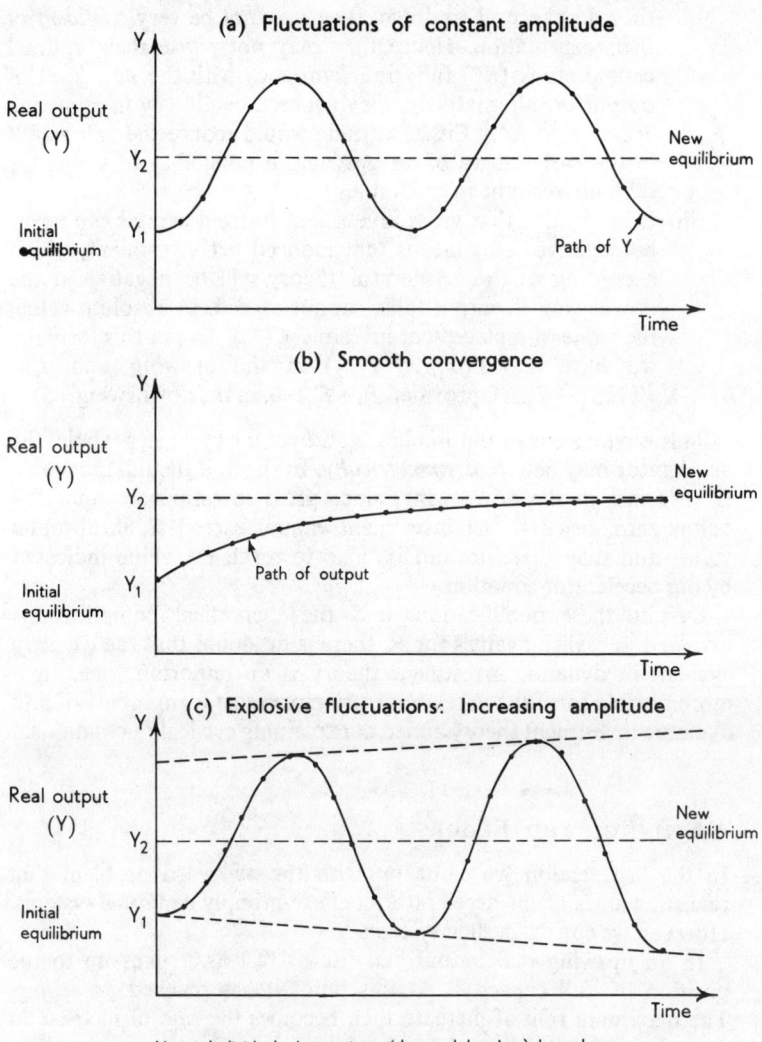

(a) Fluctuations of constant amplitude

Real output (Y)

Y_2 — — — — — — — — — New equilibrium

Initial equilibrium Y_1

Path of Y

Time

(b) Smooth convergence

Real output (Y)

Y_2 — — — — — — — — — New equilibrium

Initial equilibrium Y_1

Path of output

Time

(c) Explosive fluctuations: Increasing amplitude

Real output (Y)

Y_2 — — — — — — — — — New equilibrium

Initial equilibrium Y_1

Time

Note: Individual observations (denoted by dots) have been
linked by a smooth curve

FIG. 20.iv Classification of dynamic paths of output: multiplier accelerator model

they may not *expect* the new level of output to persist or, if
they do expect it to do so, they may not be very *confident* of
their expectation. Hence they may not revise their optimal
capital stock (K^*) fully in accordance with the new level of
output or, alternatively, may proceed cautiously in adjusting
actual K to K^*.† Either attitude would reduce the value of V
in the early stages of an upswing, a possibility of which we
take no account in our table.

(iii) It is obvious that gross investment in fixed capital can never
be negative. This means that induced net investment, which
according to the accelerator theory will be negative in the
downswing if output falls, cannot exceed, in absolute value,
the value of replacement investment (R_t). To put this formally
we have $I_t = V(Y_{t-1} - Y_{t-2})$ in the upswing and $I_t =
V(Y_{t-1} - Y_{t-2})$, provided $R_t + I_t \geqslant 0$, in the downswing.

This obvious constraint implies that, over the cycle as a whole, the
accelerator may behave *asymmetrically*. In short, if the fall in income
is very fast in the downswing, since gross investment cannot fall
below zero, negative net investment cannot exceed R_t in absolute
value, and may therefore not be able to reach the value indicated
by our accelerator equation.

Despite these qualifications and the theoretical complications
involved in realistic values for V, there is no doubt that the *capacity*
element in dynamic investment theory is an important one. In a
more flexible form the accelerator principle must form a part of any
dynamic investment theory aimed at explaining cyclical fluctuations.

4 CEILINGS AND FLOORS

In the last section we came up with the awkward problem that
realistic values of the accelerator coefficient imply *explosive* systems.
How can we constrain such systems?

In an upswing real output can rise as fast as it likes up to the
position of 'full capacity'. At this point it has reached its *ceiling*.
The maximum rate of increase then becomes the rate of increase in
capacity – in the U.K. rather more than 3 per cent per annum. This
rate of increase must be less than the rate enjoyed during the upswing
for, if it were not, 'full capacity' would never be reached. Hence, the
annual percentage increments in real output *along* the *ceiling must* be

† Our Tables assume $\lambda \equiv$ speed of response parameter to be a constant
equal to unity. In fact λ may vary over the cycle.

less than those in the upswing. Hence accelerator-induced investment must fall and a downswing begin.

The existence of a full capacity ceiling thus serves two purposes in our theory. First it explains why a theoretically explosive system cannot proceed upwards without limit. Second it explains why, if the economy attempts to 'crawl along the ceiling' it will eventually turn downwards: that is it explains why there will be an upper turning point. In practice, in the United Kingdom, booms are sometimes checked by official action before the ceiling is reached. This happened in 1960. A check of this kind slows the rate of growth and this, via the accelerator, reduces induced net investment and a down turn begins.

Why does the downswing not proceed for ever? What checks this? In the first place though gross investment *can* fall to zero it is unlikely to do so for this implies that *all* firms in the economy have zero gross investment. This is improbable. If some do not have zero gross investment then since none can have *negative* gross investment, gross investment as a whole will be positive. Moreover, even if gross investment *does* fall to zero, there will still be a floor to income since, on our usual consumption function hypothesis there will be some level of income so low that, for the community as a whole, all income will be consumed (i.e. $C_p = Y$). In the second place some net investment is, in our terminology, *autonomous*: that is unaffected by the recent behaviour of output. A part at least of this will continue even in depressions. Hence gross investment will not, in general, fall to zero in a depression but to some positive value which we may call I_{min}. It follows that, with a given consumption function, the minimum level of output is:

$$Y_{min} = \left[I_{min} \cdot \frac{1}{1-c} \right] + \frac{A}{1-c},$$

where $A \equiv$ autonomous consumption, and c, as usual, denotes the marginal propensity to consume.

Once Y reaches Y_{min} it ceases to fall. Hence the induced net investment due to the accelerator, which was *negative* when income was falling, *rises* to zero. As a result output rises above Y_{min} and, probably after some time lag, accelerator induced investment becomes positive.

Thus even when the value of the accelerator coefficient implies, mathematically, an explosive system, there are good reasons for thinking that the existence of (i) a full capacity ceiling; and (ii) a minimum level of output, will not only constrain fluctuations in a manner more in accordance with experience but also explain both the upper and lower turning points. The plausibility of this line of reasoning is strengthened by the observation that, in recent years (e.g. 1960), the British authorities have intervened to check booms before they reach the ceiling and to restart growth or check recessions (1959, 1963 and 1972).

5 Growth and Fluctuations

In this chapter, by means of a rather brief excursion into dynamics, we have sought to set out the elements of a theory which explains cyclical fluctuations in aggregate demand and thus in output and the proportion of productive capacity employed. In the previous chapter we discussed some aspects of the rate at which, in the long-run, 'full capacity' output grew over time. This separation of the related problems of growth and fluctuations is legitimate up to a point. It carries, however, a risk that the reader may unconsciously assume that the two problems are independent. To see the importance of this consider the proposition:

if we could eliminate the cyclical fluctuations in output then we could grow just as fast as we have done in the past.

This implies that the long-term 'trend' rate of growth in capacity is entirely independent of the cyclical process. This may or may not be the case. At present economists cannot give a very confident answer one way or the other. It is *possible* that, by reducing or eliminating fluctuations, we *might* grow faster. Equally it is *possible* that we might, as a result, grow more slowly. The cycle *may* be the cost of growth: or it may not. Our discussion throws no light on this issue. Nor does it imply one answer rather than another. Two things are, however, sure. The first is that in *estimating* the long-term rate of growth in capacity we are using observations obtained from the fluctuating path followed by the U.K. economy. Our estimate is, therefore, not independent of the cycle. The second point is that the question is one of considerable practical importance for, during the last few years, the elimination of the cycle, and the maintenance of steady, sustainable growth, have become avowed objectives of official policy.

6 The Balance of Payments in the Cycle

So far, in discussing the cycle, we have virtually ignored external considerations. What is likely to happen to the balance of payments during a cycle?

Suppose aggregate demand goes through a cycle due in the main to fluctuations in gross investment. Exports, we may assume, expand throughout the cycle at a rate governed primarily by the rate of growth in output in the rest of the world. For simplicity assume this to be constant at (say) 4 per cent per annum. In the upswing of domestic output imports will rise for two reasons. First the rate of imports, per annum, depends upon incomes via the marginal propensity to import. This we saw in Chapter 13. Hence as the level of income rises so does the level of imports. In the second place as output expands there will be induced investment in inventories. In the U.K. inventories have a significant import content – possibly of the order of 0·3 or 0·4. Hence there will be an accelerator-induced rise in imports. It follows that the import function which we developed earlier ignores some important *dynamic* elements in import demand. Instead of writing – and thinking of – our import function in the form:

$$\text{imports}_t = F + z\,Y_t - 1,$$

which is a dynamic version of our earlier function, we *should* write and think of a function of the form:

$$\text{imports}_t = F + z\,Y_{t-1} + z'V'[Y_{t-1} - Y_{t-2}],$$

where

$z \equiv$ marginal propensity to import

$z' \equiv$ marginal share of imports in inventory investment

$V' \equiv$ inventory investment accelerator coefficient.

Given an import function of this form it is clear that imports are likely to rise very fast in an upswing. The rise is likely to be considerably faster than that in either gross domestic product or exports. Hence upswings in U.K. output are likely to be accompanied by a sharp deterioration of the balance of payments on current account.

In Figure 20.v we have set out data for two post-war upswings which lend some support to this theory.

This analysis, brief as it is, is still suggestive. It explains why U.K. upswings have tended to cause balance of payments difficulties which have sometimes compelled the authorities to intervene to check the boom. It also shows that one way of *temporarily* easing the external position is to halt expansion. For if the growth in output is stopped inventories cease to rise and perhaps even fall. Either way the import

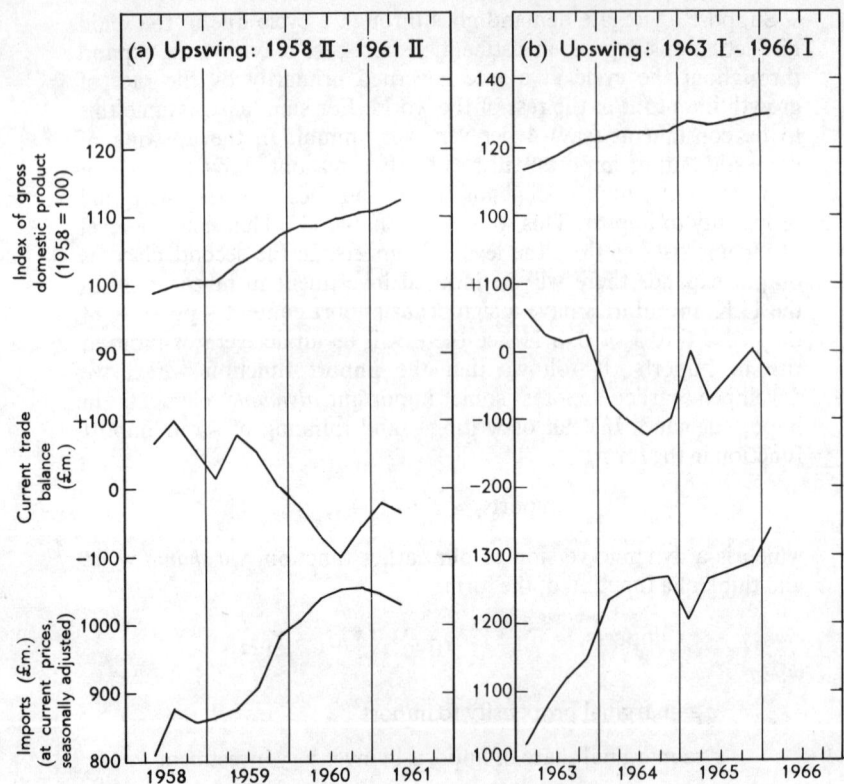

FIG. 20.v   Imports and the current balance in U.K. expansions

Source: Index gross domestic product: *National Institute Economic Review* (Nov 1967) Current trade balance (£m): *Economic Trends* (Sep 1967) Imports (£m): *Economic Trends* (Sep 1967)

bill is sharply reduced and the balance of payments strengthened. This policy which has been called, somewhat tartly, 'strength through stagnation' was essentially that of Mr Selwyn Lloyd in 1961–2 and Mr Callaghan in 1966–7. It is, of course, a temporary expedient and no more. For once a further upswing begins, as it did in early 1963, the mechanism begins again to operate, the import bill rises sharply and external difficulties reappear – as they did dramatically in 1964 and 1965, and in 1972.

7 MORE ABOUT THE CEILING

In our rather formal discussion of the cycle we have sketched a theory which (i) regards the dynamic structure of the economic system as *explosive*, but (ii) *constrains* the system within a 'ceiling' and a 'floor'. Hitherto we have interpreted the upper constraint as being the 'capacity' of the economy to produce output. However, once we admit the possibility of official intervention, 'capacity' becomes only one of a number of possible upper constraints. We must now ask, with the U.K. economy particularly in mind, is 'capacity' the relevant upper constraint?

The first alternative upper constraint may, rather loosely, be referred to as, the 'balance of payments' constraint. If, as we argued in Section 6, the U.K.'s current account balance, and indeed overall balance, on external account deteriorates sharply in upswings, the government may, in order to protect the country's overseas reserves and preserve the rate of exchange, intervene to check the upswing of the cycle *before* full capacity is reached. In such a case it is *not* the 'capacity' constraint which is effective but the 'balance of payments' constraint.

The second possible upper constraint may be thought of, again rather loosely, as the 'inflation' constraint. We shall discuss the problem of rising prices more fully in the next chapter and in this discussion seek to make the notion of 'inflation' rather more precise. Nevertheless, without anticipating the work of Chapter 21, we can argue that if, as the economy approaches full 'capacity' in the upswing, the rate of increase of prices *either* accelerates *or* is expected by the government to accelerate, the authorities may again take action to check the upswing before 'capacity' is reached. If the government acts in this way, because it regards 'rapidly' rising prices as objectionable in themselves or fears their impact on the balance of payments (or for both reasons together), then the effective constraint is *not* 'capacity' but 'inflation'.

There is little doubt that the U.K. authorities have acted to check expansions before the economy has reached 'full capacity'. In practice, therefore, it has not always been the 'capacity' constraint which has imposed the upper limit of British expansions. Indeed, since the expansion of 1958–9 it is probably true to say that the 'balance of payments' has been the effective one.

It would, of course, be entirely wrong to interpret the U.K. cycle as though the role of the government in seeking to conduct macro-economic policy was limited to checking expansions. Presumably, on the assumption that the 'balance of payments constraint' is effective, the aim of the authorities would be to manage the economy, by fiscal and monetary means, so that it moves through time as nearly as possible along the line *bb* in Fig. 20.vi which is drawn to represent the notion of the 'balance of payments constraint'. This, of course, is simply its *short-run stabilisation objective* and amounts to attempting to reduce the amplitude of the cycle. Its *long-run* objective is to ensure that the 'constraint lines' *ff*, *bb* and *pp* (which represents the inflation constraint) coincide while *ff* has the maximum attainable slope.

Stabilisation involves managing aggregate demand *counter-cyclically*. Thus in the later stages of upswings, the authorities, if they aim to reduce the amplitude of the cycle, should use fiscal and monetary means to restrain demand: conversely in downswings they should aim to expand demand. This raises difficult problems of *timing*. If the authorities impose restraint too late, it may make its impact when the economy has already reached (or even passed) its upper turning point. If this happens it will serve only to steepen the downswing. Conversely if the authorities expand demand too late – after the lower turning point is passed – they may cause the expansion to become unmanageably fast. The road to increasing instability is paved with good intentions. We know, in quantitative

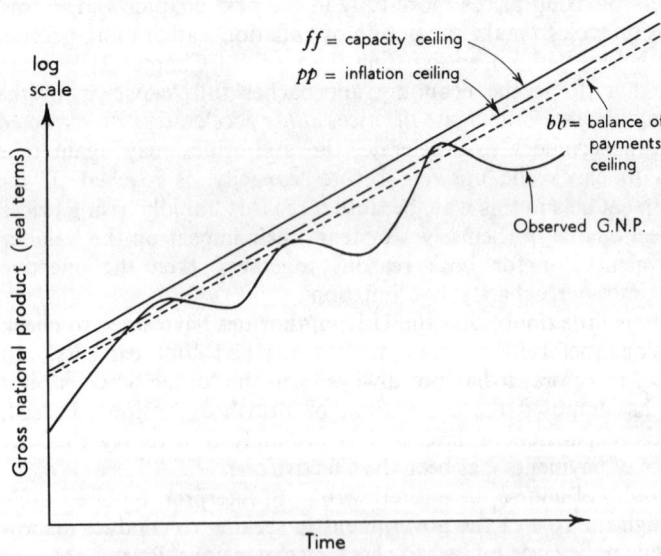

FIG. 20.vi The growth cycle: schematic presentation

terms, far too little about the parameters of the economic system including the way in which it responds through time (its dynamic properties) to make stabilisation simple. As a result there have almost certainly been important errors by the authorities in both the magnitude and timing of their interventions. Hence the observed behaviour of U.K. output, and hence the U.K. cycle, is probably at least in part the result of government intervention which has, on occasions, been destabilising rather than stabilising.

Government intervention, even in the short-run, is not only concerned with stabilisation: that is with seeking to dampen the cycle. Governments aim at re-election and it is difficult for a government to preserve its parliamentary majority at the polls in a recession or depression.† Doubtless part of the explanation of the observed cycle in U.K. output lies in this. The reader, if he records the dates of general elections on Fig. 20.i, may find the results suggestive though precisely what they suggest is a matter of considerable controversy.

If the government did not intervene (sometimes misguidedly) to promote stabilisation or to restore its popularity, would the economy still exhibit a 'growth cycle'? To answer this question we need a quantitatively estimated and relevant model of the economic system. No such model for the U.K. economy as yet exists though models which may give us some indication as to the probable answer to our questions are being constructed. Given such a model we could conduct experiments (on a computer) to see how the economy would respond to a government policy which did not either aim at stabilisation or re-election.‡ This would give us an answer to our problem.

The theory we have sketched suggests, as the reader will recall, that the economic system is potentially explosive (in the sense of Table 20.2 and Fig. 20.iv). As we know this depends on the values of certain parameters. What values these parameters take is a question of fact. They might be such as to give rise to a system characterised by damped fluctuations (Table 20.1). In this case the observed cycle can be explained by the impact on such a system of a series of exogenous *shocks* occurring in a random manner over

---

† We might, perhaps, think of a 'political' or 'unemployment' constraint and represent this by a line parallel to *ff* drawn at a level of output in relation to capacity representing the maximum percentage of excess capacity which is 'politically tolerable'.

‡ Simulation studies of this type have been conducted for models of the U.S. economy.

time. These *shocks* could take any form. A war in the Middle East, a shift in the world's demand schedule for U.K. exports, a shift in the domestic M.E.I. schedule or an increase in government expenditures are some of the numerous possibilities. Whether such a system – or the one we have outlined – is a more accurate explanation of the U.K. cycle is a question of fact and we do not know enough, in quantitative and dynamic terms about the U.K. economy, to form a confident judgment as to the answer. In either system, however, there are good grounds for thinking that government action is a significant contributory factor to the observed cycle.

8 SUMMARY

The aim of this chapter has been to explain why 'mixed-capitalist' economies in general, and the United Kingdom in particular, experience fluctuations in the level of economic activity which may, rather loosely, be termed 'cyclical'. To do this we sketched a dynamic theory of investment based, in large measure, upon the accelerator hypothesis. Since the accelerator hypothesis suggested an unstable economic system we found reasons for thinking that the fluctuations of the system were constrained by (i) the ceiling of 'full capacity' growth; and (ii) the floor provided by a minimum level of output. In discussing the accelerator hypothesis we provided an illustration of the distinction between dynamic and static economic models, for though both our accelerator models (of Tables 20.1 and 20.2) yielded identical static equilibrium results, the first model (with $V = 0.8$) was *stable* while the second (with $V = 3.0$) was *unstable*. From this it is possible to deduce that a wide range of dynamic models, with differing *dynamic* behaviour, nevertheless yield *the same equilibrium results*. From this it may be inferred that the *comparative static* method of analysis employed in earlier chapters is valid if, and only if, the model being discussed is *dynamically stable*. Then, because it is a matter of great importance to the United Kingdom, we examined the likely behaviour of the balance of payments on current account during the cycle and developed a dynamic import function. This led us to postulate a 'balance of payments' constraint which could become effective *before* the 'capacity' constraint. The whole analysis was conducted in real terms and assumed constant prices and interest rates.

QUESTIONS AND EXERCISES

1. Interpret the following two models. Give a verbal explanation of each equation.

<table>
<tr><td align="center">Model I</td><td align="center">Model II</td></tr>
<tr><td>$Y_t = C_t + I_t$</td><td>$Y_t = C_t + I_t$</td></tr>
<tr><td>$C_t = A + cY_{t-1}$</td><td>$C_t = A + cY_t$</td></tr>
<tr><td>$I_t = H_t + R_t + v(Y_t - Y_{t-1}).$</td><td>$I_t = H_t + R_t + v(Y_{t-1} - Y_{t-2}).$</td></tr>
</table>

Using the values of c, v, H_t, R_t given in the text construct tables showing the behaviour of both systems from periods t to $t+8$. What are the static equilibria of the two systems? Do they differ? Are both systems stable?

2. 'The accelerator coefficient is simply the marginal capital/output ratio.' Do you agree? If not, why not?

3. 'Since the accelerator depends on the ratio K/Y while K is a *stock* independent of the length of the period for which Y (which is a *flow*) is defined, the accelerator coefficient with respect to monthly income is *four times* as large as the accelerator with respect to annual income. It is therefore meaningless to talk of stability in terms of the accelerator coefficient.' Examine this view.

4. How would you attempt to test the accelerator hypothesis? Write down a function for investment in fixed capital incorporating the accelerator hypothesis and any other hypotheses which seem to you to be worth investigating.

5. Plot on a graph the quarterly figures for real investment in inventories in the U.K. from 1957 to 1970. What difficulties are there in interpreting this series? Is it consistent with the hypothesis that businessmen seek to maintain a constant ratio of stock to output? What leads you to take your view? [Use data from *Monthly Digest of Statistics*.]

6. 'Booms in investment in fixed capital reflect waves of innovation. Hence if there were no investment booms there would be no technical progress.' Do you agree?

7. In the market for peanuts we have (i) a relation between the quantity demanded and price of the form: $Q_t^D = A + bP_t$ where $b < 0$; and (ii) a relation between the quantity supplied and price of the form: $Q_t^S = Z + gP_{t-1}$, where $g > 0$; $P(t) \equiv$ price in period t.

Find the equilibrium price in terms of A, Z, g and b. Since the equilibrium price must be positive what must be the sign of $A-Z$ and what does this mean in economic terms?

Assign numerical values to A, b, Z and g and plot the resulting demand and supply curves on a graph. Assume that, in some period $t = 0$ price departs from equilibrium. Trace out the subsequent movements of price and quantity. Is your system stable? What is the economic interpretation of the lag between supply and price?

8. 'In the United Kingdom, investment turns up after output and turns down after output has flattened out.' Is this so? If it is, what kind of investment theory does it suggest? What starts U.K. expansions and what stops them?

9. 'Observed investment in stocks consists of both planned and unplanned elements. Since we can never identify these two components we can never hope to test any theory of planned investment in inventories.' Do you agree? Can you suggest any way of estimating unplanned inventory accumulation?

10. 'The desired ratio of stocks to output must, if businessmen are rational, depend significantly upon the cost of borrowing.' Explain. If this is so what implications has it for our inventory accelerator?

11. Assume that K_t^* (the desired level of inventories at the end of period t) responds both to output (Y_t) and the rate of interest (r_t). So that

$$K_t^* = f[Y_t, r_t].$$

Assume further that planned investment in inventories in period t (I_{pt}) depends upon the difference between the inventories desired at the end of period t (K_t^*) and actual inventories at the end of period $t-1$ (K_{t-1}) so that

$$I_{pt} = \lambda[K_t^* - K_{t-1}].$$

Unplanned inventory accumulation (I_{ut}) is simply the difference between output in period t (Y_t) and demand in period t (D_t) so that

$$I_{ut} = Y_t - D_t.$$

Since businessmen adjust output to expected demand D^* we have

$I_{pt} + I_{ut} \equiv$ observed investment in inventories

$$\equiv \lambda[K_t^* - K_{t-1}] + D_t^* - D_t.$$

Which of these variables are observable?

What is the meaning of λ?

Can you offer an explanation of D_t^* in terms of observable variables? (Hint: refer to the beer production model of Chapter 2.)

In the light of your answers reconsider Questions 9 and 10.

12. What is meant by 'autonomous' investment? What kinds of investment do you think are likely to fall into this category? If you can think of none, does this mean that you think that all investment is 'induced'?

13. 'The U.K. economy expands only in election years. The cycle is primarily political. The solution is to compel one quarter of the House of Commons to seek re-election each year.' Discuss, assembling your evidence with care.

14. Examine Fig. 20.vi carefully. On what assumptions are the slopes of pp and bb lines the same as those of the ff line? Do you consider these assumptions realistic?

15. 'The pursuit of "strength through stagnation" was carried out not only by Mr Selwyn Lloyd but also by Mr Reginald Maudling, Mr James Callaghan, Mr Roy Jenkins and Mr Anthony Barber.' Extend Fig. 20.i to the fourth quarter of 1972 and use your amended figure to discuss this statement. Is the policy defensible?

16. 'U.K. governments in their attempts to manage demand invariably intervene too late and usually intervene too sharply.' Examine the record of the last four U.K. Chancellors and seek to establish or refute this contention.

17. Compare the *dynamic* investment theory of Section 2 with the theory advanced in Chapter 10. Can you reconcile the two approaches? What difficulties do you meet in making a reconciliation? Is the accelerator coefficient a function of the interest rate? If so why?

18. It is stated in the text that V ($\equiv$ the accelerator coefficient) is equal to the marginal capital/output ratio. On what assumptions is this correct? In the text what unstated assumption is being made about the value of λ ($\equiv$ speed of response)? What is the relation between V and $\partial Y/\partial K$?

19. 'The case for the devaluation of sterling is stronger the greater the gap between the ff line and the bb line of Fig. 20.vi.' Elucidate.

20. Using the hypothetical cycle of Fig. 20.vi write a memorandum to the Chancellor of the Exchequer (an ex-Professor of Sanskrit) which explains the objectives of short and long-term economic policy. What value judgments underlie your memorandum?

21. Use the theory of the production function to relate the coefficient
    α of equation (20.I) to the marginal product of capital ($\partial Y/\partial K$).
22. To the model of page 441 [Equation (20.II.xi)] add the hypo-
    thesis of an output lag such that

$$Y(t) = D(t-1)$$

$$D(t-1) \equiv C(t-1) + I(t-1) + H(t-1) + R(t-1).$$

Construct a revised version of Table 20.1. Does it modify the
general conclusions derived from Table 20.1? If so, how and
why?

SUGGESTED READING

R. C. O. Matthews, *The Trade Cycle* (Cambridge, 1959) particularly
chs i–iii.

A. H. Hansen, *Business Cycles and National Income* (Allen &
Unwin, 1964) chs ix–xii.

J. C. R. Dow, *The Management of the British Economy, 1945–60*
(Cambridge, 1964) chs xiv–xv.

F. W. Paish, *Studies in an Inflationary Economy* (Macmillan, 1966)
ch. xvii.

F. R. Brechling and J. N. Wolfe, 'The End of Stop-Go', *Lloyds Bank
Review* (Jan 1965).

J. M. Keynes, *The General Theory of Employment, Interest and
Money* (Macmillan, 1936) ch. xxii.

P. N. Junankar, *Investment: Theories and Evidence* (Macmillan,
1972) chs 3, 6.

G. Haberler,† *Prosperity and Depression* (United Nations, 1946)
introduction, chs i, viii.

† More advanced reference.

21 Rising Prices and Inflation

IN this chapter we examine the problem of *rising prices* – commonly called the problem of *inflation*. In Chapter 17 we developed, as part of our *short-run static* model, a theory which explained the determination of *equilibrium level* of prices. In that chapter we did not discuss inflation although we did characterise *one* situation described in that chapter as an inflationary one.

The reasons for our self denial in Chapter 17 were two in number. In the first place, inflation – by definition – involves a *rate of change of prices*. It follows that in attempting to explain the rate of change of prices – *a concept which essentially involves time* – we need a *dynamic* theory not a *static* theory of the kind we set out in Chapter 17. In the second place if the economic system is such that the concept of an equilibrium *level* of prices is relevant, it follows that situations in which prices are rising (inflation) or falling (deflation) are *disequilibrium* situations. In short inflation (deflation) are, on this view, processes which occur during the transition, over time, from one equilibrium price level to another. What is involved is, essentially, the time path of prices. It follows that, methodologically speaking, any theory of inflation must be analogous to our theory of cycles in the sense that

(i) it must be concerned with the *time path* of a variable (in this case the price level);

(ii) it must ask, if a disequilibrium arises such that prices start to rise (fall),

    (*a*) *whether* the price level moves to a new equilibrium level (the system is 'stable');

    (*b*) *what path* it takes to the new equilibrium (if there is one); or

    (*c*) *whether* if the price level starts upwards (downwards) it will go upwards (downwards) forever.

Clearly the place for an analysis of this kind is after we have made, in our examination of cycles, some acquaintance with dynamic theories.

In Chapter 20 we saw that it is possible to construct two models which, though they yield the same equilibrium value of the dependent variable, display radically different dynamic behaviour. This was the case with the models illustrated in Tables 20.1 and 20.2 of that chapter, the former of which was *stable* (i.e. approached a new equilibrium), the latter of which was *unstable* (exploded upwards and never reached any new equilibrium). So it is with inflation models. This is the analytical justification for propositions (i) and (ii) above. It is, one may infer from this argument, not difficult for economic theorists to construct a virtually endless array of theories of inflation. The aim, of course, is to construct that theory which best explains the facts. What are the facts? In the figure below we have plotted against time annual percentage changes in an index number of final (factor) prices of output and an index number of the average money wage and salary per employee.

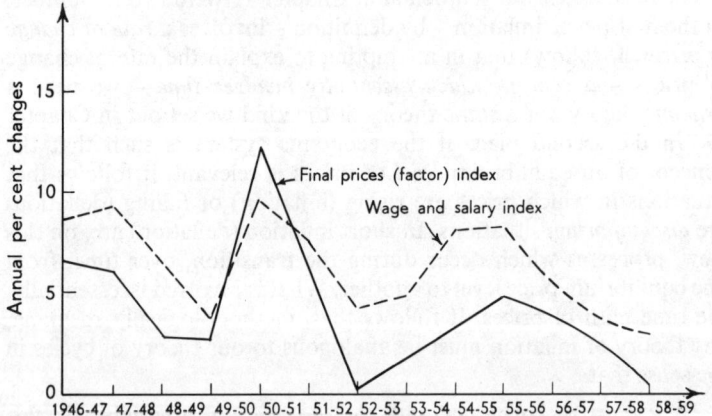

FIG. 21.i   Annual percentage changes in the index of average wage and salary per employee and of final prices (of factor sales). 1946 = 100

Source: Dicks-Mireaux, 'The Interrelationship Between Cost and Price Changes, 1946–1959', *Oxford Economic Papers*, 1961.

From this figure we can derive a number of conclusions, some familiar, others less so. They may be summarised as follows:

   (i) for the whole of the period prices and earnings have risen at approximately the following average annual rates:

      (*a*) prices at 3·6 per cent;
      (*b*) wages at 6·7 per cent;

   (ii) neither series has risen steadily: the rate of increase has varied;

(iii) there is some evidence if we refer back to the timing of U.K. cycles to suggest that the rate of price increase has tended to be *slower* in the *upswings* of output than in the downswings;

(iv) there is also some evidence to suggest that, *during* upswings, the rate of price increase has tended to become relatively *greater* as the system approaches its *upper turning point*;

(v) conversely it seems that, *during* downswings, the rate of price increase has become relatively *slower* as the system approaches its *lower turning point*;

(vi) neither prices nor earnings have, since 1946, fallen appreciably in any period;

(vii) the rate of increase in earnings seems to be appreciably faster near the *upper turning point* (*whether the system is in an upswing or not*).

These observations suggest two important conclusions.

First, the rate at which prices rise in the United Kingdom seems to depend on the stage of the output cycle. *This suggests that any theory of inflation we try to develop must be closely integrated with our theory of the cycle.*

Second, it does not seem to be true that what goes up must come down. Prices apparently do not. Nor do money earnings. It looks therefore as if both the price level and the rate of money earnings may be very 'sticky' downwards relative to their apparent upwards 'flexibility'. Both, to put matters simply, seem to be on a ratchet.

In developing our theory of inflation we shall need to take full account of these points.

1 INFLATION AND MARKET BEHAVIOUR

Since inflation is a process of price increase we can best begin our enquiry at the beginning by asking in what circumstances prices will rise. This clearly depends upon the way in which prices get determined which, in its turn, depends upon the nature of the markets involved. At a very abstract level of analysis two types may be distinguished. They are (i) those in which prices are said to be *flexible*; (ii) those in which prices are said to be *cost determined*. As we shall formulate them, these two are limiting cases. Many prices will be *partly flexible* and *partly cost determined*.

Flexible prices are said to exist when price is determined by the demand and supply situation. The typical case is shown in Figure 21.ii which represents the market for peanuts. *DD* is the demand curve showing the planned purchases of households at each price: *SS* the planned supplies of enterprises. The equilibrium price is p_0.

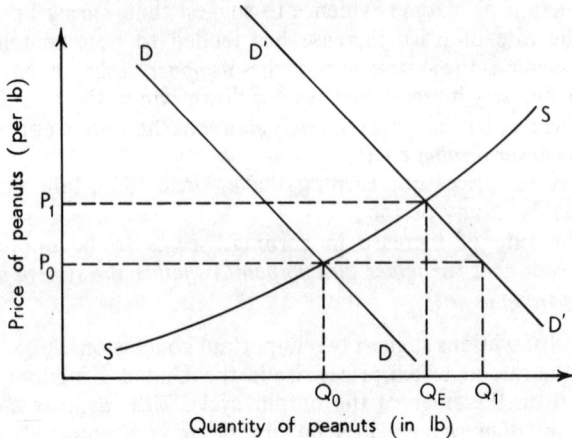

The market for peanuts

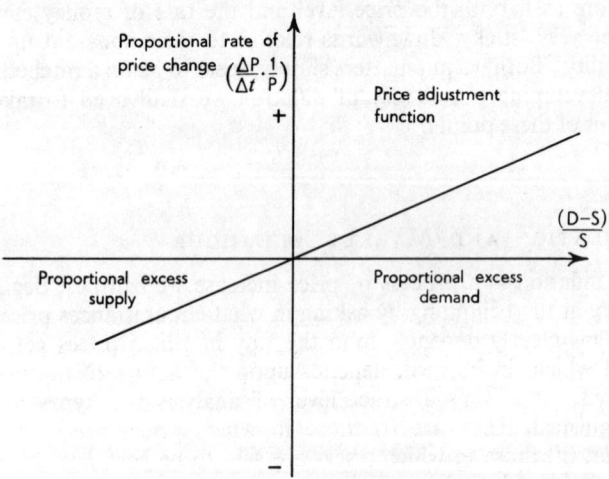

FIG. 21.ii   The market for peanuts: excess demand and the rate of price change

Suppose now the demand curve drifts to $D'D'$. There is now *excess demand* at the price p_0 amounting to Q_0Q_1. Hence prices rise; they are bid up or pulled up and firms expand output until a new equilibrium is reached at p_1. It follows that where prices are *flexible* in this sense then

(i) *prices will rise if and only if excess demand is present*;
(ii) *excess demand can occur only if the demand curve shifts to the right, the supply curve shifts to the left, or some combination of the two occurs.*

How *fast* will prices rise? This depends upon the dynamic characteristics of the theory which we have not specified. A simple assumption, however, is that, in any given market, the rate of change of prices will be greater, the greater is the excess demand. In proportionate terms, this assumption can be expressed formally thus:

$$\frac{\Delta p}{\Delta t} \times \frac{1}{p} = f\left[\frac{D-S}{S}\right]_t, \quad \text{and} \quad \frac{\Delta p}{\Delta t} \gtrless 0 \text{ if } D-S \gtrless 0 \qquad (21.\text{I})$$

where

$\frac{\Delta p}{\Delta t} \cdot \frac{1}{p} \equiv$ proportionate price change

$D \equiv$ quantity demanded at the initial market price in period t

$S \equiv$ quantity supplied at the initial market price in period t

Strictly speaking the proposition that prices are *cost determined* requires businessmen to set prices by adding a 'conventional' mark-up to costs. The price charged is now independent of demand, at least over a relatively wide range of demand/supply situations, and this theory can therefore be expressed in formal terms as follows:

$$p = (1+q)C, \qquad (21.\text{II})$$

where

$C \equiv$ costs

$q \equiv$ percentage mark-up.

It follows straightforwardly that, if prices are *cost determined*, they can change if and only if (i) costs change; (ii) the mark-up changes. If, to simplify exposition, we think of a closed economy, then for output as a whole the only cost is labour cost per unit of output. Writing this as W we have

$$p = (1+q)W. \qquad (21.\text{II(a)})$$

The rate of change of prices is therefore given by:†

$$\frac{\Delta p}{\Delta t} \cdot \frac{1}{p} = \frac{\Delta W}{\Delta t} \cdot \frac{1}{W} + \frac{\Delta q}{\Delta t} \cdot \frac{1}{1+q}, \tag{21.III}$$

that is, the rate of change of prices is equal to the rate of change of wage cost *plus* the rate of change of the mark-up.

We now think of an economy possessing two highly aggregative markets:

(i) the market for commodities (output);
(ii) the market for factors (labour input).

In developed western type economies there is little doubt that, *in general*, output prices are *cost determined*: that is, the relevant method of commodity price formulation is given by (21.II). The possible market structure can therefore be tabulated as follows:

Method of Price Formulation

	Commodity market	Factor market
Type 1	Cost determined	Flexible
Type 2	Cost determined	Cost determined

† To see this put $1+q \equiv K$ so that:

$$P = KW.$$

Now assume that K increases in period t by $\Delta K/\Delta t$ and W by $\Delta W/\Delta t$. We have

$$P + \frac{\Delta P}{\Delta t} = \left[K + \frac{\Delta K}{\Delta t}\right]\left[W + \frac{\Delta W}{\Delta t}\right]$$

$$= KW + K \cdot \frac{\Delta W}{\Delta t} + W \cdot \frac{\Delta K}{\Delta t} + \frac{\Delta K}{\Delta t} \cdot \frac{\Delta W}{\Delta t}.$$

So
$$\frac{\Delta P}{\Delta t} = KW + K \cdot \frac{\Delta W}{\Delta t} + W \cdot \frac{\Delta K}{\Delta t} + \frac{\Delta K}{\Delta t} \cdot \frac{\Delta W}{\Delta t} - KW$$

$$= K \cdot \frac{\Delta W}{\Delta t} + W \cdot \frac{\Delta K}{\Delta t} + \frac{\Delta K}{\Delta t} \cdot \frac{\Delta W}{\Delta t}$$

and
$$\frac{\Delta P}{\Delta t} \cdot \frac{1}{P} = \frac{\Delta W}{\Delta t} \cdot \frac{1}{W} + \frac{\Delta K}{\Delta t} \cdot \frac{1}{K} + \frac{\Delta K}{\Delta t} \cdot \frac{1}{K} \cdot \frac{\Delta W}{\Delta t} \cdot \frac{1}{W}$$

The formula in (21.III) thus assumes that the last term $\Delta K/K \cdot \Delta W/W$ is negligibly small and can be neglected. This, as the reader can readily verify, will be so for reasonably small values of $\Delta K/\Delta t \cdot 1/K$ and $\Delta W/\Delta t \cdot 1/W$. Thus if $\Delta K/\Delta t \cdot 1/K = 3 \cdot 0\%$ and $\Delta W/\Delta t \cdot 1/W = 2 \cdot 0\%$ their product will be 3 % of 2 % – that is 0·06 %.

This table, of course, is an oversimplification since it insists on only the limiting forms of price determination. In practice, as we shall see, both these markets, and in particular the labour/factor market, contain elements of both systems of price determination. Postponing this refinement for the moment we may now ask what processes of inflation are compatible with these systems.

2 AN INFLATIONARY PROCESS: TYPE 1

In a model with a market structure of Type 1, prices will rise if either (i) businessmen raise the mark-up percentage or (ii) costs (= labour cost per unit of output) rise. There is little evidence to suggest that mark-up inflation has ever occurred in the United Kingdom. Hence case (ii) is the plausible case. We can then ask:

  (i) how do labour costs rise?
  (ii) how will the system behave if they do?

The labour cost of a unit of output is the money earnings† of a unit of labour (W) divided by the productivity of a unit of labour (output per man employed) which we shall call X. Hence the rate of change (per cent per annum) of labour costs is:

$$\frac{\Delta(W/X)}{\Delta t} \cdot \frac{1}{(W/X)} \equiv \frac{\Delta W}{\Delta t} \cdot \frac{1}{W} - \frac{\Delta X}{\Delta t} \cdot \frac{1}{X} \qquad (21.\text{IV})$$

rate of change of   rate of change of
≡ money earnings − productivity
per employee   per employee.

For a moment let us take the rate of change in productivity as given and constant at zero. Then to explain the rate of change of wage costs per unit of output we need only explain the rate of change in money wage earnings.

Wages are the price of labour. According to our market assumptions the labour market operates according to our *flexible* model. Hence money wage earnings should rise if *excess demand* for labour is present. Suppose excess demand appears in the labour market. Then W rises and with it the rate of change of W/X which now becomes positive. Employers, confronted by the rise in costs, simply mark up prices in proportion. Prices therefore rise in the same proportion as money wages. This, if it occurs, will leave real wages

---

† Money wage earnings must be sharply distinguished from the money wage rate which is the subject of union bargaining.

unaltered. Suppose this happens and, in real terms, the demand for output is unaffected. Output will then be what it was in the original situation. So will the demand for labour. The rise in money wages and prices will have done nothing to eliminate the excess demand for labour. Hence wages, and as a result prices, will go on rising at the same rate and the process will repeat itself *ad infinitum*.

Let us put this argument down step by step in the form of a series of propositions:

 (i) the rate of change in prices is equal to the rate of change in wage costs per unit of output;
 (ii) the rate of change in wage costs is equal to the rate of change in (money) wage earnings per employee;
 (iii) the rate of change in (money) wage earnings is determined by the excess demand for labour;
 (iv) the process of wage/price *increases* does not modify (in either direction) the excess demand for labour.

In this form the model is (i) *explosive* with respect to the price level; (ii) *compatible* with any rate of change (positive or negative) in prices depending upon the degree of excess demand (supply) in the labour market. Clearly this model is unrealistic in that, first, it treats (implicitly) price behaviour as symmetric (wages rise with excess demand, fall with excess supply), and second, it takes the demand for output, and the derived demand for labour, as independent of the absolute level of prices and wages. Let us look at the second point first.

According to our static model any increase in the price level, by raising the demand for transaction balances will, unless the money supply rises *pari passu* with the price level, tend to raise the rate of interest and so reduce investment. Again, if prices rise the *real* value of households' assets, the nominal value of which is fixed in terms of the unit of account (e.g. P.O.S.B. deposits, bank deposits, notes, coin, building society deposits), will fall. This may reduce household consumption.† Finally if income tax is *progressive* with respect to money income, as it usually is, in the sense that the proportion of money income paid in tax rises with money income, then personal disposable income in real terms will fall as prices rise. Hence consumption will tend to fall.

Thus even in a closed economy there are at least three reasons why proposition (iv) should not hold. It is indeed reasonable to argue that the inflationary process, by reducing aggregate demand in

† The reader will recognise this as an extension of the 'cash-balance' effect.

relation to supply in real terms will reduce the derived demand for labour and so eliminate the excess demand and halt the price rise. If this is so the system is, in principle, *stable*. The price rise must have a stop. The stop, however, may be a long time in coming for it may require a very large increase in prices to reduce aggregate demand significantly. Hence an inflationary process of the type under review may be persistent.

Let us now look at the first element of criticism, the apparent symmetry of behaviour.

Our labour market hypothesis is that the rate of change of money wages depends upon the degree of excess demand for labour. Formally:

$$\frac{\Delta W}{\Delta t} \cdot \frac{1}{W} = f_w\left(\frac{N^D - N^S}{N^S}\right)_t, \qquad (21.\text{V})$$

where $N^D \equiv$ demand for labour, $N^S =$ supply of labour. Is this plausible? Can we test it?

Obviously the left-hand side of (21.V) is measurable in principle. It is also measurable in practice since statistical data for wage and salary earnings per employee are available. Can we measure the right-hand side?

One plausible index would be the difference between the number of vacancies (V) as a percentage of the work-force (N^S) and the number of unemployed (U) as a percentage of the work-force. That is, we might use

$$\left[\frac{V}{N^S} - \frac{U}{N^S}\right]\frac{100}{1} \text{ as an index of } \frac{N^D - N^S}{N^S}. \qquad (21.\text{VI})$$

This can be done, and in fact has been done, but data on vacancies is available only for recent years. As a result, since it can be shown that on quite reasonable assumptions, writing $U \equiv$ registered unemployed

$$\frac{N^D - N^S}{N^S} = f_n\left(\frac{U}{N^S}\right) \qquad (21.\text{VII})$$

in the sense that the lower is U/N^S the *higher* is $N^D - N^S/N^S$, the percentage of the work-force unemployed is commonly used as an index of excess demand in the labour market. In other words, in order to test the hypothesis

$$\frac{\Delta W}{\Delta t} \cdot \frac{1}{W} = f_w\left[\frac{N^D - N^S}{N^S}\right] \qquad (21.\text{VIII})$$

we argue that

$$\frac{N^D - N^S}{N^S} = f_n\left[\frac{U}{N^S}\right], \qquad (21.\text{VII})$$

and plot

$$\frac{\Delta W}{\Delta t} \cdot \frac{1}{W} \quad \text{against} \quad \frac{U}{N^S} \quad \text{per cent.} \qquad (21.\text{IX})$$

The resultant curve is of the form shown in Figure 21.iii, below.†
This shows that, on the basis of empirical evidence,‡ there is a
relation between the pressure of demand in the labour market and
the rate of change of money wage earnings.

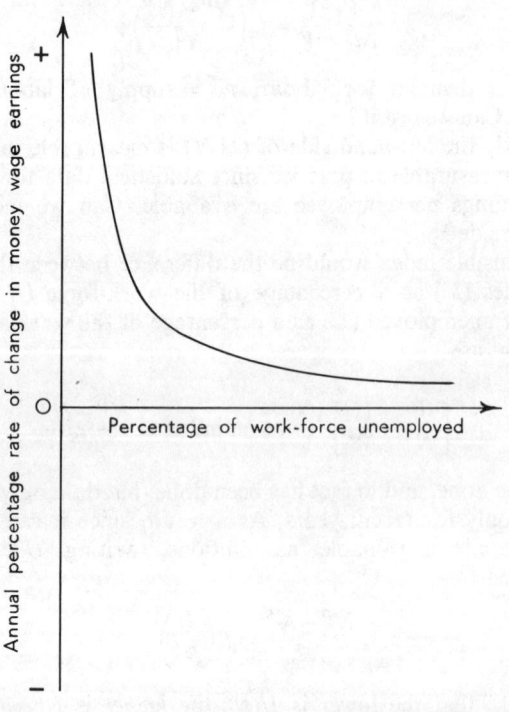

FIG. 21.iii   Wage adjustment curve (hypothetical)

† It is left to the reader to explain the shape of this function theoretically
and in particular why the form shown is plausible even if (21.V) is linear.
‡ See references at the end of this chapter.

Assuming this relationship – *which reflects the working of the labour market* – to be a stable one, the essence of our theory of inflation Type 1 is to be found in the following propositions:

(i) the rate of change of prices depends upon the rate of change of money wage earnings and the rate of change of productivity;

(ii) the rate of change of wage earnings depends upon the percentage of unemployment;

(iii) the rate of change of productivity is given.

Now in the *upswing* of the output cycle the percentage of unemployment will, initially, be relatively *high* – as we saw in Chapter 17. Hence the rate of change of wages will be relatively *low*. Productivity rises relatively fast in *upswings* – partly because, in the early stages at least, output, because of excess capacity, can be expanded fairly quickly without expanding employment proportionately. Hence in upswings we tend to get a relatively *low* rate of price increase. In *downswings* output ceases to expand and even falls. Unemployment, however, is initially *low* and the rate of change of wages relatively *high*. Productivity is likely to remain constant or fall. Hence wage costs and therefore prices tend to rise relatively fast.

This simple theory of inflation Type 1 thus seems to fit the observed facts fairly well in that (i) its wage determination hypothesis is supported by observation; and (ii) given the cyclical behaviour of the rate of change of productivity it (iii) produces a cyclical pattern of price increases for which evidence exists and (iv) is compatible with the observation that price increases occur, and indeed tend to be faster, when output is constant or falling.

Nevertheless the theory in its present form is unsatisfactory – or at least demands further enquiry – for at least two reasons. The first is that it does not seem entirely plausible that the rate of change of wages should be determined *exclusively* by the percentage of unemployment. Unions commonly base wage demands upon *past* price changes. But if past price changes influence union claims our hypothesis that what happens to wages depends only on the demand/supply position in the labour market would appear to imply that the whole process of wage bargaining is nothing but a charade – 'shadow boxing' as one authority has called it. For according to this theory it does not matter whether unions are militant or mouselike or employers tough or timid. What employees get, on average, in any round of wage increases, depends *only* on the percentage of unemployment. This seems a very strong assumption.

In the second place is it correct to assume that the curve in Fig. 21.iii is completely stable? The curve reflects employers' attitudes (demand curve), employees' attitudes (supply curve) and the institutional framework and political climate within which bargaining takes place. All four *can* change. The curve therefore seems quite likely to shift. We must then ask whether the curve ever has shifted and, if it has, whether we can formulate any meaningful theory as to what brought the shift about?

3 An Inflationary Process: Type 2

In this model *both* commodity prices *and* factor prices (wage earnings) are assumed to be *cost determined*. We know what cost-determined prices mean. What is the meaning of cost-determined wages?

In terms of the rates of change of money wages this assumption can be taken to mean that (i) the rate of change of money wages is *independent*, at least over the range experienced recently, of the state of demand in the labour market and (ii) depends only upon the past rate of change in prices which are the 'costs' of living to the wage recipient. Suppose these assumptions to be correct. How would the inflationary process proceed?

Since *all* prices are now independent of demand then, in a closed economy where, since there are no imports, a rise in import costs cannot start an inflationary process, only three possibilities exist. An inflation may be started by

(i) *employers* raising their percentage *mark-up*;
(ii) a sudden *fall in productivity* thus raising wage costs;
(iii) an *increase in money wages* which is *autonomous with respect to past price changes*.

Of these three possibilities, the third is the one which most people seem to have in mind. Suppose such an *autonomous* increase in money wages occurs. What will happen? If wages rise prices rise. But if prices rise this results in further wage increases which in turn raise prices. These again raise wages which raise prices and so on seemingly *ad infinitum*. This model, in short, provides the classic wage-price-wage spiral.

We ask first is this spiral *explosive* or will it eventually die away? Clearly the answer depends upon two marginal response co-efficients. The first of these is the marginal response coefficient linking the percentage increase in prices to the percentage increase in wages. The second is the marginal response coefficient linking the percentage increase in wages to the percentage increase in prices. If *both* these coefficients are equal to or greater than unity the spiral will be explosive. If their product is less than unity the spiral will be *damped* that is, like the multiplier, it will die away. In case this is not intuitively obvious we can easily demonstrate it thus:

According to our hypothesis the rate of change in prices will depend linearly upon the rate of change in wages probably with a lag which we shall take to be one period. Hence

$$\frac{P_t - P_{t-1}}{P_{t-1}} = \alpha \left[\frac{W_{t-1} - W_{t-2}}{W_{t-2}} \right], \qquad (21.\text{X})$$

where $\alpha \equiv$ the marginal (and average) response of proportionate price change to proportionate wage change: in other words the wage elasticity of prices.

Our second hypothesis can now be written, again assuming a lag and a linear relationship,

$$\frac{W_{t-1} - W_{t-2}}{W_{t-2}} = B \left[\frac{P_{t-2} - P_{t-3}}{P_{t-3}} \right] \qquad (21.\text{XI})$$

Combining we obtain:

$$\frac{P_t - P_{t-1}}{P_{t-1}} = \alpha B \left[\frac{P_{t-2} - P_{t-3}}{P_{t-3}} \right] \qquad (21.\text{XII})$$

which tells us that the proportionate change in prices in the current period is always αB times the change in price *two* periods before. Obviously if $\alpha B < 1$ the rate of price increase *must* be diminishing. Hence it must eventually die away altogether. In short the system behaves very much like the dynamic multiplier. That is, it converges to a new equilibrium provided $\alpha B < 1$ just as the multiplier converges to a new equilibrium if the marginal propensity to consume is less than 1.

Empirical evidence† suggests that in the short run both α and B are less than unity. Hence inflationary process Type 2 is unlikely to be explosive even if, as the model suggests, it is plausible to make the strong assumption that prices and wages are wholly independent of demand. This complete independence is, of course, a very strong assumption. In practice we should expect both α and B – the two marginal response coefficients – to respond in some degree to the demand/supply situation in the commodity and labour markets. If they do, then the three stabilising elements of process 1 apply and our tentative conclusion that a Type 2 inflationary process is unlikely to explode is strengthened.

Can we learn anything from this model?

The model of Type 2 inflation differs from that of Type 1 only in

† See references at the end of the chapter.

virtue of its labour market hypothesis. According to model Type 1 we have, writing our familiar hypothesis in dynamic form,

$$\frac{W_t - W_{t-1}}{W_{t-1}} = f_1 \left[\frac{N^D - N^S}{N^S} \right]_{t-1}, \tag{21.V*}$$

while the hypothesis of model Type 2 is:

$$\frac{W_t - W_{t-1}}{W_{t-1}} = f_2 \left[\frac{P_{t-1} - P_{t-2}}{P_{t-2}} \right]. \tag{21.XI}$$

There is good empirical evidence in favour of *both* these hypotheses. For a more satisfactory model we need to combine both by making the rate of change of wages a function of *both* variables. We thus write:

$$\frac{W_t - W_{t-1}}{W_{t-1}} = f_3 \left[\left(\frac{N^D - N^S}{N^S} \right)_{t-1}, \frac{P_{t-1} - P_{t-2}}{P_{t-2}} \right], \tag{21.XII}$$

A model of this kind is developed in the next section and estimates are given of its parameters. These are (i) the marginal response coefficients, and (ii) the lag pattern. Though we have no *a priori* expectation regarding (ii) we do expect both marginal response coefficients to be positive.

4 THE INFLATIONARY MECHANISM IN THE UNITED KINGDOM

The minimum requirement of any inflationary model is, as we have seen, a price determination hypothesis and a cost determination hypothesis. In the United Kingdom imports amount to about 24 per cent of output. Most of these are raw materials. Hence any change in import prices will affect costs. Accordingly we write our price determination hypothesis thus:

$$P_t = a + bW_t + cM_{t-\frac{1}{4}} + eX_t \tag{21.XIII}$$

where

$P_t \equiv$ annual percentage increase in prices in year t

$W_t \equiv$ annual percentage increase in wage earnings in year t

$M_{t-\frac{1}{4}} \equiv$ annual percentage increase in import prices *one quarter of a year previously*: that is, the percentage change in the year ending one quarter of a year before the current year.†

$X_t \equiv$ annual percentage change in productivity per man hour in year t

$a \equiv$ autonomous annual percentage price change.

† This lag is not, of course, based on any theoretical expectations but on empirical findings.

Comparison of this hypothesis with that of model 1 makes it clear that, apart from notational changes and the introduction of imports the two systems are identical. The marginal response coefficients are

$\dfrac{\partial P_t}{\partial W_t} = b$ which we expect to be > 0 but less than 1

$\dfrac{\partial P_t}{\partial M_{t-\frac{1}{4}}} = c$ which we expect to be close to the value of imports in G.D.P. i.e. around 0·20–0·25

$\dfrac{\partial P_t}{\partial X_t} = e$ which we expect to be negative and $\leqslant 1$ in absolute value.

The wage-determination hypothesis is, essentially, a synthesis of our hypotheses in models 1 and 2. It states that the rate of change of wages depends upon the rate of price increase in the current period, the rate of price increase in the period immediately past, and the level of the excess demand for labour. Formally:

$$W_t = q + fP_t + gP_{t-1} + h\left[\frac{N^D - N^S}{N^S}\right]_{t-\frac{1}{4}}, \qquad (21.\text{XIV})$$

where W_t, P_t are defined as before and

$P_{t-1} \equiv$ annual percentage change in prices in the year immediately past

$\left[\dfrac{N^D - N^S}{N^S}\right]_{t-\frac{1}{4}} \equiv$ percentage excess demand for labour in the twelve months ending one quarter of a year before the current year

$q \equiv$ autonomous annual percentage wage increase.

In this equation the marginal response coefficients are f, g and h. If P_t is equal to P_{t-1} then $(f+g)$ corresponds to the B of model 2. Hence we expect $(f+g)$ to be greater than zero but $\leqslant 1$; while, from the Fig. 21.iii, it is clear that we must also expect $h > 0$.

Now in this model we have six variables all of which can be observed in principle and measured in practice. They are P_t, P_{t-1}, W_t, $M_{t-\frac{1}{4}}$, $[(N^D - N^S)/N^S]_{t-\frac{1}{4}}$ and X_t. We also have six marginal response coefficients which, by the use of statistical techniques, can be estimated. The model is therefore *operational* as we require. Such a model has been put forward and statistically estimated by L. A. Dicks-Mireaux.† His results were:

$$P_t = 2·47 + 0·27W_t + 0·21M_{t-\frac{1}{4}} - 0·54X_t \qquad (21.\text{XIIIn})$$

$$W_t = 3·90 + 0·30P_t + 0·16P_{t-1} + 2·78\left(\frac{N^D - N^S}{N^S}\right)_{t-\frac{1}{4}} \qquad (21.\text{XIVn})$$

† 'The Interrelationship between Cost and Price Changes 1946–1959.'

These results are interesting for a number of reasons.

First the marginal response coefficient of wages to prices $(f+g)$ is substantially less than unity – in fact 0·46 – while the marginal response coefficient of prices to wages is also very small (0·27). If these values are correct, inflation of Type 2 would be very rapidly convergent, i.e. would die away quickly or, as it is usually stated, be heavily damped.

Second the excess demand for labour $[(N^D-N^S)/N^S]$ has a high coefficient – as we would expect from Fig. 21.iii. A one percentage point change in this variable (say from 3 to 4 per cent) – which is roughly equivalent to a one per cent change in the percentage of unemployment – adds getting on for 3 per cent to the rate of wage increase.

Third the rate of change in productivity has a significant and immediate influence on the rate of price increase.

In interpreting this element of the model we must remember that productivity is measured by output divided by the number of persons employed. Sometimes this measure is made rather more precise by allowing for variation in the hours per week worked by the average employee. Suppose output is constant (at the upper turning point of the growth cycle) then, if employment is constant so is productivity. Hence the rate of change of productivity is zero. For productivity to increase *constant* output would require *falling* employment. Hence if employers adjust employment to output with a lag or, what amounts observationally to the same thing, 'hoard labour' in recessions, the rate of change of observed productivity will follow a cyclical pattern even though the long-term (trend) rate of growth of productivity (reflecting technical progress and capital accumulation) is constant. There is good reason to believe that a lag *does* exist between output and employment. Initially, when demand increases, employers take on no more workers: they simply take up existing slack. From this the reader should find it simple to work out the cyclical path of the rate of change of productivity (as measured) and hence its cyclical influence on the rate of price increase.

How well this model fits the data is shown by two diagrams reproduced from Dicks-Mireaux's paper. The calculated P_t and W_t are, of course, obtained from equations (21.XIIIn) and (21.XIVn).

Looking at these figures it seems we can draw some additional conclusions.

(i) Until 1953/4 it looks as if the dominating factor in determining the rate of U.K. inflation was the behaviour of import prices. After 1953/4 this has not been so.

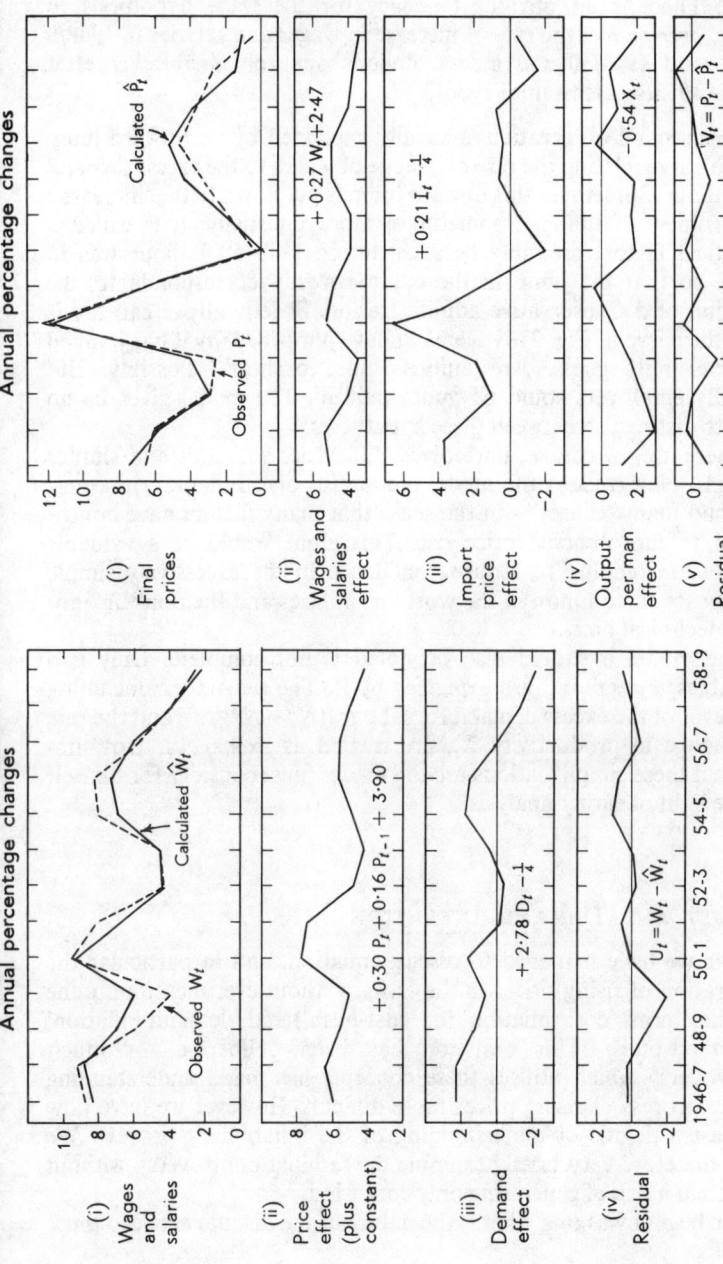

FIG. 21.iv The interrelationship between cost and price changes in the U.K., 1946-59

Source: L. Dicks-Mireaux: 'The Interrelationship between Cost and Price Changes, 1946-1959', *Oxford Economic Papers*, 1961.

(ii) There is an obvious tendency for the wage hypothesis to *over-predict* the rate of increase in wages and salaries in 1948/9 and 1949/50 and a less obvious one to *underpredict* after 1953/4 at least until 1956/7.

This second observation is usually explained by an upward jump in the curve relating the rate of change of wages to the excess demand for labour. Sometimes this upward jump is put down to the 'increased pushfulness of unions': sometimes, more unusually, it is called a 'political factor' probably because during 1948–50 Labour was in office so that the jump in the curve roughly corresponds to the election of a Conservative administration. Strictly all we can say is that the curve of Fig. 21.iv seems to have jumped. *Why* it has jumped we can only guess. Are unions 'more pushful'? Possibly. But equally employers could be 'more pullful'. The model gives us no way to distinguish between these hypotheses.

There are, of course, unresolved difficulties with this and similar models. Nevertheless the model is a useful one. Inflation, it seems, has had many 'causes' – in the sense that many factors have contributed to the observed price rise. This alone would be a valuable conclusion tending to reduce confidence in the excessively simple diagnoses so common in the world of politics and the non- or only semi-technical press.

The model it should also be noted is not complete. Only two variables, P_t and W_t, are *explained* by it. The remainder, including the level of the excess demand for labour $[(N^D - N^S)/N^S]$ and the rate of change in productivity X_t, are treated as *exogenous*. How important these simplifications are the reader must consider for himself in the light of earlier analysis.

5 COST AND DEMAND INFLATION

So far we have managed to discuss inflation, and in particular the generation of rising prices in the U.K., without ever mentioning the familiar terms 'cost inflation' (or 'cost-push') and 'demand inflation' ('demand-pull'). This omission has been deliberate for much controversy which utilises these concepts has made understanding of the process of rising prices more difficult. However we have now at least a degree of understanding of the inflationary process. We may therefore very briefly examine the familiar controversy without too great a risk of generating only confusion.

We begin by asking what is the nature of the dispute between those

who argue that inflation is due to 'demand pull' and those who assert
that it is due to 'cost push'? Rather surprisingly this is a difficult
question to answer basically because there are many different
versions of both theories. All we can do is define what we shall mean
by them in this discussion. In accordance with our general approach
we shall do this by asking:

(i) what predictions do the two types of theory generate?
(ii) which predictions are better supported by the facts?

We shall initially identify the demand-pull theory with the
proposition that prices rise because excess demand is present in
either the goods market or the factor market or both. To fix our
ideas let us assume that in the commodity market prices are *cost
determined* and the economy is closed. Then the demand-pull theory
consists of the two hypotheses:

$$\frac{P_t - P_{t-1}}{P_{t-1}} = f_1\left[\frac{W_{t-1} - W_{t-2}}{W_{t-2}}\right] \qquad (21.\text{III})$$

and

$$\frac{W_t - W_{t-1}}{W_{t-1}} = f_2\left[\frac{N^D - N^S}{N^S}\right]_{t-1}. \qquad (21.\text{V})$$

Its prediction, obtained by substituting (21.V) into (21.III) is

$$\frac{P_t - P_{t-1}}{P_{t-1}} = f_3\left[\frac{N^D - N^S}{N^S}\right]_{t-2} \qquad (21.\text{XI})$$

which, using our usual approximation for the excess demand for
labour, gives:

$$\frac{P_t - P_{t-1}}{P_{t-1}} = f_4\left[\frac{U}{N^S}\right]_{t-2}. \qquad (21.\text{XIa})$$

As we have seen this prediction is well supported by the facts.

As against this formulation the cost-push theory would accept the
price determination hypothesis of (21.III). Cost-push theorists,
however, would argue that, in the labour market, money wages are
not *pulled up* by excess demand manifesting itself in the competitive
bidding of employers (as demand-pull suggests), but are, on the
contrary, pushed up by *union action*. In general they go further and
hypothesise that union 'pushfulness' will be greater the lower is the

percentage of the work-force unemployed. This hypothesis can be written:

$$\frac{W_t - W_{t-1}}{W_{t-1}} = f_5\left(\frac{U}{N^s}\right)_{t-1}. \qquad (21.\text{X})$$

Hence the prediction of the cost-push theory, obtained by substituting (21.X) into (21.III) is:

$$\frac{P_t - P_{t-1}}{P_{t-1}} = f_6\left[\frac{U}{N^s}\right]_{t-2}, \qquad (21.\text{XI(b)})$$

which is identical with that of the demand-pull theory.

In short both theories hypothesise *the same type of labour market adjustment function though the reasoning underlying the hypotheses differs in each case.* Hence both generate the same prediction. As we have specified them the two theories are indistinguishable because, though they differ about how the labour market operates, they agree on the results.

Accordingly our (Dicks-Mireaux) model can be *interpreted* either as a *demand-pull* model or a *cost-push* model. This is because the 'wage' market adjustment curve of Fig. 21.iii merely relates the rate of change of wage earnings to *excess demand*. It does not tell us whether the excess demand is due to employers bidding up wages (demand-pull) or to unions pushing them up (cost-push) or some combination of the two.

Some investigators have found evidence to suggest that the labour market adjustment function (21.V) has shifted. Cost inflation theorists explain these apparent shifts by appeals to changing degrees of union pushfulness. Two investigators have found increased pushfulness after 1951 and explained this by a 'political factor'. But demand theorists would have no difficulty in finding explanations for these shifts though some of these might not, at first sight, seem very plausible.† Unless some way of distinguishing between 'increased pullfulness' and 'increased pushfulness' can be specified, the apparent shifts are not evidence either way. Clearly, from the nature of the dispute, any test needs to be related to the working of the labour market. One such test is available.

Suppose the demand theory to hold. Then earnings are *pulled* up by employers bidding against one another for scarce labour. This bidding, which is undertaken by firms, will not usually take the form of an offer of an increased wage *rate* but the offer of a wage in excess of the negotiated rate by, for example, guaranteed overtime or

---

† One possibility is a shift in the commodity composition of demand and thus the industrial distribution of the demand for labour.

special allowances and bonuses.† According to this view the process of wage bargaining merely *consolidates*, into the negotiated wage *rate*, the level of wage *earnings* which has *previously* emerged from the market process.

In short (i) the market determines the rate of increase in wage *earnings*; and (ii) the process of wage rate negotiation merely brings wage *rates*, after some time lag, into line with *earnings*. According to an extreme version of this view of the labour market the wage bargaining process between *groups* of employers and employees is simply shadow-boxing.

What does this theory predict that is testable? Surely that wage *rates* follow and are determined by wage *earnings*. Formally:

$$\frac{Wr_t - Wr_{t-1}}{Wr_{t-1}} = f.\left[\frac{We_{t-1} - We_{t-2}}{We_{t-2}}\right] \qquad (21.\text{XV})$$

where

$Wr_t \equiv$ money wage *rate* in period t

$We_t \equiv$ money earning per employee in period t.

By contrast the cost-push theory predicts the *reverse*. It regards the *rate* bargaining process as significant, and thus union and employer attitudes as significant and argues that:

$$\frac{We_t - We_{t-1}}{We_{t-1}} = f_a\left[\frac{Wr_{t-1} - Wr_{t-2}}{Wr_{t-2}}\right]. \qquad (21.\text{XVI})$$

These two predictions have been tested by Dicks-Mireaux. He found that the evidence was strongly in favour of hypothesis (21.XVI) – the cost-push hypothesis as we have called it.

This test is interesting though not necessarily conclusive since weaker versions of the demand-pull theory could probably be made compatible with (21.XVI). Nevertheless Dicks-Mireaux's finding does show that the process of wage *rate* determination is *not* shadow-boxing. If it can be assumed, and this does not seem a very strong assumption, that union and employer attitudes influence the outcome of the wage *rate* bargain then, for reasons we shall now discuss, this has an important bearing on policy to control inflation.

6 The Control of Inflation

Assuming a closed economy with cost determined prices the avoidance of inflation requires that the rate of change of wage earnings per employee be equal to the rate of change of productivity per employee.

† From this arises what is known as 'wage drift'. This can be defined as: the rate of change of wage earnings *minus* the rate of change of wage rates.

If this holds then at a formal level labour costs per unit of output do not change. Hence if prices are cost determined they should be invariant. Now if what we have called the demand-pull theory were correct, since the rate of change of wage earning depends only on $(N^D - N^S)/N^S$ which clearly depends, in its turn upon the level of aggregate demand in relation to capacity output, the proper method of controlling inflation would be to control demand. Put briefly, the aim of policy should be to find, *and maintain*, that percentage of unemployment (or excess capacity or excess demand for labour) which satisfied the following condition:

$$\frac{We_t - We_{t-1}}{We_{t-1}} - X_t = 0. \qquad (21.\text{XVIII})$$

This view, or a more sophisticated version of it, is the core of proposals to stabilise prices by maintaining continuously 2 to $2\frac{1}{2}$ per cent unemployment. For this is the level of unemployment which according to some estimates of the curve in Fig. 21.iii satisfies 21.XVIII when X_t is taken to be the *trend* rate of increase in productivity, i.e. about $2\frac{1}{2}$ per cent.

Note that this approach strictly requires a *constant* percentage of unemployment to be maintained continuously. *It thus requires the elimination of the output cycle we discussed in Chapter 20.* Moreover it will work only if the maintenance of what is, for the U.K. in the post-war period, a rather high level of unemployment does not shift the labour (wage) 'market adjustment curve' upwards or adversely affect the rate of change of productivity.

By contrast the cost-push theory suggests that the appropriate method of controlling inflation is to aim at shifting, *downwards*, the wage 'market adjustment curve' by bringing about a change in *the attitudes* of both unions and employers. This is essentially the so-called 'incomes policy' approach. According to the demand theorists if aggregate demand is kept in the appropriate relation to capacity an 'incomes policy' is unnecessary. Demand theorists thus emphasise the *stability* of the wage 'market adjustment curve'. According to the cost theorists this policy might fail because an attempt to move along the curve, *as a deliberate act of policy*, might bring about an *upward shift* in the curve. Cost theorists thus tend to emphasise the *instability* of the curve pointing, as evidence, to apparent shifts in 1950 and 1954 and arguing that if the (Labour) government could contain wages in 1948–50 this suggests the possibility of doing so again.

We shall discuss policy issues more fully in the next three chapters. It is clear, however, that the controversy between demand-pull and cost-push theories is of major importance for policy.

7 EXPLOSIVE INFLATIONS AND EXPECTATIONS

In this chapter we have so far argued that what evidence there is about the U.K. economy suggests that neither the price level, nor its rate of increase, are likely to be explosive. Against this we must set the familiar view that once the community learns, from experience, to *expect* prices to rise by (say) 3 per cent per annum, it will take action which will *accelerate* the rate of price increase continuously so that eventually a *hyper-inflation* emerges.

There are certainly examples of explosive inflations – mainly at the end of unsuccessful wars. In some of these the rate of price increase has exceeded 100 per cent per month. Equally there is evidence of countries which have, for many years, had a rate of price increase of 10 per cent per annum without the rate of inflation showing any obvious tendency to accelerate.

Why should explosions occur? If inflation is generally anticipated, money is seen to be a deteriorating asset. So are all tokens of debt the value of which is defined in terms of the unit of account. To hedge against inflationary losses in real wealth it is necessary to hold goods or legal titles to real capital such as equities. Moreover it is profitable, when price increases are confidently anticipated for long periods in the future, to borrow to buy such assets since the real value of the debt falls as the price level rises. On these grounds it is argued that, once inflation is confidently anticipated, the consumption and investment functions shift upwards in real terms. This raises demand which raises prices faster, again shifting the consumption and investment functions and so on. Hence, as a consequence of expectations, the inflation explodes into *hyper-inflation*.

Plainly such a process *may* occur and in some cases *has* occurred. But in a number of cases in which this argument leads us to expect it to occur it has *not* occurred. The evidence drawn from inflationary experience in *general* is therefore indecisive. Possibly there is some 'critical' rate of price increase above which inflations tend to *explode* and below which they tend to be *damped*. But there is no established theory to explain either why this should be so or the forces determining the 'critical' rate. Our examination of British price increases does not suggest that the system is explosive. Hence, in the absence of either a well developed theory of expectations or very strong evidence that there is an inherent tendency for inflations to accelerate, we are justified in adopting a position of scepticism.

8 RECENT EXPERIENCE AND EXPECTATIONS

The view that inflations have no necessary tendency to explode and the associated view that there exists some relatively stable relation between the rate of change of wage earnings, the excess demand for labour and past rates of price change are now both the subject of considerable debate. This debate has been intensified by the tendency of models of the type we have discussed to *underpredict* – sometimes by as much as 6–7 per cent – the rate of change of wage earnings in the United Kingdom in 1969, 1970 and 1971. One common explanation is that these models understate the contemporary role of expected price changes in wage bargaining. In its most extreme form this implies that the wage adjustment curve (depicted in Fig. 21.iii) is a short-run phenomenon and that in the long run it is essentially a vertical line. And this, in its turn, implies that in the long run the authorities cannot choose, as Fig. 21.iii seems to suggest, to have a little less inflation at the cost of a little more unemployment (or vice versa).

To illustrate the nature of the argument, consider Fig. 21.v in which the wage adjustment curve has been redrawn and now has superimposed upon it a line which defines the secular rate of change in productivity per head. Since the two curves cut at X we may regard U_X as defining the percentage of unemployment at which

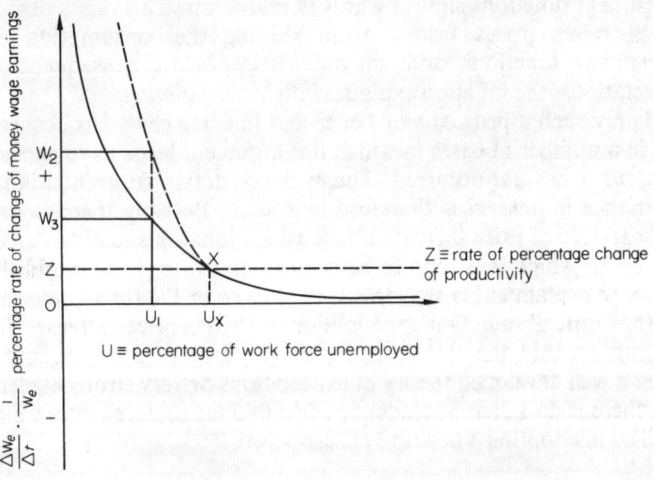

FIG. 21.v The wage adjustment curve and productivity.

the rate of change of wage costs per unit of output – and hence the rate of change of prices – is zero.

We now assume that employees expect *full* compensation for expected price changes. Hence the wage adjustment *function* is

$$w(t) = f(U) + \alpha \hat{p}(t),$$

where

$w(t) \equiv$ percentage change in wage earnings

$\hat{p}(t) \equiv$ expected percentage rate of price change

$U \equiv$ unemployment

and $\quad \alpha \equiv$ wage response to expected price change.

We are assuming $\alpha = 1$. Hence the relation can be rewritten as

$$w(t) - \hat{p}(t) = f(U)$$

that is, the expected change in real wage earnings is a function of the percentage of unemployment.

Now suppose we assume for simplicity that $\hat{p}(t) = p(t-1)$ and that the authorities raise aggregate demand so that U falls from U_X to U_1. By assumption the value of $\hat{p}(t) = p(t-1) = 0$. But at U_1 we have $w(t) >$ the rate of growth of productivity. Hence wage costs per unit of output rise and employers mark up prices. In the next period, if U is maintained at U_1, employees demand compensation for the price increase. The rate of change of wage earnings at U_1 now becomes w_2. That is, we are on a new short-run wage adjustment curve shown by the dotted line. In the next period the process repeats itself. The result, illustrated in Table 21.1, is continuously accelerating inflation.

Table 21.1 *Expectations and the Wage Adjustment Curve: Hypothetical Data*

$U_X = 6 \cdot 0$ per cent

Period	Rate of change of productivity %	Percentage unemployment %	Rate of change of money wages %	Rate of change of wage costs %	Rate of change of prices %	Expected change in real wage %	Actual change in real wage %
0	3·0	4·0	6·0	3·0	3·0	6·0	3·0
1	3·0	4·0	9·0	6·0	6·0	6·0	3·0
2	3·0	4·0	12·0	9·0	9·0	6·0	3·0
3	3·0	4·0	15·0	12·0	12·0	6·0	3·0
4	3·0	4·0	18·0	15·0	15·0	6·0	3·0
5	3·0	4·0	21·0	18·0	18·0	6·0	3·0

If this analysis is correct the apparent 'trade-off' between w and U defined by the original wage adjustment curve is a short-run phenomenon. Moreover, the only long-run *equilibrium* situation, in the sense of giving an invariant rate of price change (which may or may not be zero), can easily be shown to require $U = U_X$. This is the sense in which the 'long-run' wage adjustment curve is a vertical straight line passing through U_X.

Empirically, the important issue is the size of α – the expected price elasticity of wage earnings. Recent research suggests that both in the United Kingdom and the United States α is well below unity – indeed in the neighbourhood of the results suggested by the Dicks-Mireaux model.

These results, however, need to be treated with great caution – particularly in relation to very recent experience – for expected rates of price increase are difficult to measure and the simple forms of model employed may obscure the possible influence of 'critical' values to which we have already referred. Nevertheless, until further evidence appears, we are entitled to retain the cautious scepticism on the expectations issue which we expressed in Section 7.

Nevertheless, since the price/wage models of the type discussed in Section 4 perform poorly in recent years, it is clear that we cannot be very confident that we have, as yet, any reliable theory of wage/price behaviour.

9 SUMMARY

In this chapter we have set out an operational theory which seeks to explain the rate at which prices have increased in the U.K. in the post-war period. The resultant theory consists in the following propositions:

   (i) the rate of change of prices depends upon the rate of change in:

     (*a*) wage earnings;
     (*b*) import prices;
     (*c*) productivity;

  (ii) the rate of change of wage earnings depends upon the rate of change in the wage rates;

 (iii) the rate of change of wage rates depends upon the excess demand for labour and past rates of price increase.

Stated thus the theory can be made compatible with either *cost-push* or *demand-pull* interpretations. Of the two we have preferred the former. *The choice, as we have seen, is a critical one for policy.*

In this theory three variables, the rates of change in import prices and productivity and the *level* of excess demand for labour, are treated as exogenous. There is no analysis of any feedback from the rate of price/wage increase to excess demand for labour (aggregate demand) or the rate of change in productivity. The system must therefore be interpreted as incomplete. Contrary to many familiar arguments there is no strong evidence to suggest that inflations, if left unchecked by discretionary action, tend to accelerate or that the price level will, if inflation once begins, rise for ever. Modern economies, even where they do not engage extensively in international trade, contain a number of automatic stabilisers though these may be slow to operate.

Finally recent experience in the United Kingdom suggests that the theory set out above is unsatisfactory and that a more complex theory needs to be developed.

QUESTIONS AND EXERCISES

1. 'If we operated the economy *continuously* at around $2\frac{1}{2}$ per cent unemployment we would have a slower rate of price increase, faster growth and fewer balance of payments problems.' What assumptions are necessary to justify this statement? Do you agree with them? Have you any *evidence* for doing so?

2. 'Even if we kept the annual rate of increase in earnings exactly equal to the trend rate of increase in productivity, the 'cycle' and the 'ratchet' would still give us rising prices.' Explain and discuss.

3. 'Our price indexes make no allowance for improvements in the quality of goods. If proper allowance were made for this the apparent rate of price increase might easily be halved.' Discuss. If this proposition was correct would it be important? If so, in what contexts?

4. 'According to equation (21.XIVn) wage earners require in the short-run only about 0·5 per cent increase in money wages as a result of a 1·0 per cent increase in prices. Those who will believe this will believe anything.' Discuss the Dicks-Mireaux estimate in the light of this criticism. What is your interpretation of the constant term (3·90) in equation (21.XIVn)? Does it modify your view?

5. 'Full employment and union wage bargaining inevitably entail wage-inflation. One must go. The real question is which.' Discuss.

6. 'Ultimately – unless the nominal money supply is persistently increased – inflation of whatever kind must come to a stop.' Do you agree?

7. 'Inflation makes no-one better off.' Do you agree?

8. Reconstruct the curve in Fig. 21.v in terms of the rate of change of real wage earnings. Must it cut the horizontal line defining the secular growth in productivity? Examine the consequences of its failing to do so. What are the distributional implications?

9. 'The rate of price increase depends crucially upon the rate of increase in productivity. This is what we should be worrying about – not the rate of wage increases.' (trade union official). Discuss.

10. How would you seek to calculate the annual cost of operating the economy at $2\frac{1}{2}$ per cent rather than $1\cdot6$ per cent unemployment? Use your answer to calculate the annual cost of seeking price stability by the methods proposed in Question 1.

11. The value $U = U_X$ in Fig. 21.v is frequently referred to as the 'natural' rate of unemployment. What would you understand by this? What is the relation between this model and the 'classical' macro-economics of Chapter 18?

12. 'The effect of a wages increase on prices is far less important than the effect of a price increase on wages.' Is it?

13. 'Inflations inevitably accelerate.' Use the price data for various countries published by the International Monetary Fund in *International Financial Statistics* to discuss this contention.

14. 'If the rate of change of wages depends upon the past behaviour of prices as well as the percentage of unemployment then, since this is certainly a cost element, the demand-pull theory is refuted.' Do you agree? Show how a demand-pull theory can be formulated to take account of this relationship.

15. 'What goes up usually comes down – a proposition which holds even for prices.' Discuss. What does the historical behaviour of British prices show?

16. 'Prices and money wages are more flexible upwards than downwards.' Do you agree? If so is this finding compatible with the Dicks-Mireaux model? If not what modifications does it suggest?

17. 'Inflation is the scarecrow of modern times. There is no objection to rising prices provided we permit a flexible rate of exchange and allow the pound to fall appropriately as prices rise.' Elucidate. Do you agree? What is meant by *appropriately*?

18. 'Eventually the "cash-balance" effect will stop any inflation.' Elucidate and appraise.

19. 'If aggregate demand is properly managed, an incomes policy is unnecessary: if it is not properly managed an incomes policy is unworkable.' Elucidate. Do you agree? Is the underlying theory testable?

20. 'Meaningful disputes about inflation are about mechanisms – not about what caused a particular period of rising prices.' Do you agree? Illustrate the distinction by an example.

21. 'The initials T.U.C. stand – as they have always stood – for Trust Us Conservatives. It is not the sober, cautious, responsible union officials who push up wage rates: it is the employers, rendered rapacious and irresponsible by the competitive system, who pull them up. Controlling inflation means controlling the employers who cause it.' Discuss.

22. 'Even if money wage earnings always rose precisely at the rate recommended, since the rate of change of productivity differs between industries, prices would still rise. Two equation models of rising prices are too aggregative to be helpful.' Elucidate and discuss.

23. 'More output has been wasted in attempts to moderate inflation than in any other single way.' Examine this contention in the light of U.K. experience in 1970–2.

24. The model sketched in Section 8 can be written:

$$p(t) = w(t) - X$$
$$w(t) = f(U) + \alpha \hat{p}(t)$$
$$\hat{p}(t) = p(t-1)$$

where $X \equiv$ secular rate of change of productivity.

Show that for a constant rate of price change ($p(t) = p(t-1)$) we must, with $\alpha = 1$, have $U = U_X$. Investigate and explain the consequences of $\alpha < 1$.

25. What, if anything, do you understand by the term 'incomes policy'? What is its relevance (i) in theory and (ii) in practice, to the problem of rising prices?

26. Suppose the model of Section 8 holds *and* $U = U_X$ in all periods. Does it then follow that $p(t) = p(t-1) =$ zero? If so, why? If not, what mechanisms would you recommend to ensure it?

SUGGESTED READING

J. C. R. Dow, *The Management of the British Economy, 1945–1960* (Cambridge, 1964).

F. W. Paish, *Studies in an Inflationary Economy* (Macmillan, 1962) ch. xvii.

A. Marin, 'The Phillips Curve (Born 1958 – Died?)', *The Three Banks Review* (Dec 1972).

'Some Aspects of the Present Inflation', *N.I.E.S.R. Review* (Feb 1971) pp. 38–49.

O.E.C.D., *Inflation, the Present Problem* (Paris, 1970).

J. Burton, *Wage Inflation* (Macmillan, 1971).

O.E.C.D., *The Problem of Rising Prices* (Paris, 1961).

J. C. R. Dow and L. A. Dicks-Mireaux, 'Price Stability and the Policy of Deflation', *N.I.E.S.R. Review* no. 3 (1959).

W. B. Reddaway, 'Rising Prices for Ever?', *Lloyds Bank Review* (Jul 1966).

L. A. Dicks-Mireaux and J. R. Shepherd, 'The Wage Structure and Some Implications for Incomes Policy', *N.I.E.S.R. Review* no. 22 (1962).

R. G. Lipsey, *An Introduction to Positive Economics* (Weidenfeld & Nicolson, 1971) appendix to ch. xxxiii.

J. C. R. Dow,† 'An Analysis of the Generation of Price Inflation', *Oxford Economic Papers* (Oct 1956).

J. C. R. Dow and L. A. Dicks-Mireaux,† 'The Determinants of Wage Inflation: U.K., 1946–56', *Journal of the Royal Statistical Society Series A*, vol. 122 (1959).

L. A. Dicks-Mireaux,† 'The Interrelationship between Cost and Price Changes, 1946–1959', *Oxford Economic Papers*, vol. 13 (Oct 1961).

R. M. Solow,† *Price Expectations and the Behaviour of the Price Level* (Manchester Univ. Press, 1969).

† More advanced reference.

22 Economic Analysis and Economic Policy

IN Chapters 1–21 of this book we have tried to do two things. The first is to show *how* economists seek to develop – and test – theories which explain the way the economic system operates. The second is to set out those parts of macro-economic theory which, as the result of the work of many economists, now command a broad measure of general support. In short we have tried to display the methods and some of the results of positive economics.

As we saw in Chapter 2 positive economics is concerned with propositions of the form '*if X* occurs in a specified context *q then Z* occurs.' In this chapter and the next we discuss economic policy. Policy recommendations are, of course, propositions about what the authorities, or some other body, *ought* to do. In terms of Chapter 2 they are *normative propositions*. And, as we saw in that chapter each *normative proposition* concerning policy consists of three parts: first, a *value judgment* which defines the objectives considered to be desirable; second, a *theory or model* of how the economic system behaves; and third, a *recommended act of policy* which, *if* the model is correct, will in specified circumstances attain the desired objective. It follows from this that, in examining any policy recommendation, we need to ask three questions:

(i) what model or theory of *positive economics* does it assume and what reasons are there for thinking this model to be tenable?
(ii) what *value judgments* underlie the recommendation?
(iii) is the recommendation *consistent* with *both* the model *and* the desired objective? That is *if* we take the recommended action *and* the model correctly specifies the working of the economic system *will* the recommendation ensure the desired result?

Strictly speaking all policy proposals should be set out so as to distinguish clearly the objective and the model and the reasons for thinking that the recommended course of action is consistent with both. Unfortunately they usually are not. One is constantly meeting statements of the kind 'A capital gains tax would be economic folly' in which the whole process of reasoning supporting the recommendation (if there is one) has been, deliberately or inadvertently, suppressed. Occasionally the statement is put in a form in which it is alleged that (positive) economics *proves* a particular policy to be wrong. This is particularly often the case where a policy is highly controversial. For example 'Economics makes it clear that quantitative import restrictions are unsound' or 'To reimpose rent control at this time would be economic retrogression of the worst type'. This kind of statement implies something which is obviously erroneous for, as we well know, *positive economics* is simply concerned with the way in which the economic system will respond to a given stimulus. This is ultimately an issue which can be decided only by appeal to observation. In contrast we cannot tell whether the results of applying a particular stimulus are 'sound' or 'unsound', 'progressive' or 'retrogressive' by observation alone. To do this we must know the *value judgments* defining these terms. It follows that statements of the type quoted are either made in ignorance or with a deliberate intention to mislead. Whichever explanation of their origin is correct, they are plainly potentially dangerous and, as such, should be viewed with the deepest suspicion. As a *preliminary test*, whenever he meets one of them, the reader should immediately ask the questions set out at (i), (ii) and (iii) above.

Suppose we are confronted with a particular policy recommendation – let us say that in a given context S the Chancellor of the Exchequer should take some action we will call A in order to achieve some objective we call B. We then ask:

if A is done in context S will B follow?

This is an issue in positive economics. Suppose our knowledge of the working of the economic system leads us to feel confident that if A is done in context S then B *will* follow. This does not end the matter. We must also ask:

(iv) what *other results*, apart from B, will follow from action A?

(v) are *these other results* desirable or undesirable in terms of the value judgment on the basis of which policy A was recommended?

Almost invariably these two questions will show that though policy A will produce result B which is (by assumption) desirable it will also produce results B_1, B_2, B_3 which, in terms of the original value judgment, are *not* desirable. This raises two further questions.

(vi) Is result B sufficient, in terms of the value judgment scale, to compensate for the disadvantages B_1, B_2, B_3?

This, of course, is ultimately a question of value judgments – not of positive economics.

(vii) Is there some other conceivable policy (say A') which, while producing the desired result B, produces less of the undesirable results B_1, B_2, B_3.

This latter question as the reader will recognise, is again a question of *positive economics*. What we are asking is, given our knowledge of the workings of the economic system, is there a more *efficient policy* than A for producing the desired result B.

To sum up the argument thus far, confronted with a policy recommendation we must ask; first, will this policy, if carried out, produce the desired result and second, if it will, is there a more *efficient* way of producing the desired result? Looked at in this light a further conclusion of great importance emerges. This is:

all policy recommendations ultimately involve *quantitative* not merely *qualitative* estimates of their consequences.

To see this we merely have to extend our earlier example. Suppose policy A produces desirable result B and undesirable results B_1, B_2, B_3 and that policy A' produces desirable result B and undesirable results B_1, B_2, B_3. Assume that B is *defined* quantitatively – say an increase in the 'trend' rate of growth in capacity output from 3 per cent to $3\frac{1}{4}$ per cent. Then both policies are equally efficient in producing B. We cannot, however, begin to estimate their *relative overall efficiencies* until we know the *extent* to which they generate the undesirable results B_1, B_2, B_3. To choose effectively between A and A' the Chancellor must be given a full, which means a quantitative, description of the results of each. Given this, then on the basis of his value scale – which will, in some degree, reflect the value scale of the electorate – the Chancellor can make a reasoned choice between A and A'.

What then is the role of *positive economic analysis* in relation to the formation of economic policy?

Given the objective of policy, positive economic analysis is concerned to specify, in quantitative terms, the full consequences of the various courses of action which will attain the desired objective.

As we have seen an informed choice between alternative policies requires, strictly speaking, a quantitative statement of their results derived from a quantitatively estimated economic model. This explains why it is so difficult for economists to agree on policy matters even when they are agreed as to the objective at which policy is to be aimed. For, in the present state of economic knowledge, we simply do not know enough about the workings of the economic system, to make, with a high degree of confidence, precise quantitative predictions about economic behaviour and thus about the consequences of different policies. This does not make it less necessary to strive after precision. On the contrary it makes it more necessary. Where there can, legitimately, be differences in opinion as to how the economic system works, it is plainly a matter of the first importance to analyse, as precisely as possible, the nature of such differences. Indeed, only by doing this, can a test, designed to resolve the disagreement, be specified.

1 THE AIMS OF MACRO-ECONOMIC POLICY

In the United Kingdom the broad aims of economic policy, in macro-economic terms, have been and are

   (i)   the maintenance of 'full employment';
  (ii)   the maintenance of an average rate of growth in gross domestic product of 4 per cent per annum;†
 (iii)   the maintenance of 'reasonable stability' in the price level.

These aims, since the United Kingdom is very far from being a closed economy, must be pursued subject to the constraint that, over the 'cycle' in output (say $4\frac{1}{2}$–$5\frac{1}{2}$ years), the overall balance of payments must be in balance. This means that there must be no long-run tendency to external deficit and preferably, since any surplus we run is the deficit of some other country, no long-run tendency to accumulate any significant surplus.

What do we mean by 'overall balance'? Hitherto, in an attempt to achieve simplicity, we have discussed the balance of payments primarily in terms of the balance of payments on current account. In the present context, however, we need to be a little more sophisticated.

We begin by classifying the items in the balance of payments as either *autonomous* – meaning independent of the state of the balance of payments as a whole – or *accommodating* – meaning resulting from the state of the balance of the autonomous items. Exports, imports and long-term capital movements are clearly *autonomous* in this sense. Equally clearly the change in reserves and borrowing from foreign central banks under 'stand-by' or 'swap' agreements are *accommodating*. Private short-term capital movements are an awkward case since in many situations they occur precisely because the balance of the autonomous items has raised the fear of a

† This target has now passed into history.

devaluation (or the hope of an appreciation) of the rate of exchange. Nevertheless they also occur for reasons such as a variation in the interest rates ruling in London and overseas money markets which can be quite independent of the balance of autonomous items. Also outflows of 'hot' money are certainly not accommodating. Hence we shall treat them as autonomous though we need to remind ourselves that though not accommodating in the sense in which we have defined the term, they may well be influenced indirectly by the balance of other autonomous items.

In tabular form our classificatory scheme appears in Table 22.1: In this tabulation we have

$$\begin{matrix} \text{balance of} \\ \text{autonomous} \\ \text{items} \end{matrix} \equiv \begin{matrix} \text{visible} \\ \text{balance} \end{matrix} + \begin{matrix} \text{invisible} \\ \text{balance} \end{matrix} + \begin{matrix} \text{balance of} \\ \text{long-term} \\ \text{capital} \\ \text{transactions} \end{matrix} + \begin{matrix} \text{balance of private} \\ \text{autonomous short-} \\ \text{term capital flows,} \end{matrix}$$

and identify the balance of autonomous items with the concept of 'overall balance'.

Now *ex post* the balance of payments necessarily balances by definition. That is a negative balance of autonomous items (such as existed in 1966) must, to have occurred at all, have been financed *somehow* – either by borrowing abroad (involving an increase in the U.K.'s external liabilities), running down reserves or some combination of both. As part (2) of the Table shows the U.K. borrowed, in 1966, some £640 m., of which nearly £500 m. came from the International Monetary Fund and a further £104 m. from central banks in non-sterling area countries. A part of this (some £270 m.) was used to repay debt. The remainder financed the deficit (net of the balancing item) on autonomous items (−£126 m.) and an increase in reserves amounting to £246 m.

The balancing item (which is simply a residual error) arises because not all payments made to and receipts from overseas are identifiable. Hence *identifiable* receipts and *identifiable* payments do not balance. Since receipts and payments are equal by definition, the unidentified net payments (or receipts) constitute a residual error called, by convention, the 'balancing item'. Since this item arises precisely because its components *cannot* be identified, it is impossible to be dogmatic about its origin. It seems probable, however, that a positive item of some £50–£70 m. per year arises from underestimation of the current account position. The remainder probably reflects unidentified private short-term capital movements.†

† Cf. references at end of this chapter.

Table 22.1 *United Kingdom Balance of Payments, 1966*

£m.

1. Autonomous transactions
   (i) Current account

Exports	4,784	
Imports	−5,053	
Visible balance		−269
Government	−449	
Transport	29	
Travel	−97	
Other services	260	
Interest, profits and dividends	451	
Transfers	34	
Invisible balance		+160
Current account balance		−109

   (ii) Capital account

Long-term capital (a) private (net)	−84	
(b) official (net)	−155	
Balance of long-term capital transactions		−239
Short-term capital: private		
Increase in hire purchase and local authority liabilities (in sterling)	77	
Increase in U.K. banks liabilities (in sterling)	63	
Increase in trade credit received (in sterling)	12	
Increase in U.K. banks non-sterling liabilities	−30	
Balance of private short-term capital flows		122
Balance of autonomous capital items		−117
Balance of all autonomous items		−226
Residual error (balancing item)		100

2. Accommodating items

Borrowing from international organisations (mainly I.M.F.)	493
Increase in liabilities in non-sterling area currencies	−107
Increase in borrowing from foreign central banks in sterling:	
(i) sterling area countries	−163
(ii) non-sterling area countries	104
Miscellaneous official short-term capital	45
Increase in U.K. reserves	−246
Balance of accommodating items and residual	226

The reader should note that this table, though constructed from the official estimates, differs from them in that it contains an estimate of autonomous private short-term capital flows. This estimate may, or may not, be approximately correct. It has been obtained by classifying certain identifiable types of transactions as reflecting autonomous short-term capital movements. Since there is obviously room for legitimate differences of opinion as to which transactions *should* be classified in this way, alternative estimates could readily be constructed.

Our table, which the reader should carefully compare with the official balance of payments figures for 1966 and the N.I.E.S.R.'s own treatment of the balance of payments, serves to bring out a number of useful points.

It is clear that, in seeking to maintain a balance of the autonomous items on average over the cycle, the authorities have to consider the behaviour not only of the balance of visible and invisible items (the current account balance) but also the balance on long-term and short-term capital accounts. There are thus three elements in the problem of the external constraint of which one at least, the balance of private short-term capital movements, is potentially extremely volatile. It may also be destabilising in the sense that, for reasons we have already mentioned, a deficit of any magnitude on current and long-term capital account together may well generate a massive short-term outflow of what is sometimes called 'hot' money'.

Following this argument a stage further, we can see that the balance of payments constraint not only requires the autonomous items to balance on average over the cycle, but also that in any short period, say of 12 months, the *cumulative deficit* must not be such as to encourage fears of devaluation. The Macmillan expansion of 1958–60 probably brought such fears. So too did the Maudling expansion of 1963–4. In short the external constraint is doubly important for the U.K. for not only is she heavily dependent on international trade but she is also, probably to her disadvantage, an international banker subject, like any ordinary banker, to the threat of a run on the bank but, unlike most ordinary bankers, denied certain access to a reliable lender of last resort.

Thus, though we shall continue to speak of the balance of payments constraint as requiring only a balance of autonomous items over the cycle, the reader should be aware that this formulation conceals a number of awkward issues which, in practice, raise a number of correspondingly awkward problems for the authorities as they seek to control the overall balance.

Apart from the growth rate, none of Britain's economic objectives has been given an official quantitative definition. Simply to fix our ideas we shall therefore provide ourselves with arbitrary definitions as follows:

(i) 'full employment' is defined as 1·6 per cent of the work-force unemployed;

(ii) 'reasonable stability in the price level' is defined as an annual average rate of price increase ⩽ 2 per cent.

What does our knowledge of positive economics tell us about these objectives?

The first point we can derive from our model of the economy is that the objectives may be inconsistent either with each other or with the balance of payments constraint. An example, made all too familiar in recent years, readily serves to illustrate the possibility. Suppose the economy is operating at a level of unemployment of $2\frac{1}{2}$ per cent with the balance of payments in slight surplus and a rate of price increase of (say) $2\frac{1}{2}$ per cent per annum. Assume further that capacity is growing by 3 per cent per annum and productivity at $2\frac{1}{2}$ per cent – both 'trend' rates. In these circumstances to attain 'full employment' – as defined – demand must be increased in relation to capacity. Suppose this is done. The economy starts on an upswing. *During* the upswing the rate of price increase may fall below $2\frac{1}{2}$ per cent for reasons set out in Chapter 21. When 'full employment' is reached, however, the rate of price increase *must* increase for (i) the rate of productivity increase *at* full employment will not exceed $2\frac{1}{2}$ per cent for any appreciable length of time; while (ii) the rate of increase of wage earnings will be significantly greater *at* 'full employment' than at $2\frac{1}{2}$ per cent unemployment. Hence the maintenance of (as opposed to the movement to) 'full employment' may be inconsistent with 'reasonable price stability' as we have defined it.

As output rises imports rise both because of the operation of the marginal propensity to import and the import accelerator. Hence the movement *to* 'full employment' will produce a sharp deterioration on current account and possibly a large deficit on current and long-term capital account.† At 'full employment' output will again be growing at the capacity rate and 'accelerator' imports will be less than in the upswing. Imports as a whole, however, will be considerably higher, because output is higher, than they were at $2\frac{1}{2}$ per cent unemployment. The result may be a *continuing* deficit.‡

† As we have seen such a deficit may generate an outflow of short-term capital.

‡ Cf. the discussion above.

Hence *both* the maintenance of, *and* the movement to, 'full employment' may, even in the *short run*, infringe the balance of payments constraint while, if the U.K. 'full employment' rate of cost and price increase exceeds that of foreign competitors, 'full employment' will involve a persistent *long-run* tendency towards a deterioration in the external position.†

This example, derived directly from our earlier analysis, shows that in pursuing their chosen aims the U.K. authorities are rarely confronted with a simple choice. In general, aims tend to be inconsistent. The authorities therefore have to choose what priority to assign to each objective. Not everyone will accept their choice which gives, obviously enough, a considerable range for disagreement.

In the paragraph above we have introduced two new elements into the analysis. First we have spoken, without definition, of 'the authorities'. Second, we have implicitly assumed that it is the responsibility of 'the authorities' to seek to control the economy so as to achieve what we have called the *aims* of macro-economic policy. To fix our ideas we shall define the authorities as the 'central government' and interpret this latter term to include the Bank of England. Armed with this definition what of our implicit assumption?

In Chapters 7–17 we developed a static theory of aggregate demand which led to the conclusion that there was no automatic mechanism tending to bring about equilibrium at 'full employment' or any particular level of unemployment. In Chapter 20 we developed a dynamic theory of the cycle which sought to explain why, in the absence of purposeful intervention, the economy was likely to follow a fluctuating path through time. It is these two theories which provide the justification for purposeful intervention. And it is their general acceptance throughout society which has placed upon the authorities the responsibility for controlling the workings of the economic system.

In placing this responsibility upon the authorities society has also tended to make a *further* assumption much more dubious than the first. This is that, given the weapons at their disposal (which we shall discuss presently) and *the present state of positive economic analysis*, it is *possible* for the authorities to manage the economy 'successfully'. What this implies we shall consider later. At this stage it is sufficient for the reader to note that an assumption about the *capacity* of the authorities is implied in the decision to place responsibilities upon them. This brings us to our next question: what devices do the

† See the discussion of the determination of exports and imports in Chapter 13.

authorities have at their disposal by the exercise of which they may hope to attain their objectives?

2 THE INSTRUMENTS OF POLICY

It is customary to classify the means of influencing the economy at the authorities' disposal as:

  (i) monetary policy;
 (ii) fiscal policy;
(iii) exchange policy;
(iv) other forms of intervention.

(i) *Monetary policy* is defined as discretionary action undertaken by the authorities (usually through the Bank of England) designed to influence (a) the *supply* of money; (b) the *cost* of money (or interest rates); and (c) the ease with which, at any given interest rates, money can be borrowed – usually called the 'availability' of money.†

(ii) *Fiscal policy* is defined as discretionary action by the authorities to vary

(*a*) the level of government expenditure on goods and services and transfer payments; and

(*b*) the yield of taxation at any given level of output.

(iii) *Exchange policy* consists simply in discretionary variation in the rate of exchange between the pound sterling and other currencies.

(iv) *Other forms of intervention* is simply a 'catch all' which covers those forms of intervention not falling under the other three heads. The range of possibilities is considerable. At present the most important form of such intervention is the attempt to introduce, and make effective, what is called an 'incomes policy'.‡ Other policies falling under this head which are sometimes advocated are the introduction of quantitative restrictions on imports or an import surcharge.

Qualitatively speaking our analysis in Chapters 7–17 has already shown us *how* these policies influence the *equilibrium* levels of the dependent variables in the system. But, as we saw in Chapter 20, the economic system requires dynamic as well as static analysis. Qualitative information is therefore not sufficient for the successful

† For a more comprehensive discussion see the next chapter.
‡ Written in 1972.IV.

conduct of policy. The authorities, in framing their discretionary action, therefore need to know (i) the *quantitative* response of the economic system to any given stimulus; and (ii) the way in which this response develops *over time* – sometimes called the time form of the response – or the time lags. An example may help to make this clear. Suppose the economy exhibits over time a cycle of roughly regular periodicity and amplitude as well as a constant 'trend' rate of growth and that the aims of the authorities are to eliminate the cycle and to maintain 'full employment'. In terms of the Figure this means so managing the economy that, instead of moving along the heavy line *YY*, it moves along the dotted line *ff* – the 'full employment' growth curve line.

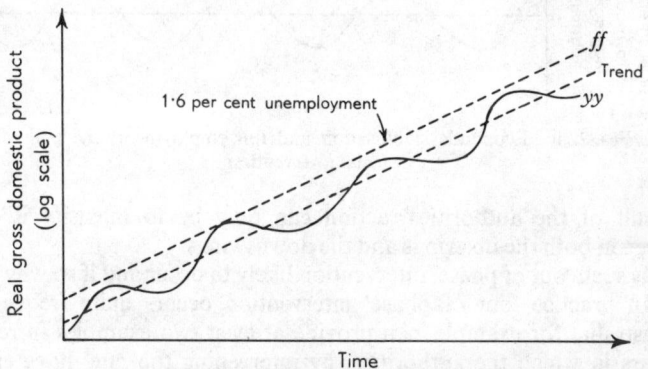

FIG. 22.i Economic stabilisation and full employment

First the authorities must raise the average level of demand so that the trend line of the future corresponds to *ff*. Then since output fluctuates with aggregate demand, to achieve their stabilisation objective the authorities must intervene, during what would otherwise be downswings, to raise aggregate demand and if the booms show any signs of generating aggregate real demand substantially in excess of full employment supply, to reduce aggregate demand. This is obvious enough. The resultant curve of necessary cyclical intervention might look something like Fig. 22.ii.

It is also obvious that the authorities must *time* their policies correctly. For if they do not there is a risk that their action will be *out of phase* with the system with the result that they intervene and *reduce* demand when it is already falling and *increase* demand when it is already rising. If this occurs, far from eliminating the cycle the

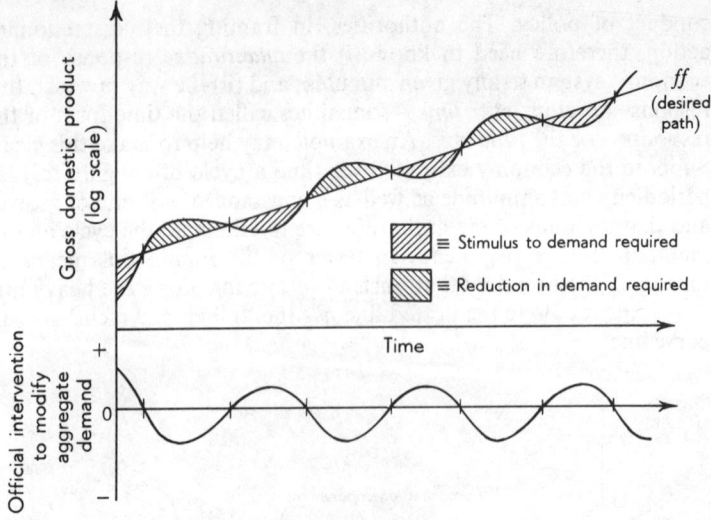

FIG. 22.ii Economic stabilisation and full employment: the path of official intervention

result of the authorities' action can only be to intensify it – to steepen both the upswings and the downswings.

Is such 'out of phase' intervention likely to occur and if so why?

In practice 'out of phase' intervention occurs quite frequently. Australia, for example, can provide at least two examples in recent years in which the authorities, by intervening too late, have either permitted inflationary booms to develop further than they need or unnecessarily deepened recessions. Why does such 'out of phase' intervention occur?

The short answer is that the conduct of economic policy in a dynamic world involves at least two types of lag. In the first place there is often a *lag* between the time at which the economy reaches a certain undesirable situation and the implementation of policies designed to correct it. This is sometimes called the 'inside lag'. In the second place there is a lag between the time at which a policy is implemented and the time at which the economic system begins to respond to official intervention – sometimes called the 'outside lag'.

An example may help to get all this clear. Suppose the authorities are attempting to stabilise the economy of Fig. 22.i by the anti-cyclical use of monetary policy. To formulate and implement intervention they must first assess the existing state of the economy: i.e., where it is in the cycle. This involves a complicated assessment of many different statistical series which are themselves only available a considerable time after the events they describe have occurred. Then they must plan – which will take further time – and obtain cabinet approval for – the monetary measures thought appropriate. Finally, they carry out the measures.

On this formulation the authorities intervene to correct an already existing deviation from the required path *ff*. That is, in terms of Fig. 22.iii they

(i) *diagnose* – at Z – the position of the economy at some past date for which statistics are available say Z_0;

(ii) *plan* intervention;

(iii) *intervene* at (say) Z_2.

If, however, the economy responds to these measures only after a significant lapse of time – that is with a significant lag – the intervention may not become effective until say Z_3. By this time, as in our Figure, it may be quite inappropriate for, in our example, the authorities will be *decreasing* demand (by decreasing the money supply and raising Bank rate) at Z_2 on the basis of a deviation from *ff* at Z_0 although, by Z_3, the time the measures take effect, the economy will have moved into its *downswing*. It follows that if the total lag involved (the sum of the 'inside' and 'outside' lags) is at all long then the authorities must act on the basis of a *forecast*. Only in this way can action be taken sufficiently in advance of the events it is planned to control.

In terms of our diagram the authorities may have to plan over, say, the period ZZ_2 to increase the money supply, reduce interest rates

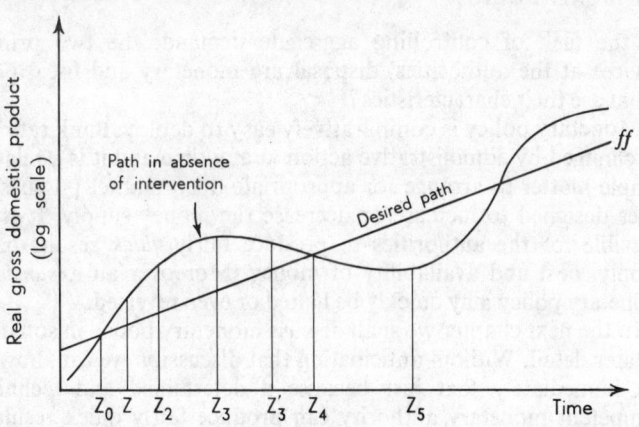

FIG. 22.iii The timing intervention

and encourage the banks to lend at Z_3 in order that aggregate demand may respond, partly through increased investment and partly through increased purchases of durable consumers' goods financed by hire purchase, at point Z_4. In short, (i) in period ZZ_2, on the basis of statistics giving (say) the situation up to and including Z_0 the authorities must *forecast* where the system would be at time Z_4 if they did *not* intervene; (ii) in period ZZ_2 they must *calculate*, on the basis of this forecast, how much and what kind of intervention to undertake; (iii) intervention must be *timed* to occur not later than Z_3 so that (iv) *after the operation of the 'outside lags'* the economy begins to respond at Z_4. Moreover, this process of diagnosis, planning intervention and actually intervening must be continuous for, as a reference to Fig. 22.iii confirms, the extent of intervention required at Z_4 is not the same as at Z_5. Hence unless the intervention at Z_4, let us say via the multiplier/accelerator, provides just the right degree of anti-cyclical impetus at Z_5 – which is unlikely – there must be further intervention at Z'_3 affecting the aggregate demand at Z_5. Hence given (i) the lag of statistical time behind calendar time; (ii) the difficulties of economic forecasting; (iii) our lack of precise quantitative knowledge regarding the 'outside lags' and (iv) the mass of ill-informed and politically motivated criticism that invariably accompanies any change in policies, it is scarcely surprising that we find instances of inadequately adjusted – or even 'out of phase' – intervention.

3 CONTROLLING AGGREGATE DEMAND: MONETARY AND FISCAL POLICY

In the task of controlling aggregate demand, the two principal devices at the authorities' disposal are monetary and fiscal policy. What are their characteristics?

Monetary policy is comparatively easy to deploy. Bank rate† can be changed by administrative action at any time and it is a relatively simple matter to arrange for appropriate open market purchases or sales designed to increase or decrease the money supply. It is thus possible for the authorities to produce fairly *quick* results on the supply, cost and availability of money. Moreover an *expansionary* monetary policy may quickly be halted or even reversed.

In the next chapter we shall discuss monetary policy in somewhat greater detail. Without anticipating that discussion we can, however, see immediately that just because a determined and technically competent monetary authority can produce fairly quick results on

† Since 1972, Minimum Lending Rate.

the supply, cost and availability of money, this does *not* ensure that the effect on the economy will be either quantitatively significant or rapid. The economic outcome must depend on the relevant parameters of the system (which are specified by our theory) including, as a matter of course, the lag parameters.

By contrast fiscal policy is more difficult to deploy. Any substantial change requires a Budget and Budgets, by tradition, occur only once a year. In special emergencies Interim Budgets are possible and have occurred. Nevertheless the political processes involved in fiscal changes are both awkward and time consuming. Fiscal policy is thus, like heavy artillery, rather slow to deploy. And it is also hard to reverse at all quickly for a Chancellor who had lowered (or raised) taxes in April would certainly face considerable political difficulties if, by August or September, he wished to raise (or lower) them again as he might well need to do.

On the other hand fiscal policy changes probably make fairly rapid impact on aggregate demand. Increases in transfer payments and reductions in direct taxation quickly affect personal disposable income and this, with perhaps a short lag, should bring about a change in consumption and start the multiplier process. Increases in government expenditure on goods and services should also have quick results. Moreover it seems possible that we can calculate the quantitative consequences of a given change in fiscal policy rather more easily than those of a given change in monetary policy simply because we know more, quantitatively, about the consumption function than the investment function. It follows that fiscal policy though harder and *slower* to deploy probably makes a more rapid and more readily predictable impact on aggregate demand. Moreover though fiscal policy, for political reasons, may be hard to reverse, if it is reversed its effects on the economy should also reverse quickly.

Since we have sadly little reliable quantitative knowledge about the characteristics of these two devices, there has been a tendency for their popularity to follow swings in fashion. Monetary policy, for example, was relatively little used between 1948 and 1951. After 1951 it enjoyed a revival. However, following the Report of the Radcliffe Committee in 1959, monetary policy has suffered in prestige and, in recent years, more emphasis has been placed upon fiscal policy. This cycle in fashion is of some interest. *But its main lesson is that we know too little about either device to reach any well supported conclusions.* Moreover monetary policy and fiscal policy are not sensibly viewed as alternatives any more than it is sensible to view the accelerator and the steering wheel as alternative devices for controlling a car. Apart from the impact of hire purchase controls monetary policy is a device or set of devices which act primarily upon planned investment in fixed capital. By contrast apart from such measures as variations in the depreciation allowances chargeable against tax, fiscal policy acts primarily upon planned consumption through variation in direct or indirect taxes. The two devices should therefore be considered as complementary rather than competitive and the problem of selection that of choosing, in any given situation, the 'best' balance of the two.

4 SUMMARY

In this chapter we have principally tried to show

  (i) the relationship between positive economic analysis and economic policy;
 (ii) the theoretical justification for official intervention in the workings of the economy; and
(iii) the difficult dynamic problems raised by any attempt at macro-economic control.

Beyond this we have sketched the objectives of British economic policy and the principal devices which the authorities can use to achieve these objectives. Finally we have given a broad outline of the principal characteristics of the two main devices by which the authorities attempt to control aggregate demand.

In the next two chapters of this book we present a particular policy *calculation*. This is designed not to show, with full benefit of hindsight, how the authorities might have done better than they did but *what is involved in determining upon a policy at all*. It is, in fact, an illustration of *method* conducted throughout in terms of the positive economic analysis we have developed. In short, now that we have devoted twenty-one chapters to developing a theory of macro-economics (and one chapter to explaining the relation of this theory to economic policy) we devote our final chapters to using it.

QUESTIONS AND EXERCISES

 1. 'The best way to encourage technological advance in Britain would be to reduce Surtax since it is those who suffer from this

tax who provide our managerial initiative.' Prepare a memo-randum for the Chancellor on this proposal setting out (i) the points you consider relevant; (ii) the kind of empirical evidence which would support (or weaken) the argument.

2. 'Since government expenditure cannot be turned on and off like a tap anti-cyclical fiscal policy is mainly a matter of varying tax rates.' Do you agree? Which taxes (or tax allowances) do you think most 'suitable' in this connection? What do you mean by 'suitable'?

3. 'Controlling output and employment is relatively easy. Controlling the balance of payments is far harder.' Discuss.

4. Prepare a Memorandum for the Prime Minister setting out the consequences of a 10 per cent devaluation of the pound.

5. 'The modern doctrine that, to check inflation, indirect taxes should be raised, is palpable nonsense. Only a lunatic or a politician would argue that the way to halt inflation is to *raise* prices. It is surprising that economists can be found to support this nonsense.' Write a reasoned defence of the 'politicians and lunatics'. Are any of the implied criticisms of their position valid?

6. 'The government ought to spend at least £100 m. a year more on education than it does for education is the most important factor making for a higher rate of economic growth.' Analyse this recommendation. What can an economist say about it?

7. 'Any attempt to increase the equality of income distribution by fiscal means would, by slowing growth, do more harm than good. Indeed there is a stronger case, if growth is a major objective, for increasing inequality.' Analyse this from the point of view of (i) positive economics; (ii) value judgments.

8. 'The rates of income tax should be capable of variation each quarter.' Do you agree? What is the relevance of this proposal to economic stabilisation?

9. 'The U.K. output cycle is due almost entirely to intervention which is from the economic point of view mis-timed. Its timing is bad because the real objective of intervention is not economic stabilisation but winning elections.' Discuss.

10. 'The best guarantee of good stabilisation policy would be to require one quarter of the House of Commons to seek re-election every 9 months.' Discuss.

11. What special difficulties for the authorities' conduct of monetary policy would arise if the 'outside lag' was half a cycle? Draw a diagram to illustrate your result.

12. Prepare (using official data) balance of payments statements

along the lines of Table 22.1 for each quarter of 1965–71. Explain and defend your method of estimating private short-term capital movements.

13. Does your statement (for Question 12) identify any periods of rapid short-term capital outflow? If it does, compare your findings with those of the N.I.E.S.R. and the official comments in *Economic Trends* and the *Bank of England Bulletin*. Are you satisfied?

14. The official balance of payments statements classify transactions by reference to the type of good, service or claim which is traded. Table 22.1 tries to classify some transactions by *motive* and is thus forced to identify certain motives with certain types of transaction. Is this so? Explain and discuss.

15. 'Table 22.1 is misleading because, in many cases, it presents estimates of *net* flows whereas, for policy purposes, what is relevant are *gross* flows.' Elucidate by using official data to compare gross and net flows. Is the distinction important for policy? Why? Give a reasoned example.

16. 'We are forced to speak of the "availability" as well as cost of money because financial institutions do not allocate funds by price but by more or less crude rationing devices.' Explain with particular reference to the concept and definition of 'availability'. Can you define a measurable index of availability?

17. Analyse the components of U.K. private long-term capital outflow. What is meant by 'portfolio' and 'direct' investment? What is the relation of each to the U.K.'s overseas capital?

18. Are the U.K.'s exports independent of her investment abroad? Can you suggest a way of obtaining evidence on this point?

19. 'Since we know so little about its working and are so reluctant to devote resources to finding out how it works, we really run the economy pretty successfully.' Do you agree?

20. 'Annual budgets are as out-of-date as sedan chairs and central bankers.' Discuss.

Suggested Reading

Radcliffe Report (H.M.S.O., 1959) ch. vi.

J. C. R. Dow, *The Management of the British Economy, 1945–1960* (Cambridge, 1964) chs, i iv, v, xiv.

P. M. Oppenheimer, 'Is Britain's Worsening Trade Gap due to Bad Management of the Business Cycle?', *Oxford Institute of Statistics Bulletin* (Aug 1965).

'The Balance of Payments: Methods of Presentation', *Bank of England Bulletin* (Dec 1964).

'Which Balance of Payments?', *Westminster Bank Review* (Dec 1964).

'Short-Term Economic Forecasting',† *Economic Trends* (Aug 1964).

M. C. Kennedy, 'How well does the National Institute forecast?', *N.I.E.S.R. Review* no. 50 (1969).

O.E.C.D., *Techniques of Economic Forecasting* (Paris, 1965) chs i, vi.

C. Drakatos,‡ 'Leading Indicators for the British Economy', *N.I.E.S.R. Review* no. 24 (1963).

R. M. Solow and J. Karecken‡ in *Stabilization Policies*§ (Prentice-Hall, 1963) pp. 1–13.

A. Ando and E. Cary Brown‡ in *Stabilization Policies*.

R. E. Caves and associates, *Britain's Economic Prospects* (Allen & Unwin, 1968) chs i–iii.

M. J. Surrey,‡ *The Analysis and Forecasting of the British Economy* (Cambridge, 1970).

† Reprinted as ch. vi of *Techniques of Economic Forecasting*.
‡ More advanced reference.
§ The remainder of this reference (pp. 14–149) is technically difficult.

23 The Model in Action: Economic Stabilisation

In the first twenty-two chapters of this book we have aimed at the gradual development of a macro-economic model sufficiently simple to be manageable without recourse to either higher mathematics or electronic computers but, at the same time, sufficiently realistic to enable us to use it to throw light upon some of the problems presently facing the British economy. In Chapter 22, we set out, in broad outline, the relationship between macro-economic models of economic behaviour and policy recommendations. In this chapter and the final two chapters of the book, we now employ the model, and the techniques of analysis which we used in building it, to analyse a particular policy problem.

We know, from Chapter 22, that the generally accepted aims of policy – which are not necessarily consistent with one another – are

(i) the maintenance of a high and stable level of employment;
(ii) the maintenance of a reasonable and steady rate of growth in domestic output;
(iii) the maintenance of a reasonable degree of price stability.

We also know that these aims have to be pursued subject to what we have called the 'balance of payments' constraint. Our method will be to look, in a specific and defined context, at one of the above problems. Our purpose in doing this is to show the model in action: to make clear what it can tell us and what it cannot.

1 ECONOMIC STABILISATION AND AGGREGATE DEMAND: CONDITIONAL FORECASTING

As we saw in Chapter 19 the attainment of the 'full employment' objective involves, strictly interpreted, the elimination of the output cycle. Less strictly interpreted it requires the damping of the cycle. This entails the control of aggregate demand by the authorities in such a way as to prevent the emergence of excess demand (or supply) for output (and hence labour) when employment is 'full' or within a defined range above or below 'full employment'. Diagrammatically our aim is to move through time as close as we can to the 'target line'

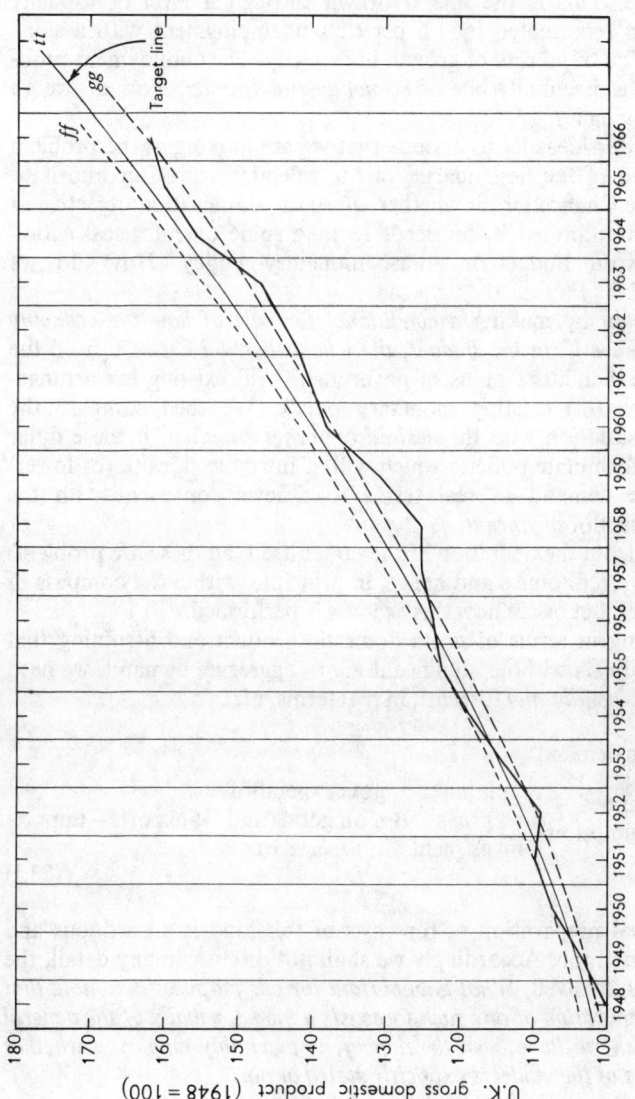

FIG. 23.i The 'target line' of the economy with a given level of unemployment at 1·6 per cent

Source: *The British Economy*

of Fig. 23.i – somewhat below the *ff* line but somewhat above the old trend line. This is the line *tt* drawn through a level of capacity utilisation represented by 1·6 per cent unemployment with a slope equal to the trend rate of growth in capacity. The employment problem is thus essentially one of *economic stabilisation*. How do we go about solving it?

To fix our ideas let us assume that we are looking at the problem at the end of the first quarter of the calendar year. Our aim is to advise the Chancellor on whether, *given* the stabilisation objective as we have interpreted it, he needs to take some overall fiscal action in his April Budget or adjust monetary policy. How do we proceed?

We begin by making *a conditional forecast of how the economy would behave if, in the Budget, the Chancellor did not modify* (i) the existing expenditure plans of government; (ii) existing tax arrangements; or (iii) existing monetary policy. We then compare the *forecast* situation with the *desired* or *target situation. If* these differ we next formulate policies which will, if introduced, raise (or lower) aggregate demand in real terms to a level consistent with the achievement of the *target*.

Apart from the definition of the target itself, all these are problems in positive economics and hence, in principle, within the compass of our model. Let us see how this exercise is performed.

Working in terms of gross domestic product and assuming that output adjusts without significant lag to aggregate demand, we need to make a *conditional* forecast, in real terms, of:

aggregate demand

$$\equiv \begin{array}{c} \text{planned} \\ \text{consumption} \end{array} + \begin{array}{c} \text{planned} \\ \text{gross} \\ \text{investment} \end{array} + \begin{array}{c} \text{govt expenditure} \\ \text{on goods and} \\ \text{services} \end{array} + \text{exports} - \text{imports}$$

(23.I)

The actual preparation of forecasts of this kind is an arduous and complicated job. Accordingly we shall not discuss, in any detail, the processes involved. *What is important for our purposes is to note that in the preparation of any such forecasts a model, usually of the general type which we have been developing, is inevitably employed whether the nature of the model is explicitly stated or not.*

To give an example. Our first task is to forecast consumption. Our theory already suggests to us that

$$C_p \equiv f[(Y - D - T + R), r, A, Q],$$

where

$Y - D \equiv$ net domestic output

$D \equiv$ depreciation

$T \equiv$ direct taxes on income

$R \equiv$ transfer receipts on income account

$r \equiv$ the rate of interest

$A \equiv$ the real value of households' assets

$Q \equiv$ an index of the availability of hire purchase finance

$C_p \equiv$ real planned consumption.

In our development of the model we found reasons for thinking that r, the rate of interest, is rather unimportant in determining C_p while A, the real value of households' assets, changes only rather slowly. Accordingly our model gives us, for a start, the *qualitative* information that we should begin our attempt to forecast consumption by forecasting personal disposable income $(Y - D - T + R)$ and the availability of H.P. finance (Q). Suppose we do this. We need also to know the *quantitative* relationship between C_p, $(Y - D - T + R)$ and Q. In short we must have a consumption hypothesis which is specified both as to form and as to the quantitative significance of the marginal response coefficients relating consumption to $(Y - D - T + R)$ and Q. If we have such a hypothesis then, from the *forecast changes* in $(Y - D - T + R)$ and Q, we can *forecast* the change in C_p. Moreover, even if we proceed directly by, say, guessing that C_p – at the end of 10 months – will be 2 per cent above its current level – we are nevertheless implicitly assuming a model and, hence, a quantitatively specified consumption hypothesis. For, to find what this is, we have only to forecast $(Y - D - T + R)$ and Q to ask, given these forecast changes in C_p, $(Y - D - T + R)$ and Q, what consumption hypothesis is implied.

Proceeding along these lines we gradually build up *conditional* forecasts of the five items on the right-hand side of (23.I). To see this process carried out in detail the reader should study carefully the *National Institute Economic Review* published by the National Institute of Economic and Social Research – particularly those (February) issues which immediately precede the April budgets. Since the N.I.E.S.R. does not explicitly specify its model, it is also a useful exercise to try to construct the N.I.E.S.R. model from its forecasts. The result of this work is a *conditional* forecast of the following kind:

Table 23.1

	1962 IV (£m. at quarterly rate)	Forecast changes		
		1962 to 1963 (per cent)	1962 IV to 1963 IV £m.	(per cent)
1. Consumers' expenditure:	4,257†	2½	110	2½
durables	(365)†	(9)	(15)	(4)
non-durables	(3,892)†	(2)	(95)	(2½)
2. (i) Gross fixed investment	1,107‡	½	35	3
(ii) Stock building	55‡		15	
3. Public authorities' current expenditure	1,070‡	5½	70	6½
4. Exports	1,345†	2½	40	3
5. Total final expenditure	7,834	3	270	3½
6. Less (i) imports	1,440†	3½	55	4
(ii) factor cost adjustment	785‡		10	
7. Gross domestic product based on expenditure estimates	5,609	3	205	3½

† Provisional estimates.
‡ Forecast or guess.

Source: Based on table 9, p. 18, in *Economic Review* (Feb 1963).

This table tells us that, in February 1963, the N.I.E.S.R. staff forecast, *assuming no change in government policy*, that gross domestic product, by the fourth quarter of 1963 would be running at a rate, in real terms, some $3\frac{1}{2}$ per cent above the rate of the fourth quarter of 1962. In terms of a diagram the situation is shown in Fig. 23.ii.

We must now *compare* the forecast G.D.P. for 1963.IV with the target G.D.P. This involves a judgment as to what the rate of expansion *ought* to be.

2 THE TARGET RATE OF EXPANSION

At first sight it seems relatively easy to calculate what the target rate of expansion *ought* to be. We possess, for example, an *estimate* of the rate of growth of capacity. Hence we might calculate the target rate

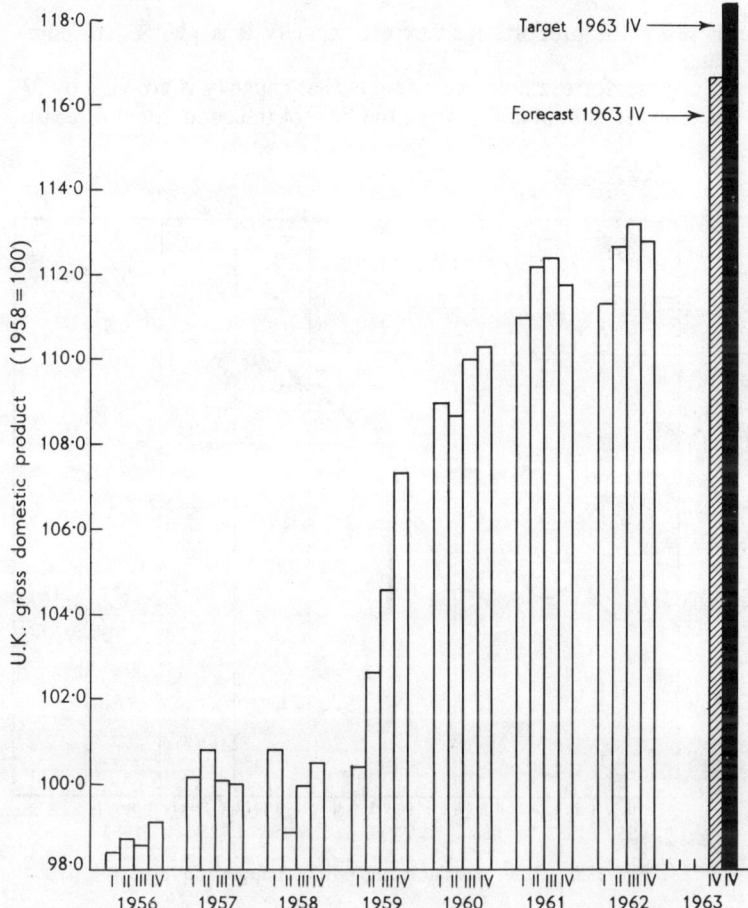

FIG. 23.ii Conditional forecast and target of U.K. gross domestic product

Sources: *National Institute Economic Review* (Feb 1963) and Godley and Gillion, *N.I.E.R.* (Feb 1964)

of growth of demand at this estimated rate. On the other hand if some part of existing capacity is not in use, it seems reasonable to add to the target rate some allowance for the desired reduction in excess capacity. Hence we have

$$\begin{array}{l} \text{target rate} \\ \text{of growth} \end{array} \equiv \begin{array}{l} \text{estimated rate} \\ \text{of growth of} \\ \text{capacity} \end{array} + \alpha \left[\begin{array}{l} \text{target capacity} \\ \text{utilisation} \end{array} - \begin{array}{l} \text{existing capacity} \\ \text{utilisation} \end{array} \right]$$

where $\alpha \equiv$ the proportion of excess capacity it is planned to eliminate.

Suppose, for example, we estimate that capacity is growing by $3\frac{1}{2}$ per cent per annum and that, at the time of the conditional forecast,

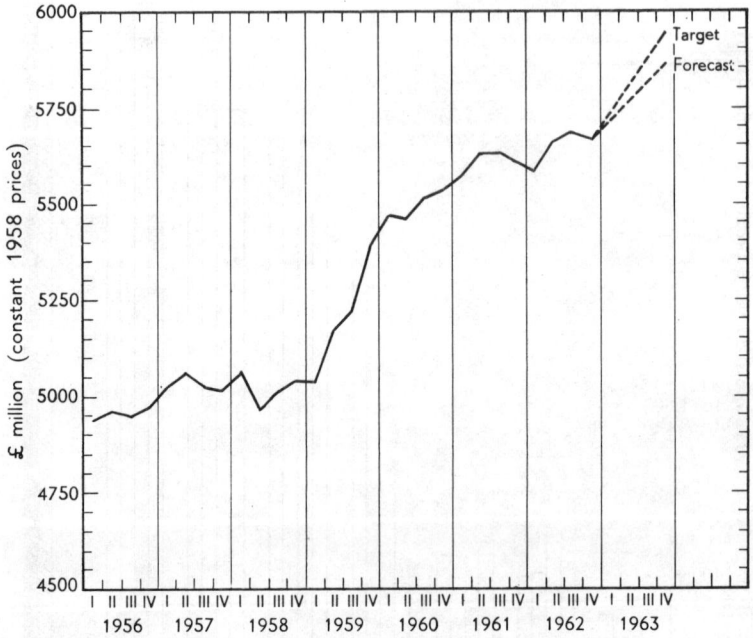

FIG. 23.iii U.K. gross domestic product: target and forecast

Source: Calculations based on Godley and Gillion, *National Institute Economic Review* (Feb 1964)

the difference between target excess capacity (zero by definition) and existing excess capacity is $1\frac{1}{2}$ per cent. Then *if* we seek to eliminate the whole of the excess capacity (by increasing demand and reducing unemployment)† we shall need to aim at 5 per cent growth over the period. Thus, given our target line (*tt* in Fig. 23.i), the estimated rate of growth of capacity (the slope of the line) and the extent to which

† i.e. put $\alpha = 1$.

the economy is currently operating *below* the line *tt*, we can calculate, simply as a piece of arithmetic, the target rate of expansion in G.D.P. for the period for which we are concerned. This calculation, of course, is no better than the value judgment (the position of *tt*) and data on which it is based. However given this target rate of growth (which for the period we are discussing, N.I.E.S.R. put at 5 per cent) we can now calculate that to meet it demand (and hence G.D.P.) should, by the fourth quarter of 1963, be 5 per cent above its level in the fourth quarter of 1962 and thus $1\frac{1}{2}$ per cent above our conditional forecast of the level which will rule in the fourth quarter of 1963 if the authorities maintain their existing policies. If we accept this target then clearly the problem for the authorities is to change their policies (monetary and/or fiscal) in such a way that, over the ten months between the 1963 Budget and the fourth quarter of 1963, demand (and hence output) expands by an additional $1\frac{1}{2}$ per cent.† The conditional forecast has thus defined, given the target, the qualitative and quantitative changes that are needed in demand.

3 THE EXTERNAL CONSTRAINT

As we have earlier pointed out the growth and unemployment (or capacity) objectives of policy have to be pursued subject to the external constraint – namely that, on average over the cycle, autonomous items in the balance of payments must balance and, in any short period, the cumulative deficit must not be such as to raise expectations of a devaluation and thus promote the outflow of 'hot' money.

A conditional balance of payments forecast can be made along lines similar to those employed to construct the G.D.P. forecast. Indeed a conditional forecast of the current account balance is *implied* in the conditional G.D.P. forecast. To this must be added conditional forecasts of (i) the balance on long-term capital account and (ii) the balance of autonomous short-term capital movements. We have, in earlier chapters, developed no theory to explain either of these elements and to attempt to do so now would take us too far afield. It is plausible, however, to argue that autonomous short-term capital movements (i.e. non accommodating and non 'hot' money) will depend upon what is called the 'covered interest margin' between

† The reader should note that we are here assuming that there is no output lag.

London and overseas financial centres. This 'covered interest margin' between London and, say, New York consists in three elements:

    (i) the short-term rate ruling in London;
   (ii) the short-term rate ruling in New York; and
  (iii) the cost of exchange cover.

For example if the short-term rate in London is 5 per cent per annum and in New York 3 per cent per annum while the forward premium on dollars in terms of pounds (discount on pounds in terms of dollars) is 2 per cent per annum, then the covered interest margin is zero. We then have the definition:

$$\begin{matrix} \text{covered interest} \\ \text{margin} \end{matrix} \equiv \begin{matrix} \text{short rate in} \\ \text{London} \end{matrix} - \begin{matrix} \text{short rate in} \\ \text{New York} \end{matrix} - \begin{matrix} \text{cost of exchange} \\ \text{cover} \end{matrix}$$

$$\equiv 5 \cdot 0\% \qquad -3 \cdot 0\% \qquad -2 \cdot 0\%$$

This cost of exchange cover simply arises because, say, a U.S. bank moving 2·4 million dollars to London today to take advantage of a differential in short rates over a period of, say, 3 months, must, in order to be sure of maintaining its dollar holding intact at the end of the period, *sell* an equivalent (£1 m.) of sterling for dollars to be delivered in *three months' time*. If these forward dollars can only be purchased at a *premium* (in terms of pounds) – that is at a rate *less* than $2·40 to the £1 – then the capital loss incurred, in terms of dollars, is the cost which the bank must pay to cover the exchange risk. Once the sterling proceeds of the dollar inflow have been sold forward for dollars to be delivered in three months, the risk of exchange loss is removed.

For any given value of interest rates and the cost of exchange cover – that is for a given covered interest margin – it is possible in principle to make an estimate of what we have called autonomous short-term capital movements. This is a conditional forecast similar to those already made for current account items. Assuming conditional forecasts of net movements of long-term capital also to be available, we can then construct a conditional forecast of the balance of autonomous items. Because of the cumulative nature of one aspect of the external constraint conditional forecasts are not usually presented simply as a rate ruling in some single period, in this case the fourth quarter of 1963, but over the period which elapses up to and including the target period – in this case the year 1963.

To give an illustration of this process we present in Table 23.2, a conditional forecast of the balance of autonomous items on external account for the first and second halves of 1963. This forecast, for consistency, assumes the same unchanged policies as the G.D.P. forecast of Table 23.1.

Table 23.2   *U.K. Balance of Payments, Conditional Forecast*

	1963		
	First half	Second half	Year
Autonomous transaction			
(i) Current account			
Exports	2,100	2,130	4,230
Imports	2,100	2,175	4,275
Visible balance	nil	−45	−45
Invisible balance	60	40	100
Current account balance	60	−5	55
(ii) Capital account			
Long-term capital (net)	−60	−100	−160
Private short-term capital (net)	−50	−45	−95
Balance of autonomous capital items	−110	−145	−255
(iii) Balancing item	100	80	180
(iv) Forecast balance of autonomous transactions	50	−70	−20

Source: Author's forecasts.

According to this forecast, which has been constructed in a manner very similar to that used by N.I.E.S.R., the outcome of 3½ per cent growth in G.D.P. should, over 1963, be an approximate balance of autonomous items. However, if policy is to be adjusted to obtain the 5 per cent growth calculated as the target rate of expansion for G.D.P., there will clearly be an increase in imports both on account of the higher level of G.D.P. in the fourth quarter and on account of the operation of the stock accelerator. Hence if policies were to be adjusted to meet the G.D.P. target, the balance of autonomous items over 1963 would probably be negative and the deficit of the order of £50–£70 m.

At this point a judgment has to be made as to whether, given the conditional forecast of the balance of payments, the external constraint permits acceptance of 5 per cent growth or even 3½ per cent growth in G.D.P. This judgment involves not only the forecasts and their accuracy but also the precise interpretation placed on and importance assigned to the external constraint. To put the same point in a slightly different way, it involves balancing the risk of a small overall deficit in 1963 (and a rate of expenditure which implies a deficit in the fourth quarter of 1963) against the attraction of an additional 1½ per cent of growth. Quite apart from the question of the value judgments of the authorities, the margin of uncertainty attaching to these forecasts – and particularly those of the balance of payments – means that a decision on this issue cannot be made with any measure of dogmatism. Even between persons with an *identical* relative valuation of the importance of growth and external balance (that is an identical value scale) diametrically opposed views may legitimately prevail. Positive economics can be used to generate conditional forecasts of what will occur in certain specified circumstances. But because of our lack of quantitative knowledge about the workings of the economy, the range of error in these forecasts is considerable. Our estimate of the deficit for 1963 is, for example, £50 m. Equally plausible estimates might raise this to £100 m. or reduce it to zero. It is not, therefore, as is all too frequently assumed, always a simple matter to determine what, qualitatively and quantitatively, *ought* to be done. The reader, in short, should not be misled, by the appearance of Tables 23.1 and 23.2, into assigning to the forecasts they record a degree of precision which they do not possess.

Though in practice, as we have seen, the decision may not be an easy one to make, we shall assume that, on the basis of our two conditional forecasts, (i) it is reasonable to accept the rate of external deficit which we forecast as the result of the 5 per cent growth in G.D.P., and hence (ii) the essential problem is to devise appropriate methods of adjusting demand so as to raise G.D.P. in the fourth quarter of 1963 to a level 1½ per cent above its forecast value.

4 THE SELECTION OF POLICIES

As a result of our conditional forecasts and the relative importance we attach to growth and external balance we now agree that we need a policy which will increase G.D.P. in the fourth quarter of 1963 by 1½ per cent: that is, from the conditionally forecast quarterly rate of £5,804 m. to £5,891 m. For simplicity we shall interpret this increase in round numbers as £90 m. We now have to select policies which will increase demand by this amount.

Clearly the number of possible ways of doing this are infinite. Thus, for example, since we can use either monetary policy alone, fiscal policy alone or any combination of the two, the theoretically possible 'mixes' are endless. We already know, from our earlier discussion in Chapter 12 that there are an infinite variety of fiscal policies alone which can bring about a given increase in demand. Hence at the theoretical level, though we now have a qualitative and quantitative specification of our problem, we are a long way from being able to decide precisely what policy to recommend.

As we have argued before, the authorities can only make a

sensible choice between alternative policies if the full outcome of each is specified qualitatively and quantitatively. In accordance with this line of thought, we shall devote the next two Chapters to examining, first, what is involved in formulating monetary (or fiscal) policies compatible with the G.D.P. target, and second, how the consequences of these policies can be compared.

QUESTIONS AND EXERCISES

1. Are 'conditional forecasts' testable in whole or in part? If so, how? What do you think is meant by the 'accuracy' of conditional forecasts?
2. Suppose the economy, because of appropriate policy changes, reaches the target level of G.D.P. What would you expect to happen to (i) unemployment; (ii) the rate of change in productivity; (iii) the rate of change of prices? Give your reasons. Would you still accept the target of 5 per cent growth in G.D.P.?
3. If the growth of the economy along the line *tt* of Fig. 23.i involved a permanent excess of autonomous external payments over receipts what policy or policies would you advocate? Why?
4. Write an essay setting out the reasoning on which the N.I.E.S.R. staff produced the G.D.P. forecasts set out in Table 23.1. What account can you give of (i) the structure, and (ii) the marginal response coefficients of the N.I.E.S.R. model?
5. What are the main lessons to be derived from N.I.E.S.R.'s review of its own forecasts? [*Economic Review*, no. 15 (1961)].
6. Construct a table showing the last four quarters' rates of private investment in fixed capital. Prepare conditional forecasts for the quarter a year ahead of the last quarter for which you have data. Explain carefully how your forecasts were obtained. On what conditions (assumptions) are they based?
7. You are asked to advise a Swiss banker as to whether he should hold £10 m. of short-term funds in sterling, dollars or Swiss francs over the next 12 months. Write a memorandum setting out your reasons for offering the advice you do. You may assume that your banker is not necessarily opposed to speculation – if the conditions are right.
8. From the *Bank of England Bulletin* construct a graph showing (i) the covered interest margin in favour of (or against) sterling; and (ii) the interest margin neglecting the cost of exchange cover. Interpret the results.

9. Suppose short-rates in London to be raised by 2 per cent. What consequences would you forecast for the balance of payments? Which items would be affected? Give your reasons.

10. 'A rise in Bank Rate discouraged "hot" money outflows.' Discuss with particular reference to the meaning of 'hot' money.

11. Write a short account of the sterling crisis of 1957. Does this throw any light on your answer to Question 10?

12. 'The forward price of dollars depends on the willingness of the British authorities to sell dollars forward whenever they are required. Hence official intervention in the forward market is an alternative to raising short-term interest rates in London.' Elucidate and discuss with particular reference to the Radcliffe Report.

13. In view of the incidence of capital gains (and losses) on the stock market how far is an assumption that the real value of household assets changes only slowly in the short-run valid? How would you seek to estimate capital gains (losses)?

14. Apply the methods of Chapter 23 to the N.I.E.S.R. forecasts and policy discussions in 1971 and 1972. (February issues in each year.)

15. On the basis of your answer to Question 14, put forward what you believe to be an appropriate macro-economic policy for 1971–2 and 1972–3. Compare your recommendations with (a) the policies recommended by N.I.E.S.R. and (b) the policies followed by the authorities.

SUGGESTED READING

J. C. R. Dow, *The Management of the British Economy, 1945–1960* (Cambridge, 1964) chs i–vi.

N.I.E.S.R. Review, annual surveys of the economy in February issues.

J. M. Fleming and R. C. Tress, 'Waiting for Exports', *London & Cambridge Economic Bulletin* (Jun 1962).

O.E.C.D., *Techniques of Economic Forecasting* (Paris, 1965) chs i, vi.

M. J. C. Surrey,† *The Analysis and Forecasting of the British Economy* (Cambridge, 1971).

J. Tinbergen,† *Economic Policy: Principles and Design* (Amsterdam, 1956) chs i–iii.

E. Lundberg,† *Business Cycles and Economic Policy* (Allen & Unwin, 1957) ch. viii and appendix.

† More advanced reference.

24 Economic Stabilisation: The Use of Monetary Policy †

OUR purpose in this chapter is to consider the way in which monetary policy influences aggregate demand and how far monetary measures can be used to generate the additional £90 m. of demand we require in the fourth quarter of 1963.

Let us begin by recalling (i) how monetary policy operates: that is, the variables which the monetary authority can influence; and (ii) the ways in which, according to our theory, manipulation of these variables may influence aggregate demand and the balance of payments.

1 MONETARY VARIABLES

As we outlined earlier, monetary policy works by influencing (i) the supply of money; (ii) the interest rate (or cost of money); and (iii) the availability of money.

The money supply we have already defined. And in earlier chapters we defined the rate of interest as the rate of return on British government irredeemable bonds. This definition, useful enough in developing our simple model, we must now elaborate distinguishing in particular between rates of interest which are determined administratively (i.e. fixed by some financial institution such as a bank) and those which are determined by the daily inter-action of demand and supply in a market (such as the rate on irredeemables). The former, by convention, are often related to Bank Rate and respond only slowly, if at all, to situations of excess demand or supply. The latter are explained by market processes. This does *not* mean that we regard the two sets of rates as entirely independent of one another. But simply that, over a limited range, a measure of independence probably exists. Thus we can argue that (i) market rates are related to the demand for and supply of money – as explained in Chapter 11 – and can be identified with the rate on British government irredeemables, while (ii) administered rates respond little to excess demand (supply) situations and are often related to Bank Rate. The significance of this distinction is that in operating upon them the monetary authority has to take different

† This chapter relates to the situation before September 1971.

actions and its degree of immediate control is probably greater over the latter than the former.

The 'cost of money' thus reflects both types of rate.

The 'availability of money' we define as the ease with which, at any given rate of interest, money can be borrowed from financial institutions. We need to introduce this concept because the market for loans is not perfect. When a bank, for whatever reasons, is curtailing loans and advances, it rations advances, at a (broadly) invariant interest rate, between competing borrowers. A borrower denied an advance when the overdraft rate is 6 per cent will not get one by offering to pay 8–9 per cent. The rate charged (i.e. the price of the loan) is not an allocative device as it is in a competitive market where, in accordance with the usual demand and supply apparatus, the available funds go to those who (assuming that they are equally acceptable risks) are able and willing to pay a price sufficiently high to clear the market. 'Availability', in short, reflects the degree of severity of rationing in the loan market. It is the counterpart of the concept of 'administered' rates which do not respond quickly, if at all, to the usual forces of demand and supply.

These then are the principal variables (which we shall call the 'monetary variables') through which the monetary authority may seek to influence aggregate demand and the balance of payments. Before we ask how the monetary authority can vary them, let us recall how, according to our model, variation of them would effect aggregate demand and the external position. In examining this problem we shall, consistently with the theory of Chapter 11, treat the market rate of interest as being determined by the supply of and demand for money. Hence the influence of the former variable will be assumed to make its impact on expenditure mainly through market interest rates.

If the money supply influences expenditure mainly via interest rates what is the logic of listing it as a separate monetary variable? To this question there are two answers. The first is that *mainly* does not mean *exclusively*. As we shall see later, the availability of bank advances may depend on the money supply and there are other less direct and obvious ways in which the money supply may exert an influence. The second answer is that the explicit inclusion of both market rates and the money supply reminds us that the monetary authority can control one or the other but not both. In practice, therefore, the monetary authority will have to choose between aiming at a target set of market rates (and providing the public with whatever money supply it demands at these rates) or aiming at a target money supply (and letting the public determine the rates at which the target supply will be held). Explicit mention of both variables is a constant reminder of this awkward and very real policy dilemma.

2 MONETARY VARIABLES AND AGGREGATE DEMAND: A PRELIMINARY SKETCH

Of the variables which make up aggregate demand, our theory suggests that exports and imports will certainly be unaffected directly by variations in the supply, cost and availability of money. Of course if monetary policy changes aggregate demand (through some other component) imports will certainly be affected and exports may be.† But the issue here is whether a change in one or more of the monetary variables will *shift* the import function. According to our theory there is no reason to expect such an outcome. Nor is there any reason to expect a change in export demands.

What of government expenditure on goods and services? This is usually taken to be an exogenous variable determined by policy considerations. It is, indeed, unlikely that the authorities will seek to restrain their own expenditure on goods and services by raising the rate of interest against themselves. We may thus neglect the influence of monetary measures on public sector expenditure on goods and services.‡

In addition to government expenditure on goods and services we also have to consider the possible influence of monetary policy on:

$T \equiv$ direct taxation receipts

$R \equiv$ transfer payments

$T_i \equiv$ indirect tax receipts.

As we know, personal disposable income is defined as $(Y - D - T + R)$. Hence, since consumption is a function of P.D.I., if changes in the monetary variables affect T and/or R they will, via P.D.I., influence the consumption/national income relationship. There seems, however, no good reason to expect transfers (R) to respond to changes in the monetary variables since like government expenditure on goods and services, these are determined primarily by social policy. A small, quantitatively insignificant effect exists because any rise (fall)

† These are, in our earlier terminology, *induced* effects.
‡ It is possible, although the evidence is sketchy, that local authorities' expenditure may respond to changes in the interest rate.

in interest rates which *includes* short-term rates must cause a rise (fall) in the amount paid out as national debt interest. However unless the government covers these additional payments by taxation the overall budget position must change – which is logically part of fiscal policy. In any case since interest receipts are subject to tax, the net effect is likely to be small. Hence, even if we do not, as a matter of logic, classify this possibility as falling under fiscal policy we can argue that, in practice, it is likely to be quantitatively insignificant.

The yield of indirect taxes (T_i) depends as a first approximation upon the structure of indirect taxes and gross national expenditure. Changes in the latter can only be *induced*; hence the relevant variation in T_i is restricted to that arising out of changes in the indirect tax structure arising out of changes in monetary variables. This tax structure is, of course, a matter of fiscal policy. We can therefore regard it as invariant.

In our earlier sketch of the operation of the public sector we treated receipts from direct taxes (T) as an exogenous element in our model, determined exclusively by government policy. In practice, of course, tax receipts are more plausibly taken to be dependent upon (i) the tax structure – an exogenous variable determined by policy – and (ii) the net national product. That is why it is common to encounter functions relating tax receipts to income. It does not seem a strong assumption to regard such a function as independent of our monetary variables.

We have now argued that imports, exports, government expenditure on goods and services and government transfers and tax receipts are all independent of monetary policy. Two conclusions follow:

(i) since imports, exports and government expenditure on goods and services are *not* influenced by monetary variables then, if monetary policy is to influence aggregate demand at all in the short-run it must be by influencing consumption and/or private investment;

(ii) since government expenditure on transfers and government tax receipts are also likely, in the short-run, to be invariant with respect to monetary policy, any influence the latter exerts on consumption cannot come about through a shift in the relationship between personal disposable income and national product.

We now look at the potential influence of monetary policy on consumption and private investment in somewhat greater detail.

3 MONETARY POLICY AND CONSUMPTION

Our consumption hypothesis can be written:

$$C_p = H + c(Y - D - T + R) + d.r^* + e.Q + f.A,$$

where

$H \equiv$ autonomous consumption

$Y \equiv$ gross national product (at factor cost)

$D \equiv$ depreciation

$R \equiv$ transfer payments to households

$T \equiv$ direct taxes on persons

$r^* \equiv$ an index of interest rates reflecting both market rates (r_m) and administered rates (r_a)

$Q \equiv$ an index of the availability of hire purchase finance

$A \equiv$ real value of household assets

$(Y - D - T + R) \equiv$ personal disposable income,

and the marginal response coefficients are

$\dfrac{\partial C_p}{\partial (Y - D - T + R)} \equiv c \equiv$ marginal propensity to consume out of personal disposable income

$\dfrac{\partial C_p}{\partial r^*} \equiv d \equiv$ marginal response coefficient relating consumption to interest

$\dfrac{\partial C_p}{\partial Q} \equiv e \equiv$ marginal response coefficient relating consumption to the index of the availability of hire-purchase finance

$\dfrac{\partial C_p}{\partial A} \equiv f \equiv$ marginal propensity to consume out of changes in the real value of household assets.

By our earlier reasoning personal disposable income $(Y - D - T + R)$ is unaffected by monetary policy. Hence *if* monetary policy influences C_p (real planned consumption) it must do so through its influence on r^*, Q and A. Looking at the problem in terms of a static analysis – we shall consider the dynamic complications later – two issues are involved, namely (i) the technical ability of the monetary authority to manipulate r^*, Q and A; and (ii) the magnitude of the marginal response coefficients. For the moment we shall postpone consideration of the technical capacity of the monetary authority. We now look at the marginal response coefficients.

Suppose the monetary authority succeeds in raising r^*, what are the consequences? For a household with no assets ($A = $ zero) an increase in r^* amounts to an increase in the rate of return on saving which is held in a form other than money. We have already argued that there is no *a priori* reason for such a change to increase rather than decrease the rate of saving. Hence where $A = $ zero by assumption our theoretical expectation is that d (the marginal response coefficient) is of uncertain sign and probably very small in absolute value. There is no very systematic statistical evidence on this point in the United Kingdom. Nevertheless it is supported by studies in the U.S.A. and it was substantially the conclusion of the Radcliffe Committee.

In general, of course, A will be positive and will consist in households' holdings of financial claims and real assets. To simplify let us assume that the real value of households' assets is given by:

$$A \equiv \frac{M_h}{p} + \frac{NM_h}{p} + \frac{B_h}{p} + \frac{E_h}{p} + K_h,$$

where

$M_h \equiv$ households' nominal money holdings

$NM_h \equiv$ households' nominal near-money holdings

$B_h \equiv$ the market value of households' bond holdings

$E_h \equiv$ the market value of households' equity holdings

$K_h \equiv$ households' real assets

$p \equiv$ the price level.

Now M_h, NM_h and K_h will be invariant with respect to r^* since they have a fixed monetary value. B_h and E_h on the contrary will not be. As regards B_h since the price of a bond is inversely related to r_m, an increase in r_m reduces B_h and thus the real value of bond holdings. What determines the market value of equity shares? As a first approximation we can regard this as being dependent upon the expected profits of companies and the rate at which the market capitalises these profits. This implies that the value of an equity in the market is given by:

$$E = \frac{Q_1}{1+\hat{r}} + \frac{Q_2}{(1+\hat{r})^2} + \dots + \frac{Q_n}{(1+\hat{r})^n},$$

the familiar present value formula of Chapter 10. If, as seems reasonable, the subjective rate $(\hat{r})$ employed by the market *varies* with r_m, then a rise in r_m *must* reduce E_h by raising the subjective discount rate $(\hat{r})$ and *may* reduce E_h by reducing the expected profits Q_1, $Q_2...Q_n$. In short a rise in r_m probably inflicts capital losses (which may or may not be realised) on those who hold marketable claims. The effect of r_m thus depends not only on the marginal response coefficient (d) (which assumes A to be constant) but also the marginal response coefficient (f) and the extent to which A falls as r_m rises.

Estimates (according to J. C. R. Dow) suggest that in some years the change in A due to the change in the rate of interest has been large. In 1951, for example, A *declined* on this account by an estimated £1500 m. while in 1959 it rose by an estimated £750 m. Thus even if the marginal response coefficient (f) is quite small – say of the order of 0·1, consumption in 1951 would have fallen on this account by £150 m. and in 1959 risen by £75 m. These are sizeable effects for £150 m. was more than $\frac{1}{2}$ percent of gross domestic product on an annual basis.

Unfortunately we have no very convincing evidence about the magnitude of the relevant marginal response coefficient. The prevailing view seems to be that it is small but the evidence on which this is based is slender. A reasonable tentative hypothesis would suggest that $f \equiv \partial C_p / \partial A \leqslant 0\cdot1$ and is certainly greater than zero. This issue certainly merits further research.

Now consider the variable Q which we have defined as the availability of hire-purchase finance.† This is varied, as the reader will know, by increasing (decreasing) the minimum deposit which must be made by the purchaser and decreasing (increasing) the maximum period over which the purchaser may repay. At the same time the rate of interest payable on his purchase borrowing also responds to changes in the market rate.

As regards the impact of a change in r^* on Q we can safely be agnostic. The 'true' rate of interest on hire purchase loans is roughly *twice* the quoted rate – a fact of which most hire purchase borrowers seem to be unaware. Moreover the interest element in the hire purchase 'interest' charge is comparatively small – much of the latter being accounted for by administrative costs and risk premia. Hence the impact of the change in r^* is negligible. On the other hand there is considerable evidence that a change in deposit and

† The reader should notice that strictly this is a matter not of 'availability' but of the *demand* for h.p. finance. We have called it 'availability' simply for convenience.

repayment terms, which we have defined as a change in 'availability', has a quantitatively significant effect. This view is supported by the Radcliffe Committee and by studies by Dow and Ball. Does this mean that the marginal response coefficient $e(\equiv \partial C_p/\partial Q)$ is large? Here we have a problem of units. Q we recall, has been defined as an index number which is presumably designed to reflect deposit and repayment terms. C_p is defined as the annual rate of consumption expenditure. The marginal response coefficient thus depends upon the construction of the index (Q) and the units in which it is expressed. This conceptual problem, however, need not detain us. The substantial conclusion is that variation in hire-purchase terms (availability) can bring about variation of the order of £100 m. or more in consumption at annual rates.

Strictly, of course, the availability of hire-purchase finance is not the only channel through which availability can influence consumption. Change in the availability of bank advances is a second potential source of influence. In formal terms the consumption hypothesis can readily be extended to include this influence though we have not done so. What is its practical importance?

The difficulty in answering this question is the difficulty (never so far satisfactorily surmounted) of defining a measurable index of the availability of bank finance. It is no use using actual advances since a fall in these may just as well reflect a reduced *demand* by the private sector as a more stringently rationed supply. Because of this awkward problem we can only follow prevailing opinion in suggesting that the quantitative impact of a reduced availability (and probably a higher price) of bank advances on consumption is probably rather small.

We can now summarise our conclusions in the form of a table.

Table 24.1

Change in monetary variable	Direction of effect on consumption (theoretical)	Quantitative estimate	Evidence
Rise in market rate of interest	(i) Direct effect: dubious	Very small	Dubious
	(ii) Capital loss effect: negative	None available Could be significant	Weak
Reduced availability of		Significant	Fairly strong
(i) hire-purchase finance	Negative	£100 m.–£150 m.	
(ii) bank finance	Negative	Small	Virtually none
Rise in administered rates on:			
(i) Hire-purchase loans	Negative	Negligible	Fair
(ii) bank advances	Negative	Negligible	Virtually none

If this table is even approximately correct two conclusions emerge:

(i) in so far as monetary policy can influence consumption at all it must be through hire-purchase availability and possibly capital losses;

(ii) despite the voluminous writings of financial journalists, the labours of the Radcliffe Committee and the endeavours of British monetary economists, we really know very little indeed about the quantitative impact, even in the static sense, of monetary policy on consumption.

In assessing any policy we need to know not only its direct effect on the target variable (in this case consumption) but its other effects for, if we do not, we cannot choose the most efficient policy but merely a feasible or workable policy. What are the principal indirect effects of the two potentially significant monetary measures?

As far as hire purchase availability is concerned, restriction falls in the main, upon the purchase of consumer durables such as cars, washing machines, T.V. sets and so on. Its industrial impact is therefore severely concentrated: in the language of the Radcliffe Committee it has *severe directional effects industrially*. In addition it has its greatest impact on the relatively less well off for, in general, the rich, even if they need to borrow to purchase consumer durables, have no need to pay the very high interest rates charged by hire-purchase companies. Hire-purchase restriction thus has severe directional effects *socially* for if the poor cannot borrow through hire-purchase it is unlikely that they can borrow at all.

There is no reason and no evidence to lead us to expect industrial directional effects from capital gains or losses. Socially, however, since the ownership of property in the U.K. is very unequally distributed, their impact is mainly on the relatively rich.

4 MONETARY VARIABLES AND PRIVATE INVESTMENT

The problem here falls into two parts: the impact of monetary policy on investment in fixed capital and its impact on investment in inventories. We begin with the former.

Our elementary theory regarded investment as being determined by the marginal efficiency of investment schedule and the market rate of interest. A slightly less elementary version introduced lenders' risk and, more significant, borrowers' risk. Our theory, however, was quite compatible with a very low interest elasticity of investment.

What we are now searching for is some evidence concerning the actual magnitude of this elasticity.

Two points are immediately clear. If firms in general calculate the marginal efficiency of capital on the basis of a short expected economic life of capital assets, the influence of the interest rate on their investment decisions will be small. For example, if funds are to be borrowed only for a week a rise in the annual rate of interest from 4 per cent to 8 per cent (a 100 per cent increase) adds less than £0·10 to the cost of a £100 loan. The second point is that where uncertainty (borrowers' risk) is at all considerable, firms will undertake investment only if the expected rate of return very considerably exceeds the interest rate. What evidence there is suggests that, for most private investment in fixed capital other than houses, the life used in calculating the marginal efficiency is rather short: probably of the order of 5–10 years. On this ground alone then we may expect a rather small response of fixed investment to interest rate changes. In addition there is evidence that firms, in order to undertake investment, require the 'expected rate of return'† to be of the order of 15 per cent or more – a figure which typically substantially exceeds the interest rate at which they can borrow. Hence on this count too, we may expect the interest elasticity of fixed investment to be small.

For a considerable time the view that the response of fixed investment to variation in the market rate of interest and to variation in administered rates was quantitatively insignificant – certainly in the *short run* and probably in the long – received general acceptance. This assessment also enjoyed considerable support from sophisticated statistical investigations. Relatively recently, however, studies in the U.S.A. have suggested that the interest elasticity of investment in fixed capital may be of the order of $-0·4$, *but that the speed of response of expenditures on investment in fixed capital to changes in the rate of interest may be very slow.* This accords well with the conclusion of the Radcliffe Committee and Dow and we shall accept it.

In assessing the effect of variations in the availability of funds from institutional lenders – such as banks, life offices and the new issue market – we meet again the difficulty discussed earlier of defining an index of availability. Moreover since it is empirically likely that

† This 'expected rate' is not, in general, calculated by firms in accordance with the marginal efficiency of capital formula but by arbitrary and often irrelevant procedures. However if businessmen compare the 15 % (however calculated) with the interest rate, our conclusion retains its acceptability.

availability declines as interest rates rise it is probable that any statistically estimated interest elasticity takes account of some of the availability effects.

Hence in sum we are left with the awkward conclusion for monetary policy that private investment in fixed capital does respond to changes in interest rates and availability but only so slowly as to make its response rather useless for the type of short-run stabilisation policy under discussion. Moreover, since investment does respond, though only very slowly, short-run variation in interest rates may have awkward longer-run consequences.

We should expect this conclusion to be modified in the case of investment in housebuilding because the expected economic life of houses is relatively long. In general the evidence supports this conclusion. However, in the United Kingdom, about half the investment in dwellings is undertaken by local authorities who are directly under government control. The investment by private developers is, however, certainly influenced both by interest rates and by the availability of funds from building societies. This restriction of availability seems to follow a rise in interest rates with a lag, principally because the building societies are slow to adjust their own rates to changes in market rates. But nevertheless it seems reasonable to expect private investment in dwellings to respond to a change in rates faster than private investment in other forms of fixed capital.

We turn now to investment in inventories. A major difficulty here is that observed fluctuations in inventories – and thus the observed rates of investment or disinvestment in inventories – reflect in part *unplanned* changes in stocks and thus *unplanned* investment. The problem is significant for stocks amount, on average, to about 45 per cent of gross domestic product. Hence if the planned level of stocks changed by (say) 1 per cent the resultant investment (or disinvestment) would be of the order of £140 m. If this adjustment was carried out in, say, two quarters it would amount on average to a change in expenditure of £70 m. per quarter – more than 1 per cent of quarterly gross domestic product. It thus becomes important to estimate the response of *planned* investment in inventories to changes in the rate of interest and availability.

Theoretically it is the desired level of stocks which should be functionally dependent on the interest rate and the ease of obtaining finance – not the rate of planned investment in stocks. Thus if the desired level of stocks at time t is $K^*(t)$ we have:

$$K^*(t) = f[Y, r^*, A_f],$$

where $r^* \equiv$ the rate of interest and $A_f \equiv$ the availability index. Then

$$I_{p(t)} \equiv \text{planned investment in inventories} = \lambda[K^*(t) - K(t-1)],$$

where $K(t-1)$ is the actual level of stocks at the beginning of period t and λ is a speed of response coefficient. It follows that any change in r^*, by changing K^*, produces a planned change in stock holdings. The rate of planned investment in stocks then depends on how *fast* businesses seek to adjust actual stocks to planned stocks. Notice that this adjustment is once and for all in the sense that, once it is complete, planned investment in stocks drops to zero.

We have rewritten the desired level of stocks ($\equiv K^*$) as a function of $Y(\equiv$ gross national product), $r(\equiv$ the interest rate) and $A_f(\equiv$ the availability index). It is intuitively acceptable that K^* should depend upon Y with a positive marginal response coefficient. The argument with respect to r is, however, less clear cut. However, putting this argument at its crudest, we may say that, where stockholding is financed by borrowing, one cost of stockholding is the rate of interest payable on the borrowed funds. Hence the greater is this rate, the greater the incentive to economise in stockholding – that is reduce K^*. Where funds are not borrowed the interest rate enters the calculation not as a cost but as an opportunity cost. We may thus expect the marginal response coefficient relating K^* to r^* to be *negative*. This argument is readily extended to availability – a concept which, as the reader will recall – is designed to reflect imperfections in the market for funds. Hence, speaking only *qualitatively*, we are entitled to expect

$$\frac{\partial K^*}{\partial Y} > 0 \qquad \frac{\partial K^*}{\partial r^*} < 0 \quad \text{and} \quad \frac{\partial K^*}{\partial A_f} > 0.$$

However the policy issue turns not on the *signs* of $\partial K^*/\partial r$ and $\partial K^*/\partial A_f$ but their magnitudes and this is a matter for empirical enquiry.

In general the attitude of British economists (other than Sir Ralph Hawtrey) has been that K^* is not significantly responsive to the interest rate. More evidence to this effect exists in the United States where econometric work typically finds no influence of the interest rate on inventory investment.† Though some U.K. studies do suggest some influence and U.S. studies may not be applicable to

† But note that, if changes in r^* influence Y, they will *indirectly* influence planned investment in inventories. In practice this effect is important.

the United Kingdom, recent work supports the view that K^* exhibits a negligible response to r^*: that is $\partial K^*/\partial r^* \approx$ zero.

This discussion of the response of private investment has been necessarily brief and presents no more than a sketch – and doubtless a controversial one at that – of the conclusions to be tentatively derived from a vast and rapidly expanding literature. We can summarise it in Table 24.2.

Table 24.2

Changes in monetary variable	Direction of change in investment component (theoretical)	Quantitative estimate	Evidence
Rise in market rate of interest Rise in administered rates Decrease in availability of finance	1. Investment in fixed capital: negative	Significant but very slow	Fairly strong
	2. Investment in stocks: negative	Insignificant	Fair – but mainly based on U.S.
	3. Investment in dwellings: negative	Significant	Fair

We must now enquire as to the principal secondary effects of using monetary policy to influence investment expenditure in the short run.

Clearly there will be some industrial directional effects – primarily through item 3. Equally, through the same item, there may be some social directional effects. Finally, if item 1 is affected, the capital goods industries as a whole will suffer. These conclusions refer, of course, to the short run. In the longer run, in so far as growth depends upon capital accumulation, variation in the rate of investment in fixed capital will influence the rate of growth.

5 MONETARY POLICY AND THE BALANCE OF PAYMENTS

Now that we have given a brief sketch of the impact of changes in monetary variables on consumption and private investment, what is the impact on the balance of payments? We begin by looking at the current account.

We have already argued that neither the import function nor foreigners' demand for exports should react to monetary changes. Hence the balance of visible trade should be invariant. Of the invisible items the only component which seems certain to be affected is 'Interest, Profits and Dividends (net)' for, clearly, if the U.K. monetary authorities raise British interest rates including short-term rates then in so far as foreigners hold British short-term assets the interest payable to them will increase. The extent of this increase will depend upon the extent to which short-term rates rise and the quantity of short-term assets foreigners hold. On this basis it has been estimated that the cost to the U.K. balance on current account of a 1 per cent rise in U.K. short-rates (from say 4 per cent to 5 per cent) is of the order of £15 m.–£18 m. a year. Thus the direct (impact) effect of a domestic rate increase is a small deterioration in the current account.

We have unfortunately no developed theory to explain the net outflow of British capital at long term. However in so far as this consists of portfolio investment (the purchase of foreign shares and securities by domestic nationals) we should expect a rise in U.K. interest rates to *diminish* the outflow of U.K. portfolio investment. By the same token the inflow of portfolio investment by foreigners should increase. This assumes, of course, that overseas rates do not react to the change in U.K. rates. As regards *direct* investment, we can be much less sure. Perhaps the wisest assumption, in the almost complete absence of knowledge, is to assume a negligible change. A rise in U.K. rates should thus bring some benefit to the U.K. long-term capital account though we have no information on which to base a quantitative estimate.

As regards autonomous short-term capital flows the situation is more complicated. Clearly if the cost of exchange cover and rates ruling overseas are unaltered, a rise in rates in London makes it more attractive to hold balances there. Hence there should be an increased rate of inflow (or diminished rate of outflow) of foreign short-term funds.

In addition it is sometimes argued that a rise in rates (if it includes as it invariably will a rise in Bank Rate), increases overseas confidence in sterling. If this happens the premium on forward dollars (the cost of exchange cover) may fall, reinforcing the effect we have discussed. Also some foreigners may be prepared to speculate (in the sense of bringing short-term funds to London *without* covering the exchange risk) thus generating a speculative inflow of short-term funds. The Bank of England argued along these lines to the Radcliffe Committee and the Radcliffe Committee, with some reluctance and scepticism, accepted the Bank's view. It is, however, only too clear that the 'confidence effect' could just as well go the other way. A rise in rates *could* be interpreted as a sign that the pound was under pressure and the risk of devaluation severe. In which case the cost of exchange cover (the forward premium) would probably widen and the inflow of covered foreign funds decline and a speculative outflow develop or increase. Since what matters here is essentially the reactions of foreign bankers and traders, the outcome probably depends upon the circumstances in which the rise in rates occurs and upon how dramatic the rise is. In the context of our specified problem a rise (or fall) in rates in 1963 would take place against the background of approximate balance on external account. In such a situation any change in rates – and the most likely direction is downward since we need to increase aggregate demand – would probably have no significant confidence effect. We should not, however, forget that in certain circumstances the 'confidence effect' can be large and either stabilising (as the Bank of England asserts) or destabilising.

These tentative conclusions are tabulated below.

Table 24.3

Change in monetary variable	Direction of change in dependent variable		Quantitative effect	Evidence
1. Capital account				
Rise in short-rates	Short-term capital inflow (covered)	Positive	?	Virtually none†
Rise in long-rates	Long-term capital movements:			
	(i) portfolio:	Positive	?	} Virtually none
	(ii) direct:	Positive(?)	?	
Rise in Bank Rate	Short-term capital inflow (covered) }	Probably depends on circumstances	Unknown but could be large }	Virtually none
	Short-term capital inflow (speculative) }			
2. Current account				
Rise in short-rates	Interest payments to foreigners	Positive	1 per cent increase in rates costs £15 m.–£18 m. a year	Good

† It is virtually impossible to distinguish statistically 'covered short-term inflows'.

6 THE TECHNIQUE OF MONETARY POLICY

Our examination hitherto has proceeded on the convenient assumption (which has never been made explicit) that the monetary authorities (Bank of England and Treasury) can vary the supply, cost and availability of money at will and are prepared to do so. This, as it were, produces a mental picture of the Governor of the Bank confronted by three levers marked 'supply', 'cost', and 'availability' which he can pull – or push – according to the dictates of policy. Such a picture is entirely fanciful. For the Bank, as our elementary discussion in Chapters 14–16 makes clear, has very little *direct* influence on the three variables we have defined.

To see this consider the money supply. If the Bank wishes to vary this it must operate on bank reserves by open market purchases or sales or by calling (or releasing) special deposits. The change in commercial bank reserves then depends, given the quantitative extent of the Bank's operations, on the change in the public's demand for cash. Given the change in this, total bank deposits will adjust to the reserves and liquid asset holdings of the banks. The magnitude of the money supply will then depend upon the public's preference for holding deposits as current account or time deposits. Thus, even if, as is sometimes disputed, the Bank can control the cash and liquid assets of the banks, the banks may *choose* to hold cash and liquid assets above their minimum requirement† or, particularly in the case of an expansion, adjust to their equilibrium position only rather slowly. There is, in short, a technical and dynamic problem in controlling the money supply which is swept under the carpet in the simple equilibrium model of our earlier chapters.

Suppose, however, the Bank *does* succeed in varying the money supply as it wishes. Then, according to our static theory of Chapter 11, an equilibrium set of interest rates will emerge, depending on the liquidity preference schedule of the public. How *quickly* will they emerge? Short-rates will doubtless adjust fast since the market is dominated by professionals and closely supervised by the Bank. But the adjustment of long-rates, which depends upon the portfolio decisions of many wealth owners, may take much longer. Once again a dynamic difficulty is involved which is less susceptible to official solution because of the known reluctance of the Bank to carry out extensive operations in the long-term market.

The Bank's influence on administered rates, provided they are linked to Bank Rate by convention, is, of course, direct. There *is*, as it were, a lever marked Bank Rate in the Governor's office, but further difficulties arise with the control of availability.

To see this, consider the control of bank advances. Even if operating on bank reserves and liquid assets controls bank deposits, it simply restricts the banks to a given total of investments (bonds) *plus* advances.‡ To expand the latter, the banks can *sell* the former. Hence the Bank usually supplements its control over total deposits by requests to the banks to observe certain priorities in granting advances or by setting an advances target or ceiling. Priorities are difficult to operate and, where the ceiling which is set involves a *reduction* in advances, reducing the advances total will take time. Again we have a lag to consider.

† This was originally set at 30% of deposits but later reduced to 28%.
‡ Frequently called 'risk' or 'earning' assets.

Apart from the availability of hire purchase finance, the terms of which can be varied administratively, the availability of funds from other financial institutions (e.g. building societies, the new-issue markets, insurance companies) is only indirectly affected by Bank actions and only as market rates respond. If the latter respond slowly so will availability.

We may thus conclude that though monetary policy can be varied quickly in the sense that Bank Rate can be rapidly raised or lowered and open market sales can easily be replaced by open market purchases, there may be considerable lags before market interest rates and availability respond. Moreover the quantitative response of market rates and availability is far from certain.

The nature of the problem may be made simpler by a highly schematic diagram (see overleaf).

The arrows indicate the direction of influence which issues from the monetary authority's instruments (top line) to the money supply, market interest rates and availability (bottom line). Lags in the system are not shown and it is left as an interesting exercise for the reader to decide where they should be inserted. The lags which do exist – defined as the period between the monetary authority's use of its instruments and the resulting changes in the three monetary variables of supply, cost and availability of money – we call the 'financial lags'.

Ordinarily, of course, some time will elapse between the *need* for a change in policy and the monetary authority's use of its instruments. This, following the terminology of Chapter 23, we call the 'inside lag' of monetary policy. Hence the sum of the 'inside lag' and the 'financial lag' define the period which must elapse between the time at which the monetary authority appreciates the *need* for a change in policy and the response of those variables through which it seeks to influence aggregate demand. Empirical work in the U.S.A. and Canada, which may or may not be relevant to the U.K., suggests that these lags together may be quite long.

The object of this section has been to sketch the principal technical and dynamic problems which are inseparable from the conduct of monetary policy in any given environment (in this case the U.K.) and which tend to be obscured by the equilibrium models (necessarily simplified for exposition) used earlier in this book. Clearly all that we have said is consistent with the theoretical principles underlying our earlier account. For example the monetary authority cannot determine *both* the money supply *and* market interest rates, and banks still adjust to their preferred asset ratios. All that we have done is introduce some of the complications, including time, of the real

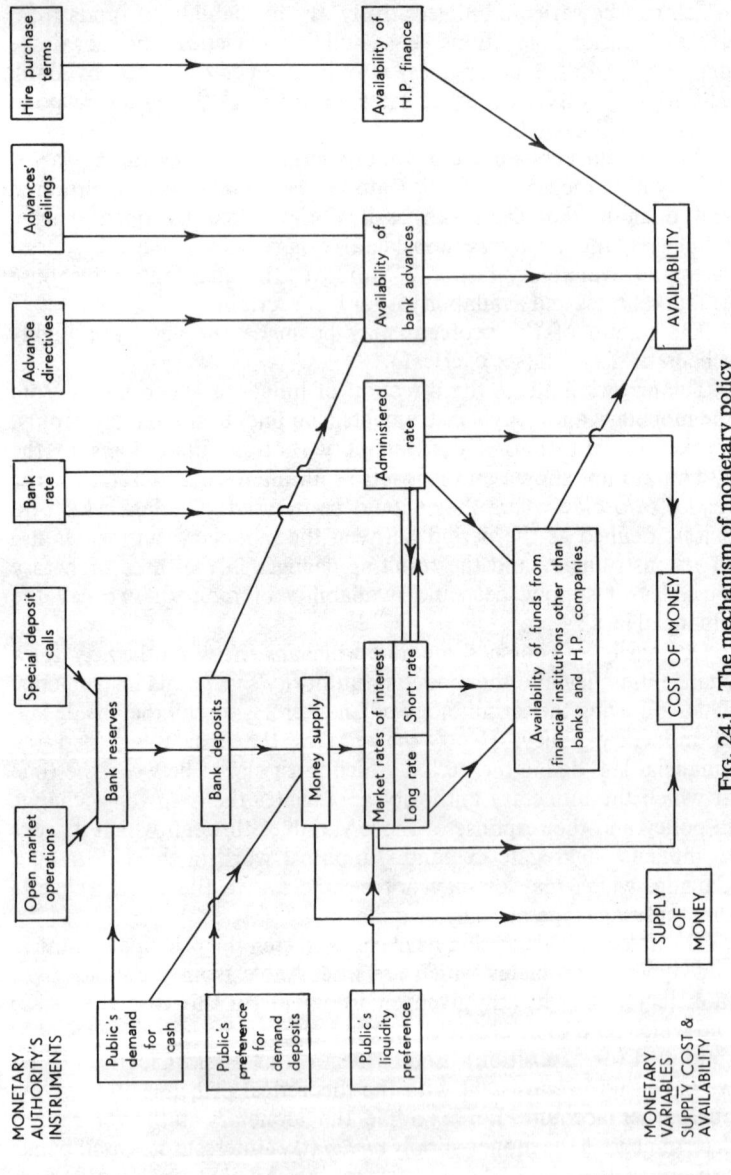

MONETARY
AUTHORITY'S
INSTRUMENTS

MONETARY
VARIABLES
SUPPLY, COST &
AVAILABILITY

Fig. 24.i The mechanism of monetary policy

world in which policy must be conducted. Undoubtedly many authorities would dispute aspects of the schematic outline of Fig. 24.i and some of the empirical judgments made in this and earlier sections. But those who do so are under the obligation to produce an alternative outline (or model – for that is what it is) and systematic evidence showing its superiority. At the moment our lack of knowledge is such that no single model can be identified as the best. By the same token, estimates of lag patterns and marginal response coefficients are still very much matters of individual opinion.

7 MORE DYNAMICS

We are now in a position to draw together the threads of our analysis, first recalling that the object of our policy exercise is to operate in the first quarter of a given year (1963) so as to add some £90 m. to the level of demand ruling the fourth quarter of the same year. Suppose now (in February 1963) the monetary authority accepts this objective and makes what it believes to be an appropriate adjustment of its instruments. What happens? Let us proceed in stages.

Stage I: after the *financial lag* has worked itself out the monetary variables have adjusted to their new values;

Stage II: consumption and investment then adjust, *again with a lag*, to the new values of the monetary variables;

Stage III: the dynamic multiplier comes in to operation and, *subject to its lags*, gradually works itself out so that by

Stage IV: the level of gross domestic product is within some calculable distance of its new final equilibrium.

Now Stages III and IV will occur whether we use monetary or fiscal policy – or some combination of the two – to bring about the initial injection of demand. We shall therefore discuss them in the next Chapter. The dynamic and quantitative problems peculiar to monetary policy essentially relate to Stages I and II.

What do we need to know to conduct an effective monetary policy in these circumstances? Our requirements are considerable. We need information on

(i) the quantitative impact on the monetary variables of any given change in the instruments and the lags involved;

(ii) the quantitative impact on consumption and private investment of changes in the monetary variables and the lags involved; and

(iii) the magnitude and dynamic characteristics of the multiplier.

Ignoring (iii) for the time being, it is clear from our earlier discussion that we have far too little information on (i) and (ii) to place
much reliance on monetary policy as a short-term stabiliser.
Moreover not only do we know remarkably little, but some of the
things we *think* we know are decidedly disquieting. Thus, for example,
if it is correct that private investment in fixed capital responds
considerably but only very slowly to change in interest rates, a
monetary policy which adds £90 m. to investment demand by the
fourth quarter of 1963 would have far greater repercussion on
demand in 1964 and possibly 1965 even if the multiplier effects are
not considered. And these might very well be inappropriate and
difficult to offset by monetary means.

In short our analysis, if correct, suggests that, apart from
variation in the terms of hire purchase credit, which has awkward
social and industrial consequences, there is no monetary device
which, in the short run, has any claim to be considered as a *reliable*
means of macro-economic control. This, as the reader will recognise,
is substantially the Radcliffe Committee's conclusion.

Conversely because interest policy *does* have medium and long-
term effects on private fixed investment, it probably has significance
for growth. It would therefore seem inappropriate to vary interest
rates for short-term reasons and rational to manage interest rates
(and thus the money supply) to conform to long-term objectives.
Again this is substantially the Radcliffe view.

8 MONETARY POLICY: CONCLUSIONS

For a long time it used to be fashionable to refer to monetary policy
as a 'delicate' and 'flexible' means of influencing both aggregate
demand and the balance of payments. If these adjectives are thought
to have any clear economic meaning – as opposed to being simple
emotive devices – our analysis suggests that both are inapplicable.
This is so because 'delicacy' presumably implies a precise and finely
controllable economic impact (which our argument suggests to be
absent) while 'flexibility' suggests an economic impact which is
readily reversible (which in our account is equally absent). From
where, then, does the view, which is still widely held in the U.K., that
'discretionary monetary policy' is a useful short-run stabilisation
device draw its strength?

The answer seems to be that, in the U.K. at least, monetary policy
derives its appeal partly from a habit of thought; partly from the
prestige it acquired in the nineteenth century in dealing, with relative

success, with problems which were quantitatively and qualitatively very different from those of today and which occurred in an economic and financial environment which was equally different, and partly from the obscurity, even mystery, with which its operations are surrounded.

Those who conduct monetary policy, that is central bankers, possess (not very surprisingly since discretionary monetary policy is the *raison d'être* of central banking) a firm belief in its value including its value as an economic stabiliser. The theory on which this belief is based they rarely state clearly. And a theory which is not stated clearly cannot easily be tested. Because most central bankers prefer to operate more like high priests than social scientists and because they see no need to set out their views in a form economists can readily understand and test, monetary policy in general and central banking in particular remains something of a mystery. Indeed, as Sir Robert Hall, for many years Economic Adviser to the British Government, once wrote: '... there is still a tendency to speak in magical rather than scientific terms of the use of interest rates and of monetary controls generally. The economy is to be given a potion or dose and wonderful results will follow'. Just why or how the 'wonderful results' will follow is, it seems, an untold and certainly untested story.

In the next Chapter we shall examine the capacities of fiscal policy. Our present assumption is that monetary policy will not be used in attempting to reach our target.

QUESTIONS AND EXERCISES

1. 'Everything we know suggests that the rate of interest is a pretty unimportant price.' Elucidate and discuss.
2. The central theoretical concept of the Radcliffe Report is that of 'liquidity'. Where, if anywhere, is 'Radcliffe liquidity' to be found in our discussion? If you can find it, do we really need it? If you cannot find it, would its inclusion significantly change the analysis?
3. 'Monetary policy is far from useless. Because its effects, and their time lags, are so uncertain it is almost certainly positively harmful.' Discuss in the light of the analysis of Chapter 22.
4. 'Central bankers think monetary policy works. We know it

doesn't; but we use it in times of crisis because when crises occur our real problem is to reassure overseas central bankers not control the economy.' Discuss.

5. Review U.K. experience of investment in stocks. Is there any evidence of interest elasticity?

6. Explain the Radcliffe contention that 'the supply of Treasury Bills and not the supply of cash has come to be the effective regulatory base of the domestic banking system'. In what circumstances, if any, is the proposition correct?

7. What reasons did the Bank of England give to the Radcliffe Committee for its reluctance to operate in the long-term market? What do these reasons imply about the public's liquidity preference?

8. 'As newly-created money finds its way into the economy as a whole, it makes it easy for potential demands...' (speech of Governor of the Bank of England). Elucidate. What theory do you think the Governor had in mind? Is there evidence to support it?

9. '... as the demand which has to be held back (by a credit squeeze) would not have been there in such force had it not been for the circulation of new money, it has always seemed to me that our difficulties would be greatly eased if restraint were to be placed on the creation of new money.' (Governor's speech.) Analyse this statement. What assumptions are necessary to connect 'monetary circulation' with 'money creation'? Can they be tested?

10. Use the identity

$$Y \equiv MV_y,$$

where

$Y \equiv$ G.N.P. at market prices

$M \equiv$ nominal money supply

$V_y \equiv$ measured income velocity of money,

to show how far increases in Y in the U.K. are to be explained by increases in the British money supply. Use your results to re-examine Questions 8 and 9.

$$\left[\text{Hint: assume } \frac{\Delta Y}{Y} = \frac{\Delta M}{M} + \frac{\Delta V_y}{V_y}. \right]$$

11. Our discussion in Chapter 24 makes no explicit reference to 'debt-policy'. What is 'debt policy'? Why did the Radcliffe Committee think it so important? Can you incorporate it into our analysis? If you do, does it modify the conclusions?

12. 'An increase in the money supply raises the ratio of money to other assets in private portfolios. This makes the portfolios more liquid and so, even if wealth does not vary, raises spending.' Discuss. Is this an aspect of Radcliffe liquidity?

13. 'Administered rates depend on market rates and market rates on administered rates.' Discuss with special reference to the rates charged (and paid) by hire purchase companies and building societies.

14. 'A fall in market interest rates encourages investment by making firms "more liquid".' Elucidate. On what does this effect depend? In what way is it analogous to the wealth (asset) effect discussed in relation to households?

15. If the interest elasticity of U.K. private fixed capital investment was $-0\cdot5$ what would be its approximate response to: (i) a rise in r_m from 4 per cent to 5 per cent; (ii) a fall in r_m from 10 per cent to 9 per cent. Use the average of quarterly values recorded for the U.K. from 1960 to 1970 to calculate your results.

16. Suppose that the proportion of the response occurring in the quarter in which interest rates changed is given by λ, that in the next quarter by $\lambda(1-\lambda)$ and the quarter following by $\lambda(1-\lambda)^2$ and so on. Construct a table showing the proportion of the equilibrium result which would have occurred after 10 periods when (i) $\lambda = 0\cdot9$; (ii) $\lambda = 0\cdot5$; (iii) $\lambda = 0\cdot3$. Which pattern of response do you think most nearly describes the analysis of this Chapter? What is the sum of the series λ, $\lambda(1-\lambda)$, $\lambda(1-\lambda)^2$... $\lambda(1-\lambda)^n$?

17. The following table shows the proportion of the equilibrium response occurring in each quarter (interest changes in quarter 0).

Quarter	0	1	2	3	4	5	6	7	8	9	10
Proportion of equilibrium response	2	5	6	12	20	30	10	6	5	3	1

Apply this information to your answer to Question 15. Plot the results on a graph. What are the implications of this response pattern for monetary policy?

18. 'The rules for British monetary policy are: (i) set the long-term rate to maintain an appropriate growth rate; (ii) keep the short-rate in line with short-rates abroad; (iii) let Bank rate *follow* the short-rate; (iv) let the public determine the money supply. For the rest, rely on the Chancellor.' Discuss.

19. 'If the Bank of England conducted open market operations in bonds in an attempt to control the long-rate, the result could

only be irreparable damage to the credit of the British government.' Elucidate. Compare with the Bank's published statements.
What validity (if any) do you assign to this statement? Give your
reasons.
20. Re-read the whole of this chapter and make a list of the empirical
propositions asserted in it. Of these select those which seem to
you to be the most *contentious*. Prepare a second list of those
which seem to you to be the most *dubious*. Are the lists related?
How would you attempt to test the asserted propositions?
21. In view of the relationships between the desired level of stocks
and monetary variables is it still correct to assert (on p. 523) that
'the import function will not react to monetary changes'? Discuss
carefully distinguishing between dynamic and static forms of the
function and equilibrium and disequilibrium situations.

SUGGESTED READING

Radcliffe Report (H.M.S.O., 1959) chs vi, vii, xii.
J. C. R. Dow, *The Management of the British Economy, 1945–1960*
(Cambridge, 1964) chs ix, xii.
J. C. R. Dow, 'Fiscal Policy and Monetary Policy as Instruments of
Control', *Westminster Bank Review* (May, Aug and Nov 1960).
D. C. Rowan, 'Radcliffe Monetary Theory' in *Money and Banking*
(Penguin, 1973).
Bank of England in *Money in Britain* (Oxford, 1970).
R. E. Caves and associates, *Britain's Economic Prospects* (Allen &
Unwin, 1968) ch. ii.
W. T. Newlyn, *The Theory of Money* (Oxford, 1962) chs xi, xii.
M. Gaskin, 'Liquidity and the Monetary Mechanism', *Oxford
Economic Papers* (Oct 1960).
P. M. Oppenheimer, 'Forward Exchange Intervention: the Official
View', *Westminster Bank Review* (Feb 1966).
H. M. Goldstein, 'Forward Exchange Intervention: Another View
of the British Experience', *Westminster Bank Review* (Aug 1966).
T. Mayer,[†] 'The Inflexibility of Monetary Policy', *Review of Economics
and Statistics* (Nov 1958).
W. H. White,[†] 'The Flexibility of Anti-Cyclical Monetary Policy',
Review of Economics and Statistics (May 1961).

[†] More advanced reference.

ADDENDUM

In the summer of 1971 the Bank of England initiated, under the general title of 'Competition and Credit Control', a new set of monetary techniques. Later, Bank Rate was abolished and, in its place, a new rate, defined as the Bank's 'minimum lending rate', was introduced. This new rate will *follow* the Treasury bill rate and be set, each week, at $\frac{1}{2}$ per cent above the rate ruling on Treasury bills.

In very general terms, the new proposals of the Bank:

    (*a*) define required 'reserve' ratios for all banks ($12\frac{1}{2}$ per cent);

    (*b*) define required 'reserve' ratios for instalment finance houses (10 per cent);

    (*c*) apply the Special Deposits procedure to all these institutions equally;

while, since 'reserves' are now defined to include such items as call money, Treasury bills, Local Authority bills, government securities with less than one year to run to maturity and (within defined limits) commercial bills, the new system is essentially a generalisation of control via a 'liquid assets ratio'.

The Bank now envisages that it will follow a more flexible interest-rate policy regarding both short- and longer-term securities and will seek to influence both lenders and borrowers – though principally the former – via interest rates.

At the moment of writing (November 1972) we have too little experience of the new system to assess its effectiveness. Chapter 24 has therefore been left largely unaltered but must now be interpreted as referring to the system in operation *until* mid-1971. For details of the new arrangements and an assessment of their implications the reader is referred to the following publications.

'Competititon and Credit Control', *Bank of England Quarterly Bulletin* (June 1971), and ibid. (Sep 1971).

Governor of Bank of England, 'Key Issues in Monetary and Credit Policy', *Bank of England Quarterly Bulletin* (June 1971).

'Reserve Ratios and Special Deposits', *Bank of England Quarterly Bulletin* (Sep 1971).

A. B. Cramp and Norman Gibson, *The Bankers' Magazine* (July 1971).

M. J. Artis, J. M. Parkin and H. G. Johnson, *The Bankers' Magazine* (Sep 1971).

D. C. Rowan, 'The Evolution of British Monetary Policy 1951–1972', *Manchester School* (Feb 1973).

25 Economic Stabilisation: The Use of Fiscal Policy

OUR examination of monetary policy led us to discard it as a short-run stabilisation device. We thus assume monetary policy to be unchanged and have to select a fiscal policy appropriate to raising gross domestic product to the target level by the fourth quarter of 1963. What are the issues involved?

Our earlier discussion of fiscal action (Chapter 12) made it clear that there are four variables, with differing equilibrium multipliers, which the authorities may manipulate namely:

$G \equiv$ government expenditure on goods and services

$T \equiv$ receipts from direct taxes

$R \equiv$ transfer payments

$T_i \equiv$ receipts from indirect taxes.

We need, therefore, to discuss the consequences of adjusting each and show how, given the properties of the dynamic multiplier, an appropriate adjustment of the chosen variable (or variables) will permit us to reach our target. Since, as we already know from Chapter 12, there are an infinite number of possible changes in G, R, T and T_i which will enable us to reach our target, the example finally discussed is only an illustration; for the choice of variable to change must rest on criteria other than the manipulation of demand – and the systematic discussion of these would take us too far afield.

1 THE CHARACTERISTICS OF FISCAL POLICY

After the quantitative and dynamic uncertainties of monetary policy, fiscal policy has a reassuring appearance of precision. An increase in taxation put forward in the Budget becomes effective immediately and is debated later. In short the government's legislative plans are carried out. Since what is legislated is a tax structure *not* a quantity of tax receipts the impact of, say, a reduction in the standard rate of income tax on tax receipts (a shift in the tax structure) must depend on what happens to the level of national income and its distribution.

Our problem, however, is to enquire into the consequence of a change in the tax structure *given* an unchanged level of income. In practice the authorities are usually able to make calculations of this kind with an acceptable degree of accuracy. Since much the same situation exists with regard to the main forms of transfer payments, we can assume that the authorities can calculate the consequences, given national income, for the variables T and R, of any proposed change in the legislation relating to tax rates or transfer rates. This is extremely important for it means that, if the authorities select changes in T and R which are designed to influence consumption through changing personal disposable income, they are already freed from a form of uncertainty which afflicted monetary policy.

To see this consider an example. Suppose tax rates are lowered in such a way that, given the value of national income, the value of personal disposable income, at annual rates, will be raised by £100 m. (the amount that the direct tax bill falls). The consequences of this for demand now depend on two factors: (i) how quickly personal disposable income responds to the tax change which, with P.A.Y.E. may be very rapid; and (ii) the dynamic multiplier process. In the alternative approach of monetary policy the authorities were unsure what response – and with what lags – the monetary variables would make to the instruments and what response, say, investment in fixed capital (and again what lags would be involved) would make to changes in the monetary variables. We may conclude that provided direct tax and transfer changes are made with the object of influencing consumption through a function of the familiar form:

$$C_p = H + c(Y - D - T + R) + d \cdot r + e \cdot Q + f \cdot A$$

the impact effect depends only on the marginal propensity to consume about which we know, or think we know, a good deal more than we do about the parameters involved in the monetary policy calculation.

Alternatively if the government decides to act through increasing government expenditure in real terms by a given amount, it can be reasonably confident (i) that its plans will be carried out; and (ii) of the directional impact of its additional expenditure. We may thus conclude that, in so far as the authorities choose to operate along these lines they have a greater measure of certainty about the outcome than in any monetary policy case save perhaps that of variation in hire purchase terms. Moreover where the authorities choose to vary T and/or R they can make useful calculations of the social impact of their policies. Fiscal policy changes can then be used to bring about changes in income distribution which the authorities regard as desirable.

There are, however, two forms of fiscal action about which it is less easy to make quantitative calculations.

The first of these relates to official attempts to stimulate (or more rarely retard) private investment in fixed capital by improving depreciation rates. The income derived from any investment is subject to tax. However the depreciation of the capital asset is an allowable tax deduction. Thus, given the interest rate, the present value of any capital asset is given by the sum of (i) the present value of the incomes expected over its lifetime *after tax*; and (ii) the present value of the depreciation allowance tax offsets allowed over its life. Formally:

$$\text{Present value} = \frac{Q_1 + D_1}{1+r} + \frac{Q_2 + D_2}{(1+r)^2} + \ldots + \frac{Q_n + D_n}{(1+r)^n}, \quad (25.\text{I})$$

where $Q_1 \ldots Q_n$ are incomes *after* tax and $D_1 \ldots D_n$ are the depreciation tax concessions in years $1 \ldots n$.

For a given set of $Q_1 \ldots Q_n$ and a given interest rate, the present value of the capital asset can be increased (and hence its purchase made more attractive) in two ways. To see this we recall that if C is the cost of the asset then, in general, the rates of depreciation accepted for tax purposes satisfy the condition:

$$\sum_{i=1}^{i=n} D_i \equiv \text{sum of depreciation allowances} = C. \quad (25.\text{II})$$

To stimulate investment, therefore, the authorities, while maintaining this equality, can arrange for the bulk of the depreciation to be charged in the early years of life. The limiting case of this is when *all* depreciation is charged in the first year: that is $D_1 = C$ and D_2, $D_3 \ldots D_n = 0$. The reader can easily satisfy himself, by a numerical example, that the earlier depreciation can be charged off, the higher, *ceteris paribus*, is the present value of the asset. Hence what is called 'accelerating depreciation' is a stimulus to investment – at least in theory. An alternative procedure is to abandon the constraint and introduce legislation which sets

$$\sum_{i=1}^{i=n} D_i > C.$$

This in effect provides a subsidy to investment. Both methods can, of course, be combined.

Tax incentives of both kinds have been commonly used in the

United Kingdom. Their effect on private investment in fixed capital is believed by some to be considerable. However the precise quantitative impact on investment for any given decrease in tax revenue derived from companies by such means is hard to estimate. Moreover, because of the lags involved in the investment process, whatever response there is may take place slowly. This type of tax change has, therefore, many of the uncertainties of monetary policy.

The second form of tax change which is subject to uncertainties is the variation of rates of indirect taxes – such as purchase taxes – a technique which is more and more being used by British Chancellors. If the rate of sales tax is identical for all goods and services the effect is, in terms of our model, simple to calculate. Suppose a 10 per cent sales tax is imposed. Then market prices are now 10 per cent above factor cost from the identity:

$$\text{market price} \equiv \text{factor cost} + \text{indirect taxes}$$

$$\equiv \text{factor cost} + 10 \text{ per cent factor cost}$$

$$\equiv \text{factor cost } [1 \cdot 10].$$

In money terms personal disposable income is unaltered. Hence real personal income has *fallen* by 10 per cent. The consequence now depends, as before, on the marginal propensity to consume – a parameter about which we have some information.

In general, however, the rate of sales (or purchase) tax is *not* the same for all commodities. On many it is zero. Hence an increase in tax rates raises the price of commodities which *are* taxed relative to those which are not. In so far as the latter are substitutes for the former, consumers to avoid the tax may switch their purchases. The result *could* be simply to direct real expenditure from taxed to untaxed commodities without reducing the real demand for all commodities in the least. For example if a purchase tax was placed on butter and margarine left untaxed, consumers might very largely give up butter in favour of margarine. If they did, the increase in tax revenue might be miniscule. Hence there would be no decrease in aggregate demand. Thus while the imposition of a general sales tax, or an increase in an existing general sales tax, will have reasonably predictable effects, operations which affect only single commodities would not unless the elasticity of demand for the taxed commodity was known.

In practice, therefore, in varying indirect taxes in order to control aggregate demand, governments tend (i) to select commodities the demand for which responds very little to changes in their relative prices (i.e. those with price inelastic demands). Typical examples are beer, tobacco, cigarettes and petrol; and/or (ii) to vary the rates of indirect taxes on rather wide groups of commodities. The object of these tax changes is not, of course, to reduce the demand for the commodities taxed but, by taking greater indirect taxes from consumers, to reduce their capacity to purchase commodities in general: that is their real planned consumption. Obviously where little is known about the relevant elasticities of demand, the increase in tax receipts, and thus the amount of purchasing power 'mopped up', may be miscalculated. In practice the British authorities' estimates of the results of changing indirect tax rates are usually good. The method of control, however, is less certain in its impact than variation in direct taxes and may also have unwanted implications for income distribution.

In what follows we shall assume that, on the basis of its chosen criteria, the government decides to operate on aggregate demand by means of a reduction in the rates of direct tax on persons. Its target is to raise output by £90 m. over a period from February 1963 to December 1963 – ten calendar months. We shall also assume that the tax cut affects personal disposable income without an appreciable lag.

According to the simple fiscal multiplier of Chapter 12 we know that the effect of tax cuts on output is given by:

$$\Delta Y = -\Delta T \frac{c}{1-c}, \qquad (25.\text{III})$$

so that if $c = 0.5$ and the target value for ΔY is £90 m. the required *reduction* in taxes is £90 m. Unfortunately this result, though formally correct, is too simple to help us. In the first place it is a (timeless) equilibrium result. The multiplier is a dynamic process. We need to know not by how much output will rise *eventually* but how much it will rise *over the ten months we have at our disposal*. To do this we must know the multiplier's dynamic properties.

In addition to its dynamic shortcomings, the simple multiplier set out above neglects many features of the real world which are relevant for our problem. For example as Y rises, so will tax liabilities (formally T is a function of Y). Our multiplier formula does not allow for this nor does it allow for the fact that a part of domestic consumption expenditure will be devoted to imports. Accordingly, in the section which follows we develop an elementary model of the dynamic multiplier process, assuming (the reader should recall) the absence of an output lag, which takes account of the complications ignored by the simple, static formulation of (25.III).

2 THE DYNAMIC MULTIPLIER AND FISCAL POLICY

Our first need is to specify the dynamic form of the consumption relation. Is there a lag between consumption and personal disposable income or is there not? Should we write

$$C_t = f(Y - D - T + R)_{t-1} \qquad (25.\text{IV(a)})$$

or

$$C_t = f(Y - D - T + R)_t. \qquad (25.\text{IV(b)})$$

On the whole the former assumption seems slightly more plausible. Hence we assume a consumption lag of one period. Remember we have already assumed that there is no output lag.

The next question is how long, in terms of calendar time, is a period? There is some evidence suggesting that, *if* there is a consumption lag at all, it is probably less than one quarter. Let us put it at two months. Hence we may expect about 5 periods to elapse between the introduction of the Budget and the fourth quarter of 1963. Accordingly we want to know how far the multiplier process will have gone by the fifth period.

In formulating the multiplier we need to make allowances for the fact that some part of consumption expenditure by households will be devoted to imports and another part be taken by the government in the form of indirect taxes. We may thus write a marginal propensity to consume *domestic output* as:

$$c_d \equiv c - m - t' \qquad (25.\text{V})$$

where

$c \equiv$ marginal propensity to consume out of disposable income
$c_d \equiv$ marginal propensity to consume domestic output
$m \equiv$ marginal propensity to import
$t' \equiv$ marginal propensity to pay indirect taxes.

Once consumption expenditure increases, if there is no output lag, output increases and, if income payments do not lag behind output, so do incomes. But as incomes rise, so, given the tax function, will *direct taxes* paid out of incomes. Let us call the marginal propensity to pay direct taxes t. Then $\partial C_d / \partial Y = c_d(1 - t)$ as long as D and R are independent of Y.

Armed with this information let us look at what happens in our multiplier series.

In period 1 personal disposable incomes rise by (say) £100 m. but, because there is a consumption lag, consumption is unchanged.

In period 2 consumption of domestic output rises by $c_d \times$ £100 m. and so does output and income.

In period 3 consumption of domestic output rises by $c_d \times$ the increase in personal disposable income i.e. by $c_d \cdot c_d(1-t)$£100 m.

In period 4 consumption of domestic output rises by

$$c_d \cdot c_d \cdot c_d(1-t)(1-t)\text{£100 m.}$$

In period 5 consumption of domestic output rises by

$$c_d \cdot c_d \cdot c_d \cdot c_d(1-t)(1-t)(1-t)\text{£100 m.}$$

The total change in output is, assuming 5 periods elapse, the sum of these elements. Let us work the problem arithmetically. According to the N.I.E.S.R. the numerical values of the parameters we need to know are approximately as follows:

$$c = 0.80$$
$$m = 0.15$$
$$t' = 0.12 \text{ so that } c_d = 0.53$$
while $t = 0.06$.

Hence we have, for injection of £100 m. per period, the following approximate results:

Period	ΔC_d	ΔY	$\Delta(Y-D-T+R)$
1	nil	nil	£100 m.
2	£53 m.	£53 m.	£50 m.
3	£26·5 m.	£26·5 m.	£24·9 m.
4	£13.1 m.	£13·1 m.	£12·3 m.
5	£6·5 m.	£6·5 m.	£6·1 m.
Total	99·1	99·1	

This gives a truncated multiplier, over the five periods, of 0·991 – which we may take, as a convenient approximation, to be unity. It follows that, if we *reduce* the rate of direct taxation by £100 m. per period then, 10 months later, the level of income per period will have risen by about £100 m.

Our aim is to raise gross domestic product by about $1\frac{1}{2}$ per cent: that is, from a forecast quarterly rate of £5804 m. to a forecast quarterly rate of (say) £5900 m. Since our period is two calendar months rather than three a reduction of £100 m. per period in direct taxation is equivalent to a reduction, at annual rates, of £600 m. or £150 m. per quarter. Such a reduction would yield about £150 m. increase in quarterly output by the fourth quarter of 1963. This would be too much. We need, on a quarterly basis, an increase in personal disposable income of about £90 m. per quarter or £360 m.

per year. Converting back to our two months period yields a required injection into personal disposable income of about £60 m. per period. Thus by specifying:

(i) the form of the *dynamic* consumption function relating real consumption of domestic output to personal disposable income;

(ii) the length of the *period* in terms of calendar time; and

(iii) the magnitude of the marginal propensities involved;

we have

(iv) calculated the size of the injection into personal disposable income per period (and so per quarter or per annum) necessary to reach the *target* level of gross domestic product by the fourth quarter of 1963.

No particular claim is made for the model of the dynamic multiplier used in this Section. It is, indeed, simply one of a number of possible variants of that used by the N.I.E.S.R. in performing the same exercise to which the reader should now refer. It was introduced only to show, first, what is involved in attempting to specify the dynamic multiplier process; and, second, how our theory helps us with the task of specification. We have now reached the position that

(i) *if* our conditional forecast is correct;

(ii) *if* our dynamic multiplier is of the right order of magnitude; and

(iii) *if* the appropriate method of stimulating the economy is by fiscal changes making their impact through personal disposable income then,

(iv) *given* our target, we

(v) need an injection of about £60 m. per period into personal disposable income or, in annual terms, an injection of £360 m.

This, of course, does not tell us *how* to operate on personal disposable income. We *could* reduce the rate of direct taxes. There are several ways of doing this. We could lower the basic Rate or the higher Rates; we could raise the earned income allowance. Or we could choose some combination of all three. Alternatively we *could* raise transfer payments (*R*), and leave tax rates alone or even pursue some mixture of both policies. This rather obvious conclusion restates a point we made much earlier namely that short-run demand forecasting of this kind can, at best, even when given a *defined* target, only specify the *quantitative* adjustment to aggregate demand necessary to produce the desired result. To tell us *how* 'best' to bring about the necessary quantitative adjustment we need other criteria.

3 OTHER OBJECTIVES AND THE EXTERNAL CONSTRAINT

Once we have calculated what we need to do to reach our output target for 1963.IV we should, recalling our arguments in Chapter 21, consider (i) whether an injection of £360 m. per annum into personal disposable income would, if made, adversely effect the rate of price increase; and (ii) whether the injection and its consequences are compatible with satisfying our external constraint. Since the purpose of this chapter is to illustrate the uses of the model and the methods of short-run forecasting rather than conduct a sustained exercise, we shall leave problems (i) and (ii) to the reader. In considering them he should, of course, apply the model we have already developed and, in particular, the model of rising prices set out in Chapter 21. After setting out his own arguments and conclusions the reader is then strongly recommended to refer to the *N.I.E.S.R. Review* where both these problems are given considerable attention.

4 SUMMARY

In Sections 1 and 2 we set out *one* way of putting our model to work in a policy context. Essentially what we did was to feed information on the existing (1962.IV) state of the economy into the model to obtain a conditional forecast of where the system would be in 1963.IV *if policies remained unaltered*. We then compared this conditional forecast with a *target* and, after postulating a particular dynamic multiplier, calculated the injection necessary to raise gross domestic product from its (conditionally) forecast value to the given *target* value. Exercises of this type are no doubt continually being conducted by the Chancellor's expert advisers in the Treasury. They are also conducted from time to time by individual economists and financial commentators as well as research organisations such as N.I.E.S.R. What are their limitations?

The *conditional forecast*, on which the whole process is based, depends upon

   (i) the statistical data relating to the *present* situation of the system and its behaviour in the immediate past which may be incomplete or even incorrect;

  (ii) the *model* explicitly or implicitly employed in making the forecast. This may be wrongly specified;

 (iii) *quantitative estimates* of the marginal response co-efficients and other parameters of the model about which very little is known.

The dynamic multiplier, from which the final quantitative estimate is derived, depends upon (ii) and (iii) and also

(iv) the *dynamic characteristics* of the system – about which also very little is known.

In view of these technical weaknesses – arising out of our lack of understanding of the economic system – it is hardly surprising that we have not – during the post-war years – succeeded as well as we might like in stabilising the economic system by damping down the cycle. Positive economics it seems, like meteorology, is not yet a reliable predictive science. In what sense, if any, is this a sensible judgment?

Any prediction, in whatever field, is subject to error. The progress of any discipline which aims at prediction, may from this point of view, be looked at as a progressive narrowing of the range of error. How large an error is 'tolerable' depends upon the purpose for which a prediction is made. Applying this argument to macro-economics we may say that if economics is unreliable it means that economists, as yet, do not know enough about the economic system to predict, even in the short-run, within a 'tolerable' margin of error. This statement, however, only has meaning if 'tolerable' is defined. Now what is 'tolerable' in this context depends upon the purpose for which prediction is made. If our aim is to stabilise output within a margin of error of ± 0.25 per cent then, with this objective in mind, it may be correct to say that macro-economics can generate only rather unreliable short-run predictions. On the other hand if our 'acceptable' margin of error is $= \pm 5$ per cent, then macro-economic predictions of output and its principal sub-aggregates *are* reliable. Moreover, the reader should notice that the 'tolerable' margin of error in any period is closely influenced by the success of predictions in the past. It is not only golfers who grow more ambitious as they grow better. Once we have learned how to predict within ± 5 per cent we aim at ± 4 per cent; this achieved we look for ± 3 per cent and so on. Putting the problem in this light it is not in the least implausible to argue that the very success of macro-economic analysis – and the predictions and policies derived from it – has led people to demand from economics and economists a degree of predictive precision which cannot yet be attained.

How successful has macro-economic analysis been? The development of macro-economics in its present form derives very largely from the work of Lord Keynes. Keynes's theory not only showed that the economic system was *not* self-regulating (and thus provided a justification for purposeful attempts at economic control) but also provided the framework upon which modern macro-economics could be developed. We may gain some rough idea of the importance of this work if we compare, by means of a graph, Britain's economic experience in the years 1920 to 1937 with her experience in the years 1945 to 1970.

If we look at the years from 1920 to 1938 we note first that the rate of growth in gross domestic product was relatively low – in fact only of

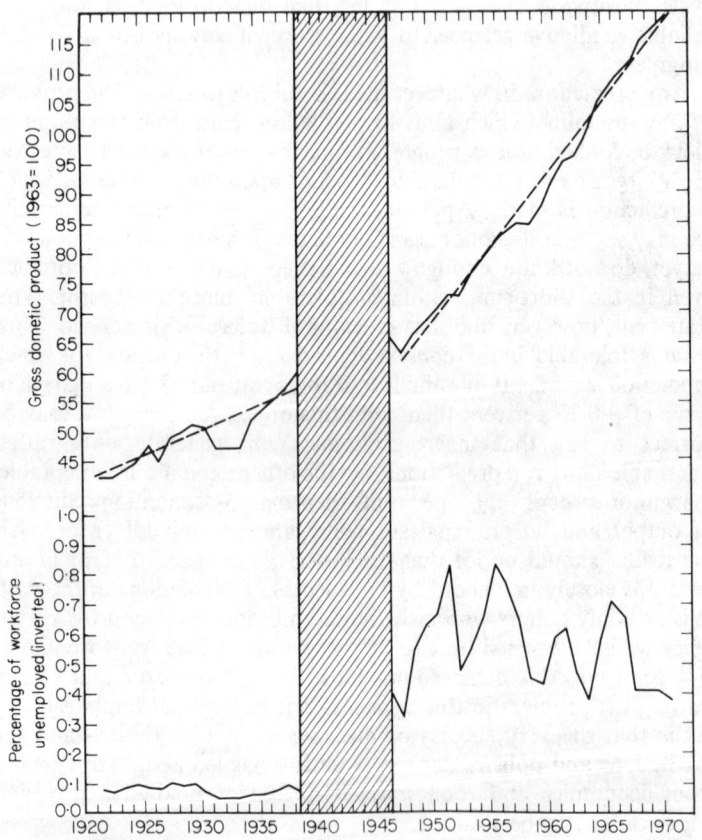

FIG. 25.i   Gross domestic product (1963 = 100) and the percentage of unemployment of the U.K., 1921–70

Sources: (1) Unemployment: 1921–47, *The British Economy*;
1947–70, *Economic Trends*. (2) Gross domestic product: *The British
Economy*, Blue Book and *Monthly Digest*

the order of 2¼ per cent per annum. This compares with a post-World War II rate of growth of about 3 per cent per annum.

Turning now to fluctuations, it is easy to see that movements about the trend in the first period were far more severe. The U.K. went into an early post-war depression in 1920–1. The unemployment percentage rose from 2·5 per cent in 1920 to 15·6 per cent in 1921. Moreover, over the next seventeen years there was no substantial recovery. Indeed at the peak of the 1937–8 'boom' the percentage of the work force unemployed was still of the order of 10 per cent. In 1930 came the 'Great Depression'. Gross domestic product fell very sharply. The percentage of unemployment rose again – this time to over 22 per cent.

Thus even on the graphs the two inter-war decades present a depressing picture of the waste of resources – both human and material. And no graph can show the misery and sense of futility which two decades of chronic unemployment brought to many men, women and children.

Clearly, compared with the inter-war years, we have, since 1945, been far more successful in running the economy close to full employment and far more successful in damping down our cyclical fluctuations. Moreover our post-war rate of growth in gross domestic product, though low in relation to many other countries, is somewhat above that of the period 1920–38, while our rate of growth in output per man year seems also to be greater. Thus, we have, since 1945, managed the economy far more successfully than we contrived to do in the inter-war years. This is shown in Table 25.1 which summarises, in a convenient form, much of the data presented in Fig. 25.i.

Table 25.1   *U.K. Economic Performance: 1920–38, 1946–63 and 1963–70*

	1920–38	1946–63	1963–70
1. Unemployment (percentage of workforce)			
Average	14·3	1·8	2·1
Maximum	22·1	3·1	2·6
Minimum	2·5	1·2	1·4
2. Output			
Percentage rate of growth	2·0	2·4	3·0
3. Output per man year			
Percentage rate of growth	0·8	1·5	2·6

It is, no doubt, precisely our relatively great post-war success with economic intervention which has led to the contemporary demand for still better results – both in terms of stabilisation and in growth –

and thus to a derived demand for prediction within even narrower limits of acceptable error.

No doubt not *all* of the relative economic success in the post-war years is to be explained by the emergence of Keynesian macroeconomics. But a great deal of it is. Major depressions, in which the level of unemployment rises to (say) 20 per cent of the work-force – as it did in the thirties – are no longer a problem. We know enough to avoid them if we wish. As a result we are now trying to stabilise unemployment between percentages such as 1·6 and 3·0 – a level and a range which, in the inter-war years, would have seemed ridiculously over-ambitious.

The root of the contemporary unreliability of positive macroeconomics is not far to seek. It arises from our inadequate quantitative knowledge of the functional relations which specify the economic system and our inadequate quantitative knowledge of the system's dynamic properties.

In the United Kingdom attempts are now being made to improve both – mainly by the construction of relatively large-scale models of the economy which yield numerical estimates of the crucial parameters including the lag forms. The success of research can never be guaranteed. However, if, as the result of the application of research results to the management of the economy, we were able to operate even one-quarter of 1 per cent closer to 'full capacity', this would give us, on the basis of 1970 prices and gross domestic product, about £110 m. of additional output in each year. The potential 'pay-off' of such research is therefore very great.

The present inability of economists to predict, within the range of error which we can permit if we are to dampen the cycle, has led some economists to propose that the system should be *made* self-correcting. What is proposed is, in essentials, that we should arrange matters so that if, at any time, some variable, say gross domestic product, deviates from its target value, there is an automatic adjustment to aggregate demand of a type appropriate to eliminating the error. The simplest analogy is with an automatic pilot which is so constructed that, if the aircraft deviates from its *target course,* a correction is automatically brought into play. In short there is a 'feed back' from the error to the correction designed to eliminate it.

There are various types of correction which may be applied. A simple economic example would be as follows. Let us define $t \equiv$ average = marginal propensity to pay taxes out of personal income. We might then formulate a correcting device by writing

$$t = f(Y - Y_{target}), \qquad \text{(25.VI)}$$

where $Y \equiv$ actual gross domestic product; $Y_{target} \equiv$ desired level of gross domestic product.

This would work as follows. Suppose $Y = Y_{target}$; then t would take some given value. If $Y < Y_{target}$, t would *fall, raising* personal disposable incomes and hence consumption.

Various types of correction compatible with the general idea behind (25.VI) can easily be constructed. So far the only official proposal for any such device is the suggestion, made many years ago and never acted upon, that rates of National Insurance contributions might vary inversely with the percentage of unemployment. This, in effect, is simply a special case of (25.VI) as the reader can easily see.

The aim of this approach is to avoid the need to forecast and the errors arising from it. The drawback of the approach is that, in order to specify devices which, *if* built in to the system, *would* stabilise it within defined limits, we need very much the same sort of quantitative information about the economy's dynamic working which, if we had it, would probably remove most of the errors arising through the use of *forecasting* and *discretionary action*. As far as the economic system is concerned *forecasting* and *automatic control* are thus likely to be equally good (or bad). It seems, therefore, that if the 'automatic control' approach is to be preferred it can only be because of the political constraints which may, only too easily, inhibit discretionary action, or because of the reduction in uncertainty which unavoidably arises from the need to forecast what discretionary action will turn out to be.

QUESTIONS AND EXERCISES

1. In the illustrative calculation of the dynamic multiplier what assumptions have (implicitly) been made regarding (i) gross private investment in fixed capital; (ii) investment in inventories? Are they sensible? How would any changes of them you propose modify your calculation of the necessary 'injection' to aggregate demand?

2. The 'truncated' (five period) multiplier for direct tax reductions is calculated at approximately unity. What is the corresponding 'five period' multiplier for an increase in government expenditure on goods and services?

3. Suppose output takes one period (two months) to adjust to demand (i.e. there is an output lag of one period). Recalculate the truncated multipliers. What would be the unplanned decline

in inventories over the five periods? Would this decline cause you to modify the inventory investment assumption and thus the size of the 'injection' necessary to reach the target?

4. In the light of the N.I.E.S.R. conditional forecasts for the years 1970, 1971 and 1972 discuss the appropriateness (or otherwise) of the Budgets introduced in these years.

5. 'To increase exports we must reduce demand.' Discuss. On what hypotheses is this contention tenable?

6. What is the equilibrium value of the multiplier used in this Chapter? Find an expression for it from the multiplier series and interpret your result in terms of Equation (25.V).

7. How 'flexible' is fiscal policy?

8. 'According to some commentators, Britain is the "sick man" of Europe.' Do you agree? If so how would you diagnose – as opposed to describe – the 'British disease'?

9. Prepare a memorandum for the Governor of the Bank of England setting out the relationship between the percentage of the work-force unemployed and the balance of autonomous receipts and payments. State your assumptions carefully and include in your memorandum an estimate of the percentage of unemployment required to maintain external balance.

10. 'The reason why tax concessions do not stimulate investment in Britain is that British businessmen do not understand how to calculate the present value of capital assets.' Discuss.

11. 'Businessmen make investment plans too far ahead to change them if depreciation allowances are adjusted.' Discuss with particular reference to the views of J. C. R. Dow.

12. 'To make fiscal policy effective we need to give the Chancellor authority to raise or lower direct taxes by up to 10 per cent in any quarter *without* having to present a Budget.' Discuss. What are the administrative difficulties involved?

13. Calculate the present value of the following two projects:

Project 1		Project 2	
Income before tax	Depreciation allowance	Income before tax	Depreciation allowance
500	100	500	300
400	100	400	100
300	100	300	75
300	100	300	20
300	100	300	5

Assume $r = 0.05$, i.e. 5 per cent; $t \equiv$ tax rate $\equiv 0.5$.

14. How would you seek to estimate the effect on consumption of a 5 per cent increase in taxes on cigarettes and tobacco?
15. Discuss the effectiveness of the indirect tax 'regulator'.
16. How far do you agree that U.K. fiscal policy during the period 1950–60 was destabilising rather than stabilising? Give your reasons and suggest ways in which Britain's fiscal performance, if defective, might be improved. Was it improved between 1961 and 1972?
17. Analyse the causes of the rising unemployment from mid-1969 to mid-1972. What was the role of fiscal policy?
18. Examine Mr Barber's budgets of March 1971, July 1971 and March 1972. What stimulus did they provide to demand and how would you account for the slow response of unemployment?
19. Examine the rate of change in the money supply between mid-1969 and mid-1972 in relation to the behaviour of interest rates. What do the series suggest about monetary policy?
20. Explain the relationship between the fiscal policies of 1971–2 and the change in the U.K.'s current balance between 1971.I and 1973.II.

SUGGESTED READING

J. C. R. Dow, *The Management of the British Economy, 1945–1960* (Cambridge, 1964) chs vii, viii, xiv–xvi.

P. M. Oppenheimer, 'Is Britain's Worsening Trade Gap due to Bad Management of the Business Cycle?', *Oxford Institute of Statistics Bulletin* (Aug 1965).

J. M. Fleming and R. C. Tress, 'Waiting for Exports', *London & Cambridge Economic Bulletin* (Jun 1962).

W. A. H. Godley and J. R. Shepherd, 'Long-Term Growth and Short-Term Policy', *N.I.E.S.R. Review* (Aug 1964).

R. E. Caves and associates, *Britain's Economic Prospects* (Allen & Unwin, 1968) chs i–iii and particularly i.

N.I.E.S.R., *National Institute Economic Review*, annual surveys of the economy in February issues.

C.S.O., *Economic Trends* (published monthly by H.M.S.O.).

Bank of England, *Quarterly Bulletin*.

Index

accelerator
  interaction with the multiplier, 440–5
  investment theory and, 436–46
actual values
  definition of, and relation to planned values, 140–55
  synonyms for, 150
aggregate consumption function, 159–162
aggregate demand
  control of, 502–4
    fiscal policy and, 259–61, 403, 502–4, 546–59
    forecasting and, 508–19
    monetary policy and, 521–41, 545
  definition of, 142, 148
  international trade and, 261–70
  public sector and, 253–8
aggregate demand curves, derivation of, 366–72
aggregate demand function, price level and, 333–8, 346–54
aggregate demand–supply analysis, 335–51, 355–7, 358–61
aggregate demand–supply schedules, construction of, 338–46
aggregate supply, definition of, 142, 148
aggregate supply function, 331–3, 335, 355
aggregates, examples of, in macroeconomics, 24
assets
  capital, see capital asset
  real value of and consumption, 159–160
  see also liquidity; money, asset demand for
average propensity to consume, 165
average propensity to save, 165
  role in capital accumulation, 419–20

balance of payments
  autonomous and accommodating items, 492, 494
  Bank Rate and, 534–5
  current account, 102–5
  cycles and, 105, 448–50, 451–2
  domestic investment and, 268
  exchange rates and, 262–3, 498
  forecasts of, 515–18
  international trade multiplier and, 266–8, 269–70
  monetary policy and, 533–5
  money supply and, 310–13
  policy aims and, 492–7
  See also foreign exchange
balanced budget, 255–6, 260–1
Ball, R. J., 528
Bank of England
  note issue and, 277, 278–9
  See also central bank
Bank Rate, (minimum lending rate), 319, 502, 521, 534, 535, 536, 537, 545
banks, cash holdings, 280–90
  cash ratio, 290, 295
  central, see Bank of England; central bank
  commercial, 282, 285, 287–301
  definition of, 287
  deposits, 277–81
    creation of, 291–9
    freezing of, 313, 314–15
  secondary reserves and, 290
behaviour, equilibrium and, 130–2
behaviour equations, 129
behaviour hypotheses, 31–6, 37, 39, 391
'Blue Book', definition of, 57n.
bond prices, rate of interest and, 210–11
bonds, definition of, 212
boom, definition of, 433
borrowers' risk premium, marginal efficiency of investment schedule, 198–200